Medical Treatment: Decisions and the Law

The Mental Capacity Act in Action

Second Edition

Editor:
Christopher Johnston

Authors:
Robert Francis QC
James Berry
Bridget Dolan
Christopher Johnston
Nicholas Mullany
Michael Mylonas
Fiona Paterson
Richard Partridge
Edward Pleeth
Debra Powell
Sarah Simcock
Amy Street
Claire Watson
Oliver Williamson
Leanne Woods

All from 3 Serjeants' Inn, London: www.3serjeantsinn.com/mtdl/
First edition by: Robert Francis QC & Christopher Johnston
Thanks to: Adrian Hopkins QC, Timothy Meakin, Joanna Warwick

Bloomsbury Professional   **3 SERJEANTS' INN**

Bloomsbury Professional Ltd
Maxwelton House
41–43 Boltro Road
Haywards Heath
West Sussex
RH16 1BJ

© Bloomsbury Professional Ltd 2010
Previously published by Tottel Publishing Ltd

British Library Cataloguing-in-Publication Data
A CIP Catalogue record for this book is available from the British Library.

ISBN 978 1 84592 424 9

Printed and bound in Great Britain by Polestar UK print limited – Wheatons division

To John Grace QC

Introduction

How the law deals with the issues surrounding medical treatment decisions speaks volumes about the values and morals of our society. It relates to the very essence of life. How rigorously do we protect people's autonomy? Who do we choose to protect from themselves? Who do we leave free to make what may be irrational decisions about their bodies or their very existence? What matters to us in defining whether a life is worth living? And, fundamentally, what is life? When does it begin? When does it end?

This book tells how the courts and lawyers wrestle with and resolve these problems, not in the abstract but in real – often desperate, often urgent – situations. The story told represents an unsung success for the courts and lawyers. Legal imagination conjured up the common law declaratory jurisdiction[1] to address Parliament's inept and accidental abolition of the ancient *parens patriae* jurisdiction (which protected adults without capacity). Disguised by the fiction that the courts were simply 'declaring' what treatment would be lawful, vital legal decisions were made to protect those whom the politicians had forgotten: incompetent adults. This fiction deserves to stand shoulder to shoulder in the legal history textbooks with the creations of the Courts of Equity[2] in previous centuries.

The jurisdiction so imaginatively carved out by the common law has now been codified in the Mental Capacity Act 2005 ('MCA'): the cogent common law test for capacity now takes statutory form in section 3 of the MCA; the MCA reflects the reality that a judge will determine not simply what treatment would be *lawful* for a patient, but what treatment would be *best*; and the *parens patriae* jurisdiction, revived by the High Court's declaratory fiction, has been formally reconstituted in the new Court of Protection. The Human Rights Act 1998 has ensured an intense focus on the rights of the individual. As to substantive rights, the common law has not been found wanting: the concept of autonomy rigorously protected by the law on capacity and consent developed in the twentieth century easily satisfies the fundamental human right to a private life. Where the common law and UK legislation have been found wanting is in the procedural safeguards necessary to ensure that those substantive rights are defined with appropriate certainty and are policed fairly. Those failings have been addressed in the new procedural framework enacted for medical treatment decisions in the High Court and Court of Protection, and set out in the 'Deprivation of Liberty Safeguards'. It is to be hoped that these new – and sometimes labyrinthine processes – will at no time distract judges from the key goal that the common law ultimately achieved so well, namely protecting the incompetent patient. It is fair to say that the authors' court experience to date has been that, both substantively and procedurally, judges have retained their focus on the best interests of the patient and child.

This book is in three sections. First, we consider general principles and procedures. We provide a guide to the legal principles underlying patient autonomy, advance decisions and the treatment of those without capacity (whether children or adults). We explain the legal tests and processes should a treatment dilemma reach court. To address the new procedural safeguards, chapters have been included on going to court, and deprivation of liberty and restraint. Secondly, fully updated specialist chapters then address the particular problems the authors have dealt with in the High Court and Court of Protection including cases involving sterilisation, abortion, caesarean sections, feeding, religious objections to treatment, permanent vegetative state and suicide. New chapters consider end of life decisions and human tissue and organ donation. Thirdly, appendices set out the key precedents, materials and forms relating to each chapter.

This is a practical guide. Our aim is simply to set out the law. As lawyers we do not seek to set out our view on the ethics underlying the decisions the courts have taken and on the statutory approach adopted by Parliament. I simply say here that, in my opinion, the law as it currently stands reflects a mature democratic compromise between the need to protect those who cannot protect themselves and the fundamental human right of personal autonomy. With the rare exception (such as the high profile decision of the conjoined twins' case, *Re A*), the approach to the development of medical ethics' law by the High Court and Court of Protection, in the face of ever increasing challenges posed both by medical science and the development of human rights jurisprudence, has achieved the right balance between patient autonomy and patient protection.

We will post the hyperlinks referred to in each chapter, and updates in this ever changing area of law, on our website www.3serjeantsinn.com/mtdl. A large part of this book is comprised of the insight its authors have gained through practical experience. If you have any suggestions for the updates or for the next edition of the book please email mtdl@3serjeantsinn.com.

Finally, thank you to my publishers for their support. Thanks to all the contributors to the book for their work and their prompt and polite responses to my continual late night email queries. Thanks also to all of those who have helped our thinking about the issues and procedures considered in this book and, at the risk of singling out one person, thanks to Beverley Taylor at the Official Solicitor's for her discussion of procedure with Amy Street. Suffice to say, however, that all the views expressed are entirely those of the authors and not those who gave us their time so freely. I would note the continual work and enthusiasm of our clerks in helping us manage these challenging medical ethics cases in court, often having to arrange hearings or communications at very unsociable times. Last, heartfelt thanks to my wife, Joanna, not only for casting the eye of a professional editor and (as importantly) non-lawyer over the text, but also for her endless patience.

Christopher Johnston

3 Serjeants' Inn

November 2009.

1   Part of which has been described as 'one of the most remarkable developments of modern British administrative law': Zamir & Woolf, *The Declaratory Judgement* (2nd ed, Sweet & Maxwell, 1993), p 8.
2   See A Diamond, *The Victorian achievement of Sir Henry Maine: a centennial reappraisal* and in particular chapter 15, *Fictions, equity and legislation: Maine's three agencies of legal change* (Cambridge University Press, 1991).

Introduction from Previous Edition

This book owes its genesis to the recent expansion of court involvement in the medical decision-making process. A glance through the table of cases we have referred to will indicate that the vast majority were decided within the last 15 years. Before then the common law appeared to concentrate on the application of the law of negligence to medical treatment. Indeed, until the publication of *Medical Law: Text and Materials* by Professors Kennedy and Grubb in 1989 many lawyers might have been forgiven for being somewhat sceptical as to whether there was such a subject, as opposed to medical negligence law. The reasons are not hard to find. Until relatively recently – at least in this country – the standards to be applied to medical treatment were left almost entirely to the medical profession. The courts intervened rarely, and then reluctantly. The standard of care imposed on the medical profession, as a result of the *Bolam*[1] case was largely the standard they thought it right to adopt. Behind this stand-offish approach was a desire not to inhibit medical progress to the disadvantage of the community as a whole:

> 'we should be doing a disservice to the community at large if we were to impose liability on hospitals and doctors for everything that happens to go wrong. Doctors would be led to think more of their own safety than of the good of their patients. Initiative would be stifled and confidence shaken. A proper sense of proportion requires us to have regard to the conditions in which hospitals and doctors have to work.'[2]

Since then the immense and rapid advances in medical science have provoked a more anxious and less trusting reaction to medical matters. Patients have become accustomed in other fields to having and being able to exercise rights, to express their views, however inexpert, and to being able to pick and choose between options which they demand they are given. They see no reason why they should not be able to do so in relation to medical treatment. The law has responded slowly and often tortuously to these concerns. It has advanced way beyond the ability retrospectively to examine the standard of care applied in the case of treatment which has gone wrong, and is now willing to intervene in matters of medical treatment and care before it is given or during it. Often this has the result of, quite literally, placing the lawyer at the bedside at the shoulder of the doctor. Not everyone welcomes this, but there is no doubt that we are only at the beginning of this development.

At the front line of these developments is the process whereby decisions are made about medical treatment. In most cases what is to be done is decided between doctor and patient without the intervention of any third party and without the shadow of any special legislation falling upon them. In matters of difficulty or controversy, however, recourse is now made on an increasingly regular basis to the courts.

The purpose of this book is modest. Some types of treatment cause day-to-day challenges for doctors, hospital managers, patients, their families as well as lawyers. Often problems arise in these areas at very short notice; many require application to the court for approval in one form or another. We have identified those areas where reference to the courts is most likely to be needed. We have sought to set out relatively briefly, and, we hope, without an excessive degree of academic analysis, what we understand to be the law applicable to these problems, first by reference to the general principles, and secondly by applying those principles to each problem in the subsequent chapters. Where we have thought it helpful to do so we have appended informative material relevant to the subject and precedents.

We hope this will prove of use not only to lawyers who are asked to advise any client involved in a difficult treatment decision, but also to doctors and medical managers, who may need to have available an easily accessible reference to a particular topic. For these reasons the book is more of an anthology of different situations, rather than an attempt at an exhaustive survey of all circumstances in which medical treatment decisions have to be made. For example, we have not sought to deal with the generality of the Mental Health Act 1983, an area already well covered by established texts, or matters coming within the remit of the Human Fertilisation and Embryology Authority, a subject worthy of a book to itself. Readers will no doubt think of other areas which are not covered. We hope that they may find some assistance from the general principles described in these pages in any event, and, if they do not, can only hope they find consolation in the comparative brevity of this work!

As we hope the book may be of help to the layman as well as the lawyer it is necessary to make clear a few caveats about the content of this book. As will be readily apparent, medical science continually springs new ethical and legal challenges on the world which throw new light on previously accepted legal principles. While the law is often rightly accused of lagging behind scientific and social developments, it is capable of producing novel solutions very rapidly indeed. The development of the declaratory jurisdiction to assist patients lacking the capacity to authorise their own treatment in *Re F (mental patient: sterilisation)*[3] is one example; the resolution offered to the challenges presented by the PVS patient in *Airedale NHS Trust v Bland*[4], in litigation which was concluded from the beginning of the first instance hearing to judgment in the House of Lords in 12 weeks, is another. Therefore, great care should be taken to avoid being tempted to assume that principles set out in previous cases, and described here, will be followed in the future, even in a similar case, if the result is seen to be undesirable or unjust. In this of all areas of law, a flexibility of approach is constantly required, and a responsiveness to the needs of society likely to be shown by the courts. This is, of course, why it is such an exciting and productive part of the law in which to study and work.

We cannot end this introduction without expressing our heartfelt thanks to Lord Justice Thorpe for kindly agreeing to write the foreword. We must also acknowledge the assistance from many of our colleagues who – often unwittingly – have helped us develop some of the ideas in this book. Last, but certainly not least, we must acknowledge our indebtedness to our families who have had to suffer the absences and late hours known to all those who are foolish enough to attempt producing any publication.

1   *Bolam v Friern Hospital Management Committee* [1957] 1 WLR 582.
2   *Roe v Minister of Health* [1954] 2 QB 66 at 83 per Denning LJ.
3   [1990] 2 AC 1.
4   [1993] AC 789.

Contents

Introduction   vii
Introduction from Previous Edition   xi
Table of Statutes   xxvii
Table of Statutory Instruments   xxxi
Table of Cases   xxxv
Table of European Legislation   xlvii
Table of International Legislation   xlix

Part 1   General principles

1   Consent – General
A   Framework   1.1
       Introduction   1.1
       Proposal to treat   1.3
            Formulation of proposal   1.3
            Risks of treatment   1.4
            Alternative forms of treatment   1.5
            Compelling a doctor to treat   1.6
            Irrational decisions by care providers to refuse treatment   1.7
            Resources   1.8
            Treatment demanded by the patient   1.9
       Communication of the proposal   1.10
       Consent – state of mind   1.13
            Intention   1.13
            Comprehension   1.14
       Communication of consent   1.15
            Written consent   1.16
            Oral consent   1.17
            Conduct   1.18
B   Information about risks   1.19
       No doctrine of informed consent   1.19
       Duty of care – common law position   1.20
       Article 8   1.21
       Other jurisdictions   1.22
       Current practice in the UK   1.23

Contents

Delegation 1.25
Duty to answer questions 1.26
Information about alternative forms of treatment 1.28
Known comparative outcomes 1.29
C Vitiating factors 1.30
Fraud 1.31
Duress and undue influence 1.32
Capacity 1.33
D Scope of authority 1.34
E Duration of authority 1.35
F Withdrawal of authority 1.37
G Conclusion 1.38

2 **Consent – Adults**
A Adult 2.1
B Capacity 2.2
Definition of capacity and its assessment 2.2
The person consenting must have the relevant mental capacity
to do so 2.2
How much capacity 2.6
Temporary incapacity 2.7
Presumption of capacity 2.8
The absolute nature of an adult's consent 2.9
Treatment must be lawful 2.10
C Refusal 2.11
D Change of mind 2.12
E Advance directives/decisions 2.13
General principle 2.13
Requirements 2.14
Form 2.15
Informed refusal? 2.16
Knowledge 2.17
Duration 2.18
Records 2.19
F Conclusion 2.20

3 **Deciding for Others – Adults**
A The court's power to order treatment 3.1
B Taking decisions for adults 3.2
General rule 1: A capable adult's wishes must be respected 3.2
General rule 2: There is only limited proxy of consent for others 3.3
General rule 3: Power to treat in an incapable person's best
interests 3.4
C Decisions in relation to adults with capacity 3.5
The obligation to treat in accordance with expressed wishes 3.6
Obstetric treatment in the interests of a viable foetus no exception 3.7

D   Deciding for adults without capacity   3.8
    Treatment out of necessity   3.8
    The Mental Capacity Act 2005   3.9
    Temporary incapacity   3.10
    Records – the basis of any application   3.11
    Scope of power to treat   3.12
    Determination of best interests   3.13
    The medical issues   3.14
    What are the interests to be considered?   3.15
    The use of force and restraint   3.16
    Advance decisions and best interests   3.17
E   Conclusion   3.18

4   Deciding for Others – Children
A   Framework   4.1
B   Capacity to consent to treatment   4.2
    Children of 16 years of age and over   4.2
    Children under the age of 16   4.3
    Parents and those with parental responsibility   4.4
C   Power to refuse treatment   4.5
    Children over the age of 16 or possessing *Gillick* competence   4.6
    Compulsory treatment and children's rights   4.7
    Children under the age of 16 not possessing *Gillick* competence   4.8
    Parents   4.9
    The court   4.10
D   Special considerations in the treatment of severely ill infants   4.11
    Deliberate killing   4.12
    Withholding and withdrawing life-sustaining treatment   4.13
        Withholding treatment   4.13
        Withdrawing treatment   4.14
    Best interests: the court's approach   4.15
    Practical guidance   4.16
E   Conclusion   4.17

5   Going to Court
A   Introduction   5.1
B   Identifying the right court for medical treatment cases   5.2
    Courts with jurisdiction to deal with medical treatment cases   5.2
    The jurisdiction of the Court of Protection   5.3
        Cases in which the Court of protection lacks jurisdiction   5.4
        16 to 17 year olds: overlap of the jurisdiction of the Court of
        Protection and the High Court   5.5
        Different age cut-offs for different types of case   5.6
        Summary   5.7
C   Procedural points common to the Court of Protection and the High
    Court   5.8
    Public law issues 5.8

Contents

The timing of proceedings   5.9
How urgent is it?   5.10
Introduction to the Official Solicitor and CAFCASS   5.11
Who should bring proceedings?   5.13
   What does the party bringing the proceedings want?   5.15
Family Division Practice Direction on Bundles   5.16
Final hearings   5.17
Typing up the order   5.18
D The Court of Protection   5.19
The Court of Protection generally   5.19
   Constitutional issues   5.19
   Location and judges   5.20
   Sources of procedural rules and guidance   5.21
   The court's general approach   5.22
   The court's powers to make medical treatment decisions   5.23
Serious medical treatment: *Practice Direction 9E*   5.24
   Definition of 'serious medical treatment'   5.25
   Procedural matters   5.26
What cases should be brought to court?   5.27
Privacy and publicity   5.28
Points to consider before starting proceedings   5.29
   Litigation friend   5.29
   Is permission required?   5.30
   Who should be named as respondents and who should be notified of
   the proceedings?   5.31
   Level of judge and initial directions   5.32
   Deprivation of liberty   5.33
Starting proceedings – non-urgent   5.34
   How are proceedings begun?   5.34
Starting proceedings – urgent   5.35
First hearing and subsequent directions hearings   5.36
Final hearings   5.37
Costs   5.38
Costs of Official Solicitor   5.39
Appeals   5.40
E The High Court's jurisdiction in relation to minors   5.41
The High Court generally   5.41
   The High Court's jurisdiction   5.41
   Regional hearings   5.42
   Procedure and rules   5.43
   What cases should be brought to court?   5.44
   Who should be the defendants?   5.49
Starting proceedings – non-urgent   5.53
Starting proceedings – urgent   5.56
Privacy and publicity   5.57
First hearing and subsequent directions hearings   5.58
Final hearings   5.59
Costs   5.60
Appeals   5.61

F   The High Court's inherent jurisdiction – in relation to
     'vulnerable adults'   5.62
G   Conclusion   5.63

6   Restraint and Deprivation of Liberty
A   Introduction   6.1
B   Restraint   6.6
     Restraint authorised under the MCA   6.8
     Restraint and Article 3 ECHR   6.11
     Proportionality and restraint   6.15
     Practical issues   6.22
C   Deprivation of liberty   6.27
     Background: the '*Bournewood* gap'   6.27
     What is 'deprivation of liberty'?   6.31
     Identifying a deprivation of liberty   6.37
     Authorising a deprivation of liberty   6.38
     Court authorisation   6.39
     The DOLS procedure   6.41
     MCA or MHA?   6.45
D   Conclusion   6.49

Part 2   Specific problems

7   Sterilisation
A   General   7.1
B   The competent patient7.2
     General rule   7.2
     Informed consent   7.3
     The role of partner/spouse   7.4
     Procedure   7.5
C   Adults7.6
     Competent adults   7.6
     Adults lacking capacity to consent   7.7
          Capacity   7.7
          Best interests   7.8
          General application of 'best interests' principle in
          sterilisation cases   7.9
          The immediacy of the risks   7.18
     Procedure   7.19
D   Children   7.20
     General principle   7.20
          Children with no learning disabilities   7.20
          Children with learning disabilities   7.21
     Best interests   7.22
     Procedure   7.23
E   Conclusion   7.24

Contents

8   Abortion
A   Statutory framework   8.1
     Offences Against the Person Act 1861   8.2
     Infant Life (Preservation) Act 1929   8.3
     Abortion Act 1967   8.4
     Human Fertilisation and Embryology Act 1990   8.5
B   Particular issues of compliance with the Abortion Act 1967
     conditions   8.6
     Conscientious objection   8.6
     Multiple foetuses   8.7
     Does the procedure have to be successful to be lawful?   8.8
     Does the procedure have to be performed by a medical
        practitioner?   8.9
     Certification of medical opinion   8.10
     The grounds   8.11
          Risk of injury to the mother greater than if pregnancy terminated:
          s 1(1)(a)   8.11
          Termination is necessary to prevent grave permanent injury:
          s 1(1)(b)   8.15
          Risk to life of pregnant woman greater than if the pregnancy were
          terminated: s 1(1)(c)   8.16
          Substantial risk of the child being seriously handicapped from
          physical or mental abnormalities: s 1(1)(d)   8.17
     The place of treatment   8.18
C   The patient's consent   8.19
     Competent adults   8.20
     Children   8.21
     Incompetent adults   8.22
          Determining competence: termination of pregnancy   8.23
          Best interests: termination of pregnancy   8.24
          Use of force: non-consensual incompetent patients   8.25
     Procedure and evidence   8.26
          Making an application   8.26
          Timing of the application   8.27
          Important considerations for the court   8.28
D   Conclusion   8.31

9   Managing Pregnancies
A   Introduction   9.1
B   The legal background   9.2
     Patient and foetal rights in obstetrics   9.2
     Compulsory obstetrics   9.3
     The caesarean section cases   9.4
          Tameside and Glossop Acute Services NHS Trust v CH   9.5
          Needle phobias: *Re L*   9.7
          A solution? *Re MB*   9.8
          Re MB Capacity   9.9
          Re MB Reasonable force   9.10

Re MB Interests of foetus   9.11
Re MB Procedure   9.12
The solution imposed – *St George's Healthcare NHS Trust v S*   9.13
C   The Court of Appeal guidelines   9.14
The Mental Capacity Act 2005   9.15
Advance decisions   9.16
Management of pregnancy in women who are comatose or in a permanent vegetative state   9.17
D   A suggested procedure for obstetric units   9.18
Assessment of capacity   9.19
Advice to patients about nature of possible treatment   9.20
Discussion with patient about possible loss of capacity   9.21
Advance decision   9.22
Psychiatric referral and assessment where capacity in doubt   9.23
Contingency planning for court application   9.24
Compliance with Court of Appeal guidelines   9.25
Continual advice to patient   9.26
E   Procedure for patients   9.27
F   Conclusion   9.28

10   Feeding
A   Introduction   10.1
B   Children   10.2
General principles   10.2
Children under the age of 16   10.2
Children aged 16 and 17   10.3
Effect of disorder on *Gillick* competence   10.4
Exercise of court's jurisdiction   10.5
Procedure   10.6
C   Adults   10.7
Competent adults – general rule   10.7
Adults lacking the capacity to consent   10.8
Competent adults detained under the Mental Health Act 1983   10.9
Procedure – declaration   10.10
Procedure – injunction   10.11
D   Conclusion   10.12

11   Religious Objections to Treatment
A   Introduction   11.1
B   Competent adults   11.2
General principle   11.2
Steps to be taken   11.3
Confirmation that the patient is mentally competent   11.4
Counselling   11.7
Undue influence   11.8
Scope of the decision   11.9
The role of relatives and close friends   11.10

Contents

Recording of decision against medical advice   11.11
C   Incapacitated adults   11.12
General principle   11.12
Advance decisions   11.13
Reported oral advance decisions   11.14
The effect of uncertainty   11.15
Written declarations   11.16
D   Children   11.17
General principle   11.17
Best interests   11.18
The 'Gillick competent' child   11.19
E   Procedural issues with children's applications   11.20
Anticipation   11.20
Notice and consultation   11.21
Evidence   11.22
Change of circumstance   11.23
F   Conclusion   11.24

12   Permanent Vegetative State
A   Introduction   12.1
B   Legal principles   12.2
The Bland decision   12.3
The problem with 'act' and 'omission'   12.4
European Convention on Human Rights   12.5
Continuing treatment is an assault   12.6
Extending Bland to other cases   12.7
Advance directives/prior consent   12.8
Summary   12.9
C   Medical issues   12.10
Imaging   12.11
Rehabilitation and time to allow for a recovery   12.12
Cases outside the RCP guidelines   12.13
D   Role of the family   12.14
E   Is an application to court required?   12.15
Consequences of withholding nutrition and hydration without court
approval   12.16
F   Application to court   12.17
Confidentiality   12.18
Evidence   12.19
G   Emergency cases   12.20
Critique of Frenchay approach   12.21
H   Children   12.22
I   Doctors who disagree in principle   12.23
J   Conclusion   12.24

13   Treatment of Suicidal Patients
A   Introduction   13.1

B   Basic definition 13.2
What is suicide? 13.2
    An act 13.3
    An intention to act 13.4
    An understanding of the likely consequences 13.5
C   Statute 13.6
European Convention on Human Rights 13.7
D   Refining the definition of suicide: failure to treat or feed 13.16
E   General principles 13.19
F   Practical problems 13.23
G   Autonomy v liability for failing to act 13.28
H   European Convention on Human Rights: duty to preserve life 13.39
I   General guidance 13.47
Emergency situations 13.49
    Inadequate time to assess capacity 13.49
    Preventing a jump from a window 13.52
J   European Convention on Human Rights: the balance to be struck 13.54
K   Compulsorily detained patients 13.56
Legal test in criticising a doctor's determination under s 63 of the Mental Health Act 1983 13.64
L   Guidance on approach to treatment 13.66
M   Conclusion 13.67

14   The End of Life
A   The definition of 'death' 14.1
B   The diagnosis of death 14.12
Brain stem death 14.13
Death following cessation of cardio-respiratory function 14.14
Certification 14.17
The 'process of dying' 14.18
C   After death 14.26
D   Application of 'work and skill' exception 14.29
E   Right of possession and disposal 14.35
F   The use and storage of human bodies and tissues 14.38
G   Conclusion 14.39

15   Human Organ and Tissue Donation
A   Introduction 15.1
B   The common law 15.2
C   The Human Tissue Act 2004 15.3
Donations by living persons 15.8
    'Domino' transplants 15.9
    Consent 15.10
    Incompetent adults 15.11
    Children 15.12
    Best interests 15.13
    Approval by the Human Tissue Authority 15.14

Contents

Types of donations by living donors   15.15
Consent – children   15.16
Consent – adults   15.17
Preservation of organs after death   15.18
Preparatory steps taken before death   15.19
D   Conclusion   15.20

Appendix 1.1 Mental Capacity Act 2005   325
Appendix 1.2 DOH Consent Form 1   332
Appendix 1.3 DOH Consent Form 2   336
Appendix 1.4 DOH Consent Form 3   340
Appendix 1.5 DOH Consent Form 4   343
Appendix 1.6 DOH: Information to assist in amending consent forms   347
Appendix 1.7 GMC: Good Medical Practice   353

Appendix 2.1 NHS: My advance decision to refuse treatment   354

Appendix 4.1 Draft Originating Summons for Child Treatment
Decision   358
Appendix 4.2 Code of Practice Mental Health Act 1983 (revised 2008)   359
Appendix 4.3 Balance Sheet in *An NHS Trust v MB* [2006] EWHC 507
(Fam)   362

Appendix 5.1 Practice Direction Family Proceedings: Court Bundles
(Universal Practice to be applied in all Courts other than the Family
Proceedings Court)   366
Appendix 5.2 List of Court of Protection Forms   372
Appendix 5.3 List of Court of Protection Practice Directions   374
Appendix 5.4 Court of Protection Practice Direction 9E – How to start
proceedings   376
Appendix 5.5 Court of Protection Practice Direction 10B – Applications
within proceedings   380
Appendix 5.6 Suggested directions to seek in an application form before the
first directions hearing in a medical treatment case in the Court of
Protection   383
Appendix 5.7 Sample draft order for first directions hearing in a medical
treatment case in the court of protection   384
Appendix 5.8 Originating summons form   387
Appendix 5.9 Example of information likely to be required in
Acknowledgment of Service of Originating Summons   389
Appendix 5.10 President's Direction (Representation of Children in Family
Proceedings Pursuant to Family Proceedings Rules 1991, rule 9.5)   390
Appendix 5.11 CAFCASS and the National Assembly for Wales Practice
Note (Appointment of guardians in private law proceedings)   392
Appendix 5.12 President's Practice Direction (Applications for Reporting
Restriction Orders)   395
Appendix 5.13 Practice Note (Official Solicitor: Deputy Director of Legal
Services: CAFCASS: Applications for Reporting Restriction Orders)   396
Appendix 5.14 Practice Note (Official Solicitor: Appointment in Family
Proceedings)   404

Appendix 5.15 Practice Note (Official Solicitor, CAFCASS and the National Assembly for Wales: Urgent and Out of Hours Cases in the Family Division of the High Court)   407

Appendix 5.16 Sample draft order for first directions hearing in a medical treatment case concerning a minor in the High Court   420

Appendix 6.1 Order authorising a deprivation of liberty for rehabilitative treatment in a registered care home   422

Appendix 6.2 Interim Order providing for Court of Protection reviews of deprivation of liberty pending MCA DOLS authorisation   424

Appendix 6.3 Order permitting use of restraint   426

Appendix 6.4 Overview of deprivation of liberty safeguards   428

Appendix 7.1 Previous Consent Form (Sterilisation or Vasectomy) (DoH)   429

Appendix 7.2 Extracts from Previous Practice Note (Official Solicitor: Sterilisation)   432

Appendix 7.3 Draft Order for Declaration that Sterilisation of Adult is Lawful   434

Appendix 7.4 Draft Order Under Inherent Jurisdiction for Sterilisation of Child   435

Appendix 8.1 Abortion Act 1967   436

Appendix 8.2 Abortion Regulations 1991   440

Appendix 8.3 Form of Certification under the Abortion Regulations 1991   443

Appendix 8.4 Form of Certification under the Abortion Regulations 1991: Emergency Case   445

Appendix 8.5 Abortion Regulations 1991 Schedule 2   446

Appendix 8.6 Form of Notification for pregnancies terminated in England and Wales: Form HSA4   448

Appendix 8.7 Sample text for sections 5.1 and 5.2 of the COP 1 Application Form, in relation to an application for a declaration that the court determine whether a termination is in an adult's best interests: 454

Appendix 8.8 Draft order that it is in an adult's best interests to undergo a termination   455

Appendix 8.9 The law and ethics of abortion BMA Views   456

Appendix 8.10 Royal College of Obstetricians and Gynaecologists Joint Guidance Further Issues Relating to Late Abortion, Fetal Viability and Registration of Births and Deaths   470

Appendix 9.1 Court of Appeal Guidelines: *Re MB* Guidelines and *St George's Healthcare v S* Guidelines   472

Appendix 9.2 Witness statement for patient opposing imposition of caesarean section   476

Appendix 9.3 Draft order preventing a caesarean section   477

Appendix 9.4 Witness statement for declaration that lawful to perform caesarian section   478

Appendix 9.5 Draft declaration permitting caesarean section   479

Contents

Appendix 9.6 Draft Order Permitting Administration of Blood Products and Caesarean Section in the Case of a Minor – assume that the hearing has been in private   481
Appendix 9.7 ROCG Guidelines 2006 Law and ethics in relation to court-authorised obstetric intervention   483

Appendix 10.1 Draft Injunction Restraining Force-Feeding   504
Appendix 10.2 DSM-IV: Diagnostic criteria for eating disorders   505

Appendix 11.1 Draft Form for Refusal of Treatment to be Signed by the Patient   507
Appendix 11.2 Draft Record of Refusal of Treatment to be Signed by Doctor   508
Appendix 11.3 Draft Specific Issue Order for Administration of Blood Products to Child   510

Appendix 12.1 End-of-life decisions   512
Appendix 12.2 Treatment of patients in persistent vegetative state   520
Appendix 12.3 The Vegetative State   527
Appendix 12.4 The process for making best interest decisions in serious medical conditions in patients over 18 years   543

Appendix 13.1 DPP Interim policy for prosecutors in respect of case of assisted suicide   544

Appendix 14.1 Extracts from 'A code of practice for the diagnosis and confirmation of death' (Academy of Medical Royal Colleges, 2008)   548
Appendix 14.2 A code of practice for the diagnosis and confirmation of death   554
Appendix 14.3 Extracts from 'Withholding or withdrawing life sustaining treatment in children' A framework for practice   556

Index   579

Table of Statutes

PARA

Abortion Act 1967 .... 2.10, 8.4–8.10,
    8.12, 8.13, 8.17, 8.18, 8.22,
    8.28, 8.31, 9.2, 9.11, App 8.1,
    App 8.2, App 8.3, App 8.4,
    App 8.9
ss 1–7 .... App 8.1
s 1 ...... 8.22, 8.25, 9.2, App 8.2, App
    8.9
    (1) ..... 8.4, App 8.2, App 8.3, App
    8.5
    (a)–(d) .... App 8.2, App 8.5
    (a) ... 8.5, 8.11, 8.12, 8.15, 8.17,
    App 8.9
    (b) .... 8.6, 8.15, App 8.9
    (c) .... 8.16, App 8.9
    (d) ... 4.12, 8.7, 8.17, 8.31, App
    8.9
    (2) 8.13
    (3A) 8.18
    (4) .... 8.18, App 8.2, App 8.4, App
    8.5
    2 .... App 8.2
    4 .... 8.6, App 8.9
    (1) 8.6
    (2) 8.6
    5(2) .... 8.7, App 8.9
Administration of Justice
    Act 1960—
    s 12(1) 5.28
    (a) 5.56
Adoption and Children
    Act 2002 .... 5.56
Anatomy Act 1984 .... 14.38
Children Act 1989 .... 4.6, 5.40, 5.42,
    5.56, 10.5, App 4.2
    s 1(1) 4.9
    ss 2–4 .... 4.4
    s 2(7) 4.4
    4 .... App 4.2

PARA

Children Act 1989 – contd
    s 5 .... 4.4
    8 .... 5.4, 5.5, 5.40
    (1) 5.40
    (7) 5.40
    9 .... 5.40
    22 .... App 4.2
    33(3)(b) .... App 4.2
    97 .... 5.56
    100(3) 5.46
    105(1) 5.40
    Sch 1, para 16 .... 5.40
Children Act 2004 .... App 4.2
Children and Young Persons
    Act 1933—
    s 39 .... 5.56
    (1) 5.56
Children and Young Persons
    Act 1963—
    s 57(4) 5.56
Congenital Disabilities (Civil
    Liability) Act 1976 .... 9.2, 9.11
Criminal Justice (Northern
    Ireland) Act 1929 .... App 8.9
Criminal Justice and Court
    Services Act 2000—
    s 11 .... 5.11
Electronic Communications
    Act 2000 .... App 8.2
Family Law Reform Act 1969 .... 4.3,
    4.6, App 4.2
    s 8 .... 4.2, 8.21, 10.3
    (3) 10.3
Gender Recognition Act 2004 .... 1.9
Human Fertilisation and
    Embryology Act 1990 ..... 8.4, 8.5,
    9.2, App 8.9
    s 37 .... 8.4
    (5) .... 8.7, App 8.9

PARA

Human Organs Transplant
  Act 1989 .... 14.38

Human Rights Act 1998 ... 4.1, 4.4, 4.7,
  7.1, 8.22, 8.31, 12.1, 12.5,
  App 4.2
s 8 .... 2.17

Human Tissue Act 1961 .... 14.38

Human Tissue Act 2004 ... 14.28, 14.38,
  15.1–15.4, 15.6, 15.8–15.11,
  15.13, 15.17–15.19
s 1(1)(b) 15.16
  (d) 15.10
  (e) 15.16
  (f) 15.10
  2(2) 15.13
  (3) 15.13
  (7) 15.17
  3 .... 15.18
  (3) 15.18
  (4) 15.18
  (6)–(8) 15.18
  (6) 15.18
  4 .... 15.18
  33 .... 15.9
  53 .... 14.38
  54(1) 15.13
  (9) 15.17
  Sch 1, para 7 .... 15.10

Incapacity (Scotland) Act 2000 ..... App
  8.9

Infant Life (Preservation)
  Act 1929 ..... 8.3, 8.5, 8.8, 8.9, 9.2,
  App 8.1, App 8.9
s 1(1) 8.3
  (2) 8.3

International Headquarters and
  Defence Organisations
  Act 1964—
Sch .... App 8.1

Matrimonial and Family
  Proceedings Act 1984—
s 32 .... 5.42, 5.52, 5.61

Medical Act 1983 .... 8.9

PARA

Mental Capacity Act 2005 ...... 1.1, 2.1,
  2.2, 2.3, 2.14, 2.20, 3.1, 3.3,
  3.4, 3.9, 3.10, 3.12, 3.14, 3.16,
  4.2, 4.4, 5.3, 5.4, 5.6, 5.8,
  5.21, 5.22, 5.27, 6.4–6.6, 6.8,
  6.15, 6.30, 6.37, 6.41, 6.44,
  6.45, 6.47, 6.49, 8.22, 8.25,
  9.9, 9.15, 9.19, 10.5, 10.6,
  10.10, 12.1, 14.19, App 1.1,
  App 4.2, App 8.9
ss 1–7 .... App 1.1
s 1 .... 3.9, 4.2, 4.4, App 1.1
  1(2) 1.30, 2.6, 3.5
  (3) 2.3, 2.7, 2.20, 3.10
  (4) 2.6, 3.10
  (5) 2.7, 3.13, 5.22, 6.10
  2 ...... 8.23, 8.27, 8.29, App 1.1
  (1) 2.2, 5.6
  (2) 2.2, 2.7
  (3) 2.2
  (b) 9.15, 9.16
  (4) 2.2
  (5) .... 2.1, 4.2, 5.3, App 1.1
  (6) 4.2
  3 .... 2.2, 4.2, 4.3, 8.23, 13.51
  (2) 2.3
  (3) 2.4
  (4) 2.3
  4 .... 3.13, 8.24, 9.16, 9.17, App 1.1
  (2) 3.13
  (4) 3.13
  (6) .... 3.13, 11.10, App 1.1
  (a) 2.17, 4.6
  (7) 11.10
  4A .... 6.38, App 1.1
  (1) 6.10
  (3), (4) 5.6
  4B .... App 1.1
  5 ...... 1.33, 1.34, 1.36, 2.1, 2.8, 3.4,
  3.12, 3.14, 5.27, 6.8, 6.48,
  8.25, 10.8, 11.8, App 1.1
  (1) 11.12
  6 .... 3.16, 6.5, 6.8, 8.25
  (4) 6.6
  (6) .... App 1.1
  7 .... 3.9
  (6) 3.9
  9(1)(a) 3.9
  (2)(c) 5.6
  12 .... 2.8
  (2) 2.8
s 15 .... 5.3, 5.23, App 1.1

PARA

Mental Capacity Act 2005 – *contd*

s 15(1) 5.3
16 .... 5.3, 5.6, App 1.1
(2) .... 3.14, App 1.1
(a) 5.6, 5.23, 5.33, 6.10,
6.38, App 1.1
(b) 3.9
16(6) 5.23
16A 6.45
(1) 6.45
18(2) 5.6
(3) .... 5.3, 5.6, App 1.1
21A 5.30, 5.33, 5.34
ss 24–26 .... 2.14, 12.8, App 1.1
s 24(1)–(5) 2.14
(1) 5.6, 11.19
(1)(a) .... App 1.1
(5) 11.11
(6) 11.11
25 .... 2.15
(2)–(6) 2.14
(2) 12.8
(b) .... App 1.1
(4) 2.16, 12.8
(c) 11.15
(5) .... 12.8, App 1.1
(a) 12.8
(6) .... 12.8, App 1.1,
26 .... 2.15, 9.16
(2) 2.17
(3)–(5) 2.14
(3) 12.8
(5) 11.9
35 .... 5.34
37 .... 5.25
42(4) 2.2
44 .... 5.6
45(1) 5.19
(5) 5.20
(6) 5.19
46 .... 5.20
(3)–(4) 5.20
(3) 5.17, 5.20
47(1) 5.19
48 .... 5.23, 5.29, 5.32, App 1.1
(a) 8.24
49 .... 5.22, 5.36
50 .... 5.30
(1) 5.30
(1A) 5.30, 5.33
(2) 5.30
(3) 5.30
51 .... 5.21

PARA

Mental Capacity Act 2005 – *contd*

Sch A1 ...... 3.12, 5.6, 5.33, 6.5, 6.10,
6.38, 6.41, 10.5, App 1.1
para 13 .... 5.6
1A 6.4, 6.38, 6.41, 6.44, 6.46
Code of Practice 2.2, 2.4, 2.8, 3.1,
3.9, 3.10, 5.3, 5.8, 5.21, 5.27,
5.43, 12.3
Ch 5 .... 3.13
9 .... 2.15, 12.8
12 .... 5.3
para 2.7 .... 2.3
4.4 .... 2.5
4.12 .... 2.2
4.20 .... 2.4
4.26 .... 3.10
4.27 .... 3.10
4.44 .... 2.8
4.45 .... 2.8
5 .... 5.27
5.13 .... 2.8
5.28 .... 3.10
6.18 .... 15.12
6.32 .... 2.8
6.34 .... 2.8
8.1 .... 5.3
8.7 .... 5.3, 5.13
8.18 .... 5.27, 5.43
9.19 .... 2.15
9.49 .... 11.15
12.7 .... 5.5, 5.8
12.24 .... 5.5
Code of Practice,
supplementary Deprivation
of Liberty Safeguards 5.21
Mental Health Act 1983 .... 3.2, 3.5,
3.16, 6.2, 6.27, 6.28, 6.30,
6.43–6.46, 8.22, 9.6, 9.13,
9.14, 10.5, 10.8–10.10, 13.22,
13.47, 13.54, 13.56, 13.58,
13.60, 13.61, 13.66, App 4.2,
App 9.1
s 2 .... 6.30, 9.13, 10.5
3 .... 6.30, 8.24, 9.5, 10.5, 13.41,
13.56, 13.57, 13.59, 13.60
7 .... 6.46
12(2) .... App 9.1
17 .... 6.46
17A 6.46
57 .... 3.5, 10.8, 13.56
58 .... 3.5, 10.8, 13.56, 13.64
58A 10.8

PARA

Mental Health Act 1983 – *contd*
s 63 .... 3.5, 6.5, 6.48, 9.5, 10.8, 10.9,
13.37, 13.56–13.60, 13.62–
13.65
118 .... 4.4
118, Code of Practice 4.4, 13.62,
App 4.2
para iv 4.4
33 .... 4.4
36.3–36.15 .... App 4.2
36.10–12 .... 4.4
s 131 .... 3.12, 6.27, 10.5
(2)–(5) 4.6
(4) 10.5
145(1) 8.6, 13.58
Mental Health Act 2007 .... 3.1, 10.8
National Health Service
Act 1977 .... 1.7
National Health Service
(Scotland) Act 1978 .... App 8.1
National Health Service
Act 2006 .... App 8.1
Offences Against the Person
Act 1861 .... 8.2, 8.8, 8.18, App 8.9
s 58 .... 8.2, 8.18, 9.11, App 8.1
59 .... 8.18, App 8.1

PARA

Senior Courts Act 1981 .... 3.1
s 19 .... 3.1
(2)(b) 3.1
61 .... 5.52
90(1) 5.11
116 .... 14.36
Sch 1 .... 5.52, 5.61
para 3(b)(ii) 5.40, 5.42
Solicitors Act 1974—
s 1 .... App 8.2
Statistics and Registration Service
Act 2007—
s 1 .... App 8.2
5 .... App 8.2
Suicide Act 1961 .... 13.6, 13.7
s 1 .... 13.6
2 .... 13.6–13.9, 13.11, 13.15, 13.17
(1) 13.9, 13.11
(4) 13.9
Theft Act 1968 .... 14.27
s 4 .... 14.31
Unfair Contract Terms
Act 1977—
s 2(1) 11.11
Visiting Forces Act 1952—
Pt 1 .... App 8.1

Table of Statutory Instruments

PARA

Abortion (Amendment) (England)
Regulations 2002,
SI 2002/887—
reg 6 .... App 8.5
Schedule .... App 8.5
Abortion (Amendment) (Wales)
Regulations 2002,
SI 2002/2879—
reg 6 .... App 8.5
Schedule .... App 8.5
Abortion Regulations 1991,
SI 1991/499 .... 8.10, App 8.2, App
8.3, App 8.4, App 8.5
regs 1–6 .... App 8.2
reg 3(1) 8.10
(a)(ii) 8.10
(2), (3) .... App 8.2
4(1) 8.10
Sch 1 .... 8.10
Pt I .... App 8.2
II .... App 8.2
2 .... 8.10, App 8.2
2, paras 1–15 .... App 8.5
3 .... App 8.2
Civil Procedure Rules 1998,
SI 1998/3132 ...... 5.21, 5.22, 5.42,
5.61
r 2.1(2) 5.42, 5.61
Pt 7 .... 5.34, 5.61
PD 7A, paras 8, 9 .... 5.34
Pt 8 .... 5.34, 5.61
r 8.1(2)(a) 5.61
PD 9A 5.34
9A, para 14 .... 5.34
9B 5.31
para 3 .... 5.31
4 .... 5.31
7 .... 5.31
9E 5.25–5.28, 5.32, 5.44

PARA

Civil Procedure Rules 1998,
SI 1998/3132 – contd
PD 9E, paras 3–7 .... 5.25
para 8 .... 5.26, 5.29, 5.35
10 .... 5.31
paras 11–16 .... 5.26
11–13 .... 5.32
para 11 .... 5.34
12 .... 5.35
paras 14–16 .... 5.36
para 16 .... 5.28
paras 17, 18 .... 5.37
10A 5.33
para 3.5 .... 5.33
8.2 .... 5.33
10B 5.9, 5.35, 5.55
para 2 .... 5.35
3 .... 5.35
4 .... 5.35
5 .... 5.35, 5.55
9 .... 5.35
13A 5.28
Pt 2 .... 5.28
paras 10–11 .... 5.28
Pt 2, paras 12–21 .... 5.28
24–26 .... 5.28
paras 24–25 .... 5.28
para 27 .... 5.28
28 .... 5.28
14A 5.36, 5.37
Annex 2 .... 5.37
15A 5.36
17A 5.29
fn 1 .... 5.29
19A 5.38
19B 5.38
20A 5.39
Pt 23 .... 5.34
r 39(2) 5.61

	PARA
Civil Procedure Rules 1998,	
SI 1998/3132 – *contd*	
Pt 43	5.59
44	5.59
r 44.3(2)	5.59
44.9–44.12	5.59
Pt 47	5.59
48	5.59
Court of Protection Rules 2007,	
SI 2007/1744	5.21, 5.22, 10.11
r 3(1)	5.22
3(3)	5.22
4	5.22
5(1)	5.22
(2)	5.22
9	5.21, 5.22
Pt 5	5.22
r 25	5.22
26	5.22
27	5.22, 5.23
(1)	5.22
28(a)	5.22
(b)	5.22
33(b)	5.22
49	5.32, 5.34
Pt 8	5.30, 8.30
rr 50–60	5.30
51–53	5.30
r 51(3), (4)	5.30
54(1)	5.34
Pt 9, PD E	8.22, 12.15, 12.17
(5)	8.22
(c)	7.19
(14)(b)	12.19
r 61(2)	5.34
(1)	5.32
63	5.32, 5.34
63(c)(iii)	5.31
64	5.34
66	5.34
69	5.34
70	5.34
71	5.24
72	5.34
(6)	5.31
73	5.31
(1)–(4)	5.31
(4)	5.32
74	5.31
75	5.31
76	5.31
Pt 10	5.28, 5.34
r 78(1), (5)	5.28

	PARA
Court of Protection Rules 2007,	
SI 2007/1744 – *contd*	
r 82	5.23
Pt 10A	5.33
r 82A	5.33
Pt 13	5.28
rr 90–93	5.28
r 90	5.31
(1)	5.28
(2)	5.28
(3)(a), (b)	5.28
91(2), (3)	5.28
(3)(a), (b)	5.28
92(1)(a)–(c)	5.28
(2)	5.28
r 93(1)(a)–(c)	5.28
Pt 14	5.36, 5.37, 7.19
rr 94–118	5.36, 5.37
117–118	5.36
Pt 15	5.36, 7.19
rr 119–131	5.36
Pt 16	5.36
rr 132–139	5.36
Pt 17	5.29
rr 140–149	5.29
r 140	5.30
141(1)	5.29
(1)(a), (c)	5.29
(2)(b)	5.29
147	5.29
Pt 19	5.38
rr 155–168	5.38
156–158	5.38
r 157	5.38
159(1), (2)	5.38
163	5.38
167	5.38
Pt 20	5.39
rr 169–182	5.39
r 170	5.31
172(1)	5.39
(2)	5.31
(8)	5.39
180	5.39
Court of Protection (Amendment)	
Rules 2009, SI 2009/582	5.33
Family Proceedings Rules 1991,	
SI 1991/1247	5.28, 5.42
r 1.2	5.42, 5.52, 5.61
1.3	5.42
(1)	5.42, 5.52, 5.53
9.2A	5.49
9.5	5.49

PARA

Family Proceedings Rules 1991,
SI 1991/1247 – *contd*
r 10.28 .... 5.28
(1) 5.59
(3)(f) 5.56
(4) 5.56
(8) 5.56
Human Tissue Act 2004 (Persons
who Lack Capacity to
Consent and Transplants)
Regulations 2006,
SI 2006/1659—
reg 3(1) 15.12
3(2)(a) 15.12
9 .... 15.8
10 .... 15.10
11 .... 15.15
(8), (9) 15.15
12 .... 15.15
13 .... 15.15
14 .... 15.15
Pt 3 .... 15.9, 15.10
Mental Capacity Act 2005
(Independent Mental
Capacity Advocates)
(General) Regulations 2006,
SI 2006/1832—
reg 4 .... 5.25

PARA

Mental Capacity Act 2005
(Transfer of Proceedings)
Order 2007, SI 2007/1899 ...... 5.5

Mental Capacity Act 2005
(Transitional and
Consequential Provisions)
Order 2007, SI 2007/1898—
art 3 .... 11.11

Non-Contentious Probate
Rules 1987, SI 1987/2024—
r 22 .... 14.36

Prescriptions Only Medicines Act
(Human Use) Amendment
(No 3) Order 2000,
SI 2000/3231 .... 8.18

Rules of the Supreme Court 1965,
SI 1965/828 .... 5.42, 5.52

Rules of the Supreme Court
(Revision) 1965,
SI 1965/1776 .... 5.52
Pt 2, Order 7, r 2 .... 5.53
r 3(1) 5.52
5 .... 5.53, 5.60
10, Appendix A 5.53
Sch 1 .... 5.52, 5.53

Table of Cases

PARA

A

A, *Re* [1992] 3 Med LR 303 .... 12.2, 12.3, 14.6

A (children) (conjoined twins: surgical separation), *Re* [2000] 4 All ER
    961, [2000] 3 FCR 577, [2000] 1 FLR 1, [2001] Fam Law 18, CA 4.7, 4.9,
    4.12

A (medical treatment: male sterilisation), *Re*, sub nom A (male
    sterilisation), *Re* [2000] 1 FCR 193, 53 BMLR 66,
    [2000] 02 LS Gaz R 30, [2000] 1 FLR 549, CA 3.13, 3.14, 6.21, 7.9, 7.13,
    7.17

A v A Health Authority and Another [2002] 3 WLR 24, [2002] EWHC 18
    (Fam) 5.7

A Hospital v SW & A PCT [2007] EWHC 425 (Fam), [2007] LS Law
    Medical 273 .... 5.38, 12.3, 12.6

A PCT & P v AH & A Local Authority [2008] EWHC 1403 (Fam),
    [2009] 1 FCR 567 .... 3.15

A PCT v TB [2009] EWHC 1737 (Fam), [2009] Fam Law 1032 .... 6.47

AB and others v Leeds Teaching Hospitals NHS Trust & Cardiff and Vale
    NHS Trust [2004] EWHC 644 (QB), [2005] QB 506 .... 15.19

AC, *Re* (1987) 533 A 2d 611 .... 9.11

AC, *Re* (1990) 573 A.2d 1235 .... 9.4

Abbas v Kenney [1996] 7 Med LR 47 .... 1.11

Airedale NHS Trust v Bland [1993] AC 789, [1993] 2 WLR 316,
    [1993] 1 FLR 1026, [1993] AC 865, [1993] AC 883, HL 3.14, 4.14, 10.7,
        10.9, 12.1, 12.3, 12.4, 12.6–12.10, 12.12, 12.14, 12.16, 12.19,
            12.21, 12.24, 13.16–13.18, 13.25, 14.2, 14.8, 14.19

Al Hamwi v Johnston and North West London Hospitals NHS Trust
    [2005] Lloyd's Rep Med 309, [2005] EWHC 206 (QB) 1.21

Andronicou and Constantinou v Greece (1997) 25 EHRR 491,
    [1998] Crim LR 823 .... 13.54

Associated Provincial Picture Houses Ltd v Wednesbury Corporation
    [1948] 1 KB 223, [1947] 2 All ER 680 .... 1.7, 13.64, 13.65

Attorney General's Reference (No 3 of 1994) [1998] AC 245,
    [1997] 3 All ER 936, [1997] 3 WLR 421, [1998] 1 Cr App Rep 91,
    [1997] Crim LR 829, HL 9.2, 9.11

Attorney General's Reference (No 6 of 1980) [1981] All ER 715 .... 1.9

Austin and Saxby v Metropolitan Police Commissioner [2009] UKHL 5,
    [2009] 1 AC 564 .... 6.36

PARA

B

B (a minor) (treatment and secure accommodation), sub nom A
Metropolitan Borough Council v DB, *Re* [1997] 1 FCR 618,
[1997] 1 FLR 767 .... 10.5
B (a minor) (wardship: medical treatment), *Re* [1990] 3 All ER 927, [1981]
[1981] 1 WLR 1421, CA 4.10, 4.13
B (a minor) (wardship: sterilisation), *Re* [1988] AC 199, [1987] 2 All ER
206, HL 7.11, 7.12, 7.14, 7.21
B (a Minor), *Re* [2009] LS Law Med 214 .... 5.9, 5.46
B (Adult: Refusal of Medical Treatment), *Re* [2002] EWHC 429 (Fam),
[2002] 2 All ER 449, Fam D 4.7
B (child: termination of pregnancy), *Re* [1991] FCR 889, [1991] 2 FLR
426, [1991] Fam Law 379, Fam D 8.24
B v An NHS Hospital Trust, [2002] Lloyd's Rep Med 265 .... 3.5
B v Croydon Health Authority [1995] Fam 133, [1995] 2 WLR 294,
[1995] 1 All ER 683, (1994) 22 BMLR 13, CA 3.5, 6.5, 8.6, 9.5, 9.6, 10.7–
10.9, 13.17, 13.57, 13.59, 13.61, 13.63
B NHS Trust v J [2006] EWHC 3152 (Fam), (2007) 94 BMLR 15, [2006]
All ER (D) 290 (Nov), Fam D 3.14, 12.3, 12.14
Baby Boy Doe, *Re* (1994) 632 NE 2d 32 .... 9.11
Banks v Goodfellow (1870) LR 5 QB 549, 39 LJQB 237,
[1861–73] All ER Rep 47, Ct of QB .... App 9.1
Barr v Matthews (1999) 52 BMLR 217, QBD 8.6
Bassilious v General Medical Council [2008] EWHC 2857 (Admin),
[2008] All ER (D) 205 (Nov), Admin Ct 1.23
Bellinger v Bellinger (Lord Chancellor intervening) [2003] UKHL 21,
[2003] 2 AC 467, [2003] 2 All ER 593, HL 1.9
Birch v University College London Hospital NHS Foundation Trust
(2008) 104 BMLR 168 .... 1.28
Bolam v Friern Barnet Hospital Management Committee [1957] 1 WLR
582; [1957] 2 All ER 118 .... 1.20, 1.23, 1.28, 1.38, 3.14, 7.8, 12.3, 12.6, 12.16
Bolton Hospitals NHS Trust v O [2003] 1 FLR 824, [2003] Fam Law 319,
Fam D 9.13
Bournewood case, *See HL v UK—*
Bronda v Italy (Application 22430/93) (1998) 33 EHRR 4, [1998] ECHR
22430/93 [1998] EHRLR 756, ECtHR 4.9
Bruggeman and Scheuten v Federal Republic of Germany (1978) 10 DR E
Com HR 100, ECommHR 9.11
Buchanan v Milton [1999] 2 FLR 844 Fam Div 14.36
Buck v Bell 247 US 200 .... 7.1
Burrows v HM Coroner for Preston [2008] EWHC 1387 (QB),
[2008] 2 FLR 1225, QBD 14.27, 14.36
Burton v Islington Health Authority [1993] QB 204, [1992] 3 All ER
833, CA. 9.2, 9.11

C

C (a child) (HIV testing), *Re* [2000] Fam 48, [2000] 2 WLR 270,
[1999] 3 FCR 289, Fam D 4.9
C (a minor), *Re* [1990] Fam 26, [1989] 2 All ER 782, [1989] 3 WLR
240, CA 4.10
C (a minor) (detention for medical treatment), *Re* [1997] 3 FCR 49,
[1997] 2 FLR 180, Fam D 10.5

C (a minor) (medical treatment), *Re* [1998] 1 FCR 1, [1998] 1 FLR 384,
[1998] Lloyd's Rep Med 1, [1998] Fam Law 135 .... 4.10, 14.21
C (Adult: Refusal of medical treatment), *Re* [1994] 1 All ER 819,
[1994] 1 WLR 290, 15 BMLR 77, [1993] NLJR 1642, Fam D ... 4.7, 9.9, 11.8,
13.61, App 9.1
C (Welfare of Child: Immunisation), *Re* sub nom C (a Child)
(Immunisation: Parental rights), *Re*; Re F (a Child) (Immunisation:
Parental rights) [2003] EWCA Civ 1148, [2003] 2 FLR 1095 .... 4.4, 4.9
C v S [1988] QB 135, [1987] 2 WLR 1108, [1987] 1 All ER 1230,
[1987] 2 FLR 505, [1987] Fam Law 269 .... 2.9, 8.20, 8.24, 9.2, 9.11, 14.31
Canterbury v Spense 464 F 2d 772 (1972) (USA) 1.22
Case Number EA/2008/0074; ICO Decision Reference FS50122432 (heard
on 29 May–3 June 2009) 8.31
Chatterton v Gerson [1981] QB 432, [1981] 1 All ER 257, QBD 1.4, 1.19, 1.31,
2.3
Ciarlariello v Schacter 100 DLR (94th) 609 (1983) (SCC), (1994) 5 Med
LR 213, Can SC 2.12
City of Sunderland v PS and CA (2004) 40 EHRR 761, 81 BMLR 131,
ECtHR 3.16
Clift v Schwabe (1846) 3 CB 437, 17 LJCP 2, 7 LTOS 342, Ex Ch 13.2
Corr (Administratrix of Corr decd) v IBC Vehicles Ltd [2008] UKHL 13,
[2008] 1 AC 884, [2008] 2 All ER 943, HL 13.30
Cossey v UK (1990) 13 EHRR 622, [1993] 2 FCR 97, ECtHR 1.9
Costello-Roberts v United Kingdom (Application 13134/87)
(1993) 19 EHRR 112, [1994] 1 FCR 65, ECtHR 4.3
Crouse Irving Memorial Hospital v Paddock 485 NYS 2d 443 (1985) 9.11
Curran v Bosze (1990) 566 NE 2d 1319 .... 15.14

D

D (a minor) (wardship: sterilisation), *Re* [1976] Fam 185, [1976] 1 All ER
326, Fam D 4.6, 4.10, 7.10–7.12, 7.21
D (adult: medical treatment), *Re* [1988] 1 FCR 498, [1998] 1 FLR 411,
(9 November 2000, unreported) 12.13, 12.19, 12.21
D (Medical treatment: Mentally Disabled Patient), *Re* [1998] 2 FCR 178,
[1998] 2 FLR 22, Fam D 6.19
DS v JS & An NHS Trust, [2002] EWHC 2734 (Fam), [2003] 1 FLR 879,
Fam D 3.14
Davis (deceased), *Re* [1968] 1 QB 72, [1967] 1 All ER 688, CA 13.2
Dehler v Ottawa Civic Hospital (1980) 25 OR (2d) 748, (1979) 29 OR (2d)
677 .... 9.2
Deriche v Ealing Hospital NHS Trust [2003] EWHC 3104 (QB), [2003]
All ER (D) 373 (Dec), QBD 1.27
Director of Public Prosecutions v Kebilene, *see R v Director of Public
Prosecutions v Kebilene—*
Dobson v North Tyneside Health Authority and Another (1997) Med LR
110, [1997] 1 WLR 596, (1998) Med LR 6(2) 247 .... 14.30, 14.31, 14.35
Dodsto v Sweden (2007) 45 EHRR 22, ECHR 14.36
Doodeward v Spence (1908) 6 CLR 406, 15 ALR 105, 95 R (NSW) 107,
Aust HC 14.29–14.31, 14.33, 15.19

PARA
E
E (a minor), *Re* [1992] 2 FCR 219, [1993] 1 FLR 386, [1993] Fam Law
116, Fam D 4.3, 4.6, 4.9, 4.10, 11.17, 11.19
E (a minor) (medical treatment), *Re* [1991] FCR 771, [1991] 2 FLR 585,
[1992] Fam Law 15, 7 BMLR 117, Fam D 7.8, 7.21

F
F (in utero), *Re* [1988] Fam 122, [1988] 2 All ER 193, CA 9.2, 9.4
F (mental patient: sterilisation), *Re* [1990] 2 AC 1, [1988] AC 199 ..... 3.8, 3.14, 7.8,
7.9, 7.11, 7.12, 7.14, 7.15, 7.21, 8.22, 9.2, 9.3, 9.6
F v F (unreported), *The Times*, April 29, 1991 .... 7.8
F v Riverside Mental Health NHS Trust [1994] 2 FCR 577, [1994] 1 FLR
614, Fam D 10.8
Freeman v Home Office (No 2) [1984] QB 524, [1984] 1 All ER
1036, CA 1.4
Frenchay Healthcare NHS Trust v S [1994] 1 WLR 601, [1994] 2 All ER
403, [1994] 1 FLR 485, [1994] 3 FCR 121, [1994] Fam Law 320 ... 12.3, 12.20

G
G (persistent vegetative state), *Re* [1995] 2 FCR 46, Fam D 12.14
GF, *Re* [1991] FCR 786, [1992] 1 FLR 293, Faqm D 7.8
G-U (a minor) (wardship), *Re* [1984] FLR 811; [1984] Fam Law 248 .... 8.21
Garcia v Switzerland, Application No 10148/82 .... 4.9
Gillick v West Norfolk and Wisbech AHA [1986] AC 112, [1985] 3 WLR
830, [1985] 3 All ER 402, HL 4.3, 4.4, 4.6, 4.7, 4.9, 4.17, 7.21, 7.23, 8.21,
10.2, 10.4–10.6, 13.22, 13.66, 15.13, App 8.9, App 9.1
Glass v United Kingdom [2004] 1 FLR 1019, (2004) 39 EHRR 15 .... 4.9, 4.13
Gold v Haringey Health Authority [1988] QB 481, [1987] 2 All ER 888 .... 1.5, 1.20
Gonzales v Carhart (2007) 550 US 124 .... 8.31
Goodwin v UK (2002) EHRR 18, [2002] IRLR 664 .... 1.9

H
H (adult: medical treatment), *Re* [1998] 2 FLR 36, [1998] 3 FCR 174 .... 12.13
H v Norway (1992) 73 DR 155, E Com HR 9.11
HE v A Hospital NHS Trust [2003] 2 FLR 408, [2003] EWHC 1017
(Fam) 2.14
Hartstone v Gardner [2008] 2 FLR 1681, [2008] Fam Law 985 .... 14.36
Haughian v Paine [1987] 4 WWR 97, 37 DLR (4th) 624 (Sask CA) 1.28
Herczegfalvy v Austria (1992) 15 EHRR 437, 18 BMLR 48 .... 6.12
HL v United Kingdom (Application 45508/99) ('the Bournewood case')
(2005) 40 EHRR 32, (2004) 40 EHRR 761, [2004] All ER (D) 39
(Oct), ECtHR 3.16, 6.27, 6.30, 6.31, 6.33
HM v Switzerland [2002] MHLR 209 .... 6.34
Hoffman v Austria (1993) 17 EHRR 293, [1994] 1 FCR 193 .... 4.9

I
In the matter of P [2009] EWHC 163 (Ch), [2009] 2 All ER 119 .... 3.13
In the matter of SA (A Local Authority v (1) MA (2) NA and (3) SA (by
her children's guardian LJ) [2006] 1 FLR 867, [2005] EWHC 2942
(Fam) 5.2, 5.61
In the matter of Unborn Baby D (Bury Metropolitan Borough Council v D)
[2009] EWHC 446 (Fam), [2009] All ER (D) 266 (Mar) 5.2

J

J (a minor) (child in care: medical treatment), *Re* [1993] Fam 15,
[1992] 4 All ER 614 .... 1.6, 1.7, 1.16, 2.11, 2.12, 12.23
J (a minor) (wardship: medical treatment), *Re* [1991] Fam 33,
[1991] 2 WLR 140, [1990] 3 All ER 930, [1990] 2 Med. LR
67, CA 4.4, 4.10, 4.15, 6.21, 8.6, 14.22
J (Specific Issue Orders: child's religious upbringing and circumcision), *Re*
[2000] 1 FLR 571 .... 4.4, 5.45, 11.17
JE v DE and Surrey County Council [2007] MHLR 39 .... 6.32, 6.36
JR, GR, RR & YR v Switzerland No 22398/93 Dec 5/4/95, DR 81 .... 4.7
JS C and CH C v Wren [1987] 2 WWR 669 .... 8.21
Janaway v Salford Area Health Authority [1989] AC 537, [1988] 2 WLR
442 .... 8.6, 8.9
Jefferson v Griffin Spalding County Hospital Authority (1981) 274 SE 2d
457 .... 9.4, 9.11
Jepson v Chief Constable of West Mercia Police Constabulary
[2003] EWHC 3318 (Admin) 8.17
Johansen v Norway (1996) 23 EHRR 33, [1996] ECHR 17383/90 .... 4.9
Joyce v Merton and Sutton and Wandsworth Health Authority [1995] 6
Med LR 60 .... 12.16

K

K (a Child), *Re* [2006] 2 FLR 883, [2006] EWHC 1007 (Fam) 14.22
K, W and H (minors) (consent to treatment), *Re* [1993] 1 FLR 854,
[1993] 1 FCR 240 .... 4.6
KB, *Re* [1997] 2 FLR 180, [1997] Fam Law 474 .... 3.5
Keegan v Ireland (1994) 18 EHRR 342 .... 4.3
Keenan v United Kingdom (Application 27229/95) (2001) *Times*, 18 April,
10 BHRC 319, [2001] ECHR 27229/95, (2001) 33 EHRR 38,
(2001) 33 EHRR CD 362 .... 13.36, 13.40–13.42, 13.44

L

L (A Child) (Medical Treatment: Benefit), *Re*, sub nom Winston-Jones (a
child) (medical treatment: parent's consent), *Re* [2004] EWHC 2713
(Fam), [2005] 1 FLR 491, [2004] All ER (D) 313 (Oct), Fam D 4.15
L (an adult: non-consensual treatment), *Re* [1997] 1 FCR 609,
[1997] 2 FLR 837 .... 9.7
LC (medical treatment: sterilisation), *Re* [1997] 2 FLR 258,
[1997] Fam Law 604 .... 3.14, 7.9, 7.11, 7.18
LLBC v TG, JG and HR (and others) [2007] EWHC 2640 (Fam), [2007]
MHLR 203 .... 5.36, 5.57, 5.58, 6.36
Little v Little (1979) 576 W 2d 493 .... 15.14
Local Authority X v (1) MM (by her Litigation Friend the Official
Solicitor) (2) KM [2007] EWHC 2003 (Fam), (2009) 1 FLR 443 .... 2.2, 2.5,
11.4
Lybert v Warrington Health Authority [1996] 7 Med LR 71, 25 BMLR
91 .... 1.21

M

M (Child: Refusal of Medical Treatment), *Re* [1999] 2 FCR 577,
[1999] FLR 1097 .... 4.6
M (Wardship: Sterilisation), *Re* [1988] 2 FLR 497, [1988] Fam Law 434 .... 7.22

PARA

MB (an adult: medical treatment), *Re* [1997] 2 FCR 541, [1997] 2 FLR
    426, [1997] Fam Law 542, [2002] EWHC 2781 (Fam), [1997] 8 Med
    LR 217, 38 BMLR 175, [1997] NLJR 600, [1998] 3 WLR 936,
    [1998] 3 All ER 673, CA ... 2.2, 2.5, 2.7, 3.7, 3.13, 3.16, 4.12, 4.13, 5.17, 6.22,
                    8.24, 8.25, 8.27, 8.29, 9.8, 9.12–9.14, 11.4, 11.6, App 9.1
McCann v UK (1995) 21 EHRR 97, [1995] ECHR 18984/91 .... 13.54
MacFarlane v Tayside Health Board [2000] 2 AC 59, [1999] 3 WLR
    1301 .... 7.3
Mabon v Mabon [2005] 3 WLR 460, [2005] EWCA Civ 634 .... 4.3, 4.7
Madyun, *Re* (1986) 573 A 2d 1259 .... 9.4, 9.11
Malette v Shulman [1991] 2 Med LR 162, (1990) 67 DLR 321 ..... 2.17, 11.2, 13.66
Medhurst v Medhurst 46 OR (2d) 263 (1984) 9.2
Moore v Regents University of California (1990) 793 P 2d 479 .... 14.27
Mouisel v France (2004) 38 EHRR 34, [2002] ECHR 67263/01, ECtHR 6.14

N

NK (No 2). Re (4 April 1990, unreported) 3.14
National Assembly for Wales Practice Note (Appointment of guardians in
    private law proceedings), June 2006 [2006] 2 FLR 143 .... 5.49
NHS Trust (An) v (1) MB (a Child by CAFCASS as guardian ad litem) (2)
    Mr and Mrs B [2006] 2 FLR 319, [2006] EWHC 507 (Fam) 14.20, 14.21
NHS Trust (An) v (1) A (adult patient: withdrawal of medical treatment),
    (2) SA [2005] EWCA Civ 1145, [2005] All ER (D) 07 (Sep),
    [2006] Lloyd's Rep Med 29, CA, *affirming* [2005] All ER (D) 110
    (Aug), Fam D 3.14, 4.15
NHS Trust (An) v B, *sub nom* An NHS Trust v MB [2006] EWHC 507
    (Fam), [2006] 2 FLR 319, Fam D .... 4.14–4.16, App 4.3
NHS Trust (An) v D [2000] 2 FLR 677, [2000] 2 FCR 577 .... 4.14, 14.22
NHS Trust (An) v D [2003] EWHC 2793 (Fam), [2004] 1 FLR 1110;
    [2004] Lloyd's Rep Med 107 .... 8.22, 8.26
NHS Trust (An) v H [2001] WL 483013 .... 12.10
NHS Trust (An) v M [2001] Fam 348, [2001] 1 All ER 801 .... 4.14
NHS Trust (An) v Mrs 'M' and An NHS Trust 'B' v Mrs 'H'
    [2001] 1 All ER 801, [2001] 1 FCR 406 .... 12.1–12.3, 12.21
NHS Trust (An) v SA [2006] EWCA Civ 1145, [2006] Lloyd's Rep Med
    29 .... 3.14
NHS Trust (An) v T [2005] 1 All ER 387, [2004] EWHC 1279 (Fam) 10.10
Nevmerzhitsky v Ukraine (2006) 43 EHRR 32, [2005] ECHR 54825/00 .... 13.39
Nielsen v Denmark (1988) 11 EHRR 175 .... 4.9, 10.5, App 4.2
Norfolk & Norwich Healthcare (NHS) Trust v W [1996] 2 FLR 613,
    [1997] 1 FCR 269 .... 8.25, 9.6

O

O (a minor) (medical treatment), *Re* [1993] 1 FCR 925, [1993] 2 FLR
    149 .... 11.17
OT, *Re* [2009] EWHC 633 (Fam) 3.13, 4.14, 4.16, 5.9, 5.17, 5.55
O'Brien v Cunard SS Co (1891) 28 NE 266 .... 1.18
Open Door and Dublin Well Woman v Ireland (1992) 15 EHRR 244 .... 9.11
Orange v Chief Constable of West Yorkshire [2001] EWCA Civ 611,
    [2002] QB 347 .... 13.30
Organ Retention Group Litigation, *Re* (AB v Leeds Teaching Hospital
    NHS Trust) [2004] EWHC 644 (QB), [2005] QB 506 .... 14.31, 14.33, 14.35

P

P (A Minor) (Wardship: Sterilisation), *Re* [1989] 1 FLR 182,
[1989] Fam Law 102 .... 7.22
P (Adult patient) (Consent to medical treatment), *Re* [2008] EWHC 1403
(Fam), [2009] 1 FCR 567, ... 6.5
P (Minor), *Re* [2004] 2 FLR 1117 .... 4.6, 11.19
Paton v British Pregnancy Advisory Service Trustees [1979] QB 276,
[1978] 3 WLR 687, [1978] 2 All ER 987, QBD 2.9, 7.4, 8.20, 8.24, 9.2,
9.11, App 8.9
Paton v United Kingdom (1980) 3 EHRR 408, EComHR 7.4, 8.24, 9.2, 9.11
Pearce v United Bristol Healthcare NHS Trust (1999) 48 BMLR 118 .... 1.4
Peters v Netherlands (1994) 77A DR 75 .... 1.21, 4.7, 4.9
Portsmouth NHS Trust v Wyatt, *See Wyatt (a child) (medical treatment:
parents' consent)*—
Practice Direction [2002] 1 WLR 325 .... 5.61
Practice Direction (Family Proceedings: Court Bundles), 27 July 2006
[2006] 2 FLR 199 .... 5.16
Practice Direction 20 April 2009, Attendance of Media Representatives at
Hearings in Family Proceedings 5.56
Practice Note (CAFCASS) [2006] 2 FLR 143 .... 5.12
Practice Note (Official Solicitor: Appointment) [2001] 2 FLR 155 .... 5.11, 5.50
Practice Note (Official Solicitor: Declaratory Proceedings: Medical and
Welfare Decisions for Adults who Lack Capacity) [2001] 2 FLR
158 .... 7.23
Practice Note (Official Solicitor: Declaratory Proceedings: Medical and
Welfare Decisions for Adults who Lack Capacity) [2006] 2 FLR
373 .... 7.23
Practice Note (Official Solicitor: Deputy Director of Legal Services
CAFCASS – Applications for reporting restriction orders') 18 March
2005, [2005] 2 FLR 120 .... 5.56
Practice Note (Official Solicitor: Sterilisation) [1996] 2 FLR 111 .... 7.23
Practice Note (Out of Hours) [2006] 2 FLR 354 .... 5.9, 5.55
President's Direction (Representation of Children in Family Proceedings
pursuant to Family Proceedings Rules 1991, Rule 9.5), 5 April 2004
[2004] 1 FLR 1188 .... 5.49
Pretty v United Kingdom (Application 2346/02) [2002] 2 FCR 97,
[2002] 2 FLR 45 .... 4.7
Prince v Massachusetts (1944) 321 US Reports 158 .... 4.9

R

R (a minor) (medical treatment), *Re* (Camden London Borough Council v
R (a minor)) [1993] 2 FCR 544, [1993] 2 FLR 757 .... 11.17
R (a minor) (wardship: consent to treatment), *Re* [1992] Fam 11,
[1991] 4 All ER 177, CA 4.3, 4.6, 8.21, 10.2, 11.19
R v Bourne [1939] 1 KB 687, [1938] 3 All ER 615, CCA .... 8.2, App 8.9
R v Bournewood Community Mental Health NHS Trust, *ex parte* L
[1999] AC 458 , [1998] 1 All ER 634, CA 3.16
R v Bristol Coroner,ex parte Kerr [1974] QB 652, [1974] 2 All ER
719, DC 14.28, 14.37
R v Brown [1994] 1 AC 212, [1993] 2 All ER 75, [1993] 2 WLR
556, HL 1.9, 2.10, 12.8

PARA

R v Cambridge Health Authority,ex parte B [1995] 2 All ER 129,
[1995] 1 WLR 898, CA 1.8

R v Cundick (1822) Dow & Ry NP 13 .... 15.8

R v HS Dhingra [1991] Birmingham Crown Court Judgment 24 January
1991 .... App 8.9

R v Director of Public Prosecutions, *ex parte* Kebeline, sub nom R v DPP,
ex parte Kebeline [2000] 2 AC 326, [1999] 4 All ER 801,
[1999] 3 WLR 972, DC 13.7

R v Dr Collins and Ashworth Hospital Authority, *ex parte* Brady
(2001) 58 BMLR 173, [2000] 1 MHLR 17, [2000] LS Law Medical
355, [2000] Lloyd's Med LR 355, QBD 2.5, 10.7, 10.9, 13.37, 13.53, 13.64,
13.66, 13.67

R v Emmett *Times*, October 15, 1999 .... 1.9

R v Gibbins and Proctor (1918) 13 Cr App R 134 .... 12.3

R v Gwynedd County Council, *ex parte* B [1992] 3 All ER 317,
[1991] FCR 800, CA 14.36

R v Iby [2005] NSWCCA 178 .... 14.4

R v Kelly [1999] QB 621, [1998] 3 All ER 741, [1999] 2 WLR 384, 51
BMLR 142 .... 14.27, 14.31, 14.33, 15.19

R v Kirklees Metropolitan Borough Council, *ex parte* C (a minor)
[1992] 2 FCR 321, [1992] 2 FLR 117 .... 10.5

R v Leonard Arthur (1981) 12 BMLR 1, Ct tbc 4.13

R v Lynn (1788) 1 Leach 497, 2 Term Rep 733, pre-SCJA 1873 .... 15.8

R v Malcherek; R v Steel [1981] 2 All ER 422, [1981] 1 WLR 690, CA 14.5

R v McDonald [1999] N I 150 .... 8.3

R v Ministry of Defence,ex parte Smith [1996] QB 517, [1996] 1 All ER
257, CA 13.64

R v North and East Devon Health Authority, *ex parte* Coughlan
[2000] 3 All ER 850, [1999] Lloyd's Rep Med 306 .... 1.7

R v North Derbyshire Health Authority, *ex parte* Fisher [1997] 8 Med LR
327, (1997) 38 BMLR 76 .... 1.8

R v North West Lancashire HA, *ex parte* A [2000] 1 WLR 977,
[2000] 2 FCR 525, CA 1.7

R v Portsmouth Hospitals NHS Trust, *ex parte* Glass (1999) 50 BMLR
269 .... 5.7

R v Richardson [1999] QB 444, [1998] 3 WLR 1292, CA 1.31

R v Secretary of State for Health & (1) Schering Health Care Ltd (2)
Family Planning Association (Interested Parties), ex parte John
Smeaton (on behalf of the Society for the Protection of the Unborn
Child) [2002] EWHC 2410 .... App 8.9

R v Secretary of State for Social Services, *ex parte* Hincks
(1980) 1 BMLR 93, CA 1.8

R v Sharp (1857) Dears & Bell 160 .... 14.27

R v Smith [1973] 1 WLR 1510, [1974] 1 All ER 376 .... 8.10

R v Tabassum [2000] Crim LR 686, [2000] All ER (D) 649, CA 1.31

R v United Kingdom. (1983) 33 DR 270 .... 13.7

R v Wilson [1997] QB 47, [1996] 3 WLR 125, [1996] 2 Cr App Rep
241, CA (Crim Div) 1.9, 2.10

R (on the application of Axon) v Secretary of State for Health and Family
Planning Association [2006] EWCA 37 (Admin), [2006] All ER (D)
148, (Admin) 4.3, 4.7, 4.9, 8.21

PARA

R (on the application of Burke) v General Medical Council and Disability
Rights Commission and Others [2006] QB 273, [2005] QB 424,
[2005] EWCA Civ 1003, CA 2.11, 3.13, 4.14, 4.15, 9.16, 14.23, 14.24
R (on the application of C) v Secretary of State for Justice [2008] EWCA
Civ 882, [2009] 2 WLR 1039, CA 6.11
R (on the application of G) v Mental Health Review Tribunal
[2004] EWHC 2193 (Admin), [2004] All ER (D) 86 (Oct) 6.36
R (on the application of Gillan) v Metropolitan Police Commissioner
[2006] UKHL 12, [2006] 2 AC 307, HL 6.36
R (on the application of Graham) and R (on the application of Allen) v
Secretary of State for Justice [2007] EWHC 2940 (Admin), [2007] All
ER (D) 383 (Nov) 6.14
R (on the application of Middleton) v West Somerset Coroner
[2004] UKHL 10, [2004] 2 AC 182, HL 13.40
R (on the application of Oliver Leslie Burke) v GMC [2006] QB 273,
[2005] 3 WLR 1132, [2005] EWCA Civ 1003 .... 3.6
R (on the application of Pretty) v Director of Public Prosecutions
[2002] 1 AC 800, (2002) 35 EHRR 1 .... 13.8, 13.10
R (on the application of PS) v Responsible Medical Officer & others
[2006] EWCA Civ 28, [2006] 1 WLR 810, CA [2003] EWHC 2335
(Admin) 3.5
R (on the application of Purdy) v Director of Public Prosecutions,
[2009] UKHL 45, [2009] 3 WLR 403, HL 13.9, 13.10, 13.15, 13.69
R (on the application of Rogers) v Swindon NHS Primary Care Trust
[2006] 1 WLR 2649, (2006) 89 BMLR 211 .... 1.8
R (on the application of Sacker) v West Yorkshire Coroner [2004] 2 All ER
487, [2004] 1 WLR 796, HL 13.40
R (on the application of Smeaton) v Secretary of State for Health
[2002] 2 FLR 146, [2002] EWHC 610 (Admin), (No 2)
[2002] EWHC 886 (Admin), [2002] All ER (D) 147 (May), Admin
Ct 8.18
R (on the application of Takoushis) v Inner North London Coroner
[2005] EWCA Civ 1440, [2006] 1 WLR 461, CA 13.40
R (on the application of Wilkinson) v RMO Broadmoor Hospital
[2002] 1 WLR 419, [2001] EWCA Civ 1545 .... 6.18, 13.64
R (on the application of Williamson and others) v Secretary of State for
Education [2005] UKHL 15, [2005] 2 AC 246, HL 4.3
Rance v Mid-Downs Health Authority [1991] 1 QB 587, [1991] 2 WLR
159, [1991] 1 All ER 801 .... 7.3, 8.3
Rand v East Dorset Health Authority (2000) 56 BMLR 39 .... 7.3
Raninen v Finland (1998) EHRR 563 .... 6.14
Rasmussen v Fleming (1987) 154 Ariz 207, P 2d 674 .... 12.1
Rees v Darlington Memorial Hospital NHS Trust [2004] 1 AC 309,
[2003] 3 WLR 1091 .... 7.3
Reeves v Metropolitan Police Commissioner [2000] 1 AC 360,
[1999] 3 All ER 897, HL 13.27, 13.29–13.33, 13.35, 13.38, 13.53
Reibl v Hughes (1980) 114 DLR (3d) 1 (Canada) 1.22
Rochdale Healthcare NHS Trust v C [2000] 1 AC 360, [1999] 3 All ER
897, HL 9.6
Rodriguez v British Columbia (1994) 107 DLR (4th) 342 .... 13.7
Rogers v Whitaker (1992) 109 ALR 625, (1993) 4 Med LR 79
(Australia) 1.22

PARA

Royal College of Nursing of the United Kingdom v Department of Health
and Social Security [1981] AC 800, [1981] 2 WLR 279 .... 8.8, 8.9

S

S, *Re* (30 November 1994, unreported), ... 12.21
S (a minor) (refusal of medical treatment), *Re* [1995] 1 FCR 604 .... 11.17
S (Adult Patient: Sterilisation), *Re* [2000] 3 WLR 1288, [2000] 2 FLR
389 .... 8.22
S (adult sterilisation), *Re* [1999] 1 FCR 277, [1998] 1 FLR 944 ...... 3.14, 7.9, 7.11,
7.18
S (adult: refusal of treatment), *Re* [1993] Fam 123, [1993] 1 Med L
Rev 92, (1992) 142 NLJ 1638 .... 9.4, 9.11, App 9.1
S (hospital patient: court's jurisdiction), *Re* [1996] Fam 1, [1995] 3 WLR
78, [1995] 3 All ER 290, CA 3.12, 12.17
S (hospital patient: foreign curator). Re [1996] Fam 23, [1995] 4 All ER
30, Fam D 3.14, 3.15
S (sterilisation), *Re* [2000] 2 FLR 389, [2000] 2 FCR 452,
[2000] Fam Law 711 .... 7.8, 7.12, 7.19
S & S sub nom C v V (2009) LS Law Medical 97 .... 3.13, 5.22, 5.29
S & S; W v Official Solicitor (or W) [1972] AC 24, [1970] 3 All ER
107, HL 2.11
SA (Vulnerable Adult with Capacity: Marriage), *Re* [2006] 1 FLR 867,
[2005] EWHC 2942 (Fam) 3.1
SG (a patient), *Re* [1991] 2 FLR 329, [1993] 4 Med LR 75 .... 8.22
SL (adult patient) (medical treatment), *Re* [2000] 1 FCR 361,
[2000] 2 FLR 389, (2000) Lloyds Law Reports (Medical) 339, CA ... 3.13, 3.14
SS (An Adult: Medical Treatment, Late Termination), *Re* [2002] 1 FLR
445, [2002] 1 FCR 73 .... 8.22, 8.24
Salford City Council v GJ [2008] 2 FLR 1295 .... 6.39
Savage v South Essex Partnership NHS Foundation Trust [2008] UKHL
74, [2009] 2 WLR 115, HL 13.27, 13.30, 13.41–13.43, 13.45, 13.50, 13.54,
13.55, 13.68
Secretary of State for the Home Department v JJ [2007] UKHL 45,
[2008] 1 AC 385, HL 6.34, 6.35
Secretary of State for the Home Department v Mental Health Review
Tribunal [2003] MHLR 202 .... 6.34
Secretary of State for the Home Department v Robb [1995] Fam 127,
[1995] 1 FLR 412, [1995] 1 All ER 677 ... 10.7, 12.8, 13.3, 13.16–13.18, 13.38
Sidaway v Board of Governors of the Bethlem Royal Hospital and the
Maudsley Hospital [1985] AC 871, [1985] 2 WLR 480, [1985] All ER
643 .... 1.4, 1.10, 1.20, 1.21, 1.23, 1.26–1.28, 3.14, 7.3, 9.2, App 9.1
Smiley v Home Office [2004] EWHC 240 (QB) , [2004] All ER (D) 243
(Feb), QBD 13.30
South West Hertfordshire Health Authority v KB, sub nom KB (Adult)
(Mental Patient: Medical Treatment), *Re* [1994] FCR 1051,
(1994) 19 BMLR 144 .... 10.8
St George's Healthcare NHS Trust v S, R v Collins,ex parte S (No.2)
[1999] Fam 26, [1998] 3 All ER 673, [1998] 3 WLR 936,
[1998] 2 FCR 685, [1998] 2 FLR 728, [1998] Fam Law 526, 44
BMLR 160, [1998] NLJR 693, CA 2.8, 2.11, 2.19, 3.7, 4.12, 8.24, 9.13,
9.14, App 9.1
Strunk v Strunk 445 SW 2d 145 (1969) 15.14

PARA

Swindon & Marlborough NHS Trust v S [1995] 3 Med LR 84, (1994)
 Guardian, 10 December 5.13

T

T (a Minor) (Wardship: Medical Treatment), *Re* [1997] 1 All ER 906,
 [1997] 1 WLR 242, CA 3.15, 4.9, 4.15, 11.18
T (adult: refusal of treatment), *Re* , [1992] 4 All ER 649 [1993] Fam
 95, CA 1.31–1.33, 2.6, 2.14, 7.7, 9.4, 9.11, 11.8, 11.9, 11.11, 11.13, 11.15,
                      App 9.1
T v T [1988] Fam 52, [1988] 1 All ER 613, Fam D 7.14, 9.3
TC, *Re* (A Minor) High Court (NI) [1994] 2 Med L Rev 376 .... 14.7
Tameside and Glossop Acute Services NHS Trust v CH [1996] 1 FCR 753,
 [1996] 1 FLR 762, (1996) 146 NLJ 1385 .... 8.25, 9.5, 9.6
Taylor v Shropshire Health Authority [1998] Lloyd's Rep Med 395 .... 1.16
Thor v Superior Court 5 Cal 4th 725 (1993) 13.37
Trust A and B v H (an Adult patient) [2006] EWHC 1230 (Fam) ,
 [2006] 2 FLR 958, Fam D 3.16, 6.5, 6.21
Trust A v M [2005] EWHC 807 (Fam), [2005] All ER (D) 198 (Apr), Fam
 D 12.14

U

University Hospital Lewisham NHS Trust v Hamuth [2006] EWHC 1609
 (Ch), [2006] Inquest LR 141 .... 14.37
Uyan v Turkey (Application no 7496/03), 8 January 2009 .... 6.14

V

VS (Adult: Mental Disorder), *Re* [1995] 3 Med L Rev 292 .... 13.59
Van Colle v Chief Constable of the Hertfordshire Police [2008] UKHL 50,
 [2009] 1 AC 225, HL 13.44
Villar v Sir Walter Gilbey [1907] AC 139, [1904–7] All ER Rep 779, HL 9.11
Vo v France (2005) 10 EHRR 12, [2005] Inquest Law Reports 128 .... 8.24, 9.2

W

W, *Re* [1993] 2 FCR 187, [1993] 1 FLR 381, Fam D 7.9, 7.11
W (a minor) (medical treatment: court's jurisdiction), *Re* [1993] Fam 64,
 [1992] 3 WLR 758, [1992] 2 FCR 785, [1992] 4 All ER 627, CA 4.1, 4.6,
                10.2, 10.4, 10.5, 11.19
W (Adult: Refusal of Treatment), *Re* [2002] EWHC 901 (Fam) 3.5, 13.34
W Healthcare NHS Trust v (1) KH, (2) H and (3) PH [2004] EWCA Civ
 1324, [2005] All ER (D) 94 (Jan), CA 3.13, 3.17
Washington v Glucksberg 521 US 702 (1997) 13.54
Wheatley v Lodge [1971] 1 All ER 173, [1971] 1 WLR 29, DC 1.14
Williams v Williams (1882) 20 Ch D 659, [1881–5] All ER Rep 840, Ch
 D 14.29, 14.35
Wyatt (a child) (medical treatment: parents' consent), *Re*, sub nom
 Portsmouth NHS Trust v Derek Wyatt and others [2004] EWHC 2247
 (Fam), [2005] 1 FLR 21, [2005] 2 FLR 480, [2004] All ER (D) 89
 (Oct) [2005] EWCA Civ 1181, Fam D 4.15, 5.56
Wyatt v (1) Portsmouth Hospital NHS Trust (2) Charlotte Wyatt (by her
 Guardian CAFCASS) [2005] EWCA Civ 1181, [2005] 1 WLR
 3995, CA 14.20

PARA

Wyatt v Dr Curtis and Central Nottinghamshire Health Authority
 [2003] EWCA Civ 1779, [2003] All ER (D) 493 (Oct), CA 1.27
Wyatt, *Re*, sub nom Portsmouth NHS Trust v Derek Wyatt and others
 [2005] EWHC 2293 (Fam), [2005] 4 All ER 1325, [2006] 1 FLR 652,
 [2005] All ER (D) 246 (Oct), Fam D 4.11

X

X (adult sterilisation), *Re* [1999] 3 FCR 426, [1998] 2 FLR 1124, Fam D 7.9,
 7.11, 7.18
X v Austria and the European Court of Justice fnn 1 and 2 of Nys, (1999)
 7(2) Med L Rev 7 209 .... 1.21, 4.7
X v Germany (1984) 7 EHRR 152, EComHR 13.39
X v Germany (8741/79) (unreported, March 10, 1981, Eur Comm HR) 14.36
X and Y v The Netherlands (1985) 8 EHRR 235, [1985] ECHR 8978/80,
 ECtHR 1.21, 4.7, 4.9

Y

Y (mental patient: bone marrow donation), *Re* [1997] Fam 110,
 [1997] 2 WLR 556, [1996] 2 FLR 787, [1997] 2 FCR 172 .... 3.15, 4.12, 15.14
Yearworth v North Bristol NHS Trust [2009] EWCA Civ 37,
 [2009] 2 All ER 986, (2009) LS Law Medical 126, CA 14.27, 14.31, 14.34
Yousef v Netherlands (2003) EHRR 345 [2002] 3 FCR 577, [2003] 1 FLR
 210, ECtHR 4.9

Z

Z (a minor) (identification: restrictions on publications), *Re* [1997] Fam 1,
 [1995] 4 All ER 961, CA 4.9
Z (an adult: capacity), *Re*; Local Authority v Z [2004] EWHC 2817 (Fam),
 [2005] 3 All ER 280, *The Times*, December 9, 2004, Fam D 13.20, 13.34
Z (medical treatment: hysterectomy), *Re* [2000] 1 FLR 523, [2000] 1 FCR
 274, Fam D 7.8, 7.12

Table of European Legislation

PARA

European Convention for the
Protection of Human Rights
and Fundamental Freedoms
1950 ...... 1.38, 4.7, 4.9, 5.28, 5.56,
6.11, 11.2, 13.7, 13.39, 13.46,
13.54
Art 2 .... 4.7, 4.14, 8.17, 8.24, 9.2,
12.1, 12.5, 13.8, 13.30, 13.39,
13.41, 13.43, 13.45, 13.46,
13.49, 13.54, 13.68, 14.2
(1) 13.54
3 .... 3.16, 4.7, 6.11–6.14, 6.16,
13.39
5 .... 4.7, 6.27, 6.29, 6.30, 6.32,
6.34, 6.36–6.38, 6.40, 6.49,
10.5
(1) 3.16, 6.28
(4) 3.16, 6.28, 6.40
8 ... 1.21, 1.34, 1.38, 4.4, 4.7, 4.9,
4.13, 4.17, 5.47, 7.1, 8.22,
11.2, 11.17, 13.7–13.11,
13.15, 13.46, 13.68, 14.36

PARA

European Convention for the Protection
of Human Rights and Fundamental
Freedoms 1950 – contd
Art 8(1) 1.21, 4.7, 8.22, 11.2, 13.8
(2) 4.7, 4.9, 8.22, 11.2, 13.8,
13.10
9 .... 11.2, 11.17
(1) 11.2
(2) 11.2
10 .... 13.7
12 .... 7.1
14 .... 4.7
United Nations Convention on the
Rights of the Child 4.3
Art 3(1) 4.9
7 .... 4.3
8 .... 4.6
12 .... 4.7
(1) 4.3
14(1) 4.3
(2) 4.3
16 .... 4.3

Table of International Legislation

PARA

Death (Definition) Act 1983
(South Australia)—
s 3 .... 14.4

Human Tissue Act 1983 (New
South Wales) 14.4

Human Tissue Act 1985
(Tasmania)—
s 27A 14.4

Human Tissue Transplant Act
(Northern Territories)—
s 23 .... 14.4

PARA

Human Tissues Act 1982
(Victoria)—
s 41 .... 14.4

Transplantation and Anatomy
Act 1979 (ACT)—
s 45 .... 14.4

Transplantation and Anatomy
Act 1979 (Queensland)—
s 45 .... 14.4

United Nations Convention on the
Rights of the Child .... App 4.2

Uniform Determination of Death
Act (1980) USA 14.3

Part 1

General principles

Chapter 1

Consent – General

A   Framework 1.1
       Introduction 1.1
       Proposal to treat 1.3
             Formulation of proposal 1.3
             Risks of treatment 1.4
             Alternative forms of treatment 1.5
             Compelling a doctor to treat 1.6
             Irrational decisions by care providers to refuse treatment 1.7
             Resources 1.8
             Treatment demanded by the patient 1.9
       Communication of the proposal 1.10
       Consent – state of mind 1.13
             Intention 1.13
             Comprehension 1.14
       Communication of consent 1.15
             Written consent 1.16
             Oral consent 1.17
             Conduct 1.18
B   Information about risks 1.19
       No doctrine of informed consent 1.19
       Duty of care – Common law position 1.20
       Article 8 1.21
       Other jurisdictions 1.22
       Current practice in the UK 1.23
       Delegation 1.25
       Duty to answer questions 1.26
       Information about alternative forms of treatment 1.28
       Known comparative outcomes 1.29
C   Vitiating factors 1.30
       Fraud 1.31
       Duress and undue influence 1.32
       Capacity 1.33
D   Scope of authority 1.34
E   Duration of authority 1.35

F   Withdrawal of authority 1.37
G   Conclusion 1.38

A FRAMEWORK

Introduction

1.1   The legality of all medical treatment is founded on the existence of consent or some other lawful authority. The general principle is that no form of medical treatment can be given without either the consent of the capable patient; or, if the patient is a child or an incapable adult, either the consent of someone with the authority to give consent on the patient's behalf or the authority of the court;[1] or, if the patient is incompetent and aged over 16, by reason of the common law doctrine of necessity (as applied within the statutory regime of the Mental Capacity Act 2005 ('MCA')[2]). The very structure of the last sentence displays the convoluted nature of the law in this area, which is a result of its piecemeal, largely accidental development.

1   If the patient is a child, the court can consent on their behalf; if the patient is an incompetent adult, a court can declare that proposed treatment would be lawful, being in their best interests.
2   See **APPENDIX 1.1**: Mental Capacity Act 2005.

1.2   This chapter addresses those cases in which consent is or can be obtained. Although the provision of medical treatment and the consent to it may form a legal contract, it need not do so. The process, however, is similar: there must be a proposal to treat (or 'offer' in contractual parlance); a communication of that proposal or offer; understanding of what is proposed; consent to or acceptance of it; and communication of the consent or acceptance by a patient possessing the relevant capacity. The ingredients necessary for a contract which will often be missing in the context of the National Health Service will be consideration for the offer of treatment, and intention to form legal relations in the contractual sense.

Proposal to treat

Formulation of proposal

1.3   It is axiomatic that no treatment will be undertaken unless a medical practitioner proposes to provide it. This is not the place to examine the medical thought process that leads to a decision to offer treatment, but it will usually be necessary for the doctor to have examined the patient, undertaken any preliminary investigations and enquiries, including the taking of a history, and, on the basis of the material so obtained, come to a diagnosis, provisional or firm. From this he[1] will deduce the appropriate form of treatment to offer.

1   Throughout the masculine form is used generically for 'he'/'she' and 'him'/'her'.

Risks of treatment

1.4 A doctor owes a duty of care to inform a patient about those risks of which any competent medical practitioner undertaking such treatment would warn a patient.[1] It will usually be the responsibility of the doctor to inform a patient of 'a significant risk which would affect the judgment of a reasonable patient'.[2] Further, there will be a duty to warn of any risk which is so grave that it is obvious that the patient has the right to know of it, whatever may be the accepted medical practice.[3] However, a failure to give such a warning does not render the treatment unlawful in the sense of being an assault, so long as the patient is given a general understanding of the nature of the treatment being proposed.[4] Any action would be in negligence.[5]

1 *Sidaway v Board of Governors of the Bethlem Royal Hospital and the Maudsley Hospital* [1985] AC 871. See also **CHAPTER 3**: Deciding for Others – Adults **PARA 3.14**; **APPENDIX 9.1** Court of Appeal Guidelines: RE MB Guidelines and St George's Healthcare v S Guidelines: para 3.
2 *Pearce v United Bristol Healthcare NHS Trust* (1999) 48 BMLR 118.
3 *Sidaway* (**N1** above).
4 *Chatterton v Gerson* [1981] QB 432; *Freeman v Home Office (No 2)* [1984] QB 524.
5 See **PARA 1.20** below: Duty of care.

Alternative forms of treatment

1.5 If there are alternative forms of treatment available, the doctor will need to consider which of those is in the best interests of the patient. Sometimes there is little to choose in terms of outcome, in which case he will doubtless decide to offer the treatment with which he is most familiar or which is most readily available. Whether he has to give the patient a choice may depend on the demands of competent medical practice in the precise circumstances. It was confirmed in *Gold v Haringey Health Authority*[1] that there was no duty to advise of alternative forms of treatment when not doing so was in accordance with a responsible body of opinion. However, the latest GMC guidance, which replaces and expands upon previous guidance, states baldly that:

'You must give patients the information they want or need about: ... (c) options for treating or managing the condition, including the option not to treat.'[2]

In effect, this guidance means that competent professional practice now requires advice to be given on the alternative forms of treatment, subject only to the qualifications mentioned in the guidance.[3] It is therefore likely to be negligent not to offer such advice.[4]

1 [1988] QB 481.
2 GMC: Consent: patients and doctors making decisions together (http://www.gmc-uk.org/guidance/ethical_guidance/consent_guidance/Consent_guidance.pdf), (2 June 2008) para 9.
3 *Ibid*, paras 13–17: Reasons for not sharing information with patients.
4 See **PARA 1.28** below: Information about alternative forms of treatment.

Compelling a doctor to treat

1.6 A doctor generally cannot be compelled to provide treatment which he does not consider to be in the patient's best interests.[1] This is so even if other practitioners consider the treatment desirable. This sensible rule is necessary: it would clearly be highly undesirable for both doctor and patient if an unwilling doctor could be forced to provide treatment he believed to be harmful to the patient or the effectiveness of which he doubted. The rule is consistent with the contractual rule that specific performance will not be granted to enforce the provision of personal services. However, doctors do need to be aware of the requirement to refer a patient for a second opinion if it is obvious that the patient wishes to receive treatment which is known to be available in other responsible and competent hands. A doctor is not entitled to restrict a patient's choice of treatment to satisfy his own conscience and might be found liable in an action for negligence if his advice did not conform to responsible and accepted medical practice or was not sustainable on rigorous logical scrutiny.[2]

1   *Re J (a minor) (child in care: medical treatment)* [1993] Fam 15. See also GMC: Consent: patients and doctors making decisions together (http://www.gmc-uk.org/guidance/ ethical_guidance/consent_guidance/Consent_guidance.pdf), para 5(d). But note **PARA 1.7** below.
2   The duties of a doctor as defined by the GMC include an obligation to make sure that personal beliefs do not prejudice patients' care; see **APPENDIX 1.7**: GMC: Good Medical Practice, (13 November 2006) paras 7 and 8. For a discussion about using a refusal of consent as a backdoor method of securing treatment which a doctor does not wish to provide see **CHAPTER 2**: Consent – Adults **PARA 2.11**. And for a discussion about a doctor's position who is in principle against withdrawal of feeding/hydration for a patient in a Permanent Vegetative State see **CHAPTER 12**: Permanent Vegetative State **PARA 12.23**.

Irrational decisions by care providers to refuse treatment

1.7   There is no English authority on whether a doctor can be required to provide treatment which he refuses to give on irrational or discriminatory grounds. Two principles would appear to clash: the rule against forcing someone to provide personal services[1] and the public law principle requiring rational decisions to be made by those exercising public administrative functions.[2] The courts have jurisdiction to compel a health authority to provide treatment where an irrational or, in some circumstances, unfair decision to refuse it has been made.[3] If such a refusal arose because of an irrational decision of the only doctor available to provide treatment, then it is likely that the courts would act to ensure that treatment was provided, if this was practicable.

1   *Re J (a minor) (child in care: medical treatment)* [1993] Fam 15.
2   *Associated Provincial Picture Houses Ltd v Wednesbury Corpn* [1948] 1 KB 223; *R v North and East Devon Health Authority, ex p Coughlan* [1999] Lloyd's Rep Med 306.
3   *Ex parte Coughlan* (**N2** above); *R v North West Lancashire HA, ex p A* [2000] 1 WLR 977, CA (health authority had acted unlawfully in the rigid operation of a policy which resulted in a refusal to provide gender reassignment surgery under the National Health Service Act 1977).

Resources

1.8   Problems may arise where the form of treatment the doctor would like to offer is unavailable in his hospital or practice because of a lack of resources over which he has no control. Generally, health authorities are at liberty to allocate resources in the best way they see fit in the fulfilment of their statutory duties.[1] This power is, nevertheless, under constant challenge in the courts.[2] An individual doctor is unlikely to be criticised where he is not given the relevant resources, but in such circumstances he will have to consider whether the patient should be referred to a centre which has them.

1   *R v Secretary of State for Social Services, ex p Hincks* (1980) 1 BMLR 93; *R v Cambridge Health Authority, ex p B* [1995] 1 WLR 898.
2   For example, *R v North Derbyshire Health Authority, ex p Fisher* [1997] 8 Med LR 327, (1997) 38 BMLR 76, CA per Dyson J (health authority refusal to fund beta interferon treatment on the ground of insufficient resources successfully challenged on ground that health authority policy failed to pay sufficient heed to NHS Executive circular asking Health Authorities to facilitate introduction of the drug); and *R (Rogers) v Swindon NHS Primary Care Trust* [2006] 1 WLR 2649, (2006) 89 BMLR 211 (Primary Care Trust's policy of refusing funding for treatment with unlicensed drug Herceptin, save where there were exceptional personal or clinical circumstances, successfully challenged on the ground that it was irrational as it was not possible to envisage what such circumstances would be).

Treatment demanded by the patient

1.9   There are limits to the extent to which consent is capable of providing a defence in criminal law to offences of assault.[1] It is generally accepted that 'reasonable surgical interference' is lawful and would not render the surgeon open to a criminal prosecution. This so-called 'medical exception' has been justified on the ground of the public interest[2] or for therapeutic purposes.[3] But what about surgery which has no therapeutic purpose, such as surgery solely for cosmetic purposes, which cannot be justified on the basis of public interest but, it seems, has always been accepted as lawful where a patient with capacity gives consent? And what is to be regarded as 'reasonable surgical interference'? Gender reassignment surgery, which involves the removal of healthy body parts and is irreversible, has always been regarded as lawful.[4] In contrast, there is much controversy over the position of patients who suffer from body dysmorphic disorder[5] and who wish the amputation of a healthy limb.[6] There is debate over the categorisation of the condition and its appropriate treatment. It is suggested it is at least strongly arguable that, given that the criminal law does not interfere with cosmetic surgery, it should not do so in cases where the amputation of a healthy limb would lead to the alleviation of a patient's suffering and reduce the risk of them harming themselves.[7] Such cases will have to be carefully defined: we would suggest they would comprise the rare cases where a patient with capacity has given fully informed consent and where all other avenues for treatment have proved unsuccessful. In practice a surgeon contemplating such surgery would certainly wish to take specific legal advice (as recommended by the BMA) and in any event may run into the practical obstacle that hospitals may refuse to provide the facilities for such operations to be carried out.

1   *R v Brown* [1994] 1 AC 212; *R v Wilson* [1996] 3 WLR 125; and *R v Emmett* Times, October 15, 1999. See also **CHAPTER 2**: Consent – Adults **PARA 2.10**.
2   *Attorney General's Reference (No 6 of 1980)* [1981] All ER 715 per Lord Lane CJ at 1059.
3   Law Commission, *Consent and Offences against the Person: A Consultation Paper*, Consultation Paper No 134 (HMSO, 1994), para 2.4.
4   For example, *Cossey v UK* (1990) 13 EHRR 622; *Goodwin v UK* (2002) EHRR 18; *Bellinger v Bellinger* [2003] 2 AC 467; and the Gender Recognition Act 2004.
5   *Diagnostic and Statistical Manual of Mental Disorders* (4th edn, text revision Arlington, 2000), pp 507–510.
6   Elliott, 'Body dysmorphic disorder, radical surgery and the limits of consent' (2009) 17 Med L Rev 1.

7   We are aware of no prosecutions having been brought in the UK against surgeons who have undertaken such surgery.

Communication of the proposal

1.10   No consent can be obtained without the nature and effect of the proposed treatment being communicated to the patient or other person giving proper consent.[1] The treatment need not be described in complete detail, but sufficient must be stated to enable the person consenting to understand in broad terms what is to be done.[2]

1   See **CHAPTER 2**: Consent – Adults: on the capacity of a patient to understand the information communicated to them.
2   *Sidaway v Board of Governors of the Bethlem Royal Hospital and the Maudsley Hospital* [1985] AC 871.

1.11   The communication may be oral or in writing: in practice it is nearly always oral, but may be supplemented by something in writing. Where a surgical or other invasive procedure is contemplated it is usual and prudent practice for a consent form to be used. The standard NHS form[1] is a useful tool to remind health care staff to obtain and record consent and can also provide subsequent evidence that some discussion of (and at least apparent consent to) the proposed procedure did take place. Such forms are not, nevertheless, a substitute for a thorough discussion with the patient about what is proposed. Even so, care should be taken to ensure that the treatment is accurately described on the form.[2] Whether or not a form is used, a note should be made in the patient's medical records of what the patient was told. It is no longer of any assistance in risk management for the doctor to enter 'consent' ✓ in the notes and expect this to be accepted as proof that an adequate description of the procedure was given.

1   See **APPENDIX: 1.2**: DOH Consent Form 1 for the standard form which is likely to be the most commonly used, that relating to adults who have capacity to consent. See also **APPENDICES 1.3 TO 1.5** for the relevant forms relating to a child or young person, procedures where the patient's consciousness will not be impaired and adults who lack capacity to consent, respectively.
2   However, note *Abbas v Kenney* [1996] 7 Med LR 47 per Gage J who held that, on the facts, a patient had consented to a more extensive operation being performed if the need arose, despite it not being referred to expressly in the consent form.

1.12   It should be noted that the duty to communicate a proposal to provide treatment applies to all forms of treatment, not only operations and major medical treatment. A pulse should not be taken before the intention to do so has been communicated or without the patient's consent. The more radical or serious the treatment, the greater the detail required.

Consent – state of mind

Intention

1.13   For treatment to be provided lawfully to a competent adult patient, he must consent, that is, agree to and acquiesce in the treatment being proposed. This requires an intention on the part of the patient to consent. However, intention may be inferred from words or conduct which the reasonable observer would construe as manifesting intentional consent.

Comprehension

1.14   Does the requirement that the patient be given sufficient information to enable him to understand the nature and effect of the proposed treatment import a requirement that he must actually understand everything he has been told? We think not. Capacity to understand is required[1] but to require proof of actual understanding of what has been said is to create a dangerously high hurdle to overcome before necessary treatment is given.[2] So long as the patient realises that some form of treatment is proposed and that this will be as described by the doctor and he agrees to submit to this, we consider that a sufficient intent to consent has been established. That a patient is unable to or will choose not to understand the full technical detail of what is being proposed will not invalidate consent, provided he has the requisite capacity.

1   See **CHAPTER 2**: Consent – Adults: **PARA 2.3**.
2   In the context of information to be given by police officers on arrest, the Divisional Court in *Wheatley v Lodge* [1971] 1 WLR 29 determined that what is required is not that the person being arrested actually comprehends what is being said but merely that the officer has acted reasonably on the basis of the information he knew about the person being arrested. (The officer – reasonably – had failed to realise that he was deaf.)

Communication of consent

1.15   A consent which is not communicated is no consent at all. A doctor's authority to act is based upon awareness of the capable patient's consent. Consent can be manifested to the person seeking consent in three ways.

Written consent

1.16   First, in practice, consent for all elective invasive treatment of any significance is obtained in writing signed by the patient.[1] This is not a legal requirement, but is clearly a matter of prudence.[2] The discipline of being required to present a form to the patient and to explain the need for it provides some assurance that the patient has been provided with details of what is proposed and has actually consented to it. However, while it is a prudent step to take, the existence of such a form is no guarantee that consent has in fact been obtained. The patient may have been asked to sign a form without reading it or without an adequate or any explanation being given. Thus, such a form has evidential value but is not conclusive proof of a proper consent procedure.[3]

1   *Re J (a minor) (child in care: medical treatment)* [1993] Fam 15.
2   For example, Department of Health's *Reference Guide to Consent for Examination or Treatment* (6 April 2001): (http://www.dh.gov.uk/en/Publicationsandstatistics/Publications/PublicationsPolicyAndGuidance/DH_103643). For further key documents on consent from the Department of Health, see http://www.dh.gov.uk/en/Publichealth/Scientificdevelopment geneticsandbioethics/Consent/Consentgeneralinformation/index.htm.   See   also   GMC: Consent: patients and doctors making decisions together (http://www.gmc-uk.org/guidance/ethical_guidance/consent_guidance/Consent_guidance.pdf), paras 44–50. For hyperlinks related to this chapter, see: www.3serjeantsinn.com/mtdl/consent .

3   Popplewell J in *Taylor v Shropshire Health Authority* [1998] Lloyd's Rep Med 395 said: 'For
    my part I regard the consent form immediately before operation as pure window dressing in this
    case and designed simply to avoid the suggestion that a patient has not been told. I do not regard
    the failure to have a specialised consent form at the time to be any indication of negligence.'.

Oral consent

1.17   Secondly, most routine medical treatment is given by virtue of consent
which has been obtained informally and orally. There is nothing objectionable
in law about this and everything to commend it in practice and common sense in
relation to treatment and care which carries minimal risks or is repetitive and
routine.

Conduct

1.18   Thirdly, consent can often be inferred from the patient's conduct. An
arm proffered to a nurse brandishing a syringe is sufficient consent – even if the
patient insists on looking the other way.[1] Before conduct – whether active or
acquiescent – can be taken to be consent, however, it must be shown that, by
words or conduct, the practitioner has informed the patient of the nature and
effect of what he wishes to do, and that the patient's conduct is an intentional
response to that information; for example, a patient opening his mouth in
response to a request to undertake an oral examination.

1   *O'Brien v Cunard SS Co* (1891) 28 NE 266 Supreme Judicial Court of Massachusetts
    (passenger on a boat who stood in a line of passengers waiting to see a surgeon and who held
    her arm out for a smallpox inoculation was held to have consented).

B INFORMATION ABOUT RISKS

No doctrine of informed consent

1.19   No information about the risks of the proposed treatment is required in
order for a legally valid consent to be obtained. A failure to give any or any
adequate information about the possible adverse effects of treatment or about
its likelihood of success or failure does not render the practitioner liable to an
allegation of assault, criminal or civil, even where competent professional
practice requires such information to be given.[1] The common law purpose of
the doctrine of consent is to provide a framework for justifying medical
treatment rather than to enforce a requirement that proper information be given
to the patient. The question of the adequacy of the information falls within the
realm of the duty of care and the cause of action of negligence.

1   *Chatterton v Gerson* [1981] QB 432. See also **CHAPTER 2**: Consent – Adults **PARA 2.3**.

Duty of care – common law position

1.20   The obligation to provide proper information about risks is protected
by the law of negligence. The doctor owes a duty to his patient to provide such

information about the risks of the proposed treatment as would be provided by any competent and responsible practitioner in the circumstances.[1] This application of the *Bolam* test has been the subject of much criticism, but has survived to date. There is no distinction between advice given in relation to therapeutic and non-therapeutic procedures.[2] There are circumstances in which the risk is so obviously important that any prudent doctor would warn of it: then the courts are entitled to hold that there was a duty to do so, even if the medical practice was not to do so.[3]

1   *Sidaway v Board of Governors of the Bethlem Royal Hospital and the Maudsley Hospital* [1985] AC 871.
2   Such as sterilisations: *Gold v Haringey Health Authority* [1988] QB 481.
3   *Sidaway* (N1 above).

Article 8

1.21   Following the incorporation of Art 8 of the European Convention on Human Rights into English law by the Human Rights Act 1998, the doctor-centred focus of *Sidaway* may now, however, be vulnerable to attack. Article 8(1) states that:

'Everyone has the right to respect for his private and family life.'

It has been held that this extends to protecting the moral and bodily integrity of a person from unjustified assault: thus, it protects a patient's right to self-determination and autonomy.[1] It is a fundamental right. In our opinion, for this right to have real meaning, a true doctrine of informed consent is required. It is inappropriate to judge the extent of information provided by doctors pre-operatively or pre-treatment by the standards set by doctors (as required by *Sidaway*). Hence the level of information required should be judged from what, objectively assessed, a patient should be entitled to know.

Support for a more patient-centred approach to consent can be found in *Al Hamwi v Johnston and North West London Hospitals NHS Trust* in which Simon J[2] confirmed that:

-   a clinician must take reasonable care to give a warning which is adequate in scope, content and presentation and take steps to see that the warning is understood;[3]
-   the counselling should be balanced; and
-   the counselling should also be tailored to the individual patient.

The then GMC guidance on consent[4] was referred to with approval: it was deemed 'useful guidance'.

1   *X and Y v The Netherlands* (1985) 8 EHRR 235. See also *Peters v Netherlands* 77A DR 75 (1994) at 79, indicating that unwanted medical intervention (the taking of urine samples) is an infringement of Art 8; and reference to the *X v Austria and the European Court of Justice* decision in the HIV case cited at footnotes 1 and 2 of Nys, 'Physician Involvement in a Patient's death – a Continental European Perspective' (1999) 2 Med L Rev 7(2) 209. For a discussion of compulsory treatment and children's rights see **CHAPTER 4**: Deciding for Others – Children **PARA 4.7**. See also **CHAPTER 7**: Sterilisation **PARA 7.1**; **CHAPTER 11**: Religious Objections to Treatment; and **CHAPTER 13**: Treatment of Suicidal Patients **PARAS** 13.7 to 13.15.
2   [2005] Lloyd's Rep Med 309 at paras 43–45.

3   With reference to *Lybert v Warrington Health Authority* [1996] 7 Med LR 334.
4   November 1998.

Other jurisdictions

1.22   In other jurisdictions[1] there is imported into the duty an element of objectivity which permits the court to reject accepted medical practice where this offends against its notions of reasonableness. The duty has been expressed as a requirement to warn of such risks as it would be reasonable to expect of a doctor in the circumstances and which a patient would reasonably expect to receive.

1   *Rogers v Whitaker* (1992) 109 ALR 625, (1993) 4 Med LR 79 (Australia); *Canterbury v Spense* 464 F 2d 772 (1972) (USA); *Reibl v Hughes* (1980) 114 DLR (3d) 1 (Canada).

Current practice in the UK

1.23   Although UK law does not currently have a true doctrine of informed consent, it should be noted that the latest GMC guidance accepts that patients have a right to information and requires doctors to give them a wide range of information, tailored to their needs and priorities.[1] Thus, this standard of disclosure to patients amounts in practice to compliance with the doctrine of informed consent as understood in other jurisdictions. A paternalistic view of what it is right for the patient to know has been decisively rejected. The standard form of consent suggested by the Department of Health requires the professional to declare that the benefits and risks of any available alternative treatments (including no treatment) have been explained.[2] In our view, then, the doctrine of 'informed consent' rejected by the House of Lords[3] has effectively been incorporated in English law by way of accepted professional practice:[4] 'informed consent' is now the *Bolam* required standard. [5]

1   GMC: Consent: patients and doctors making decisions together (http://www.gmc-uk.org/ guidance/ethical_guidance/consent_guidance/Consent_guidance.pdf, (2 June 2008) paras 7–12.
2   See **APPENDIX: 1.2**: DOH Consent Form 1: Patient agreement to investigation or treatment (DoH 9 February 2007).
3   *Sidaway v Board of Governors of the Bethlem Royal Hospital and the Maudsley Hospital* [1985] AC 871.
4   For example, *Bassilious v General Medical Council* [2008] EWHC 2857 Admin 4.
5   See **PARA 1.20** above. And for a discussion of informed consent in the context of sterilisation, see **CHAPTER 7**: Sterilisation **PARA 7.3**.

1.24   It is suggested that, in an age of increasing demands for patient autonomy, the prudent practitioner or NHS Trust will ensure that there is a constant review of the information that is given to patients in respect of common procedures, and perhaps the less common but complex ones, and that steps are taken to ensure that patients are informed of all significant risks. It would also be prudent for any specific risks that are mentioned to be recorded in the patient's medical records. This is not merely a legal defence precaution, but, in a busy hospital with different doctors attending patients, will help to avoid needless repetition of alarming facts to the patient. It also recognises that the courts will give increasing emphasis to an objective standard of reasonableness in preference to a professionally created standard.

Delegation

1.25   Where the treating doctor with overall responsibility for the care of the patient, or the operating surgeon, delegates the task of obtaining consent from the patient to a more junior colleague, it will be prudent practice to ensure that the person explaining the risks involved has an adequate understanding of them. For a doctor to be able to obtain real informed consent he must have sufficient knowledge of the treatment or surgery proposed, its risks and benefits and any alternative treatment options available (such that he is able to explain these adequately to the patient and answer any questions).

Duty to answer questions

1.26   There is a very clear duty on the part of those seeking a patient's consent to answer truthfully and accurately any questions asked.[1] This is so even where it is feared that the answers may dissuade the patient from treatment thought to be in his best interests or will give rise to unhelpful anxiety. Lord Bridge in *Sidaway* stated:

> ' ... when questioned specifically by a patient ... about risks involved in a particular treatment proposed, the doctor's duty must, in my opinion, be to answer both truthfully and as fully as the questioner requires.'[2]

The GMC's latest guidance states: 'You must answer patients' questions honestly and, as far as practical, answer as fully as they wish.'[3]

1   *Sidaway v Board of Governors of the Bethlem Royal Hospital and the Maudsley Hospital* [1985] AC 871 per Lord Diplock at 895D and per Lord Bridge at 898.
2   *Sidaway* (N1 above) at 898.
3   GMC: Consent: patients and doctors making decisions together (http://www.gmc-uk.org/ guidance/ethical_guidance/consent_guidance/Consent_guidance.pdf), para 12.

1.27   The Court of Appeal has considered the duty of care in the contrasting situations where a question has been expressly asked of a clinician by a patient against the lack of such a question either expressly or impliedly put. In *Wyatt v Dr Curtis and Central Nottinghamshire Health Authority*[1] a patient who presented with chicken pox had not been warned by her GP about the consequent risk to her unborn child. The GP claimed a contribution against the Hospital Trust whose SHO had, some weeks later, failed to warn of the same risk. The GP argued that it was incumbent upon the SHO to ascertain what advice the patient had been given by the GP and to correct it. The court held that such a duty went well beyond that established in *Sidaway* and, after being told that the patient was aware of the risks and was not worried about them, the SHO was entitled to assume that the correct advice had been given to her by a competent GP. In *Deriche v Ealing Hospital NHS Trust*[2] Buckley J distinguished *Wyatt* in similar factual circumstances, but where a specific question had been asked of the doctor concerning termination of the pregnancy. It was held that there had been a breach of duty to the patient in failing to ensure that she fully understood the nature of the risks under discussion. The doctor had warned that there was a very small risk to the unborn child, but he had not satisfied himself that the patient understood that the nature of the risk concerned potentially devastating abnormalities.[3] Thus, the duty to inform may –

13

depending on the particular factual circumstances – be considerably wider where the doctor has been asked a question by the patient.

1   [2003] EWCA Civ 1779.
2   [2003] EWHC 3014 (QB).
3   It should be noted, however, that Buckley J was careful (1) to endorse the views of the judges in *Wyatt* (paras 48 and 51); (2) to point out the factual differences between the two cases (para 47); and (3) to stress that his conclusions were based on the specific agreement in the expert evidence given in the case (paras 34 and 42). Thus, it can be argued that *Deriche* has not in fact significantly extended the duty.

Information about alternative forms of treatment

1.28   The courts may impose a duty to inform of alternative procedures in circumstances where the risks of the alternative procedure are substantially lower than the procedure in fact proposed or where the procedure proposed carries a risk of a particularly severe complication which would be avoided using the alternative procedure. In those circumstances, even if a body of medical opinion would support not informing the patient about the alternative, the case could be considered as falling into the exception set out in *Sidaway* as being so grave a risk that the patient is entitled to know of it regardless of 'accepted' medical practice. Alternatively, the courts may be prepared to carve out a second *Bolam* exception based on the need to inform patients of alternative procedures in the circumstances outlined above.[1] In *Birch v University College London Hospital NHS Foundation Trust*[2] the court held that, by logical extension of the principle that there was a duty to inform a patient of significant risks that would affect the judgment of a reasonable patient, such duty would not be discharged unless and until the patient was made aware that fewer or no risks were associated with another available and alternative treatment. In that case the patient had been informed of the risks involved with catheter angiography but not the comparative risks of MRI. She would have undergone the less invasive procedure had she been properly apprised of the comparative risks. She had therefore been subjected to an unnecessary procedure that had caused her stroke and the Trust was held liable. In any event, medical practice, as reflected by the advice of the General Medical Council, is likely to be in favour of the available alternatives being offered to patients.[3]

1   In *Haughian v Paine* [1987] 4 WWR 97 the Saskatchewan Court of Appeal (albeit applying the doctrine of informed consent) held that a surgeon should advise the patient of the consequences of leaving an illness untreated and of alternative means of treatment and their risks. As this was not done, the patient did not give informed consent to his surgery.
2   (2008) 104 BMLR 168.
3   GMC: Consent: patients and doctors making decisions together (http://www.gmc-uk.org/guidance/ethical_guidance/consent_guidance/Consent_guidance.pdf), paras 9(c), 29 and at 42: 'You should do your best to make sure that such patients have considered the available options and reached their own decision.'

Known comparative outcomes

1.29   Should a doctor put himself forward to perform treatment if there is a practitioner elsewhere who does it better or is known to have a better record of outcome? If a centre has a higher mortality or morbidity rate than others, should it cease the treatment in question? How much (if anything) should doctors inform patients about such comparative outcomes? The medical profession has been struggling towards ethical answers to these difficult questions, and these issues were at the centre of a public inquiry in 2001.[1] The following principles, which take account of the Inquiry's recommendations, are suggested as forming the basis of prudent practice:

- Doctors and all those responsible for the provision of health services ought to keep their results under review and apply to them accepted clinical audit systems.
- Where it is possible to compare outcomes with a national or other accepted standard, this should be done.
- Where the performance of the doctor or the centre is below a generally accepted deviation from the standard, serious consideration should be given to whether it is in the interests of patients to be offered treatment by that doctor or at that centre or whether patients should be referred elsewhere until the cause of the deviation has been identified and remedied.
- Comprehensible information about performance of the trust, of the specialty and of the consultant and his team should be available for patients, even where the outcomes are within the accepted range. Indeed, consideration should be given to referring the patient to this information.

1   The Bristol Royal Infirmary Inquiry (http://www.bristol-inquiry.org.uk/). In Ashcroft, Dawson, Draper and McMillan, *Principles of Health Care Ethics* (2nd edn, Wiley, 2007), p 320, the authors stated: 'There was a failure of informed consent in [the Bristol Royal Infirmary] cases, not because the procedures turned out badly, but because it is obviously relevant to patients to know about the manifest inadequacies of those surgeons. In placing themselves or their loved ones in the hands of these surgeons they were unwittingly making themselves or their loved ones vulnerable to the lethal consequences of surgical incompetence.' Interestingly, they argue further that in the context of a proper 'informed consent' doctrine, information about a surgeon's relative performance is vital: 'What creates an ethical obligation to disclose a risk is not the magnitude or probability of the risk itself, but whether that particular risk is material to the patient and whether the doctor could reasonably be aware that this risk was material to this patient.'

C VITIATING FACTORS

1.30   A consent is not valid if it is obtained:

(i)   by fraud;
(ii)   by duress;
(iii)   from a person who lacks capacity.

A doctor should satisfy himself that none of these factors applies.[1]

1   A person over the age of 16 years is presumed to have capacity unless the contrary is shown: MCA, s 1(2). Where there is no evidence about a patient's capacity, the presumption applies. In practice, then, a doctor does not need to perform a capacity test in every case, but where there is some concern as to a patient's capacity, for whatever reason, further investigation must be made. See **CHAPTER 2**: Consent – Adults, **PARA 2.8** for further discussion.

Fraud

1.31   Consent obtained by a fundamental deception – such as to the nature of the act or the identity of the person who is to provide the treatment – is no consent at all and provides no justification for treatment which would otherwise be an assault.[1] The test is whether the deception is of a nature which means that the decision is not really that of the patient at all.[2]

Thus, any consent given by a patient, who in doing so relies on a false representation on these matters made by the person seeking consent, is invalid. The deception must be material; that is, must be one on which the patient might reasonably be expected to rely or which is made knowing he is in fact relying on it. It must also relate to the nature of the treatment or the identity of the person to provide it. Examples might be:

- Consent obtained by or for a person pretending to be a doctor.
- A materially inaccurate account of the surgeon's outcome figures.
- A false description of the procedure, for example, stating that the patient is to have her appendix removed, when the intention is to perform a hysterectomy.
- Consent obtained for an ulterior motive, such as an indecent assault or to bolster research results.

However, surprisingly, a deception about the entitlement to practise of the practitioner has been held by the Court of Appeal (Criminal Division) in *R v Richardson*[3] not to vitiate consent. The appellant was a registered dental practitioner until 30 August 1996, but was suspended from practice by the General Dental Council. While still suspended, she carried out dentistry on a number of patients in September 1996. The Court of Appeal held that the deception concerning her status as a registered practitioner was not a deception as to the 'identity' of the person who was to provide treatment. Therefore it did not vitiate consent in criminal law.

However, in the later case of *R v Tabassum*[4] the Court of Appeal refused to quash three convictions of indecent assault where three women had taken part in a breast cancer survey carried out by the appellant which involved him touching their breasts in order to demonstrate how they should examine themselves. The women believed him to be medically qualified and that the touching was for medical purposes when in fact he had no medical qualifications. In distinguishing *Richardson*, Rose LJ said:

> 'In *Richardson*, the case proceeded solely by reference to the point on identity ... In the present case the motive and intent of the defendant were irrelevant ... The nature and quality of the defendant's acts in touching the breasts of women to whom, in sexual terms he was a stranger, was unlawful and an indecent assault unless the complainants consented to that. On the evidence ... consent was given because they mistakenly believed that ... the touching was for a medical purpose. As this was not so, there was no true consent. They were consenting to touching for medical purposes, not to indecent behaviour, that is, there was consent to the nature of the act but not its quality.'

The decision in *Tabassum* shows that the unfortunate view of the court in *Richardson* may be very narrowly confined.

1   In *Chatterton v Gerson* [1981] QB 432, Bristow J said that to prove trespass to the person it had to be shown that the consent was 'unreal'.
2   Lord Donaldson in *Re T (adult: refusal of treatment)* [1993] Fam 95 at 113.
3   [2000] Crim LR 686, [2000] All ER (D) 649, CA.
4   *Ibid.*

Duress and undue influence

1.32   Consent cannot be validly obtained from a person not acting under their own free will; that is, where the will of the patient is overborne by circumstances over which he has no control.[1]

Thus if the patient is detained against his will and feels forced to consent to treatment in order to escape detention, the consent will not be recognised. Similarly, if undue influence is brought to bear by a third party, consent will not be valid. Doctors need to be aware of social and other factors in the patient's background which may render him vulnerable to pressure either to submit to or to refuse treatment. This may be a far from easy task. The matters to be considered were set out by Lord Donaldson of Lymington MR:

> 'A special problem may arise if at the time the decision is made the patient has been subjected to the influence of some third party. This is by no means to say that the patient is not entitled to receive and indeed invite advice and assistance from others in reaching a decision, particularly from members of the family. But the doctors have to consider whether the decision is really that of the patient. It is wholly acceptable that the patient should have been persuaded by others of the merits of such a decision and have decided accordingly. It matters not how strong the persuasion was, so long as it did not overbear the independence of the patient's decision. The real question in each such case is "Does the patient really mean what he says or is he merely saying it for a quiet life, to satisfy someone else or because the advice and persuasion to which he has been subjected is such that he can no longer think and decide for himself?" In other words "Is it a decision expressed in form only, not in reality?"
>
> When considering the effect of outside influences, two aspects can be of crucial importance. First, the strength of the will of the patient. One who is very tired, in pain or depressed will be much less able to resist having his will overborne than one who is rested, free from pain and cheerful. Second, the relationship of the "persuader" to the patient may be of crucial importance. The influence of parents on their children or of one spouse on the other can be, but is by no means necessarily, much stronger than would be the case in other relationships. Persuasion based upon religious belief can also be much more compelling and the fact that arguments based upon religious beliefs are being deployed by someone in a very close relationship with the patient will give them added force and should alert the doctors to the possibility – no more – that the patient's capacity or will to decide has been overborne. In other words the patient may not mean what he says.'[2]

1   *Re T (adult: refusal of treatment)* [1993] Fam 95.
2   *Re T* (N1 above) at 113.

Capacity

1.33   The person consenting must have the relevant mental capacity to do so. The test for and assessment of capacity are dealt with in detail in subsequent chapters.[1] Consent given by a person not possessing the relevant capacity is invalid and cannot be used to justify the provision of treatment.

Previously, at common law, it was not clear whether a doctor who mistakenly, but in the circumstances reasonably, believed that the patient had capacity committed an assault if he provided treatment relying on that belief.[2] The position is now clarified with the introduction of the MCA, s 5 which provides that there will be no liability where, prior to carrying out a particular proposed act in relation to the care and treatment of the patient, a doctor has taken reasonable steps to establish whether the patient lacks capacity in relation to it and when carrying out the act the doctor reasonably believes that the patient lacks capacity and the act is in the patient's best interests.[3]

1   See **CHAPTERS 2**: Consent – Adults, **3**: Deciding for Others – Adults and **4**: Deciding for Others – Children.
2   In *Re T (adult: refusal of treatment)* [1993] Fam 95 at 122 Staughton LJ doubted that such a belief would be a defence in the case of a purported refusal:
    'Some will say that, when there is doubt whether an apparent refusal of consent is valid in circumstances of urgent necessity, the decision of a doctor acting in good faith ought to be conclusive. In this case there was an application at the judge's lodgings at 11 o'clock at night, a procedure which may not always be available. However, I cannot find authority that the decision of a doctor as to the existence or refusal of consent is sufficient protection, if the law subsequently decides otherwise. So the medical profession, in the future as in the past, must bear the responsibility unless it is possible to obtain a decision from the courts.'
3   See **CHAPTER 3**: Deciding for Others – Adults.

D SCOPE OF AUTHORITY

1.34   Treatment may be carried out as authorised by the consent. This justifies the provision only of the treatment actually described in the consent. Unless the consent expressly or impliedly allows for it, no variation is authorised.

This is not to say that no different treatment may be carried out even though no consent has been given for it:

*   If it emerges that the proposed treatment is not possible – for example, where a cancerous tumour proves to be inoperable – the doctor may stop the procedure which has been authorised and undertake conservative treatment consequent on his inability to pursue the procedure originally contemplated.
*   If an emergency arises while the patient is unconscious during an authorised procedure, and it is necessary to act immediately to save life or prevent a deterioration in health, the doctor may provide the treatment necessary to this end.[1] What he may not do is to extend the scope of what has been authorised merely because he finds an

unexpected condition which he considers it to be in the patient's interests to deal with. Many consent forms contain an expression designed to permit a surgeon to perform any extra procedures which may become necessary during the procedure specified; the surgeon is also asked to specify these other procedures.[2] Only very cautious reliance should be placed on such a provision. It cannot be a justification for embarking on treatment of a type not discussed with the patient, and only remotely connected with what was authorised. It should be regarded as authorisation for no more than treatment necessarily ancillary to that which has been authorised. In our view this has always been the position at common law, but it is further reinforced by the right to autonomy over one's body under Art 8.[3]

1   MCA, s 5.
2   See **APPENDIX 1.2**: Consent form 1: Patient agreement to investigation or treatment (DoH 9 February 2007).
3   See **PARA 1.21** above, on Art 8.

E DURATION OF AUTHORITY

1.35   Consent is inevitably intended to cover some future event: retrospective consent can have no legal effect.[1] The consent may be for an injection to be offered almost immediately or it may be for an operation to be performed in several weeks' time. In either case the consent may be presumed to be intended to last until the procedure is performed, unless the patient has specified some time limit or condition under which the consent will be revoked. Where this is done, and it will be an unusual occurrence, the doctor taking the consent must be careful to record what is required.

A consent will not survive a material change of circumstance. The following are examples where the consent might cease to be valid:

- Where the consent specifies a particular doctor to perform the procedure and he is unavailable.
- Where new information, either generally about the procedure, or specifically about the patient, comes to light which fundamentally alters the risks of the procedure of which the patient has or ought to have been told.[2]
- Where the clinical condition of the patient changes or the diagnosis changes so that in the opinion of the responsible doctor the procedure consented to is no longer necessary in the patient's interests.

1   It may have an evidential effect in relation to a causation issue in a civil negligence claim, by showing that the patient would have consented if asked.
2   The effect on the legal validity of the consent will depend on whether the information on the risks is of such a character that ignorance of it results in the consent not being real and see discussion on information about risks above at **PARAS 1.19–1.24**.

1.36   Consent will survive a patient's loss of capacity[1]. Indeed, this rule is applied in all surgical procedures under general anaesthetic: the consent to the operation remains valid although the patient has been rendered unconscious by the anaesthetic. A difficulty may arise if, following a loss of capacity, circumstances change to an extent where usually a further consent would be required. A doctor may undertake different treatment only if it is necessary as a matter of urgency and it is not possible to wait until the patient has recovered capacity. If the patient is unlikely to recover capacity at all, then the doctor may act immediately in the patient's best interests,[2] subject to the principles governing the treatment of incapacitated patients.[3]

1   See **CHAPTER 2**: Consent – Adults, **PARA 2.13**.
2   MCA, s 5.
3   See **CHAPTERS 3**: Deciding for Others – Adults, and **4**: Deciding for Others – Children below, on deciding for others.

F WITHDRAWAL OF AUTHORITY

1.37   A patient possessing the appropriate mental capacity may withdraw a consent at any time before the treatment so authorised has been given. The consent ceases to have effect from that moment.[1]

1   See **CHAPTER 2**: Consent – Adults, **PARA 2.12** for a discussion of withdrawal of consent once treatment has started.

G CONCLUSION

1.38   The ostensible common law negligence position that there is no doctrine of informed consent jars both with accepted clinical practice and with the requirements of the ECHR. Whatever the courts have said in the past about the lack of such a doctrine, it would be foolhardy of a clinician to rely on such an approach today. The latest guidance for practitioners on consent from the GMC and publications on consent from the Department of Health place greater emphasis on the autonomy of the patient in receiving information from clinicians on treatment, alternatives, risks and outcomes. This reflects the general desire of more progressive clinicians to involve patients in decision-making rather than dictate to them. The practical consequence of this guidance has been to ensure that the courts are likely to consider informed consent as *de facto* the required *Bolam* standard. Further, the principles of autonomy at the forefront of Art 8 of the ECHR, in our opinion, mandate such an approach.

> For updating material and hyperlinks related to this chapter, see: www.3serjeantsinn.com/mtdl/consent

Chapter 2

Consent – Adults

A   Adult 2.1
B   Capacity 2.2
     Definition of capacity and its assessment 2.2
          The person consenting must have the relevant mental capacity
          to do so 2.2
          How much capacity? 2.6
     Temporary incapacity 2.7
     Presumption of capacity 2.8
     The absolute nature of an adult's consent 2.9
     Treatment must be lawful 2.10
C   Refusal 2.11
D   Change of mind 2.12
E   Advance directives/decisions 2.13
     General principle 2.13
     Requirements 2.14
     Form 2.15
     Informed refusal? 2.16
     Knowledge 2.17
     Duration 2.18
     Records 2.19
F   Conclusion 2.20

A ADULT

2.1   An adult is considered to be a person aged 18 years or more. Certain aspects of the law of consent apply only to adults. However, the qualifying age for the application of the Mental Capacity Act 2005 ('MCA') is now 16 years or more.[1]

---

1   MCA, s 2(5), save for the provisions in respect of the Deprivation of Liberty Safeguards that apply only to those over 18.

B CAPACITY

Definition of capacity and its assessment

The person consenting must have the relevant mental capacity to do so.

2.2   Capacity for those 16 years or over is to be determined by reference to the principles set out in the MCA.[1] The MCA and the accompanying Code of Practice[2] (which *must* be taken into account by those assessing capacity and caring for someone who lacks capacity)[3] emphasise the need to involve and assist patients and those close to them in the decision-making process with regard to medical treatment. The MCA codifies and expands upon pre-existing common law principles in respect of the determination of capacity and provides a framework for decision making for those who lack capacity in respect of medical treatment.

Although the test for determining capacity is now enshrined in s 3 of the MCA, there is no relevant distinction between the test as set out in the MCA and the previous common law test approved by the Court of Appeal in *Re MB* (*an adult: medical treatment*).[4] As much of the MCA draws upon the existing common law principles, the pre-2007 jurisprudence remains relevant to determination of matters under the MCA.

The MCA makes clear that a person can only lack capacity because of a disturbance of mental or brain function. Refusal of treatment because of obstinance or belligerence will not suffice. As stated in s 2(1) and (2) MCA, a person lacks capacity in relation to a matter if at the material time:

'there is a temporary or permanent impairment of or disturbance in the functioning of the person's mind or brain; **and**

that impairment or disturbance is sufficient to render the person incapable of making a decision for himself'.

The phrase '*at the material time*' is of importance: capacity must be considered at the time the relevant decision is to be made and in the context of the specific decision that has to be made.

Some examples of an impairment or disturbance in the functioning of the brain are given in paragraph 4.12 of the Code of Practice and include mental illness, dementia, organic brain injury, significant learning disabilities and intoxication.

The statutory test for capacity is found in s 3 MCA which provides that:

'(1)   … a person is unable to make a decision for himself if he is unable –
      (a)   to understand the information relevant to the decision,
      (b)   to retain that information,
      (c)   to use or weigh that information as part of the process of making the decision, or
      (d)   to communicate his decision (whether by talking, using sign language or any other means).'

Any question of capacity falls to be determined on the balance of probabilities.[5]

Discrimination must be avoided – lack of capacity cannot be established by reference to:

(a)   a person's age or appearance; or

(b)   a condition of his, or an aspect of his behaviour, which might lead others to make unjustified assumptions about his capacity.[6]

1   This came into force in October 2007 and has been amended by the Mental Health Act 2007.

2   The Code of Practice can be found at: http://www.publicguardian.gov.uk/docs/code-of-practice-041007.pdf . For hyperlinks related to this chapter, see: www.3serjeantsinn.com/mtdl/consent-adults .

3   MCA, s 42(4).

4   [1997] 2 FLR 426; *Local Authority X v (1) MM (by her Litigation Friend the Official Solicitor) (2) KM* [2007] EWHC 2003 (Fam), (2009) 1 FLR 443 at para 74.

5   MCA, s 2(4).

6   MCA, s 2(3).

(a) Understanding the information

2.3   The MCA capacity test applies to decisions such as where to live and who to have contact with, as well as whether or not to have medical treatment; thus it is unsurprising that there is no prescriptive guidance in the statute or the Code of Practice as to what exactly must be understood to demonstrate capacity.

The MCA states in s 3(4) that:

'The information relevant to a decision includes information about the reasonably foreseeable consequences of—

(a)   deciding one way or another, or

(b)   failing to make the decision.'

In respect of medical treatment decisions the amount and complexity of information that must be understood will vary widely, depending upon the illness or condition under consideration. For example, deciding whether or not to have a decayed tooth extracted will involve understanding of far less detailed information than whether to accept radiotherapy and/or chemotherapy and/or surgery for breast cancer.

To be considered capable it is likely to be sufficient if the patient is able to understand in 'broad terms':

- the nature of their diagnosis and prognosis;
- the nature of the proposed treatment;
- the anticipated benefits of treatment;
- the potential risks associated with treatment;
- the risks associated with not having the proposed treatment;
- any alternative treatment options and the risks and benefits of those.[1]

Unlike the previous common law position, the MCA specifically requires that steps should be taken to enhance a patient's capacity. Section 1(3) states:

'a person is not to be treated as unable to make a decision unless all practicable steps to help him have been taken without success'.

Section 3(2) emphasises the need to facilitate understanding:

> 'A person is not to be regarded as unable to understand the information relevant to a decision if he is able to understand an explanation of it given to him in a way that is appropriate to his circumstances (using simple language, visual aids or any other means).'

The steps which could be taken to help a patient understand the decision they are being asked to take include:

- the use of simple language;
- the use of an interpreter so that the explanation can be given in the patient's first language;
- the use of sign language;
- the use of visual aids such as pictures, diagrams or anatomical models;
- treatment of an underlying medical condition to enable the person to regain capacity.[2]

1   *Chatterton v Gerson* [1981] QB 432; see **CHAPTER 1**: Consent – General, **PARA 1.4**: Risks of treatment.
2   Code of Practice, para 2.7; and see **CHAPTER 3**: Deciding for Others – Adults at **PARA 3.1**: Temporary incapacity.

(b) Retaining the information

2.4   As capacity is specific to the decision to be made at the particular time, it is perhaps unsurprising that the information relevant to the decision need be retained only for as long as it takes for that particular decision to be made. MCA, s 3(3) states:

> 'The fact that a person is able to retain the information relevant to a decision for a short period only does not prevent him from being regarded as able to make the decision.'

Therefore, even those with memory difficulties (such as early-stage dementia) will still not necessarily be deemed incapable in respect of all decisions. However, the greater the complexity of the relevant information about the decision, the greater the degree of retention that will be required to hold all the information in mind while weighing it up to decide.

As with understanding, all practicable steps should be taken to help a person retain information and make a decision. The Code of Practice suggests that aids such as notebooks, posters, photographs, videos and voice recorders can be used to help people retain and record information.[1]

For example, in the case of a patient with short-term memory loss caused by dementia, it would be prudent for the doctor assessing capacity to consent to treatment to record in the patient's medical records:

- the fact that the person was able to retain the information for a short period or periods only;
- the reason for the short period of retention, if known;
- the steps taken to assist the patient to retain the information; and

- any objective evidence that the information has been retained long enough to allow the person to make the decision as to treatment.

1   Code of Practice, para 4.20.

(c) *Weighing information as part of a decision-making process*

2.5   Once relevant treatment information has been understood and retained, the person must also be able to use or weigh the information in order to reach a decision. This is sometimes described as the 'rational decision-making ability' stage of the capacity test. The ability to use or weigh information does not always follow from the ability to understand and retain that information. For example:

- A person who suffers with anorexia nervosa may understand and retain all the information given as to the consequences of not eating and the physiological need for nutrition to survive: that patient may, nevertheless, be unable rationally to weigh up that information when deciding whether or not to eat because their illness makes them place inappropriate importance upon achieving extreme thinness.
- A psychotically deluded patient who believes psychiatric medication will cause him to shrink will of course fail the 'understanding' stage of the capacity test, but he may well demonstrate the ability rationally to weigh information in the balance when he declares he will not take his pills because he does not wish to become extremely small.

This limb of the capacity test was considered by the court in *R v Collins & Ashworth Hospital Authority, ex parte Brady.*[1] The applicant, Mr Brady, who was suffering from a personality disorder, went on hunger strike when he was moved from one ward to another under restraint. A decision was taken to commence force feeding and Brady applied for judicial review of that decision on the basis that his refusal of food was unrelated to his mental disorder and was a rational decision by a competent person. In giving judgment Maurice Kay J confirmed that:

> 'It is common ground that a mentally disordered patient may nevertheless have capacity … '

but in this case he was:

> ' … satisfied on a balance of probabilities that the Applicant has been incapacitated in relation to all his decisions about food refusal and force feeding since his attitude hardened when he refused blood tests and medication on 25 October. Since then, notwithstanding the fact that he is a man of well above average intelligence, he has engaged in his battle of wills in such a way that, as a result of his severe personality disorder, he has eschewed the weighing of information and the balancing of the risks and needs to such an extent that, from that time until this, his decisions on food refusal and force feeding have been incapacitated. As a result, the doctors have been legally empowered to supply medical treatment in his best interests.'

An assessment of capacity must be based on a person's ability to make a specific decision at the time it needs to be made and not his ability to make decisions in general. While some patients, such as those with very severe learning difficulties, will in fact be so globally impaired that they lack capacity in respect of all medical treatment decisions, an 'all or nothing' approach to the assessment of capacity must be avoided. The anorexic patient who will probably be incapable of making decisions about accepting nutrition may well have capacity to decide whether to consent to an appendectomy.[2]

The importance of assessing capacity for specific decisions was emphasised in *Local Authority X v (1) MM (by her Litigation Friend the Official Solicitor (2) KM:*

> 'capacity is "issue specific", so someone may have capacity for one purpose but lack capacity for another purpose. That is why in cases of this kind it has now become the practice to grant separate declarations (for example) as to a vulnerable adult's capacity (i) to litigate, (ii) to decide where she should reside, (iii) to decide whom she has contact with, (iv) to decide on issues concerning her care, (v) to consent to sexual relations, (vi) to consent to marry and (vii) to manage her financial affairs ...

> '... capacity is not merely issue specific in relation to different types of transaction; capacity is also issue specific in relation to different transactions of the same type. Thus a vulnerable adult may have capacity to consent to a simple medical procedure but lack capacity to consent to a more complex medical procedure. In the same way a vulnerable adult may have capacity to conduct some simple piece of litigation but lack the capacity to conduct more complex litigation ...[3]'

1   (2001) 58 BMLR 173 at paras 57–65; *Re MB (an adult: medical treatment)* [1997] 2 FCR 541, [1997] 2 FLR 426, [1997] 8 Med LR 217.
2   Code of Practice, para 4.4.
3   [2007] EWHC 2003 (Fam), [2009] 1 FLR 443 per Munby J at paras 64 and 65.

How much capacity?

2.6   While capacity is to be considered either present or absent (on the balance of probabilities), the requisite decision-making ability will vary according to the gravity of the decision to be taken:

> 'What matters is whether at that time the patient's capacity was reduced below the level needed in the case of a refusal of that importance, for refusals can vary in importance. Some may involve a risk to life or of irreparable damage to health. Others may not.'[1]

A patient with capacity is not obliged to arrive at a rational decision: indeed a patient is entitled to refuse treatment, and therefore to consent to it, for any reason, good or bad, rational or irrational. This is just as well, as many patients doubtless consent to necessary and beneficial treatment on entirely illogical or unjustified grounds.

In *Re T (Adult: Refusal of Treatment)* Lord Donaldson of Lymington MR stated:

> 'Prima facie every adult has the right and capacity to decide whether or not he will accept medical treatment, even if a refusal may risk permanent injury to his health or even lead to premature death. Furthermore, it matters not

whether the reasons for the refusal were rational or irrational, unknown or even non-existent. This is so notwithstanding the very strong public interest in preserving the life and health of all citizens.'[2]

This principle is confirmed in s 1(4) MCA which provides that:

'A person is not to be treated as unable to make a decision merely because he makes an unwise decision.'

All those over 16 years old are presumed to possess the capacity to consent to medical treatment unless the contrary is shown.[3] Where there is no evidence about a patient's capacity, the presumption will apply.

1   *Re T (adult: refusal of treatment)* [1993] Fam 95 at 113.
2   *Ibid.*
3   MCA, s 1(2).

Temporary incapacity

2.7   Capacity may be lost temporarily.[1] Obvious examples are intoxication or temporary unconsciousness. Less obviously, extreme panic or pain can result in a temporary loss of capacity, as can a phobia precipitated by a specific stimulus. Such phenomena will not necessarily lead to incapacity, but they may do where they cause such a serious impairment or disturbance of mental functioning as to render a patient incapable of weighing information rationally and making a decision.[2]

In *Re MB*[3] a woman with a needle phobia consented to a caesarean section, but – when she was exposed to the needle required for anaesthesia – her phobia led her then to refuse the intervention. The Court of Appeal found that her refusal of treatment when in the grip of her phobia was the product of a temporary loss of capacity.

Doctors need to exercise considerable caution before providing treatment when a temporary phenomenon of this type has given rise to a loss of capacity. The circumstances which are likely to provoke extreme pain, panic or even a phobia are usually predictable, and the wishes of the patient in such an eventuality often can and, whenever possible, should be established at a time when calm and rational discussion is possible and the patient is more likely to have capacity. A doctor who knows that a patient has a needle phobia, but fails to discuss with the patient in advance the need for the intervention requiring the use of a needle, and thus fails to ascertain what his capable wishes might be, is probably failing in his duty to advise the patient of the treatment required and to obtain his consent in advance. Further, it would be a potential breach of MCA, s 1(3).[4] Such a breach may expose the doctor to liability in negligence, if not assault.

The concept of temporary incapacity allows for a degree of subjective judgment in emergencies which could very substantially undermine the autonomy of patients. Temporary incapacity should not be used as an excuse for running a patient's life without his consent. While pain might impair capacity, it will not necessarily destroy decision-making capacity. It would doubtless surprise many women in labour to be told that they might be deprived of their freedom to make decisions about the management of that labour by reason of the pain they were suffering. Indeed it is in just such circumstances that a patient most values the right to decide what should be done to her body. It is also in just such circumstances that the pressure is greatest on the attending doctor – or midwife – to 'do something' and thus to regard any hesitation on the part of the patient as evidence of an inability to make a decision rather than of reluctance on the patient's part to allow something abhorrent to be done to her. Therefore it is suggested that over-reliance on temporary incapacity is dangerous and should be avoided if at all possible by intelligent anticipation of the circumstances in which it might arise and by careful consideration of the likely duration of such incapacity and the possibility of either putting off the decision until the person can make it himself or of taking action which is less restrictive of a person's rights and freedom of action[5] pending the person regaining or developing capacity.

1   MCA, s 2(2).
2   *Re MB (an adult: medical treatment)* [1997] 2 FLR 426, [1997] 2 FCR 541, [1997] 8 Med LR 217; and Code of Practice, para 4.12. For a detailed analysis see **CHAPTER 9**: Managing Pregnancies.
3   *Ibid.*
4   'a person is not to be treated as unable to make a decision unless all practicable steps to help him have been taken without success.'
5   MCA, s 1(5).

Presumption of capacity

2.8   Health care professionals are entitled to rely upon the presumption of capacity such that there is no need for a practitioner to perform a capacity test on every patient they meet before acting upon the patient's apparent assent to the proposed treatment. However, if there is anything in the patient's presentation or demeanour which gives rise to a question of whether that patient does have the relevant capacity, then the doctor must investigate capacity further.[1] In practice capacity of a patient is rarely questioned until they disagree with their doctor. A doctor, nonetheless, cannot ignore the possibility of incapacity and expect to be able to rely on the patient's consent if it transpires that there was no capacity.

Section 5 of the MCA gives those who act in connection with the care and treatment of a patient protection from liability if:

•   before providing care/treatment, the health care worker took reasonable steps to establish whether the person lacked capacity in relation to the matter in question; and
•   when providing care/treatment, the health care worker reasonably believed the patient lacked capacity and it was in their best interests to provide the care/treatment.[2]

What comprises 'reasonable steps' will depend upon the facts of each case. A doctor should undertake as full an assessment of capacity as possible in the circumstances, making a record in the patient's clinical notes of the grounds which justify a reasonable belief of lack of capacity.

As to who should undertake the assessment of capacity, *Re F* makes the important point that an initial assessment of capacity – in order to give the court jurisdiction to make initial directions under MCA s 48 – need not be from a psychiatrist or other specialist. It may well be appropriate and desirable for a general practitioner to provide at least an initial assessment, so that the court can assume jurisdiction without delay.[3] However, where there is any doubt as to capacity, it is suggested that a second opinion should be sought and consideration should be given to requesting a s 12 Mental Health Act approved doctor to undertake a formal assessment of capacity in accordance with the guidance given by the Court of Appeal in *St George's NHS Healthcare Trust v S*. This states:

'Concern over capacity

(iv) The authority should identify as soon as possible whether there is concern about a patient's competence to consent to or refuse treatment.

(v) If the capacity of the patient is seriously in doubt it should be assessed as a matter of priority. In many such cases the patient's general practitioner or other responsible doctor may be sufficiently qualified to make the necessary assessment, but in serious or complex cases involving difficult issues about the future health and well-being or even the life of the patient, the issue of capacity should be examined by an independent psychiatrist, ideally one approved under section 12(2) of the Mental Health Act. If following this assessment there remains a serious doubt about the patient's competence, and the seriousness or complexity of the issues in the particular case may require the involvement of the court, the psychiatrist should further consider whether the patient is incapable by reason of mental disorder of managing her property or affairs. If so the patient may be unable to instruct a solicitor and will require a guardian ad litem in any court proceedings. The authority should seek legal advice as quickly as possible. If a declaration is to be sought the patient's solicitors should be informed immediately and if practicable they should have a proper opportunity to take instructions and apply for legal aid where necessary. Potential witnesses for the authority should be made aware of the criteria laid down in Re: MB and this case, together with any guidance issued by the Department of Health, and the British Medical Association.

(vi) If the patient is unable to instruct solicitors, or is believed to be incapable of doing so, the authority or its legal advisers must notify the Official Solicitor and invite him to act as guardian ad litem. If the Official Solicitor agrees he will no doubt wish, if possible, to arrange for the patient to be interviewed to ascertain her wishes and to explore the reasons for any refusal of treatment.'[4]

Further guidance as to what amounts to 'reasonable steps' is given in the Code of Practice[5] and includes:

- involving the person who lacks capacity and trying to ascertain their wishes and feelings, beliefs and values;
- asking other people's opinions where practical and appropriate (such as

carers, close relatives, friends and those who take an interest in the person's welfare);

- working to a person's care plan;
- applying the best interests checklist at paragraph 5.13 of the Code of Practice.

1   Code of Practice, para 4.34
2   See **CHAPTER 3**: Deciding for Others – Adults, **PARA 3.4**.
3   Court of Protection case no 11649371, 28 May 2009 (available at http://www.public guardian.gov.uk/docs/judgement-re-f-28-may-2009.pdf) per Her Honour Hazel Marshall QC at para 40: 'There is a danger, with the current spotlight on the new and more sophisticated approach to mental capacity contained in the Act and the very extensive Code of Practice, that general practitioners will think that that they cannot or should not complete such an assessment for the court because of lack of supposed expertise – as happened in this case. This would be likely to lead to their declining to do so in the very cases which are problematic, because there is doubt whether the borderline has been crossed, between decisions which are the product of impaired powers of reasoning, or are merely eccentric unwise or unreasonable decisions in the opinion of others. It would be unfortunate if a conclusive specialist assessment came to be regarded as necessary before the court would accept jurisdiction at all.' As to the court's interim jurisdiction under MCA s 48 see **CHAPTER 5**: Procedure at **PARA 5.23**: The court's power to make medical treatment decisions.
4   [1999] Fam 26; [1998] 3 WLR 936. For a detailed analysis see **CHAPTER 9**.
5   Paras 4.44, 4.45, 6.32 and 6.34.

The absolute nature of an adult's consent

2.9   The consent of an adult patient is always enough to justify a willing doctor providing lawful treatment. It cannot be challenged by anyone else, whatever legal or moral claim to interest in the outcome they may have. Thus it is clearly established that the father of a foetus has no right to seek to prevent the mother consenting to the termination of the pregnancy.[1] The court cannot override a capable adult's consent, if the proposed treatment would otherwise be lawful.

1   *Paton v British Pregnancy Advisory Service Trustees* [1979] QB 276; *C v S* [1988] QB 135. See **CHAPTER 9**: Managing Pregnancies, **PARA 9.2**.

Treatment must be lawful

2.10   The mere demand by a patient for a particular treatment which the doctor is willing to give does not automatically render it lawful. Treatment will be considered unlawful if it is deemed so by statute; for example, a termination of pregnancy not authorised by the Abortion Act 1967.[1] Further, treatment will be unlawful at common law if it is against public policy.[2] This is more difficult to define, but it may be thought that the amputation of a limb purely for some claimed psychological need would offend against public policy. As a matter of general principle, any form of physical mutilation is unlawful unless it is for good reason. Obviously, bona fide medical treatment provides such a reason. However, consensual sado–masochistic practices leading to serious injury do not.[3] While this is a problem unlikely to be encountered in routine medical practice, there may be questions over cosmetic treatment intended to disfigure the patient in some way which is considered to be unacceptable in the public interest. It is not easy to determine which activities fall on which side of the line, but consensual tattooing, even if undertaken by unqualified individuals, appears to be lawful.[4] This principle will have to be kept in mind when consideration is given to new and ethically controversial treatments such as advanced techniques for reproduction and cloning.

1 See **CHAPTER 8**: Abortion.
2 See, by way of analogy, *R v Brown* [1994] 1 AC 212.
3 *Ibid* and see **CHAPTER 1, PARA 1.9**: Treatment demanded by the patient.
4 *R v Brown* (see **N2**) and see *R v Wilson* [1997] QB 47, [1996] 3 WLR 125, [1996] 2 Cr App Rep 241, CA (Crim Div) (accused branded his wife's buttocks with his own initials at her instigation and with her consent: held that the action taken by the accused could be seen as similar to tattooing, which did not attract a criminal sanction).

C REFUSAL

2.11   It is the corollary of the right to authorise treatment that there is a right to refuse it. To the extent that the right to refuse treatment is denied, so is the autonomy of the individual.[1] A refusal may be for any reason, good or bad, or for no reason at all. The fact that the refusal is considered by others to be irrational or morally repugnant in no way invalidates it or avoids the need to respect it.[2]

The only qualification to the right to refuse treatment is that a refusal cannot be used as a backdoor method of insisting on treatment which the doctor is unwilling to provide. No doctor, and no health authority, can be required to provide a patient with treatment which is not clinically indicated and is not considered by them to be in the patient's interests.[3] Thus, a patient who is advised to have a treatment consisting of two inseparable elements cannot, by consenting to only one of them, require the doctor to provide it.[4]

This does not excuse the treating doctor from dealing with the patient as he finds him. If he starts a treatment with the patient's consent, and the consent is subsequently withdrawn, the treatment cannot proceed, and the doctor must provide whatever proper treatment the patient allows him to undertake in order to ameliorate the position. A patient who refuses a blood transfusion which is needed for an operation to proceed cannot be forced to have the operation or the transfusion, and conservative treatment must be resorted to, even though, in the opinion of the surgeon, surgery is the best treatment.

1 *S & S; W v Official Solicitor (or W)* [1972] AC 24, HL at 43 per Lord Reid: 'The real reason is that English law goes to great lengths to protect a person of full age and capacity from interference with his personal liberty. We have too often seen freedom disappear in other countries not only by coups d'etat but by gradual erosion: and often it is the first step that counts. So it would be unwise to make even minor concessions.'
2 *St George's Healthcare NHS Trust v S* [1999] Fam 26, CA and *Re W (Adult: Refusal of Treatment)* [2002] EWHC 901 (Fam) where a secure prisoner who intentionally cut his own leg and kept it open by forcing objects into it was found to have capacity to refuse treatment notwithstanding that he was likely to contract septicaemia and die. See also **CHAPTER 13**: Treatment of Suicidal Patients, **PARA 13.34**.
3 *Re J (a minor) (child in care: medical treatment)* [1993] Fam 15; *R (Burke) v General Medical Council* [2006] QB 273 at paras 31, 50 and 51. For further discussion of *Burke* see **CHAPTER 14**: The End of Life, **PARAS 14.23–14.24**.
4 See **CHAPTER 1**: Consent – General, **PARA 1.6**: Compelling a doctor to treat.

D CHANGE OF MIND

2.12   An adult with full capacity is entitled to withdraw a consent already given at any time before the treatment concerned has been provided. Even if the treatment has started, and the patient retains capacity, he may demand that it be stopped.[1] While, as stated above, the doctor cannot be required to treat the patient so as to leave him in an unacceptable state, it is doubtful whether he can insist upon finishing a procedure he has started if a patient still possessing full capacity requires him to stop. There may be a difference between the doctor being required to *do* something which will have an unacceptable result and being required to *stop* doing something which will avoid it. In practice, of course, this is unlikely to arise, and a doctor reasonably believing that a patient is likely to act in this way if provided with treatment is justified in refusing to do so.

For a withdrawal of consent to have effect it is necessary for it to be communicated to the person providing treatment. A surgeon who continues to operate in ignorance of a withdrawal communicated to a junior doctor on the ward is unlikely to attract personal liability, although the junior doctor, and his employer, most certainly will – for a breach of the duty of care to the patient.[2]

Withdrawal of consent will also depend upon the patient's capacity which may well be affected by sedation or other medication given prior to or during the procedure. Thus where a patient demands that treatment which has been started should be stopped, an assessment of capacity will be required and it is suggested the right to withdraw consent is therefore not absolute and may be overruled where the effects are life-threatening or pose a serious risk to the patient's health and this cannot be appropriately weighed by the patient once the treatment is underway.

1   *Ciarlariello v Schactr* 100 DLR (94th) 609 (1983) (SCC), (1994) 5 Med LR 213: the claimant suffered an adverse reaction following a diagnostic cerebral angiogram and sued the doctor for battery, having asked him to stop during the procedure. Cory J stated: 'An individual's right to determine what medical procedures will be accepted must include the right to stop a procedure. It is not beyond the realm of possibility that the patient is better able to gauge the level of pain or discomfort that can be accepted or that the patient's premonitions of tragedy or mortality may have a basis in reality. In any event, the patient's right to bodily integrity provides the basis for the withdrawal of a consent to a medical procedure even while it is underway. Thus, if it is found that the consent is effectively withdrawn during the course of the procedure then it must be terminated.'
2   *Re J (a minor) (child in care: medical treatment)* [1993] Fam 15.

E ADVANCE DIRECTIVES/DECISIONS

General principle

2.13   Consent is often given in advance of the proposed treatment. In the case of surgery under general anaesthetic, it has to be. Equally, it is possible for a patient to express a present intention to refuse treatment in specified circumstances. There is now no doubt that if certain conditions are fulfilled, doctors and others are bound in law to comply with such statements. In other words, to proceed with treatment prohibited by a valid and applicable advance directive is unlawful and renders those providing the treatment liable to a charge or claim for assault and battery.

Requirements

2.14   Sections 24–26 of the MCA give statutory recognition to advance decisions refusing treatment and specify the conditions which must be fulfilled before such a decision or directive is considered to be valid and applicable.

An advance decision is a decision to refuse specified treatment in the future which is to have effect if the person making the advance decision lacks the capacity to consent to or refuse treatment at that point in the future.

To be valid, an advance decision must:

- be made by a person aged 18 or over;
- be made at a time when a patient has capacity;
- specify the treatment which is to be refused. [1]

It is not necessary to specify the treatment covered by the advance decision in medical language[2] nor is it necessary to specify the circumstances in which the refusal is to apply, although s 24(1) MCA provides that this 'may' be done. Although not expressed in the Act, it must follow that there must have been no vitiating influence such as duress, undue influence or fraud.[3]

A person may withdraw or alter an advance decision at any time when he has capacity to do so and such a withdrawal (including a partial withdrawal) or alteration need not be in writing, unless the alteration relates to an advance decision refusing life-sustaining treatment.[4]

An advance decision is not valid:

- if withdrawn while the patient has capacity;
- where the patient has created a lasting power of attorney after the decision was made in which he has conferred authority to give or refuse consent to the specified treatment to the donee;
- if the patient has done anything clearly inconsistent with the advance decision.[5]

In *HE v A Hospital NHS Trust*[6], a woman who suffered from a congenital heart problem had made an advance directive refusing blood products at a time when she was a practising Jehovah's Witness. She had subsequently become engaged to a Muslim and was professing that she would live by the principles of that faith when she was taken seriously ill and rushed to hospital. Her father applied to the court for an order that the hospital give her a blood transfusion in order to save her life, as the advance decision no longer reflected her intentions. Munby J held that:

'Since it is quite clear that the Advance Directive was founded entirely on [HE's daughter's] AE's faith as a Jehovah's Witness — that is made clear beyond argument by the very terms of the Advance Directive itself — it seems to me that it cannot have survived her deliberate, implemented, decision to abandon that faith and to revert to being a Muslim. When the entire substratum has gone, when the very assumption on which the advance directive was based has been destroyed by subsequent events then, as Lord Donaldson put it in *In re T*, "the refusal ceases to be effective". The advance directive ceases to have effect, whether or not expressly revoked by the patient. AE's rejection and abandonment of her faith as a Jehovah's Witness deprives the Advance Directive of any continuing validity and effect … '[7]

An advance decision is not applicable if:

- the patient retains capacity to give or refuse consent to the specified treatment at the time it is provided;
- the treatment in question is not that specified in the advance decision;
- any circumstances which have been specified in the advance decision are absent;
- there are reasonable grounds for believing that circumstances exist which the patient did not anticipate at the time of the advance decision and which would have affected his decision had he anticipated them.[8]

The patient must have been in possession of knowledge of the nature and effect of the decision being taken. Therefore an advance refusal made in ignorance that the effect of withholding the treatment objected to would mean certain death will not bind the doctors unless there is clear evidence that the patient was aware of this consequence, or was at least clearly willing to take that risk.

Further specific safeguards have been provided by s 25(5) and (6) of the MCA for advance decisions applicable to life-sustaining treatment. These provide that the decision must:

- include a statement by the patient that it is to apply to the treatment specified even if life is at risk;
- be in writing;
- be signed by the patient or another person in the patient's presence and by the patient's direction; and
- be witnessed.

A doctor or any other person, who reasonably believes that an advance decision is valid and applicable to treatment, does not incur liability if the treatment is withheld or withdrawn in accordance with that decision.[9]

Provision is made for the court to make a declaration as to the existence, validity and applicability of an advance decision.[10] Importantly, nothing in an advance decision stops a person from providing life-sustaining treatment or doing any act he reasonably believes to be necessary to prevent a serious deterioration of a patient's condition while a decision in respect of 'any relevant issue' is sought from the court.[11]

The principle behind s 26(5) is that where there is genuine doubt either about the patient's capacity to have made his advance refusal of treatment or about whether the terms are sufficiently specific then the paramount consideration will be preservation of life and health pending the court's determination of the issue. Section 26(5) is unqualified and so will allow treatment apparently inconsistent with the terms of an advance decision to be given in an emergency situation pending determination by the court as to the existence, validity or applicability of that advance decision. It therefore begs the question: can the mere issue of proceedings change the status of the act, for example giving a blood transfusion to a card-carrying Jehovah's Witness, rendering lawful what would otherwise be unlawful? If strictly construed, this may be the case. However, it is suggested that this would be difficult to reconcile with basic common law principles and the thrust of the MCA, which is to safeguard the fundamental principle of personal autonomy or self-determination. An emergency application could be made to the court to validate that autonomy. The authors are aware of such an application being made by a hospital seeking the court's approval for *not* providing a blood transfusion to a Jehovah's Witness even though the material advance directive could not be found.

1   MCA, s 24(1).
2   MCA, s 24(2).
3   See **CHAPTER 1, PARAS 1.30–1.32** for a discussion of factors vitiating consent.
4   See **PARA 2.15**: Form below; MCA, s 24(3), (4) and (5).
5   MCA, s 25(2).
6   [2003] EWHC 1017 (Fam), [2003] 2 FLR 408.
7   *Ibid* at para 49
8   MCA, s 25(3) and (4).
9   MCA, s 26(3).
10 MCA, s 26(4).
11 MCA, s 26(5).

Form

2.15   An advance statement may be oral or in writing, save where the decision is applicable to life-sustaining treatment when it must be in writing as specified in ss 25 and 26 of the MCA. There is no legal requirement as to form so long as the requirements referred to above are met. It is obviously prudent for any patient desiring to ensure that his wishes are respected to record his intentions in writing and to give a copy of the document to any doctor likely to be treating him in the future, and also to his general practitioner. Any doctor receiving such a document should ensure that a copy is lodged with the patient's records, and that all doctors who may be treating the patient are informed.

While any form of words will suffice if it makes the intentions of the patient clear, many patients will want to be offered some form on which they can indicate their choices. Chapter 9 of the Code of Practice provides a list of suggested information which could be included in a written advance decision at paragraph 9.19 and further guidance can be obtained from the NHS Advance Decisions to Refuse Treatment (ADRT) website.[1]

1   www.adrtnhs.co.uk ; A form of directive published by the ADRT is illustrated in **APPENDIX 2.1**: Draft Advance Directive; Draft Advance Directives can be found at: http://www. adrtnhs.co.uk/pdf/EoLC_appendix1.pdf and http://www.christie.nhs.uk/patients/booklets/pdf/ Living_Wills.pdf .

Informed refusal?

2.16   Where consent is being obtained for treatment the doctor will be under a duty to warn the patient of the risks involved.[1] Failure to do so may render the doctor liable in negligence, but does not invalidate the consent, unless the doctor deceives the patient in a way which results in his true will not being expressed. It is unclear whether the same principle applies to advance refusals. A patient may express an advance refusal to specific treatment under mistaken beliefs as to the risks and benefits of the treatment, either because he has not asked any qualified person for advice or because erroneous advice has been given. For example, an advance directive may be signed because of a false rumour relayed by a friend that a particular form of treatment was very dangerous, without having discussed the matter with a person qualified to know. A person with strong religious beliefs may hold views about the effects of certain types of treatment quite at odds with the opinions of the medical profession. There is no direct authority on the point. Applying s 25(4) of the MCA, it is arguable that an intention to refuse treatment expressed under a mistaken belief as to the facts is invalid because it is not a statement intended to govern the actual factual situation at the time when the perceived need for treatment arises. However, to override an advance refusal on this ground would be to deny the individual's right to make decisions for himself on whatever information he chooses to base them. If, therefore, the doctor wishes to ignore an advance directive because he is aware that the statement was made under a belief as to the risks and benefits of the treatment, which he considers to have been mistaken, he may be exposing himself to criticism. In view of the uncertainty it would seem essential to seek a court declaration before proceeding. It is suggested it may be easy to persuade the court in those circumstances that the advance refusal did not cover the factual situation facing the doctor, in particular if failing to treat will result in death.

1   See **CHAPTER 1, PARA 1.4**: Risks of Treatment and **PARA 1.28**: Information about alternative forms of treatment.

Knowledge

2.17   In order for an advance directive to be effective, in practice, the doctor confronted with the incapacitated patient must obviously be aware of its existence. It has been suggested above that patients wishing to make such statements should ensure they are in writing and disseminated to all those likely to need to know about them. What action should doctors take when presented with a patient and they do not know whether a directive has been made?

Section 4(6)(a) MCA requires that when considering what action is in an incapable person's best interests one must consider, so far as is reasonably ascertainable—

'the person's past and present wishes and feelings (and, in particular, any relevant written statement made by him when he had capacity)'.

Therefore any doctor proposing to treat an incapacitated patient is obliged by law to make reasonable enquiries into their previous wishes and this will include whether a formal advance directive has been made.

What is reasonable will depend on the nature of the patient's condition and the proposed treatment. It is more easily anticipated that some patients will be reluctant to accept treatment for some conditions, for example radical surgery to palliate an inevitably fatal cancer, than for others. Greater efforts to establish whether the patient has left any statement might be required in such a case than in a case of more routine care.

Section 26(2) of the MCA now allows a doctor to raise as a defence to any charge of assault the assertion that he acted in good faith in ignorance of an advance refusal of treatment. However, it is suggested that it remains incumbent on doctors and health managers to have in place systems which minimise the chance of an advance statement being missed. It is sometimes argued that the risks involved in treating in ignorance of an advance directive are less than not providing treatment to an ill person because damages for the latter could never be more than nominal. This is not so: first, to treat in such circumstances could lead to criminal charges; secondly, as the act is unlawful, damages are at large and could arguably be assessed on the basis that the injury was the invasive treatment itself.[1] Further, where the treatment gave rise to complications, even non-negligent ones, there would undoubtedly be a right to compensatory damages in both tort and under s 8 of the Human Rights Act 1998.

1   In *Malette v Shulman* [1991] 2 Med LR 162, a Jehovah's Witness was in an accident. She had a card requesting no blood transfusions which was shown to the treating doctor. Nonetheless he administered blood transfusions to the patient. The transfusion probably saved her life. She made a good recovery from her injuries. The Ontario Court of Appeal affirmed the first instance judge's determination that the doctor's actions constituted an assault and that the award made of $20,000 was appropriate (about $28,000 or £16,000 at today's rates).

Duration

2.18   In theory, an advance directive is of indefinite duration. In practice, its life will be limited by the requirement that it is intended to cover the circumstances as they are at the time treatment is being considered. Many such statements are intended to cover specific illnesses and will expire if the patient either fails to develop the feared condition or recovers from it unexpectedly. The emergence of new forms of treatment may also invalidate the directive. Accordingly, patients who make directives should be advised of the need to review them on a regular basis, preferably in conjunction with their general practitioner or other appropriate medical adviser.

Records

2.19   The Court of Appeal has made clear that, for their own protection, health authorities and doctors should seek unequivocal assurances in writing that a refusal represents an informed and settled decision and that the patient understands the nature of the proposed treatment, the reasons for it being recommended, the risks, and likely prognosis involved in the decision to refuse it.[1] Where the patient is not prepared to provide such a written assurance, a careful record must be made of the advice given to the patient about the need for treatment and the risks of refusing it, together with the patient's reasons for refusal.

1   *St George's NHS Healthcare Trust v S* [1999] Fam 26, [1998] 3 WLR 936.

F CONCLUSION

2.20   While it has always been well established that an adult who lacks capacity cannot give valid consent to treatment, the MCA places a renewed emphasis on the autonomy of the patient and imposes a clear requirement to involve patients and those close to them in the decision-making process in relation both to medical treatment and to the assessment of capacity (where this is in doubt). Clinicians must undertake reasonable steps to establish whether a patient has capacity to make a specific decision. If legal proceedings arise, the courts will assess assiduously whether practical steps have in fact been taken in a particular case to enhance the patient's capacity.[1] If they have not, this will have serious ramifications for clinicians and hospital trusts alike. It is therefore important that protocols are put in place in hospitals to guide healthcare workers through steps which can be taken with more challenging patients who may traditionally have been treated in a paternalistic fashion. Trusts would be well advised to seek input from organisations such as Mencap, the Mental Health Foundation and MIND as to how better to communicate with such patients. The goal should be to ensure that, where capacity to take a particular decision is present, it is genuinely respected regardless of the preconceptions which may be held about certain 'types' of patient.

1   MCA, s 1(3).

For updating material and hyperlinks related to this chapter, see www.3serjeantsinn.com/mtdl/consent-adults

---

Chapter 3

Deciding for Others – Adults

A The court's power to order treatment 3.1
B Taking decisions for adults 3.2
 General rule 1: A capable adult's wishes must be respected 3.2
 General rule 2: There is only limited proxy of consent for others 3.3
 General rule 3: Power to treat in an incapable person's best interests 3.4
C Decisions in relation to adults with capacity 3.5
 The obligation to treat in accordance with expressed wishes 3.6
 Obstetric treatment in the interests of a viable foetus no exception 3.7
D Deciding for adults without capacity 3.8
 Treatment out of necessity 3.8
 The Mental Capacity Act 2005 3.9
 Temporary incapacity 3.10
 Records – the basis of any application 3.11
 Scope of power to treat 3.12
 Determination of best interests 3.13
 The medical issues 3.14
 What are the interests to be considered? 3.15
 The use of force and restraint 3.16
 Advance decisions and best interests 3.17
E Conclusion 3.18

A THE COURT'S POWER TO ORDER TREATMENT

3.1 Traditionally, the High Court has exercised its inherent jurisdiction when making declarations or orders in relation to medical treatment issues.[1] However, on 1 October 2007 the Mental Capacity Act 2005 ('MCA')[2] came into force. It provides a statutory framework to assist with the decision-making process for people who lack capacity. Although the MCA covers a much broader compass than medical and treatment decisions alone, it is particularly useful for those involved in and advising on those and related issues. The MCA should be read in conjunction with the Mental Capacity Act 2005 Code of Practice ('the Code')[3] which provides a useful explanation of the principles and of the suggested approach to consideration and assessment of the relevant issues. The way in which the MCA impacts upon individual aspects of the decision-making process is explored in greater detail below.[4] The specific issue of deprivation of liberty under MCA is dealt with in **CHAPTER 6**.

1   Section 19 of the Senior Courts Act 1981 and s 19(2)(b) confirm that the civil jurisdiction it exercised prior to the SCA coming into force was to continue. Munby J in *Re SA (Vulnerable Adult with Capacity: Marriage)* [2006] 1 FLR 867 at paras [38]–[43] and specifically at paragraph 37 stated: 'It is now clear … that the court exercises what is, in substance and reality, a jurisdiction in relation to incompetent adults which is for all practical purposes indistinguishable from its well-established *parens patriae* or wardship jurisdictions in relation to children. The court exercises a "protective jurisdiction" in relation to vulnerable adults just as it does in relation to wards of court.'.
2   Amended by the Mental Health Act 2007.
3   See www.justice.gov.uk/guidance/mca-code-of-practice.htm and in particular sections 1–6, 8 and 9.
4   For a detailed analysis of the development of the 'best interests' test and a discussion of the potential impact of the MCA, see M Donnelly, 'Best interests, patient participation and the Mental Capacity Act 2005' (2009) 17 Med L Rev 1.

B TAKING DECISIONS FOR ADULTS

General rule 1: A capable adult's wishes must be respected

3.2   Regardless of how wise or unwise the patient's decision may appear to others, there is no power to impose or withhold treatment contrary to the competent patient's election. The only exception is treatment for mental disorder that may be provided under the Mental Health Act 1983 ('MHA') despite a competent refusal.

General rule 2: There is only limited proxy of consent for others

3.3   There is a frequently held misconception that the incompetent patient's next of kin have a right to be consulted or even to decide on treatment. This is not so. Prior to the MCA coming into force, no-one other than the patient could give or refuse consent to the treatment proposed for that patient so long as he was an adult. There was no proxy of consent for the capable or incapable adult. The High Court had common law powers to make declarations that the provision of treatment in the absence of consent would be lawful, but the introductory wording of those orders typically made clear that the person being treated did not have capacity and could not consent.[1] Even with the advent of the MCA, proxy consent in decision-making for others lies with only a limited group of people, namely those with a lasting power of attorney over treatment and welfare decisions and deputies appointed by the court to decide on behalf of the incapable patient.[2]

1   Typically the declaratory orders made by the courts commenced with the words 'IT IS DECLARED that (a) X lacks capacity; and (b) Notwithstanding X's inability to consent to treatment, it shall be lawful for the clinicians at Y Hospital to [and the relevant treatment was then described)'.
2   See further below at **PARA 3.9**.

General rule 3: Power to treat in an incapable person's best interests

3.4   Where an adult patient is incapable, then prior to the MCA the common law doctrine of necessity could be relied upon to permit doctors to provide such treatment to an incapable person as was in their best interests. Since the MCA that common law defence is now on a statutory footing in s 5 of the Act which states:

'Acts in connection with care or treatment

(1) If a person ("D") does an act in connection with the care or treatment of another person ("P"), the act is one to which this section applies if—

    (a)   before doing the act, D takes reasonable steps to establish whether P lacks capacity in relation to the matter in question, and

    (b)   when doing the act, D reasonably believes—

        (i)   that P lacks capacity in relation to the matter, and

        (ii)   that it will be in P's best interests for the act to be done.

(2) D does not incur any liability in relation to the act that he would not have incurred if P—

    (a)   had had capacity to consent in relation to the matter, and

    (b)   had consented to D's doing the act.'

C DECISIONS IN RELATION TO ADULTS WITH CAPACITY

3.5   Section 1(2) of the MCA provides the starting point for the consideration of capacity which must come before any decision-making in respect of another:

'A person must be assumed to have capacity unless it is established that he lacks capacity.'[1]

This includes the capacity to take a decision as to whether information should be shared with others. Before any steps are taken to involve family members in any decision-making process, all reasonable steps should be taken to ascertain whether the person in respect of whom a decision is being taken consents to or has capacity to consent to that sharing of information. Disclosures that were necessarily made to clinicians in the ordinary course of treatment would not amount to a breach.

Regardless of how wise or unwise the patient's decision may appear to others, there is – save for one exception – no power to impose or withhold treatment where the competent patient has made an election. Thus, where a prisoner intentionally cut his own leg then contaminated the wound and refused medical treatment with the result that he was likely to contract septicaemia and die, the court refused to intervene.[2]

In *B v An NHS Hospital Trust*,[3] B suffered an intracranial haemorrhage which caused her to be admitted to hospital. She was warned of the possibility of a further bleed and took the decision to prepare a living will asking that treatment be withdrawn if she was subsequently admitted suffering from any life-threatening condition, mental impairment or permanent unconsciousness. Her condition improved and she was discharged. She later suffered a dramatic deterioration, was admitted and then put on a ventilator. She made a second living will. In the course of proceedings, the President took evidence from B, found her 'a most impressive witness' and determined that at all material times she had capacity. It followed that the hospital's treatment of her had been unlawful and she was entitled to damages, although in the circumstances only a very modest sum was awarded.

The isolated exception to the autonomy that competent patients enjoy over the way in which they are to be treated is contained within s 63 of the Mental Health Act 1983 which provides that:

> 'The consent of a patient shall not be required for any medical treatment given to him for the mental disorder from which he is suffering, not being treatment falling within section 57 or 58 above, if the treatment is given by or under the direction of the responsible medical officer.'

In *PS*,[4] the patient (PS) suffered from schizophrenia but it was common ground that he had capacity to refuse treatment. Silber J determined that it was lawful under the MHA and in his best interests to receive psychotropic medication, despite PS's competent refusal to accept the treatment.

Section 63 will not only permit treatment for the core mental disorder, but may also cover treatment for physical symptoms consequent upon the mental disorder despite capable refusal of the same. In *B v Croydon Health Authority*, the Court of Appeal concluded that relieving the symptoms of the mental disorder is just as much a part of treatment under s 63 as relieving its underlying cause.[5] Thus an anorexic patient can be force fed and the self-inflicted wound of someone who self-harms as a consequence of a personality disorder may be sutured pursuant to s 63 MHA powers.[6]

1   See **CHAPTER 2**: Consent – Adults at **PARA 2.8**: Presumption of Capacity.
2   *Re W (Adult: Refusal of Treatment)* (2002) EWHC 901 (Fam).
3   [2002] Lloyd's Rep Med 265.
4   *R (on the application of PS) v Responsible Medical Officer & others* [2003] EWHC 2335. See also the CA at [2006] EWCA Civ 28, [2006] 1 WLR 810.
5   [1995] Fam 133, [1995] 1 All ER 683 following *In re KB (Adult) (Mental Patient: Medical Treatment)* (1994) 19 BMLR 144 at 146 and *Riverside Mental Health NHS Trust v Fox* [1994] 1 FLR 614 at 619.
6   *Re KB* [1997] 2 FLR 180.

The obligation to treat in accordance with expressed wishes

3.6   Most of the cases coming before the courts involve patients who either refuse treatment or cannot consent to treatment being provided. Interesting questions arise where a competent patient makes it clear that he expects life-saving treatment to be provided in future. In *Burke*, the patient was suffering from a progressive degenerative disorder and sought clarification of the circumstances in which treating staff might lawfully withdraw artificial nutrition and hydration in the future. In dealing with a variety of complex issues, the Master of the Rolls noted:

> 'We have indicated that, where a competent patient indicates his or her wish to be kept alive by the provision of [artificial nutrition and hydration] any doctor who deliberately brings that patient's life to an end by discontinuing the supply of [artificial nutrition and hydration] will not merely be in breach of duty but guilty of murder. Where life depends on the continued provision of [artificial nutrition and hydration] there can be no question of the supply of [artificial nutrition and hydration] not being clinically indicated unless a clinical decision has been taken that the life in question should come to an end. That is not a decision that can lawfully be taken in the case of a competent patient who expresses the wish to remain alive.'[1]

1 *R (on the application of Oliver Leslie Burke) v GMC* [2006] QB 273, [2005] 3 WLR 1132 at para 53.

Obstetric treatment in the interests of a viable foetus no exception

3.7   It has long been established that the competent adult patient's right to personal freedom from physical invasion extends to cases where the exercise of that freedom may prejudice the well-being of a viable foetus.[1]

1 *Re MB (an adult: medical treatment)* [1997] 2 FLR 426, [1997] 8 Med LR 217; and *St George's Healthcare NHS Trust v S* [1998] 3 WLR 936. See **CHAPTER 9**: Managing Pregnancies.

D DECIDING FOR ADULTS WITHOUT CAPACITY

Treatment out of necessity

3.8   The law requires a doctor to provide such treatment and care as would be in the incapable patient's best interests. This principle is derived from the legal doctrine of necessity and translates into the medical context by requiring the doctor to provide such treatment as he considers to be both in the patient's best interests and necessary in relation to the preservation or improvement of his health.[1]

1 *Re F (mental patient: sterilisation)* [1990] 2 AC 1.

The Mental Capacity Act 2005

3.9   The advent of the MCA has not changed the underlying basis on which treatment may be provided but it does 'enshrine in statute current best practice and common law principles concerning people who lack capacity and those who take decisions on their behalf'.[1] The MCA is underpinned by the five key principles set out in s 1:

● unless and until it is established that a person lacks capacity, he shall be presumed to have capacity;

- a person should not be treated as being unable to make a decision until all practicable steps have been taken to help him make a decision yet he still lacks the necessary capacity;
- a person should not be taken to lack capacity simply because he takes an unwise decision;
- any act done or step taken on a person's behalf under the MCA must be taken in his best interests;
- where action is taken on behalf of a person who lacks capacity, care should be taken to ensure that the course which is followed is the least restrictive of that person's rights.

Where a patient lacks the capacity to make a decision for himself, only those with a lasting power of attorney ('LPA')[2] or a court-appointed deputy ('CAD')[3] have a power in law to consent or refuse treatment on his behalf. In particular, the next of kin or other close family members have no such power. Prior to the MCA coming into force, a court would have expected to see evidence that steps had been taken to establish from the family any relevant background information that might assist in deciding what the person's view as to treatment would probably have been. The usual starting point would have been to consult family members. Section 7 of the MCA now specifically directs that where a person takes a decision for another:

'He must take into account, if it is practicable and appropriate to consult them, the views of:

(a)   Anyone named by the person as someone to be consulted on the matter in question or on matters of that kind,

(b)   Anyone engaged in caring for the person or interested in his welfare,

(c)   Any donee of a lasting power of attorney granted by the person, and

(d)   Any deputy appointed for the person by the Court,

as to what would be in the person's best interests and, in particular, as to the matters mentioned in sub-section 6.'

Sub-section 6 requires consideration of the person's previously expressed views, his beliefs and values and any other factors he would likely have taken into account when reaching a decision had he been able to do so.

In some cases a person may have an appointed Independent Mental Capacity Advocate. Where serious medical treatment is contemplated and there is no-one who falls within the categories above but an Independent Mental Capacity Advocate has been appointed, the person seeking to take a decision should instruct him to prepare a report.[4] Importantly, though, while part of the Independent Mental Capacity Advocate's role is to represent and put forward the views of the incapable patient, he has no power to consent to or refuse treatment on their behalf.

---

1   Summary of the Act by the Department of Constitutional Affairs: http://www.dca.gov.uk/legal-policy/mental-capacity/mca-summary.pdf .

2   MCA, s 9(1)(a).

3   MCA, s 16(2)(b).

4   Code of Practice, para 5.50.

Temporary incapacity

3.10   Where the patient is permanently incapacitated then, subject to consideration of best interests under the framework provided by the MCA, a doctor may provide any treatment he considers necessary and in the patient's best interests. In such circumstances, once an assessment of best interests has been carried out there is no point in delaying treatment. However, where a person's incapacity is or may be temporary, s 1(3) of the MCA requires any person seeking to take a decision on behalf of another to consider:

(a)   whether it is likely that the person will at some time have capacity in relation to the matter in question; and

(b)   if it appears likely that he will, when that is likely to be.

Section 1(4) imposes a further obligation to ensure that all reasonably practicable steps are taken to permit and encourage a person to participate or improve his ability to participate in any decision affecting him. While this is of general application, it has particular importance where there is a possibility that incapacity may be only temporary. In such circumstances it would be good practice to ascertain in advance and provide evidence of:

- the cause of the incapacity;
- how long the person has lacked capacity;
- whether this is an isolated event or a more frequent occurrence;
- whether the person's ability to comprehend, retain, weigh up and communicate has deteriorated, improved or remained consistent and whether, absent any treatment, any change is anticipated;
- whether medical opinion suggests that any particular course of treatment might provide a return to capacity;
- if so, what sort of treatment is involved; how invasive would it be; what are the prospects of an improvement in capacity; and how long would it take before any improvement was likely to manifest itself;
- whether and, if so, how the underlying medical condition requiring treatment is likely to deteriorate while steps are being taken to provide the person with capacity.

In a case of temporary incapacity where urgent treatment is necessary and there is no time to undertake consultation, the medical team may provide only that treatment or care which is necessary before the likely recovery of capacity. The Code of Practice provides additional assistance on this issue.[1]

1   Code of Practice, paras 4.26, 4.27 and 5.28. See **CHAPTER 2**: Consent – Adults, **PARA 2.7**: Temporary incapacity.

Records – the basis of any application

3.11   Medical treatment decisions will frequently have an impact on the life (or death) of a person. There may be ramifications upon a person's liberty. In some cases a court will authorise sedation and restraint so that treatment can be provided. The provision of some types of treatment may lie against a person's fundamentally held religious belief and could impact upon their standing within a family or society. For all these reasons it will be important that assessments of capacity are recorded. The source of any information as to capacity should be queried and noted. In particular, it should not be assumed that medical staff (including psychiatrists) have focused on the necessary elements of capacity unless and until this has been expressly confirmed. The ability of the adviser to confirm such information will depend upon the urgency of any given situation. However, the advocate making an application to court for a declaration on treatment issues bears a heavy burden to ensure the accuracy of the information upon which any declaration is granted. The difficulties faced both by legal representatives and by the court only increase when applications are made out of hours and by telephone. It would be wise for anyone advising in such cases, and in particular those who make representations to the court, to take a detailed note of the evidence relied upon at the time that it is received. If facilities permit, a copy of that information should be e-mailed or faxed to the court prior to the hearing, thereby reducing the chances of any misunderstanding. If there is any obvious gap in the evidence available then that feature also should be emphasised to the court. Thus, for example, the court should be informed if a patient has a partner or close family member who would be expected to provide some information about what the patient would have considered to be in his best interests but whom it has been impossible to locate (along with a description of the steps undertaken and the chances of making contact in the near future).

Scope of power to treat

3.12   The general power to act under s 5 MCA, as described above, which must include the concept of necessity,[1] provides sufficient justification for all forms of treatment and care required for an incapacitated adult patient.[2] Thus a decision as to the location in which a mentally incompetent stroke victim should be cared for is to be decided by those responsible for his care by reference to his best interests[3] in the same way as a decision to perform surgery. The MCA is not restricted in application to medical decisions and applies equally to decisions concerning property and affairs and other everyday decisions about personal care.[4]

A patient lacking the capacity to consent to treatment who has been admitted informally to a mental hospital under s 131 of the MHA may be provided with such treatment for their condition as is in their best interests. However, if the circumstances of the patient's admission for treatment amount to a deprivation of liberty, that detention, even if in the patient's best interests, must be further authorised under Schedule A1 to the MCA.[5]

---

1   Section 5 MCA simply refers to 'best interests'. However, the principle of necessity must continue to have an important role, but is now subsumed into the meaning of 'best interests'. If 'necessity' has no role, it would mean that a surgeon could extend the scope of an operation based on his assessment of the patient's best interests simply because the patient was unconscious. The law must remain that in emergency situations the doctor can only provide treatment which is strictly necessary in relation to the preservation or improvement of his health.

2   Save for treatment and care requiring a deprivation of liberty – for which see CHAPTER 6: Restraint and Deprivation of Liberty.

3   *Re S (hospital patient: court's jurisdiction)* [1996] Fam 1, [1995] 3 WLR 78, [1995] 3 All ER 290.

4   These decisions fall outside the scope of this book.
5   See **CHAPTER 6**: Restraint and Deprivation of Liberty.

Determination of best interests

3.13   The issue of best interests is central to any decision taken on behalf of another person. Section 1(5) of the MCA requires that any decision taken on behalf of a person must be in his best interests, while s 4 provides a detailed framework for assessment of best interests in each case. Any assessment of best interests must be carried out in accordance with the provisions of s 4 and in particular:

- The person conducting the assessment must ensure that all 'relevant' circumstances are taken into account.[1] The scope of 'relevant' issues will vary from case to case. It may well include religious beliefs or previously expressed views as to treatment which have not been recorded formally in an advance decision. The person conducting the assessment must inquire into the issues that would likely have been considered relevant by the person in respect of whom decisions are being taken. The particular importance previously applied by a person to family ties or living in a certain style will be relevant and should be noted. The sources of information should be considered carefully, particularly where decisions will have an impact on life or death issues. In general, and in particular when dealing with life or death decisions, care must be taken to ensure that advice from family members is not tainted by self-interest. Of necessity, these issues must be approached discreetly and with sensitivity.
- All reasonable steps must be taken to ensure that the person in respect of whom the decision is taken is encouraged and enabled to participate.[2] If the decision is not urgent this may involve providing treatment or therapies to encourage communication. Where there are issues arising out of a person's inability to understand advice, circumstances may warrant the instruction of a speech and language therapist to assist in comprehension and communication.
- A person's previously held beliefs and feelings will be central to a decision as to best interests.[3] As discussed above, family members and relatives will usually be a source of those views and opinions. It is often the case that a person in respect of whom a decision is being taken will have had previous experience of incapacity or disability in a friend or family member and may have been heard to express views about the prospects of life in such circumstances (such as 'I couldn't stand a life like that'). Such expressions will be more or less useful depending on the specific circumstances in which they were made. Where a person has spent many years looking after a partner suffering from a progressive debilitating illness and has witnessed first hand and for an extended period of time the physical and mental deterioration involved then a court will rightly apply weight to an expression that the carer would not wish under any circumstances to be in a similar position. However, there will be significant caution over expressions of desire as to future treatment based on less substantial grounds and information.[4]

Chapter 5 of the Code of Practice provides detailed guidance as to the assessment of best interests but the Act has not altered the basic approach that the court will take when assessing best interests. The courts have long accepted that 'best interests are not limited to best medical interests'.[5] Best interests encompass 'medical, emotional and all other welfare issues'.[6] As Thorpe LJ stated in *Re SL (adult patient) (medical treatment)*:

> 'In deciding what is best for the disabled patient the judge must have regard to the patient's welfare as the paramount consideration. That embraces issues far wider than the medical. Indeed it would be undesirable and probably impossible to set bounds to what is relevant to a welfare determination.'[7]

At one stage there was a focus on defining the 'best interests' test by reference to the concept of 'intolerability'. In *Burke*,[8] Munby J considered the authorities in some detail and attempted to provide guidance for those assessing 'best interests' decisions. In conducting that exercise he said:

> 'There is a very strong presumption in favour of taking all steps which will prolong life and save in exceptional circumstances, or where the patient is dying, the best interests of the patient will normally require such steps to be taken. In case of doubt that doubt falls to be resolved in favour of the preservation of life. But the obligation is not absolute. Important as the sanctity of life is, it may have to take second place to human dignity. In the context of life-prolonging treatment the touchstone of best interests is intolerability. Thus, if life-prolonging treatment is providing some benefit it should be provided unless the patient's life, if thus prolonged, would from the patient's point of view be intolerable.'[9]

However, when *Burke* reached the Court of Appeal, that approach found little favour. The Master of the Rolls reviewed the guidance provided and said:

> 'We do not think that any objection could have been taken to this summary had it not been for the final two sentences … The suggestion that the touchstone of "best interests" is the "intolerability" of continued life has, understandably, given rise to concern. The test of whether it is in the best interests of the patient to provide or continue [artificial nutrition and hydration must depend on the particular circumstances] …
>
> As to the approach to best interests where a patient is close to death, it seems to us that the judge himself recognised that "intolerability" was not the test of best interests. At paragraph 104 he said: "where the patient is dying, the goal may properly be to ease suffering and, where appropriate, to 'ease the passing' rather than to achieve a short prolongation of life"
>
> We agree. We do not think it possible to attempt to define what is in the best interests of a patient by a single test, applicable in all the circumstances.'[10]

When a court weighs up arguments as to best interests it may be assisted by the preparation of a 'balance sheet', as suggested by Thorpe LJ in *Re A: Male Sterilisation*:

' ... it seems to me that the first instance judge with the responsibility to make an evaluation of the best interests of a claimant lacking capacity should draw up the balance sheet. The first entry should be of any factor or factors of actual benefit ... on the other sheet the judge should write any counter-balancing dis-benefits to the applicant ... then the judge should enter on each sheet the potential gains and losses in each instance making some estimate of the extent or possibility that the gain or loss might accrue. At the end of that exercise the judge should be better placed to strike a balance between the sum of the certain and possible gains against the sum of the certain and possible losses. Obviously only if the account is in relatively significant credit will the judge conclude that the application is likely to advance the best interests of the claimant.' [11]

Carrying out an assessment in such a way will tend to avoid undue weight being applied to relatively hypothetical outcomes – a problem that Thorpe LJ considered had affected the judgment of the court at first instance in *Re A*.

When representing a party where a 'best interests' decision is to be made, it will usually be helpful to provide the judge with a proposed draft of Thorpe LJ's 'best interests checklist' either as part of one's opening skeleton/position statement or in final submissions.[12]

1   MCA, s 4(2).
2   MCA, s 4(4).
3   MCA, s 4(6). The weight to be attached to previous wishes has been considered in *In the matter of S & S sub nom C v V* (2009) LS Law Medical 97, as qualified by *In the matter of P* [2009] EWHC 163 (Ch).
4   The Court of Appeal in *W Healthcare NHS Trust v (1) KH, (2) H and (3) PH* [2004] EWCA Civ 1324 acceded to an application by the Trust that it was lawful to insert a PEG feeding tube despite strong evidence from the family that the patient had expressed views which would not have supported such action.
5   *Re MB (an adult: medical treatment)* [1997] 8 Med LR 217 at 225 per Butler-Sloss LJ. See **CHAPTER 9**: Managing Pregnancies **PARA 9.8FF**.
6   *Re A (medical treatment: male sterilisation)* [2000] 1 FCR 193, 53 BMLR 66, [2000] 02 LS Gaz R 30, *sub nom Re A (male sterilisation)* [2000] 1 FLR 549, CA.
7   *Re SL (adult patient) (medical treatment)* [2000] 2 FLR 389, (2000) Lloyds Law Reports (Medical) 339; See also Thorpe LJ in *Re A Male Sterilisation* [2000] FLR 549.
8   *Burke v GMC* [2006] QB 273.
9   *Ibid*, at para 116.
10 *Ibid* at para 62.
11 *Re A* (N 7 above) at 560E.
12 For example, the checklist prepared by counsel and adopted by Parker J in *OT* [2009] EWHC 633 Fam at paras 109–145; see **CHAPTER 5**: Going to Court.

The medical issues

3.14   In general, the doctor is obliged to assess the patient's best medical interests in accordance with a competent and responsible standard of medical practice, that is, in the same way as he performs all other parts of his duty to his patient. If he proceeds to treat the patient in accordance with his own assessment (without obtaining a declaration from the court) and any question subsequently arises about the chosen course of treatment, the standard against which he will be judged is that set out in *Bolam*.[1] In codifying many of the principles and processes which the courts used to assess best interests previously, the MCA provides clarity, guidance and reassurance where medical treatment decisions are being taken on behalf of persons without capacity. There will nevertheless be some cases where precedent, medical practice or general prudence require that a declaration is obtained from the court.[2]

In some cases the court will be prepared to sanction relatively controversial treatment where the balance of competing factors supports such a course. In *B NHS Trust v J*,[3] J had suffered a brain haemorrhage and entered a persistent vegetative state some three years prior to the case coming before the court. The Trust made an application, supported by the family, that it was lawful for life-saving treatment to be withdrawn. The Official Solicitor opposed the application and suggested that J be given a short course of Zolpidem – a drug which had, in three isolated cases, produced some improvement in patients in a similar state. Despite the views of the Trust and family, the President declared that it would be lawful for a three-day course of the drug to be administered, within which time any beneficial effects could be expected to have been demonstrated.

In *DS v JS & An NHS Trust*,[4] two sibling patients suffered from variant Creutzfeldt Jakob disease which caused progressive neurological deterioration and inevitable death. There was no known cure and no medication recognised to defer the onset of symptoms or death. On application by the parents, the court granted a declaration that it was lawful for pioneering treatment to be attempted which comprised the intracerebral infusion of pentosan polysulphate, although this had never previously been attempted on human beings.

The Court of Protection has power to consent to treatment in respect of an incapable adult.[5] Additionally, the court may make declarations about the lawfulness of any treatment. It was previously arguable, on the basis of House of Lords authority, that the court was meant to do no more than satisfy itself that the doctors had assessed the patient's interests in accordance with the standards of the medical profession, as opposed to imposing its own view of the case.[6] The difficulty with that approach was that it did nothing to resolve a disagreement between two conflicting responsible views, competently formed.[7] Both points of view will be found to be lawful, and no decision will have been taken for the patient unable to decide for himself.[8]

The Court of Appeal in *Re SL*[9] resolved this problem. In cases where a declaration is sought, the court should adopt a two-stage approach. First, it should consider whether the treatment proposed is *Bolam* reasonable, namely whether a responsible body of medical practitioners would accept this treatment as being appropriate for this patient. Secondly, the court should determine whether in fact the treatment is in the patient's best interests. The President stated:

> 'In these difficult cases where the medical profession seeks a declaration as to lawfulness of the proposed treatment, the judge, not the doctor, has the duty to decide whether such treatment is in the best interests of the patient. The judicial decision ought to provide the best answer not a range of alternative answers. There may, of course, be situations where the answer may not be obvious and alternatives may have to be tried. It is still at any one point the best option of that moment which should be chosen.[10]

... The question ... for the judge, was not was the proposed treatment within the range of acceptable opinion among competent and responsible practitioners, but was it in the best interests of S?

It is submitted that this approach is in accordance with the practice followed in cases where there has been a real dispute about the correct result.'[11]

Thus the court can and does impose its own view as to what will be in the patient's best interests: it is obliged to determine the case on the facts and the evidence before it. These may be very different to those known to the doctors at the time of their initial decision. Nonetheless, a doctor who acts in accordance with recognised and accepted medical practice is unlikely to find himself open to criticism. The *Bolam* test is useful to medical practitioners and other professionals as a standard by which they go about their business, and the court can judge retrospectively whether they have complied with that standard. Further, and importantly, *Bolam* will be central to the assessment of whether a doctor has complied with the obligation imposed by s 5 of the MCA to take reasonable steps to establish a lack of capacity and the lawfulness of his assessment of best interests.[12] However, where the court has to make a finding as to the patient's best interests, the judge will look at all the evidence before the court and make an unequivocal finding as to where those interests lie, in just the same way as a finding of more concrete fact is made.

It has been said that the true analysis is that doctors owe not one duty but two duties to their patients: to treat them with the standard of care required by *Bolam* and to treat them in their best interests.[13] It may be questioned whether this is consistent with the speeches in *Sidaway*,[14] in which it was emphasised that the doctor owes just one duty. It is in any event difficult to conceive of circumstances in which the *Bolam* standard of care required the doctor to act other than in the patient's best interests.

1 *Bolam v Friern Hospital Management Committee* [1957] 1 WLR 582.
2 See **CHAPTER 7**: Sterilisation; and **CHAPTER 12**: Permanent Vegetative State.
3 [2006] EWHC 3152 (Fam).
4 [2002] EWHC 2734 (Fam).
5 s 16(2).
6 *Re F (mental patient: sterilisation)* [1990] 2 AC 1 at 52 per Lord Bridge, at 66–68 per Lord Brandon, at 69 per Lord Griffiths and at 78 per Lord Goff. See also the speech of Lord Browne-Wilkinson in *Airedale NHS Trust v Bland* [1993] AC 789 at 884.
7 *An NHS Trust v SA* [2005] EWCA Civ 1145 and [2006] Lloyd's Rep Med 29 at para 83, where Waller LJ firmly rejected the suggestion made on behalf of SA that it could not be in a patient's best interests if even one medical opinion opposed the proposed course: 'That in my view simply cannot be right ... It overlooks ... the role of the Court completely. It is for the court ultimately to judge in a case of this sort what is in the best interests of the patient and that must involve the court in the exercise of assessing the medical evidence that it has.'
8 One judge of the Family Division in a treatment case concerning a proposed hysterectomy has indeed made declarations that two opposing courses of action would be lawful: *Re NK (No 2)* (4 April 1990, unreported) per Scott Baker J.
9 [2000] 1 FCR 361, CA.
10 Smith Bernal Transcript, p 13.
11 *Re S (hospital patient: foreign curator)* [1996] Fam 23 per Hale J; *Re LC (medical treatment: sterilisation)* [1997] 2 FLR 258 per Thorpe J; and *Re S (adult sterilisation)* [1999] 1 FCR 277, [1998] 1 FLR 944 per Johnson J.
12 MCA, s 5.

13 *Re A (medical treatment: male sterilisation)* [2000] 1 FCR 193, 53 BMLR 66, [2000] 02 LS Gaz R 30, *sub nom Re A (male sterilisation)* [2000] 1 FLR 549, CA.
14 *Sidaway v Board of Governors of the Bethlem Royal Hospital and the Maudsley Hospital* [1985] AC 871. At p 893 Lord Diplock said emphatically: 'In English Jurisprudence the doctor's relationship with his patient which gives rise to the normal duty of care to exercise his skill and judgment to improve the patient's health in any particular respect in which the patient has sought his aid, has hitherto been treated as single comprehensive duty covering all the ways in which a doctor is called upon to exercise his skill and judgment in the improvement of the physical or mental condition of the patient for which his services either as a general practitioner or specialist have been engaged. This general duty is not subject to dissection into a number of component parts to which different criteria of what satisfy the duty of care apply, such as diagnosis, treatment, advice (including warning of any risks of something going wrong however skilfully the treatment is carried out).'.

What are the interests to be considered?

3.15   Doctors will be proposing treatment or care, first, because of their assessment of the patient's medical interests and needs. This will be derived from their examination, investigation and diagnosis in the usual manner. Just as a judge in addressing the question of best interests also considers broader welfare and social issues, so must a treating doctor. A competent patient will consider these for himself when deciding whether or not to consent to treatment. It is relevant to consider the patient's domestic circumstances in determining, for example, whether an appropriate level of family or domestic support for the treatment is available to allow for a reasonable chance of recovery.[1]

There may be situations where tensions between family members and treating staff mean that the all-encompassing 'best interests' assessment produces a different solution to that which would prevail if the assessment were limited to best medical interests alone. In *A PCT & P v AH & A Local Authority*,[2] P was an adult male epileptic who lived with his mother and carer. He suffered from frequent fitting which gave rise to a significant danger of brain damage and possible death if untreated. His mother would have impeded any treatment with which she did not agree, including treatment at the local community hospital that was available immediately. An alternative treatment option existed at a specialist unit some distance away but treatment would be delayed for at least a week. Recognising the difficulties with providing treatment in the face of objection from P's mother, the President made a declaration instead allowing treatment at the specialist unit despite the delay and potential for further deterioration of P's condition in that time.

In rare cases the interests of others may be a factor, but only in so far as these are of potential benefit to the patient: thus, organ donation may be appropriate if it is likely to ensure a close bond with a caring relative or indeed the survival of the carer.[3]

The financial interests of the patient are unlikely to be a legitimate factor to take into account, but it is possible to envisage rare cases where this might be so: if there was a choice between two equally valid forms of treatment, one of which would make fewer demands on the patient's estate in terms of the cost of care to be provided, it might be acceptable to take this into account. However, it would be unwise in most cases for the doctor to become involved in such matters. This is not to suggest that they should be unaware of the dangers of others having ulterior motives for the views they express about the patient's interests.[4] What will always be unacceptable is seeking to adjust the timing of treatment or its withdrawal for the convenience, financial or otherwise, of others.

1   For example *Re T (a minor) (wardship: medical treatment)* [1997] 1 WLR 242. Although this case concerned a child, the court took into account the practical difficulties caused by the parents' reluctance to allow the proposed operation to be performed.
2   [2008] EWHC 1403 (Fam).
3   *Re Y (mental patient: bone marrow donation)* [1997] Fam 110.
4   For example, *Re S (hospital patient: foreign curator)* [1996] Fam 23.

The use of force and restraint[1]

3.16   Difficult questions arise when a patient is unco-operative. The court has made it clear that in such circumstances:

'... it is lawful to impose treatment despite the absence of consent and even to overcome non-co-operation of a resisting patient by the sedation and a moderate and reasonable use of restraint in order to achieve it if the treatment is in the patient's best interests. The lawfulness of such restraint has to be carefully considered when assessing the balance of benefit and disadvantage in the giving of the proposed medical treatment and where the interest of the patient truly lies. A patient ... has, like any other, the right not to be subjected to degrading treatment under Article 3 of the European Convention on Human Rights.'[2]

The MCA authorises the use of restraint under s 6 only where it is reasonably believed that it is necessary to restrain to prevent harm to the patient and such restraint is a proportionate response to (a) the likelihood of the patient suffering harm, (b) the seriousness of that harm.

The extent of force required and the balance of advantage to detriment is as much a matter for professional judgment as any other aspect of treatment in such a case.[3]

In *R v Bournewood*,[4] the House of Lords found by a 3 to 2 majority that a 48-year-old autistic man who had been admitted to hospital and deprived of his liberty for a four-month period had not been 'detained'. Lord Steyn said:

'The general effect of the decision of the House is to leave compliant incapacitated patients without the safeguards enshrined in the Act of 1983. This is an unfortunate result. The Mental Health Act Commission has expressed concern about such informal patients in successive reports. The common law principle of necessity is a useful concept, but it contains none of the safeguards of the Act of 1983. It places effective and unqualified control in the hands of the hospital psychiatrist and other health care professionals. It is, of course, true that such professionals owe a duty of care to patients and that they will almost invariably act in what they consider to be the best interests of the patient. But neither habeas corpus nor judicial review are sufficient safeguards against misjudgments and professional lapses in the case of compliant incapacitated patients. Given that such patients are diagnostically indistinguishable from compulsory patients, there is no reason to withhold the specific and effective protections of the Act of 1983 from a large class of vulnerable mentally incapacitated individuals. Their moral right to be treated with dignity requires nothing less. The only comfort is that counsel for the Secretary of State has assured the House that reform of the law is under active consideration.'

The House went on to find unanimously that even if a 'deprivation of liberty' had occurred then it had been in the patient's best interests. However, when the *Bournewood* case[5] came before the European Court of Human Rights, it declared both that there had been a 'deprivation of liberty' and that the detention was unlawful under Art 5(1). The Strasbourg Court echoed the concerns voiced earlier by Lord Steyn and found that the inherent jurisdiction provided insufficient safeguards such as compliance with Art 5(4).[6] The questions of deprivation of liberty and of restraint are considered in more detail later.[7]

1 See **CHAPTER 6**: Restraint and Deprivation of Liberty.
2 The President in *Trust A and Trust B v H* [2006] EWHC 1230 at para 27.
3 *Re MB (an adult: medical treatment)* [1997] 8 Med LR 217 at 225 per Butler-Sloss LJ.
4 *HL v United Kingdom* (45508/99) (2005) 40 EHRR 32; *R v Bournewood Community Mental Health NHS Trust* [1999] AC 458.
5 *HL v UK* (2004) 40 EHRR 761.
6 For an analysis of relevant authorities see Munby J in *City of Sunderland v PS and CA* (2004) 40 EHRR 761. These issues are considered in detail in **CHAPTER 6**: Restraint and Deprivation of Liberty.
7 See **CHAPTER 6**: Restraint and Deprivation of Liberty.

Advance decisions and best interests

3.17   Prior to the MCA, advance directives provided a source of considerable difficulty both for patients and for those entrusted with treating them. In the absence of a clear framework there was uncertainty as to the precise form of words that would be required to ensure that a court would not interfere with a patient's desire to be treated (or not treated) in a certain way in the future.

In *W Healthcare NHS Trust v (1) KH, (2) H and (3) P,*[1] KH was a 59-year-old woman who had suffered from multiple sclerosis for 25 years. It was agreed that she had lacked capacity to take decisions for herself for the last 20 years. Ten years prior to the hearing, her condition deteriorated and she was admitted to a nursing home. She had been fed, for the five years preceding the application to court, through a percutaneous endoscopic gastrostomy ('PEG') feeding tube directly into her stomach. That tube had come free and the Trust applied for a declaration that it was lawful to re-insert the tube in order to continue to provide nutrition and so prolong her life. She was said to be in a 'pitiful state'. Most of her bodily functions had ceased to work, she required 24-hour care, her swallowing was unsafe, she was doubly incontinent and, although conscious, she was disoriented in time and space and could recognise no-one. The family opposed the application. Their evidence was that KH had made clear statements that she did not wish to be a burden on the family and that she would not want to be kept alive by machines. While recognising the force of those general expressions of her hopes for the future, the Court of Appeal acceded to the

Trust's application because it was not satisfied that those expressions covered the specific situation that KH now found herself in. Brooke LJ said:

> 'I am of the clear view that the judge was correct in finding that there was not an advance directive which was sufficiently clear to amount to a direction that she preferred to be deprived of food and drink for a period of time which would lead to her death in all the circumstances. There is no evidence that she was aware of the nature of this choice, or the unpleasantness or otherwise of death by starvation and it would be departing from established principles of English law if one was to hold that there was an advance directive which was established and relevant in the circumstances in the present case, despite the very strong expression of her wishes which came through in the evidence.'[2]

The position in relation to advance directives now is set out in **CHAPTER 2**: Consent – Adults and provides for far greater certainty in the law. For a directive to be valid, the patient must have had capacity at the relevant time. However, in a situation where it is determined that the patient did not have capacity, the clinicians – and ultimately the court – must take the expressed views of the incapable patient into account when assessing what is in his best interests.

1   [2004] EWCA Civ 1324.
2   *Ibid.* at para 21.

E CONCLUSION

3.18   For as long as professionals have sought declarations as to best interests, the courts have emphasised the importance of bringing such cases as soon as it becomes clear that a determination will be required. Notwithstanding repeated entreaties, applications are still made out of hours or on short notice for declarations in respect of treatment which should have been anticipated weeks, sometimes months, in advance. In the case of advance decisions, one of the issues central to the court's assessment will be whether or not a person had capacity at the time the decision was made. Often it will be possible for the case to be notified to the Official Solicitor and for a formal assessment of capacity to be undertaken before a person lapses into unconsciousness or otherwise loses capacity. The effect of any delay in properly assessing the relevant issues in such a case may well be determinative of the court's assessment as to validity. Courts will expect a high standard of vigilance and anticipation of the issues that arise in relation to the validity of advance decisions. A failure properly to investigate issues such as capacity at an early stage may well result in treatment being provided against a patient's valid advance decision. To the extent that the authors of this book can add any further encouragement to those involved in advising on or taking medical treatment decisions then we urge that early and proper assessments of all the relevant issues are conducted and that timely notification of cases to the Official Solicitor (or CAFCASS) is made so that if and when a case comes before the court, an informed decision can be taken as to best interests and future treatment.

For updating material and hyperlinks related to this chapter, see:
www.3serjeantsinn.com/mtdl/deciding-for-others-adults

Chapter 4

Deciding for Others – Children

A   Framework 4.1
B   Capacity to consent to treatment 4.2
      Children of 16 years of age and over 4.2
      Children under the age of 16 4.3
      Parents and those with parental responsibility 4.4
C   Power to refuse treatment 4.5
      Children over the age of 16 or possessing *Gillick* competence 4.6
      Compulsory treatment and children's rights 4.7
      Children under the age of 16 not possessing *Gillick* competence 4.8
      Parents 4.9
      The court 4.10
D   Special considerations in the treatment of severely ill infants 4.11
      Deliberate killing 4.12
      Withholding and withdrawing life-sustaining treatment 4.13
          Withholding treatment 4.13
          Withdrawing treatment 4.14
      Best interests: the court's approach 4.15
      Practical guidance 4.16
E   Conclusion 4.17

A FRAMEWORK

4.1   In English law a child is any person under the age of 18. As might be expected, the law recognises that children do not possess the same capacity to make decisions as adults. As will be seen, however, much depends on the age of the child.

Consent to medical treatment of a child can be obtained from a number of sources and treatment should not be undertaken without obtaining consent or authority from one of the following:

- those with parental responsibility – usually one or both of the parents, unless the responsibility has been allocated by the court in some different way or to a third party;[1]

- the child in question if he is over the age of 16 or is otherwise of sufficient maturity and comprehension to take a decision of the relevant gravity;
- the court exercising its inherent or statutory jurisdiction over children.

In the absence of any such authority it is unlawful to treat a child unless the circumstances are of such urgency that it is impossible to obtain such consent *and* it is in the child's best interests to have the treatment: the treatment will be justified by the doctrine of necessity.

Whereas consent by any of those with the capacity to do so will be sufficient authority to proceed with the treatment, the same is not so with a refusal. The effect of a refusal of consent to treatment depends on who makes it. The case law currently indicates the following hierarchy of authority:

- the refusal of the child patient, of whatever age, will not prevail in law against the consent of a person with parental responsibility or the court;
- the refusal of the parent will not prevail against the consent of a child of 16 and over, or even of a younger child of sufficient maturity and understanding to consent to the treatment in question;
- the refusal of the child (of any age) or of the parents will not prevail against the authority of the court exercising its inherent or statutory jurisdiction.[2]

It follows that it is much easier to obtain authority to treat of a child than to prohibit treatment. As English law stands, it is permissible with the relevant authority to treat a child against his will and to use the restraint reasonably necessary for that purpose.[3] The continued legitimacy of this position under the Human Rights Act 1998 is questionable and remains untested.

1   However, note that certain categories of procedure should not be performed without the court's permission: see, for example, **CHAPTER 5**: Going to Court **PARA 5.24** and note, in relation to circumcision and immunisation that if parents are in dispute, the approval of the court must be sought: see below **PARA 4.4** and **CHAPTER 7**: Sterilisation **PARA 7.19**.
2   *Re W (a minor) (medical treatment: court's jurisdiction)* [1993] Fam 64, [1992] 3 WLR 758, [1992] 4 All ER 627, CA; and *Re P (Minor)* [2003] EWHC 2327 (Fam), where the competent wishes of a boy aged 16 years and 10 months and of his parents that he should not receive blood or blood products necessary for his post-operative survival were overridden by the court on application of the 'best interests' test.
3   For children aged 16 to 18, while a competent refusal to undergo medical treatment can be overridden, competent refusal to be admitted to hospital for mental health treatment cannot: see below **PARA 4.4** onwards.

B   CAPACITY TO CONSENT TO TREATMENT

Children of 16 years of age and over

4.2   The Family Law Reform Act 1969, s 8 provides:

'(1) The consent of a minor who has attained the age of 16 years to any surgical, medical or dental treatment which, in the absence of consent, would constitute a trespass to his person, shall be as effective as it would be if he were of full age; and where a minor has by virtue of this section given an effective consent to any treatment it shall not be necessary to obtain any consent for it from his parent or guardian.

(2) In this section 'surgical, medical or dental treatment' includes any procedure undertaken for the purposes of diagnosis, and this section applies to any procedure (including, in particular, the administration of an anaesthetic) which is ancillary to any treatment as it applies to that treatment.

(3) Nothing in this section shall be construed as making ineffective any consent which would have been effective if this section had not been enacted.'

The consent of a child over the age of 16 is therefore as valid as if it were given by an adult. Parliament has created the presumption that such children have the relevant capacity.[1] For a child over the age of 16, the test of capacity is the same as for adults under the Mental Capacity 2005 ('MCA').[2] Reference should be made to **CHAPTER 2**: Consent – Adults. A child over the age of 16 who does not pass the test of capacity in s 3 of the MCA will not be able to provide valid consent and the provisions of the MCA apply.[3] Until such a child reaches the age of 18, his parents will be able to provide consent for him.

1   This presumption has been reinforced by the MCA, s 1. The Code of Practice states that '[t]he Act's starting point is to confirm in legislation that it should be assumed that an adult (aged 16 or over) has full legal capacity to make decisions for themselves (the right to autonomy) unless it can be shown that they lack capacity to make a decision for themselves at the time the decision is made. This is known as the presumption of capacity' (Department of Constitutional Affairs, Mental Capacity Act 2005 MCA Code of Practice (TSO, 2007), p 15, para 1.2).
2   MCA, s 2(5). A person may not exercise powers over another person under the Act which may be exercised in relation to a child under the age of 16, save for decisions about a child's property and financial affairs, where the court considers that the child will still lack capacity to make decisions in respect of these matters when he reaches 18 (s 2(6)). See further **CHAPTER 5**: Going to Court, **PARA 5.3**.
3   Reference should be made to **CHAPTER 3**: Deciding for Others – Adults.

Children under the age of 16

4.3   Even prior to the implementation of the Family Law Reform Act 1969, the assumption was that a sufficiently mature minor was able to give effective consent to treatment without the need for doctors to obtain parental approval.[1] However, in the early 1980s the controversy surrounding the provision of contraceptive advice to children caused the capacity of children to be considered in detail by the House of Lords in *Gillick v West Norfolk and Wisbech AHA*.[2] That case confirmed that children of any age may have the capacity to consent to treatment without the involvement of their parents. What is required is that they are of sufficient maturity and understanding to take a decision of the seriousness in question.[3] In other words, they must be able to understand the general nature and effect of what is proposed and be able to balance the factors for and against the treatment in the same way as an adult. As stated by Lord Scarman:

'I would hold that as a matter of law the parental right to determine whether or not their minor child below the age of 16 will have medical treatment terminates if and when the child achieves a sufficient understanding and intelligence to enable him or her to understand fully what is proposed. It will be a question of fact whether a child seeking advice has sufficient understanding of what is involved to give a consent valid in law. Until the child achieves the capacity to consent, the parental right to make the decision continues save only in exceptional circumstances.'[4]

In *Re R (a minor) (wardship: consent to treatment)* Lord Donaldson MR summarised the *Gillick* competence test, stating that:

'What is involved is not merely an ability to understand the nature of the proposed treatment ... but a full understanding and appreciation of the consequences both of the treatment in terms of intended and possible side effects and, equally important, the anticipated consequences of a failure to treat.'[5]

This seems to suggest that in fact the *Gillick* competence test may be more difficult to pass than the adult capacity test under s 3 of the MCA.

The closer a child is to the age of 16, the more likely the determination that he is *Gillick* competent.[6] However, it must be stressed that – as with the test for an adult's competence[7] – the level of cognitive ability required to demonstrate *Gillick* competence varies according to the nature and gravity of the decision which is to be taken: the more serious the decision and the more serious the consequences of receiving or not receiving treatment, the greater the level of comprehension and rational decision-making ability that will be required. As with adults, capacity is specific to the particular decision to be made, hence *Gillick* competence must be assessed discretely for each separate investigation or course of treatment proposed.

Re E (a minor)[8] provides an example where the nature of the treatment decision was such that a high degree of cognitive ability was required to satisfy the court that an otherwise apparently intellectually able child – who was nearly 16 – had sufficient competence in relation to a particular decision.

E was a 15-year-old Jehovah's Witness. He refused to consent to blood transfusions which were a necessary part of conventional treatment for leukaemia. His parents also refused to consent. In relation to *Gillick* competence Ward J concluded[9] that E was a:

'boy of sufficient intelligence to be able to take decisions about his own well-being, but I also find that there is a range of decisions of which some are outside his ability fully to grasp their implications'.

He did not have full understanding of the implications of a refusal of blood transfusions. Thus, he was not of sufficient understanding, intelligence and maturity to give full and informed consent.

The House of Lords has emphasised that it expected that doctors would consult parents in most cases. However, such consultation would be permissible only with a *Gillick* competent child's consent: if such a child wishes to keep the matter confidential, that is his entitlement.[10]

If a child has the relevant competence, he can then exercise his power to consent in any particular manner he chooses. As with adults, a competent child may make an unwise decision. However, unlike with adults, the legal effect of a refusal of consent by a competent child is circumscribed.

Who is to judge whether the child has the relevant capacity? In the first place this can only be the attending doctors who must form an opinion on the matter in accordance with accepted practice. Practitioners should be cautious when dealing with assertions by medical staff that a patient lacks capacity. It will be important to confirm that the doctor concerned has experience and understanding of the issues considered by the court to be relevant to such an assessment; secondly it is critical to ensure that the assessment of capacity has been rigorously conducted and carefully documented. Where the decision is that a patient lacks capacity then the doctor performing the assessment must identify and note the specific reason for such a conclusion. This is especially so where urgent applications are made, often by telephone, late in the evening.

If parents or others with a legitimate interest disagree with the medical assessment of a child's capacity, then the final arbiter will be a court. However once a court is seized of the matter, the issue of the child's capacity will rarely be the determining factor in the final outcome. In such a case, the reality is that the court will make the final decision about what is in the child's best interests.[11] There may be cases of particularly serious treatment where the doctors may feel doubt about whether the child has the capacity to make the decision even if the parents do not disagree with the proposed treatment. Again, the doctors may wish to refer the matter to court.

1   D Skegg, 'Consent to Medical Procedures on Minors' (1973) 36 MLR 370.
2   [1986] AC 112, [1985] 3 WLR 830, [1985] 3 All ER 402.
3   The United Nations Convention on the Rights of the Child, by Art 12(1), requires that contracting states 'shall assure to the child who is capable of forming his or her own views the right to express those views freely in all matters affecting the child, the views of the child being given due weight in accordance with the age and maturity of the child'. Article 14(1) requires respect for 'the right of the child to freedom of thought, conscience and religion'. This Convention has been increasingly referred to as an aid to interpretation in both domestic and Strasbourg decisions. In the domestic courts, see, for example, *Mabon v Mabon* [2005] 3 WLR 460 and *R (on the application of Williamson and others) v Secretary of State for Education* [2005] 2 AC 246; in Strasbourg, see, for example, *Keegan v Ireland* (1994) 18 EHRR 342, referring at para 50 to Art 7 (right to be cared for by his parents); *Costello-Roberts v United Kingdom* (1993) 19 EHRR 112 European Court of Human Rights, referring at para 35 to Art 16 (right to respect for private life).
4   [1986] AC 112 at 188H, HL.
5   [1992] Fam 11 at 26A, CA.
6   The UN Convention on the Rights of the Child, Art 14(2): 'States Parties shall respect the rights and duties of the parents and, when applicable, legal guardians, to provide direction to the child in the exercise of his or her right in a manner consistent with the evolving capacities of the child.' See **N3** above.
7   See **CHAPTER 2**: Consent – Adults.
8   [1993] 1 FLR 386 (per Ward J).
9   *Ibid* at 391A.
10   In relation to advice and treatment related to abortion, contraception and reproductive health: *R (on the application of Axon) v Secretary of State for Health and Family Planning Association* [2006] EWCA 37 (Admin), [2006] All ER (D) 148 (Admin).
11   See below: **PARA 4.10FF**.

Parents and those with parental responsibility

4.4   The mother of a child (and – if married to the mother, or an order of the court has so provided – the father)[1] has the power to consent to treatment unless deprived of it either through lack of her own capacity or because the entitlement has been modified or removed by order of a court.

The duty of such a person is to give or withhold consent in the best interests of the child and without regard to their own interests.[2]

A parent's capacity to consent to the treatment of their child will be assessed in the same way as for a patient personally. A parent aged 16 and above therefore will be presumed to have capacity unless shown not to satisfy the test of capacity under the MCA.[3] A parent under the age of 16 will be assessed by reference to the *Gillick* test. If a parent lacks capacity then he will be unable to give valid consent.

Where someone other than a parent has been awarded parental responsibility, such as another relation or a public authority,[4] doctors should approach that person for authority to treat rather than the natural parents.[5] Depending on the circumstances, it may be good practice to approach the latter to consult them in any event, but they are unable to give valid consent.

While the general position is that the consent of one parent is sufficient, the position concerning certain irreversible treatment is different. Before a doctor can perform circumcision on a child, the consent of both parents or the approval of the court is essential:

> 'in the absence of agreement of those with parental responsibility, [it] ought not to be carried out or arranged by a one-parent carer although she has parental responsibility … Such a decision should not be made without the specific approval of the court'.[6]

In *Re C*[7] two sets of parents disagreed over whether their children aged 4 and 10 should receive the MMR vaccine. The court ordered that the children should undergo the immunisations and the Court of Appeal dismissed their mothers' appeal against this order. The court stated that immunisations should be added to the 'small group of important decisions' that includes circumcision where the consent of both parents or an order of the court is required.[8]

We would argue that as parental agreement is required before a child undergoes a disputed circumcision or immunisation, it is strongly arguable that intersex and non-therapeutic cosmetic surgery should also require parental consensus or a court order.

Consideration of the potential implications of Art 8 of the ECHR has led to further guidance being issued to health professionals as to whether they should rely upon parental consent in all circumstances. The recently revised Code of Practice to the Mental Health Act 1983[9] suggests that there is a 'zone of parental control' for treatment of children, outside which court approval may be required. To establish whether a decision falls within the 'zone of parental control' the doctor must ask two 'key questions'.

First:

'… is the decision one that a parent would be expected to make, having regard to what is considered to be normal practice in our society and to any relevant human rights decisions made by the courts?'.

Second:

'are there no indications that the parent might not act in the best interests of the child or young person?'.[10]

If the doctor cannot answer both questions confidently in the affirmative, it is suggested that the decision may fall outside the 'zone of parental control' and any consent given by the parent will be invalid.[11] The Code advises that '[t]he more extreme the intervention, the more likely it will be that it falls outside the zone'.[12] Referring to situations where parents have overridden their child's refusal to consent to treatment, the Code advises that:

'… [t]here is no post-Human Rights Act decision on this, and the trend in recent cases is to respect greater autonomy for under-18s in law. In the Department of Health's view it is not wise to rely on the consent of a person with parental responsibility to treat a young person who refuses in the circumstances'.[13]

1   Children Act 1989, ss 2–4.
2   *Re J (a minor) (wardship: medical treatment)* [1991] Fam 33. For an alternative view that the parent's own views should form part of the treatment decision and that this is prevented by an undue focus on individual patient autonomy see J Herring 'Where are the Carers in Healthcare Law and Ethics' (2006) and J Hardwig 'What about the Family?' (1990) 20 Hastings Centre Report 5.
3   MCA, s 1; see **APPENDIX 1.1**: Mental Capacity Act 2005 and see **CHAPTER 2**: Consent – Adults.
4   See Children Act 1989, s 5.
5   Although, in the authors' experience, where the proposed treatment has serious consequences or involves irreversible surgery, some local authorities holding parental responsibility will not give their consent, preferring instead for the matter to be fully considered and authorised by the High Court.
6   *Re J (Specific Issue Orders: child's religious upbringing and circumcision)* [2000] 1 FLR 571 at 577 per Butler-Sloss P.
7   *Re C (Welfare of Child: Immunisation)* [2003] 2 FLR 1095.
8   *Ibid* per Thorpe LJ at para 17.
9   Department of Health, Code of Practice to the Mental Health Act 1983 (TSO, 2008). The relevant sections are reproduced at **APPENDIX 4.2**. The Code is issued under s 118 of the Mental Health Act 1983. While s 118 imposes no legal duty to comply with Code, the introduction (para iv) states that registered medical practitioners, approved clinicians and approved mental health professionals must have regard for the Code and record any departures from it: 'Departures from the Code could give rise to legal challenge, and a Court, in reviewing any departures from the Code, will scrutinise the reasons for the departure to ensure that there is sufficiently convincing justification in the circumstances.'
10   Code, s 36.10.
11   Code, s 36.11.
12   Code, s 36.12.
13   Code, s 36.33.

C   POWER TO REFUSE TREATMENT

4.5   The uninformed observer might be forgiven for expecting that, as with adults, the principles governing refusal of treatment would be the same as those for authorising treatment. However, this is not the case. The fundamental principle is that the authority of any one party with the power to consent trumps the refusal of any other, unless a court directs otherwise. There is logic in this position because the consequences of refusing treatment recommended by a doctor will usually be far more serious than accepting such treatment.

The system is biased in favour of children receiving treatment, to avoid their being deprived of care which, objectively, it is in their best interests to receive.

Children over the age of 16 or possessing *Gillick* competence

4.6   Unlike the position with competent adults, a refusal by children recognised by the law as having the capacity to authorise treatment (whether given by a child over the age of 16[1] or a younger, *Gillick* competent child[2]) is not binding on the doctors if another person with the capacity to consent to treatment does so.[3] In effect this means that any person with parental responsibility can authorise the imposition of medical treatment on an unwilling child, as can the courts. The Court of Appeal has felt able to confine the effect of *Gillick* to a restriction on the power of veto a parent has over the treatment given to his child, and to confine the effect of the Family Law Reform Act 1969 to the power to consent rather than the power to refuse treatment. The situation is attenuated for the treatment of mental disorder as capable 16 and 17 year olds may now validly refuse admission to hospital for such treatment.[4]

The age of the child will certainly be a relevant consideration and, in particular, difficult decisions face the court where the child in question is approaching the age of 18. Once a child reaches 18, validly he has capacity to refuse consent to medical treatment and that refusal will be determinative. In *Re W*, Balcombe LJ suggested that the fact that there was nothing to preclude the court from exercising its inherent jurisdiction in relation to 16 year olds did not mean that the court should exercise its discretion in a moral vacuum:

> 'Undoubtedly, the philosophy ... is that, as children approach the age of majority, they are increasingly able to take their own decisions concerning their medical treatment. In logic there can be no difference between an ability to consent to treatment and an ability to refuse treatment ... Accordingly the older the child concerned the greater the weight the court should give to its wishes, certainly in the field of medical treatment.'[5]

Balcombe LJ saw this approach as an application of the principle of the paramountcy of the child's welfare, noting that it will normally be in the best interests of a child of sufficient age and understanding to make an informed decision. that the court should respect the child's integrity as a human being and should:

> '... not lightly override its decision on such a personal matter as medical treatment, all the more so if that treatment is invasive.'[6]

He concluded that:

'... the court exercising the inherent jurisdiction in relation to a 16 or 17 year old child who is not mentally incompetent will, as a matter of course, ascertain the wishes of the child and will approach its decision with a strong predilection to give effect to the child's wishes ...' [7]

In *Re P (Minor)* Johnson J went further, observing that where the court has to decide whether to authorise treatment required for continued life by a child approaching the age of 18, it must consider whether to override the wishes of a child:

'... when the likelihood is that all that will have been achieved will have been deferment of an inevitable death and for a matter only of months.' [8]

Nevertheless, an underlying inelasticity in the court's approach to medical treatment decisions involving children approaching their 18th birthday is confirmed by Johnson J's conclusion in *Re P (Minor)*, where guided by the words of Nolan LJ in *Re W*, [9] he stated that:

'In general terms the present state of the law is that an individual who has reached the age of eighteen is free to do with his life what he wishes, but it is the duty of the court to ensure so far as it can that children survive to attain that age.' [10]

In *Re W*, Balcombe LJ explained that:

'... if the court's powers are to be meaningful, there must come a point at which the court, while not disregarding the child's wishes, can override them in the child's own best interests, objectively considered. Clearly such a point will have come if the child is seeking to refuse treatment in circumstances which will in all probability lead to the death of the child or to severe permanent injury.' [11]

Of course, the fact that someone other than the patient can authorise treatment does not necessarily mean that it would be right, let alone obligatory, to do so in respect of an unwilling patient. Whether or not a child is competent will not ultimately determine the application, but the judge must give due weight to the child's views when approaching their best interests. This will include consideration of the effect upon the child of their views being overridden and of the child's Art 8 right to autonomy: a competent refusal must weigh heavily in the scales. Thus there may be cases in which the balance may be tipped in favour of refusal of treatment because the child's refusal is a competent refusal. [12]

Lord Donaldson MR said in *Re W (a minor) (medical treatment: court's jurisdiction)*:

'Hair-raising possibilities were canvassed of abortions being carried out by doctors in reliance upon the consent of parents and despite the refusal of consent by 16 and 17 year olds. Whilst this may be possible as a matter of law, I do not see any likelihood taking account of medical ethics, unless the abortion was truly in the best interests of the child. This is not to say that it could not happen ... [13] ...[and] the inherent jurisdiction of the court could still be invoked ...to prevent an abortion which was contrary to the interests of the minor. [14]

Thus there will be cases where it is considered in the child's best interests to impose treatment, such as where his life can only be saved by it, despite the child's competent objection to the treatment.[15] Equally, there will be cases where it is considered impracticable or unethical to impose the treatment.[16] In most such situations, difficult though they are, it will be possible for the doctors and the parents between them to work out what is best for the child. In rare cases there will remain a sufficient degree of dispute or doubt to justify a reference to the court.

1 *Re W (a minor) (medical treatment: court's jurisdiction)* [1993] Fam 64.
2 *Re R (a minor) (wardship: consent to treatment)* [1992] Fam 11.
3 For example, *Re K, W and H (minors) (consent to treatment)* [1993] 1 FLR 854 per Thorpe J.
4 Mental Health Act 1983 (as amended), s 131(2)–(5).
5 *Re W* (see **N1** above) at 88.
6 *Ibid.*
7 *Ibid.*
8 *Re P (Minor)* [2004] 2 FLR 1117 at 9. Such a case was *Re E (A Minor)* [1993] 1 FLR 386 where a 15-year-old boy's refusal of blood products was overridden by the court. When E reached 18 he exercised his unassailable right to refuse blood products and died (as noted by Johnson J in *Re P (Minor) ibid. at 8).*
9 *Re W* (see **N1** above) at 94 per Nolan LJ.
10 *Re P (Minor)* (see **N8** above) at 9. It was surprising that there was no mention of the European Convention on Human Rights in Johnson J's judgment.
11 *Re W* (see **N1** above) at 88.
12 Even where a child patient is not competent to consent, this does not prevent doctors from attempting to elicit the child's views and, where possible, agreement or co-operation with the proposed treatment. The effect on the child both in terms of his well-being and the efficacy of treatment undertaken in spite of his refusal are factors that will be weighed in the determination of best interests. Indeed, for children over 16 who lack capacity, s 4(6)(a) MCA requires the child's views to be considered as part of the determination of best interests.
12 *Re W (a minor) (medical treatment: court's jurisdiction)* [1993] Fam 64 at 94 per Nolan LJ.
13 Lord Donaldson MR gave the example of *Re D (a minor) (wardship: sterilisation)* [1976] Fam 185 where the child concerned lacked the intelligence or the understanding to consent or to refuse consent.
14 *Re W* (see **N1** above) at 88.
15 For example, *Re M (child: refusal of medical treatment)* [1999] 2 FCR 577, [1999] FLR 1097, where Johnson J authorised doctors to carry out a heart transplant on a 15-year-old girl who refused to consent to the operation. The risks of the child's resentment against the imposition of treatment and the risks of the procedure itself had to be set against 'not simply the risk but the certainty of death'. Fortin, *Children's Rights and the Developing Law* (Butterworths, 1998: Update 4, Chap 5) has commented in support of the *Re M* approach that: 'It insults a perfectly normal teenager's intelligence to argue that she is not *Gillick* competent. She might better appreciate that the court, under its inherent jurisdiction, though obliged to consider her wishes, is also obliged to act in her best interests and keep her alive, if possible, throughout her minor status.' See also *Re P (Minor)* (see **N8** above) where the firm wishes of a boy aged 16 years and 10 months and of his parents, who were Jehovah's Witnesses, that he did not receive blood or blood products necessary for his post-operative survival were overruled by the court.
16 Compare *Re M (Child: Refusal of Medical Treatment)* (see **N15** above) (where Johnson J overruled a 15-year-old girl's refusal to undergo a heart transplant) with the *Hannah Jones* case (Hertfordshire PCT discontinued High Court proceedings to remove the 13-year-old from her parents' custody temporarily to ensure that she underwent a heart transplant over her unequivocal and emphatic refusal to be treated). See S Burns, 'The right to be kept alive', SJ 153/17, p11.

Compulsory treatment and children's rights

4.7   A proposal for compulsory treatment must now be scrutinised with the Human Rights Act 1998 in mind. Art 8(1) of the European Convention on Human Rights protects the moral and bodily integrity of a person from unjustified assault.[1] It thus includes a right not to be subjected to compulsory medical interference.[2] However, this is a right which, by virtue of Art 8(2) may be justifiably interfered with on grounds of the protection of health or morals: as stated by Kilkelly:[3]

> 'Compulsory medical treatment … will not infringe the Convention as long as there is proportionality between the interference which it creates and the need to protect the public interest which it serves. This has been found to be particularly important where children are concerned, because they have limited possibilities to protect their own rights.'[4]

The Art 8 protection should in fact mean that courts when performing the best interests' assessment will ensure that only in exceptional circumstances – for example, where it is necessary to save life – will the wishes of a child over the age of 16 or a *Gillick* competent child be overridden. Thus, the disparity between the law's approaches to a child's right of refusal and to his right to consent is likely to narrow: the courts will be more likely to accept a child's refusal of treatment in circumstances in which he has the capacity – whether by statute or *Gillick* – to consent to the same treatment.

For Fortin:

> '… splicing the Gillick competence test onto Article 8 rights suggests that mature teenagers now have complete autonomy in all matters that they fully comprehend, whether or not they are consenting to a procedure such as medical treatment or refusing it. Such an approach would accomplish a radical change in legal principles governing this area of law … Logically … it would not be enough merely to withdraw parent's legal powers over their teenagers. The courts should also lose their own right to override the wishes of a Gillick competent teenager intent on self-destruction. Consequently, they could not, for example, argue that despite the teenager having the right under Article 8 to personal autonomy and dignity, it is necessary, under Article 8(2) to force him to undergo life sustaining treatment, by virtue of his minor status'.[5]

Art 14 could also be used to bolster any argument that competent children should receive the same protection as adults against being forced to undergo medical treatment despite their refusal. The axiom of medical law that a competent adult can refuse medical treatment even if the decision to do so is objectively irrational or would result in death is protected by Art 8.[6] The court's refusal to extend the same protection to a child who is deemed competent and therefore possessive of sufficient insight and understanding to surgery can be seen as anomalous.

Outside the field of medical treatment decisions, various *dicta* in cases involving children support an increase in the court's appreciation of the child's autonomy. In *Mabon v Mabon* Thorpe LJ stated:

'Unless we in this jurisdiction are to fall out of step with similar societies as they safeguard Article 12 [of the UN Convention on the Rights of the Child][7] rights, we must, in the case of articulate teenagers, accept that the right to freedom of expression and participation outweighs the paternalistic judgment of welfare.'[8]

Citing this extract from *Mabon*, in *Axon* Silber J commented that:

'… the right of young people to make decisions about their own lives by themselves at the expense of the views of their parents has now become an increasingly important and accepted feature of family life'[9]

Nevertheless, the editors of Mason and McCall Smith doubt whether the Human Rights Act (including the application of Arts 2, 3, 5 and 8) require a change in the courts' approach to refusal of consent by a *Gillick* competent child. They point to the doctrines of the margin of appreciation and proportionality and conclude that:

'… [t]he English courts have made a concerted effort to demonstrate their desire to find a balance in the cases and there is little in [European Court of Human Rights'] jurisprudence that would lead them to upset that delicate equilibrium.'[10]

We would suggest that the level of patient autonomy protected by Art 8 means that the courts can appropriately interfere with a *Gillick* competent child's refusal of treatment in only the most exceptional circumstances. This should preferably be confined to some (but not necessarily all) cases in which overriding a child's refusal of treatment is necessary to save his life. While an adult has the absolute right to make an unwise or irrational decision which costs him his life, we can legitimately say as a society that our children do not. That desire to protect in life and death situations may justify interference with the laudable aim of affording competent children greater respect.

1   *X and Y v Netherlands* (1985) 8 EHRR 235; *Peters v Netherlands* 77A DR 75 (1994) at 79, indicating that unwanted medical intervention (the taking of urine samples) is an infringement of Art 8. And see also reference to *X v Austria* and the European Court of Justice decision in the HIV case cited at fns 1 and 2 of Nys, 'Physician Involvement in a Patient's death – a Continental European Perspective' (1999) 7(2) Med L Rev 209.

2   *Re A (children) (conjoined twins: surgical separation)* [2000] 4 All ER 961, [2000] 3 FCR 577, [2000] 1 FLR 1, [2001] Fam Law 18, CA. See **PARA 4.12**.

3   Kilkelly, *The Child and the European Convention on Human Rights* (Dartmouth Publishing, 1999).

4   *Ibid* at p 150, citing *JR, GR, RR & YR v Switzerland* No 22398/93 Dec 5/4/95, DR 81 at 61.

5   J Fortin, 'Accommodating Children's Rights in a Post Human Rights Era' (2006) 69 MLR 299.

6   Treatment in the absence of consent (including once consent has been withdrawn) will constitute an assault: *Re C (Adult: Refusal of Treatment)* [1994] 1 All ER 819; *Re B (Adult: Refusal of Medical Treatment)* [2002] All ER 449; *Pretty v UK* [2002] 2 FLR 45 and see **CHAPTER 2**: Consent, **PARA 2.11**: Refusal.   .

7   See **PARA 4.3**, N3 above.

8   *Mabon v Mabon* [2005] 3 WLR 460 per Thorpe LJ at para 28.

9   *R (on the application of Axon) v Secretary of State for Health and Family Planning Association* [2006] EWCA 37 (Admin); [2006] All ER (D) at para 79.

10 K Mason and G Laurie, *Mason and Mc Call Smith's Law and Medical Ethics* (7th ed, Oxford, 2005), p 372, para 10.53.

Children under the age of 16 not possessing *Gillick* competence

4.8   Children under the age of 16 who lack the capacity to consent to treatment also cannot validly refuse treatment which is otherwise lawfully authorised. In effect they can be compelled to accept treatment either under the authority of a person with parental responsibility or of the court exercising its inherent or statutory jurisdiction over children. Nevertheless, while such children have no veto over treatment, their views must be taken into consideration when assessing whether treatment is in their best interests. Very difficult practical issues arise when a child requires long-term treatment necessarily involving his co-operation (for example, kidney dialysis), but actively refuses to comply with that treatment. In these circumstances attempts to override the child's refusal by resorting to the court will not provide a solution to a practical medical problem. Where a child's lack of co-operation with even highly desirable treatment means that it can not be delivered effectively, it can legitimately be determined that forcing him to undergo the treatment is not in the child's best interests. In such circumstances, particularly when the treatment is life-saving, it is strongly suggested that the court should be involved.

Parents

4.9   As has been seen, parents have the power to override their children's refusal of treatment. In order to do so they must have the capacity to take such a decision. The refusal of competent parents will be accorded respect by the law, but their power to act in this way is not absolute and may be overridden by the court.[1] The court will not allow a parental refusal – albeit well informed and made in good faith – to override what it deems to be in the child's best interests. The child's interests must always be paramount.[2] The weight to be given to the parents' views will vary according to the circumstances. In *Re T (a minor) (wardship: medical treatment)* Waite LJ described a scale:

> '... at one end of which lies the clear case where parental opposition to medical intervention is prompted by scruple or dogma of a kind which is patently irreconcilable with principles of child health and welfare widely accepted by the generality of mankind; and that at the other end lie highly problematic cases where there is genuine scope for a difference of view between parent and judge.'[3]

Wherever the parents' view falls on this scale, it is the court's independent assessment of the child's best interests that will prevail. However, Waite LJ continued that:'

> '... in cases at the latter end of the scale, there must be a likelihood ... that the greater the scope for genuine debate ... the stronger will be the inclination of the court to be influenced by a reflection that in the last analysis the best interests of every child include an expectation that difficult decisions affecting the length and quality of its life will be taken for it by the parent to whom its care has been entrusted by nature.'[4]

Thus, there is a form of rebuttable presumption that the parents' views should be respected, particularly when their right to a family life under Art 8 are taken into account.[5]

Nonetheless, where a parent's views place the child's life in danger or are otherwise detrimental to his best interests, the courts will override the refusal. As stated in *Prince v Massachusetts*:

'Parents may be free to become martyrs themselves, but it does not follow that they are free in identical circumstances to make martyrs of their children before they have reached the age of full and legal discretion when they can make choices for themselves.' [6]

The courts will even override a parent's views on an issue – upon which there is no general social consensus – where those views are supported by a significant proportion of the community. The case where the court authorised the separation of conjoined twins against the parents' opposition, although the operation was bound to result in the death of the weaker twin was such a case.[7] In practice the court's view will almost invariably prevail. As a Master of the Rolls put it:

'... the decision of a devoted and responsible parent should be treated with respect. It should certainly not be disregarded or lightly set aside. But the role of the court is to exercise an independent and objective judgment. If that judgment is in accord with that of the devoted and responsible parent, well and good. If it is not, then it is the duty of the court, after giving due weight to the view of the devoted and responsible parent, to give effect to its own judgment.... [O]nce the jurisdiction of the court is invoked its clear duty is to reach and express the best judgment it can.' [8]

Nonetheless there are practical limits to the power of the court. Even where it disagrees with the parental views, in weighing the child's best interests, the court may have to accept them where treatment cannot be accomplished successfully without the parents' co-operation and they are either unwilling or unable to give it. Orders will not be made which cannot be enforced. Thus a court declined to order a mother to desist from breast-feeding her baby in spite of the risks to the baby's health caused thereby.[9]

In *Re T* three doctors had concluded that T – who had been lawfully taken out of the jurisdiction by his mother – was suitable for a liver transplant and that, even though the surgery was major and complicated, it had a good chance of success. Without surgery, T would die within 12 to 18 months; with surgery, T had a good chance of living a normal life for many years. T's mother objected to the treatment. Connell J at first instance gave consent for the treatment to be performed. The Court of Appeal overturned that decision, holding that the first-instance judge had failed to take sufficient account of T's mother's views. Permitting the treatment would have the effect of coercing T's mother into playing the 'crucial and irreplaceable' role in the aftermath of major surgery which would be essential to the success or otherwise of the treatment. The reasonableness of the mother was not the primary issue (although the Court of Appeal doubted Connell J's conclusion that she was unreasonable): what mattered in this case was the dependence of the child on the mother:

'This mother and this child are one for the purpose of this unusual case and the decision of the court to consent to the operation jointly affects the mother and son ... The welfare of this child depends upon his mother. The practical considerations of her ability to cope with supporting the child in the face of her belief that this course is not right for him, the requirement to return probably for a long period to this country, either to leave the father behind and lose his support or to require him to give up his present job and seek one in England were not put by the judge [at first instance] into the balance when he made his decision.

... I would stress that ... the court is not concerned with the reasonableness of the mother's refusal to consent but with the consequences of that refusal and whether it is in the best interests of C for this court in effect to direct the mother to take on this total commitment where she does not agree with the course proposed ... forcing the devoted mother of this young baby to the consequences of this major invasive surgery.'[10]

Butler-Sloss LJ concluded that it was not in the best interests of the child to require him to return to England for the purpose of undergoing liver transplantation, rather, that his best interests required:

'... that his future treatment should be left in the hands of his devoted parents.'

Re T has come under sustained academic[11] and judicial criticism. In *Re C* Thorpe LJ left no room for doubt that *Re T* should be confined to its facts:

'... the outcome of that appeal, denying a child life-prolonging surgery, is unique in our jurisprudence and is explained by the trial judge's erroneous focus on the reasonableness of the mother's rejection of medical opinion thus excluding other factors including the risks and consequences of the surgery, the mother's crucial role in the aftermath of surgery and the practical consideration that the judge's order would have required both parents, alternatively the mother alone, to return to this jurisdiction from a distant commonwealth country probably for the long period that the surgery and its aftermath would require.'[12]

A further limit on a parent's power of refusal is that it will be effective only if both parents agree. As the consent of either parent will validate treatment, the refusal of one will not override the consent of the other. The remedy of the parent who wishes to stop treatment being provided is to apply to the court for an order prohibiting it.

The Art 8 right to a private and family life will be relied upon by parents in order to assert that their views about their child should be respected, regardless of the prevailing medical opinion. ECHR jurisprudence has applied Art 8 in support of parents' rights to control their children.[13] However, the right is not absolute: legitimate and proportionate restrictions can be placed on parental rights and parental control when the child's health or morals are at stake or when conflicting rights come into play. As stated by the European Court of Human Rights:

'... a fair balance has to be struck between the interests of the child in remaining in public care and those of the parent in being reunited with the child ... In carrying out this balancing exercise, the Court will attach particular importance to the best interests of the child, which, depending on their nature and seriousness, may override those of the parent.' [14]

In assessing whether there has been a breach of a parent's right to family life it is also necessary to consider other potentially conflicting rights, for example, the child's own right to autonomy. Article 8 protects the moral and bodily integrity of a person from unjustified assault:[15] thus, it protects patients' right to self-determination. In order to give meaning to a child's right to autonomy the court may have to make decisions on the child's behalf which are against the wishes of parents. The confidentiality in a doctor's advice to a *Gillick* competent girl about abortion and reproductive health must be respected: the girl's Art 8 rights outweigh those of her parents.[16]

In *Glass v UK* the mother of a seriously ill child objected to his doctors' decision to administer diamorphine and to issue a 'do not resuscitate' order.[17] The relationship between the mother and the medical team had become severely compromised.[18] The hospital overrode the wishes of the mother and administered diamorphine without seeking a declaration from the court. The European Court of Human Rights ruled that the administration of diamorphine against the wishes of the child's mother violated Art 8 and she was awarded damages. Save for emergency situations, parental consent to treatment should be sought and, where it is not given, authorisation must be obtained from the court. *Glass* serves as a reminder to doctors of the importance of seeking a court order where parents will not consent to treatment and of the very restricted nature of the exception to this rule in cases of 'emergency'.

The European Court of Human Rights has allowed Member States a wide margin of appreciation in their approach to child care matters:

'In determining whether ... measures were "necessary in a democratic society" ... the Court will have regard to the fact that perceptions as to the appropriateness of intervention by public authorities in the care of children vary from one Contracting State to another, depending on such factors as traditions relating to the role of the family and to State intervention in family affairs and the availability of resources for public measures in this particular area.' [19]

In practice it is suggested that the Strasbourg approach mirrors that of the United Kingdom: the ultimate test is what is in the best interests of the child. While a parent's Art 8 rights must be respected and placed in the balance when the courts take decisions concerning a child, the overriding interest is that of the child.[20] Thus, the European jurisprudence supports a view that the Art 8 right of a parent to control his child exists not for the benefit of the parent but for the benefit of the child.

1 The GMC's guidance on consent involving children states that doctors 'must consider parents, but their patient must be the doctor's first concern' and 'should always act in the best interests of children and young people': GMC, '0–18 years: guidance for all doctors' (2007), paras 4, 8.
2 Children Act 1989, s 1(1).
3 *Re T (a minor) (wardship: medical treatment)* [1997] 1 WLR 242 at 254 per Waite LJ.

4   *Ibid.* J Fortin, *Children's Rights and the Developing Law* (Butterworths, 1998: Update 3, Chap 11), contrasts the respect given to the views of the parents in *Re T* (see N3 above) with the perfunctory dismissal of the parents' views in *Re C (Medical Treatment)* [1998] 1 FLR 384 and comments that 'one is left with the uneasy feeling that the judiciary's attitude to parents' strong convictions about their children's health care is influenced by the way in which parents are perceived, in terms of societal orthodoxy and background'.

5   See the hint to this effect by Wall J in *Re C (a child) (HIV testing)* [2000] 2 WLR 270 at 280. See also *Glass v UK* [2004] 1 FLR 1019.

6   (1944) 321 US Reports 158: quoted by Ward J in *Re E (a minor)* [1993] 1 FLR 386 at 394D, and, as stated by Ward J at 394E, the court 'should be very slow to allow an infant to martyr himself'.

7   *Re A (children) (conjoined twins: surgical separation)* [2000] 4 All ER 961, [2000] 3 FCR 577, [2000] 1 FLR 1, [2001] Fam Law 18, CA.

8   *Re Z (a minor) (identification: restrictions on publications)* [1997] Fam 1 at 32–33.

9   As was suggested in *Re T* (N3 above); see also *Re C (HIV testing)* (see N5 above).

10 *Re T* (see N3 above) per Butler-Sloss LJ.

11 Freeman describes the decision as 'the nadir of judicial thinking in this area': M Freeman, 'Whose Life Is It Anyway?' (2001) 9 Med L Rev 529; Brazier questions whether it is an 'aberration': M Brazier and E Cave, *Medicine, Patients and the Law* (4th ed, Penguin, 2007) at p 388.

12 *Re C (Welfare of Child: Immunisation)* [2003] 2 FLR 1095.

13 For example, *Nielsen v Denmark* (1988) 11 EHRR 175.

14 *Johansen v Norway* (1996) 23 EHRR 33 at para 64.

15 See above and cases cited of *X and Y v Netherlands* (1985) 8 EHRR 235; and *Peters v Netherlands* 77A DR 75 (1994) and see PARA **4.7** N 1 above.

16 *R (on the application of Axon) v Secretary of State for Health and Family Planning Association* [2006] EWCA 37 (Admin); [2006] All ER (D) 148 (Admin). See also *Yousef v Netherlands* (2003) EHRR 345 where it was held that in cases of dispute, the child's Art 8 rights should be prioritised over the parents.

17 *Glass* (see N5 above).

18 The child's mother resuscitated him herself and resorted to violence against his doctors.

19 *Johansen* (see N14 above) at para 64.

20 Article 3(1) of the UN Convention on the Rights of the Child states: 'In all actions concerning children, whether undertaken by public or private social welfare institutions, courts of law, administrative authorities or legislative bodies, the best interests of the child shall be a primary consideration.' And see, for example, *Hoffman v Austria* (1993) 17 EHRR 293; *Bronda v Italy* [1998] EHRLR 756; and in *Garcia v Switzerland*, Application No 10148/82 (DR 42, p 98) the Commission stated: 'having regard to Article 8 para 2, when as in the instant case there is a serious conflict between the interests of the child and those of one of his parents which can only be resolved to the detriment of one of these parties the interests of the child must prevail'.

The court

4.10   The court[1] has the ultimate power to prevent treatment being given, whatever the views of the child, his parents, and his treating doctors. On an application, the court will intervene where it perceives it to be in the interests of the child's welfare to do so. Thus a proposed sterilisation of a disabled 11-year-old girl was prevented on the ground that:

'A review of the whole of the evidence leads me to the conclusion that in a case of a child of 11 years of age, where the evidence shows that her mental and physical condition and attainments have already improved, and where her future prospects are as yet unpredictable, where the evidence also shows that she is unable as yet to understand and appreciate the implications of this operation and could not give a valid or informed consent, but the likelihood is that in later years she will be able to make her own choice, where, I believe, the frustration and resentment of realising (as she would one day) what had happened, could be devastating, an operation of this nature is, in my view, contraindicated.'[2]

In determining best interests the court will consider the views of both the child and the parents, but ultimately the decision is the court's alone. For example, in *Re E (a minor)*[3] Ward J, in assessing the child's and his father's view that life-saving blood transfusions should not be permitted, stated:

' … is this choice of death one which a judge … can find to be consistent with the welfare of the child? … life is precious … When therefore I have to balance the wishes of father and son against the need for the chance to live a precious life, then I have to conclude that their decision is inimical to his well-being.' [4]

The court may therefore act to preserve life even when parents feel that the point has been reached when no more life-saving efforts should be made.[5]

Conversely, when it is no longer in a child's best interests that his life be preserved at all costs, the court will authorise doctors either to take no further active treatment steps or even to withdraw treatment which is being provided.[6] It can be in a child's best interests to cease life-saving treatment even when he is not terminally ill.[7]

1   For detailed consideration of procedure, see **CHAPTER 5**: Going to Court and see **APPENDIX 4.1** for a precedent for a court application.
2   *Re D (a minor) (wardship: sterilisation)* [1976] Fam 185.
3   [1993] 1 FLR 386 per Ward J.
4   *Ibid* at 393 per Ward J.
5   *Re B (a minor) (wardship: medical treatment)* [1981] 1 WLR 1421, CA (a Down's syndrome child required a life-saving operation. The parents refused to consent. It was held that because it had not been demonstrated that the child should be condemned to die, the court would make an order that the operation should be performed).
6   *Re C (a minor)* [1990] Fam 26, CA (the court approved recommendations designed to ease the suffering rather than prolong the life of a terminally-ill hydrocephalic baby); *Re J (a minor) (wardship: medical treatment)* [1991] Fam 33, [1991] 2 WLR 140, [1990] 3 All ER 930, [1990] 2 Med. LR 67, CA (the curtailment of treatment of a severely brain damaged baby was in the baby's best interests; an 'absolutist test' should not be applied; the sole question was what is in the child's best interests); *Re C (a minor) (medical treatment)* [1998] 1 FCR 1, [1998] 1 FLR 384, [1998] Lloyd's Rep Med. 1, [1998] Fam Law 135 (C had a fatal disease. Treatment only prolonged her life and did not alleviate her suffering. The court supported the doctors' view that it was in C's best interests for ventilation to be withdrawn and for it not to be restored should C suffer a further relapse).
7   *Re J (a minor) (wardship: medical treatment)* (see **N6** above) (J was a profoundly handicapped baby who suffered intermittent convulsions. J was not terminally ill. Nonetheless the court held that consent to life-saving treatment could be withheld in the child's best interests).

D   SPECIAL CONSIDERATIONS IN THE TREATMENT OF SEVERELY ILL INFANTS

4.11   Treatment dilemmas involving seriously ill infants is an area warranting separate discussion. Questions of capacity do not arise in children so young, nor can all but their most basic wishes be inferred. Best interests, therefore, are the sole consideration for this type of child patient. The majority of reported cases in recent years have arisen because of a disagreement between parents and doctors as to where the child's best interests lie. Hedley J has provided the following analysis of the circumstances in which disagreements may result in treatment decisions coming before the court, with the 'vast majority' of disagreements falling within categories (ii) and (iii):

'(i)   where a doctor advocated treatment which parents resisted (for example, a blood transfusion), and a failure to administer such treatment would be an affront to that doctor's conscience;

(ii)   where a doctor advocated treatment which the parents resisted on grounds, that while reasonable, were contrary to the clinician's view;

(iii)   where parents wanted treatment, which the clinician could not advise, but the giving of which would not be an affront to conscience; and

(iv)   where the treatment requested would be an affront to conscience.[1]'

1   *Portsmouth NHS Trust v Wyatt* [2005] EWHC 2293 (Fam) per Hedley J at paras 29–30.

Deliberate killing

4.12   At the interface between the law of abortion and the law relating to the treatment of severely disabled newborns there is a paradox. A termination of pregnancy may be performed up to term for reason of serious foetal abnormality.[1] It is trite law that the unborn foetus has no rights.[2] Yet, once the baby is born, deliberately ending its life, for reason of disability or otherwise, will constitute murder.

The doctrine of necessity provides a possible exception to the rule against deliberate killing. It has been invoked only once in a medical treatment decision case and is likely only to apply in the case of conjoined siblings who are unable to achieve independent existence. *Re A*[3] concerned conjoined twins, the weaker of whom, (Mary), was effectively parasitic on the stronger (Jodie) for circulation of oxygenated blood. Without separation, both twins would inevitably die due to the strain on the Jodie's organs. If the twins were separated, Jodie would have a good chance of a relatively normal life. Mary, however, would die immediately after the separation.

At first instance, Johnson J determined that the reasoning in *Bland*[4] applied and therefore the separation would be lawful. In *Bland* it was held that it was lawful to discontinue artificial means of keeping a PVS patient alive. While actively administering a lethal injection would be illegal, omitting to continue prolonging life by artificial means would not. Johnson J held that that this reasoning applied because doctors proposed not a positive act but 'merely the withdrawal of Mary's blood supply', in the same way that doctors were permitted to withdraw Anthony Bland's artificial nutrition and hydration. The Court of Appeal, rightly in our view, unanimously rejected this line of reasoning. Unlike *Bland*, where life sustaining treatment could be discontinued, this did not apply in *Re A*, because Mary was not receiving treatment. Saving Jodie's life involved a positive act – an invasive operation in which Mary would be separated from Jodie with the inevitable conclusion that Mary would die.

In the Court of Appeal, only Robert Walker LJ agreed (albeit for different reasons) with Johnson J's second ground for holding that the separation would be lawful, namely that it was in both Mary's and Jodie's best interests. Stripped of the protection of the *Bland* omissions' doctrine, Johnson J's opinion that Mary's short life would be painful and to her disadvantage can be seen as a stark endorsement of active euthanasia based on quality of life principles. For Brook LJ (with whom Ward LJ concurred):

> '... by no stretch of the imagination could it be said that the surgeons would be acting in good faith in Mary's best interests when they prepared an operation which would benefit Jodie but kill Mary.'[5]

Regardless of the supposed poor quality of Mary's life, the Court of Appeal was constrained by the law of homicide and the unlawfulness of active euthanasia. The court therefore had to establish whether the act of undertaking the operation would amount to intentional killing under the law of homicide and whether that act of killing would be unlawful.

Ward and Brooke LJJ concluded that in performing the separation, the surgeons did intend to kill Mary. They searched for a legal means to convert the separation into a lawful act. Ward LJ rejected labelling Mary 'with the American terminology which would paint her to be 'an unjust aggressor', but nevertheless adopted the principles underlying that test to determine that the doctors could avail themselves of a plea of 'quasi-self-defence, modified to meet the quite exceptional circumstances nature has inflicted on the twins' in:

> '... coming to Jodie's defence and removing the threat of fatal harm to her presented by Mary's draining her lifeblood.'[6]

Brooke LJ relied upon the defence of necessity. He felt able to distinguish the conjoined twins' case from the seminal case of *Dudley and Stephens* where it was held that the defence of necessity was not available to shipwrecked sailors who killed and ate a cabin boy to avoid starvation.[7] What distinguished Mary from the cabin boy was that she was 'self designated for a very early death' in any event.[8] This distinction is tenuous. Despite Ward LJ's statement that 'this is a court of law, not of morals',[9] the decision was not based on settled legal principles (less still principles upon which their Lordships agreed). Their judgment was arguably founded on moral relativism, balancing the relative worth of two existences: an exercise that Lord Coleridge was unable to countenance in *Dudley and Stephens*.[10]

The result might have been different had there been evidence that both twins could survive longer than the 'near future'. The twins' parents did not wish to pursue an appeal to the House of Lords (despite a fully constituted Judicial Committee making itself available to hear such an appeal). We are therefore left with the opaque and unsatisfactory decision of the Court of Appeal.[11]

The heart-wrenching nature of the no-win decision to be made in this case leads us to ask whether these vanishingly rare circumstances should not form an exception to the rule that the court can trump a parental determination. Should the Art 8 right to respect for family life and/or the Art 9 right to respect for religious beliefs[12] not mean that exceptionally here the parents should have had the ultimate decision as to whether Mary should be killed to save Jodie's life?

Finally, Smith suggests that the limited ratio of *Re A*, regardless of the legal route by which it was achieved, was as follows:

'Where A is, as the defendant knows, is doomed to die in the near future but even the short continuation of his life will inevitably kill B as well, it is lawful to kill A, however free of fault he may be.'[13]

We would agree.

The specific and rare factual matrix in *Re A* means that the potential for the application of the doctrine of necessity will arise very infrequently. It seems unlikely that procedures at the expense of one child for the benefit of another will often be permitted. Indeed, it is an established principle that organ and tissue donation for the benefit of a sibling will not be permitted unless it can be demonstrated that it is in the interests of the donor child – reasoning which will invariably require the survival of both siblings.[14] Doctors faced with a situation such as that in *Re A* must seek the approval of the court before proceeding with a separation.[15]

1 Abortion Act 1967, s 1(1)(d); see **CHAPTER 8**: Abortion; **PARA 8.17**.
2 *Paton v British Pregnancy Advisory Service Trustees* [1979] 1 QB 276; *Paton v United Kingdom* (1980) 3 EHRR 408; *C v S* [1987] 1 All ER 1230. *Re MB (an adult: medical treatment)* [1997] 2 FLR 426, [1997] 8 Med LR 217; and *St George's Healthcare NHS Trust v S* [1998] 3 WLR 936. See **CHAPTER 9**: Managing Pregnancies: **PARAS 9.2** and **9.11**.
3 *Re A (children) (conjoined twins: surgical separation)* [2001] Fam 147; [2000] 4 All ER 961, [2000] 3 FCR 577, [2000] 1 FLR 1, [2001] Fam Law 18, CA.
4 *Airedale NHS Trust v Bland* [1993] AC 789, [1993] 2 WLR 316, [1993] 1 FLR 1026, HL [hereafter simply '*Bland*'], see **CHAPTER 12**: Permanent Vegetative State.
5 See **N3** above [2001] Fam 147 at 218A.
6 See **N5** above at 203D-204C.
7 *R v Dudley and Stephens* (1884–85) LR 14 QBD
8 See **N5** above at 239C-240E.
9 See **N5** above at 155D.
10 See **N5** above at 287–288.
11 Hewson cites an ITN News interview in which Ward LJ recognised that 'fifty percent of the population will agree with the decision-fifty per cent will think we have gone potty' (B Hewson 'Killing Off Mary: Was The Court of Appeal Right?' Med Law Rev (2001) (9) 281 at footnote 2).
12 See **CHAPTER 1**: Consent – General **PARA 1.21**: Article 8; **CHAPTER 4**: Deciding for Others – Children, **PARA 4.4**: Parents and those with parental responsibility; **CHAPTER 11**: Religious Objections to Treatment, **PARAS 11.2** and **11.17**, General principles.
13 J C Smith, Case Comment [2001] Crim LR 400 at 405.
14 *Re Y (mental patient: bone marrow donation)* [1997] Fam 110, [1997] 2 WLR 556, [1996] 2 FLR 787, [1997] 2 FCR 172 (an operation to transplant bone marrow from Y, a mentally and physically handicapped adult, into her terminally ill sister was in Y's best interests because this would tend to prolong the life of both her sister and her mother, and Y would thereby receive emotional, psychological and social benefit with minimal detriment to Y). See **CHAPTER 15**: Human Organ and Tissue Donation, **PARAS 15.12–15.13**.
15 In *Re A*, given the grave issues raised by the decision to undertake treatment which was predictably going to end the life of one of the infants, an application to court was inevitable. The twins' parents, who were committed Roman Catholics, refused to consent to the separation necessitating an application to the court by the medical team in any event.

Withholding and withdrawing life-sustaining treatment

Withholding treatment

4.13   Doctors are under a duty to give their infant patients medical care and attention. Where a doctor fails in his duty to treat a child patient and the child dies as a result of that failure, the doctor may be liable to prosecution under the law of homicide. Dr Arthur was charged with murder in relation to his treatment of a child born with Down's syndrome. In his summing-up the judge explained that there is:

'... no special law in this country which places doctors in a separate category and gives them special protection over the rest of us'.[1]

Nevertheless, it is accepted that in certain situations, where it is in the best interests of the child, doctors can withhold or decline to initiate treatment, even where the inevitable result will be the death of the infant.

In *Re B (a minor) (wardship: medical treatment)*,[2] a child with Down's syndrome urgently required straightforward surgery to remove an intestinal blockage, without which surgery she would die. Her parents refused to consent. The Court of Appeal held that because it had not been demonstrated that 'the life of this child is demonstrably going to be so awful that in effect the child must be condemned to die',[3] the court would make an order that the operation should be performed. Whilst it is clear now that 'best interests' forms one indivisible test, two subsidiary factors are important: first, the nature of the infant's disability and the extent to which she will be burdened by prolonged life; second, the level of suffering that will be caused by the proposed intervention.

It is impossible to be prescriptive about different levels of disability. Moreover, it should be remembered that the child's wider best interests will be determinative, rather than his purely medical interests[4] or the medical categorisation of his illness or disability. The Royal College of Paediatrics and Child Health has produced the following schema for situations where it may be ethical and legal to consider the withholding or withdrawal of life-sustaining medical treatment, which is often used as a framework by practitioners and by the court:[5]

'1 The "Brain Dead" Child[6]

In the older child where criteria of brain-stem death are agreed by two practitioners in the usual way it may still be technically feasible to provide basal cardio-respiratory support by means of ventilation and intensive care. It is agreed within the profession that treatment in such circumstances is futile and the withdrawal of current medical treatment is appropriate.

2 The "Permanent Vegetative State"[7]

The child who develops a permanent vegetative state following insults, such as trauma or hypoxia, is reliant on others for all care and does not react or relate with the outside world. It may be appropriate to withdraw or withhold life- sustaining treatment.

3 The "No Chance" Situation

The child has such severe disease that life-sustaining treatment simply delays death without significant alleviation of suffering. Treatment to sustain life is inappropriate.

4 The "No Purpose" Situation

Although the patient may be able to survive with treatment, the degree of physical or mental impairment will be so great that it is unreasonable to expect them to bear it.

5 The "Unbearable Situation"

The child and/or family feel that in the face of progressive and irreversible illness further treatment is more than can be borne. They wish to have a particular treatment withdrawn or to refuse further treatment irrespective of the medical opinion that it may be of some benefit.'

Where the infant's condition lies within this schema is inevitably a matter that falls within the treating clinician's competence. However, even skilled clinicians may have difficulty placing a particular child's situation into one or other of the specific categories. That in itself is not a substantial obstacle: the key is to ensure that the assessment of best interests focuses on the *child's* best interests and identifies each of the factors relied upon in carrying out a balancing exercise and reaching a conclusion. The decision as to where the child's best interests lie is performed in the first instance by his parents. However, the weight to be applied to the parents' assessment is not without limit. If the doctors disagree with the parents on the grounds that continuing or ending the child's life is not in his best interests, an application to the court will often be necessary.[8] Where the issue is brought before the court for determination, it is not uncommon for the parents' assessment of their child's best interests to be over-ruled, albeit with due respect for, and sensitivity to, those sincerely held views.

1   *R v Leonard Arthur* (1981) 12 BMLR 1. Dr Arthur was charged with murder. He was alleged to have ordered 'nursing care only' and prescribed an appetite-suppressant for a child born with Down's syndrome in accordance with his parents' wishes. The child died in its third day of life. It was established in evidence that the baby had not died of starvation and also suffered brain and lung damage. The judge reduced the charge to one of attempted murder and Dr Arthur was acquitted by the jury. Dr Arthur's trial occurred after the Court of Appeal's decision in *Re B (*N2 *below) although the latter was not cited in court.*

2   [1981] 1 WLR 1421.

3   Per Templeman LJ, who concluded that 'in the present case the choice ... is this: whether to allow an operation to take place which may result in the child living for 20 or 30 years as a mongoloid or whether (and I think this brutally must be the result) to terminate the life of a mongoloid child because she also has an intestinal complaint. Faced with that choice, I have no doubt ... that the child must live'. Templeman LJ's ruling has survived the test of time; his terminology has not.

4   *Re MB (an adult: medical treatment)* [1997] 8 Med LR 217 at 225 per Butler-Sloss LJ.

5   See **APPENDIX 14.3**: Royal College of Paediatrics and Child Heath, *Withholding or Withdrawing Life Sustaining Treatment* (2004), pp 10–11, 28–29.

6   For our discussion of this issue see **CHAPTER 14**: End of Life.

7   For our discussion of this issue see **CHAPTER 12**: Permanent Vegetative State.

8   See in particular the decision of the European Court of Human Rights in *Glass v United Kingdom* (2004) 1 FLR 1019, (2004) 39 EHRR 15 discussed above at **PARA 4.9**. In our view the dicta of Ward LJ in *Re A (children) (conjoined twins: surgical separation)* [2000] 4 All ER 961 that it would have been a 'perfectly acceptable response' for doctors treating conjoined twins to respect the parent's wishes and 'let nature take its course' without referral to the court because the doctors' duty of care to the children did not extended to 'a further duty to refer this impasse to the court' at 987E-F is no longer tenable (even if it was in 2000).

Withdrawing treatment

4.14   When intensive treatment has been initiated, the situation may arise where doctors or parents wish it to be withdrawn. The House of Lords decision in *Bland*[1] applies equally to infants as to adults: withdrawing life support does not constitute murder. There is in law no distinction between withholding and withdrawing life-sustaining treatment. The single test of the infant's best interests applies equally to both situations.[2]

Withdrawal of treatment will inevitably engage the Art 2 right to life. While a severely disabled infant has a 'right to life', he does not have 'a right to be kept alive' in circumstances where continued treatment would be futile.[3] Withdrawing treatment that is no longer in the child's best interests will not amount to a breach of Art 2, even where this course of action is against parental wishes.[4] In *Re OT*, having recognised this, Parker J granted a hospital trust orders and declarations allowing ventilation to be withdrawn from a seriously ill baby and offering him palliative care to allow him to die with the least possible distress.[5]

As stated at **PARA 4.9** above, in the absence of parental consent or if there are doubts as to the child's best interests, whether the parents are acting in the child's best interests, or to the legality of the proposed withdrawal of treatment generally, the matter should be referred to the court. Where there are such disagreements or doubts, treatment should be continued until agreement has been reached or the court has made a decision.

1   *Airedale NHS Trust v Bland* [1993] AC 789; see **CHAPTER 12, PARA.12.3** for detailed discussion of this case.
2   *An NHS Trust v MB* [2006] EWHC 507 (Fam) at para 20 per Holman J.
3   For example, *NHS Trust A v M* [2001] Fam 348; *Re OT* [2009] EWHC 633 [Fam].
4   For example, *An NHS Trust v D* [2000] 2 FLR 677; *R (on the Application of Burke) v GMC* [2005] EWCA Civ 1003; *Re OT* [2009] EWHC 633 [Fam].
5   [2009] EWHC 633 (Fam).

Best interests: the court's approach

4.15   The court's approach to infant treatment decisions is, by necessity, highly fact-specific and the courts have been understandably slow to set out definitive guidance on the application of the 'best interests' test.[1] The flexibility afforded to the court comes at the expense of certainty for doctors and their legal advisers.

The court is tasked with weighing up the advantages and disadvantages of providing, withholding or withdrawing the various treatment options and to balance them in order to determine what the child's best interests are.[2] The court must exercise independent and objective judgment on the basis of all of the available evidence.[3] Best interests are not limited to medical interests and it is for the court, not for a doctor, to determine what the child's best interests are. Thus, evidence will not be limited to medical evidence.[4] The views of doctors, other members of the infant's care team and his parents should be taken into account to the extent that they touch on the child's best interests, rather than their own interests or opinions.

Where the court is deciding whether to withdraw treatment it will have to conclude 'to a high degree of probability' that it is in the best interests of the child.[5] This does not mean, however, that the medical experts giving evidence must be unanimous in a proposed course of action. The court will weigh competing medical evidence and is entitled to reject one line of evidence.[6]

The courts approach the exercise of determining best interests against the background of a strong presumption in favour of preserving life. Where treatment would, however, be futile, the presumption is rebutted and it has been held that there is no obligation on the medical profession to provide such treatment.[7]

It has been suggested in the adult context that the key question to be asked is whether there is any chance of the patient recovering any quality of life so as to justify his continued discomfort.[8] Assessments of life quality should be approached cautiously and with due regard for the presumption that favours preservation of life.

The concept of 'intolerability' of the child's condition should not be invoked to usurp a comprehensive determination of best interests. It is neither a supplementary test to the 'best interests' test nor a gloss on that test.[9] Although it may be a relevant factor in the assessment of best interests, intolerability cannot provide a single determinative test as to best interests.[10]

In *NHS Trust v MB* Holman J provided a helpful summary of the application of the 'best interests' test in infant treatment decisions, noting that it was the role and the duty of the court to exercise its own independent and objective judgment:

'[1] The right and power of the court to do so only arises because the patient, in this case because he is a child, lacks the capacity to make a decision for himself.

[2] I am not deciding what decision I might make for myself if I was, hypothetically, in the situation of the patient; nor for a child of my own if in that situation; nor whether the respective decisions of the doctors on the one hand or the parents on the other are reasonable decisions.

[3] The matter must be decided by the application of an objective approach or test ... That test is the best interests of the patient. Best interests are used in the widest sense and include every kind of consideration capable of impacting on the decision. These include, non–exhaustively, medical, emotional, sensory (pleasure, pain and suffering) and instinctive (the human instinct to survive) considerations.

[4] It is impossible to weigh such considerations mathematically, but the court must do the best it can to balance all the conflicting considerations in a particular case and see where the final balance of the best interests lies.

[5] Considerable weight (Lord Donaldson ... MR referred to 'a very strong presumption'[11]) must be attached to the prolongation of life because the individual human instinct and desire to survive is strong and must be presumed to be strong in the patient. But it is not absolute, nor necessarily decisive; and may be outweighed if the pleasures and the quality of life are

sufficiently small and the pain and suffering or other burdens of living are sufficiently great …[12]

[6] All these cases are very fact specific, i.e. they depend entirely on the facts of the individual case.

[7] The views and opinions of both the doctors and the parents must be carefully considered. Where, as in this case, the parents spend a great deal of time with their child, their views may have particular value because they know the patient and how he reacts so well; although the court needs to be mindful that the views of any parents may, very understandably, be coloured by their own emotion or sentiment …

[8] It is important to stress that the reference is to the views and opinions of the parents. Their own wishes, however understandable in human terms, are wholly irrelevant to consideration of the objective best interests of the child save to the extent in any given case that they may illuminate the quality and value *to the child* of the child/parent relationship.'[13]

The difficulty faced by the court in performing a balancing exercise was highlighted in the 2009 case of *RB*, a 13 month old boy who was born suffering from a severe neuro-muscular disorder.[14] RB's condition was static but unlikely to improve. He was a 'floppy' baby with virtually no independent movement. He had required ventilating since birth and had failed all attempts to wean him from ventilation. Although it had not been possible to reach a diagnosis with any certainty, the probability was that his condition arose from a defective gene. There was some prospect of research within his lifetime identifying that gene but no realistic prospect of any treatment being developed. RB had been resident on the applicant Trust's paediatric intensive care unit for 8 months and was invasively ventilated through an endo-tracheal tube which passed through his nose. His parents and the clinicians agreed that it was not in his best interests for that to continue. The clinicians and his mother argued that RB's very poor quality of life weighed in favour of withdrawing ventilation. His father argued that a tracheostomy should be performed so as to allow his discharge home. After 6 days of evidence the father withdrew his objection to the treatment and McFarlane J granted declarations relating to the withdrawal of ventilation and the provision of palliative treatment.

In light of the consensus that was finally reached, no formal judgment was handed down although the Judge concluded the hearing with some words of endorsement which included the comment:

'… I agree with the outcome and consider that the conclusion to which they and the clinicians have come is the only tenable outcome for RB, the viability of whose life, from its first moment, has depended upon receiving intensive and invasive care from others.'[15]

1   A point which the courts routinely reiterate. For example, *NHS Trust v MB* [2006] EWHC 507 (Fam) at paras 106–107 per Holman J: 'this is a very fact specific decision taken in the actual circumstances as they are for this child and today … My sole and intense focus has been this child alone'.

2   *Re J (a minor) (wardship: medical treatment)* [1991] Fam 33, [1991] 2 WLR 140, [1990] 3 All ER 930, [1990] 2 Med. LR 67, CA.

3   *Re T (A Minor) (Wardship: Medical Treatment)* [1997] 1 WLR 242 CA.

4   *Portsmouth NHS Trust v Wyatt* [2004] EWHC 2247; *Re L (A Child) (Medical Treatment: Benefit)*
     [2004] EWHC 2713 (Fam); [2005] 1 FLR 491; *An NHS Trust v A* [2005] EWCA Civ 1145.
5   *An NHS Trust v X* [2005] EWCA Civ 1145; [2006] Lloyd's Rep Med 29.
6   *Ibid.*
7   For example: *Re L (A Child) (Medical Treatment: Benefit)* [2004] EWHC 2713 (Fam), [2005]
     1 FLR 491.
8   *An NHS Trust v X* (see **N5** above).
9   *Portsmouth NHS Trust v Wyatt* [2004] EWHC 2247 at para 24 endorsed by the Court of Appeal
     in *Wyatt v Portsmouth Hospital NHS Trust* [2005] EWCA Civ 1181 at para 76 and para 91.
10   *R (on the application of Burke) v GMC* [2005] EWCA Civ 1003, where the Court of Appeal
     emphatically rejected Munby J's assertion that in the context of life-prolonging treatment the
     'touchstone of best interests is intolerability' (paras 61–63). See, in the context of the treatment
     of infants, *Re L (A Child) (Medical Treatment: Benefit)* [2004] EWHC 2713 (Fam), [2005]
     1 FLR 491; *NHS Trust v MB* [2006] EWHC 507 (Fam) at para 17 per Holman J.
11   In *Re J* (see **N2** above) at 46
12   Holman J noted the words of Lord Donaldson MR *Re J* (see **N2** above): 'There is without doubt
     a very strong presumption in favour of a course of action which will prolong life, but it is not
     irrebuttable. Account has to be taken of the pain and suffering and quality of life which the child
     will experience if life is prolonged. Account has also to be taken of the pain and suffering
     involved in the proposed treatment. ... [T]he instinct and desire for survival is very strong. We
     all believe in and assert the sanctity of human life. Even very severely handicapped people find
     a quality of life rewarding which to the unhandicapped may seem manifestly intolerable.
     People have an amazing adaptability. But in the end there will be cases in which the answer
     must be that it is not in the interests of the child to subject it to treatment which will cause it
     increased suffering and produce no commensurate benefit, giving the fullest possible weight to
     the child's, and mankind's desire to survive'.
13   *NHS Trust v MB* (see **N1** above) at para 16 with our enumeration inserted.
14   *In the matter of RB (A Child)* [2009] EWHC B26 (Fam): http://www.bailii.org/ew/cases/
     EWHC/Fam/2009/B26.html .
15   *Ibid.* at para 10.

Practical guidance

4.16   Where an application is made to the court for a declaration that it will
be lawful for doctors to withhold or withdraw life-sustaining treatment the
courts frequently have to assess a significant amount of evidence to discern the
child's best interests under pressure of time. In recent years the use of best
interests 'balance sheets' in which parties list their submissions as to the
benefits and burdens (or disbenefits) of the proposed treatment has been
endorsed.[1] This exercise will readily assist the court in performing the best
interests balancing exercise.[2]

In preparing or opposing any application for withdrawal of treatment it will be
critical for all relevant evidence to be placed before the court. The courts may be
assisted by video evidence showing how well or badly a child is able to interact
with his surroundings. Careful scrutiny of medical records may reveal a hitherto
unrecognised ability to interact with play therapists or other carers. The oral
testimony of nurses and those with day to day management of severely injured
or disabled children is likely to provide a useful context for any balancing
exercise. If time permits, the preparation of focussed agendas and joint
meetings between the opposing experts may narrow or remove any areas of
disagreement. Perhaps most importantly, there is no need for disagreements
about best interests' decisions to become unduly contentious. Careful handling
of both medical and lay clients by legal advisors can minimise the adverse

impact on the therapeutic relationship and may well promote a consensual outcome as in *RB*.

For the appropriate procedure for taking any issues to court, see **CHAPTER 5**: Going to Court.

1   *An NHS Trust v MB* [2006] EWHC 507 (Fam) at para 59 per Holman J. An example of a best interests 'balance sheet' or 'checklist' derived from this case is reproduced at **APPENDIX 4.3**. See also the 'balance sheet' prepared by counsel and adopted by Parker J in *Re OT* [2009] EWHC 633 (Fam).

2   See **CHAPTER 3**: Deciding for others – adults and in particular the guidance at **PARAS 3.13–3.15**.

E   CONCLUSION

4.17   The law in relation to seriously ill infants is reasonably settled.[1] Complexity arises in applying the 'best interests' test to challenging facts. The volume of 'hard cases' involving critical decisions at the very beginning of life is likely to increase in correlation with advances in neonatal technology. In any event, religious convictions and the inability or unwillingness of distraught parents to accept the inevitability child's condition mean that best interests cases will continue to appear in the courts and the newspaper headlines.

The most obvious issue the courts will have to grapple with in treatment decisions involving older children is the application of Art 8 to situations where 16 and 17 year olds and indeed younger *Gillick* competent children refuse treatment that their parents and doctors insist is in their best interests. The Department of Health's 2008 guidance explicitly doubts the wisdom of relying on parental consent over a child's refusal. In an era of increased and increasing respect for child autonomy, it will be interesting to see how the courts and legislators deal with cases where parents and doctors wish to compel a child to undergo treatment against his wishes.

1   There continue to be calls for legislation or firmer professional guidelines on withholding and withdrawing life sustaining treatment. The Nuffield Council on Bioethics' 2006 report 'Critical care decisions in fetal and neonatal medicine: ethical issues' (November 2006) proposed guidelines on initiating and continuing intensive care based on gestational age which included the recommendation that below 22 weeks gestation no baby should be resuscitated save for within a clinical research study with research ethics committee approval and parental consent (p xxi para 23(f)). Contrast, also, the US situation where the Federal 'Baby Doe' Rules require maximal treatment of all impaired newborns, save where that treatment would be physiologically futile: 'Nondiscrimination on the basis of handicap; procedures and guidelines relating to health care for handicapped infants – HHS. Final rules. Fed Regist. 1985; 50: 14879 – 14892 incorporated into the US Child Abuse Prevention and Treatment Act. Pub. L. No. 42 USC 5101 and the situation in the Netherlands where neonatal euthanasia has been permissible *de facto* since the 'Groningen Protocol' became a nationwide practice in 2005. The protocol offers guidelines for neonatal euthanasia including requirements of futility, parent-physician consensus and a 'waiting period'. If protocol is followed, prosecutors refrain from taking action. E Verhagen E & P Sauer, The Groningen Protocol – Euthanasia in Severely Ill Newborns, 10 N Engl J Med 352, 959–62 (2005).

For updating material and hyperlinks related to this chapter, see:
www.3serjeantsinn.com/mtdl/deciding-for-others-children

Chapter 5

Going to Court

A   Introduction 5.1
B   Identifying the right court for medical treatment cases 5.2
     Courts with jurisdiction to deal with medical treatment cases 5.2
     The jurisdiction of the Court of Protection 5.3
          Cases in which the Court of protection lacks jurisdiction 5.4
          16 to 17 year olds: overlap of the jurisdiction of the Court of
          Protection and the High Court 5.5
          Different age cut-offs for different types of case 5.6
          Summary 5.7
C   Procedural points common to the Court of Protection and the High
     Court 5.8
     Public law issues 5.8
     The timing of proceedings 5.9
     How urgent is it? 5.10
     Introduction to the Official Solicitor and CAFCASS 5.11
     Who should bring proceedings? 5.13
          What does the party bringing the proceedings want? 5.15
     Family Division Practice Direction on bundles 5.16
     Final hearings 5.17
     Typing up the order 5.18
D   The Court of Protection 5.19
     The Court of Protection generally 5.19
          Constitutional issues 5.19
          Location and judges 5.20
          Sources of procedural rules and guidance 5.21
          The court's general approach 5.22
          The court's power to make medical treatment decisions 5.23
     Serious medical treatment: Practice Direction 9E 5.24
          Definition of 'serious medical treatment' 5.25
          Procedural matters 5.26
     What cases should be brought to court? 5.27
     Privacy and publicity 5.28
     Points to consider before starting proceedings 5.29
          Litigation friend 5.29

Is permission required? 5.30
Who should be named as respondents and who should be notified of the proceedings? 5.31
Level of judge and initial directions 5.32
Deprivation of liberty 5.33
Starting proceedings – non-urgent 5.34
How are proceedings begun? 5.34
Starting proceedings – urgent 5.35
First hearing and subsequent directions hearings 5.36
Final hearings 5.37
Costs 5.38
Costs of Official Solicitor 5.39
Appeals 5.40
E   The High Court's jurisdiction in relation to minors 5.41
The High Court generally 5.41
The High Court's jurisdiction 5.41
Regional hearings 5.42
Procedure and rules 5.43
What cases should be brought to court? 5.44
Who should be the defendants? 5.49
Starting proceedings – non-urgent 5.53
Starting proceedings – urgent 5.56
Privacy and publicity 5.57
First hearing and subsequent directions hearings 5.58
Final hearings 5.59
Costs 5.60
Appeals 5.61
F   The High Court's inherent jurisdiction – in relation to 'vulnerable adults' 5.62
G   Conclusion 5.63

A INTRODUCTION

5.1   This chapter provides guidance on procedure and practice for those taking a medical treatment case to court or considering doing so, or who find themselves involved in proceedings. It addresses the procedural issues which arise most frequently and its references to legislation and other source material should assist those requiring guidance in more unusual situations. Section B provides help in identifying the right court and jurisdiction; generic procedural points are dealt with in section C; and procedural points specific to the different courts and jurisdictions are then dealt with in sections D, E and F. Concluding thoughts are set out in section G.

B IDENTIFYING THE RIGHT COURT FOR MEDICAL TREATMENT CASES

Courts with jurisdiction to deal with medical treatment cases

5.2   An initial task for all those considering bringing a case to court is to identify the correct court. Medical treatment cases can be dealt with in three 'jurisdictions':[1]

- The Court of Protection;
- The High Court's jurisdiction in relation to minors;
- The High Court's 'vulnerable adult' jurisdiction, although its use is likely to be rare.[2]

1   Note that while the powers of the High Court to make decisions in relation to minors and vulnerable adults are considered separately here, they fall under the same inherent jurisdiction. See also (in the context of a local authority's application for a declaration as to whether it was lawful not to tell a mother in labour of its plan to remove her child at birth) the High Court's 'jurisdiction under the general law' to make an anticipatory declaration in an appropriate case 'in the public interest and for the proper protection of a public authority': *In the matter of Unborn Baby D (Bury Metropolitan Borough Council v D)* [2009] EWHC 446 (Fam) per Munby J at paras 12–13.
2   *In the matter of SA (A Local Authority v (1) MA (2) NA and (3) SA (by her children's guardian LJ))* per Munby J [2006] 1 FLR 867.

The jurisdiction of the Court of Protection

5.3   On 1 October 2007 the Court of Protection assumed jurisdiction to deal with many of the medical treatment cases which had previously been heard only in the Family Division of the High Court. The Court of Protection now has jurisdiction to hear medical treatment cases relating to people – referred to in the language of the MCA as 'P'[1] – who meet two conditions:

- *They are aged 16 or over.* On a careful reading, a general minimum age for the exercise of the court's jurisdiction is not set out expressly in the Act. There is no such limit in s 15 or s 16. While MCA s 2 (5) states that no 'power which a person ('D') may exercise under this Act . . . is exercisable in relation to a person under 16', the power of the court to take action is not expressly limited in this way. However, it is well understood in practice that the Court of Protection does not have the power to make personal welfare decisions (including medical treatment decisions) in relation to people aged under 16. This finds support in the Explanatory Note to the Act (which in contrast to s 2(5) does not distinguish between 'D' and the court),[2] implicitly in the Act itself,[3] and in the main Code of Practice.[4]

and
- *They are said to lack capacity under the MCA.* The Court of Protection's jurisdiction is not limited to cases in which the applicant asserts that the patient lacks (or may lack) capacity. It also has jurisdiction to hear an application brought by a patient (or other properly interested person)

who contends that he has capacity, in circumstances, for example, where medical treatment decisions are being taken by others on the basis that he lacks capacity.[5] It is the *dispute* about MCA-capacity which triggers the court's jurisdiction.

1   MCA, s 16.
2   Para 24 of the Explanatory Note: 'Subsection (5) makes it clear that powers under the Act generally only arise where the person lacking capacity is 16 or over . . .'.
3   For example the need for the exception in s 18(3): 'The powers under section 16 as respects any other matter relating to P's property and affairs may be exercised even though P has not reached 16, if the court considers it likely that P will still lack capacity to make decisions in respect of that matter when he reaches 18.'
4   For example para 8.1 refers to the setting up of the Court of Protection '. . . to deal with decision-making for adults (and children in a few cases) . . .'; and the beginning of Chapter 12 states: 'The Act does not generally apply to people under the age of 16.'
5   For example MCA, s 15(1): 'The court may make declarations as to— (a) whether a person has or lacks capacity to make a decision specified in the declaration; (b) whether a person has or lacks capacity to make decisions on such matters as are described in the declaration; . . .'; and the main Code of Practice para 8.7: '. . . a person wishing to challenge a finding that they lack capacity may apply to the court . . .'.

Cases in which the Court of Protection lacks jurisdiction

5.4   The Court of Protection has *no* jurisdiction to hear cases about medical treatment decisions relating to the following categories of people:

- *People under 16 years old.* Such cases must be heard by the Family Division of the High Court exercising its inherent jurisdiction in relation to minors or its jurisdiction under s 8 Children Act 1989.
- *People aged 16 or over who are not said to lack capacity under the MCA.* This category can be sub-divided as follows:
  - *Cases concerning people aged 16 and 17 who are not said to lack capacity under the MCA.* These cases must also be heard by the Family Division of the High Court exercising its inherent jurisdiction in relation to minors or its jurisdiction under s 8 Children Act 1989. There are two categories of case in which a court application might be necessary: first, if seeking to override a competent refusal of treatment; secondly, where the dispute regarding acceptance or refusal of treatment raises doubts about the wisdom or maturity (as opposed to MCA-capacity) of the adolescent patient to make the decision in question.
  - *Cases concerning people aged 18 or over who are not said to lack capacity under the MCA.* These cases can only be heard by the Family Division of the High Court – again exercising its inherent jurisdiction, in this case in respect of capable but vulnerable adults. While this is a jurisdiction occasionally invoked in respect of welfare decisions, applications in respect of medical treatment are likely to be rare[1] and would be just one part of a multi-disciplinary strategy to resolve a many-faceted problem.

1   The authors are unaware of any case where this jurisdiction has been invoked only to deal with a specific medical treatment issue, although in one unreported case the provision of pressure sore care to a capable but vulnerable physically disabled women arose as part of the consideration of wider welfare issues. In theory one can perhaps foresee that this jurisdiction

might be invoked where family members prevented a capable but vulnerable person from undergoing some elective operation (such as sterilisation).

16 to 17 year olds: overlap of the jurisdiction of the Court of Protection and the High Court

5.5 In relation to medical treatment decisions about people aged 16 or 17, the Court of Protection and the High Court both have jurisdiction and the applicant must choose in which court to issue proceedings.

Overlap between COP & High Court for 16–17 year olds

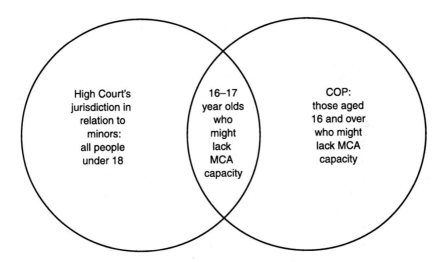

The main Code of Practice indicates that the Court of Protection may often be the appropriate court. Paragraph 12.7 of the Code states:

- 'It may be appropriate for the Court of Protection to make a welfare decision concerning a young person who lacks capacity to decide for themselves (for example, about where the young person should live) if the court decides that the parents are not acting in the young person's best interests.

- It might be appropriate to refer a case to the Court of Protection where there is disagreement between a person interested in the care and welfare of a young person and the young person's medical team about the young person's best interests or capacity.'

Paragraph 12.24 of the Code states that the Family Division may be more appropriate for one-off cases:

'If a case might require an ongoing order (because the young person is likely to still lack capacity when they are 18), it may be more appropriate for the Court of Protection to hear the case. For one-off cases not involving property or finances, the Family Division may be more appropriate.'

The authors would suggest that practitioners should be wary about categorising many medical treatment cases as 'one-off' given the length of time which proceedings can take, the variable course of many clinical conditions, the potential for the matter to return to court for 'review' even after the 'final' hearing and provisions granting the parties 'liberty to apply'.

Whichever jurisdiction is invoked, the 16 or 17 year old will usually need to be represented in the proceedings as follows:

- In the High Court: under the court's inherent jurisdiction in relation to minors or its jurisdiction under s 8 Children Act 1989: by a guardian *ad litem* appointed through CAFCASS.
- In the Court of Protection: by the Official Solicitor as litigation friend.

Where circumstances permit it is advisable to consult both CAFCASS and the Official Solicitor about any proposed application concerning a 16 or 17 year old and consider their views as to venue.

If it becomes apparent that a case which has already been issued in the Court of Protection is best dealt with in the High Court (or vice versa), the matter can be transferred.[1]

1 The Mental Capacity Act 2005 (Transfer of Proceedings) Order 2007 (SI 2007/1899) provides for such transfers in the case of a person under 18 years old.

Different age cut-offs for different types of case

5.6 The age cut-off for the exercise of powers under the MCA is not consistent throughout the Act. While some of the powers set out below may be irrelevant in a medical treatment decision case, practitioners should be aware that there are varying age limits in the following provisions:

The Deprivation of Liberty Safeguards in MCA, Schedule A1 cannot be used by either managing authorities or supervising authorities to authorise the deprivation of liberty of under 18-year-olds.[1] However, the Court of Protection may make an order authorising the deprivation of liberty of a 16 or 17 year old who lacks capacity under the MCA.[2]

In the following respects the MCA applies to people under 16:

- The Court of Protection may make a decision in relation to the person's property and affairs, or appoint a deputy to do so, if the person lacks capacity and the court considers it likely that he will still lack capacity to make decisions in respect of that matter when he reaches 18.[3] As Jones puts it:[4]

  'This provision enables the court to take a long term view where a brain damaged child has been awarded a large sum of damages and there is no prospect of the child ever gaining the capacity to manage that money.'

- The offence of ill-treating or wilfully neglecting a person lacking capacity[5] does not specify the minimum age of the victim. See the main Code of Practice at the beginning of Chapter 12[6] and Jones at paragraph 1–371.[7]

In the following respects the MCA applies only to people aged 18 years old and over, that is, not to 16 and 17 year olds:

- Only a person aged 18 or over can make a lasting power of attorney.[8]
- Only a person aged 18 or over can make an advance decision to refuse treatment.[9]
- The Court of Protection may make a statutory will only for a person aged 18 or over.[10]

1 See the 'age requirement' in MCA, Schedule A1, para 13.
2 Under MCA, s 4A(3) and (4) and s 16(2)(a).
3 MCA, s 18(3): 'The powers under section 16 as respects any other matter relating to P's property and affairs may be exercised even though P has not reached 16, if the court considers it likely that P will still lack capacity to make decisions in respect of that matter when he reaches 18.' It appears that the word 'other' in 'any other matter' may be superfluous.
4 Jones R, *Mental Capacity Act Manual* (3rd ed, Sweet & Maxwell, 2008), para 1–175.
5 MCA, s 44.
6 ' . . . Offences of ill treatment or wilful neglect of a person who lacks capacity within section 2(1) can also apply to victims younger than 16 (section 44) . . .'.
7 Jones, (N4 above).
8 MCA, s 9(2)(c).
9 MCA, s 24(1).
10 MCA, s 18(2).

Summary

5.7
- Medical treatment decision cases concerning children under 16 must be issued in the High Court only.
- For those who are 18 years old or over the Court of Protection is the appropriate court where MCA-capacity is or may be lacking. A medical treatment (or even welfare) decision in relation to a vulnerable adult who clearly has MCA-capacity will warrant a court application only rarely. Any such applications must be issued in the High Court.
- If there is doubt about which court is appropriate, it is unnecessary to issue in both courts. Particularly in light of the provision for transferring proceedings, it is more sensible to issue in one court only and to raise the issue of which court is appropriate in the application documents and at the first directions hearing.
- In relation to 16 to 17 year olds the choice of court is likely to be fact-specific but the authors suggest the following general guidelines.
  - The tenor of the Code of Practice is that the Court of Protection may often be appropriate. Practitioners considering an application to the High Court should attempt to identify reasons why this jurisdiction is more appropriate than the Court of Protection in the specific circumstances of the case.
  - The High Court is likely to be appropriate for any case in which there are doubts about following the patient's expressed wishes other than those based on a lack of MCA-capacity.
  - The closer a patient gets to 18, or the longer the period of time for which the court's involvement will probably be required, the more appropriate it will be to issue in the Court of Protection.

5.7 *Going to Court*

     –   Depending on the circumstances it may be prudent to consult both CAFCASS and the Official Solicitor.

●   The following flowchart is intended to act as a guide for identifying the right jurisdiction.

Flow Chart: COP or High Court?

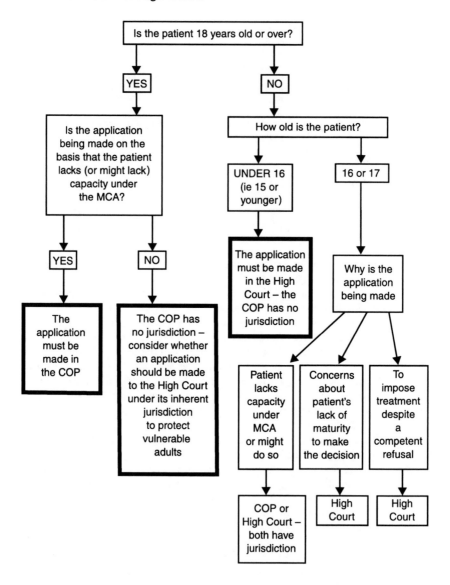

C PROCEDURAL POINTS COMMON TO THE COURT OF PROTECTION AND THE HIGH COURT

Public law issues

5.8   If a medical treatment case raises both capacity/'best interests' issues and public law issues, the proceedings should generally be brought, in the first instance at least, in the court which has jurisdiction in the capacity/'best interests' issues. An application for judicial review is not the appropriate forum for determining sensitive medical treatment issues, unless they are exclusively public law issues.[1]

1   See the judgment of Munby J in *A v A Health Authority* [2002] 3 WLR 24, in particular at para 89 onwards. As an example of a case which does raise exclusively public law issues and is appropriately brought as a judicial review application, he refers to proceedings 'brought with a view to compelling an under-resourced health authority to carry out heart surgery on seriously ill children' or challenging 'a health authority's refusal to fund experimental treatment of a 10-year old child suffering from leukaemia': para 94. As an example of a medical treatment case brought by way of judicial review which should have been brought in the Family Division, he refers *to R v Portsmouth Hospitals NHS Trust, ex p Glass* (1999) 50 BMLR 269: paras 74–75.

The timing of proceedings

5.9   Where it is the nature of the medical treatment decision which necessitates a court order (as opposed to the existence of any doubt or dispute), an application should be made as soon as it is reasonably apparent that a court order will be required. Applicants should not generally delay issuing until they have obtained all the information which they think the court will require for its final determination, not least because the early involvement of a litigation friend or guardian *ad litem* (where appropriate) is likely to be valuable in shaping the course of the proceedings and this generally requires proceedings to be started.

Where an application is made because of a doubt or dispute about a patient's capacity or best interests, there is a balance to be struck. Save in cases of obvious urgency, sufficient time must have passed – and sufficient discussion taken place – to identify a continuing doubt or dispute which may require the court's intervention. Nevertheless, it is a common mistake to delay too long to see whether the doubt or dispute can be resolved. Attempts at resolution can – and should – continue after proceedings have been issued. Moreover, investigation of the case in the context of issued proceedings is itself often conducive to resolution. For example, a patient's family may agree with a joint expert's recommendations. Other important factors which may contribute to the reaching of agreement include:

- independent consideration of the case;
- input into the expert's instructions;
- (sometimes) the ability of the expert to explain the issues better than the treating clinicians; and
- possibly new recommendations from the expert which no party had previously considered.

It is common for medical treatment cases to start as disputes and end with a position agreed between the parties.[1]

One obvious risk of delaying a case is that it may suddenly require an urgent application which could have been avoided, for example because of a sudden deterioration in the patient's condition. The court is likely to be critical of urgent cases which could have been avoided by prompt applications.[2]

When applications are brought in advance of an anticipated deterioration, the parties may have to grapple with the difficulty that the precise circumstances which the declaration will need to cover are not yet known.[3]

1   Once court proceedings have been started, such cases should generally not simply be withdrawn. Instead, the court should be notified that the final hearing will not be contested and is likely to be shorter than listed. The parties should agree a draft order for consideration by the court, along with an agreed case summary and a bundle accompanied by a list of essential reading.

2   See the express warnings of the Court of Protection (in its *Practice Direction 10B, 'Urgent and interim applications'*, see **APPENDIX 5.5 PARA 4**: 'In some cases, urgent applications arise because applications to the court have not been pursued sufficiently promptly. This is undesirable, and should be avoided. A judge who has concerns about the facility for urgent applications may have been abused may require the applicant or the applicant's representative to attend at a subsequent hearing to provide an explanation for the delay.') and the High Court (as reflected in similar terms in the *Practice Note (Official Solicitor, CAFCASS and the National Assembly for Wales: Urgent and Out of Hours cases in the Family Division of the High Court)* [2006] 2 FLR 354 (**APPENDIX 5.15**) at PARA 2).

3   While this may sometimes indicate that the application is premature (see for example the comments of Parker J in *Re OT* [2009] EWHC 633 (Fam) at para 84), in other cases it is simply inevitable if the parties are to deal properly with a situation before it becomes urgent: see for example *Re B (A Minor)* [2009] LS Law Med 214, in which Coleridge J recognised the merits of an anticipatory approach in the right case, and at para 4 proposed a practical step to help ameliorate some of the inevitable difficulties: 'A perusal of that order show that it contemplates the withholding of intensive resuscitation treatment in two particular circumstances – that the child is on a steep downward gradient because of a deteriorating illness or becomes severely unwell for other reasons. In those circumstances the treating doctors would be permitted to withhold this type of treatment. It is less specific than sometimes declarations of this kind are. Because it is less specific and because the doctors themselves in evidence candidly admitted that they could not necessarily foresee every situation in which the permission which they had obtained would be needed, I suggested that a short joint experts' report which is in the papers . . . should be attached to the order itself so that any doctor coming new to this child and to a critical situation in the future would have further guidance to enable them to make what might be a very difficult sensitive and finely balanced clinical judgment. However, I am unaware that such a course has been adopted in other cases of this kind. It may be that this is a helpful way of guiding the medical team who have care for a sick child, or a sick patient, where the medical definitions and situations which may arise in emergencies are not necessarily capable of complete contemplation . . .'

How urgent is it?

5.10   The main basis for advancing a case of urgency must be the best interests of the patient. By their very nature, most if not all medical treatment cases will have some degree of urgency about them. This must be balanced with the need to investigate the case properly through the gathering of factual and expert information. In relation to urgency, the task of the person bringing proceedings – and other parties as they become involved – is to:

- identify, through detailed discussion with treating clinicians, particular features of the case which increase the risk to the patient as time passes;
- make a decision about how quickly the case needs to be heard – first for directions and then for a final hearing; and
- provide sufficiently detailed information on this point so that the court can exercise its judgment appropriately too.

Introduction to the Official Solicitor[1] and CAFCASS[2]

5.11   The Official Solicitor may act as:

- litigation friend of last resort to P (the subject of the proceedings) in Court of Protection proceedings;[3]
- litigation friend of a party other than P (the subject of the proceedings) in the Court of Protection;[4]
- litigation friend of last resort to someone other than the subject of the proceedings (for example, a parent who is him or herself a child, or who has learning disabilities) in High Court proceedings concerning a minor;[5]
- (far more rarely) an advocate to the court in the Court of Protection or the High Court.

1   The Official Solicitor is an officer of the Senior Courts, appointed by the Lord Chancellor: Senior Courts Act 1981, s 90(1). The Official Solicitor was an officer of the Supreme Court until 1 October 2009, when reference to the Supreme Court was replaced by reference to the Senior Courts.
2   Children and Family Court Advisory and Support Service, established under Criminal Justice and Court Services Act 2000, s 11.
3   See below at **PARA 5.29**: Litigation friend.
4   The authors have been involved in cases involving both medical and welfare decisions regarding incapable adults where both the person who is the subject of the proceedings and another respondent (for example, their parent) have lacked capacity. In such cases the Official Solicitor has acted as litigation friend to both incapable parties, but has appointed separate legal teams to provide the legal representation with a 'Chinese Wall' operating in the Official Solicitor's office. See, as an example, *KD & LD v London Borough of Havering*, COP 11448388/03, 19th October 2009 in which both the subject of the application, LD, and her mother, KD, also a protected party, were represented by the Official Solicitor as litigation friend. The Official Solicitor had instructed different external solicitors and counsel to represent each.
5   See below at **PARA 5.51**: Parents? and *Practice Note (Official Solicitor: Appointment in Family Proceedings)* [2001] 2 FLR 155 (**APPENDIX 5.14**).

5.12   CAFCASS provides representation for children in High Court proceedings, by guardians *ad litem*, and can also (far more rarely) act as advocate to the court in such proceedings.[1]

1   See below at **PARA 5.50**: The child? and *CAFCASS and the National Assembly for Wales Practice Note (Appointment of guardians in private law proceedings)* [2006] 2 FLR 143 (**APPENDIX 5.11**).

Who should bring proceedings?

5.13   It will usually be appropriate for the body responsible for the patient's treatment (such as a Primary Care Trust or NHS Trust) to bring the proceedings, even if proceedings are necessary only because an objection has been raised by someone else such as a member of the patient's family.[1] The task of taking a case to court should not be left to the patient or a member of his family.[2]

1   In relation to Court of Protection proceedings, see the main Code of Practice at para 8.7: 'For cases about serious or major decisions concerning medical treatment . . . the NHS Trust or other organisation responsible for the patient's care will usually make the application.'
2   *Swindon & Marlborough NHS Trust v S* (1995) 3 Med L Rev 84.

5.14   Sometimes joint applicants[1]/plaintiffs[2]/claimants[3] might be appropriate.[4] The most straightforward way of dealing with this is often for one party to start proceedings, naming the proposed joint applicant/plaintiff/claimant as a respondent[5]/defendant,[6] explaining – and ideally including written confirmation of – this party's position in the application papers; and then to seek a direction at the first case management hearing that this party shall be the second applicant/plaintiff/claimant, as the case may be.

1   In Court of Protection proceedings the person starting proceedings is the 'applicant'.
2   In proceedings under the High Court's jurisdiction in relation to minors, the person starting proceedings is strictly speaking the 'plaintiff' because of the application of the originating summons procedure (see below at PARA 5.53: Starting proceedings – non-urgent). However, the party who brings the proceedings is often referred to as the 'applicant'.
3   In proceedings under the High Court's vulnerable adult jurisdiction, the person starting the proceedings is the 'claimant'.
4   For example, in a case concerning a proposed operation for a patient in a residential home, the Primary Care Trust might be the driving force behind the proceedings. However, the Primary Care Trust is likely to rely heavily on the evidence of the hospital clinicians who will carry out the operation, and the NHS Trust responsible for the hospital, if supportive of the proceedings, may also wish to be in the position of applicant/plaintiff/claimant as the case may be, perhaps represented by the same legal team. So long as the NHS Trust is a party, the title given to it in the proceedings will make no material difference to its rights and obligations. However, having it named as 'second applicant' (or second plaintiff/second claimant) may help the parties to understand the roles being played in the proceedings.
5   In Court of Protection proceedings.
6   In High Court proceedings – under the court's jurisdiction in relation to minors and its jurisdiction in relation to vulnerable adults.

What does the party bringing the proceedings want?

5.15   Those bringing proceedings should consider carefully and state clearly whether they are:

- putting forward a positive case on any of the issues in dispute, in reliance on medical evidence or otherwise; or
- remaining neutral and seeking the court's decision.

Either position may, depending on the circumstances, be appropriate. A party may of course change its position during the course of proceedings, as further evidence becomes available. However, it is helpful for parties to be explicit about their positions, first at the stage of bringing proceedings and then again, at the latest, before the final hearing. Those bringing proceedings should also consider and state clearly what relief they seek.

Family Division Practice Direction on Bundles[1]

5.16   The Family Division Practice Direction on Bundles requires for each hearing:

- preliminary documents:[2]
    - case summary;[3]
    - statement of the issue or issues to be determined (1) at that hearing and (2) at the final hearing;
    - position statement by each party including a summary of the order or directions sought by that party (1) at that hearing and (2) at the final hearing;
    - an up-to-date chronology, if it is a final hearing or if the case summary is insufficient;
    - skeleton arguments, if appropriate, with copies of all authorities relied on;
    - a list of essential reading for that hearing;[4]
- a bundle[5] divided into separately paginated sections.[6]

See the Practice Direction itself for more detail as to the specific requirements. There is currently no equivalent practice direction for the Court of Protection, although it is good practice to adopt the approach set out in the Family Division Practice Direction and present a bundle that will be familiar to, and hence easily navigated by, the High Court judges sitting in the Court of Protection.

Parties should attempt to agree a draft order before each hearing and supply any agreed draft to the court.

There is no magic to a 'position statement' and there is no prescribed form. It can be a very simple document, as short as the circumstances of the case will allow, setting out a party's position with a summary of the reasons for it.

1   *Practice Direction (Family Proceedings: Court Bundles) (Universal practice to be applied in all courts other than the Family Proceedings Court)*, 27 July 2006 [2006] 2 FLR 199 (**APPENDIX 5.1**). This does not apply in the Court of Protection but it is good practice to follow it.
2   *Ibid*, para 4.2.
3   *Ibid*, para 4.2(i): 'an up to date summary of the background to the hearing confined to those matters which are relevant to the hearing and the management of the case and limited, if practicable, to one A4 page.'
4   In addition a reading time estimate will assist the judge.
5   See N1, paras 3.1–3.2: agreed if possible, prepared by the applicant or, if the applicant is a litigant in person, by the first named respondent who is not a litigant in person.
6   *Ibid*, para 4.1: Section (a) Preliminary documents; (b) Applications and orders; (c) Statements and affidavits; (d) Care plans (where appropriate); (e) Experts' reports and other reports (including those of a guardian, children's guardian or litigation friend); and (f) Other documents, divided into further sections as may be appropriate.

Final hearings

5.17   Parties should ensure at the outset that it is clear whether the hearing is in public or private.[1]

Both the High Court and the Court of Protection can sit in the middle of the night[2] and/or at a hospital[3] if that is what a particularly urgent and difficult case requires.

If factual and/or expert issues are in dispute, the final hearing will run much as a trial would in any other court. If by the time of the final hearing there are no contested issues and the parties are well organised, they may be able to arrange for a judge to look at an agreed order on the papers. However, in most cases an oral hearing will still take place, although the parties should of course notify the court if the agreed time estimate has changed. In many cases of agreement, there will be no need for the court to hear any evidence, but in some cases it may still be appropriate for the court to do so. In all cases the court must exercise its own judgment to reach a decision, albeit in the light of the agreement of the parties. Practitioners should bear in mind that in the forum of both the High Court's inherent jurisdiction and the Court of Protection, they should not give the impression that they are presenting the court with a fait accompli. A draft order, whether for directions or a final order including declarations, is simply for the court's consideration and discretion, albeit that the court is likely to be strongly guided by the parties' agreement. While some judges may be happy to see – or even propose – the words 'BY CONSENT' in an agreed final order, others will deprecate this course of action because the court must exercise its independent judgment. If the parties or the court wish to reflect the agreement of the parties to the order, this could be done by a way of a recital stating 'UPON the parties agreeing to the terms of this order'.

1   See the rules in each jurisdiction at **PARAS 5.28** and **5.57** below.
2   The Court of Protection may sit at any place in England and Wales, on any day and at any time (MCA, s 46(3)), thus retaining the flexibility of the High Court's procedures: in *Re MB (an adult: medical treatment)* [1997] 2 FLR 426, [1997] FCR 541, [1997] 8 Med LR 217, the first instance hearing took place between about 8pm and 9pm, and the Court of Appeal hearing between about 11pm and 1am.
3   See, by analogy in the inherent jurisdiction, *Re OT* [2009] EWHC 633 (Fam) per Parker J at para 8.

Typing up the order

5.18   In the Royal Courts of Justice (whether High Court or Court of Protection) the practice is for the advocate acting for the party bringing proceedings to type up the order and email it to the associate[1] on the email address supplied by the associate. If a copy of the sealed order is required urgently, the associate should be alerted to this.

1   Note that this person is distinct from both the usher and the judge's clerk.

D THE COURT OF PROTECTION

The Court of Protection generally

Constitutional issues

5.19   The Court of Protection is a superior court of record created by statute.[1] The Court of Protection used to be the name for an office of the Supreme Court which has now ceased to exist.[2] In connection with its jurisdiction the Court of Protection has the same powers, rights, privileges and authority as the High Court.[3] From 1 April 2009 the Court of Protection became part of Her Majesty's Courts Service and its forms and practice directions can be found on the HMCS website.[4]

1   MCA, s 45(1).
2   MCA, s 45(6).
3   MCA, s 47(1).
4   www.hmcourts-service.gov.uk

Location and judges

5.20   The Court of Protection sits in a range of locations around the country, with a range of judges of different levels of seniority, depending on the nature of the case. The Court of Protection may sit at any place in England and Wales, on any day and at any time.[1]

The judges who sit in the Court of Protection may be district judges, circuit judges or High Court judges, but all must be nominated to do so.[2] Medical treatment cases will generally[3] be heard by a judge of the Family Division of the High Court (sitting as a nominated judge of the Court of Protection). Many financial and welfare applications are wholly dealt with at district judge – or, if not, circuit judge – level. There is a President, Vice-President and Senior Judge of the Court of Protection.[4]

The Court of Protection has a building at Archway in North London which houses its central registry. The Archway building also houses a hearing centre with resident district judges. However, Court of Protection hearings also take place in other locations in London, and in regional centres, presided over by nominated judges, in the same courtrooms in which they hear non-Court of Protection work. District, circuit and High Court judges hearing cases in their usual courts may move seamlessly to sit in the jurisdiction of the Court of Protection as the case is ushered into the courtroom.

Locations have been identified for regional hearings,[5] but no regional registries have as yet been designated.[6] This means that documents for Court of Protection proceedings being heard in, say, Manchester, must generally be filed at Archway.[7] The exception to this is documents such as bundles, position statements and skeleton arguments relating to a hearing which is listed to take place somewhere other than Archway. The arrangements for delivery of such documents should be dealt with in directions at an earlier hearing: it will generally be sensible for such documents to be delivered directly to the court where the hearing is to take place. In relation to hearings before a Family

Division judge (sitting as a nominated judge of the Court of Protection) at the Royal Courts of Justice ('RCJ') on the Strand in London, the listing of such cases is dealt with by the Clerk of the Rules at the RCJ; and the RCJ also seals orders made there.

Medical treatment cases can in appropriate circumstances be allocated to a High Court level judge sitting at a regional centre rather than at the RCJ. This tends only to happen in non-urgent cases because of the special procedures at the RCJ for dealing with very urgent hearings, and the greater availability of suitable judges in London. Regional hearings before High Court judges are common in cases concerning welfare issues such as residence, care and contact.

1   MCA, s 45(3).
2   MCA, s 46.
3   Cases which do not concern 'serious medical treatment' (as to which, see below at **PARA 5.25**) can be dealt with by a judge of any level, depending on the nature of the case. See further *Court of Protection Practice Direction 9E* (see **APPENDIX 5.4**) at **PARAS 11–12** and *Practice Direction 12A*, *'Court's jurisdiction to be exercised by certain judges'*.
4   MCA, s 46(3)-(4).
5   At July 2009 the list of court centres which may hear Court of Protection matters in addition to Archway is as follows (although it should not be assumed that all these centres will regularly hear such cases as a matter of course): Barnet County Court, Barrow in Furness County Court, Brent Magistrates' Court, Birkenhead County Court, Birmingham Civil Justice Centre, Bradford Combined Court Centre, Bournemouth County Court, Bristol County Court, Caernarfon County Court, Cambridge County Court, Cardiff Civil Justice Centre, Central London Civil Justice Centre, Chester Civil Justice Centre, Clerkenwell & Shoreditch County Court, Darlington County Court, Gloucester County Court, Ipswich County Court, Lancaster County Court, Leeds Combined Court Centre, Liverpool Civil and Family Court, Manchester Civil Justice Centre, Newcastle Combined Court Centre, Nottingham County Court, Oxford Combined Court Centre, Poole County Court, Preston Combined Court Centre, Principal Registry of the Family Division (High Holborn, London), Portsmouth Courts of Justice, Royal Courts of Justice (The Strand, London), Rhyl County Court, Southampton Courts of Justice, Sunderland County Court, Swindon Combined Court Centre, Teeside Combined Court Centre, Warrington County Court, Winchester Law Courts.
6   The Lord Chancellor has a power to do so under MCA, s 45(5).
7   The parties can take common sense steps to ameliorate the administrative difficulties this may cause, for example, invite the local judge who deals with the final hearing to indicate that it would be appropriate for applications under a 'liberty to apply' provision to be copied directly to him (perhaps even emailed if the judge is keen to receive information this way) as well as being filed at Archway.

Sources of procedural rules and guidance

5.21   Any practitioner advising or taking steps in relation to the Court of Protection should look directly at five key sources:[1]

- Mental Capacity Act 2005 ('MCA');
- Court of Protection Rules 2007[2] ('the Rules');
- the Court of Protection's Practice Directions;[3]
- Mental Capacity Act 2005 Code of Practice dated 23 April 2007 ('the main[4] Code of Practice');
- the Court of Protection forms.[5]

Further sources of procedural guidance are:

- case-law under the MCA as it develops;
- pre-MCA case-law to the extent that it is relevant;

- the Family Division Practice Direction on Bundles. While this does not strictly apply in the Court of Protection, it should be adopted unless the Court of Protection issues its own guidance on the topic.[6]
- the 'Information for Professionals' section on the Office of the Public Guardian website[7] which includes links to judgments of the Court of Protection.[8]

1 Reference may occasionally be needed to the Civil Procedure Rules. See r 9 of the Court of Protection Rules 2007: 'In any case not expressly provided for by these Rules or the practice directions made under them, the Civil Procedure Rules 1998 (including any practice directions made under them) may be applied with any necessary modifications, insofar as is necessary to further the overriding objective.'
2 SI 2007/1744, made under MCA, s 51. The Rules are the Court of Protection equivalent of the Civil Procedure Rules. They are divided into Parts. Note that the Rules have been amended and the version available on the HMCS website at www.hmcourts-service.gov.uk/cms/14705.htm may be the unamended version.
3 Given under MCA, s 52. Available on the HMCS website at www.hmcourts-service.gov.uk/cms/14705.htm . Each Practice Direction is identified with a number, a letter and a title. The number is the Part of the Rules to which it relates. The Practice Directions relevant to each Part are each given a sequential letter. A list of the Practice Directions is set out in **APPENDIX 5.3**.
4 'Main', to distinguish it from the supplementary Deprivation of Liberty Safeguards Code of Practice under the MCA dated 26 August 2008. See **CHAPTER 6**: Restraint and Deprivation of Liberty at **PARA 6.37**: Identifying a 'deprivation of liberty'.
5 See **APPENDIX 5.6**.
6 See **PARA 5.16** above.
7 http://www.publicguardian.gov.uk/forms/information-professionals.htm
8 http://www.publicguardian.gov.uk/forms/other-orders-cop.htm – although the list of judgments here should not be presumed to be exhaustive.

The court's general approach

5.22 Medical treatment cases in the Court of Protection are now subject to far more rules than was previously the case when they were dealt with under the High Court's inherent jurisdiction. It would be wrong, however, to see the many rules as an inflexible straitjacket. Key parts of the procedure are strict (for example, a prescribed application form and the need for permission in most cases). But in between there is much room for flexibility.[1] The Court of Protection Rules both maintain the flexibility of the procedures previously dealt with under the High Court's inherent jurisdiction and arguably go further in making express provision for the court to do, largely, whatever it sees fit in the best interests of the patient.

The Rules have their own overriding objective, of 'enabling the court to deal with a case justly[2] having regard to the principles contained in the Act'.[3] Importantly, the parties are required to help the court to further the overriding objective.[4] The court itself will further the overriding objective by actively managing cases.[5] The Rules include examples of active case management[6] and the whole of Part 5 is devoted to 'General case management powers'. Insofar as is necessary, the Civil Procedure Rules (and their Practice Directions) may be applied with necessary modifications to fill any gaps in the Court of Protection Rules and Practice Directions.[7] The Rules provide extreme flexibility, sensibly encouraging the court to prioritise substance over form.[8]

5.22 Going to Court

A Court of Protection case outside the medical treatment context (*In the matter of S & S*,[9] involving the appointment of deputies) is instructive as to the general approach of the Court of Protection. The judge said this of the procedures of the Court:

> 'The processes in the Court of Protection are intended to give the court wide flexibility to reach a decision quickly, conveniently and cost-effectively where it can, whilst still preserving a proper opportunity for those affected by its orders to have their views taken into account in full argument if necessary. To that end, on receiving an application, the court can make a decision on the papers, or direct a full hearing, or make any order as to how the application can best be dealt with. This will often lead to a speedy decision made solely on paper which everyone is content to accept, but any party still has the right to ask for a reconsideration.'[10]

The court's power to make summary decisions must be exercised appropriately and with restraint.[11]

The Court cannot consider best interests properly[12] unless it takes a more inquisitorial approach than the civil courts would do when deciding a case under the Civil Procedure Rules: for example, by ordering that a non-party provide evidence on a specified issue or calling for reports of its own initiative under s 49 MCA. Of course, the Court of Protection does not conduct a pure inquisitorial process as understood in other countries: when capacity and / or best interests are in dispute the parties may advocate polarised positions, and the court will be assisted by – and indeed expect – full cross-examination and argument in order to test the issues to the limit.[13] However, the court will be cautious not to lose sight of the purpose of the proceedings: whatever the disputes between – and conduct of – the parties, the court must make a decision in the patient's best interests (if he lacks capacity to make it himself). In *S v S* it was said that the first instance judge had 'fallen into error' by treating the hearing as an:

> 'adversarial contest between [the parties], rather than as the inquisitorial exercise of ascertaining which course of action was more in Mr and Mrs S's best interests ... his judgment has the clear undertone that, in his view, C did not 'deserve' the result for which she was contending because the conduct of which he disapproved ought not to be rewarded with success. Whilst it may well be a proper concern of a court exercising its discretion in an adversarial dispute between two parties, it is not an appropriate consideration where the issue is what is in the best interests of a third party. It is merely part of the context in which that issue must be decided. The dispute, however regrettable it may be, and whoever is more in the right, is simply a fact, the consequences of which have to be managed in Mr and Mrs S's best interests.'[14]

1   For example, the court may make an interim declaration in an urgent case before an application has been drafted let alone filed; and may make an order for the subsequent filing of a COP1 and 1B but dispense with the need for a COP2 or COP3.
2   r 3(3) sets out a list of considerations which 'dealing with a case justly' includes.
3   r 3(1).
4   r 4.
5   r 5(1).

6   r 5(2) and r 25.

7   r 9.

8   For example: it may dispense with the requirement of any rule (r 26); it may exercise its powers on its own initiative without representations from the parties (r 27(1) – see further the whole of r 27); and where there has been an error of procedure, the error does not invalidate any step taken in the proceedings unless the court so orders (r 28(a) – see further r 28(b)).

9   *S v S sub nom C v V* [2009] LS Law Med 97.

10 Per HHJ Hazel Marshall QC, the senior chancery circuit judge at Central London County Court, at para 61.

11 *KD & LD v London Borough of Havering*, COP 11448388/03, 19th October 2009, per HHJ Horowitz QC at para 28. See this case generally for an example of an impermissible summary approach and discussion of the principles.

12 'Dealing with a case justly includes ... ensuring that P's interests and position are properly considered': r 3(3)(b). In doing so the court must have 'regard to the principles contained in the Act': r 3(1). These include the key principle (MCA, s 1(5)) that an 'act done, or decision made, under this Act for or on behalf of a person who lacks capacity must be done, or made, in his best interests'.

13 While the usual procedure will be for witness statements (r 96(2)) and expert reports to stand as evidence in chief, the court can require all witnesses to be fully examined to elicit their evidence in chief orally. In the authors' experience this has occurred in highly disputed cases concerning withdrawal of life-saving treatment.

14 *S v S* (N9 above) para 64.

The court's powers to make medical treatment decisions

5.23   The Court of Protection's powers to make medical treatment decisions are as follows:

●   The power to make declarations as to whether a person has or lacks capacity to make a specified decision, or decisions on specified matters, and as to the lawfulness of any act done, or yet to be done, in relation to that person.[1]

●   The power to make orders making 'personal welfare' decisions on behalf of people who lack capacity to make such decisions themselves.[2]

●   The power to make interim declarations[3] which could relate to capacity and/or best interests. The court also has the power under MCA, s 48 to make orders and case management directions on an interim basis even if lack of capacity is not established on the balance of probabilities, so long as there is reason to believe that P lacks capacity in relation to the matter and it is in P's best interests for the court to make the order or give the directions, as the case may be, without delay. This provision is intended to provide for situations 'where the obtaining of a formal declaration or decision under s 15 or s 16 will take time, but common sense suggests that some action may be needed in the interim'.[4] Less evidence is required to found the court's interim jurisdiction under s 48 than that required to justify the ultimate declaration. What is required is sufficient evidence to justify a 'reasonable belief', 'good or serious cause for concern' or a 'real possibility' that P may lack capacity in the relevant regard.[5] The court must then move on to a second stage to decide what action, if any, it is in P's best interests to take before a final determination of his capacity can be made. Such action may include not only immediate safeguarding steps with regard to P's affairs or life decisions but also giving directions to enable evidence to resolve the issue of capacity to be obtained quickly. The appropriate directions will depend on the facts of the case and a balance between the importance and urgency of making the decision on the one hand, and, on the other hand, the principle that P's right to autonomy is to be restricted as little as is consistent with his best interests. Where capacity itself is in issue it may be that the only proper interim direction should be obtaining appropriate specialist evidence to determine that issue.[6]

The court will usually make such declarations and decisions in proceedings begun specifically for that purpose. However, the court may also do so on its own initiative.[7]

1   MCA, s 15.
2   MCA, s 16(2)(a).
3   r 82. *The NHS Trust v Ms T* [2004] EWHC 1279 (Fam), [2004] Lloyd's Rep Med 433, provides a pre-Court of Protection example of the High Court making an interim declaration under its inherent jurisdiction and the Civil Procedure Rules.
4   *Re F*, Court of Protection case no 11649371, 28th May 2009 (http://www.publicguardian. gov.uk/docs/judgement-re-f-28-may-2009.pdf) per HHJ Hazel Marshall QC at paras 25 and 26.
5   *Ibid.* at paras 35 and 36.
6   *Ibid.* at para 44.The district judge at the first hearing had adjourned the case for further medical evidence establishing P's lack of capacity to be obtained. She declined to make any other order to progress the case, such as joining in the relevant authorities or directing a s 49 report, on the apparent basis that she considered that the court had no jurisdiction to make an order before the evidence was sufficient (which it currently was not) to rebut the presumption of P's capacity. HHJ Hazel Marshall QC disagreed on appeal: the threshold for engaging s 48 was met. On the facts she stated at para 46: 'To my mind, the unclear situation certainly suggested a serious possibility that F *might* lack capacity in relation to decisions about her own care needs, whether temporarily or on a more long term basis. That possibility was also, in my judgment clearly sufficiently serious, or real, that the court was entitled to take jurisdiction under s 48. The obvious matter needing determination was, in particular, whether F's attitude to her care arrangements did indeed stem from lack of capacity in that regard or not. The case therefore invited a direction appropriate to the circumstances, to enable this issue to be resolved with dispatch, even though the situation might not have been serious enough to justify making any further direction or order with regard to F's living conditions at that stage.'
7   See generally r 27 and, specifically in relation to s 16(2)(a), s 16(6).

Serious medical treatment: *Practice Direction 9E*[1]

5.24   Rule 71 of the Rules enables a Practice Direction to make additional or different provision in relation to specified types of application. *Practice Direction 9E* does this 'where the application concerns serious medical treatment in relation to P'.[2]

1   See **APPENDIX 5.4**.
2   *Practice Direction 9E*, para 2.

Definition of 'serious medical treatment'[1]

5.25   Serious medical treatment means treatment which involves providing, withdrawing or withholding treatment in circumstances where: (a) in a case where a single treatment is being proposed, there is a fine balance between its benefits to P and the burdens and risks it is likely to entail for him; (b) in a case where there is a choice of treatments, a decision as to which one to use is finely balanced; or (c) the treatment, procedure or investigation proposed would be likely to involve serious consequences for P.[2] 'Serious consequences' are those which could have a serious impact on P, either from the effects of the treatment, procedure or investigation itself or its wider implications. This may include treatments, procedures or investigations which: (a) cause, or may cause, serious and prolonged pain, distress or side effects; (b) have potentially major consequences for P; or (c) have a serious impact on P's future life choices.[3] *Practice Direction 9E* gives examples of serious medical treatment.[4]

1 *Practice Direction 9E*, paras 3–7. Note that the phrase 'serious medical treatment' is also used in the rules governing the appointment of Independent Mental Capacity Advocates. See MCA, s 37 and reg 4 of the Mental Capacity Act 2005 (Independent Mental Capacity Advocates) (General) Regulations 2006 (SI 2006/1832).
2 *Ibid*, para 3.
3 *Ibid*, para 4.
4 Paras 5–7.

Procedural matters

5.26 *Practice Direction 9E* addresses specific procedural matters[1] which will be set out as they arise in this chapter.

1 Consultation with the Official Solicitor (para 8); allocation of cases to appropriate level of judge (paras 11 and 12); matters to be considered at the first directions hearing (paras 13–15) including the general rule that hearings should be ordered to be in public with restrictions on publication of information (para 16); and form of declarations as to capacity and best interests.

What cases should be brought to court?

5.27 The main Code of Practice and *Practice Direction 9E* set out the types of case which should be brought to court. The MCA and the Rules are silent on this topic.

Paragraph 8.18 of the main Code of Practice states as follows (with the addition of one point from *Practice Direction 9E* in square brackets):

'Prior to the Act coming into force, the courts decided that some decisions relating to the provision of medical treatment were so serious that in each case, an application should be made to the court for a declaration that the proposed action was lawful before that action was taken. Cases involving any of the following decisions should therefore be brought before a court:

- decisions about the proposed withholding or withdrawal or artificial nutrition and hydration (ANH) from patients in a permanent vegetative state (PVS) [or minimally conscious state][1]
- cases involving organ or bone marrow donation by a person who lacks capacity to consent
- cases involving the proposed non-therapeutic sterilisation of a person who lacks capacity to consent to this (for example, for contraceptive purposes)[2] and
- all other cases where there is a doubt or dispute about whether a particular treatment will be in a person's best interests.'[3]

The latter category of disputed cases provides the bulk of the medical treatment cases before the Court of Protection. This category will include cases concerning a wide range of medical procedures, both serious and more minor.

Where there is no dispute between the medical team and the patient's family and other carers, most medical treatment decisions will be made appropriately under MCA, s 5 without the need for an application to the Court of Protection. However, the authors suggest that, in addition to the circumstances set out above from the Code of Practice, consideration should be given to an application in the following additional circumstances:

- Where there is doubt about whether or not the patient lacks capacity;
- Where the patient may regain capacity part way through a proposed course of urgent treatment and there is reason to think they might then refuse;
- Where there is doubt about the validity of or interpretation of an advanced directive;
- Where a significant or unusual degree of restraint (whether or not amounting to a deprivation of liberty) may be necessary;
- Where a best interests assessment concerns experimental treatment or a novel ethical dilemma;
- End of life cases where the proposed withholding or withdrawal of treatment will significantly hasten death and the judgment about best interests is finely balanced or raises a difficult or controversial moral issue.

1   This is the only point which *Practice Direction 9E* (at para 5) adds to the Code of Practice. The authors would assert that, *a fortiori*, a proposal to withhold artificial nutrition and hydration from patients in any greater state of consciousness must be taken to court.
2   In the case of a termination of pregnancy for non-medical reasons, consideration should be given to whether an application is needed. See **CHAPTER 8**: Abortion, **PARA 8.22**: Incompetent adults.
3   And, the authors would add, where there is a doubt or a dispute about whether the person lacks capacity to decide this issue.

Privacy and publicity

5.28   Those involved in medical treatment cases should consider two questions:

- Is each hearing in private or public?
- To what extent (if at all) is publication of information relating to the proceedings restricted or permitted?

These issues are dealt with in Part 13 of the Rules[1] and *Practice Directions 9E* and *13A*.[2] In summary, the effect of these provisions is that:

- The general rule is that hearings are in private.[3] However, the court may order that the hearing (or part of it) be held in public.[4]
- Practice Direction 9E states that in applications concerning serious medical treatment[5] the court will ordinarily[6] order[7] that any hearing shall be held in public, with restrictions to be imposed[8] in relation to publication of information about the proceedings. In case the judge does

not have intimate knowledge of the relevant practice direction, it is incumbent on one of the parties to bring the requirement for a public hearing to the court's attention.

- Whether the hearing is in private or public the court may exclude or authorise[9] the attendance of specific people or classes of people.[10]
- In relation to a private hearing, the court may authorise the publication of specified information relating to the proceedings and/or the text or a summary of the whole or part of a judgment or order.[11] In the absence of such authorisation it is a contempt of court to publish information relating to proceedings held in private.[12] The court may give such authorisation on such terms as it thinks fit.[13] In particular it may impose restrictions on the publication of the identity of any person[14] and prohibit the publication of information that may lead to any such person being identified.[15]
- In relation to a public hearing, the court has the same power to impose restrictions on the publication of information.[16]
- The court may exercise its powers in relation to privacy and publicity at any time,[17] either on its own initiative or upon an application,[18] but only where it appears to the court that there is good reason for making the order in question.[19]
- When the court orders that a hearing be held in public, or that information relating to a private hearing may be published, the court may at the same time impose restrictions on the publication of information without having to notify the national news media of the proposed restrictions. However, if the court has already ordered that the hearing be held in public, or that information relating to a private hearing may be published, without imposing restrictions on the publication of information, the national news media must be notified before any such restrictions are subsequently imposed.[20] Parties should be alert to this and ensure that any necessary restrictions on publication are considered at the same time as a public hearing is ordered or publication of information is permitted, and not afterwards.[21]
- Restrictions on the publication of the identity of any person and prohibition of the publication of information that may lead to any such person being identified should aim to protect the patient rather than to confer anonymity on other individuals or organisations.[22] However, it may be necessary to prohibit the identification of the patient's family, carers, doctors, and treating institutions etc, where their identification might lead to the identification of the patient or be likely to prejudice their ability to care for the patient.[23] The identities of experts instructed in the proceedings (as opposed to treating clinicians) are not normally restricted in the absence of evidence giving a good reason why they should be.[24] Save in exceptional cases, the publication of material which is already in the public domain will not be restricted.[25]
- If a hearing is in private and publication of information has not been authorised, there is no legal reason for the parties' names to be anonymised.[26]

In *Independent News and Media Ltd v A*[27] the Court of Protection gave guidance on the approach to be taken to a media application to attend a hearing in relation to a person who was known to the public. This case is an important milestone in the development of the Court of Protection's jurisprudence and warrants reading in full by practitioners dealing with privacy and publicity issues. As to the presence of the media, the guidance it provides[28] is likely to be of greatest relevance to cases other than serious medical treatment cases, because in serious medical treatment cases the court will ordinarily order in any event that hearings be in public (see the reference to *Practice Direction 9E* earlier in this paragraph). As to reporting restrictions, the case demonstrates that the question of what details may be reported is likely to depend on the precise circumstances of the case. It is an example of the court allowing the media (after the disposal of / time limit for any appeal) to identify P in relation to the case and give some (but not all) further details, albeit in the specific circumstances of that case[29] in which P was already known to the public.

1   rr 90–93 – Part 13 is entitled 'Hearings'.
2   Entitled 'Hearings (including reporting restrictions)'.
3   r 90(1). Rule 90(2) sets out who (subject to any order of the court) may attend a private hearing.
4   r 92(1)(a) and (b). Care should be taken by practitioners to ensure that the most up-to-date directions and guidance are considered prior to any hearing. The issue of transparency of court processes is currently the subject of debate and rules and practice may change.
5   See above at **PARA 5.25**: Definition of 'serious medical treatment'.
6   *Practice Direction 9E*, para 16.
7   Under r 92(1)(a).
8   Under r 92(2).
9   This could in principle include the class of accredited media representatives. Note that the Court of Protection position in relation to media representatives (that is, the default position is that they are excluded from a private hearing but they may be permitted to attend) contrasts with the position under the Family Proceedings Rules 1991 in relation to minors (r 10.28: the default position is that they are permitted to attend a private hearing but they may be excluded – see further below at **PARA 5.57**: Privacy and publicity). This may create a dilemma in the (admittedly rare) cases in which the same judge may at the same time hear an adult case in the Court of Protection and a linked child case in the High Court. Generally the Court of Protection is likely to have to deal with applications by accredited media representatives to attend private hearings, as they would prima facie be entitled to in cases concerning minors. See *Independent News and Media Ltd v A* in the text above and at **N27** below for an example of such an application and the principles to be applied.
10 Authorisation of attendance at a private hearing: r 90(3)(a); exclusion from attendance at private hearing: r 90(3)(b); exclusion from attendance at public hearing: r 92(1)(c).
11 r 91(2).
12 Administration of Justice Act 1960, s 12(1).
13 r 91(3).
14 r 91(3)(a).
15 r 91(3)(b).
16 r 92(2).
17 r 93(1)(b).
18 r 93(1)(c). This provision states, 'on an application made by any person in accordance with Part 10'. But an application notice need not be filed if the court dispenses with this requirement: r 78(1) and (5). Such matters can usually be dealt with at hearings (preferably directions hearings) without the need for an application notice.
19 r 93(1)(a).
20 See Part 2 of *Practice Direction 13A*, in particular para 12. The procedures for giving notice to the national news media are set out in paras 13–20 and the *Annex to the Practice Direction*; the procedures for the media's response at para 21; and human rights considerations to be taken into account at the hearing at paras 24–26.
21 This arrangement is intended to facilitate the balancing of competing Convention rights. See, for example, paras 10–11 and 24–25 of *Practice Direction 13A*. But the trigger for notifying the national news media of proposed restrictions may be arbitrary (for example, if the court

authorises publicity while inadvertently failing to impose any restrictions on that publicity, and later wishes to rectify the mistake, the national news media must be notified; but if the court imposes restrictions at the same time as authorising publicity, no notification is required) and easy for the court and the parties to avoid (by considering restrictions on publicity at the same time as authorising publicity). The arrangements do not seem to be based on principle: whether the national news media must be notified depends not on the substance of the restriction which is sought to be imposed, but on the order in which the procedural steps occur.

22 *Practice Direction 13A*, para 27.
23 *Ibid*, para 27.
24 *Ibid*, para 27.
25 *Ibid*, para 28.
26 However, anonymisation is often prudent, not least for the purpose of the listing of the case so that the parties' names do not appear on the court lists, the danger of which is greater in regional courts than in the Royal Courts of Justice, where current practice is to list using case numbers only.
27 COP 11647854, 12th November 2009, [2009] EWHC 2858 (Fam). Note that (confusingly) some Court of Protection cases such as this one are given neutral citations for the High Court and some transcripts of Court of Protection judgments wrongly carry the High Court heading.
28 Para 27 sets out a two-stage approach. First, the court should apply a 'summary' 'gatekeeping test' and consider whether the media can show good reason for their presence at the hearing. Secondly, if 'good reason' is found the court must then carry out a balancing exercise between the Art 8 rights of the person concerned and the Art 10 rights of the media.
29 Paras 36–40.

Points to consider before starting proceedings[1]

Litigation friend[2]

5.29 P will generally – but not always – need a litigation friend. P does not need a litigation friend if he is not a party to the proceedings, although in medical treatment cases P will generally be made a party to the proceedings for the very purpose that a litigation friend can then be appointed to represent his interests. A litigation friend is not appropriate if P has litigation capacity.[3] A litigation friend may properly be appointed before lack of litigation capacity is established on the balance of probabilities, so long as there is reason to believe[4] that P lacks litigation capacity.

Consideration should also be given to the need for litigation friends for any protected parties[5] or children who are parties to the proceedings.

The pre-requisites for a litigation friend are that he can fairly and competently conduct proceedings on behalf of the person in question, and has no interests adverse to those of that person.[6]

In medical treatment cases, family members will often be unsuitable candidates for litigation friend, because of the potential conflict between their interests and P's. Where there is no other suitable person to act as litigation friend, the Official Solicitor will usually be prepared to act if invited to do so by the court.

The appointment of the litigation friend must be made by the court (that is, self-appointment is not permitted) where the litigation friend is for:

- P in all cases;[7] and
- any protected parties or children if the prospective litigation friend is the Official Solicitor.[8]

The court may appoint a litigation friend only with the consent of the person to be appointed.[9]

Applications in which the Official Solicitor may be invited to act should generally be discussed with a member of the Official Solicitor's staff in advance.[10] The Official Solicitor's current practice is that he will generally not consent to act until:

- he has been invited to act by the court;
- there is some evidence providing a reason to believe that P lacks litigation capacity;
- funding has been confirmed (whether through public funding, private resources of P or more usually in medical treatment cases the applicant (if an NHS body or Local Authority) has agreed to pay half of the Official Solicitor's costs.

1   See also the points of general application above at Section C above – Procedural points common to the Court of Protection and the High Court – **PARAS 5.8–5.19**.
2   See generally Part 17 of the Rules (rr 140–149) and *Practice Direction 17A*, 'Litigation Friend'.
3   Because the test of capacity is issue-specific (see **CHAPTER 2**: Consent – Adults at **PARA 2.5**), a person may in principle have litigation capacity but lack capacity to decide the substantive issues in question, although the Rules (see rr 141(1) and 147) do not appear to deal with the situation where P is a party to the proceedings but has capacity to litigate. For an example of this situation, see *S & S*, paras 4 and 20 (see above at **PARA 5.22**).
4   This is the test for an interim order under MCA, s 48.
5   See footnote 1 in *Practice Direction 17A*: ' "Protected party" means a party, or an intended party (other than P or a child) who lacks capacity to conduct the proceedings.'
6   r 140.
7   r 142(1)(a).
8   r 142(1)(c).
9   r 142(2)(b).
10 See para 8 of *Practice Direction 9E* at **APPENDIX 5.4**: 'Members of the Official Solicitor's staff are prepared to discuss applications in relation to serious medical treatment before an application is made. Any enquiries about adult medical and welfare cases should be addressed to a family and medical litigation lawyer at the Office of the Official Solicitor, 81 Chancery Lane, London WC2A 1DD, ph: 020 7911 7127, fax: 020 7911 7105, email: enquiries@offsol.gsi.gov.uk .'

Is permission required?[1]

5.30   An applicant in a medical treatment case will generally[2] require permission to start[3] proceedings.[4] The application for permission is made in form COP2 and is determined in accordance with MCA, s 50(3).[5]

1   See generally MCA, s 50, Part 8 of the Rules (rr 50–60).
2   Permission is required for an application to the Court of Protection save in excepted cases: MCA, s 50(1), (1A) and (2). The most important cases in which permission is not required are when the application is brought by: P himself; someone with parental responsibility for him if he is under 18; the donee of a lasting power of attorney; P's court-appointed deputy; the Official Solicitor; or P's representative in a s 21A application in relation to the Deprivation of Liberty Safeguards. For full details, see MCA, s 50 and rr 51–53. The authors are not aware of a case in which an NHS body has been refused permission for an application in a case concerning medical treatment.
3   If proceedings have already been started, and a party or someone notified of proceedings seeks a different order in the same proceedings, that person does not need permission to do so: r 51(4).

4 Permission is not required for application notices, as opposed to application forms to start proceedings: r 51(3).

5 Which states: 'In deciding whether to grant permission the court must, in particular, have regard to –

    (a)   the applicant's connection with the person to whom the application relates,

    (b)   the reasons for the application,

    (c)   the benefit to the person to whom the application relates of a proposed order or directions, and

    (d)   whether the benefit can be achieved in any other way.'

Who should be named as respondents and who should be notified of the proceedings?

5.31   The COP1 application form contains space for the identification of two categories of people: first, respondents; and secondly, other people to be notified of the proceedings.

The naming of respondents defines the parties to the proceedings. Unless the court orders otherwise, parties to the proceedings are the applicant and any person named as a respondent in the application form who files an acknowledgement of service.[1] P must not be named as a respondent unless this is ordered by the court.[2]

The applicant is required to notify other people that the proceedings have been issued.[3] The specific requirements for notification are set out in *Practice Direction 9B*.[4] There is no 'interested party' status in the Court of Protection: someone with sufficient interest to be a party is simply a respondent. Hence one of the purposes of notification is to alert those who do not obviously have a position that requires them to be a party, but who are closely enough connected with the subject of the case that they might for some reason want to apply to become a party, of the fact that the action has commenced.

The starting point for deciding whether to name someone as a respondent, or as someone merely to be notified, is that a respondent is someone – other than P – whom the applicant reasonably believes to have an interest which means that he ought to be heard[5] in relation to the application.[6] Applicants need not be unduly concerned about getting this distinction (between identifying respondents, on the one hand, and people merely to be notified) right at the application stage because there is considerable flexibility as to the addition and removal of parties once proceedings have been started.[7] There are however differences[8] in the rights and obligations as between respondents and people who have been notified.[9]

Applicants should not assume that P's family members should necessarily be named as respondents. Rather, they should consider carefully whether they reasonably believe that such relatives have an interest which means that they ought to be heard as opposed to merely notified.[10] Where the medical issue involves a dispute between relatives and clinicians about best interests then the relative will more often than not be named as a respondent. However, particularly in circumstances where there is no dispute, but the withdrawal of treatment requires court authorisation (such a in a PVS case), relatives may be worried and upset by being named as a respondent when this is unnecessary.

Where practicable, applicants should canvass with relatives their preferred level of involvement in the proceedings. If there is doubt, and the case is not urgent, the best approach will often be merely to notify the relative, explaining that if they wish to make arguments of their own to the court (and will therefore need to be a party) they should let this be known.

In serious medical treatment cases, an organisation which is, or will be, responsible for providing clinical or caring services to P should usually be named as a respondent (where it is not already the applicant in the proceedings).[11]

If joint applicants are appropriate, one could take the lead in completing the application forms and starting proceedings, naming the other as a respondent. At the first directions hearing an order can be sought making these parties first and second applicants.[12]

1 r 73(1).
2 r 73(4).
3 r 170.
4 Entitled 'Notification of other persons that an application form has been issued'. The key requirement is that the applicant must seek to identify at least three people who are likely to have an interest in being notified that an application form has been issued: para 4. Para 7 gives a 'list of people ordered according to the presumed closeness in terms of relationship to P'. There is no requirement separately to 'notify' someone who has been named as a respondent: para 3.
5 Which presumably means 'make submissions'.
6 r 63(c)(iii).
7 The court may add (r 73(2)) or remove (r 73(3)) a party; a person with sufficient interest may apply to be joined as a party (r 75); a party may apply to be removed as a party (r 76); a person notified of proceedings who wishes to take part must file an acknowledgement of notification including an indication whether he wishes to be joined as a party (r 72(6)). These matters can often be dealt with at directions hearings without the need for formal applications.
8 Respondents are entitled to 'be heard' (that is make submissions) in the proceedings whilst those who have been merely notified are not: r 63(c)(iii); under r 90, a person who has been simply notified of the proceedings is not automatically entitled to attend a private hearing or have access to documents, statements or reports filed in the case. However the court can allow such a person to attend and allow disclosure of documents to them.
9 A person who has been notified of an application form is bound by any order or directions of the court in the same way that a party to the proceedings is so bound (r 74) and may apply for permission to appeal against it (r 172(2)).
10 Support for this proposition is provided by the very fact that *Practice Direction 9B*, 'Notification of other persons that an application form has been issued', contemplates circumstances in which it will be appropriate merely to notify close relatives rather than to name them as respondents.
11 *Practice Direction 9E* at **APPENDIX 5.4, PARA 10**.
12 See above at **PARA 5.13**: Who should bring proceedings?

Level of judge and initial directions

5.32   Proceedings must be conducted by the President of the Court of Protection, or another judge nominated by the President, if the application relates to:

- the lawfulness of withholding or withdrawing artificial nutrition and hydration from a person in a persistent vegetative state, or a minimally conscious state; or
- a case involving an ethical dilemma in an untested area.[1]

In other cases concerning serious medical treatment, proceedings must be conducted by a puisne judge of the High Court.[2]

Practice Direction 9E suggests that nothing in such a case should happen in advance of a first directions hearing before the appropriate level of judge.[3] However, the practice in non-emergency cases is for the paper application to be initially placed before one of the district judges at Archway and in addition to ordering that the application be allocated to a High Court judge, these judges appear to have adopted the sensible practice of dealing with four additional matters, namely:

- Granting the applicant permission to make the application – after which the court can issue the application (so that proceedings are officially 'begun'[4]) and give it a case number.
- Joining P as a party[5] – so that he can be heard in the proceedings, either on his own account or represented by a litigation friend.
- Where there is (at least) reason to believe that P lacks capacity to litigate,[6] inviting the Official Solicitor (or another appropriate person if available) to act and, subject to his consent, appointing him as P's litigation friend – so the Official Solicitor is able to become involved in the case before the next directions hearing in the High Court.
- Dispensing,[7] if appropriate, with the requirement to notify P of the application.

Indeed in most non-urgent cases applicants could sensibly invite the court to make these four directions on paper before the first directions hearing, as well as directing that the matter be transferred to a High Court judge.

1 *Practice Direction 9E* at **APPENDIX 5.4**, para 11.
2 *Ibid*, para 12.
3 Its reference to 'proceedings' includes 'permission, the giving of any directions, and any hearing': *ibid*, paras 11 and 12; and see para 13: unless the matter is urgent the court should list the matter for a first directions hearing.
4 Proceedings are started when the court issues an application form: r 62(1). The court shall not issue the application form until permission (if required) is granted: r 63.
5 P shall not be named as a respondent unless the court orders otherwise: r 73(4).
6 This is part of the test under MCA, s 48 for making an interim order.
7 Under r 49.

Deprivation of liberty

5.33   Where a person makes an application under MCA, s 21A, challenging a standard or urgent authorisation,[1] there are specific forms[2] and a practice direction.[3] The court will aim to have the first hearing before a judge within 5 working days of the application.[4] For all applications which are not made under s 21A, the usual Court of Protection forms should be used, even if they involve deprivation of liberty issues.[5] Permission is not required for a s 21A application by the relevant person's representative.[6]

1 Made under the Deprivation of Liberty Safeguards: MCA, Schedule A1.
2 Forms with the prefix 'DL' (for 'Deprivation of Liberty'): 'DLA' (Application Form), 'DLB' (Declaration of exceptional urgency), 'DLC' (Permission), 'DLD' (Certificate of service/non-service/notification/non-notification) and 'DLE' (Acknowledgement of service/notification).

3   Practice Direction entitled *'Deprivation of liberty applications'*, made under r 82A (Part 10A) of the Rules, as inserted by the Court of Protection (Amendment) Rules 2009 (SI 2009/582) from 1 April 2009.
4   *Ibid*, para 8.2.
5   *Ibid*, para 3.5: 'Where an application seeks relief concerning a deprivation of P's liberty other than under section 21A in respect of a standard or urgent authorisation (for example, where the application is for an order under section 16(2)(a)), the dedicated DoL court forms should not be used. Rather the standard court forms should be used for such an application, but it should be made clear on them that relief relating to a deprivation of P's liberty is being sought, and the proposed applicant should contact the DoL team to discuss handling at the earliest possible stage before issuing the application.'
6   MCA, s 50(1A).

Starting proceedings – non-urgent

How are proceedings begun?

5.34   Unless permission is not required,[1] proceedings are started by filing a COP2 permission form and an application form[2] – which is technically a draft until permission is granted[3] – at the Court of Protection's registry at Archway. The COP1 application form itself indicates what information is required in it.[4]

It is advisable (although not mandatory) to file the following additional documents at the permission stage:

- COP1B: Welfare annex to application form;
- COP3: Assessment of capacity form,[5] to be completed by a medical / care professional rather than a lawyer.
- COP24: Witness statement (unless all information is provided in the other forms).
- Any other documents referred to in the forms (for example, clinicians' reports, minutes of meetings).[6]

The forms are long and repetitive. All required information must be provided, but – contrary to appearances – the substance of the information is more important than its form.[7] Applicants should not worry that they will be caught out by not having provided the information in the right place.

The permission form, application form and accompanying documents must provide sufficient detail about the case so that the parties and the court can identify the issues and decide on the case management needed to take it to a final hearing. The information required will of course vary case-by-case, but the following points will usually need to be addressed:

- P's current circumstances and the medical issue arising;
- P's background;
- views of treating clinicians as to capacity and best interests;
- any past and present wishes and feelings expressed by P;
- views of family members;
- views of any clinicians giving second opinions, or experts who have been consulted so far;
- views of any independent mental capacity advocate ('IMCA');[8]
- summary of attempts to reach agreement and why a court application is necessary;

- how urgently the case needs to be heard for (1) directions and (2) final hearing;
- whether the case concerns serious medical treatment and must therefore be heard by a High Court level judge; or whether it falls into the category of cases[9] which must be heard by the President of the Court of Protection or his nominee;
- if the case does not concern serious medical treatment, what level of judge it should be heard by;
- what directions are sought in advance of the first hearing.

The forms do not have an obvious space for a summary narrative which would make it easy for a reader to understand the nature of the case quickly. However, such a narrative can be provided, for example in a witness statement which can be referred to at appropriate points on the forms.

While the rules do not require applicants to serve respondents,[10] and notify others,[11] until permission has been granted and an application issued, it is good practice in medical treatment cases to serve and notify relevant persons on filing the application for permission (if not before), subject to considerations about the confidentiality of the information concerning P.

P must be notified that an application form has been issued, unless the requirement to do so has been dispensed with.[12] Where P is to be represented by a litigation friend in a medical treatment case it will often be appropriate to seek dispensation, particularly where providing notification to P would be either futile or distressing.[13] This can be dealt with in the application starting the proceedings, or at the first directions hearing: a separate application notice will generally be unnecessary.

Respondents and people notified of an application must file an acknowledgement of service or notification if they want to take part in proceedings.[14]

1 In which case proceedings are started by filing an application form and the documents required by r 64.
2 Standard form COP1 should be used (except in proceedings under MCA, s 21A, in which case specific Deprivation of Liberty forms should be used: see above at **PARA 5.33**: Deprivation of liberty). Note the distinction between an application form (which is used to begin proceedings and is equivalent to a Part 7 or Part 8 Claim Form under the CPR) and an application notice (COP9, which is used to make an application within proceedings and is equivalent to an application notice under CPR, Part 23).
3 r 54(1).
4 The requirements derive from r 63 and *Practice Direction 9A*, 'The application form'.
5 Note *Practice Direction 9A* at para 14: 'If the applicant is unable to complete an assessment of capacity form (as may be the case, for example, where P does not reside with the applicant and the applicant is unable to take P to a doctor, or where P refuses to undergo the assessment), the applicant should file a witness statement with the application form explaining:
  - why he has not been able to obtain an assessment of capacity;
  - what attempts (if any) he has made to obtain an assessment of capacity; and
  - why he knows or believes that P lacks capacity to make a decision or decisions in relation to any matter that is the subject of the proposed application.'
6 But note that the court will not want voluminous medical records at this stage.
7 See r 61(2): 'The appropriate forms must be used in the cases to which they apply, or with such variations as the case requires, but not so as to omit any information or guidance which any form gives to the intended recipient.'
8 See MCA, s 35 onwards.

9   *Practice Direction 9E* at **APPENDIX 5.4**, para 11 and **PARA 5.32** above – Level of judge and initial directions.

10 r 66: Applicant to serve application form and accompanying documents on named respondents, together with form for acknowledging service, and file certificate of service.

11 r 70: Applicant to notify persons other than P of an application, together with a form for acknowledging notification, and file certificate of notification.

12 r 69. Paras 8 and 9 of *Practice Direction 7A* ('Notifying P') state:

'8. The person required to notify P may apply to the court for an order either:

(a)   dispensing with the requirement to notify P; or

(b)   requiring some other person to effect the notification, [r49]

using a COP9 application notice in accordance with Part 10.

9. Such an application would be appropriate where, for example, P is in a permanent vegetative state or a minimally conscious state; or where notification by the applicant is likely to cause significant and disproportionate distress to P.'

13 Para 9 of *Practice Direction 7A* may well contemplate notification to P in more cases than is appropriate.

14 r 72 sets out the specific requirements.

Starting proceedings – urgent

5.35   *Practice Direction 10B*[1] allows an oral application at the Royal Courts of Justice before proceedings have been begun and even before any of the COP forms have been drafted. The applicant should take steps to advise the respondent(s) of the application, unless justice would be defeated if notice were given.[2] Applicants should take all reasonable steps to make even urgent applications within court hours.[3] An out-of-hours application requires a greater level of urgency. Urgent applications, especially out-of-hours, should be avoided by pursuing applications promptly.[4]

Urgent applications are generally arranged by counsels' clerks making contact with the Royal Courts of Justice.[5] Out-of-hours applications must be arranged through the RCJ duty security officer who in turn will contact the clerk to the duty judge.

If it is likely (as it usually will be) that P will need to be represented by the Official Solicitor as litigation friend, the Official Solicitor should be contacted – directly during working hours[6] and by the Royal Courts of Justice security office out of hours.[7]

Urgent hearings may take place by telephone.[8] Indeed, highly urgent out-of-hours cases are often dealt with on hearing the applicant alone. In such cases the judge's clerk will often liaise directly with counsel to arrange a telephone hearing with the judge. While the court may be prepared to proceed on the basis of less written information than it would normally require (or none at all), those involved should:

• obtain as much in writing as possible (whether witness statements, doctors' reports or even an attendance note of a lawyer's conversation with the relevant clinician);

• ensure that instructions to counsel are accurate and detailed: in some extremely urgent cases the 'hearing' may be a telephone conversation between the judge and counsel for the applicant; and the judge may have to make a decision on the basis of counsel's oral submissions, on instruction, alone;

- attempt to make potential witnesses available should the judge wish to speak to them on the telephone.

On an urgent application, especially out-of-hours, the court is likely to do the minimum necessary to protect P's position until a further hearing. For example:

- an interim declaration of incapacity to make the decision in question;
- an interim declaration that life-saving treatment (as specified in the order) is in the patient's best interests until further order;
- an order that the matter return to court within a short period of time;
- an order (or undertaking) that the applicant issue the application within a short period of time;
- if only oral information or evidence has been provided, an order requiring the applicant to file written evidence which verifies it.

Counsel for the applicant will usually also be required to draft and lodge the order made. Where the emergency application wholly deals with the matter (for example a declaration authorising a caesarean section) it may be pragmatic and proportionate to request that the order dispenses with the requirement for the COP1B, COP2 and COP3 and undertake to file the COP1 alone.

1 Entitled 'Urgent and interim applications', reproduced at **APPENDIX 5.5**. See para 9: 'Where the exceptional urgency of the matter requires, an application may be started without filing an application form if the court allows it (but where time permits an application should be made in writing). In such a case an application may be made to the court orally. The court will require an undertaking that the application form in the terms of the oral application be filed on the next working day, or as required by the court.'
2 *Ibid*, para 5. To the extent that para 1 suggests that, as a matter of course, notice will not be given to the respondent(s), it is misleading.
3 *Ibid*, para 2.
4 *Ibid*, para 4.
5 During court hours, the office of the Clerk of the Rules – 0207 947 6543 (*Practice Direction 10B*, para 2 gives the telephone number 084 5330 2900; but this is the number for the Office of the Public Guardian); out of hours, the security office – 020 7947 6000: *ibid* para 3.
6 Telephone number 020 7911 7127 (*Practice Direction 9E*, **APPENDIX 5.4**, para 8).
7 Because this is the Official Solicitor's preferred practice.
8 See *Practice Direction 10B*, **APPENDIX 5.5**, para 8.

First hearing and subsequent directions hearings

5.36   The following is a checklist of matters which should be considered and reflected in the order where appropriate:[1]

- Privacy, publicity and anonymity: Is this (and are future hearings) in private or public? Does publication of information need to be authorised or restricted? Should the proceedings be anonymised in any event?
- Level of judge: Is this appropriate for the type of case?
- Permission: Does the applicant need/have permission to make the application?
- Should P be made a party/notified of proceedings?
- Litigation friend for P/any other party
- Parties: Are the appropriate parties involved and are they appropriately designated (that is, as applicant, respondents and any interested parties)?

- Involvement of others: Does the involvement of other people (for example, family members who do not wish to be parties) need to be facilitated?
- Documents: Should anybody, whether a party or not, be required to provide documents, to whom, and by when?[2]
- Interviewing P and accessing records[3]
- Factual evidence[4]
- Expert evidence[5]
- Official Solicitor's statement[6]
- Any meeting between the parties and their lawyers to attempt to resolve issues
- Further interim hearing/s to deal with further directions or preliminary issues
- Final hearing
- Housekeeping before subsequent hearings[7]
- Interim declarations
- *Inter partes* costs (including costs of the Official Solicitor if sought)
- Liberty to apply.[8]

1 See also specifically *Practice Direction 9E*, **APPENDIX 5.4**, paras 14–16.
2 Disclosure is dealt with in Part 16 of the Rules (rr 132–139). But in medical treatment cases it is the practice to specify what category of documents should be provided by and to whom, rather than to order 'standard disclosure'. It is likely to help all concerned if records are ordered to be provided in paginated form from the outset. If there is concern that some documents should be withheld from someone, provision can be made for all the documents to be supplied to the Official Solicitor in the first instance. The Official Solicitor can then take a view about further disclosure in P's best interests; and any dispute can be raised before the court if necessary. In cases where time is of the essence, parties may seek a direction that records be sent directly to experts. Any order against someone who is not present or represented at the hearing and who has not consented to what is proposed should be subject to liberty to apply.
3 The Official Solicitor sometimes seeks a direction that he may interview P and access P's records etc. As litigation friend, this is not strictly necessary, but the Official Solicitor sometimes finds it helpful to demonstrate to others (for example, the holders of records) that he can lawfully access them. Parties sometimes seek similar orders in relation to experts.
4 Part 14 of the Rules (rr 94–118) and *Practice Direction 14A* ('Written evidence') deal with miscellaneous points about factual evidence.
5 Note that the court has the power to order reports from Court of Protection visitors and NHS bodies under MCA, s 49 and rr 117–118 ('section 49 reports'). But in medical treatment cases the parties will generally be permitted to instruct experts or a single joint expert, as to which see Part 15 of the Rules (rr 119–131) and *Practice Direction 15A* ('Expert evidence').
6 The Official Solicitor as litigation friend generally provides a statement once all the other evidence is available.
7 For example, preparation, service and filing of the bundle and position statements/skeleton arguments.
8 Note that the phrase 'liberty to apply' should not be used without explanation when it may be relevant to people who are unlikely to know what it means: *LLBC v TG (and others)* [2007] EWHC 2640 (Fam) per McFarlane J at para 56.

Final hearings

5.37   In relation to evidence at a hearing, see Part 14 of the Rules (rr 94–118) and *Practice Direction 14A* ('Written evidence'), Annex 2 of which deals with evidence by video link.

Matters to consider including in a final order are:

- Does publication of information need to be authorised or restricted?
- Final declarations[1] and orders
- Is a review hearing necessary?
- *Inter partes* costs (including costs of the Official Solicitor if sought)
- Detailed assessment of publicly funded parties' costs
- Is liberty to apply appropriate?

1   Suggested wording for declarations is set out in *Practice Direction 9E*, **APPENDIX 5.4**, para 17:
    'Where a declaration is needed, the order sought should be in the following or similar terms:
    - That P lacks capacity to make a decision in relation to (the proposed medical treatment or procedure). E.g. 'That P lacks capacity to make a decision in relation to sterilisation by vasectomy'; and
    - That, having regard to the best interests of P, it is lawful for the (proposed medical treatment or procedure) to be carried out by (proposed healthcare provider).'
    and para 18:
    'Where the application is for the withdrawal of life-sustaining treatment, the order sought should be in the following or similar terms:
    - That P lacks capacity to consent to continued life-sustaining treatment measures (and specify what these are); and
    - That, having regard to the best interests of P, it is lawful for (name of healthcare provider) to withdraw the life-sustaining treatment from P.'

Costs[1]

5.38   In medical treatment cases the general rule is that there is no order for costs.[2] However, the court may depart from the general rule.[3]

1   Part 19 (rr 155–168) and *Practice Directions 19A* ('Costs in the Court of Protection') and 19B ('Fixed costs').
2   r 157: 'Where the proceedings concern P's welfare the general rule is that there will be no order as to the costs of the proceedings or of that part of the proceedings that concerns P's welfare.'
3   In accordance with r 159(1) and (2):
    '(1)   The Court may depart from rules 156–158 if the circumstances so justify, and in deciding whether departure is justified the court will have regard to all the circumstances including –
    (a)   the conduct of the parties;
    (b)   whether a party has succeeded on part of his case, even if he has not been wholly successful; and
    (c)   the role of any public body involved in the proceedings.
    (2)   The conduct of the parties includes –
    (a)   conduct before, as well as during, the proceedings;
    (b)   whether it was reasonable for a party to raise, pursue or contest a particular issue;
    (c)   the manner in which a party has made or responded to an application or a particular issue; and
    (d)   whether a party who has succeeded in his application or response to an application, in whole or in part, exaggerated any matter contained in his application or response.'

Costs of Official Solicitor

5.39   In medical treatment cases the Official Solicitor has a practice of not consenting to act as litigation friend unless the applicant agrees to pay half the Official Solicitor's costs. If a party were to contest this, the Official Solicitor would be likely to rely on rule 163[1] and the case of *A Hospital v SW & A PCT*.[2]

SW was a decision under the High Court's inherent jurisdiction in which costs were at the general discretion of the court. The President of the Family Division heard detailed argument for and against the award of costs to the Official Solicitor in medical treatment cases and approved an approach whereby the payment of half the Official Solicitor's costs by the applicant is seen as an appropriate starting point.[3] There is no reported case dealing with the issue of the Official Solicitor's costs under the Court of Protection Rules.

1 'Any costs incurred by the Official Solicitor in relation to proceedings under these Rules or in carrying out any directions given by the court and not provided for by remuneration under rule 167 [Remuneration of a deputy, donee or attorney] shall be paid by such persons or out of such funds as the court may direct.' The effect of r 163 appears to be that the general rule (that there should be no order for costs) does not apply to the Official Solicitor's costs, and that the Official Solicitor's costs are simply within the court's discretion.
2 [2007] LS Law Med 273.
3 See para 65 ('On the assumption, as is generally the case, that the Official Solicitor acts, not as an adversary but as a facilitator, and that the part which he plays is helpful rather than obstructive in the court proceedings, it appears to me that the 'half costs' solution is, in principle at least, a reasonable starting point in cases of this kind.') and para 67 ('In my view, it is permissible for the court to adopt an initial approach in favour of 'half costs' solution …').

Appeals[1]

5.40   Permission is required to bring an appeal.[2] In determining where an appeal lies to, there is an internal hierarchy within the Court of Protection:[3]

First instance level	Appeal level
District judge	Circuit judge
Circuit judge	High Court judge
High Court judge	Court of Appeal

In the first two cases a second appeal lies to the Court of Appeal.

1 Appeals are dealt with in Part 20 of the Rules (rr 169–182) and Practice Direction 20A ('Appeals').
2 r 172(1), except for an appeal against an order for committal to prison: r 172(8).
3 r 180.

E   THE HIGH COURT'S JURISDICTION IN RELATION TO MINORS

The High Court generally

The High Court's jurisdiction

5.41   The High Court has two distinct jurisdictions under which it can make medical treatment decisions about minors.[1] First, there is its inherent jurisdiction. Secondly, it has jurisdiction[2] to make a specific issue order[3] or a prohibited steps order.[4] Under the inherent jurisdiction, the court can do anything that it could do in making either of those two types of order. Most, if not all, medical treatment cases can therefore be brought under the inherent jurisdiction.[5]

1 That is, persons under the age of 18. In relation to the Children Act 1989, see s 105(1) of that Act: 'child' means, subject to paragraph 16 of Schedule 1 [which deals with financial provision

for children], a person under the age of eighteen'. Cases under both jurisdictions are allocated to the Family Division: Senior Courts Act 1981, Schedule 1, para 3(b)(ii).

2   Under s 8 Children Act 1989. Note the restrictions under s 9 Children Act 1989 on using s 8 orders, especially sub-section (1) ('No court shall make any section 8 order, other than a residence order, with respect to a child who is in the care of a local authority.') and sub-s (7) ('No court shall make any section 8 order, other than one varying or discharging such an order, with respect to a child who has reached the age of sixteen unless it is satisfied that the circumstances of the case are exceptional.')

3   s 8 Children Act 1989: 'an order giving directions for the purpose of determining a specific question which has arisen, or which may arise, in connection with any aspect of parental responsibility for a child'. For a s 8 application there is a standard form (C100) at http://www.hmcourts-service.gov.uk/courtfinder/forms/C100_1108.pdf but, if s 8 is being relied on at all, it would be usual to issue in the inherent jurisdiction as well, and therefore simply issue one originating summons to cover both jurisdictions.

4   s 8 Children Act 1989: 'an order that no step which could be taken by a parent in meeting his parental responsibility for a child, and which is of a kind specified in the order, shall be taken by any person without the consent of the court'.

5   Although it is not unusual for proceedings to be brought both under the inherent jurisdiction and s 8 Children Act 1989, as indicated on documents by the headings, 'In the matter of the inherent jurisdiction' and 'In the matter of the Children Act 1989'.

Regional hearings

5.42   Medical treatment cases can in appropriate circumstances be allocated to a High Court judge sitting at a District Registry of the High Court rather than at the Royal Courts of Justice in London. This tends only to happen in non-urgent cases because of the special procedures at the RCJ for dealing with very urgent hearings, and the greater availability of suitable judges in London.

Procedure and rules

5.43   Both the High Court's inherent jurisdiction in relation to minors and its jurisdiction under the Children Act 1989 are subject to the Family Proceedings Rules 1991 and the Rules of the Supreme Court 1965.[1] The Civil Procedure Rules do not apply.[2] Family Division practice directions are available online.[3]

1   By virtue of s 32 of Matrimonial and Family Proceedings Act 1984 and the Senior Courts Act 1981, Schedule 1, para 3(b)(ii), both are 'family business' and therefore (see r 1.2 Family Proceedings Rules 1991) 'family proceedings'. Hence (see r 1.3 Family Proceedings Rules 1991) the relevant procedural rules are to be found in the Family Proceedings Rules 1991 and (with the necessary modifications) the Rules of the Supreme Court 1965.

2   Civil Procedure Rules, r 2.1(2).

3   http://www.hmcourts-service.gov.uk/cms/479.htm .

What cases should be brought to court?

General issues

5.44   Although the Court of Protection Main Code of Practice does not apply in the High Court, it[1] neatly identifies some of the general circumstances in which medical treatment cases should be brought to court, whether they relate to adults or minors.

1   At para 8.18, with the addition of the point in square brackets from Court of Protection *Practice Direction 9E*, **APPENDIX 5.4**. See further above at **PARA 5.27**: What cases should be brought to court? Includes both a reference to the Code of Practice and the authors' suggestions of additional categories in which consideration should be given to bringing a case to court.

5.45   The following additional categories of cases which should be brought to court arise specifically in relation to minors but not adults.

Parental issues

5.46   These are usually manifestations of the more general category of cases in which there is a dispute about best interests. For example:

- where parental consent is withheld for a procedure which treating clinicians believe to be in a child's best interests;[1]
- where a procedure is intended to be carried out for which agreement of all those with parental responsibility is required but not forthcoming.[2]

1   For example, Jehovah's Witness parents refusing consent for a child's blood transfusion.
2   For example, circumcision other than on medical grounds. See *Re J (Child's religious upbringing and circumcision)* [1999] 2 FLR 678.

Local authority issues

5.47   In cases where a local authority exercises parental responsibility over a minor, it may feel unable to agree to a proposed course of action concerning the minor's medical treatment (whether provision, withholding or withdrawal), even if it considers it to be the most appropriate course of action, and invite the relevant NHS body to make an application to court.[1] A local authority requires the consent of the court to make an application for any exercise of the court's inherent jurisdiction with respect to children.[2]

1   See *Re B (A Minor)* [2009] LS Law Med 214 per Coleridge J at para 7: 'So far as the local authority is concerned, they have invited the NHS Trust to make this application because although they do in fact have, as a matter of statutory law, parental authority from this child arising from the care order, they felt that that parental authority did not invest them with sufficient authority to consent to this declaration. That is a nice point. I think that they are probably right. Even if they are not right and they do have sufficient authority I think they are entirely right in this situation which has arisen in that they have taken the understandable line that they do not wish to consent to, or be seen to consent to, a declaration of this kind. I think in circumstances like this, where there is a child of this age in this kind of extreme situation, and where there is any uncertainty as to their position, the local authority is sensible to take the course that this one has.'
2   Children Act 1989, s 100(3).

Imposing treatment despite competent refusal

5.48   The authors suggest that an application should always be made where it is proposed to impose treatment on a minor contrary to his or her competent refusal. Such circumstances are likely to involve consideration of issues under Art 8 ECHR.

Who should be the defendants?

Body responsible for treatment or care

5.49   An organisation which is, or will be, responsible for providing clinical or caring services to the minor should usually be named as a defendant if it is not already the plaintiff in the proceedings.

The child?

5.50   Generally in medical treatment cases the child should be named as a party (although this should be confirmed by the judge)[1] and a guardian *ad litem* should be appointed to represent the child.[2] The guardian *ad litem* is usually provided by CAFCASS.[3] CAFCASS can also act as advocate to the court in appropriate cases. In some cases, CAFCASS has taken the view that its assistance is not needed.[4] However, applicants should never assume that CAFCASS will not want to become involved: all medical treatment cases concerning minors should be referred to CAFCASS legal before the application is made.

1   *President's Direction (Representation of Children in Family Proceedings pursuant to Family Proceedings Rules 1991, Rule 9.5)*, 5 April 2004 [2004] 1 FLR 1188 (**APPENDIX 5.10**) at para 3: 'The decision to make the child a party will always be exclusively that of the judge, made in the light of the facts and circumstances of the particular case. The following are offered, solely by way of guidance, as circumstances which may justify the making of an order:- ... '; and from that list, for example, paragraph 3.6 'Where there are complex medical or mental health issues to be determined or there are other unusually complex issues that necessitate separate representation of the child'.
2   Rule 9.5 of the Family Proceedings Rules 1991 provides for the appointment of a guardian *ad litem* for a child party unless the child is of sufficient understanding and can participate as a party in the proceedings without a guardian, as permitted by r 9.2A.
3   The Children and Family Court Advisory and Support Service. CAFCASS legal (as opposed to local CAFCASS offices) will often be involved in medical treatment cases. See the *President's Direction* at N 1 above, and *CAFCASS and the National Assembly for Wales Practice Note (Appointment of guardians in private law proceedings)*, June 2006 [2006] 2 FLR 143 (**APPENDIX 5.11**). Note that contact details given in para 11 should be replaced with the following: Service Manager, CAFCASS High Court Team, 6th Floor, Sanctuary Buildings, Great Smith Street, London, SW1P 3BT, Fax: 0844 353 3351, DX 157050 Westminster 3, Tel: 0844 353 3362 (direct line).
4   For example, in some cases concerning babies whose Jehovah's Witness parents refuse consent for blood transfusions CAFCASS has not considered it necessary to act, on the basis that the child does not have ascertainable wishes and there is established case-law to assist the Court as to the appropriate course of action.

Parents?

5.51   Naming parents as a party when this is not necessary may be worrying and upsetting for them. Whether or not the child's parents are named as parties should depend on their position in relation to the application and the level of involvement which they wish to have in the proceedings. If the proceedings are necessary because the parents object to treatment proposed for the child, they should generally be named as parties. However, if proceedings are necessary because, for example, experimental treatment is proposed for the child and the parents agree, it may well be unnecessary for the parents to be named as parties, although the court will expect to be kept informed of their views.

If a parent (or any other party) does not have capacity to conduct the proceedings, the Official Solicitor may be prepared to act as litigation friend to that person.[1]

1 *Practice Note (Official Solicitor: Appointment in family proceedings)*, 2 April 2001 [2001] 2 FLR 155 (**APPENDIX 5.14**) and an article about the Official Solicitor's role in children cases on the Official Solicitor's website at http://www.officialsolicitor.gov.uk/docs/parentsnet workarticle.doc.

Local authority

5.52   If a local authority is involved in the minor's life, consideration should be given to whether and to what extent it should also be involved in the proceedings.

Starting proceedings – non-urgent

5.53   Permission is not required to start proceedings.[1] Proceedings are started by way of originating summons[2] and should be accompanied by an affidavit setting out a summary of the facts and grounds relied on, attaching relevant documents such as reports or witness statements from treating clinicians. The information required will of course vary case-by-case, but the following points will usually need to be addressed:

- the minor's current circumstances and the medical issue/s arising;
- the minor's background;
- views of treating clinicians as to competence / capacity and best interests (voluminous medical records should not be included at this stage);
- any past and present wishes and feelings expressed by the minor;
- views of parents and any other family members;
- views of any clinicians giving second opinions, or experts who have been consulted so far;
- summary of attempts to reach agreement and why a court application is necessary;
- how urgently the case needs to be heard for (1) directions (2) final hearing.

1 Except by a local authority: see above. This is in contrast with most applications in the Court of Protection.
2 Rules of the Supreme Court continue to apply, with the necessary modifications, to family proceedings in the High Court (r 1.3(1) Family Proceedings Rules 1991 ('FPR')); 'family proceedings' means High Court business assigned to the Family Division and to no other Division by or under s 61 of (and Schedule 1 to) the Senior Courts Act 1981 (r 1.2 FPR and s 32 Matrimonial and Family Proceedings Act 1984); Rules of the Supreme Court 1965 (Schedule 1 to SI 1776/1965, Rules of the Supreme Court (Revision) 1965) set out the originating summons procedure in Part 2/Order 7: Originating Summons: General Provisions. Order 7, r 3(1) states: 'Every originating summons must include a statement of the questions on which the plaintiff seeks the determination or direction of the High Court or, as the case may be, a concise statement of the relief or remedy claimed in the proceedings begun by the originating summons

with sufficient particulars to identify the cause or causes of action in respect of which the plaintiff claims that relief or remedy.'

5.54 A standard form originating summons is provided by the Principal Registry of the Family Division.[1] This may require modification to make the language more reader-friendly and fit the circumstances of the case (especially so as to make them intelligible to non-lawyers such as family members who may be unrepresented).

1 **APPENDIX 5.8**. See also **APPENDIX 4.1** (Draft Originating Summons for Child Treatment Decision) for sample text to be included. The court will generate an acknowledgement of service for the defendant/s on issue. An example of the type of information which is likely to be required in an acknowledgement of service standard form is provided at **APPENDIX 5.9**.
2 Modifications are expressly permitted by r 1.3(1) of the Family Proceedings Rules 1991. For example, if, on urgent application before the issue of proceedings, an order has been made dealing with the issue in question, and no further hearing is to take place but there is liberty to apply, the originating summons should explain this and make it clear that no further action is required.

5.55 The court will list the matter for a directions hearing.

Starting proceedings – urgent

5.56 An urgent oral application may be made at the Royal Courts of Justice before proceedings have been begun and even before the originating summons has been drafted.[1] The proposed plaintiff should take steps to notify potential defendants of the application, unless justice would be defeated if notice were given.[2] It is necessary so far as possible for the parents to be in a position to address the application made.[3]

Applicants should take all reasonable steps to make even urgent applications within court hours.[4] An out-of-hours application requires a greater level of urgency. Urgent applications, especially out of hours, should be avoided by pursuing applications promptly.[5]

Urgent applications are generally arranged by counsels' clerks making contact with the Royal Courts of Justice.[6] CAFCASS should be contacted, directly during working hours;[7] by the Royal Courts of Justice security office out of hours.[8]

For further guidance, see **PARA 5.35** above (Starting proceedings – urgent) which applies equally[9] in relation to Court of Protection and High Court practice.

1 See *Practice Note (Official Solicitor, CAFCASS and the National Assembly for Wales: Urgent and out of hours cases in the Family Division of the High Court)*, 28 July 2006 [2006] 2 FLR 354, reproduced at **APPENDIX 5.15**. Paras 5–7 dealing with adult medical treatment and welfare cases have now been mostly superseded by practice and procedure in the Court of Protection.
2 See by way of analogy ourt of Protection *Practice Direction 10B*, para 5.
3 Per Parker J in *Re OT* [2009] EWHC 633 (Fam) at para 85.
4 See the *Practice Note* at **N 1** above, para 3.
5 *Ibid*, para 2.
6 During court hours, the office of the Clerk of the Rules – 0207 947 6543; out of hours, the security office – 020 7947 6000: *Ibid*, para 4.
7 The telephone number for the service manager of the High Court team is 0844 353 3362.
8 See the *Practice Note* at **N 1** above, para 8.
9 If one reads 'plaintiff' and 'originating summons' for 'applicant' and 'application'.

Privacy and publicity

5.57   Proceedings are heard in private or (less commonly) public.[1] In a private hearing, duly accredited media representatives[2] are entitled to be present[3] unless the court orders otherwise.[4]

The publication of information relating to proceedings before a court sitting in private under the exercise of the inherent jurisdiction of the High Court with respect to minors or under the Children Act 1989 will generally be a contempt of court.[5] But the court can authorise such publication with restrictions (for example, prohibiting the identification of an individual) as necessary. In relation to a public hearing, the court can restrict the publication of information.[6]

There is a practice direction governing 'any application in the Family Division founded on Convention rights for an order restricting publication of information about children'.[7] It does not appear that this procedure needs to be followed where the court, for example, simply orders restrictions on the identification of a patient and others in the case (for the purpose of protecting the patient) at the same time as ordering that a hearing shall take place in public, because such restrictions are founded on statute rather than Convention rights. However, further restrictions may be required in a case with significant media interest.[8]

If a hearing is in private and publication of information has not been authorised, there is no legal reason for the parties' names to be anonymised.[9]

1   Family Proceedings Rules 1991, r 4.16(7) states: 'Unless the court otherwise directs, a hearing of, or directions appointment in, proceedings to which this Part [Proceedings under the Children Act, etc] applies shall be in chambers.' See further *Re Child X (Residence and Contact – Rights of media attendance – FPR Rule 10.28(4))* [2009] EWHC 1728 (Fam). At paras 26–49 the President examined the principles of privacy and publicity in cases concerning children, in the context of r 10.28 of the Family Proceedings Rules 1991, which governs who may be present during a hearing in proceedings held in private. For examples of medical treatment cases concerning children which have been heard in public, see *Portsmouth NHS Trust v Derek Wyatt and others* [2005] 1 FLR 21 per Hedley J at para 1 and [2005] 2 FLR 480 at para 23; and *An NHS Trust v MB and others* [2006] 2 FLR 319. The case of *RB* (a baby with a severe neuro-muscular disorder whose doctors and mother supported the withdrawal of treatment, but whose father objected to this course of action until some way through the hearing when agreement was eventually reached) was also heard before McFarlane J in private with media attendance under r 10.28 in November 2009. http://www.bailii.org/ew/cases/EWHC/Fam/2009/B26.html. A reporting restriction order was made following the draft attached to *'Practice Note – Official Solicitor: Deputy Director of Legal Services CAFCASS – Applications for reporting restriction orders'* dated 18 March 2005, [2005] 2 FLR 120, **APPENDIX 5.13**.
2   Family Proceedings Rules 1991, r 10.28(8): 'In this rule "duly accredited" refers to accreditation in accordance with any administrative scheme for the time being approved for the purposes of this rule by the Lord Chancellor.'
3   Family Proceedings Rules 1991, r 10.28(3)(f).
4   Family Proceedings Rules 1991, r 10.28(4): ' ... where satisfied that—
    (a)   this is necessary—
          (i)   in the interests of any child concerned in, or connected with, the proceedings;
          (ii)   for the safety or protection of a party, a witness in the proceedings, or a person connected with such a party or witness; or
          (iii)   for the orderly conduct of the proceedings; or
    (b)   justice will otherwise be impeded or prejudiced.'

See *Practice Direction: 'Attendance of Media Representatives at Hearings in Family Proceedings'*, dated 20th April 2009, http://www.hmcourts-service.gov.uk/cms/files/PD-MediaAttendanceInFamilyProceedings-CountyCourtsAndTheHighCourt.doc .

5   Administration of Justice Act 1960, s 12(1)(a).

6   See Children Act 1989, s 97:

'(2)   No person shall publish [to the public at large or any section of the public] any material which is intended, or likely, to identify—

(a)   any child as being involved in any proceedings before [the High Court, a county court or] a magistrates' court in which any power under this Act [or the Adoption and Children Act 2002] may be exercised by the court with respect to that or any other child; or

(b)   an address or school as being that of a child involved in any such proceedings.

(3)   In any proceedings for an offence under this section it shall be a defence for the accused to prove that he did not know, and had no reason to suspect, that the published material was intended, or likely, to identify the child.'

And Children and Young Persons Act 1933, s 39(1) (as supplemented by Children and Young Persons Act 1963, s 57(4): s 39 '… shall, with the necessary modifications, apply in relation to sound and television broadcasts as they apply in relation to newspapers.'):

'In relation to any proceedings in any court … the court may direct that—

(a)   no newspaper report of the proceedings shall reveal the name, address, or school, or include any particulars calculated to lead to the identification, of any child or young person concerned in the proceedings, either as being the person [by or against] or in respect of whom the proceedings are taken, or as being a witness therein;

(b)   no picture shall be published in any newspaper as being or including a picture of any child or young person so concerned in the proceedings as aforesaid;

except in so far (if at all) as may be permitted by the direction of the court.'

7   *President's Practice Direction (Applications for Reporting Restriction Orders)* dated 18 March 2005, **APPENDIX 5.12**; see also application form at http://www.hmcourts-service.gov.uk/cms/files/APPLICATIONS_FOR_REPORTING_RESTRICTION_ORDERS.doc and *Practice Note (Official Solicitor: Deputy Director of Legal Services: CAFCASS: Applications for reporting restriction orders* dated 18 March 2005, [2005] 2 FLR 120, **APPENDIX 5.13**, with a draft reporting restriction order attached.

8   The President of the Family Division emphasised in *Re Child X* (see **N1** above) the importance of parties complying with the *President's Direction* dated 18 March 2005 in **N7** above by serving applications for reporting restrictions orders on the national news media where restrictions are sought which go beyond the pre-existing statutory restrictions and are therefore founded on Convention rights, for example, prohibiting the soliciting of information. See paras 71–80 of the judgment and paras 81–89 as to procedural issues. The relevant provisions in the Court of Protection are addressed at **PARA 5.28** above: Privacy and publicity.

9   However, anonymisation is often prudent, not least for the purpose of the listing of the case so that the parties' names do not appear on the court lists, the danger of which is greater in regional courts than in the Royal Courts of Justice, where current practice is to list using case numbers only.

First hearing and subsequent directions hearings

5.58   The following is a checklist of matters which should be considered and reflected in the order where appropriate:

- Privacy and publicity: Is this (and are future hearings) in private or public? Does publication of information need to be authorised or restricted? Should proceedings be anonymised in any event?
- Should the minor be made a party?
- Does a guardian *ad litem* need to be appointed for the minor?

- Parties: Are the appropriate parties involved?
- Involvement of others: Does the involvement of other people (for example, family members who do not wish to be parties) need to be facilitated?
- Documents: Should anybody, whether a party or not, be required to provide documents, to whom, and by when?[1]
- Factual evidence.
- Expert evidence.
- Interviewing P and accessing records.[2]
- Guardian *ad litem's* statement.[3]
- Any meeting between the parties and their lawyers to attempt to resolve issues.
- Further interim hearing/s to deal with further directions or preliminary issues.
- Final hearing.
- Housekeeping before subsequent hearings.[4]
- Interim declarations.
- *Inter partes* costs.
- Liberty to apply.[5]

1   In medical treatment cases the practice is to specify what category of documents should be provided by and to whom. It is likely to help all concerned if records are ordered to be provided in paginated form from the outset. If there is concern that some documents should be withheld from someone, provision can be made for all the documents to be supplied to the guardian *ad litem* in the first instance. The guardian *ad litem* can then take a view about further disclosure in the minor's best interests; and any dispute can be raised before the court if necessary. In cases where time is of the essence, parties may seek a direction that records be sent directly to experts. Any order against someone who is not present or represented at the hearing and who has not consented to do what is proposed should be subject to liberty to apply.
2   Parties sometimes seek a direction that any experts referred to in the order may examine/interview the minor and access the minor's records etc. This may not be strictly necessary but is sometimes helpful so that the expert can demonstrate to others (for example, the holders of records) that he can lawfully access them.
3   The guardian *ad litem* generally provides a statement once all the other evidence is available.
4   For example, preparation, service and filing of the bundle and position statements/skeleton arguments.
5   Note that the phrase 'liberty to apply' should not be used without explanation when it may be relevant to people who are unlikely to know what it means: *LLBC v TG* [2007] EWHC 2640 (Fam) per McFarlane J at para 56.

Final hearings

5.59   Matters to consider including in a final order are:

- Does publication of information need to be authorised or restricted?
- Final declarations;
- Is a review hearing necessary?
- *Inter partes* costs;
- Detailed assessment of publicly funded parties' costs;
- Is liberty to apply appropriate?

Costs

5.60   Costs are frequently not sought. Costs are in the discretion of the court but there is no general rule that costs follow the event.[1]

1   See r 10.28(1) of the Family Proceedings Rules 1991, applying CPR, Pts 43 and 44 (except rr 44.9–44.12), 47 and 48 but with modifications including the disapplication of CPR, r 44.3(2) (costs follow the event).

Appeals

5.61   An appeal (for which leave must be sought) lies to the Court of Appeal.[1]

1   In accordance with Part 5 of the Rules of the Supreme Court 1965.

F THE HIGH COURT'S INHERENT JURISDICTION – IN RELATION TO 'VULNERABLE ADULTS'[1]

5.62   As a matter of practice, such applications should be made to the Family Division.[2] The Civil Procedure Rules apply.[3] Depending on the circumstances, a CPR, Part 7 or CPR, Part 8 claim form should be used.[4] Parties should give consideration to whether the hearing should be in private and whether there should be an order prohibiting the disclosure of the identity of a party or witness.[5]

1   See *In the matter of SA (A Local Authority v (1) MA (2) NA and (3) SA (by her children's guardian LJ))* per Munby J [2006] 1 FLR 867.
2   By analogy with the *Practice Direction* dated 14 December 2001 [2002] 1 WLR 325 (now of no application since the subject matter has been taken over by the Court of Protection) issued by the then President of the Family Division stating that proceedings which invoke the jurisdiction of the High Court to grant declarations as to the best interest of incapacitated adults are not assigned to any division but are suitable for hearing within the Family Division.
3   These proceedings are not, by virtue of Matrimonial and Family Proceedings Act 1984, s 32 and Senior Courts Act 1981, Schedule 1 'family business' and therefore (see Family Proceedings Rules 1991, r 1.2) not 'family proceedings'. Hence CPR, r 2.1(2), disapplying the CPR to family proceedings, does not apply.
4   The Part 8 procedure will be appropriate where there are no substantial disputes of fact: CPR, r 8.1(2)(a).
5   See CPR, r 39.2.

G CONCLUSION

5.63   Whether in the High Court or the Court of Protection, judges considering medical treatment cases have as their focus the best interests of the person who is the subject of the proceedings.[1] While the procedural rules must of course be observed, the need to achieve the right result for that person requires an emphasis on substance over form. Translating parties' proposals for case-management into workable directions often requires considerable thought and imagination. Resourcefulness is also required in order to capitalise on any possibility of reaching agreement on the substantive issues. But if agreement cannot be reached, differences of opinion as to the desired outcome should not stand in the way of as much co-operation as possible in working out how best to investigate and ventilate the issues in the case.

1   Or in the rare 'vulnerable adult' case, the court's focus is protecting the interests and facilitating the choices of the vulnerable but capable adult.

For updating material and hyperlinks related to this chapter, see: www.3serjeantsinn.com/mtdl/court

Chapter 6

Restraint and Deprivation of Liberty

A   Introduction 6.1
B   Restraint 6.6
       Restraint authorised under the MCA 6.8
       Restraint and Article 3 ECHR 6.11
       Proportionality and restraint 6.15
       Practical issues 6.22
C   Deprivation of liberty 6.27
       Background: the 'Bournewood gap' 6.27
       What is 'deprivation of liberty'? 6.31
       Identifying a deprivation of liberty 6.37
       Authorising a deprivation of liberty 6.38
       Court authorisation 6.39
       The DOLS procedure 6.41
       MCA or MHA? 6.45
D   Conclusion 6.49

A INTRODUCTION

6.1   Restraint and deprivation of liberty are rarely, if ever, stand-alone issues, although they regularly arise in the context of achieving other care and treatment goals. There are many occasions when a proposed medical treatment intervention can be practicably achieved only if some degree of restraint of the patient is employed. Restraint might be required to get a patient to the hospital as well as to achieve the desired assessment and/or treatment of the patient once they arrive there. Particularly where an incapable patient cannot understand the benefits of undergoing an uncomfortable or anxiety-provoking procedure, their forcible resistance of the intervention may need to be overcome before the treatment that is deemed to be in their best interests can be safely delivered.

6.2   This chapter is not concerned with issues of restraint and deprivation of liberty in order to provide treatment for mental disorder under the Mental Health Act 1983 ('MHA'), as this subject is fully dealt with in other works. This chapter only considers restraint and deprivation of liberty for the purpose of providing medical treatment and care which cannot be provided under the MHA.[1]

1   The MHA, s 63 only permits treatment for the mental disorder from which the detained patient is suffering, although this may include physical conditions arising from the mental disorder (see *B v Croydon HA* [1995] 1 All ER 683). It does not permit treatment of physical conditions which are unrelated to the patient's mental disorder. *GJ v The Foundation Trust* [2009] EWHC 2972 (Fam) provides important guidance on the meaning of 'treatment' in MHA and how it relates to DOLS eligibility. For an update about this case and other issues relating to restraint and deprivation of liberty see www.3serjeantsinn.com/mtdl/restraint .

6.3   It has long been recognised that reasonable and proportionate restraint may be a necessary adjunct to the proposed treatment of physical disorder and hence justified under the common law doctrine of necessity if in the incapable patient's best interests. The courts providing declaratory relief, however, have been keen to scrutinise the need for and proportionality of any restraint employed.[1]

1   *Trust A and B v H (an Adult patient)* [2006] EWHC 1230 (Fam).

6.4   Previously, such matters have been considered under the High Court's inherent jurisdiction for incapable patients. However, the implementation of the Mental Capacity Act 2005 ('MCA') in October 2007 created a statutory basis for lawfully restraining an incapable adult[1] and, where the restraining measures employed amounted to a deprivation of liberty, a judge sitting in the Court of Protection had the jurisdiction to declare such acts lawful under MCA s 15.[2] Further, since April 2009, restraint which amounts to a deprivation of liberty can now only be authorised by an order of the Court under MCA s 16(2)(a) or by Primary Care Trusts and Local Authorities, under Schedule A1 of the MCA.[3]

1   The general provisions under MCA, s 6 in respect of restraint apply to those aged 16 and over; the MCA provisions relating to deprivation of liberty in Schedule A1 apply only to those aged 18 and over; see **APPENDIX 1.1**: Mental Capacity Act 2005.
2   *Re P (Adult patient)(Consent to medical treatment)* [2008] EWHC 1403 (Fam) at para 31.
3   And, in urgent situations only, by the detaining hospital or care home.

6.5   Many of the earlier common law principles will still apply to decisions regarding restraint and deprivation of liberty under the MCA. In particular issues of best interests, necessity and proportionality will still be paramount, although these are now to be addressed within the MCA's statutory framework.

B   RESTRAINT

6.6   'Restraint' is defined in MCA, s 6(4) as follows:

' ... D (a person) restrains P (a patient) if he—

(a)   uses, or threatens to use, force to secure the doing of an act which P resists, or

(b)   restricts P's liberty of movement, whether or not P resists.'

Importantly, verbal restraint as well as physical restraint will fall within the MCA definition.

6.7   For the capable patient, physical restraint in the absence of consent or other lawful authority will amount to a civil trespass to the person and may amount to a crime, depending upon the severity and impact of the restraining measure. Only the restraint of incapable persons is considered further in this chapter.

Restraint authorised under the MCA

6.8   The MCA recognises that restraint will on occasions be necessary when caring for the health and welfare of those who lack capacity and, hence, MCA s 6 extends the general authority under MCA s 5 to treat incapable patients in their best interests to include the use of restraint where two specific conditions are satisfied:

'(2)   The first condition is that D reasonably believes that it is necessary to do the act in order to prevent harm to P.

(3)   The second is that the act is a proportionate response to—
　　(a)   the likelihood of P's suffering harm, and
　　(b)   the seriousness of that harm.'

Necessary and proportionate restraint can also be authorised by someone with lasting power of attorney[1] or by a court appointed deputy, providing that the deputy is acting within the scope of the authority that has been expressly conferred on him by the court.[2]

1   MCA s11
2   MCA s 20. The welfare deputy will have had to have been given sufficient powers by the Court under MCA s 16(5) which states: 'The court may ... confer on a deputy such powers or impose on him such duties, as it thinks necessary or expedient for giving effect to, or otherwise in connection with, an order or appointment made by it under subsection (2).' And see Chapter 3: Deciding for Others – Adults para 3.3 and 3.9

6.9   Thus, restraint can lawfully be used where it is reasonably believed that it is necessary to prevent harm and the restraint used is proportionate to the likelihood and seriousness of that harm. The restraint must also be in the person's best interests.[1]

1   MCA, s 1(5); see **APPENDIX 1.1**: Mental Capacity Act 2005.

6.10   However, if there comes a point when the restriction of liberty becomes a deprivation of liberty this cannot be authorised under MCA s 5 and s 6[1] even where the purpose of the deprivation of liberty is to deliver medical treatment to an incapable person that is in their best interests. Where the circumstances amount to a deprivation of liberty then this can be lawfully effected only where either (a) the deprivation of liberty has been ordered or authorised by the Court of Protection,[2] or (b) authority has been given under the 'Hospital and Care Home Residents: Deprivation of Liberty' procedures of Schedule A1 to the MCA,[3] or (c) in an emergency whilst a court decision is obtained, but then only if the detention is necessary to provide treatment aimed at sustaining life or preventing a serious deterioration in the patient's condition.[4]

1   By virtue of MCA, s 4A(1); see **APPENDIX 1.1**: Mental Capacity Act 2005.
2   Under s 16(2)(a).
3   See further below: **PARA 6.38FF**.
4   MCA, s 4B; see **APPENDIX 1.1**: Mental Capacity Act 2005 and see **PARA 6.38** below.

Restraint and Article 3 ECHR

6.11   Forcible restraint of another, even if falling short of a deprivation of liberty, can engage rights under the European Convention on Human Rights ('ECHR')[1], particularly the Art 3 right not to be subject to inhuman and degrading treatment. As was pointed out in *R (C) v Secretary of State for Justice*:

> 'We tend to think of obligations under Art 3 in terms of extreme violence, deprivation or humiliation. Convention jurisprudence however makes clear that depending on the circumstances, Art 3 may be engaged by conduct that falls below that high level. Two circumstances that have been identified as imposing special obligations on the state are that the subject is dependent on the state because he has been deprived of his liberty; and that he is young or vulnerable.'[2]

1   For the full text see: http://www.echr.coe.int/NR/rdonlyres/D5CC24A7-DC13–4318-B457–5C9014916D7A/0/EnglishAnglais.pdf .
2   [2008] EWCA Civ 882 at para 58.

6.12   In *Herczegfalvy v Austria*[1] a mentally ill man who physically resisted being given medication was handcuffed to a bed. He was forcibly administered neuroleptics and he sustained injuries including loss of teeth, broken ribs and bruises. He complained of a violation of his Art 3 rights. The patient's challenge failed: the European Court of Human Rights found that 'according to the psychiatric principles generally accepted at the time, medical necessity justified the treatment in issue'. Nevertheless, it was stated that:

> 'The Court considers that the position of inferiority and powerlessness which is typical of patients confined in psychiatric hospitals calls for increased vigilance in reviewing whether the Convention has been complied with. While it is for the medical authorities to decide, on the basis of the recognised rules of medical science, on the therapeutic methods to be used, if necessary by force, to preserve the physical and mental health of patients who are entirely incapable of deciding for themselves and for whom they are therefore responsible, such patients nevertheless remain under the protection of Article 3 , whose requirements permit of no derogation.
>
> The established principles of medicine are admittedly in principle decisive in such cases; as a general rule, a measure which is a therapeutic necessity cannot be regarded as inhuman or degrading. The Court must nevertheless satisfy itself that the medical necessity has been convincingly shown to exist.'[2]

1   (1993) 15 EHRR 437.
2   Para 82.

6.13   When considering whether treatment was 'degrading' within the meaning of Art 3, the Strasbourg court will have regard to whether its object was to humiliate and debase the person or whether it was to meet a therapeutic need. By way of example, requiring a prisoner to wear handcuffs when he is outside the prison and there is reason to believe that he will abscond or cause injury to others will not generally amount to degrading treatment.[1] Hence, challenges to the use of restraint with prisoners have been successful only where it has been found on the specific facts of individual cases that the handcuffing of a prisoner while he underwent hospital treatment was not a proportionate response to the identified risk of absconding and violence.[2] Each case will be fact-specific and there will undoubtedly be occasions where the reasonably apprehended risks of escape or violence do justify restraint of a prisoner during the course of treatment. In assessing the nature and extent of restraint used the national and European courts will be focusing on the proportionality of the restraint when set against the identified and documented risks.

1   *Raninen v Finland* (1998) EHRR 563 at para 56; and *Mouisel v France* (2004) 38 EHRR 34.
2   *R (Graham) and R (Allen) v Secretary of State for Justice* [2007] EWHC 2940 (Admin); see also *Uyan v Turkey* (Application no 7496/03), 8 January 2009 and *Mouisel v France* (2004) 38 EHRR 34.

6.14   This principle of proportionality is the paramount consideration in decisions under MCA, even where Art 3 rights are not explicitly put in issue.

Proportionality and restraint

6.15   The majority of national case-law on the use of restraint with incapable patients pre-dates the implementation of the MCA; however, the common law principles therein will continue to apply to decisions under the MCA.

6.16   The courts have repeatedly emphasised the need for 'moderate and reasonable use of restraint' and that:

'the lawfulness of such restraint has to be carefully considered when assessing the balance of benefit and disadvantage in the giving of the proposed medical treatment ... [whilst recognising the patient's] right not to be subjected to degrading treatment under Art 3 ECHR.'[1]

1   *Trust A v H (An adult patient)* [2006] EWHC 1230 at para 27.

6.17   There will be occasions where the degree and extent of the restraint required to achieve a treatment outcome is such that, when the patient's best interests are considered, it would not be proportionate to apply such restraint over the period in question.

6.18   As Hale LJ (as she then was) stated in *R (Wilkinson) v RMO Broadmoor Hospital,* where an incapable person:

'is actively opposed to a course of action, the benefits which it holds for him will have to be carefully weighed against the disadvantages of going against his wishes, especially if force is required to do this.'[1]

1   [2002] 1 WLR 419 at para 64.

6.19   This principle applies even where the consequences of not restraining and treating the patient may be death. In *Re D (Medical treatment: Mentally Disabled Patient)* Sir Stephen Brown granted a declaration that doctors were not required to continue providing kidney dialysis for a 49-year-old man suffering from chronic renal failure and high blood pressure where the patient lacked the mental capacity to consent to or refuse treatment and was forcibly resisting dialysis. Physical restraint in the face of such resistance was not practicable for the period of the dialysis. The patient would have been subject to lengthy periods of general anaesthesia four times each week in order to permit the dialysis to be carried out. Such steps were found to be both 'impractical and dangerous'; consequently it was determined that giving the proposed restraint and treatment was not in the patient's best interests.[1]

1   (1998) 2 FLR 22.

6.20   Indeed the authors are aware of a number of unreported cases concerning patients with severe psychotic disorders where the degree of physical restraint that would be required to secure life-saving treatment in the face of the patient's forcible resistance has been such that to continue to restrain the incapable patient has been found to be not merely impracticable and unachievable, but in at least one case described as 'being tantamount to torture'. Declarations have therefore been made that it would not be in the patient's best interests to be so restrained, even though the inevitable consequence has been that the treatment could not been given and the patient has died.

6.21   No novel approach is adopted in such life and death situations; the principle of best interests remains paramount and the approach described by Thorpe LJ in *Re A (Male Sterilisation)*[1] is commonly adopted by the court. The judge will be required to conduct a balancing exercise aided by drawing up a table of the benefits and 'dis-benefits' of the proposed options and the distress, discomfort and any potential injury caused by restraint will be a relevant 'dis-benefit'. Although there is a presumption in favour of prolonging life in such a balancing exercise, this is not irrebuttable. As stated by Lord Donaldson MR in *Re J (A Minor) (Wardship: Medical Treatment)*:

'There is without doubt a very strong presumption in favour of a course of action which will prolong life, but ... it is not irrebuttable ... Account has to be taken of the pain and suffering and quality of life which the child will experience.'[2]

1   [2000] 1 FLR 549.
2   [1991] Fam 33 at 46 per Lord Donaldson of Lymington MR.

Practical issues

6.22   In recognition of the need for flexibility when dealing with human actions, the courts have not sought to be prescriptive as to precisely what degree of restraint can be used. As the Court of Appeal stated in *Re MB (Medical Treatment)*:

'The extent of force or compulsion that may become necessary in ensuring that medical treatment is provided to a mentally incapacitated patient can only be judged in each individual case and by health professionals.'[1]

1   [1997] 2 FLR 426, CA, at 439.

6.23   Whilst the court will be unlikely to 'micro-manage' the use of restraint, before endorsing its use the court (or at least the Official Solicitor representing the patient) will usually require a comprehensive care plan to be provided, setting out the type of restraint that it is anticipated may have to be used and the practical arrangements in place to achieve the desired outcome by means of the least restrictive option.

6.24   Those wishing to carry out the restraint will need to demonstrate that they have considered issues such as whether sedation will be employed and how that sedation will be administered. On occasions where a patient does not comply with oral medication, covert sedation may be the best practicable method of achieving an admission to hospital without increasing the anxiety and distress of the patient. The care plan may also need to address issues such as who will provide the transport and the escorting staff to get a patient to hospital, what liaison there will be with the ambulance service and whether carers with whom the patient is familiar will remain in attendance at the hospital throughout the admission. On occasions where a patient may need one-to-one supervision in hospital the issues of the funding for the additional staff required may need clarification before the court will endorse the proposals.

6.25   In order properly to weigh up best interests it will often be necessary for the clinical witnesses and the independent experts to have considered the psychological impact upon the patient of being restrained: will it aggravate a pre-existing mental disorder? Will any distress caused be permanent or temporary? To what extent will the therapeutic relationship with the clinical team be damaged by forcible treatment? In some cases the proposed treatment may be given under the cover of medication (for example, Midazolam) which causes short periods of retrograde amnesia, thereby minimising the recollected trauma of any restraint.

6.26   The applicant (who will usually be an NHS body) will need to provide a draft order to the court which is as specific as possible as to the extent of restraint that will be used. Examples of court orders are provided in **APPENDICES 6.1** and **6.3**. Invariably the court will require the order to include a paragraph reflecting that any restraint used will be the minimum practicable in the situation and delivered in such a way to ensure the patient suffers the least distress and retains the greatest dignity.

C   DEPRIVATION OF LIBERTY

Background: the '*Bournewood* gap'

6.27   Until the decision in *HL v UK*[1] ('the *Bournewood* case'), it was accepted practice in psychiatric hospitals to informally admit those incapable patients who did not indicate any objection to their admission or treatment. Formal powers of detention under the MHA were usually invoked only if an incapable patient refused or resisted the admission or treatment, or if they tried to leave the hospital once admitted. In *HL* the European Court of Human Rights found that the circumstances of the admission of an incapable but non-resistant man to a psychiatric in-patient unit constituted a violation of his right to liberty under Art 5 ECHR. Although he had been admitted to hospital to provide him with treatment for his mental disorder, HL had not been formally detained under the MHA but had remained a 'voluntary' patient under MHA, s 131 throughout his admission.

1   (2004) 40 EHRR 761.

6.28   Art 5(1) ECHR permits the detention of those of 'unsound mind'. However, Art 5(1) states that 'no one shall be deprived of his liberty save … in accordance with a procedure prescribed by law' and hence a legal process for the detention must be followed if a state is to protect its citizens from an arbitrary deprivation of liberty. Further, in stating that 'everyone who is deprived of his liberty … shall be entitled to take proceedings by which the lawfulness of his detention shall be decided speedily by a court and his release ordered if his detention is not lawful', Art 5(4) ECHR requires the state to provide a procedure by which any deprivation of liberty may be speedily reviewed and challenged. As HL was held 'informally' and not detained under MHA 1983, he had none of these legal protections in place.

6.29   Before petitioning Strasbourg, HL had already challenged his detention through the national courts, claiming that he had been falsely imprisoned. However the House of Lords found (by a majority) that HL was not 'detained' and, further, even if he was detained, his admission to hospital was lawful, being justified under the common law doctrine of necessity. His false imprisonment claim therefore failed. The European Court of Human Rights, however, found that HL had been 'deprived of liberty' within the meaning of Art 5 ECHR and that the absence of any procedural rules governing the hospital admission of informal incapable patients violated his Art 5 procedural rights.

6.30   The lacuna in national law (hence the *'Bournewood* gap') which meant that there were no Art 5 procedural protections for incompetent compliant patients could not be solved by formally detaining all incapable patients under MHA. Many incapable but non-resistant patients would not meet the criteria for detention under MHA, s 2 or s 3; further, a large number of incapable people reside outside psychiatric institutions in care homes in the community where they are not being treated for any mental disorder. The Government needed to provide a procedure to authorise the deprivation of liberty in situations where the MHA could not be invoked. This was eventually achieved through amendment to the MCA; in April 2009 the 'Hospital and Care Home Residents: Deprivation of Liberty' procedures (more commonly known as the Deprivation of Liberty Safeguards or 'DOLS') came into force.[1]

1   http://www.dh.gov.uk/en/SocialCare/Deliveringadultsocialcare/MentalCapacity/
MentalCapacityActDeprivationofLibertySafeguards/index.htm

What is 'deprivation of liberty'?

6.31   In the *Bournewood* case the European Court of Human Rights stated that in determining whether there is a deprivation of liberty 'the starting-point must be the concrete situation of the individual concerned and account must be taken of a whole range of factors arising in a particular case such as the type, duration, effects and manner of implementation of the measure in question'.[1] It will not be determinative whether a ward is locked or lockable, although this may be one relevant consideration.[2] The *Bournewood* court found that 'the clear intention of [the] health care professionals [was] to exercise strict control over [the patient] HL's assessment, treatment, contacts and, notably, movement and residence'. It was decided that the patient would be released from the hospital back to the care of his carers only as and when the professionals considered it appropriate. His contact with his carers was directed and controlled by the hospital, his carers having been prevented from visiting him at the beginning of his admission. 'Accordingly, the concrete situation was that the applicant was under continuous supervision and control and was not free to leave.'[3]

1   *HL v UK* (2004) 40 EHRR 761 at para 89.
2   *Ibid* at para 92.
3   *Ibid* at para 91.

6.32   In *JE v DE and Surrey County Council*,[1] Munby J (as he then was), in reliance on the case of *Storck v Germany*,[2] considered that three elements were required to constitute a 'deprivation of liberty' in Art 5 terms. First, an objective element of a person's confinement in a defined space for a not negligible period of time; secondly, a subjective element, namely that the person has not validly consented to the confinement (and where the person lacks capacity to consent it cannot be inferred by a lack of objection); and, thirdly, that the deprivation of liberty is by an agent of the state.

1   [2007] MHLR 39 para 77.
2   (2005) 43 EHRR 96 at paras 74 and 89.

6.33   The existence of the objective element is perhaps the most difficult aspect to assess, as stated in the *Bournewood* case:

'The distinction between a deprivation of, and a restriction upon, liberty is merely one of degree or intensity and not one of nature or substance.'[1]

1   *HL* (PARA **6.31** above N1).

6.34   In determining whether the circumstances might amount to a deprivation of liberty the purpose of the measures imposed can be a relevant consideration. In *Secretary of State for Home Dept v MHRT*,[1] the Court of Appeal found that restrictions on movement outside an institution which were designed principally for the benefit of the individual might not amount to a deprivation of liberty (applying *HM v Switzerland*[2]). Similarly, in *Secretary of State for the Home Dept v JJ* Baroness Hale suggested that in determining whether there has been a deprivation of liberty one can consider the effect of measures on the life the person would be otherwise living and that restrictions designed for the benefit of the person concerned are less likely to breach Art 5 than restrictions designed for the protection of society.[3] However, if the only or predominant determinant of a deprivation of liberty was the purpose of the measures imposed then very few cases of restriction of movement in the health and welfare setting could be found to be a deprivation of liberty and the DOLS provisions would be invoked only rarely. It is suggested that it is more likely that the purpose of the measures will be only one of many relevant factors considered by the courts when decisions about the existence of a deprivation of liberty are made.

1   [2003] MHLR 202.
2   [2002] MHLR 209; see also *Austin and Saxby v Commissioner of Police of the Metropolis* [2009] UKHL 5; [2009] 1 AC 564.
3   [2008] 1 AC 385 at 423, para 58.

6.35   There remains no definitive legal test of what a deprivation of liberty actually is and each case will be decided on its own (usually unique) facts. As was said by Lord Bingham in *JJ,* 'the Strasbourg jurisprudence must be used in the same way as other authority, as laying down principles and not mandating solutions to particular cases'.[1] Further, 'the Strasbourg jurisprudence is closely focused on the facts of particular cases, and this makes it perilous to transpose the outcome of one case to another where the facts are different.'[2]

1   See **PARA 6.34, N3** at 409 para 13.
2   *R (Gillan) v Commissioner of Police of the Metropolis* [2006] 2 AC 307 at para 23.

6.36   It has hence been recognised that 'there will be borderline cases when a decision either way cannot said to be wrong in law. The court must be careful not to interfere unless persuaded that the decision is wrong in law.'[1] It is perhaps, then, unsurprising that some first-instance judgments remain somewhat difficult to reconcile. In *LLBC v TG,*[2] an elderly and incapable demented man had been admitted to a care home identified by the local authority and although his relatives were unrestricted in their visits to him they were being prevented from removing him to live elsewhere. McFarlane J described this as a case that 'may be near the borderline' but nevertheless found the circumstances did not amount to an Art 5 deprivation of liberty. In contrast, in *JE v DE,*[3] Munby J found there was a deprivation of liberty where the wife of an incapable man placed in a care home was not permitted to take him back home. Munby J placed great emphasis on the fact that the local authority would not discharge DE to his wife's care, as he stated DE was not 'free to leave'.[4]

1   *R (G) v MHRT* [2004] EWHC (Admin) at para 20, [2004] MHLR 265.
2   *LLBC v TG,JG and HR* [2007] EWHC 2640 (Fam), [2007] MHLR 203.
3   [2007] MHLR 39.
4   *Ibid,* para 117.

Identifying a deprivation of liberty

6.37   An unenviable task is faced by those health professionals (and the lawyers who advise them) required to consider whether there is or is not a deprivation of liberty that will require authorisation. There is some assistance in the DOLS Code of Practice section entitled 'How can deprivation of liberty be identified?' which emphasises that 'all the circumstances of each and every case' must be considered.[1] Until a greater body of case-law in the health and welfare arena is built up, particularly clarifying how much weight should be put on a benevolent purpose in considering whether the Art 5 threshold is met, the following factors might be considered as pointing towards a deprivation of liberty:

● Restraint and/or sedation being used to admit to the person to the institution.

● Opposition of family/carers to the admission.

- Locks or restraint being used to keep to the person from leaving the institution.
- The person being kept away from an alternative home.
- Family and carers being refused access or other social contacts restricted.
- Staff deciding when the person is allowed out.
- Community access being restricted for the safety of others.
- Staff controlling several aspects of the person's life.
- Measures used for more than the short term.

1 Mental Capacity Act 2005: Deprivation of Liberty Safeguards Code of Practice to supplement the main Mental Capacity Act 2005 Code of Practice (TSO, London, 2008). See in particular para 2.6. http://www.dh.gov.uk/en/Publicationsandstatistics/Publications/PublicationsPolicy AndGuidance/DH_085476 .

Authorising a deprivation of liberty

6.38   Where a deprivation of liberty is taking place or is anticipated then authorisation will be required to uphold the incapable detainee's Art 5 rights. Section 4A MCA permits the authorisation to come either from a Court of Protection order or under the 'Hospital and Care Home Residents: Deprivation of Liberty' procedures in Schedule A1 to the MCA:

'4A Restriction on deprivation of liberty

(1)   This Act does not authorise any person ("D") to deprive any other person ("P") of his liberty

(2)   But that is subject to:
    (a)   the following provisions of this section, and
    (b)   section 4B.[1]

(3)   D may deprive P of his liberty if, by doing so, D is giving effect to a relevant decision of the court.

(4)   A relevant decision of the court is a decision made by an order under section 16(2)(a) in relation to a matter concerning P's personal welfare.

(5)   D may deprive P of his liberty if the deprivation is authorised by Schedule A1 (Hospital and Care Home Residents: Deprivation of Liberty).'

The s 4A(1) restrictions on the means by which a deprivation of liberty may be authorised are such that neither a court-appointed deputy nor someone with a welfare power of attorney can give consent to a deprivation of liberty.[2]

1 MCA s 4B authorises a deprivation of liberty necessary to provide either life-sustaining treatment or treatment aimed at preventing a serious deterioration in the patient's condition while a relevant decision is sought from the Court of Protection as to the authority under MCA s 4A. See **APPENDIX 1.1**: Mental Capacity Act 2005.

2 Although a donee of a lasting power of attorney or a Court-appointed deputy may authorise necessary and proportionate restraint MCA s 11(6) and s 20(13) state that a donee/deputy 'does more than merely restrain P if he deprives P of his liberty within the meaning of Article 5(1) of the Human Rights Convention'.

Court authorisation

6.39   Judges of the High Court acting in its inherent jurisdiction and, since October 2007, the Court of Protection, have had authority to authorise a course of action that deprives an incapable person of their liberty. It should be noted that the judges' statutory power under MCA s 16A to make a welfare order that deprives P of his liberty is different from the statutory power to make declarations conferred by MCA s 15.[1] In May 2008, prior to the implementation of the DOLS procedure, the Court of Protection considered the appropriate review structure to be put in place while an incapable person remained subject to an authorised care plan of the local authority the implementation of which would amount to a deprivation of liberty.[2]

1   *GJ v The Foundation Trust and Others* [2009] EWHC 2972 (Fam) at para 132(14).
2   *Salford City Council v GJ* [2008] 2 FLR 1295.

6.40   Munby J found that to comply with Art 5 ECHR a review hearing within four weeks after the making of the interim order was desirable as a matter of general practice (although a different time frame might be appropriate in some cases). There should be a court review at, or no later than, 12 months after the final hearing and thereafter at similar intervals, so long as the deprivation of liberty continued. Between the court reviews there needed to be regular internal reviews and provision should be made for this in the final order. Munby J stated[1] that it was vital that the Official Solicitor or other litigation friend should participate fully in internal reviews. The continuing role of the litigation friend would therefore not have concluded with the final order. However, no matter what internal review structure was put in place, evidence of any significant change had to prompt speedy consideration of the need for calling an internal review. Up-to-date reports were needed for review hearings but unless there had been any material change in the relevant circumstances they could be appropriately brief. Munby J held that Art 5(4) did not necessitate an oral hearing at every annual review.[2]

1   See **PARA 6.39 N2**, paras 27–47.
2   An example order reflecting a similar review procedure is at **APPENDIX 6.2**.

The DOLS procedure

6.41   The 'Hospital and Care Home Residents: Deprivation of Liberty' procedures ('DOLS') set out an entire new system to govern admission, detention, reviews and appeals of those incapable patients who are deprived of their liberty in hospitals or registered care homes. The DOLS procedure is found in the lengthy and complex additions to the MCA in Schedule A1 and Schedule 1A MCA 2005. The provisions set out how an application for authorisation is made; the criteria for granting authorisation; when review must take place and how reviews are to be conducted, the support and representation to which incapable people are entitled in the process; and the appeal process. The cumbersome DOLS procedure is dealt with in detail in the many textbooks dedicated to the subject and hence only a very brief summary is given here (and see **APPENDIX 6.4**).

6.42   Generally the procedure will be commenced when the 'Managing Authority' of a hospital or registered care home believes the circumstances in which someone is to be admitted to their institution are such that a deprivation of liberty may occur. The 'Managing Authority' is required to seek authorisation from its relevant 'Supervisory Body' (which will be a Primary Care Trust for a hospital or a local authority for a care home). The 'Supervisory Body' can then give standard authorisation (in advance) permitting detention of the incapable person for up to 12 months. If an emergency situation arises where the deprivation of liberty cannot be delayed pending a standard authorisation being given then the Managing Authority can self-authorise the deprivation of liberty with an interim 'urgent' authorisation which can last for up to 7 days and is renewable only once.

6.43 The standard authorisation will be given if the 'qualifying requirements' are met following six professional assessments being carried out within 21 days.[1] These are: a 'Best Interests' assessment (whether the proposed plan of care will in fact deprive P of liberty and is in the person's best interests, necessary and proportionate); a 'Mental Health' assessment (whether the person suffers with a mental disorder); a 'Mental Capacity' assessment (whether the person lacks capacity to decide whether to be accommodated as proposed) an 'Age' assessment (whether the person is over 18 years old); a 'No Refusals' assessment (whether the deprivation of liberty conflicts with a valid advance directive or valid decision of someone with power of proxy); and an 'Eligibility' assessment (whether the person is ineligible because the authorisation would conflict with a pre-existing MHA obligation or because the person is indicating objection and falls within the scope of the MHA).[2]

1   MCA DOLS standard forms can be found at: http://www.dh.gov.uk/en/Publications andstatistics/Publications/PublicationsPolicyAndGuidance/DH_089772 .
2   Schedule 1A sets out these eligibility criteria and the interaction of MCA with the MHA.

6.44 The DOLS procedure has been described by Gunn as being 'Byzantine in the extreme'[1] and:

'Given that what is being authorised is an interference less than that authorised through the Mental Health Act 1983, it is difficult to justify this complex approach. Reading any of the works on the process makes it clear that it is complex in the extreme.'[2]

1   M Gunn, 'Hospital Treatment for Incapacitated Adults' [2009] Med Law Rev 1 at 6.
2   *Ibid.* at 7.

MCA or MHA?

6.45 The existence of two apparently overlapping legislative schemes permitting detention for treatment has led to some confusion over which power to detain and treat can and/or should be relied upon in a particular case. In broad terms a DOLS authorisation will be required (because the MHA will be inapplicable) when one wishes to deprive an incapable person of their liberty for welfare reasons or for medical treatment of a physical disorder that does not arise from a mental disorder.[1] If treatment for mental disorder is to be given then with the incapable but compliant patient there is potentially a choice between the provisions of the MCA or the MHA. However, as the MHA code of practice states:

'If the MCA can be used safely and effectively to assess or treat a patient, it is likely to be difficult to demonstrate that the criteria for detaining the patient under the Mental Health Act are met.'[2]

The MHA will be required where the purpose of the detention is to treat a mental disorder in hospital and the patient is indicating any dissent to the proposed care plan. This is because in this latter case it is likely that neither a DOLS authorisation nor an order of the Court of Protection could be relied upon as the powers under the MCA are specifically curtailed by s 16A(1) of the MCA which provides that:

'If a person is ineligible to be deprived of liberty by this Act, the court may not include in a welfare order provision which authorises the person to be deprived of his liberty.'

1 See **PARA 6.2** above (**N1** *GJ v The Foundation Trust* [2009] EWHC 2972 (Fam)) and the more detailed discussion of the extent of powers to treat physical disorder under MHA, s 63 in **CHAPTER 10**: Feeding and **CHAPTER 13**: Suicide.
2 At para 4.22.

6.46   The eligibility criteria for DOLS, which are found in MCA, Schedule 1A, are complex, but in summary a person will be ineligible for DOLS authorisation if (1) they are currently subject to detention under the MHA; or (2) they are subject to an order under MHA which imposes conditions (such as guardianship (s 7), a community treatment order (s 17A) or trial leave (s 17)) and the DOLS authorisation sought would conflict with any of those conditions; or (3) the authorisation is sought to detain the person for treatment of mental disorder in a hospital (as defined in MHA) and they fall within the scope of the MHA and object (by word or action) either to being detained or to some or all of the proposed treatment under detention.

6.47   However, *A Primary Care Trust v TB*[1] clarified that if the patient's objection relates to detention for mental health treatment that is to be provided in a registered care home as opposed to in a hospital setting (such as specialist rehabilitative treatment) then the ineligibility criteria will not apply and an authorisation under MCA may be provided even where the patient objects to that detention and/or treatment.

1 [2009] EWHC 1737 (Fam).

6.48   It is important to remember that although the purpose of the authorised deprivation of liberty may be to treat the patient, the DOLS process itself does not authorise that treatment. To be lawful, the proposed assessment or treatment must still be either (1) such that it falls within MCA, s 5; or (2) the subject of a Court of Protection order; or (3) performed with the patient's capable consent [1]; or (4) performed with the consent of a welfare deputy or someone with a welfare power of attorney.[2]

1 Because capacity is issue specific (see **CHAPTER 2**: Consent – Adults at **PARA 2.5**) a patient who meets the mental capacity requirement for DOLS (because he lacks capacity to decide where he should be accommodated) may nevertheless have capacity to consent to treatment.
2 This requires that the welfare deputy has been given sufficient powers. MCA s 16(5) states: 'The court may ... confer on a deputy such powers or impose on him such duties, as it thinks necessary or expedient for giving effect to, or otherwise in connection with, an order or

appointment made by it under subsection (2).' And see **CHAPTER 3**: Deciding for Others – Adults **PARAS 3.3** and **3.9**.

D CONCLUSION

6.49   The issues surrounding restraint and deprivation of liberty are complex, not least because of the challenges involved in first identifying when a deprivation of liberty in terms of Art 5 ECHR is likely to be occurring and then attempting to disentangle the complex provisions of the MCA. The MCA DOLS provisions are at an early stage of implementation, with very few decisions yet reported. However, as a body of decided cases is built up it can be hoped that the landscape will become much clearer for lawyers (although as Gunn[1] remarks it is 'completely unrealistic' to expect health and social work professionals to be able to keep up with the relevant case-law), and it may be that many challenges of DOLS decisions can be expected for the future.

1   M Gunn, 'Hospital Treatment for Incapacitated Adults' [2009] Med Law Rev 1.

For updating material and hyperlinks related to this chapter, see: www.3serjeantsinn.com/mtdl/restraint

Part 2

Specific Problems

Chapter 7

Sterilisation

A   General 7.1
B   The competent patient 7.2
     General rule 7.2
     Informed consent 7.3
     The role of partner/spouse 7.4
     Procedure 7.5
C   Adults 7.6
     Competent adults 7.6
     Adults lacking capacity to consent 7.7
         Capacity 7.7
         Best interests 7.8
         General application of 'best interests' principle in sterilisation
         cases 7.9
         The immediacy of the risks 7.18
     Procedure 7.19
D   Children 7.20
     General principle 7.20
         Children with no learning disabilities 7.20
         Children with learning disabilities 7.21
     Best interests 7.22
     Procedure 7.23
E   Conclusion 7.24

A GENERAL

7.1   Sterilisation is one of the most fundamental forms of medical treatment that can be provided. It removes, often permanently, the ability to reproduce. Medically it is now relatively simply achieved and therefore the temptation to solve perceived social problems by this route may be increased. While the procedure is performed on men and women who consent to it as a matter of routine, this will always be a socially sensitive area, requiring meticulous attention to counselling and consent protocols if the anxieties provoked by history are to be allayed.

7.1   Sterilisation

As with any other invasive procedure, sterilisation cannot be performed without the consent of the competent patient. Usual procedures for obtaining consent apply.[1] Particular attention must, however, be paid to the need to explain to the patient the risks associated with the procedure.

Sterilisation of people unable to make their own decisions is an emotive and sensitive subject and any case involving it must be treated with considerable care and caution. There are obvious reasons for this.

The twentieth century has seen horrific policies implemented with the objective of promoting ethnic purity. The Nazis embarked on widespread sterilisation of particular groups, including the mentally disabled, as part of their overall plan of Aryanisation. Less well remembered is the policy followed by many states in the USA encouraging the compulsory sterilisation of mental patients, a policy found to be constitutional by the Supreme Court in 1927 where Holmes J felt able to declare:[2]

'Three generations of imbeciles is enough.'

Such attitudes have largely disappeared by reason of the emphasis placed on human rights now recognised in domestic law, in particular the right to a private and family life and the right to found a family.[3] The proposal to sterilise someone without their consent or even comprehension may, at first blush, seem a denial of these fundamental rights and a return to dated and repugnant attitudes.

Countervailing considerations may arise, however. Paternalistic attitudes towards the care of those with learning disabilities have to some extent been replaced with a desire to enable such people to live as independent and fulfilled lives as possible. A potential partner who lacks capacity to consent may be prevented from having sexual intercourse because of the disadvantages, both psychological and physical, of producing children. Sterilisation may, however, allow a fulfilling sexual relationship to develop without the concern associated with the trauma and damage likely to be caused through pregnancy and/or birth. In such circumstances, sterilisation, rather than being a restriction on a person's liberties, can be a means of freeing a person with learning disabilities from the constraints that would otherwise be necessary.

The last three decades have seen an increasing awareness of and concern about the vulnerability of those who cannot care for themselves, highlighted by incidences of sexual abuse by carers and others. It is in this context that the supervision of those who care for vulnerable people has become increasingly strict. Proposals for sterilisation for non-therapeutic reasons should be regarded as a final option following the attempt and failure of all other reasonable alternatives to address the concerns thought to arise in any particular case. Given the enormity of what is being sought and the competing considerations in evaluating such a proposal , the sterilisation of a patient, whether child or adult, should not be undertaken without an appropriate application being made to the court and a thorough examination of the evidence and all relevant issues.

1   See **CHAPTER 1**: Consent – General.
2   *Buck v Bell* 247 US 200 at 207 (1927).
3   Human Rights Act 1998; the European Convention on Human Rights, Arts 8 and 12.

B THE COMPETENT PATIENT

General rule

7.2   No sterilisation should be performed on a competent patient without his consent. There are likely to be very few, if any, exceptions to this rule. Where in the course of some other operation, for example a Caesarean section, it is considered necessary to perform some further operation the result of which would be to sterilise the patient, it would be most unwise to proceed without consent unless it can definitely be demonstrated that the preservation of the life or health of the patient requires immediate intervention before consent can be obtained. It should not be presumed that a patient would have consented to such a step.

Informed consent

7.3   While ostensibly the transatlantic doctrine of informed consent forms no part of English law,[1] there is a duty to abide by the practice of a body of responsible and competent professional opinion in relation to warning patients of the potential consequences and risks of the proposed procedure.

It is now general professional practice, and therefore a requirement of the duty of care, for patients to be counselled as to the risks of the sterilisation not being effective and as to any interim precautions that ought to be taken until confirmatory tests or examinations have been performed. Failure to comply with such a practice will render the medical practitioner liable in an action for negligence should the patient consent to what turns out to be an ineffective sterilisation in reliance on defective counselling. Damages awarded may include compensation for the pregnancy and birth but in general will not now include damages for the maintenance of the child.[2] In such an action, application of traditional causation principles necessitates proof that the patient would not have consented to the procedure but for the defective counselling.[3] NHS Trusts usually have standard forms of consent for sterilisation,[4] but practitioners need to be aware that the completion of a form does not necessarily amount to proof that the duty in relation to counselling has been fulfilled.[5]

1   *Sidaway v Board of Governors of the Bethlem Royal Hospital and the Maudsley Hospital* [1985] AC 871, [1985] 2 WLR 480, [1985] All ER 643; see further detailed discussion in **Chapter 1**: Consent – General.
2   *MacFarlane v Tayside Health Board* [2000] 2 AC 59, [1999] 3 WLR 1301 restricted the right to recovery of maintenance of a child. Note the subsequent decision in *Rand v East Dorset Health Authority* (2000) 56 BMLR 39. *MacFarlane* was considered in *Rees v Darlington Memorial Hospital NHS Trust* [2004] 1 AC 309, [2003] 3 WLR 1091, where a disabled mother who gave birth to a healthy child following a negligently performed sterilisation was held not to be entitled to recover the extra costs of child care attributable to her disability. However, a conventional award of £15,000 was made to mark the legal wrong and to reflect loss of the opportunity to limit the size of her family and to live life as planned. That award was in addition to any compensatory award related to the pregnancy and birth.
3   *Rance v Mid-Downs Health Authority* [1991] 1 QB 587, [1991] 2 WLR 159, [1991] 1 All ER 801. Note, however, the narrow modification of traditional causation principles introduced by majority in *Chester v Afshar* [2005] 1 AC 134 with a view to vindication of the patient's right of choice and to provide a remedy for the failure to warn of risk.

4   See **APPENDIX 7.1**: Previous Consent Form (sterilisation or vasectomy).
5   See **CHAPTER 1, PARA 1.11**.

The role of partner/spouse

7.4   As in other areas of patient care, there is no duty in law to obtain the consent of the spouse or partner of the patient who is to be sterilised. Further, the consent of the partner or spouse does not amount to legal authority for the procedure, even if the patient is unconscious or otherwise unable to give consent at the time. However, where the patient is accompanied to consultations by the partner or spouse and the patient wishes him or her to be included in the counselling and to participate in the decision, then the medical practitioner is likely to be found to owe a duty of care to the partner or spouse, as well as the patient. Family planning is, after all, a family matter, with consequences for persons other than the patient and is an area where many patients will wish to share the decision-making process.

On the other hand, there is no duty on the part of the medical practitioner to include the spouse or partner in the decision-making process, unless the patient wishes this to happen. A third party has no right to prevent a sterilisation procedure taking place any more than a termination of pregnancy.[1]

1   *Paton v British Pregnancy Advisory Service Trustees* [1979] QB 276, [1978] 3 WLR 687, [1978] 2 All ER 987; *Paton v United Kingdom* (1980) 3 EHRR 408.

Procedure[1]

7.5   While in principle there is no legal distinction between the requirements for obtaining consent to a sterilisation and the requirements for any other form of medical treatment, it would be prudent in the interests of both the patient and the medical practitioner to ensure not only that a proper counselling process has taken place, but that there is proof available of this, in a form which also provides a reminder to the patient of the advice and a corresponding entry in the clinical notes.

Therefore the following steps should be considered:

- Adequate time – well in advance of the proposed procedure (to allow those giving consent to reflect upon what they have been told and ask further questions) – should be allowed for counselling.
- The counselling should be performed by the medical practitioner who is to perform the procedure or a practitioner who is in possession of adequate knowledge of the available techniques, the proposed method, the general outcome figures for that procedure as compared with all others and, where it is known, the outcome rates of the practitioner who is to perform the operation.
- While much information may be provided in written form, it is unwise to rely solely on printed leaflets without ensuring by discussion that the patient understands the information provided.
- The patient may be encouraged to involve the spouse or partner in the discussion but the decision whether to do so is the patient's not the medical practitioner's.

- If possible, the patient should be provided with a written summary of the information provided in counselling. While general information might be in the form of a leaflet, information specific to the patient will need to be in a letter or similar form.
- The medical practitioner should keep a record of the advice given. While the record of routine information might be reduced to a common printed form, it is more convincing proof of what has been said if it is recorded at the time of the consultation (in the clinical notes) and is specific to the patient.

1 See **CHAPTER 5**: Going to Court.

C ADULTS

Competent adults

7.6   The general principles are dealt with above.

Adults lacking capacity to consent

Capacity

7.7   The mental capacity of an adult to consent to a sterilisation procedure is no different from that applicable to any other form of medical treatment.[1] As, however, the procedure is intended to be irreversible and involves the fundamental right to reproduce and found a family, the capacity must be commensurate with the gravity of the decision to be taken.[2] Therefore, although there is a presumption that patients have capacity, unless the contrary is shown, it is incumbent on those proposing to perform a sterilisation procedure to ensure that the patient has the requisite degree of capacity. Doctors who proceed on an assumption of capacity risk a subsequent retrospective finding that their patient lacked the relevant capacity. If a finding of incapacity is made it must be considered whether this is likely to be permanent or whether there is some prospect of it being regained. Sterilisation is unlikely to be an appropriate step in the interests of the patient, if capacity may be regained in the foreseeable future.

1 See **CHAPTER 2**: Consent – Adults, especially **PARA 2.1**.
2 *Re T (adult: refusal of treatment)* [1993] Fam 95 at 113.

Best interests

7.8   Where an adult lacks the mental capacity to consent to sterilisation it will be lawful for the operation to be performed if it is in the patient's best interests.[1] Where the procedure is 'non-therapeutic', that is, for contraceptive purposes and not ancillary to the treatment of some physical condition, a declaration of the court should be sought that the procedure is lawful before embarking on it: it falls into the special category of cases where such a step is required. In *Re GF*[2] it was stated that it was not necessary to apply to court where two medical practitioners are satisfied that a procedure which will sterilise the patient is:

'(1) necessary for therapeutic purposes, (2) in the best interests of the patient, and (3) that there is no practicable, less intrusive means of treating the condition.'[3]

In *Re S*[4] the Court of Appeal stressed that parties should err on the side of bringing sterilisation cases before the court. The President noted that the *Re GF* criteria should be 'cautiously interpreted and applied':[5]

'if a particular case lies anywhere near the [*Re GF*] boundary line it should be referred to the court by way of application for a declaration of lawfulness.[6]

Thus, even in 'therapeutic' sterilisation cases, the court will examine critically whether the sterilisation is in the patient's best interests.[7]

The potential for confusion about how the patient's best interests are to be judged is discussed in **CHAPTER 2** above. In sterilisation cases, as in others, in practice the court will judge for itself where the best interests of the patient lie paying all due regard to medical opinion.

'Best interests' encompasses medical, emotional and all other welfare issues. The court will examine the proportionality of the proposed treatment as against the problem to be solved. Although a doctor must assess the patient's best interests in accordance with a professional standard of care, the court will not be bound by a medical opinion but will seek the best answer from the alternatives available. In the words of Thorpe LJ:[8]

'In practice, the dispute will generally require the court to choose between two or more possible treatments both or all of which comfortably pass the *Bolam* test. As most of us know from experience, a patient contemplating treatment for a physical condition or illness is often offered a range of alternatives with counter-balancing advantages and disadvantages. One of the most important services provided by a consultant is to explain the available alternatives to the patient, particularly concentrating on those features of advantage and disadvantage most relevant to his needs and circumstances. In a developing relationship of confidence the consultant then guides the patient to make the choice that best suits his circumstances and personality. It is precisely because the patient is prevented by disability from that exchange that the judge must in certain circumstances either exercise the choice between alternative available treatments or perhaps refuse any form of treatment. In deciding what is best for the disabled patient the judge must have regard to the patient's welfare as the paramount consideration. That embraces issues far wider than the medical. Indeed it would be undesirable and probably impossible to set bounds to what is relevant to a welfare determination.'

1   *Re F (mental patient: sterilisation)* [1990] 2 AC 1.
2   [1992] 1 FLR 293.
3   At 294 per Butler-Sloss P. Note also *Re E (a minor) (medical treatment)* [1991] 2 FLR 585; *F v F* (unreported, *The Times*, April 29, 1991) where sterilisation was the incidental result of hysterectomy considered necessary.

4   *Re S (Sterilisation)* [2000] 2 FLR 389, [2000] 2 FCR 452, [2000] Fam Law 711.
5   [2000] 2 FLR 389 at 401 per Butler-Sloss P.
6   [2000] 2 FLR 389 at 405 per Thorpe LJ.
7   *Re S* (N4 above); and see *Re Z (medical treatment: hysterectomy)* [2000] 1 FLR 523, [2000] 1 FCR 274.
8   *Re S (Sterilisation)* [2000] 2 FLR 389 at 403.

General application of 'best interests' principle in sterilisation cases

7.9   While every case will obviously turn on its own facts, reference should be made to the cases that have been before the courts for guidance on the considerations that will be taken into account in deciding on the patient's best interests.[1]

It is suggested that the following factors are among those which need to be considered.

1   *Re F (mental patient: sterilisation)* [1990] 2 AC 1; *Re W* [1993] 1 FLR 381; *Re LC (medical treatment: sterilisation)* [1997] 2 FLR 258; *Re S (adult sterilisation)* [1998] 1 FLR 944; *Re X (adult sterilisation)* [1998] 2 FLR 1124; *Re A (medical treatment: male sterilisation)* [2000] 1 FLR 549, CA; sub nom *Re A (male: sterilisation)*.

The capacity of the patient

7.10   While patients may lack the capacity to consent to sterilisation, they may be able to take decisions about their sexual life, perhaps guided by skilled counselling. The disability of others may not be permanent. If there is a prospect of improvement, certainly if there is a chance that a patient will regain the capacity to consent to treatment, or to marriage, then it would be highly unlikely that the court would find sterilisation in his best interests.[1]

In *London Borough of Ealing v KS*[2] a 33 year old woman suffering from a severe learning disability and schizo-affective disorder lapsed periodically into mental illness. Following her third marriage, an issue arose as to whether she had capacity to consent to marriage. It was declared that the marriage would not be recognised as valid, that she did not have the capacity to litigate or consent to marriage and was unlikely ever to have the capacity so to do, as she did not understand the nature of the marriage contract or the duties and responsibilities that normally attach to a marriage. She also lacked capacity to make a decision about surgery to remove an ovarian cyst. Applying the best interests test, and balancing the relevant factors, it was held undoubtedly to be in her best interests for that procedure to be carried out and, if medically necessary, to proceed to an oophorectomy. However, it was held not to be in her best interest's that the hospital should carry out the insertion of an IUD contraceptive device at the same time where the hospital proposed to consider that issue at a multi-disciplinary meeting one month after the surgery. The evidence revealed a fluctuating capacity to consent to sexual intercourse. Accordingly, her carers were to be provided with a clear list of the indicators of a possible loss of capacity to make decisions about sexual intercourse or other sexual contacts, so that they might recognise them and act consistently with her other carers in establishing where the dial pointed on the barometer of capacity. The court considered it to be too early to come to a determination of the issues of capacity and best interests on the subject of contraception.

1   *Re D (a minor) (wardship: sterilisation)* [1976] Fam 185 at 195. While this case concerned a
     child, there is no reason why the factors considered would not be relevant in the case of an
     adult.
2   [2008] EWHC 636.

The risk of sexual contact

7.11   Many disabled people will be sheltered from the chance of sexual contact for their own protection and that of other disabled people they may meet in residential homes and day centres whether or not they are capable of reproduction. Others will have evinced no or little interest in such contact. Thus one of the reasons in *Re D (a minor) (wardship: sterilisation)* for the declaration being refused was that the patient:

> 'had as yet shown no interest in the opposite sex, and ... her opportunities for promiscuity, if she were so minded, were virtually non-existent, as her mother never leaves her side and she is never allowed out alone.'[1]

In *Re B (a minor) (wardship: sterilisation)*, on the other hand, the patient was showing signs of sexual awareness and drive and her carers' philosophy was to allow her as much freedom as was consistent with her disability.[2]

Similarly, in *Re F (mental patient: sterilisation)* the patient had benefited from being given a greater degree of freedom of movement within the hospital grounds and had already formed an attachment with a fellow patient which was not thought to be harmful.[3] In *Re W*[4] the presence of such a risk influenced the court in favour of the declaration. In contrast, the possibility of a risk arising in the future may not be sufficient.[5] The risk may need to be 'identifiable' as opposed to 'speculative'.[6]

1   [1976] Fam 185 at 194.
2   [1988] AC 199 at 208.
3   [1990] 2 AC 1 at 9.
4   [1993] 1 FLR 381.
5   *Re LC (medical treatment: sterilisation)* [1997] 2 FLR 258; *Re S (adult sterilisation)* [1998]
     1 FLR 944 at 949, c f *Re X (adult sterilisation)* [1998] 2 FLR 1124 at 1126–1127.
6   *Re S (adult sterilisation)* [1998] 1 FLR 944 at 949.

The availability of other methods of contraception

7.12   This is a central consideration: the sensitivity concerning sterilisation is because of its irreversibility; if reversible methods of preventing conception can be used, they should be. All practical contraceptive methods should be considered before sterilisation is canvassed. In *Re D* the judge found that other methods could be used, if contraception was necessary.[1] In *Re B*[2] and in *Re F*[3], by contrast, an oral contraceptive had been found to produce undesirable side-effects. In *Re ZM and OS*[4] the court considered the case of Z, a 19-year-old with Down's syndrome. She had menstrual periods that were heavy, painful and irregular. There was medical disagreement about what was in Z's best interests. Bennett J determined that a 'Mirena' contraceptive coil was not sufficient to achieve the aim of stopping Z's troubling periods and that it was in her best interests to undergo a laparoscopic subtotal hysterectomy.

In contrast, in *Re S*[5] the Court of Appeal over-turned the first-instance judge's determination that a subtotal hysterectomy should be performed on a 29-year-old woman with severe learning disabilities. The Court of Appeal decided that the judge had failed to give sufficient weight to the unanimous medical opinion which favoured using the less invasive 'Mirena' coil. While S's mother favoured hysterectomy, the Court of Appeal held – applying a true 'best interests' test[6] – that it was appropriate first to undertake the less invasive coil procedure and only if it failed would it be appropriate for the matter to be returned to court to consider whether hysterectomy should be undertaken.[7]

Where a patient is developing a relationship of significance, consideration should be given to the capacity and maturity of his/her partner. Thus, even if it is felt that the patient does not have the ability adequately to ensure birth control, if their partner can adequately ensure that contraception is used then there is no current need for sterilisation.

1   [1976] Fam 185 at 195.
2   [1988] AC 199 at 207.
3   [1990] 2 AC 1 at 10.
4   *Re Z (medical treatment: hysterectomy)* [2000] 1 FLR 523, [2000] 1 FCR 274.
5   *Re S (Sterilisation)* [2000] 2 FLR 389.
6   Discussed above in **CHAPTER 3**: Deciding for Others – Adults, **PARA 3.14**.
7   *Re S (Sterilisation)* [2000] 2 FLR 389 at 401 per Butler-Sloss P.

The need for counselling and preparation

7.13   Expert evidence was adduced in *Re A*[1] to the effect that sterilisation on its own was not a solution to the problems involved in allowing a patient with learning disabilities to enjoy sexual relations and that there was a need for counselling and education which it was the duty of local services to provide. The Court of Appeal commented that to expect such facilities to be available might be unrealistic. Nonetheless, it might be thought that it would be a denial of the right of the patient with learning disabilities to lead as full and rewarding a life as possible to claim that sterilisation on its own is likely to be a solution to the problems involved.

1   *Re A (medical treatment: male sterilisation)* [2000] 1 FLR 549, CA; sub nom *Re A (male sterilisation)*.

The risks of pregnancy

7.14   In some patients with mental disabilities the experience of pregnancy would be disastrous because of a lack of understanding of the process or its consequences or an inability to care for a child with consequent adverse effects on the patient's mental and physical condition.[1]

1   For example, *T v T* [1988] Fam 52, where the patient had already become pregnant and required a termination as well as sterilisation; *Re B (a minor) (wardship: sterilisation)* [1988] AC 199 at 208–209; *Re F (mental patient: sterilisation)* [1990] 2 AC 1 at 10: 'For F to become pregnant would be a disaster ... She has a much diminished ability to cope with the problems of pregnancy and would not be able to cope with labour or looking after the child once born.

Professor B ... used the word "catastrophic" to describe the psychiatric consequences of her having a child.'

Freedom of association

7.15   In some cases the patient can be given more freedom to associate with others and form friendships which might be dangerous if there was a risk of pregnancy. The patient in *Re F[1]* was clearly enjoying her relationship with a man with whom she could not be safely left on her own because the encounters risked a catastrophic pregnancy.

1   [1990] 2 AC 1.

The effect on the standard of care

7.16   It is sometimes argued that the knowledge that a patient is incapable of reproduction will cause the regime of supervision and care to be slackened, even when his or her interests would still require a high level of protection from exploitation and other dangers.

Male patients

7.17   To date we are aware of only one application to the court seeking a declaration for the sterilisation of a male.[1] This was refused as not being in his best interests, although there was evidence that he was sexually aware and might proceed to sexual intercourse if not prevented from doing so.[2] However, there was no immediate risk of his being allowed to have casual intercourse and he enjoyed no stable relationship in which this was likely to be permitted. The risks that a disabled partner might become impregnated were not taken into account as being relevant. It may also be due to the greater difficulty in identifying the advantages of sterilisation to the male patient as opposed to his carers and associates.

1   *Re A (medical treatment: male sterilisation)* [2000] 1 FLR 549, CA.
2   Mr James Munby QC (as he then was) commented in his chapter in *Principles of Medical Law* (Grubb, OUP, 2004), p 292 (fn 535) that this scarcity of cases is: 'A revealing insight into societal attitudes to gender, sexuality and contraception.'

The immediacy of the risks

7.18   The court will be slow to grant an order approving of a non-therapeutic sterilisation unless the risks identified as justifying the operation are present risks and not theoretical future risks. Evidence should be adduced which establishes that the condition which it is sought to avoid will in fact occur. For example, in the case of a contraceptive sterilisation, that there is a need for contraception because: (a) the patient is physically capable of procreation; and (b) the patient is likely to engage in sexual activity, at the present or in the near future, under circumstances where there is a real danger (as opposed to mere chance) that pregnancy is likely to result.

The cases at first instance now establish that there must be a clearly identifiable risk against which sterilisation is the only practicable means of protecting the patient. Thus, in three recent cases[1] declarations have been refused because there was no immediate realistic chance of the patient being allowed to have sexual contact whether or not there was a sterilisation. These cases emphasise that a desire to prevent a mentally disabled person procreating is no reason of itself to permit a sterilisation to be performed.

1   *Re LC (medical treatment: sterilisation)* [1997] 2 FLR 258; *Re S (adult sterilisation)* [1998] 1 FLR 944 at 944; *Re A (medical treatment: male sterilisation)* [2000] 1 FLR 549; c f *Re X (adult sterilisation)* [1998] 2 FLR 1124 at 1126–1127.

Procedure[1]

7.19   Where it is proposed to perform a non-therapeutic sterilisation operation on a patient incapable of consenting to the procedure, there should be the fullest consultation with the carers, and any close relatives who have a caring role, about the need for the procedure, the circumstances in which the patient lives and the benefits and disadvantages of proceeding.

Cases involving proposals to perform a non-therapeutic sterilisation operation on a patient incapable of consenting to the procedure are to be regarded as concerning 'serious medical treatment' for the purposes of the Court of Protection Rules and Practice Direction E – Applications Relating to Serious Medical Treatment.[2] Where it is apparent that a court application will have to be made in order to sanction the performance of the proposed procedure,[3] the application in relation to an adult will be made to the Court of Protection.[4]

It would be prudent for those making the application to have available the favourable opinion of an independent surgical expert and of a psychiatrist specialising in the rehabilitation and care of patients with learning difficulties. The court has power to control the evidence adduced including the discipline and identity of expert witnesses, whether their evidence is to be admitted only in writing and whether they are to attend for cross-examination.[5] While the court will have the power to order there to be a single expert, this is unlikely to be desirable in any other than the most clear and undisputed case in this field. The whole purpose of the matter coming before the court is to ensure that the issues are properly examined in the interests of the patient and the public; there will be a danger of the public perceiving the court as merely rubber-stamping the opinion of the appointed expert if this sort of restriction were to gain currency.

1   See **CHAPTER 5**: Going to Court.
2   Part 5(c) of *Practice Direction E – Applications Relating to Serious Medical Treatment,* reproduced at **APPENDIX 5.4**.
3   See **PARA 7.18**: no application will usually be needed when the procedure is necessary for therapeutic purposes, in the best interests of the patient, and, importantly, that there is no practicable, less intrusive means of treating the condition. If there is any doubt whether all these factors are satisfied an application should be made: see *Re S (Sterilisation)* [2000] 2 FLR 389.
4   See **CHAPTER 5**: Going to Court.
5   Court of Protection Rules 2007, Parts 14 and 15.

D CHILDREN

General principle

Children with no learning disabilities

7.20   It will obviously be rare for anyone to wish to sterilise a child who is expected to grow up into a mentally competent adult for non-therapeutic or 'social' reasons. It is difficult to think of circumstances in which any competent medical practitioner would wish to carry out such an operation or in which a person with parental responsibility would be willing to consent to it. If such a thing were contemplated, the procedures referred to in the next section would have to be considered.

On occasion it will be necessary to consider treatment required for compelling therapeutic reasons which will have the side-effect of sterilising the patient. Radiotherapy or surgery in the area of the uterus for cancer are examples. Obviously, the effects of such treatment must be discussed very carefully with those having parental responsibility and, to the extent that is appropriate having regard to the age and maturity of the child, with the patient. However, if the treatment is consented to in accordance with the general principles governing authority for treating a child, it may be performed without reference to the courts.

Children with learning disabilities

7.21   Where children with learning disabilities require treatment for therapeutic reasons which will have sterilisation as a side-effect, it may be authorised in the same way as for children without such disabilities.

Occasionally it has been thought necessary to propose sterilisation of a child with mental disabilities for the sole purpose of preventing the child becoming pregnant. This is properly to be regarded as an exceptional course of action to propose and one which will be the subject of the closest judicial scrutiny.

In the first such case to come before the English courts,[1] concerning an 11-year-old girl suffering from Sotos syndrome, whose mother was anxious, with the support of a surgeon, that she should be prevented from having children, the proposal received short shrift. As the case has conditioned much of the approach by the courts to this class of case, it is worth setting out part of the judgment in full:[2]

'Dr Gordon, however, maintained that provided the parent or parents consented the decision was one made pursuant to the exercise of his clinical judgement and that no interference could be tolerated in his clinical freedom. The other consultants did not agree. Their opinion was that a decision to sterilise a child was not entirely within a doctor's clinical judgment, save only when sterilisation was the treatment of choice for some disease, as for instance, when in order to treat a child and to ensure her direct physical well-being, it might be necessary to perform a hysterectomy to remove a malignant uterus. Whilst the side effect of such an operation would be to sterilise, the operation would be solely performed for therapeutic purposes.

I entirely accept their opinions. I cannot believe, and the evidence does not warrant the view, that a decision to carry out an operation of this nature performed for non-therapeutic purposes on a minor can be held to be within the doctor's sole clinical judgement.

It is quite clear that once a child is a ward of court no important step in the life of that child can be taken without the consent of the court, and I cannot conceive of a more important step than that which was proposed in this case.

A review of the whole of the evidence leads me to the conclusion that in a case of a child of 11 years of age, where the evidence shows that her mental and physical condition and attainments have already improved, and where her future prospects are as yet unpredictable, where the evidence also shows that she is unable as yet to understand and appreciate the implications of this operation and could not give a valid or informed consent, but the likelihood is that in later years she will be able to make her own choice, where, I believe, the frustration and resentment of realising (as she would one day) what had happened could be devastating, an operation of this nature is, in my view, contraindicated.

For these, and for the other reasons, to which I have adverted, I have come to the conclusion that this operation is neither medically indicated nor necessary, and that it would not be in D's best interests for it to be performed.'

It should be noted that the support of a responsible medical practitioner and of a caring mother advocating the procedure was insufficient to persuade the court to allow it. The sole test was whether the procedure was then and there in the best interests of the child. To the judge the answer was that the procedure was clearly not in the child's best interests.

In contrast, the House of Lords[3] permitted the sterilisation of a 17-year-old suffering from a moderate degree of mental handicap and very limited intellectual development, determining that it was in her best interests. The evidence was that she was showing signs of sexual awareness and that pregnancy would have been highly detrimental to her well-being. However, *Re D* has influenced judges in later cases to place a heavy restriction on how decisions in such cases should be taken. In a speech which was not expressly supported by the other Law Lords, Lord Templeman expressed the view that:[4]

'sterilisation of a girl under 18 should only be carried out with the leave of a High Court judge. A doctor performing a sterilisation operation with the consent of the parents might still be liable in criminal, civil or professional proceedings. A court exercising the wardship jurisdiction emanating from the Crown is the only authority which is empowered to authorise such a drastic step as sterilisation after a full and informed investigation.'

This statement cannot be taken literally. It has been since pointed out by Lord Donaldson of Lymington that an operation performed with the consent of the parents on a girl who was not a ward of court would not necessarily be unlawful. However, it laid down a practice which ought to be followed:

> 'I think he was combining two propositions. First, he was saying that no such operation ought ever to be undertaken without the court's approval even if the parents or the child consented and that if such an operation was contemplated the child should be made a ward of court and the leave of the court sought.[5] Second, he was saying that, where this was done, the decision was of such difficulty and delicacy that it should be undertaken not only by a High Court judge, but one having special experience.'[6]

In the same case Lord Griffiths said of *Re D (a minor) (wardship: sterilisation)* that:[7]

> 'it stands as a stark warning of the danger of leaving the decision to sterilise in the hands of those having the immediate care of the woman, even when they genuinely believe that they are acting in her best interests.'

The position in relation to children is, therefore, that, although a sterilisation operation for non-therapeutic reasons might be lawful if performed with the consent of a person having parental responsibility, or, if *Gillick* competent, of the child herself, no prudent practitioner or hospital would be well advised to proceed without ensuring that the permission of a Family Division judge had been obtained. Where the operation is for therapeutic reasons, no application to the court is required.[8]

1 *Re D (a minor) (wardship: sterilisation)* [1976] Fam 185 per Heilbron J.
2 [1976] Fam 185 at 196.
3 *Re B (a minor) (wardship: sterilisation)* [1988] AC 199.
4 [1988] AC 199 at 206–207.
5 It may be that it is unnecessary to make the child a ward of court. As with other treatment decisions, what is required is that the court exercises its inherent jurisdiction: it is not necessarily a wardship jurisdiction and unless there is a need for on-going wardship supervision a simple application under the inherent jurisdiction should be made.
6 *Re F (mental patient: sterilisation)* [1990] 2 AC 1 at 20.
7 [1990] 2 AC 1 at 69, at 54, 56 per Lord Brandon of Oakbrook, at 79 per Lord Goff of Chieveley.
8 *Re E (a minor) (medical treatment)* [1991] 2 FLR 585; *Re GF* [1992] 1 FLR 293.

Best interests

7.22   A sterilisation procedure for non-therapeutic reasons, like any other form of treatment, should be carried out only if it is in the best interests of the child. Clearly, such interests cannot be assessed by exclusive reference to medical factors, and, indeed, many doctors may feel that they are not well equipped to make the assessment given the social issues involved.

The factors which are taken into account in assessing the best interests of a child are much the same as those for an adult.[1]

1 See PARA **7.8** above in relation to adults and PARA **7.23** below in relation to children. See also *Re M (Wardship: Sterilisation)* [1988] 2 FLR 497, [1988] Fam Law 434; *Re P (A Minor) (Wardship: Sterilisation)* [1989] 1 FLR 182, [1989] Fam Law 102.

Procedure[1]

7.23   Where a proposal to sterilise a child irreversibly is being considered the following steps need to be taken.

It must be determined whether the procedure is merely the side-effect of treatment required for therapeutic reasons, for example to treat cancer. If it is, then the usual procedures for obtaining authority to treat a child may be adopted. It is suggested that proposals justified on the ground of the treatment of dysmenorrhoea should be examined carefully to ensure that there is no less radical treatment available pending the child's attainment of majority.

If the prime purpose of the procedure is sterilisation, and the child is not mentally disabled, it is highly unlikely that the procedure could be found to be in the best interests of the patient and careful consideration would need to be given to whether the decision should not be deferred until the child has achieved adulthood. If the child is *Gillick* competent and desires the operation, given the sensitivities described above, an application to the court should be seriously considered before proceeding.

If the child is mentally disabled and the proposed procedure is 'non-therapeutic', there should be a full discussion with those having parental responsibility. Relevant information should be obtained from social workers and others who may have views on the child's best interests.

Consideration should be given to the possibility of alternative contraceptive measures, particularly where there is a prospect of the child gaining in maturity and understanding, and to whether, even with sterilisation, sexual encounters are likely to occur or be permitted or be in the child's interests.

If it is decided, after discussions, that an operation in childhood for permanent sterilisation would be in the child's best interests, and that it would not be reasonable to wait until adulthood, an application must be made to either the Family Division of the High Court or to the Court of Protection, depending on the age of the child.[2]

The application must be supported by evidence from carers and others to explain why an irreversible operation is necessary in the best interests of the child and to describe the consideration and consultation that led to the decision. Ethical, social, moral and welfare considerations will be taken into account, as will emotional, psychological and social benefits and detriments to the patient – for example, the risk that if the patient becomes pregnant or gives birth she is likely to experience trauma or psychological damage greater than that resulting from sterilisation. The court will, in effect, prepare a balance sheet of the advantages and disadvantages for the patient. Assessment will be made of the likelihood of advantages and disadvantages in fact occurring – for example, the risk that pregnancy will occur.[3] Medical evidence will be required in relation to the risks to the patient of not being sterilised and of the operation itself. It can be expected that proceedings will usually involve a thorough adversarial investigation of all possible opinion and of the possible alternatives to sterilisation. All reasonable arguments against sterilisation will be presented and considered.

CAFCASS or the Official Solicitor will carry out their own investigations and obtain expert evidence necessary to satisfy themselves that all medical, psychological and social evaluations have been conducted and that all appropriate matters are able to be ventilated before the court. Where the patient is able to express any views, however limited, the patient will be interviewed in private by his representative.

1   See **CHAPTER 5**: Going to Court.
2   *Ibid.*
3   Although it relates to procedures concerning adults, regard may usefully be had to the short-list of factors referred to in the still in force Practice Note (Official Solicitor: Declaratory Proceedings: Medical and Welfare Decisions for Adults who Lack Capacity) [2006] 2 FLR 373, especially at [17]–[18] and to those referred to in the superseded Practice Note (Official Solicitor: Declaratory Proceedings: Medical and Welfare Decisions for Adults who Lack Capacity) [2001] 2 FLR 158 and Practice Note (Official Solicitor: Sterilisation) [1996] 2 FLR 111, all of which are reproduced at **APPENDIX 7.2** and www.3serjeantsinn.com/mtdl/ sterilisation.

E   CONCLUSION

7.24   The permanent effect of sterilisation highlights the importance of strict compliance with all preoperative protocols. The closest attention must be directed to explanation of all associated risks and alternatives, to issues of capacity where these arise and to all procedural prerequisites. Evidence must be carefully compiled and considered and competing considerations thoroughly weighed having regard to the inherent sensitivities involved. Sterilisation for non-therapeutic reasons is an especially drastic measure and proposals for such intervention are properly to be regarded as an option of final resort demanding the most meticulous scrutiny.

For updating material and hyperlinks related to this chapter, see: www.3serjeantsinn.com/mtdl/sterilisation

---

Chapter 8

Abortion

A Statutory framework 8.1
  Offences Against the Person Act 1861 8.2
  Infant Life (Preservation) Act 1929 8.3
  Abortion Act 1967 8.4
  Human Fertilisation and Embryology Act 1990 8.5
B Particular issues of compliance with the Abortion Act 1967 conditions 8.6
  Conscientious objection 8.6
  Multiple foetuses 8.7
  Does the procedure have to be successful to be lawful? 8.8
  Does the procedure have to be performed by a medical practitioner? 8.9
  Certification of medical opinion 8.10
  The grounds 8.11
   Risk of injury to the mother greater than if pregnancy terminated: s 1(1)(a) 8.11
   Termination is necessary to prevent grave permanent injury: s 1(1)(b) 8.15
   Risk to life of pregnant woman greater than if the pregnancy were terminated: s 1(1)(c) 8.16
   Substantial risk of the child being seriously handicapped from physical or mental abnormalities: s 1(1)(d) 8.17
  The place of treatment 8.18
C The patient's consent 8.19
  Competent adults 8.20
  Children 8.21
  Incompetent adults 8.22
   Determining competence: termination of pregnancy 8.23
   Best interests: termination of pregnancy 8.24
   Use of force: non-consensual incompetent patients 8.25
  Procedure and evidence 8.26
   Making an application 8.26
   Timing of the application 8.27
   Important considerations for the court 8.28
D Conclusion 8.31

A STATUTORY FRAMEWORK

8.1 The termination of pregnancy is largely governed by statute law. While this book is primarily concerned with decision-making in medicine, in this field it is necessary to be aware of the legal framework within which the decision must be taken. Any practitioner in this area must be aware of the fact that any termination of pregnancy is likely to be unlawful and a serious criminal offence unless there is a legal justification for it. By the same token, the patient's freedom of choice and decision is circumscribed by the law.

Offences Against the Person Act 1861

8.2 The procuring of a miscarriage of a foetus is a criminal offence unless some legal justification can be identified:

> 'Every woman, being with child, who, with intent to procure her own miscarriage, shall unlawfully administer to herself any poison or other noxious thing, or shall unlawfully use any instrument or other means whatsoever with the like intent, and whosoever, with intent to procure the miscarriage of any woman, whether she be or be not with child, shall unlawfully administer to her or cause to be taken by her any poison or other noxious thing, or shall unlawfully use any instrument or other means whatsoever with the like intent shall be guilty … '[1]

This offence is not committed by the termination of the life of a child in the course of delivery.[2] It is a lawful justification for procuring a miscarriage that it was done for the purpose of saving the life of the mother.[3]

1   Offences Against the Person Act 1861, s 58.
2   But see below for the offence of child destruction; PARA **8.3**: Infant Life (Preservations) Act 1929.
3   *R v Bourne* [1939] 1 KB 687.

Infant Life (Preservation) Act 1929

8.3 If a foetus is capable of being born alive, ending its life unlawfully, whether *in utero* or during delivery, amounts to the offence of child destruction:

> 'Subject as hereinafter in this subsection provided, any person who, with intent to destroy the life of a child capable of being born alive, by any wilful act causes a child to die before it has an existence independent of its mother, shall be guilty … Provided that no person shall be found guilty of an offence under this section unless it is proved that the act which caused the death of the child was not done in good faith for the purpose only of preserving the life of the mother.'[1]

Under the statute a foetus is presumed to be capable of being born alive at the gestational age of 28 weeks:

> 'For the purposes of this Act, evidence that a woman had at any material time been pregnant for a period of 28 weeks or more shall be prima facie proof that she was at that time pregnant of a child capable of being born alive.'[2]

Clearly the presumption is rebuttable by evidence that a particular child was not capable of being born alive. A foetus is capable of being born alive if it is capable of:

> 'breathing and living by reason of its breathing through its own lungs alone, without deriving any of its living or power of living by or through any connection with its mother'.[3]

The statute does not mean that a foetus of a lower gestational age cannot be proved to be capable of being born alive, and the abortion of a foetus capable of these functions, whatever its age, would be an offence of child destruction.[4]

1   Infant Life (Preservation) Act 1929, s 1(1).
2   *Ibid*, s 1(2).
3   *Rance v Mid-Downs Health Authority* [1991] QB 587, [1991] 2 WLR 159 at 188; see also *R v McDonald* [1999] NI 150 (it was not necessary for the prosecution to prove that the child would have lived for any particular period of time provided it proved that the child would have lived, even for a short period of time).
4   *Rance* (N **3** above).

Abortion Act 1967

8.4   The Act makes lawful what would otherwise be unlawful under the 1861 and 1929 Acts if certain conditions are met:

> 'Subject to the provisions of this section, a person shall not be guilty of an offence under the law relating to abortion when a pregnancy is terminated by a registered medical practitioner if two registered medical practitioners are of the opinion, formed in good faith:

> (a)   that the pregnancy has not exceeded twenty four weeks and that the continuance of the pregnancy would involve risk, greater than if the pregnancy were terminated, of injury to the physical or mental health of the pregnant woman or any existing children of her family; [1] or

> (b)   that the termination is necessary to prevent grave permanent injury to the physical or mental health of the pregnant woman; or

> (c)   that the continuance of the pregnancy would involve risk to the life of the pregnant woman, greater than if the pregnancy were terminated; or

> (d)   that there is a substantial risk that if the child were born it would suffer from such physical or mental abnormalities as to be seriously handicapped.'[2]

1   Sometimes referred to as 'the social ground'.
2   Abortion Act, s 1(1), as amended by the Human Fertilisation and Embryology Act 1990, s 37.The Act does not extend to Northern Ireland. The Act is reproduced in full at **APPENDIX 8.1**.

Human Fertilisation and Embryology Act 1990

8.5   The 1967 Act was amended to the form quoted above to achieve a number of objectives.

A time limit of 24 weeks was imposed on abortions performed on the 'social' ground'.[1]

The time limit imposed by the 1929 Act was removed from terminations on other grounds. In particular, this means that a termination of a pregnancy where there is a substantial risk that the child will be seriously handicapped may be performed at any gestational age, even if the foetus is capable of being born alive.

Since the 1990 amendments there have been calls to reduce the 24 week limit further to reflect earlier foetal viability. An amendment tabled to the Human Fertilisation and Embryology Bill 2008 which presented options of 12, 16, 20 and 22 week time limits was rejected by the House of Commons in May 2008 in what was the first vote on the time limit in 18 years.[2]

1   Abortion Act 1967, s 1(1)(a). 'Abortion Debate' MPs reject limit cut *The Daily Telegraph* 21 May 2008.
2   'Abortion Debate MPs reject limit cut' *The Daily Telegraph* 21 May 2008. The most modest cut to 22 weeks was defeated by 71 votes.

B PARTICULAR ISSUES OF COMPLIANCE WITH THE ABORTION ACT 1967 CONDITIONS

Conscientious objection

8.6   The general rule that a patient is not entitled to force a doctor to provide treatment he is unwilling to give[1] is, in the case of abortions, reinforced by a statutory exemption for those who have a conscientious objection to participation:

> 'No person shall be under any duty, whether by contract or by any statutory or other legal requirement, to participate in any treatment authorised by this Act to which he has a conscientious objection.'[2]

The exemption does not, however, cover treatment needed to save life or prevent permanent injury to the physical or mental health of the pregnant woman.[3] Therefore a doctor[4] or nurse[5] faced with circumstances in which a termination is required under s 1(1)(b), could be obliged to undertake the treatment[6] or face the relevant legal consequences, however strong his conscientious objection. The exemption does not cover activities which do not amount to participation in the procedure of termination, such as the typing of a referral letter by a secretary.[7] It is unclear whether the act of certification of grounds for a termination amounts to participation in the treatment.[8] It can be argued that it does, as the certification is the necessary legal step which initiates the process of treatment and without which it cannot take place lawfully. In other contexts the concept of treatment includes the ancillary care made necessary by it.[9] There is no reason why that should not be the position in relation to certification.[10]

The entitlement of a practitioner to take advantage of the exemption does not relieve him of all duties towards the pregnant woman who has come for advice and assistance. Unless the practitioner is able to decline to assume any duty towards the patient, a duty of care will inevitably arise under which the doctor's conscientious objection should be explained and advice offered about how to seek advice and treatment elsewhere.[11] A conscientious objection does not entitle a practitioner to seek to impose his own views on patients.[12] The practical solution for a practitioner with a conscientious objection is to make a standing arrangement with a colleague to accept referrals.

1   *Re J (a minor) (wardship: medical treatment)* [1991] Fam 33.
2   Abortion Act 1967, s 4(1).
3   Abortion Act 1967, s 4(2).
4   Including (were the situation to arise) a medical student. See, for example (although not specifically dealing with abortion), GMC, 'Personal Beliefs and Medical Practice' Supplementary Guidance (GMC, March 2008), especially para 25 and fn 9.
5   It is not only doctors and paramedical professionals who are entitled to the exemption, but anyone who participates in the termination of a pregnancy.
6   If otherwise under a relevant duty of care to the woman.
7   *Janaway v Salford Area Health Authority* [1989] AC 537.
8   The point was noted in *Janaway* (*ibid.*) but no opinion expressed on it.
9   For example, the Mental Health Act 1983, s 145(1); *B v Croydon Health Authority* [1995] Fam 133.
10 For a contrary view, see Kennedy & Grubb, *Principles of Medical Law* (2nd ed, OUP, 2004), p 771.
11 *Barr v Matthews* (1999) 52 BMLR 217 for an example of a claim – albeit unsuccessful – against a practitioner (who was opposed to abortion on ethical and religious grounds) on the ground that he had prevented an abortion in breach of his duty to the patient.
12 GMC, 'Personal Beliefs and Medical Practice' Supplementary Guidance (GMC, March 2008), especially para 19: 'You should not normally discuss your personal beliefs with patients unless those beliefs are directly relevant to the patient's care. You must not impose your beliefs on patients, or cause distress by the inappropriate or insensitive expression of religious, political or other beliefs or views. Equally, you must not put pressure on patients to discuss or justify their beliefs (or the absence of them).'

Multiple foetuses

8.7   It is on occasion necessary or desired to destroy one of multiple foetuses being carried by a pregnant woman. 'Selective reduction' has become increasingly common as a result of the greater efficacy and use of IVF technology. Prior to the amendment of the 1967 Act,[1] it might have been argued that to leave one or more foetuses to be delivered alive would not amount to a termination of pregnancy for the purposes of acquiring the protection of the 1967 Act because the pregnancy of the other foetus would continue. Now, however, where there is a substantial risk that *one* of the foetuses would, if born, be seriously handicapped,[2] anything done with intent to procure the miscarriage of that foetus will not be unlawful. Where one of the other grounds under s1 of the 1967 Act applies, anything done with intent to procure the miscarriage of any of the foetuses will be lawful.

1   Abortion Act 1967, s 5(2), as amended by the Human Fertilisation and Embryology Act 1990, s 37(5).
2   The ground specified in s 1(1)(d) of the Abortion Act 1967.

Does the procedure have to be successful to be lawful?

8.8   The 1967 Act might appear to require the actual termination to be completed for the Act to provide a defence in relation to the 1861 and 1929 Acts by use of the words 'when a pregnancy is terminated'. Where a termination procedure fails and the foetus is born alive, certainly the Act provides no defence to an act of killing or attempting to kill it. Any such act will be subject to the full rigour of the law against homicide. However, it is unlikely that the mere failure of the termination procedure to achieve its intended goal would render the procedure unlawful. Both the 1861 and 1929 Acts require a specific intent to perform an act which would amount to the offence described. That intent must be absent if the practitioner honestly believes that he is performing a procedure which will end the pregnancy in compliance with the 1967 Act. The point is not free from controversy. One Law Lord has expressed the view that the Act was not intended to cover failed terminations.[1] The better view, expressed in the same case, is that the Act legitimises the whole treatment for the termination of the pregnancy and that it cannot have been the intention of Parliament to limit the legal protection to cases where the procedure was successful.[2]

1   Per Lord Wilberforce in *Royal College of Nursing of the United Kingdom v Department of Health and Social Security* [1981] AC 800 at 823, [1981] 2 WLR 279 at 295.
2   *Ibid*, per Lord Diplock at [1981] AC 800 at 823, [1981] 2 WLR 279 at 299, with whom, on this point, Lord Edmund-Davies agreed: [1981] AC 800 at 823, [1981] 2 WLR 279 at 303.

Does the procedure have to be performed by a medical practitioner?

8.9   The Abortion Act 1967 requires the procedure to be carried out by a registered medical practitioner, that is, one who is registered by the General Medical Council under the Medical Act 1983. This does not mean that the doctor has to perform every part of the procedure personally and a procedure will be lawful if it is prescribed and initiated by a medical practitioner who remains in charge of it.[1] The requirement in the 1929 Act for a 'wilful act' may well import the requirement of an intent to act in circumstances which would be unlawful, rather than knowledge of the illegality of those circumstances. An act – albeit in accordance with a doctor's instructions and under his or her supervision – in circumstances where the doctor is acting unlawfully could be said to have been a wilful act for these purposes. It is unfortunate that there is a lack of clarity in relation to conduct which could have criminal consequences.[2]

1   *Royal College of Nursing of the United Kingdom v Dept of Health and Social Security* [1981] AC 800. The Royal College of Nursing advises: 'Nurses will be working lawfully in the limits of the Abortion Act 1967 providing they are carrying out treatment in accordance with delegated instructions from a registered medical practitioner. The medical practitioner must remain responsible for patient care throughout any treatment.': (Royal College of Nurses, *Abortion Care: RCN guidance for nurses, midwives and specialist community public health nurses* (RCN, October 2008)).
2   Kennedy & Grubb, *Principles of Medical Law* (OUP, 2nd ed, 2004), pp 750–751.

Certification of medical opinion

8.10   Except in an emergency, the two certifying doctors must give their opinion either in the prescribed form or in a 'certificate of opinion' designed by the doctor before treatment is begun.[1] Even in an emergency, the doctors must still have formed their opinion before the treatment is begun. There is no express requirement that the doctors should have examined the patient personally or that either of them is the practitioner who actually performs the procedure. It might be envisaged, however, that there would be difficulties in establishing good faith without some form of examination or at least personal knowledge of the case. Thus, medical practitioners would be well advised to examine the patient for themselves.[2]

It has been suggested that the two doctors need not agree on the ground on which termination is justified.[3] This is an overly liberal construction of the Act. While the section contemplates more than one ground being present in any one case, there would seem to be a requirement that the ground relied on should, in the opinion of at least two doctors, be present. If only one doctor considers that a particular ground is present, the wording of the section would not appear to be satisfied.

There is no requirement that the ground chosen by the medical practitioners is in fact correct. All that is required is that two doctors are of the opinion, formed in good faith, that the ground exists. As was stated in a rare criminal prosecution under the Act:

'Thus a great social responsibility is firmly placed by the law upon the shoulders of the medical profession.'[4]

1   Abortion Regulations 1991 (SI 1991/499), reg 3(1) and Schedule 1. The Regulations were amended in 2002 to allow a doctor, either individually or jointly with the second certifying practitioner, to design his own form, so long as it complies with reg 3(1)(a)(ii) and is signed and dated by each practitioner. Following the termination, a separate notice of termination and the required information under Schedule 2 must be sent to the Chief Medical Officer within 14 days of the termination, either in a sealed envelope or by an electronic communication (reg 4(1)). See **APPENDICES 8.2–8.6**.
2   The determination of whether particular actions were done in good faith is to be carried out in criminal trials by the jury, albeit guided by appropriate evidence concerning accepted medical practice: *R v Smith* [1973] 1 WLR 1510, [1974] 1 All ER 376.
3   Kennedy and Grubb, *Principles of Medical Law* (2nd ed, OUP, 2004), p 752.
4   *R v Smith* [1973] 1 WLR 1510 at 1512 per Scarman LJ.

The grounds

Risk of injury to the mother greater than if pregnancy terminated: s 1(1)(a)

8.11   The doctors must be of the opinion that the following circumstances apply:

8.12   *[1] The pregnancy has not exceeded 24 weeks – s 1(1)(a)*

The Act does not specify the precise starting date of the pregnancy for this purpose, and there is no authoritative guidance from the courts. While arguably this could mean the date of implantation, rather than the more conventional date of the last menstrual period,[1] it would be prudent for practitioners to adhere to the earlier date, bearing in mind the potentially serious consequences that might otherwise follow.

1   Kennedy and Grubb, *Principles of Medical Law* (2nd ed, OUP, 2004), pp 756–757.

8.13   *[2] There is a risk to the mental or physical health of the woman or any existing children of her family*

The Act does not quantify or describe what degree or type of risk must be present. There is no requirement that the doctors be satisfied that there will actually be physical harm or mental illness. Essentially, 'health' is likely to encompass whatever a doctor acting with professional competence and in good faith considers is a matter of health. There is no definition of 'children of her family' but it is presumably not intended to be limited to children born to her, but could include not only adopted children but any accepted by her as children of her family, by comparison with the similar concept in matrimonial law. It is the lack of definition which permits abortion on so-called 'social' grounds. This is further reinforced by the liberty given to the doctor to take into account the:

'... pregnant woman's actual and foreseeable environment.'[1]

1   Abortion Act 1967, s 1(2).

8.14   *[3] The risk identified must be thought to be greater if the pregnancy were allowed to continue than if it were terminated*

How that comparison is to be undertaken is clearly a matter for the medical practitioners to consider acting in good faith.

Termination is necessary to prevent grave permanent injury: s 1(1)(b)

8.15   This condition has no time limit attached to it. If the condition is satisfied, a termination may be carried out at any stage of the pregnancy before the baby is delivered. The condition requires more than a risk of injury: the procedure must be necessary to prevent the injury occurring. Thus, the doctors must be of the opinion that such injury will actually occur unless the pregnancy is terminated and that there is no alternative means of preventing the injury. Of course, as this can be only a matter of opinion, the doctors do not subsequently have to prove that they were indubitably correct – only that they held the opinion in good faith. The injury sought to be prevented must be both grave and permanent, and may be to mental or physical health or both. This is to be contrasted to the injury contemplated in s 1(1)(a), where any injury will suffice if there is a greater risk of it occurring than if the pregnancy were terminated. What is or is not considered 'grave' may be a matter on which there can be different opinions, and may vary from case to case. Again, therefore it is suggested that the doctor's opinion, so long as it is formed in good faith, must be conclusive.

Risk to life of pregnant woman greater than if the pregnancy were terminated: s1(1)(c)

8.16   No time limit is placed on the deployment of this condition. 'Life' in the context of this subsection must be taken literally and will not include injuries which will affect the quality of life which might be included in other conditions. The degree of risk is not quantified in the statute; therefore any level of risk will suffice to satisfy this condition, so long as the risk is greater than that which would exist if the pregnancy were terminated.

Substantial risk of the child being seriously handicapped from physical or mental abnormalities: s 1(1)(d)

8.17 There is no gestational time limit in relation to this condition. The risk involved must be 'substantial' and the handicap envisaged must be 'serious'. Neither of these adjectives is defined in the Act. Professor Grubb has argued that whether or not a risk is 'substantial' is a matter of law, and that it will not be defined by the opinion of medical practitioners, however compliant they are with accepted medical practice and however much they form the opinion in good faith.[1] If this is correct then medical practitioners run a risk: if they are found to have formed an opinion contrary to the view taken by a court as to what is properly described as substantial, they may be prosecuted for participating in an unlawful abortion because they would not, as a matter of law, have formed the requisite opinion. There is, however, a contrary argument. It must be remembered that this is a criminal statute and should be construed narrowly. It is suggested that if more were required than an honest doctor's opinion that the risk was substantial (whether or not others would agree with that opinion) then Parliament would have said so clearly. The same consideration ought to apply to the meaning of 'seriously'.

Abortions under s 1(1)(d) came under heightened scrutiny in 2003 when a curate, Rev Joanna Jepson, sought permission for judicial review of a police decision not to investigate a doctor who performed an abortion under s 1(1)(d), the 'serious handicap' being a bilateral cleft lip and palate. Rev Jepson was granted permission and intended to pursue her argument that a cleft lip and palate could not constitute a 'serious handicap' and that from 24 weeks a foetus had a right to life under Art 2. The case was suspended pending a police investigation into the doctor who performed the disputed abortion and eventually discontinued after the CPS decided that there was insufficient evidence for a realistic prospect of conviction.[2]

While the *Jepson* case does not fetter a doctor's professional judgement under s 1(1)(d), it does underline the possibility of criminal prosecution in cases where 'substantial risk' or, more importantly, 'serious handicap', are questionable. Although there is no list of qualifying 'handicaps',[3] doctors will themselves take a view of foetal abnormalities on a sliding scale from those vitiating short-term viability to the cosmetic. The availability and efficacy of treatment will be factors for consideration. However, the mother's view of the potency of the risk, the seriousness of the handicap or her willingness to bear, or to accept, a 'seriously handicapped' child is strictly of no relevance under s 1(1)(d) which requires an objective medical assessment of 'substantial risk' and 'serious handicap'.[4] In the absence of further definition in the Act or from the courts, doctors would be well advised to consult the RCOG's 2001 Guidelines on late abortion.[5]

1 Kennedy and Grubb *Principles of Medical Law* (2nd ed, OUP, 2004), p 760.
2 *Jepson v Chief Constable of West Mercia Police Constabulary* [2003] EWHC 3318 (Admin).
3 Rev Jepson intended to apply for a declaration that 'serious handicap' must be understood by reference to the remediability of the condition and that, given the availability of surgery to correct a cleft lip and palate, such condition did not constitute a 'serious handicap'.
4 For arguments why, see Kennedy and Grubb, *Principles of Medical Law* (2nd ed, OUP, 2004), p 761. For arguments as to why parents' views should receive recognition in this context, see R

Scott, 'The Uncertain Scope of Reproductive Autonomy in Preimplantation Genetic Diagnosis and Selective Abortion', (2005) 12 *Medical Law Review* 291–327. The mother's perspective will be important in a termination before 24 weeks, which can be undertaken pursuant to s 1(1)(a). The problem arises where foetal scanning is not performed until after 24 weeks and an abnormality is detected.

5   Royal College of Obstetricians and Gynaecologists, Further Issues Relating to Late Abortion, Fetal Viability and Registration of Births and Deaths (RCOG, 2001).

The place of treatment

8.18   Termination of pregnancy may be performed only in a National Health Service facility or a place approved by the Secretary of State, unless a medical practitioner forms the opinion in good faith that the termination is:

'immediately necessary to save the life or to prevent grave permanent injury to the physical or mental health of the pregnant woman'.[1]

1   Abortion Act 1967, s 1(4). The Secretary of State has the power to approve of a class of places in relation to medicinal abortions: s 1(3A). The Prescriptions Only Medicines Act (Human Use) Amendment (No 3) Order 2000 (SI 2000/3231) re-classified the 'morning after pill' (Levonelle) from a prescription-only drug to make it available over the counter to be dispensed by pharmacists. However, taking the 'morning after pill' does not amount to 'procuring a miscarriage' under the Offences Against the Person Act 1861 since it takes effect pre-implantation. In *R (on the application of Smeaton) v Secretary of State for Health* [2002] FLR 146, Munby J held that pregnancy is not established until the fertilised egg has become implanted in the endometrium of the uterus. Accordingly, until this point is reached, the provisions of the Offences Against the Person Act 1861 and hence the Abortion Act 1967 are not engaged. Munby J was emphatic that 'there is nothing in sections 58 and 59 of the [1861] Act which in any way criminalises, makes unlawful, or otherwise prohibits or inhibits the prescription, supply, administration or use of the pill, the mini-pill or the morning after pill (or, so far as the evidence before me bears on this aspect of the case, of IUDs).'

C THE PATIENT'S CONSENT

8.19   It goes without saying that the normal requirements for obtaining authority to treat a patient apply to a termination of pregnancy, and nothing in the legislation is intended to derogate from them. The following particular points should be noted.

Competent adults

8.20   No termination of pregnancy should be proceeded with unless the patient has been fully advised of the alternatives to termination, the relative risks of proceeding with the pregnancy and having the termination. In the case of an adult possessing the legal capacity to consent to the procedure, her refusal to have a termination is determinative, and it cannot lawfully be performed. No other person has any entitlement either to consent on her behalf or to prevent the procedure taking place. Therefore, the father of the foetus has no right to be consulted or to have his consent sought.[1]

1   *Paton v British Pregnancy Advisory Service Trustees* [1979] QB 276; *C v S* [1988] QB 135. See **CHAPTER 9**: Managing Pregnancies, **PARA 9.2**.

Children[1]

8.21   A child, who has attained 16 years of age,[2] or who is sufficiently mature in understanding,[3] may consent to a termination of pregnancy. Such consent will be sufficient authority even if the child's parents are unaware of the proposed treatment or actively oppose it.[4] However, the consent of the parent will provide the doctor with legal justification, even where the child refuses.[5] Where there is a dispute between parents and the child, or between the child and the doctor, the latter, in our opinion should seek the guidance of the court exercising its parental jurisdiction before proceeding to a termination of pregnancy (although there is no obligation to do so, unless the child is already a ward of court).[6]

While, theoretically, it would be possible for an abortion to be imposed on an unwilling child, the courts (and most practitioners) will be very reluctant to proceed in this way. In *Re W*, Lord Donaldson MR described the:

'[h]air-raising possibilities ... of abortions being carried out by doctors in reliance upon the consent of parents and despite the refusal of consent by 16 and 17 year olds'

adding that:

'[w]hilst this may be possible as a matter of law, I do not see any likelihood taking account of medical ethics, unless the abortion was truly in the best interests of the child.'[7]

Abortion is only likely to be imposed on an unwilling child where the pregnancy caused a serious risk to her life or health which she refused or was unable to recognise, such that an abortion (even against her wishes) was clearly in her best interests.[8] Save for the direst emergency, an application must be made to court before imposing such a termination.

1   See, generally **CHAPTER 4**: Deciding for Others – Children.
2   Family Law Reform Act 1969, s 8.
3   *Gillick v West Norfolk and Wisbech Area Health Authority* [1986] AC 112. Also *JS C and CH C v Wren* [1987] 2 WWR 669 (an Albertan court refused the parents' application seeking to prevent their daughter from having an abortion: the 16-year-old girl had sufficient intelligence and understanding to make up her own mind).
4   Doctors should provide a child who is *Gillick* competent with abortion advice and treatment in the same way they would an adult. The child's confidentiality, including from her parents, should be maintained: *R (on the application of Sue Axon) v Secretary of State for Health and Family Planning Association* [2006] EWCA 37 (Admin), [2006] All ER (D) 148.
5   *Re R (a minor) (wardship: consent to treatment)* [1992] Fam 11.
6   *Re G-U (a minor) (wardship)* [1984] FLR 811, [1984] Fam Law 248.
7   *Re W (a minor) (medical treatment: court's jurisdiction)* [1993] Fam 64 and see **CHAPTER 4**: Deciding for Others – Children, **PARA 4.6**.
8   Where doctors or parents attempt to override a child's wish not to have an abortion, the court will have to assess whether an abortion over the child's objections is truly in her best interests. The older the (competent) child is, the less credence will be accorded to the views of others in its assessment of best interests. See **CHAPTER 4**: Deciding for Others – Children, **PARA 4.5FF**.

Incompetent adults

8.22   The termination of pregnancies in women over 16 with questionable capacity to make an abortion decision is now governed by the Mental Capacity

Act 2005 ('MCA').[1] Unlike sterilisation, abortion is not included in the category of cases for which there is an obligation to seek a declaration from the Court of Protection under Practice Direction E.[2] In *Re SG (a patient)* the President decided that, in a case where a pregnant woman clearly lacked capacity, the provisions of the Abortion Act 1967 provided adequate safeguards making a declaration as to best interests unnecessary.[3] The *Re SG* decision was revisited in *An NHS Trust v D*,[4] where Coleridge J noted that if the guidance in *Re SG* were to be strictly applied, it would leave responsibility for all termination decisions for mentally incapacitated women, regardless of the circumstances, in the hands of their medical professionals. Coleridge J held that this could not be correct in all cases and provided the following guidance:[5]

- '• Where the issues of capacity and best interests are clear and beyond doubt, an application to the court is not necessary.
- • Where there is any doubt as to either capacity or best interests, an application to the court should be made.'

As to cases where there is 'doubt', Coleridge J provided a non-exhaustive list of circumstances that would ordinarily warrant the making of an application:[6]

'(i)   Where there is a dispute as to capacity, or where there is a realistic prospect that the patient will regain capacity, following a response to treatment, within the period of her pregnancy or shortly thereafter;

(ii)   Where there is a lack of unanimity amongst the medical professionals as to the best interests of the patient;

(iii)   Where the procedures under section 1 of the Abortion Act 1967 have not been followed (ie, where two medical practitioners have not provided a certificate);

(iv)   Where the patient, members of her immediate family, or the foetus' father have opposed, or expressed views inconsistent with, a termination of the pregnancy; or

(v)   Where there are other exceptional circumstances (including where the termination may be the patient's last chance to bear a child).'[6]

Coleridge J emphasised that if any case is considered to fall anywhere near the boundary line in relation to any one of the above criteria, it should be referred to the court and that the importance of a timeous application cannot be overstated.[7]

Save for (iii) above, these principles might apply to any decision to give irreversible medical treatment under the provisions of the MCA 2005. Where there is dispute or doubt, it would be wise to seek the authority of the court.

Abortion decisions about incompetent women may arise in the milieu of the psychiatric hospital, where a woman detained under the provisions of the Mental Health Act 1983 falls pregnant. In *Re SS (An Adult: Medical Treatment)* Wall J suggested that it was 'essential' that each hospital has a protocol to deal with possible terminations. Protocols should be designed to address the issue in good time so that, wherever practical and in the interests of the patient, a termination can be carried out at the earliest possible opportunity. The protocol should also ensure that the patient is referred at an early stage to independent legal advice.[8]

The court's positive duty to protect the welfare of incapable people has been fortified by the Human Rights Act 1998 and the right to respect for private and family life in Art 8(1) of the European Convention. Carrying out a termination in accordance with the requirements of the Abortion Act 1967, in circumstances where an incapacitated patient's best interests require it, will not breach Art 8. Whilst it will constitute an 'interference' with the woman's Art 8(1) rights, the interference will be permissible under Art 8(2) because it is necessary and proportionate to the legitimate aim of protection of the woman's health.[9]

1   For detailed treatment of capacity and best interests, see **CHAPTER 3**: Deciding for Others – Adults.

2   Court of Protection *Practice Direction E – Applications Relating to Serious Medical Treatment*, s 5 reproduced at **APPENDIX 5.4**; and see **CHAPTER 7**: Sterilisation and **CHAPTER 5**: Going to Court **PARAS 5.24–5.26**.

3   *Re SG (a patient)* [1991] 2 FLR 329, [1993] 4 Med LR 75. Note also *Re X, The Times*, June 4, 1987 (an abortion would not be unlawful merely because the patient lacked the capacity to give informed consent).

4   *An NHS Trust v D* [2003] EWHC 2793 [2004] 1 FLR 1110, [2004] Lloyd's Rep Med 107.

5   Butler-Sloss P authorised Coleridge J expressly to record her agreement with his guidance for 'doubt' cases (at 38).

6   Based on the matters listed by Lord Brandon in *Re F (Medical Patient: Sterilisation)* [1990] 2 AC 1.

7   Echoing the guidance of Thorpe LJ in *Re S (Adult Patient: Sterilisation)* [2000] 3 WLR 1288, [2000] 2 FLR 389 and Wall J in *Re SS (An Adult: Medical Treatment)* [2002] 1 FCR 73.

8   *Re SS (An Adult: Medical Treatment)* [2002] 1 FCR 73. The source of the 'independent legal advice' suggested by Wall J was to be the Official Solicitor or the solicitor who represented the patient at her Mental Health Review Tribunal. The guidance in *Re SS* was followed in *An NHS Trust v D* [2003] EWHC 2793; [2004] 1 FLR 1110; [2004] Lloyd's Rep Med 107 (see **N4** above).

9   *An NHS Trust v D* [2003] EWHC 2793; [2004] 1 FLR 1110; [2004] Lloyd's Rep Med 107 (see **N4** above).

Determining competence: termination of pregnancy

8.23   Complex questions arise when consideration is given to capacity in the context of a refusal to undergo a termination of pregnancy. The test of capacity is as set out in ss 2 and 3 of the MCA and is no different for terminations than for any other medical procedure. At the very least, capacity requires a woman to have the ability to understand that she is carrying a foetus which is likely to be born alive if there is no termination, and that she will not have this baby if she has a termination of pregnancy. She should understand the nature of the procedure to be performed; for example, suction, or induction of labour. The extent to which the courts will require wider considerations to be brought into play is unclear. While the bar of capacity should not be set too high, we would suggest that consideration should be given to whether the patient understands more than the proximate medical issues of pregnancy and childbirth and appreciates the wider social consequences including that she may have to look after the child (or might be prevented from doing so). However, whilst there may well be wider psychological, physiological, social and economic consequences of the decision, a requirement of the ability to understand fully the latter would prevent a far wider range of patients having the relevant capacity to consent to this sort of decision than would be desirable.

Best interests: termination of pregnancy

8.24   Where a termination decision reaches the court and the court decides that the woman lacks capacity, or that there is reason to believe that the woman lacks capacity,[1] in relation to the termination decision it will be appropriate also to seek an order:

> 'That the Respondent's best interests in relation to the termination or continuation of her current pregnancy be determined.'

This will particularly apply if there has been no certification prior to the hearing of grounds for lawful termination.

While decisions in this area are fraught with moral and ethical difficulties, practitioners must strive to divorce their own views from the objective assessment of 'best interests' required by s 4 of the MCA.. In considering the 'best interests' test, the interests of persons other than the patient (even those of the baby[2] *a fortiori* those of society as a whole) are irrelevant. Nonetheless it might be argued that the patient's ability to consider the interests of others is relevant to the assessment of her capacity.

In *Re SS (Medical Treatment, Late Termination)*[3] a schizophrenic woman was detained in a psychiatric hospital under s 3 of the Mental Health Act 1983. An application for a declaration that SS lacked capacity to make an abortion decision and that a termination would be in her best interests was made when she was nearly 24 weeks pregnant. The expert evidence was that the procedure used for late a termination (foeticide followed by induction of labour, typically taking 24 hours) would be no less traumatic than normal birth followed by removal of the child for adoption. Wall J contrasted the observations that late abortion procedure required SS's co-operation which she may not give and that it was unlikely that she would have any real understanding of the procedure with the fact that SS had given birth to four children by straightforward labour. Wall J decided 'on fine balance' that the continuation of the pregnancy carried the lesser detriment to the applicant and that a termination was not in her best interests.

The courts have applied the 'best interests' test in favour of allowing children to undergo abortions. For example, in *Re B*[4] a mother opposed her 12-year-old daughter undergoing an abortion. The child, the putative father and her maternal grandparents supported the procedure. The court agreed with the local authority's view that it was in the child's best interests to have the abortion as continuation of the pregnancy involved greater risks to her mental and physical health.

1   MCA, s 48(a).
2   See **CHAPTER 9**: Managing Pregnancies, **PARA 9.11**. In the first edition of this book, the question of whether an unborn child's interests would have to be considered when addressing the 'best interests' tests in view of Art 2 of the European Convention on Human Rights was posed (and doubted, given the approach adopted in *Paton v United Kingdom* (1980) 3 EHRR 408). In *Vo v France* (2005) 10 EHRR 12 at 81–82, [2005] Inquest Law Reports 128, the European Court of Human Rights held (by majority) that (i) the issue of when the right to life begins comes within the margin of appreciation which Member States should enjoy; (ii) that there is no European consensus on the scientific and legal definition of the beginning of life. The court decided that 'it is neither desirable nor even possible as matters stand, to answer in the abstract the question whether the unborn child is a person for the purposes of Article 2'. Given the court's reasons for taking a firm stand and bearing in mind the expansion of the EU, it

is suggested that the court's position is unlikely to change for the foreseeable future. The position in England and Wales, within the domestic court's margin of appreciation, is tolerably clear: a foetus does not have any independent legal rights or status. See, in the abortion context, *Paton v British Pregnancy Advisory Service Trustees* [1979] 1 QB 276; *C v S* [1987] 1 All ER 1230 and, in the context of a mother's refusal of treatment during pregnancy, *Re MB (An Adult: Medical Treatment)* (1997) 38 BMLR 175; *St George's Healthcare Trust NHS Trust v S (No2); R v Collins, ex parte S (No.2)* [1998] 3 All ER 673.

3   [2002] 1 FLR 445, [2002] 1 FCR 73.
4   *Re B (child: termination of pregnancy)* [1991] 2 FLR 426.

Use of force: non-consensual incompetent patients

8.25   If an incompetent patient is reluctant to undergo a termination, it may be that it will have to be performed under sedation or restraint.

In the case of a patient over the age of 16 who lacks capacity, the provisions of s 6 of the MCA apply and the test set out there must be met.[1] For children under the age of 16, the common law continues to apply. See **CHAPTER 4, PARAS 4.5–4.10**.

There are no reported post-MCA cases. However, under s 6, any restraint must be proportionate to the 'harm' it is seeking to avoid. 'Harm' is not defined in the Act and can include both the physical and psychological harm arising from the continuation of pregnancy. The restraint must also be in the patient's best interests under s 5. In two cases decided before the MCA came in force, *Tameside and Glossop Acute Services Trust v CH*[2] and *Norfolk & Norwich Healthcare (NHS) Trust v W*,[3] it was held that the mothers lacked capacity. The obstetricians wished to bring delivery forward in time by, if necessary, caesarean section. It was held that it would be lawful to use reasonable force to achieve this in the best interests of the patient. This principle was affirmed in *Re MB (an adult: medical treatment)*.[4] The court held that it followed from the determination that treatment was in the patient's best interests that treatment could be given forcibly despite the her objections, although difficult questions arose as to how to strike the balance between continuing treatment which is forcibly opposed and deciding not to continue with it. The same principle would apply in the case of the termination of the pregnancy of a patient lacking the capacity to refuse such a procedure, but who was resisting it. In all such cases, the doctors will have to decide whether the proposed termination is compliant with the Abortion Act 1967, s 1 and in the patient's best interests under the MCA.

1   For more detailed consideration of the use of restraint, see **CHAPTER 6**: Restraint and Deprivation of Liberty.
2   [1996] 1 FLR 762 at 773–774.
3   [1996] 2 FLR 613.
4   [1997] 2 FLR 426, (1997) 8 Med LR 217.

Procedure and evidence

Making an application[1]

8.26   Decisions about whether to make an application to the court for a declaration should be made using the guidance in *An NHS Trust v D*.[2] Where there is any doubt as to capacity or best interests, the presumption should be in favour of seeking a declaration.

1   See **CHAPTER 5**: Going to Court and also **APPENDIX 8.7**: Sample text for sections 5.1 and 5.2 of the COP and **APPENDIX 8.8**: Draft order that it is in an adult's best interests to undergo a termination.
2   *An NHS Trust v D* [2003] EWHC 2793 [2004] 1 FLR 1110, [2004] Lloyd's Rep Med 107.

Timing of the application

8.27   Applications to the court in relation to termination of pregnancy where the patient's capacity and/or best interests are in question should be made as soon as practicable and, so far as possible, well before the 24th week of pregnancy. [1]

A report, preferably from two consultant psychiatrists, that the patient lacks capacity to form or withhold consent should be obtained. Care must be taken to ensure that the psychiatrists consider the test as set out in s 2 of the MCA and *Re MB*.[2]

1   *See* **PARA 8.22** above and *Re SS (An Adult: Medical Treatment)* [2002] 1 FCR 73.
2   See **APPENDIX 9.1**: Re MB Guidelines.

Important considerations for the court

Statutory position

8.28   The views of any treating doctors and in particular their opinion about the existence of grounds for a termination under the Abortion Act 1967 and whether such a procedure was appropriate for the patient.

Capacity

8.29   The basis on which it is asserted that the patient lacks the ability to weigh treatment information in the balance. For example, the mere fact that a patient is unwilling to discuss the pregnancy with psychiatric staff and is frightened cannot of itself be sufficient to show lack of capacity for this particular decision.

The information which has been put to the patient about the advantages and disadvantages of pregnancy/termination and her response to it.

The patient's comprehension of:

(i)   the consequence of sexual intercourse in leading to pregnancy;
(ii)   the nature and extent of the physical and emotional stress associated with childbirth and responsibilities of having a child;
(iii) if relevant, the risk of her child being mentally impaired.

Whether the possibility of foetal abnormality has been put to the patient and, if so, the manner in which this was done and her response.

Evidence from a speech and language therapist may assist, where there are issues concerning the patient's ability to comprehend. His view on the patient's understanding of everyday vocabulary and complex adult language may assist.

A view as to her ability to understand is crucial to a determination under s 2 of the MCA and the *Re MB* test.

Best interests

8.30 A report should be obtained from the relevant Care Manager, if Social Services have been involved, on:

- The ability of the patient to care for the baby after the birth, with or without support.
- The availability of such support, if it is needed.
- The likelihood of the baby being taken into care immediately after birth and the impact this would have on the patient.
- The risk of the baby being born disabled.
- Any difficulties foreseen in getting the patient to hospital, and persuading her to stay there. Evidence should be sought on this from any community nurses involved in the patient's care.
- If the patient is undergoing other forms of treatment, the impact the termination will have on her relationship with her treating physicians and the risk of permanent damage to this relationship.
- The likely difference between termination and continuing to full term on the patient's future (1) mental state; and (2) relationship with therapeutic staff.
- The physical risks of the patient continuing with the pregnancy, as assessed by the gynaecology team.
- If the patient is young, the attitude of her parents or close family to the pregnancy.
- If the patient is attending a school or college the views of any tutor with detailed knowledge of her abilities, personality and needs.
- If the patient is likely to abscond, the available supervision options.
- The nature of the relationship with the father of the unborn child, and, where this is continuing, his attitude to the pregnancy, and likely affect on the relationship of a termination.
- The maturity of the pregnancy and any associated urgency.

In the authors' experience, courts faced with an application for an order that an abortion is in a woman's immediate best interests have required the parties to address more wide-ranging questions about how she became pregnant in the first place and what steps have been put in place to avoid similar situations recurring. Those representing parties at such applications should be fully prepared to deal with the broader questions of the woman's ongoing capacity and best interests in relation to her sexual and reproductive health.

If an application is being considered, the Official Solicitor should be informed of the case immediately. If there are issues concerning what would happen to the baby after delivery it would be important to consider adding Social Services as a party.

It is suggested that a declaration should be sought in the following terms:[1]

'(a) The Respondent [patient] lacks the capacity to consent to [or refuse] a termination of her current pregnancy.

181

(b) It is in her best interests that it should be terminated.

(c) In the present circumstances it is lawful for the Respondent's current pregnancy to be terminated in spite of her inability to consent to this procedure.'[2]

1　By way of an originating summons for a child and (currently) by way of Part 8 procedure for an adult. See **CHAPTER 5**: Going to Court: **PARAS 5.53 – 5.54**.

2　See generally **CHAPTER 5**: Going to Court.

D　CONCLUSION

8.31　Notwithstanding the advent of the Human Rights Act 1998 and recent cases at the fringes of the Abortion Act 1967, abortion law in this jurisdiction remains settled. It has not attracted the sustained legal challenge or political centre stage that the equivalent jurisprudence has in the United States. The key battleground for abortion campaigners has been, and will remain, the time limit for 'social' abortions. The time limit was lowered from 28 weeks to 24 in 1990 and attempts at further reduction in 2008 failed. A reason for this failure was that despite significant advances in neonatal technology in the 1980s, since 1990 the threshold of viability has not been reduced appreciably. By the same token, any significant advances in the threshold of viability will spark renewed calls for a reduction in the 24-week limit.[1] The second area of dispute is 'late term' abortions which can technically be performed just minutes before birth and – as the petitioner in the US case of *Gonzales v Carhart*[2] argued – sometimes by necessarily barbaric procedures. It should be noted, however, that late abortions are rare: of the 195,296 abortions performed in 2008, 2,899 were after 20 weeks and only 124 were performed at 24 weeks and over.[3] Furthermore, late-term abortions are available only *in extremis*. The vaguely worded law relies upon a doctor's good faith which is subject to little scrutiny. However a decision by the Information Tribunal,[4] required the Department of Health to publish its table of medical conditions for abortions under s 1(1)(d) might change the course of the debate and see renewed calls for specific conditions to be excluded from the definition of 'serious handicap'. It is still the case for all abortions that the requirement for certification by two doctors means that the medical profession remains the 'gatekeeper' of a woman's 'free choice'.

1　The Nuffield Council on Bioethics' 2006 report 'Critical care decisions in fetal and neonatal medicine: ethical issues' (November 2006) noted the following (para 24) 'At the time of writing, most babies born at 23 weeks die or survive with some level of predicted disability even if care is given. Survival and discharge from invasive care for babies born between 22 and 23 weeks is rare. The Working Party has no evidence of any therapeutic developments likely to improve the prospects of babies born before 22 weeks in the near future.'.

2　550 US 124 (2007).

3　The vast majority (142,645) were performed at 3–9 weeks (Office for National Statistics and Department of Health, Abortion Statistics, England and Wales 2008 (May 2009)).

4　*Department of Health v The Information Commissioner v The Pro Life Alliance (Additional Party)* (Appeal No EA/2008/0074, 15 October 2009).

For updating material and hyperlinks related to this chapter, see: www.3serjeantsinn.com/mtdl/abortion

Chapter 9

Managing Pregnancies

A   Introduction 9.1

B   The legal background 9.2

Patient and foetal rights in obstetrics 9.2

Compulsory obstetrics 9.3

The caesarean section cases 9.4

    The mentally competent adult patient: Re S (Adult: refusal of treatment) 9.4

    Tameside and Glossop Acute Services NHS Trust v CH 9.5

    Needle phobias: *Re L* 9.7

    A solution? – *Re MB* 9.8

    Re MB Capacity 9.9

    Re MB Reasonable force 9.10

    Re MB Interests of foetus 9.11

    Re MB Procedure 9.12

    The solution imposed – *St George's Healthcare NHS Trust v S* 9.13

C   The Court of Appeal guidelines 9.14

The Mental Capacity Act 2005 9.15

    Advance directives 9.16

    Management of pregnancy in women who are comatose or in a permanent vegetative state 9.17

D   A suggested procedure for obstetric units 9.18

Assessment of capacity 9.19

    Advice to patients about nature of possible treatment 9.20

    Discussion with patient about possible loss of capacity 9.21

    Advance decisions 9.22

    Psychiatric referral and assessment where capacity in doubt 9.23

    Contingency planning for court application 9.24

    Compliance with Court of Appeal guidelines 9.25

    Continual advice to patient 9.26

E   Procedure for patients 9.27

F   Conclusion 9.28

A INTRODUCTION

9.1   The use of surgical deliveries has long been a controversial and sensitive subject. Concerns have been raised about a perceived increase in the incidence of such procedures and suggestions made that this is due to excessively 'defensive' medical practice as opposed to a proper consideration of the interests of the patient.[1]

On the other hand, some medical opinion has viewed the movement in favour of natural birth with scepticism, doubting whether it is in the true interests of mother and child. Given that background, it is not surprising that there was controversy in the past when – in a small number of instances – patients were subjected to non-consensual surgical delivery. In most cases this occurred in the context of women who were, or were at least perceived to be, lacking in the mental capacity to decide whether or not to undergo such a procedure. In at least two cases, however, women who did not lack capacity were forced to have their babies surgically. Following the appearance of this type of case in the United States' courts, it was not surprising that the English courts were drawn into the search for a legal sanction for non-consensual surgical deliveries. The development of legal thinking in this class of case is worth recounting as an object lesson of what can happen when the courts are placed under the pressure of demands to take urgent action to save life, and to demonstrate the dangers of assuming that the conclusions of previous cases can always be relied upon. The cases concerning caesarean section provide a useful guide to many of the principles involved in the application of the declaratory jurisdiction to medical treatment decisions and are therefore considered in some detail.

B THE LEGAL BACKGROUND[1]

Patient and foetal rights in obstetrics

9.2   An obstetrician continually faces the dilemma caused by the perception of an ethical duty to both the mother and her foetus as separate entities. The Royal College of Obstetricians and Gynaecologists' own guidelines state that:

> 'The aim of those who care for pregnant women must be to foster the greatest benefit to both the mother and foetus with the least risk to both. Obstetricians must recognise the dual claims of the mother and her foetus. The mother may have separate interests from her future child. Obstetricians must inform and advise the family, using their training and experience in the best interests of both parties.'[2]

The common law has not, in general, recognised this dual obligation. On several occasions the courts have refused to recognise the foetus as having any legal personality giving the court jurisdiction to intervene. Thus, a husband may not apply for an injunction to restrain the abortion of a foetus of which he is the father.[3] It has been made clear that in such a case the foetus has no rights:

'The first question is whether this plaintiff has a right at all. The foetus cannot, in English law, in my view, have a right of its own at least until it is born and has a separate existence from its mother. That permeates the whole of the civil law of this country (except the criminal law, which is now irrelevant), and is, indeed, the basis of the decisions in those countries where law is founded on the common law ... there can be no doubt, in my view, that in England and Wales the foetus has no right of action, no right at all, until birth.'[4]

An action cannot be brought on behalf of an unborn child to prevent an abortion:

'The authorities, it seems to me, show that a child, after it has been born, and only then, in certain circumstances, based on he or she having a legal right, may be a party to an action brought with regard to such matters as the right to take, on a will or intestacy, or for damages for injuries suffered before birth. In other words, the claim crystallises upon the birth, at which date, but not before, the child attains the status of a legal persona, and thereupon can then exercise that legal right.'[5]

There is no jurisdiction to make an unborn child a ward of court, even to protect it from damage likely to be caused by its mother.[6]

Although the Royal College guidelines describe the dual claims of the mother and foetus, they nevertheless recognise the overriding control of the mother:

'For the duration of pregnancy, the woman is the only person who can directly control what is done to her foetus. The foetus is totally reliant on the mother so long as it remains in utero. The protection of the foetus stands on her performance of her moral obligations, not on any legal right of its own.'[7]

This is not to say that acts and omissions before birth may not have consequences after birth. Thus the common law recognises that an action in negligence may be brought by a child once born alive in respect of injuries inflicted as a result of ante-natal acts or omissions.[8] A charge of homicide will follow an assault on a pregnant woman which causes the death of the child, if he or she is initially born alive:

'Murder or manslaughter can be committed where unlawful injury is deliberately inflicted either to a child in utero or to a mother carrying a child in utero in the circumstances postulated in the question. The requisite intent to be proved in the case of murder is an intention to kill or cause really serious bodily injury to the mother, the foetus before birth being viewed as an integral part of the mother. Such intention is appropriately modified in the case of manslaughter ...

The fact that the death of the child is caused solely in consequence of injury to the mother rather than as a consequence of injury to the foetus does not negative any liability for murder and manslaughter provided that the jury are satisfied that causation is proved.'[9]

A similarly ambivalent view is taken by the English legislature. On the one hand, the Abortion Act 1967 authorises terminations of pregnancy in a wide range of cases. On the other, the Infant Life (Preservation) Act 1929 prohibits the destruction of any child capable of being born alive.[10] The Congenital Disabilities (Civil Liability) Act 1976 clarifies the common law position in relation to liability to the child born alive in respect of injuries *in utero*. Turning to the mother, the law has to resolve the conflict between the principle that a competent adult patient cannot be forced to submit to medical treatment, however well intentioned, and however necessary to preserve life or health[11] and the principle that treatment could be given to a patient incapable of consenting if it was in her best interests.[12] As will be seen, the perceived imperative to save life, foetal and maternal, resulted in what may be considered surprising developments in the definition of mental capacity and of patients' best interests.

1   This section is drawn in part from an article by one of the authors published in the Catholic University of America's *Journal of Public Health Law*.
2   See **APPENDIX 9.7**: Royal College of Obstetricians and Gynaecologists, 'Law and Ethics in Relation to Court-Authorised Obstetric Intervention' (2006), para 5.3.
3   *Paton v British Pregnancy Advisory Service* [1979] QB 276; *Paton v United Kingdom* (1980) 3 EHRR 408.
4   *Paton (ibid.)* at 279 per Sir George Baker P.
5   *C v S* [1988] QB 135 per Heilbron J at 140, citing Canadian authorities *Medhurst v Medhurst* 46 OR (2d) 263 (1984); and *Dehler v Ottawa Civic Hospital* 25 OR (2d) 748 (1979), 29 OR (2d) 677 (1980). See also the European Court of Human Rights' neutral stance on whether the foetus has any rights under Art 2 in *Vo v France* (2005) 10 EHRR 12, discussed in **CHAPTER 8**: Abortion, **PARA 8.24**.
6   *Re F (in utero)* [1988] Fam 122.
7   See **N2** para 5.1.
8   *Burton v Islington Health Authority* [1993] QB 204, CA.
9   *A-G's Reference (No 3 of 1994)* [1998] AC 245.
10   This is subject to an exception under the Abortion Act 1967 in relation to a foetus of 24 weeks or more likely to be seriously handicapped on birth: Abortion Act 1967, s 1 (as amended by the Human Fertilisation and Embryology Act 1990); and see **CHAPTER 8**: Abortion, **PARA 8.3**.
11   *Sidaway v Board of Governors of the Bethlem Royal Hospital and the Maudsley Hospital* [1985] AC 871.
12   *Re F (mental patient: sterilisation)* [1990] 2 AC 1.

Compulsory obstetrics

9.3   Until 1988 no case appears to have been brought before the English courts in which an attempt was made to authorise the imposition of obstetric management on a woman without a lawful consent. The extension of the declaratory jurisdiction[1] by the cases of *T v T*[2] and *Re F (mental patient: sterilisation)*[3] to include issues of mental capacity and best interests – combined with a practical requirement for 'sensitive' cases to be referred to court – inevitably set the scene for obstetric cases to be the subject of applications. Although this chapter focuses on caesarean sections, as the Royal College guidelines state:

'The legal and ethical principles that apply to caesarean section also apply to other possible interventions, such as intrauterine transfusion, cervical cerclage or medication in pregnancy.'[4]

1   Part of which has been described as 'one of the most remarkable developments of modern British administrative law': Zamir & Woolf, *The Declaratory Judgment* (2nd ed, Sweet & Maxwell, 1993), p 8.
2   [1988] Fam 52.
3   [1990] 2 AC 1; see the judgments of Lord Brandon at 56–57 and 62–65; Lord Griffiths at 70–71; Lord Goff at 79–80, 83. The practice is now followed in sterilisation cases (see **CHAPTER 7**: Sterilisation and **APPENDIX 7.2**: Superseded Practice Note (Official Solicitor: Sterilisation)) and for the withdrawal of life-sustaining nutrition and hydration (see **CHAPTER 12**: Permanent Vegetative State and **APPENDIX 12.1**: Superseded Practice Note (Official Solicitor: Vegetative State)).
4   See **APPENDIX 9.7**: Royal College of Obstetricians and Gynaecologists, 'Law and Ethics in Relation to Court-Authorised Obstetric Intervention' (2006), para 2.

The caesarean section cases

9.4   While they have provoked considerable controversy, there have in fact been very few cases in which courts in this country have been asked to consider a proposal to deliver a baby by caesarean section against the will of the mother. It might be presumed that before the advent of the declaratory jurisdiction referred to above, doctors did not consider it necessary to seek such a safeguard, relying on some form of medical paternalism to justify their actions. In the case of competent patients it is more likely that it did not occur to doctors to perform such procedures if their persuasive powers failed to convince the patient of the need for it. In any event, as will be seen from the cases that have come before the courts, such problems usually arise in circumstances of great urgency and it may not have been thought practicable to involve the machinery of justice in addressing the issues. It may be possible that the ever-increasing threat of litigation arising out of obstetric accidents has been a powerful motivating force behind the modest flow of cases in this area.

The mentally competent adult patient: *Re S (adult: refusal of treatment)*[1]

This was the first case brought before the courts for a declaration that it would be lawful to perform a caesarean section delivery on a woman in labour. The circumstances in which the case was brought were extraordinary and unlikely to produce reasoned jurisprudence. A 30-year-old woman was in labour with her third pregnancy, being six days overdue with the foetus in a transverse lie and a foetal elbow projecting through the cervix. For deeply held religious reasons the mother refused to consent to delivery by caesarean section although she had been advised and understood that without such a procedure she and the baby were in mortal danger. An application was made to the court by the hospital for a declaration that surgical delivery would be lawful. The mother was not represented, but the court was assisted by an *amicus curiae*.[2] It was clear on the basis of the information provided to the judge, Sir Stephen Brown P, that the mother and child would die within hours, if not minutes, if no intervention took place. The judge noted that there was no English authority on the point, although it had been said that it might be possible to override the will of a competent woman to save a viable foetus.[3] However, he considered there was American authority[4] suggesting that in a case like this the American courts would be likely to favour the grant of a declaration. The President then granted a declaration that:

'the operation of caesarean section and necessary consequential treatment which the Plaintiff, by its servants or agents proposes to perform on the Defendant at [the hospital] is in the vital interests of the Defendant and the unborn child she is carrying and can lawfully be performed despite the Defendant's refusal to give her consent'.[5]

The case had many unsatisfactory features. The court had found it to be lawful for doctors to override the clearly expressed will of a mentally competent woman and to perform invasive surgery on her. While time did not permit a reasoned judgment, it is clear that the justification cannot have been any perceived irrationality of the decision: a competent adult has an absolute right to choose whether or not to undergo medical treatment.[6] In fact, the foetus died before delivery and the doctors proceeded – in reliance upon the order – to undertake a caesarean section against the patient's wishes.

A more leisurely study of the American authority relied upon in *Re S* indicated that it very strongly suggested that the will of a mentally competent woman should in fact never be overridden. Two further arguments against overriding the patient's objections were contained in the authority, namely that, first, it destroyed the necessary trust between patient and doctor and might drive high-risk mothers out of the health care system, and, secondly, in this type of case the urgency rendered justice almost impossible to achieve (for reasons which applied even more cogently in *Re S* itself).[7]

Re S was the subject of considerable academic[8] and feminist[9] criticism. A competent adult's refusal of invasive surgery had been overridden in part in the interests of her foetus but, the foetus having died, in favour of her interests as determined by others. This momentous step was taken without any representation on her behalf and with only the most rudimentary evidence. In so far as the decision was taken to protect the interests of the foetus, it would seem to have conflicted with the powerful *obiter dictum* of Balcombe LJ in *Re F (in utero)*:

'If the law is to be extended in this manner, so as to impose control over the mother of an unborn child, where such control may be necessary for the benefit of that child, then under our system of parliamentary democracy it is for Parliament to decide whether such controls can be imposed and, if so, subject to what limitations or conditions ... If Parliament were to think it appropriate that a pregnant woman should be subject to controls for the benefit of her unborn child, then doubtless it would stipulate the circumstances in which such controls may be applied and the safeguards appropriate for the mother's protection. In such a sensitive field, affecting as it does the liberty of the individual, it is not for the judiciary to extend the law.'[10]

Following this case, the Royal College of Obstetricians issued guidelines[11] which concluded by suggesting a practice of respecting the competent mother's wishes in these circumstances:

'A doctor must respect the competent pregnant woman's right to choose or refuse any particular recommended course of action whilst optimising care for both mother and fetus to the best of his or her ability. A doctor would not then be culpable if these endeavours were unsuccessful.'

Building on this, the 2006 Guidelines expressly provided:

'It is inappropriate to invoke judicial intervention to overrule an informed and competent woman's refusal of a proposed medical treatment, even if it seems to others to be irrational.'[12]

1   [1993] Fam 123.
2   The judge, Sir Stephen Brown P, has described in detail what occurred in 'Matters of Life and Death' (Lecture to the Medico–Legal Society, 14 October 1993) (1994) 6 Med Leg J 52). This is quoted in *Medical Treatment Decisions and the Law* (1st ed).
3   *Re T (adult: refusal of treatment)* [1993] Fam 95.
4   *Re AC* 573 A.2d 1235, 1240, 1246–1248, 1252 (1990).
5   The text is taken from the official transcript, as it does not appear in the report.
6   See **CHAPTER 2**: Consent – Adults.
7   There was in fact some US authority in favour of non-consensual deliveries, some of which was cited in *Re AC*, namely: *Jefferson v Griffin Spalding County Hospital Authority* 274 SE 2d 457 (1981); *Re Madyun* 573 A 2d 1259 (1986). However, following the final decision in *Re AC*, the family of AC sued for malpractice in a suit settled on terms which included a statement endorsed by the American Medical Association and American College of Obstetricians and Gynecologists, including the following: 'A judicial proceeding is the least desirable manner to obtain authorization for treatment and should be utilized only in the absence of other surrogates ... Judicial authorization to override a patient's competent decision is virtually never justified' ((1992) 142 NLJ 1638).
8   Note commentary by Professor Grubb at [1993] 1 Med L Rev 92.
9   (1992) 142 NLJ 1638.
10 [1988] Fam 122 at 144.
11 *A Consideration of the Law and Ethics in relation to Court-Authorised Obstetric Intervention* (Royal College of Obstetricians and Gynaecologists, 1996). This has been repeated in the 2006 guidelines (referred to at **PARA 9.2** above) at para 7 (summary) and set out at **APPENDIX 9.7**.
12 See **APPENDIX 9.7**: Royal College of Obstetricians and Gynaecologists, 'Law and Ethics in Relation to Court-Authorised Obstetric Intervention' (2006).

Tameside and Glossop Acute Services NHS Trust v CH[1]

9.5   After an interval of over three years the Family Division was called upon in circumstances of slightly less urgency to consider the case of a female paranoid schizophrenic who was compulsorily detained in a mental hospital under s 3 of the Mental Health Act 1983. Such detention does not carry any necessary implication that the patient has lost the mental capacity to consent to or refuse medical treatment.[2] The patient wanted to have her baby and care for it, but suffered from a delusional belief that the doctors caring for her were evil and wished to harm the baby. She had a history of resisting treatment. The treating doctors became concerned at intra-uterine growth retardation and concluded that delivery by caesarean section was necessary to safeguard the baby. They feared that the patient, whom they considered incapable of understanding the advice she received, would resist. They sought a declaration that it would be lawful to provide such treatment and to use reasonable restraint to the extent necessary for that purpose. Thorpe J concluded that s 63 of the Mental Health Act 1983 permitted a caesarean section to be imposed on the patient without her consent on the ground that it was treatment for the mental disorder from which she was suffering. The evidence before him was that without surgical delivery, the foetus would die, but there would be no physical harm to the mother. However, the birth of a stillborn baby would have had a profoundly deleterious effect on her mental health and would have impeded recovery.

This interpretation of the statute is controversial,[3] but there would seem to be a pragmatic argument in favour of it in this type of case. On the evidence, the mother wished to protect her baby, but – by reason of her serious mental disorder – believed that the very act which would save it was intended to do it harm. If such a patient cannot be protected from such serious consequences of her illness, it might be thought that the mental health legislation was deficient.

1   [1996] 1 FCR 753.
2   *B v Croydon Health Authority* [1995] Fam 133, [1995] 2 WLR 294, [1995] 1 All ER 683, CA; and see **CHAPTER 10:** Feeding.
3   Professor Grubb ((1996) 4 Med L Rev 194–198) argues that it is 'incredible'. Barbara Hewson wrote: 'A cynic's response might be: women (at any rate whilst pregnant or in labour) are a species of inferior being, who are not the same as, and are therefore not entitled to claim the same fundamental rights as men' ((1996) 146 NLJ 1385).

An attack on the competence of pregnant women?

9.6   Two cases heard urgently on the same day also caused controversy. In the first, *Rochdale Healthcare NHS Trust v C,*[1] the patient apparently objected to a caesarean section because she had suffered backache and pain after a previous similar procedure. She had said she would rather die than have a caesarean section again. After a rudimentary hearing[2] the judge stated that the patient was in:

'the throes of labour with all that is involved in terms of "pain and emotional stress" and concluded that a patient who could, in those circumstances, speak in terms which seemed to accept the inevitability of her own death, was not a patient who was able properly to weigh up the considerations that arose so as to make any valid decision, about anything of even the most trivial kind, surely still less one which involved her own life'.

Accordingly, he found that it was in the patient's best interests to undergo the operation and made a declaration that such a procedure would be lawful. In fact, by the time news of the declaration had been transmitted to the hospital, the patient had changed her mind and she consented to the operation which was performed successfully.

The decision caused concern because not only had an order been made on an *ex parte* basis, but the judge also appeared to suggest in the passage that a woman 'in the throes of labour' was incapable, by reason of that fact, of making any decision, however trivial. Such a view is unlikely to appeal to labouring mothers or, indeed, women in general. Indeed, there appeared to be no evidence, of even an informal kind, to justify the finding. While the mother's decision may well be thought to be irrational, general principles preclude deciding competence on the basis of the absence of good reasons for a decision.

The other case decided on the same day – *Norfolk & Norwich Healthcare NHS Trust v W*[3] – concerned a woman who, although she was in the second stage of labour, denied she was pregnant. She had a history of psychiatric treatment. The consultant wished to effect delivery by forceps, but wanted authority to deliver by caesarean section in the event that this failed. He considered that the foetus would die if not delivered within 1¼ hours of the time the application began. The attending consultant psychiatrist considered that, although the patient was not suffering from a mental disorder warranting detention under the Mental Health Act 1983, she was incapable of balancing treatment information given to her so as to make a choice. The judge could have found her incompetent on that ground alone, but he chose to go further:

> 'I held that although she was not suffering from a mental disorder within the meaning of the statute, she lacked the mental competence to make a decision about the treatment that was proposed because she was incapable of weighing up the considerations that were involved. She was called upon to make that decision at a time of acute emotional stress and physical pain in the ordinary course of labour made even more difficult for her because of her own particular mental history.'[4]

He went on to find that the proposed method of delivery would be in her best interests to prevent damage to her uterus, and because the death of the foetus would have detrimental psychological effects on her. He also ruled that at common law reasonable force could be used as a necessary incident of treatment, thus deciding the point left open in *Tameside*, on the ground that it was in accordance with the doctrine of necessity enunciated in *Re F (mental patient: sterilisation)*.[5]

Many would agree that a patient who for reasons of mental disorder[6] was incapable of believing she was pregnant in the circumstances of this case should in some way be protected from danger. The judge in this case, however, seems to have been influenced by a particular view of the abilities of labouring women, and by the dangers posed to a viable foetus. Furthermore, the court was prepared to make an order which effectively authorised compulsory invasive surgery and restraint at a hearing of which the patient appears to have had no notice and at which she was unrepresented, without any formal evidence.

Barbara Hewson suggested:

> 'The assumption ... seems to [have been] that pregnant women are not really autonomous individuals entitled to equal protection, but merely a subdivision of what the courts once called infants and lunatics, incapable of making decisions for themselves, for whom doctors and courts should be surrogate decision-makers.'[7]

1   [1997] 1 FCR 274.
2   For a fuller description see *Medical Treatment Decisions and the Law* (1st ed).
3   [1996] 2 FLR 613.
4   [1996] 2 FLR 613 at 616 (emphasis added).
5   *Re F (mental patient: sterilisation)* [1990] 2 AC 1.
6   As Professor Grubb stated at (1996) 4 Med L Rev 197: 'it is difficult to believe that her denial of the obvious was based upon a difference of opinion or values rather than having a psychiatric history'. It was clearly important for the court to be satisfied that the inability is caused by mental disorder rather than: 'the tendency most people have when undergoing medical treatment to self-assess and then puzzle over the divergence between medical and self-assessment'. See *B v Croydon Health Authority* (1994) 22 BMLR 13 at 25 per Thorpe J.
7   (1996) 146 NLJ 1385 at 1386 – Women's rights and legal wrongs.

Needle phobias: *Re L*

9.7 In *Re L*[1] the patient, in her twenties, was in labour at full term, but progress was obstructed. The consultant considered that, without intervention, deterioration in foetal health and eventual death were inevitable. The patient wanted to have her child safely, but suffered from an extreme needle phobia and would not consent to any injection such as would be necessary for an anaesthetic. The alternative of inducing anaesthesia by gas inhalation carried a 60 per cent chance of causing the patient's death, and the anaesthetist considered this unacceptable.

It was reported that the consultant obstetrician considered the patient to be incapable of weighing treatment information to make a choice. The judge ruled that the patient lacked the capacity to make treatment decisions on the ground that:

'her extreme needle phobia amounted to an involuntary compulsion that disabled L from weighing treatment information in the balance to make a choice. Indeed it was an affliction of a psychological nature that compelled L against medical advice with such force that her own life would be in serious peril'.[2]

The judge was willing to make such a finding despite the absence of any psychiatric evidence or even reported opinion. However, where an urgent situation arises, it might be argued that it is better for the matter to receive some form of judicial review than for doctors to proceed without any external reference.

1   *Re L (an adult: non-consensual treatment)* [1997] 1 FCR 609.
2   *Ibid* at 612E.

A solution? – *Re MB*

9.8 The concerns raised by the previous cases were to some extent resolved in *Re MB*.[1] The case was heard in circumstances of considerable urgency: an application was made by telephone to a Family Division judge, Hollis J, between 9.25 and 9.55 pm, when he granted a declaration in the following terms:

'It shall be lawful for 2 days from the date of this order, notwithstanding the inability of [the patient] to consent thereto:

(i)   for the [hospital's] responsible doctors to carry out such treatment as may in their opinion be necessary for the purposes of the [patient's] present labour, including, if necessary, caesarean section, including the insertion of needles for the purposes of intravenous infusions and anaesthesia;

(ii)   for reasonable force to be used in the course of such treatment;

(iii)   generally to furnish such treatment and nursing care as may be appropriate to ensure that the [patient] suffers the least distress and retains the greatest dignity.'[2]

The patient was represented by counsel who had had some opportunity to take instructions from her, if only by telephone. The Official Solicitor's representative was present as *amicus*. No formal evidence was available and, as in previous cases, information gleaned by counsel for both parties by telephone was relayed to the judge.

The case concerned a woman with a 33-week pregnancy with a footling breech presentation and an extreme needle phobia. If normal labour was allowed to proceed there was a considerable risk of harm to the foetus, but little danger to the mother herself. She did not oppose a caesarean section as such, but adamantly refused to allow the insertion of a needle for any purpose. In this case the anaesthetist was prepared to take the risks involved in the gas inhalation technique, but the patient continually changed her mind as to whether she would consent to this. Her consultant psychiatrist's opinion was:

'Away from the need to undergo the procedure, I had no doubt at all that she fully understood the need for a caesarean section and consented to it. However in the final phase she got into a panic and said she could not go on. If she were calmed down I thought she would consent to the procedure. At the moment of panic, however, her fear dominated all.'[3]

Hollis J found that she lacked the mental capacity to make treatment decisions and made the declaration set out above. An appeal was immediately launched against the decision and the Court of Appeal convened to hear it in open court at 11.00 pm. The hearing concluded at 1.00 am with the dismissal of the appeal. As this was the first occasion on which a case of this type had been before the Court of Appeal, judgment was reserved. This judgment should be read in full by anyone proposing to undertake a non-consensual operation or apply to the court in connection with one.[4] Many of the problems seen above were addressed. In summary, the court addressed the following points.

1 *Re MB (an adult: medical treatment)* [1997] 2 FLR 426.
2 *Ibid.* at 432.
3 *Ibid.* at 431.

Re MB: Capacity

9.9   It was emphasised that every adult is presumed to have the capacity to make decisions about treatment unless and until that presumption is rebutted, and that a competent person is entitled to make a decision:

'for religious reasons, other reasons, for rational or irrational reasons or for no reason at all ... [to] choose not to have medical intervention, even though the consequences may be the death or serious handicap of the child she bears, or her own death. In that event the courts do not have the jurisdiction to declare medical intervention lawful and the question of her own best interests objectively considered does not arise'.

The irrationality in which the competent patient was entitled to indulge was defined in very wide-ranging terms:

'a decision so outrageous in its defiance of logic or of accepted moral standards that no sensible person who had applied his mind to the question to be decided could have arrived at it'.

However, it was suggested that:

'Although it might be thought that irrationality sits uneasily with competence to decide, panic, indecisiveness and irrationality in themselves do not as such amount to incompetence, but they may be symptoms or evidence of incompetence. The graver the consequences of the decision, the commensurately greater the level of competence required to take the decision.'

The court approved of the then test for capacity,[1] but added the gloss that temporary factors, such as confusion, shock, fatigue, pain or drugs, or panic induced by fear, might destroy or erode capacity. It was emphasised that careful examination of the evidence was required to determine whether fear had destroyed capacity as opposed to being a rational reason for refusal. Applying these principles to the facts,[2] the court held that the patient had lost her capacity by reason of her needle phobia dominating her thinking.

1   *Re C* test; now supplanted by the MCA; see **CHAPTER 2**: Consent – Adults.
2   By the time the Court of Appeal delivered its reserved judgment, affidavit evidence verifying the information given at the hearing had been filed.

Re MB: Reasonable force

9.10   The court affirmed the previous decisions on this point and held that reasonable force could be used where necessary in the best interests of the patient. It was accepted that the issue may need to be examined in greater depth on a future occasion.[1]

1   For the detail of the current law on restraint and detention, see **CHAPTER 6.**: Restraint and Deprivation of Liberty.

Re MB: Interests of foetus

9.11   After a thorough consideration of statute and case law, including human rights cases and US authorities,[1] it was held emphatically that there was no jurisdiction at common law to declare non-consensual medical intervention to be lawful to protect the interests of the unborn child:

'The law is, in our judgment, clear that a competent woman who has the capacity to decide may, for religious reasons, other reasons, or no reasons at all, choose not to have medical intervention, even though … the consequence may be the death or serious handicap of the child she bears or her own death. She may refuse to consent to the anaesthesia injection in the full knowledge that her decision may significantly reduce the chance of her unborn child being born alive. The foetus up to the moment of birth does not have any separate interests capable of being taken into account when a court has to consider an application for a declaration in respect of a caesarean section operation.'[2]

Thus the court dealt a mortal blow to the validity of *Re S* as an authority and emphatically restored the primacy of the competent adult woman's autonomy, while seeking to maintain a level of protection for those who are incapable of making a decision for themselves.

1   *Re T (adult: refusal of treatment)* [1993] Fam 95; *Paton v British Pregnancy Advisory Service Trustees* [1979] QB 276; *C v S* [1989] QB 135; *Burton v Islington Health Authority* [1993] QB 204; *A-G's Reference (No 3 of 1994)* [1998] AC 245, HL; *Villar v Sir Walter Gilbey* [1907] AC 139; Offences Against the Person Act 1861, s 58; Abortion Act 1967; Congenital Disabilities Act 1976; *Bruggemann and Scheuten v Federal Republic of Germany* (1978) 10 DR E Com HR 100; *Paton v United Kingdom* (1980) 3 EHRR 408; *H v Norway* (1992) 73 DR 155, E ComHR); *Open Door and Dublin Well Woman v Ireland* (1992) 15 EHRR 244; *Jefferson v Griffin Spalding County Hospital Authority* (1981) 274 SE 2d 457; *Crouse Irving Memorial Hospital v Paddock* 485 NYS 2d 443 (1985); *Re Madyun* 573 A 2d 1259 (1986); *Re AC* 533 A 2d 611 (1987); *Re Baby Boy Doe* 632 NE 2d 32 (1994).
2   Transcript, p 28.

Re MB: Procedure

9.12   Procedural guidelines were offered in *Re MB*.[1] While it was said that the court was unlikely to entertain an application for a declaration of this type unless capacity was in issue, it was suggested that 'for the time being at least' doctors ought to seek a ruling on the issue of competence. It was unclear whether this related only to cases where there was a dispute on that issue. It was made clear that it was highly desirable for this type of case to be brought as soon as a potential problem was identified rather than at the last, desperate, minute, and that the hearing should be *inter partes*, with the mother being represented in all cases if she wished to be. It was preferable for evidence on competence to be given by a psychiatrist.

1   [1997] 2 FLR 426.

The solution imposed – *St George's Healthcare NHS Trust v S*

9.13   *St George's Healthcare NHS Trust v S*[1] brought together the most unfortunate features of the cases which preceded *Re MB* and resulted in firm guidelines being laid down by the Court of Appeal. A young adult woman of full mental capacity, who was 36 weeks pregnant and who suffered from pre-eclampsia, rejected medical advice that she needed urgent attention and an induced delivery in the interests of the health of herself and her baby. She refused, insisting on a natural delivery. A social worker and two doctors approved her detention in hospital under s 2 of the Mental Health Act 1983 for assessment. A few hours later, an *ex parte* application was made to a Family Division judge sitting in chambers. No evidence was presented, but erroneous information was given to the court. The judge granted a declaration which purported to dispense with the patient's consent to treatment. Later the same day she was subjected to delivery of her baby by caesarean section without her consent. No judicial consideration was given to the issue of the patient's capacity. In combined actions for judicial review and damages the Court of Appeal held:

- An adult of full mental capacity cannot be ordered to undergo surgery or any form of medical treatment against his or her wishes.

- An unborn child is not a separate person from its mother and its need for medical assistance does not prevail over the mother's right to refuse treatment.

- No person may be detained under the Mental Health Act 1983 unless the patient falls within the conditions prescribed by the Act: detention for the purpose of providing non-consensual obstetric treatment, as opposed to assessment or treatment of a mental disorder, does not come within the Act.

- A person detained under the Act still possessing full mental capacity cannot have medical treatment imposed on him unless it is permitted by the Act. Treatment other than for the mental disorder for which the patient is detained can be administered only with the consent of the patient.

- A declaration made on an *ex parte* application which the defendant could not oppose and of which he knew nothing has no effect and, in particular, is no defence to an action by the patient for damages for trespass to the person, once set aside on appeal.[2]

In *Bolton Hospitals NHS Trust v O*[3] a woman at 39 weeks' gestation found herself in a similar position to the mother in *Re MB*.[4] She had given birth by caesarean section four times before. Without a caesarean on this occasion there was a greater than 95 per cent chance of failure which would result in the death of mother and baby. While the patient consented to the operation, on four separate occasions she had withdrawn her consent after having gone down to the theatre to have the operation, experiencing panic in the operating theatre at the last moment. The patient had been diagnosed as suffering from post-traumatic stress disorder arising from her previous caesareans. The hospital, supported by the woman, sought a declaration from the court to override any last-minute withdrawal consent.

Butler-Sloss P recognised that the patient wanted to go home with her baby, but wanted the decision to be taken out of her hands. The President held that, while a patient was entitled to refuse treatment even if she did not give good reasons for so doing, there was a point at which refusal and irrationality, as others might see it, tipped the usually competent person over into a situation where the capacity to see through the consequences was inhibited by the panic situation in which the patient found herself. The patient was able to accept anaesthetic in the ward, but panic prevented her from accepting it in the operating theatre. Thus, the President held, at the crucial point when she went down to the operating theatre, the patient was temporarily without capacity to consent or to refuse the surgery proposed, or the anaesthesia that was an essential prerequisite of the surgery, because of overwhelming psychological fear and anxiety. In the premises it was held that it was lawful, notwithstanding her inability to consent, to provide her with medical treatment in connection with her present labour, including if necessary caesarean section and, *inter alia*, anaesthesia, and for reasonable force to be used for such purposes.

Butler-Sloss P noted that the consultant who gave evidence had read the decisions in *Re MB* and *St George's Healthcare NHS Trust v S* and had applied the requirements of those cases to the facts. This undoubtedly impressed the President and doctors who might find themselves in the position of having to make an emergency application are well advised to have digested the guidance and be ready to apply it.[5]

1   [1999] Fam 26, [1998] 3 WLR 936, [1998] 3 All ER 673.
2   Note the ability now under the MCA to seek interim orders and declarations: see **CHAPTER 5**: Going to Court, **PARA 5.23**.
3   [2003] 1 FLR 824.
4   [2002] EWHC 2781 (Fam).
5   See **PARA 6.16** and **APPENDIX 9.1**.

C THE COURT OF APPEAL GUIDELINES

9.14   In the *St George's Healthcare* case the Court of Appeal issued guidelines[1] after consultation with the President of the Family Division, the Official Solicitor and further submissions by the parties, who had themselves taken soundings from a wide range of professional bodies. These replaced guidelines given at the time of the original judgment. Although principally aimed at obstetric cases, they apply to all instances of proposed invasive treatment of a patient lacking the capacity to consent to or refuse treatment. These are set out in full in the Appendix below.[2] These guidelines should be read in light of the new procedural framework outlined in **CHAPTER 5**. In summary, the court stated that:

- It is pointless making an application to the court if the patient has full mental capacity.
- Refusals should be recorded and authenticated in writing wherever possible.
- A patient lacking the relevant mental capacity should be treated and cared for according to the hospital authority's judgment of his best interests.
- A competently made advance directive should be respected; if there was doubt about its validity, an application should be made to the court.
- Any problem about mental capacity to consent to treatment should be identified as soon as possible and assessed as a priority. While assessment by a general practitioner or other non-specialist might suffice, in serious or difficult cases it should ideally be performed by a consultant psychiatrist approved under the Mental Health Act 1983.
- If, on assessment, there was a serious doubt about competence, the patient's capacity to manage his own property or affairs should also be considered. If this is in doubt, legal advice should be sought as soon as possible, as a guardian *ad litem* may need to be appointed and the Official Solicitor notified.
- The patient's solicitors must be informed immediately of any intention to make an application for a declaration, and an opportunity given to take instructions and obtain legal aid.
- Potential witnesses for the health authority must be made aware of the

guidance in *Re MB*,[3] *St George's Healthcare NHS Trust v S*, and any guidance issued by the DoH and the BMA.

- Any application for a declaration should be *inter partes*, as any other form of proceeding will not bind the patient.

- Although the Official Solicitor will not act for a patient capable of instructing a solicitor, he can be called upon by the court to act as *amicus curiae*.

- On any such application the court must be supplied with all accurate and relevant information, including the reasons for the treatment, any alternatives, and any ascertainable reason why the patient is refusing the treatment.

- The terms of the order must be recorded and approved by the judge before they are communicated to the health authority. The patient must be informed of the precise terms.

- Applicants for emergency orders made without issuing and lodging the relevant documents have a duty to comply with proper procedure and pay the relevant court fees.

- There might be cases which are so urgent that it is impracticable to apply to the court at all: where delay might damage the patient's health and rigid adherence to the guidelines may be inappropriate.

The practical problem for all practitioners and authorities left by this guidance is to know in what type of case it is desirable or obligatory to make an application to the court for a declaration, and in what cases it is acceptable to provide treatment without such an application in what is assessed to be the best interests of the patient. The original case was concerned with a caesarean section, as was *Re MB*. The guidance, however, is deliberately designed to cover any form of surgical or invasive treatment. It would appear that it is not every case which ought to be referred to court, but that a judgment must be made. It is suggested that consideration must be given to making an application in every case where it is considered that the patient lacks capacity to consent to or refuse treatment and is actively refusing the proposed treatment. The guidance should not be read as meaning that such consideration should only be given when there is a serious doubt about competence in the sense that there is a professional disagreement between practitioners on the issue. In every case where the patient refuses or claims the right to refuse treatment he is asserting the right, and prima facie claiming the capacity, to do so. In that important sense the question of competence is in dispute and a serious doubt is raised where a properly qualified practitioner seeks to override that refusal. It is suggested that it would be prudent, at least for the time being, to make an application in the case of any such patient on whom it is proposed to perform a caesarean section or other form of surgical or assisted delivery against the patient's will. The cases demonstrate that such circumstances are almost inevitably serious and complex.[4]

1   [1998] 3 WLR 936 at 968, [1998] 3 All ER 673 at 702.
2   See **APPENDIX 9.1**: *St George's Healthcare v S* Guidelines.
3   [1997] 2 FLR 426, [1997] 8 Med LR 217; see also **APPENDIX 9.1**: *Re MB Guidelines* [1998] 3 WLR 936, [1998] 3 All ER 673.
4   For further discussion of when to go to court, see **CHAPTER 5**: Going to Court.

The Mental Capacity Act 2005

9.15   Management of pregnancy in a woman (aged 16 or over) who has questionable capacity is now governed by the Mental Capacity Act 2005.

The Act requires demonstration that the patient is unable to make a decision as a result of an impairment or disturbance in the functioning of the mind or brain. The fact of a woman's pregnancy or her behaviour during pregnancy cannot establish a lack of capacity.[1] Since capacity is judged at 'the relevant time', temporary incapacity during pregnancy (or labour) can be established under the Act as it could under the common law.

1   Section 2(3)(b).

Advance decisions[1]

9.16   The situation might arise where a competent woman (over 18) has made an advance decision detailing how she should (or should not) be treated in the event that she loses capacity during pregnancy. Under s 26 of the Mental Capacity Act 2005, where an individual lacking capacity at the time of the proposed treatment has made a written advance decision at a time when she had capacity, the decision stands as if it were being made at the relevant time. The Royal College Guidelines[2] advise practitioners that generally they are under a duty to respect, in an advance directive, the refusal of any procedure debarred to them by a patient's refusal of consent.[3] However, doctors are reminded that they are not obliged to honour a request for specific treatment in an advance decision that they would hold to be contrary to professional judgment or personal conscience.[4] In any event, the court has the power to make declarations as to the validity of an advance decision. In *R (Burke) v GMC* the Court of Appeal held that: 'While section 26 … requires compliance with a valid advance decision to refuse treatment, section 4 does no more than require this to be taken into consideration when considering what is in the best interests of a patient.'[5]

1   Section 2(3)(b).
2   (2006) See **PARA 9.2, N5.**
3   Para 4.1.
4   *Ibid.*
5   [2005] EWCA Civ 1003.

Management of pregnancy in women who are comatose or in a permanent vegetative state

9.17   Save where she has prepared an advance decision of sufficient particularity, health care professionals and the courts face a complex decision where a mother enters a coma but her pregnancy remains intact. A woman in this condition will lack capacity. In the absence of a formal advance decision or other expressions of her wishes, treatment decisions will be based on the assessment of best interests. It could be argued that where a woman is brain stem dead, with no prospects of recovery, her foetus, which could enjoy a full life, has a greater (or at least equal) claim to rights and interests. This seems to be the approach taken in the Royal College Guidelines, as it is stated that where the mother is brain stem dead:

'the interests of the fetus would predominate. It would, thus, be appropriate to defer any decision to withdraw life support until intact independent survival was likely.'[1]

However, this would run contrary to the long line of authority that the foetus has no independent legal status[2] and it is doubted whether this statement reflects the true legal position. In those rare cases where the interests of the foetus may be in opposition to those of the mother, the mother's interests are not usurped. The assessment of best interests should be limited to those of the mother and a number of different considerations pertain.[3] First, what are the mother's prospects of recovery? If she is likely to recover, it will more easily be said that an invasive procedure will be in the mother's best interests. She will, eventually, gain the pleasure of a having child and avoid the trauma of knowing that her pregnancy failed. Secondly, will the continuance of pregnancy to the point at which a viable baby can be born or an invasive procedure to effect that birth be detrimental to the woman's short-term health or long-term prospects of recovery? If the pregnancy is not yet at a viable stage, will a decision to withhold or withdraw life-sustaining treatment, its continuation not being in the mother's best interests, have to be postponed until a caesarean section is possible?[4]

There may also be situations where the mother lacks capacity at the time of the proposed treatment but prior to this, and at a time when she did have capacity, she indicated that she did not want the treatment. Assuming that this does not amount to a valid advance directive, s 4 of the Mental Capacity Act 2005 would then come into play and any act done or decision made for or on behalf of the mother lacking capacity must again be done or made in her best interests. In assessing those best interests the person making the decision must consider, so far as is reasonably ascertainable:

- the person's past and present wishes and feelings (and, in particular, any relevant written statement made by her when she had capacity);
- the beliefs and values that would be likely to influence her decision if she had capacity;
- the other factors that she would be likely to consider if she were able to do so.

It is supposed that, while the first two factors would often lead doctors to follow the mother's indication that she did not want treatment, the third may allow for inferences about how the mother would have acted if she had known her unborn child may be in grave danger. However, the Royal College Guidelines do acknowledge that:

'The mother's wishes should be respected in the same way as if she were conscious and competent. This may be at the expense of the fetus.'[5]

---

1 See **APPENDIX 9.7**: Royal College of Obstetricians and Gynaecologists, 'Law and Ethics in Relation to Court-Authorised Obstetric Intervention' (2006), para 4.4.
2 See **PARA 9.2** above.
3 It should also be noted that the Royal College Guidelines (see **N1**), advise practitioners that where there is no valid advance directive relevant to the situation, the obstetrician 'being uncertain of the intentions of the mother, would be free to allow more weight to the interest of the fetus' (at para 4.3).

4   For discussion of PVS generally, see **CHAPTER 9:** Permanent Vegetative State.
5   See **N1** para 4.2.

D A SUGGESTED PROCEDURE FOR OBSTETRIC UNITS

9.18   While it is impossible to legislate for all circumstances, it would be prudent for all obstetric units to develop a practice for detecting and dealing with cases where a problem of capacity may arise. A simple and properly applied practice is likely to alleviate many of the problems which are illustrated in the cases described above, including the stress on and distress to patients and their families, unnecessary prejudice to the health of mothers and their babies, and exposure of doctors and others to litigation.

Assessment of capacity

9.19   On first referral or admission, the responsible consultant should ensure that an assessment is made of the patient's capacity to make decisions on obstetric issues. All examiners should be aware of the test for capacity set out in the MCA.[1] Such an initial assessment can probably be made from the patient's reaction to a careful explanation of the likely course of the pregnancy and requirements for management of labour. It must always be remembered that patients must be presumed in law to have the relevant capacity until the contrary is shown.

1   See **CHAPTER 2:** Consent – Adults.

Advice to patients about nature of possible treatment

9.20   In the light of the experience of the courts, it would be prudent to ensure that a patient is made aware as soon as is practicable of any possible need to administer injections or intravenous fluids or to insert needles for other purposes to establish whether she suffers from any form of needle phobia.

Discussion with patient about possible loss of capacity

9.21   If there is a real possibility of a transient loss of capacity occurring in the future due to a phobia or pain, or panic, this should be discussed with the patient well before the event arises, in order to agree with her, while she retains capacity, what should be done in that eventuality.

Advance decision

9.22   The patient should be asked whether she has an existing advance decision specific to her pregnancy in place. If not, consideration should be given to suggesting to a woman with a history suggestive of possible temporary losses of capacity that she put an advance directive in writing while she retains capacity.

Psychiatric referral and assessment where capacity in doubt

9.23 If, on initial assessment or at any subsequent time, a real doubt emerges about the patient's competence, she should be referred to a consultant psychiatrist for an opinion on her capacity.

Contingency planning for court application

9.24 If it is established that the patient lacks or is likely to lack the relevant capacity, is likely to refuse invasive treatment required for the health of herself or her baby, and there is a reasonable possibility of such treatment being required, legal advice should be sought at the earliest opportunity. This should enable a decision as to whether a court application should be made and, if so, when and in what circumstances that ought to be done.[1]

1 See **APPENDICES 9.2–9.6** for precedents for a court application.

Compliance with Court of Appeal guidelines

9.25 If an application is to be made, the Court of Appeal's guidance must be followed as applied in the context of the Court of Protection.[1]

1 See **CHAPTER 5:** Going to Court.

Continual advice to patient

9.26 At all stages the patient should be advised of what is being done and of her rights to obtain her own advice and representation. To this end hospital authorities and their legal advisers should be in a position to assist patients to contact a lawyer when this is required.

E PROCEDURE FOR PATIENTS

9.27 Where a patient fears that doctors are likely to try to impose an unwanted surgical delivery on her, she has the right to seek an injunction restraining them from doing so. If she retains the capacity to make her own decisions, or has made her wishes clear when in possession of her full capacity, or such an operation is not in her best interests, the court is likely to grant an injunction or a declaration that the proposed treatment would be unlawful, whichever remedy is appropriate. A declaration is appropriate where the hospital is prepared to give an undertaking to abide by the decision of the court, and that appears to give sufficient protection to the patient in the circumstances of the case.

The evidence on which those seeking to impose treatment rely should be obtained at the earliest opportunity. A request by a solicitor on behalf of the patient for disclosure of such information should be acceded to by any reasonable hospital authority.[1]

For the best prospect of mounting a successful application, those advising the patient should seek evidence on the following matters:

- the woman's mental capacity to make decisions for herself – generally this will have to be given by a psychiatrist. In theory the patient could rely on the presumption of capacity, but it is likely that the hospital authority will adduce some evidence of incapacity which will require rebuttal;
- any evidence of previously declared wishes in relation to the mode of delivery;
- the intentions of the attending hospital staff;
- the patient's reasons for refusing the proposed mode of delivery; and
- any reasons why it is not in her interests to undergo the proposed mode of delivery (generally this should be supported by independent medical opinion).

Usually, time will be short and the court must be notified immediately of the need for an urgent hearing.[2]

1   The procedure is set out in **CHAPTER 5**: Going to Court.
2   Some general precedents are contained in **APPENDICES 9.2–9.6** below.

F CONCLUSION

9.28   The principles underpinning the assessment of capacity during pregnancy and childbirth are now straightforward. Whilst pregnancy may increase the personal responsibility of a woman, it in no way diminishes her entitlement freely to accept or to reject medical treatment. An unborn child is not in law a separate person from its mother: until born, its interests are subservient. The competent mother can reject any invasion of her body whether necessary for the preservation of the life of her baby or herself. In managing potential capacity issues in pregnancy, the key for healthcare professionals is anticipation. Questions about the possible incapacity of a mother need to be addressed as early as possible. Timely, compassionate and clear communication between health professionals and pregnant women about potential issues in childbirth would obviate a significant number of the litigation issues which the authors have experienced. Greater use should be made of advanced decisions to deal with the very small number of cases in which there is the possibility that a mother will suffer from a temporary loss of capacity in the face of particular procedures.

For updating material and hyperlinks related to this chapter, see:
www.3serjeantsinn.com/mtdl/pregnancies

Chapter 10

Feeding

A   Introduction 10.1
B   Children 10.2
     General principles 10.2
          Children under the age of 16 10.2
          Children aged 16 and 17 10.3
          Effect of disorder on *Gillick* competence 10.4
          Exercise of court's jurisdiction 10.5
     Procedure 10.6
C   Adults 10.7
     Competent adults – general rule 10.7
     Adults lacking the capacity to consent 10.8
     Competent adults detained under the Mental Health Act 1983 10.9
     Procedure – declaration 10.10
     Procedure – injunction 10.11
D   Conclusion 10.12

A INTRODUCTION

10.1   Refusal of nutrition and hydration is often associated with mental disorder. The compulsion not to eat or drink can in some cases be so severe as to be life-threatening. These cases must be distinguished from those who capably and deliberately refuse to take food or drink, such as the rational prisoner who wishes to go on hunger strike in protest at his conviction or someone who wishes not to prolong their life in the face of the onset of a devastating illness.

The principal diagnostic category where the sufferer exhibits self-starvation is anorexia nervosa. However, food refusal manifests itself as a symptom in a number of other mental disorders, including psychotic disorders and personality disorders. Most notably in cases of borderline personality disorder, it is not uncommon for the patient to become compelled to harm himself and this may on occasions take the form of deprivation of food.

Disorders of eating tend to be suffered more by women than men, and the onset is generally in the teenage years. Distorted beliefs about eating are a pathognomonic feature of anorexia nervosa and hence if this clinical diagnosis[1] has been satisfactorily established there will often be no dispute that the patient lacks the requisite capacity to decide whether or not to eat. However, the prevalence of the disorder among those who are just on the point of attaining their majority and releasing themselves from even the theoretical control of parents adds to the challenges of ensuring that treatment given is legally justified.

This section principally addresses the problems posed by those who do not wish to receive nutrition or ancillary treatment and inevitably concentrates on cases of involuntary feeding.[2] As lawyers, we do not seek to pass an opinion on when such treatment might be medically or ethically justified.

1   For example, see **APPENDIX 10.2**: DSM-IV: Diagnostic criteria for eating disorders.
2   Those opposing such treatment will often use the phrase 'force-feeding'. This is avoided here as it carries connotations which do not necessarily correspond to the reality of what is actually done.

B CHILDREN

General principles

Children under the age of 16

10.2   In the case of *Gillick v West Norfolk and Wisbech Area Health Authority*[1] the court held that children who have sufficient understanding and intelligence to comprehend fully what is proposed in terms of medical treatment will have the competence to consent to that treatment. When a child is '*Gillick* competent' their refusal to consent to treatment can be overridden by a person having parental responsibility or by the court.[2]

1   [1985] 3 All ER 402, HL.
2   Re *R (a minor) (wardship: consent to treatment)* [1992] Fam 11; *Re W (a minor) (medical treatment: court's jurisdiction)* [1993] Fam 64. See **CHAPTER 4**: Deciding for Others – Children, **PARA 4.6**.

Children aged 16 and 17

10.3   While statute creates a presumption that a competent consent given by a 16 or 17 year old is as valid as if given by an adult,[1] it does not follow that a refusal by such a patient is a bar to treatment. A refusal by the patient does not amount to a veto of treatment if someone with parental responsibility has consented.[2]

1   Family Law Reform Act 1969, s 8: see **CHAPTER 4:** Deciding for Others – Children, **PARA 4.2**.
2   As is made clear by s 8(3) (see **N1** above): 'Nothing in this section shall be construed as making ineffective any consent which would have been effective if this section had not been enacted.'

Effect of disorder on *Gillick* competence

10.4   The views of the child are an important fact to be taken into account by parents and doctors in deciding whether treatment should proceed. However, it has been pointed out that in anorexia nervosa these views may be of less significance:

'I have no doubt that the wishes of a 16 or 17 year old or indeed a younger child who is "Gillick competent" are of the greatest importance both legally and clinically ... I personally consider that religious or other beliefs which bar any medical treatment or treatment of particular kinds are irrational, but that does not make minors who hold those beliefs any the less "Gillick competent." They may well have sufficient intelligence and understanding fully to appreciate the treatment proposed and the consequences of their refusal to accept that treatment. *What distinguishes W from them ... is that it is a feature of anorexia nervosa that it is capable of destroying the ability to make an informed choice. It creates a compulsion to refuse treatment or only to accept treatment which is likely to be ineffective. This attitude is part and parcel of the disease, and the more advanced the illness, the more compelling it may become.* Where the wishes of the minor are themselves something which the doctors reasonably consider need to be treated in the minor's own best interests, those wishes will clearly have a much reduced significance.'[1]

In other words, the disorder itself may deprive (and in cases of anorexia nervosa usually will deprive) the patient of the capacity to make a decision about eating for himself.

1   *Re W (a minor) (medical treatment: court's jurisdiction)* [1993] Fam 64 at 80 per Lord Donaldson of Lymington MR (emphasis added).

Exercise of court's jurisdiction

10.5   In practical terms, if the court's jurisdiction is invoked, and there is evidence before it that a continued refusal of treatment will probably lead to death or serious injury, the refusal of a child, however near majority, is likely to be overruled:

'[1] It will normally be in the best interests of a child of sufficient age and understanding to make an informed decision that the court should respect its integrity as a human being and not lightly override its decision on such a personal matter as medical treatment, all the more so if that treatment is invasive.

[2] In my judgment, therefore, the court exercising the inherent jurisdiction in relation to a 16 or 17 year old child who is not mentally incompetent will, as a matter of course, ascertain the wishes of the child, and will approach its decision with a strong predilection to give effect to the child's wishes.

[3] ... The case of a mentally incompetent child will present different considerations, although even there the child's wishes, if known, must be a very material factor ...

[4] Nevertheless, if the court's powers are to be meaningful, there must come a point at which the court, while not disregarding the child's wishes, can override them in the child's own best interests, objectively considered.

[5] Clearly such a point will have come if the child is seeking to refuse treatment in circumstances which will in all probability lead to the death of the child or to severe permanent injury.'[1]

The inherent jurisdiction of the court in respect of children extends to authorising the detention of a child patient in a place where treatment can be provided, so long as the court's jurisdiction is not ousted by the accommodation being secure accommodation under the Children Act 1989.[2] The court has power to direct that reasonable force be used if necessary. However, it is important that careful attention should be paid to the safeguards under the Act, and any order made is likely to be made of limited duration and subject to review.[3]

While the Mental Capacity Act 2005 ('MCA') can be applied to those between 16 and 17 years old, it is important to consider whether the circumstances in which treatment will be given will amount to a deprivation of liberty in Art 5 terms. The deprivation of liberty provisions in Schedule A1 to the MCA apply only to those aged over 18.[4] However, where what is sought to be achieved is the detention of a mentally disordered 16 to 17 year old in hospital for involuntary feeding, it is likely that the provisions of the Mental Health Act 1983 ('MHA') could be used in any event.

Previously, the position was that a child aged 16 to 17 could have been detained in hospital for treatment of mental disorder as an 'informal' patient under s 131 MHA on the basis of the consent of someone with parental responsibility. However, that position changed with the recent enactment of s 131(4) MHA which provides that where a child aged 16 to 17 does not consent to an admission to hospital for psychiatric treatment, such an admission cannot be authorised on the basis of parental consent. Thus, for those patients aged 16 to 17 who either do not consent or are incapable of consenting to the admission to hospital for the treatment of their mental disorder either (a) a court order will be required or (b) a compulsory detention power under s 2 or s 3 MHA will need to be implemented.

1 *Re W (a minor) (medical treatment: court's jurisdiction)* [1993] Fam 64 at 88 per Balcombe LJ (enumeration added).

2 *Re C (a minor) (detention for medical treatment)* [1997] 2 FLR 180; see also *Re B (a minor) (treatment and secure accommodation)* [1997] 1 FCR 618, sub nom *A Metropolitan Borough Council v DB* [1997] 1 FLR 767 per Cazalet J.

3 *Re C (a minor) (detention: medical treatment)* (see N2 above). It must be doubtful whether doctors, acting on the authority of parents, can detain a *Gillick* competent child against his will without the authority of the court. Such a step might well contravene the requirement of Art 5 of the ECHR that any deprivation of liberty must be in accordance with a procedure prescribed by law. However, see *Nielsen v Denmark* (1988) 11 EHRR 175, where the Court of Human Rights held (by 9 votes to 7) that detention of a child in a psychiatric ward on his mother's authorisation did not bring into play Art 5 because the deprivation of liberty was not by the authorities of the State. It may be doubted whether the court would adopt the same stance today and, unless such action is authoritatively established to be lawful, the authors' view is that a court application should invariably be made if involuntary detention is thought to be necessary. See, for example: *R v Kirklees Metropolitan Borough Council, ex p C (a minor)* [1992] 2 FLR 117, where it was held that a 12-year-old child had been validly detained in a mental hospital even though not under the Mental Health Act 1983, on the authority of those having parental responsibility, but where the court made it clear that the child was not *Gillick* competent.

4 See **CHAPTER 6**: Restraint and Deprivation of Liberty.

Procedure

10.6   Where it is desired to obtain approval for treatment for which the child is unwilling or unable to give consent, the following steps need to be taken:

- Unless the child is *Gillick* competent and refuses to allow his parents to be involved in the decision-making process – and even then if it is in the child's best interests – the parents or those having parental responsibility should be consulted about the proposed treatment and, if possible, their consent obtained. If such consent is obtained, that is sufficient legal authority to proceed with treatment despite the child's refusal. The position will obviously have to be explained carefully to the child, whose co-operation should be sought if at all possible.

- If no parental consent can be obtained, or the doctors are met with a parental refusal, and it is considered that it remains in the child's best interests that the treatment should be given – unless the case is of such extreme urgency that there is no time to do so – an application should be made to the Family Division of the High Court under the inherent jurisdiction of the court for an order giving permission for the treatment in question to be given. If the child is already a ward of court then the application should be made in the wardship proceedings.

- In preparing for such an application those seeking the order should be prepared with evidence of the medical history, the present condition and prognosis of the patient, the need for treatment, the capacity and views of the patient, the views of the parents or those having parental responsibility, the risks and benefits of the treatment, and the possible results if treatment is not given. Independent expert opinion is always helpful, and should be obtained if at all possible.

- It is always important that the most up-to-date information be available to the court. Therefore applicants should not merely rely on evidence even a few weeks old, but must be prepared to inform the court of the current position.

- In determining the application the court will weigh up the child's best interests on the same basis as it would for an adult. Although the MCA does not apply to children under 16, the principles are still likely to be applied.[1]

1   See **CHAPTER 4**: Deciding for others: Children.

C ADULTS

Competent adults – general rule

10.7   As in any other sphere of medical activity, the general rule is that a competent adult has the absolute right to refuse any form of treatment. Competent adults are fully entitled to refuse to take food or drink for any reason or for no reason at all. A mentally competent adult prisoner who chooses to go on hunger strike and to refuse any form of life-saving care must, therefore, be allowed to do so.[1]

'The right of the defendant to determine his future is plain. That right is not diminished by his status as a detained prisoner ... against the specific right of self determination held by the defendant throughout his sentence there seems to me in this case to be no countervailing state interest to be set in the balance.[2]

Even if the refusal to eat is tantamount to suicide, as in the case of a hunger strike, he cannot be compelled to eat or be forcibly fed.'[3]

In the authors' experience this principle has been upheld in a number of unreported cases where the conscious decision of a prisoner to starve himself to death has not been interfered with by the court.[4]

1   *Secretary of State for the Home Department v Robb* [1995] Fam 127; (discussed in **CHAPTER 13**: Treatment of Suicidal Patients at **PARA 13.16**).
2   *Robb* (**N1** above) per Thorpe J.
3   *B v Croydon Health Authority* [1995] Fam 133 at 137 per Hoffman LJ: for a patient to allow himself to die by declining food has been said not to amount to suicide: see *Robb* (**N 1** above); Lord Goff in *Airedale NHS Trust v Bland* [1993] AC 789 at 864. See also **CHAPTER 6**: Restraint and Deprivation of Liberty, **PARA 6.2**.
4   And see *Brightwater Care Group v Rossiter* [2009] WASC 229 (20 August 2009) discussed in **CHAPTER 13**: Treatment of Suicidal Patients, **PARA 13.34**.

Adults lacking the capacity to consent

10.8   In practice, if a patient suffers with anorexia nervosa he/she is likely to lack the requisite capacity due to fixed, distorted beliefs about eating. Anorexics are, however, often treated under s 63 MHA which permits treatment for mental disorder to be given to the incapable patient and also even in the face of a capable refusal.[1] So far as anorexia is concerned, it has been held that naso-gastric feeding is treatment for the mental disorder for the following reasons:

'it is pointed out that the mental disorder from which she is suffering is anorexia nervosa which is an eating disorder and relieving symptoms is just as much a part of treatment as relieving the underlying cause. If the symptoms are exacerbated by the patient's refusal to eat and drink, the mental disorder becomes progressively more and more difficult to treat and so the treatment by naso-gastric tube is an integral part of the treatment of the mental disorder itself. It is also said that the treatment is necessary in order to make psychiatric treatment possible at all.

This argument, in my judgment, is correct and makes it clear that feeding by naso-gastric tube in the circumstances of this type of case is treatment envisaged under s 63 and does not require the consent of the patient.'[2]

Thus, if the patient is lawfully detained under the MHA for treatment for an eating disorder, it will be possible, under s 63 MHA, to impose the physical treatment of naso-gastric tube feeding on the patient. It will be a matter of medical judgment whether this is appropriate or not, even where the patient has the mental capacity to consent to or refuse treatment. While there have been a number of cases in which declarations have been sought from the court to sanction treatment in such circumstances,[3] this is not a category of case where court proceedings are necessary in every case. It is suggested that they are only required where there is likely to be controversy, such as where friends or family of the patient support the patient's opposition to treatment.

Where an adult patient suffering from an eating disorder lacks the capacity to consent to treatment, and it is not possible to provide that treatment under the MHA, such treatment as is necessary in the patient's best interests may be given under s 5 of the MCA.

1 'The consent of a patient shall not be required for any medical treatment given to him for the mental disorder from which he is suffering, not being a form of treatment to which section 57, 58 or 58A above applies, if the treatment is given by or under the direction of the approved clinician in charge of the treatment' (as amended by Mental Health Act 2007).
2 *South West Hertfordshire Health Authority v KB* [1994] 2 FCR 1051 at 1053 per Ewbank J.
3 *F v Riverside Mental Health NHS Trust* [1994] 2 FCR 577; *South West Hertfordshire Health Authority v KB* (see **N2** above) *B v Croydon Health Authority* (see **PARA 10.7, N3** above).

Competent adults detained under the Mental Health Act 1983

10.9   Adults will often retain their legal capacity to consent to or refuse medical treatment despite being lawfully detained under the MHA.

Involuntary feeding under s 63 MHA will be lawful, in spite of the patient's competent refusal of treatment, if:

- The steps to be taken are properly described as medical treatment. Naso-gastric feeding is medical treatment.[1]
- The treatment is for the mental disorder for which the patient is being detained.

While it may seem surprising that a patient who is compelled by a mental disorder to deprive himself of food to the point of death might have the mental capacity to refuse treatment designed to alleviate the consequences, there is no necessary connection between such a disorder and incapacity. In *B v Croydon Health Authority* a woman who had a borderline personality disorder as a result of which she had starved herself to a near lethal extent, and who was refusing treatment, was found to have the mental capacity to entitle her at common law to refuse the treatment designed to save her life, although treatment was permitted under s 63 MHA.[2] Had she not been detained under the Act, there would have been no means of requiring her to have treatment. Careful consideration of the facts, however, will be required in every case to establish whether the patient does have the relevant capacity, as there may sometimes be more than one possible view. It was said by an appeal judge in *B v Croydon Health Authority*:

'I am bound to say that I have some difficulty with the judge's conclusion ... I am as impressed as the judge was by her intelligence and self-awareness. It is, however, this very self-awareness and acute self-analysis which leads me to doubt whether at the critical time, she could be said to have made a true choice in refusing to eat ... I find it hard to accept that someone who acknowledges that in refusing food at the critical time she did not appreciate the extent to which she was hazarding her life, was crying inside for help but unable to break out of the routine of punishing herself, could be said to be capable of making a true choice as to whether or not to eat.' [3]

While the issue of lack of capacity over accepting nutrition may be relatively easily determined where the core disorder is anorexia nervosa, more difficult decisions about capacity can arise in cases of personality disorder. In *R v Collins and Ashworth Hospital Authority, ex parte Brady*,[4] a detained patient had commenced a hunger strike in protest at being moved wards and subsequently expressed the view that he wished to die as there was nothing for him to live for, as he accepted that he would die in custody. The hospital commenced enforced naso-gastric tube feeding which he challenged. Understanding the intentions and motivations of the patient caused the expert psychiatrists and the judge some difficulty:

'It is not possible for me to arrive at a certain conclusion as to what the Applicant's present intention is. That is one of the consequences of trying to assess the workings of such a disordered personality and mind ... In my judgment, this is probably correct and the likelihood (but not the certainty) is that the Applicant is playing the system ... there is at least a reasonable possibility that the present intention of the Applicant is to protest and/or to win a power struggle but not to die.'[5]

Having found that he was 'playing the system' and engaging in a battle of wills with his clinical team rather than wishing to die, the court found that the decision to continue the hunger strike was a manifestation of the personality disorder from which the prisoner suffered. Further, on the balance of probabilities, this battle of wills and his personality meant that he was not properly able to make a decision as to the risks involved in refusing food and so was incapacitated in relation to that issue. As the feeding amounted to treatment for his personality disorder, it could be given without his consent under s 63 MHA.

1 *Airedale NHS Trust v Bland* [1993] AC 789.
2 See **PARA 10.7, N3** above.
3 *Ibid*. at 140–141 per Hoffmann LJ.
4 [2000] 1 MHLR 17 and see **CHAPTER 13**: Treatment of Suicidal Patients, **PARA 13.37**.
5 [2000] 1 MHLR 17 at 25, para 51.

Procedure – declaration

10.10   Where a patient lacks the capacity to consent to or refuse life-saving treatment rendered necessary by an eating disorder, it may be given without reference to the court unless there is a dispute among those wishing to provide the treatment and others who seek to represent the interests of the patient. If there is a substantial dispute, those proposing to treat the patient against his will need to consider whether to apply to the court for a declaration that it is lawful to give the proposed treatment. An application should be made only if it is thought necessary to protect those providing the treatment from later criticism or litigation. Generally, the professionals should, having taken care to ensure that their views are in accordance with the best contemporary practice, proceed on their own judgment, just as they would in any other case. However, an application for a declaration should be made where (a) it is thought likely that proceedings will be taken against those providing the treatment or (b) there is a genuine and substantial dispute about capacity or what the interests of the patient require.

Given the predictability of a refusal of treatment during a crisis, preparatory steps should be taken as long beforehand as possible. These include:

- A full discussion with the patient, where this is practicable, to consider the options which will confront the patient and the carers if, and when, there is a crisis.
- An assessment at as early a stage as possible of the patient's capacity to consent to or refuse medical treatment. The patient may have capacity to make advance decisions about treatment for a crisis before that event occurs, even if capacity is likely to be lost at that time. However, it should be noted that advance directives cannot prevent compulsory treatment under the MHA. If possible, patients should be encouraged to decide for themselves, when capable of doing so, what should happen. Full records of any such decision must be made and if possible approved by the patient. If these steps are taken, many legal difficulties will be avoided.
- If the point comes when treatment considered to be necessary to save life is being refused and no prior advance consent or refusal is available, an assessment must be made as to the urgency of the case. This should be realistic. False alarms help no-one but, on the other hand, delay should not be allowed where the patient's life is at risk.[1]
- A decision should be made as to whether the case is suitable for treatment under the MHA. If this is appropriate, the necessary steps to detain the patient and provide treatment should be undertaken. In general, no court application will then need to be made by those treating the patient.[2]
- If MHA treatment is inappropriate,[3] consideration must be given to the patient's capacity to refuse the proposed treatment. If the patient is found to possess legal capacity, then his wishes must be respected. If there is a substantial dispute about capacity it will be appropriate to make an application to the court for a declaration as to capacity, but in general doctors should proceed on their clinical judgment.
- If the patient lacks capacity, but treatment under the MHA is not available, an assessment should be made of whether the treatment is nonetheless in the patient's best interests. Factors taken into account will include: the wishes and views of the patient expressed during interludes when he had the relevant capacity; the views currently expressed by the patient; the views of close family or partners on what they perceive the patient would have wanted; the likely effectiveness of the treatment; the availability of alternatives; and the risks and benefits of the treatment proposed.[4]
- If it is agreed by those responsible for the care of the incapacitated patient that treatment is required, generally no court application will be required, but if force is required to administer such treatment it would be prudent to seek the approval of the court[5] and if physical detention is required either the authority of the court or DOLS ('deprivation of

213

liberty') authorisation under the MCA must be obtained if the MHA is not applicable.[6]

- If an application is to be made, however urgent the case, evidence of the need for treatment, the patient's incapacity, and the reasons why the treatment is in the patient's best interests will be required. Appropriate statements of the relevant evidence should, therefore, be prepared.

- If it is decided to make an application to the court, as much notice as possible should be given to the patient and practical assistance given to enable him to obtain legal advice and assistance. The Official Solicitor should be notified and, unless there is an obvious alternative, invited to become the patient's litigation friend.

- Interim declarations can be granted[7] and hearings can be conducted by telephone where appropriate, and at any time of the day or night.

1 See **CHAPTER 2**: Consent – Adults **PARA 2.7** and **2.13–2.15** and in relation to pregnancy see: **CHAPTER 9**: Managing Pregnancies, **PARA 9.16**.
2 See **PARA 10.9** above.
3 There may well be occasions when the view is taken that an adolescent patient should not be stigmatised by an MHA section at such a young age.
4 See **CHAPTER 3**: Deciding for Others – Adults, **PARA 3.13–3.17**.
5 See **CHAPTER 5**: Going to Court.
6 See **CHAPTER 6**: Deprivation of liberty & restraint.
7 See **CHAPTER 5**: Going to Court: **PARA 5.23**.

Procedure – injunction

10.11   Where the carers intend to proceed with treatment without first applying to the court, the patient may wish to contest that decision either because he does not accept that there is a lack of capacity or that the treatment is necessary or in his best interests. In such circumstances, the patient, or a litigation friend acting on his behalf, is likely to need to apply to the court for an injunction. The following procedure may be followed:[1]

- The Court of Protection can grant an interim declaration and the court can grant an interim injunction, and in an urgent case will frequently do so, in order to preserve the status quo until the full merits of a case have been able to be considered. Obviously, where there is an urgent need to decide whether or not life-saving treatment should be given, the court will be more likely to make a substantive decision preserving life at the first hearing on the evidence available. However, the first step on behalf of a patient should be to commence proceedings and seek an interim injunction restraining the carers from proceeding with the proposed treatment under Court of Protection Rules. This may be brought before the commencement of an action, but generally a Court of Protection application should be issued if this is possible and, where not possible, any order will include an undertaking to issue forthwith.

- Evidence in the form of statements verified with a statement of truth should be obtained to support any assertion that the patient has the capacity to refuse treatment, and from expert witnesses that it is not in the patient's interests to have the treatment imposed against his will.

- Urgent steps should be taken to have the interim application heard in private as soon as possible.

- Depending upon the nature of the case, it may not be necessary to proceed to a substantive trial, as the issues will have been sufficiently resolved by the interim hearing. However, given the ongoing nature of food refusal, a substantive hearing with evidence from all parties and perhaps a jointly instructed independent expert may be required.

1 See **CHAPTER 5**: Going to Court and see **APPENDIX 10.1**: Draft Injunction Restraining Involuntary Feeding.

D CONCLUSION

10.12   Disorders of eating and consent to treatment are complicated by the prevalence of the disorder amongst teenagers and young adults. This adds to the challenges of ensuring that treatment given is legally justified. It is clear from the procedural requirements outlined above that a medical practitioner is not under an obligation to seek a declaration from the court in every situation. It is, however, essential that legal and medical practitioners constantly refer back to the general obligation to consider the best interest of the patient of whatever age. It must be recognised that in a controversial field such as this medical and professional practice will be constantly under review, and it should not, therefore, be assumed in any case that involuntary treatment is necessarily the appropriate solution.

For updating material and hyperlinks related to this chapter, see: www.3serjeantsinn.com/mtdl/feeding

---

Chapter 11

Religious Objections to Treatment

A   Introduction 11.1
B   Competent adults 11.2
     General principle 11.2
     Steps to be taken 11.3
          Confirmation that the patient is mentally competent 11.4
     Counselling 11.7
     Undue influence 11.8
     Scope of the decision 11.9
     The role of relatives and close friends 11.10
     Recording of decision against medical advice 11.11
C   Incapacitated adults 11.12
     General principle 11.12
     Advance decisions 11.13
          Reported oral advance decisions 11.14
          The effect of uncertainty 11.15
     Written declarations 11.16
D   Children 11.17
     General principle 11.17
     Best interests 11.18
     The '*Gillick* competent' child 11.19
E   Procedural issues with children's applications 11.20
     Anticipation 11.20
     Notice and consultation 11.21
     Evidence 11.22
     Change of circumstance 11.23
F   Conclusion 11.24

A INTRODUCTION

11.1   On occasions, patients will object to proposed medical treatment on religious grounds. The circumstance in which this has arisen most frequently has been in relation to the administration of blood transfusions. The best-known religious objectors to the use of blood in treatment are Jehovah's Witnesses.

They believe that the use of blood and some blood products is prohibited by laws laid down in the Bible, such as:

> 'You shall not partake of the blood of any flesh, for the life of all flesh is its blood. Anyone who partakes of it shall be cut off.'[1]

Where the refusal of treatment involves, in the view of the medical attendants, the inevitability of death, very difficult choices and decisions face all concerned, whether the patient is a young child whose parents are seeking to limit medical treatment or a competent adult with a settled and principled view.

This chapter seeks to set out the considerations which will apply in such cases. While the emphasis is on the administration of blood transfusions, the same principles will obviously apply to any refusal of potentially life-saving medical treatment on religious grounds. It is essential in any well-run medical institution, where treatment which might be objected to on religious grounds is offered, for the practitioners and management to have considered the problem in advance, to have ensured that the staff are informed of the issues, and to have developed a general policy for the handling of such cases. Often problems in this field can be foreseen and managed with sensitive counselling, discussion and consideration of alternative approaches to treatment. Nothing can be more destructive of the necessary confidence between doctor and patient than a hurried decision to impose treatment on a patient against his will or against the demands of the parents of a child.

1 Leviticus 171:10. This is not the place for study of the grounds for this belief or the controversy that surrounds it. It is suggested that practitioners who may have to confront the very real problems thrown up by it need to acquaint themselves with the arguments for and against it. It should not be assumed that all Jehovah's Witnesses adhere to the same beliefs.

B COMPETENT ADULTS

General principle

11.2   As considered in detail elsewhere,[1] the competent adult has the absolute right to refuse invasive treatment for any reason, good or bad, or for no reason at all, even where that refusal may lead to serious injury, deterioration in health or death. Clearly, a refusal based on religious grounds is a reason that must be respected, however much others may disagree with it. The right to privacy and physical inviolability[2] and the right to freedom of religious belief[3] are fundamental human rights. As stated by the European Court of Human Rights:

> 'Freedom of thought, conscience and religion is one of the foundations of a 'democratic society' within the meaning of the Convention. It is, in its religious dimension, one of the most vital elements that go to make up the identity of believers and their conception of life, but it is also a precious asset for atheists, agnostics, sceptics and the unconcerned. The pluralism indissociable from a democratic society ... depends upon it.'[4]

The imposition of invasive treatment on a mentally competent adult patient without his consent will render those doing so liable to civil and criminal proceedings for assault and trespass to the person.[5] Any decision to override a choice apparently made by a mentally competent adult, therefore, must be taken with great care and not a little hesitation for full consideration of the issues.

1 See **CHAPTER 2**: Consent – Adults, **PARA 2.11**.
2 European Convention on Human Rights: Article 8 – Right to respect for private and family life:
   '(1) Everyone has the right to respect for his private and family life, his home and his correspondence.
   (2) There shall be no interference by a public authority with the exercise of this right except such as is in accordance with the law and is necessary in a democratic society in the interests of national security, public safety or the economic well-being of the country, for the prevention of disorder or crime, for the protection of health or morals, or for the protection of the rights and freedoms of others.'
   And see **CHAPTER 1**: Consent – General, **PARA 1.21**; **CHAPTER 4**: Deciding for Others – Children, **PARA 4.4**; **CHAPTER 7**: Sterilisation **PARA 7.1** and **CHAPTER 13**: Treatment of Suicidal Patients **PARAS 13.7–13.15**.
3 European Convention on Human Rights: Article 9 – Freedom of thought, conscience and religion:
   '(1) Everyone has the right to freedom of thought, conscience and religion; this right includes freedom to change his religion or belief and freedom, either alone or in community with others and in public or private, to manifest his religion or belief, in worship, teaching, practice and observance.
   (2) Freedom to manifest one's religion or beliefs shall be subject only to such limitations as are prescribed by law and are necessary in a democratic society in the interests of public safety, for the protection of public order, health or morals, or for the protection of the rights and freedoms of others.'
   And see Art 18 of the Universal Declaration of Human Rights and Art 10 of the EU Charter of Fundamental Rights.
4 *Kokkinakis v Greece* [1993] ECHR 20; (1994) 17 EHRR 397 para 31 quoted in the interesting article by E Wicks, *Religion, Law and Medicine: Legislating on Birth and Death in a Christian State* (2009) 17 Med L Rev 410 at 411.
5 In *Malette v Shulman* 67 DLR 321 at 336 (1990), [1991] 2 Med LR 162 Robins JA said in a blood transfusion case in the Ontario Court of Appeal: 'The right to determine what shall be done with one's own body is a fundamental right in our society. The concepts inherent in this right are the bedrock upon which the principles of self-determination and individual autonomy are based. Free individual choice in matters affecting this right should, in my opinion, be accorded very high priority.' And see also in relation to this case: **CHAPTER 2**: Consent – Adults, **PARA 2.17** and **CHAPTER 13**: Treatment of Suicidal Patients, **PARA 13.66**.

Steps to be taken

11.3   The will of the competent adult patient refusing a blood transfusion must be respected, even where the result is likely to be fatal. The following steps need to be taken in the interests of both the patient and those providing medical care.

Confirmation that the patient is mentally competent

11.4   The attending practitioners must satisfy themselves that the patient is competent to make the very serious decision of refusing life-saving medical treatment by reference to the principles set out in s 1 of the MCA 2005 and the test for incapacity set out in s 3.[1] The statutory test is, in essence, the same as the test developed under the common law, set out in *Re MB (an adult: medical treatment).*[2] In the context of a refusal of treatment for religious reasons, various points require emphasis:

219

1   See **CHAPTER 2**: Consent – Adults.
2   [1997] 2 FCR 541, [1997] 2 FLR 426, [1997] 8 Med LR 217 (See **APPENDIX 9.1**: Re MB Guidelines and St George's Healthcare v S Guidelines); *Local Authority X v MM and KM* [2007] EWHC 2003 (Fam) per Munby J at para 92.

Ability to understand the information relevant to the decision

11.5   In order to assess whether the patient can 'understand' treatment information, it will have been necessary to ensure that the patient has been given all the relevant information. As the patient may believe, from information given by other adherents of his church, for example, that there are other equally effective forms of treatment to those being proposed, it is necessary to ensure that the patient is able to understand information on the effectiveness of alternatives as well as of the treatment being advocated.

Ability to use or weigh the information as part of the process of making the decision

11.6   The requirement that the patient is able to use or weigh the information should not be taken as an excuse to define as incompetent those who reject treatment advice on religious grounds. It could be argued that a patient who believes that he will die spiritually if he submits to the proposed treatment is incapable of using or weighing the information that it will save his life. The temptation to do so should be resisted. A patient can be quite capable of understanding that a doctor is genuinely of the opinion that the treatment is life saving while disagreeing – having weighed that information – that it is in his interests to submit to it. A competent woman who has the capacity to decide may for religious reasons, other reasons, for rational or irrational reasons or for no reason at all, choose not to have medical intervention, even though the consequence may be the death or serious handicap of the child she bears, or her own death.[1]

1   *Re MB* (see **PARA 11.4, N1** above).

Counselling

11.7   There is an obvious need both in the interests of the patient and those offering treatment that the options and their risks are clearly and calmly laid out for the patient to enable a balanced and informed judgment to be made, if that is the patient's wish. This requires anticipation of the particular problems likely to be thrown up by the patient's condition and the proposed treatment in the light of his known beliefs and discussion of these by all concerned. A doctor or other carer is clearly entitled, where appropriate, to give advice in strong and clear terms, but should not act in a way which might be interpreted as bringing undue influence to bear on the patient. Any decision taken by a patient whose will has been dominated by a doctor will be as invalid as if the undue influence had been exerted by a relative or friend. It is always important to ensure that the decision is a product of an exercise of the patient's own free will.

Undue influence

11.8   Religious and similar beliefs are held with differing strength of conviction by different people. Some, faced with the prospect of death, will retreat from the apparent consequences and change their views; others will find their stand strengthened.[1] Whatever the position is in an individual case, it is important that those attending the patient are satisfied that the patient's own views and wishes are being communicated, not those of relatives or other interested individuals or groups such as church representatives. A patient's decision arrived at under duress or undue influence is not a valid decision and need not be followed by the attending doctors:

'A special problem may arise if at the time the decision is made the patient has been subjected to the influence of some third party. This is by no means to say that the patient is not entitled to receive and indeed invite advice and assistance from others in reaching a decision, particularly members of the family. But the doctors have to consider whether the decision is really that of the patient. It is wholly acceptable that the patient should have been persuaded by others of the merits of such a decision and have decided accordingly. It matters not how strong the persuasion was, so long as it did not overbear the independence of the patient's decision. The real question in each such case is "Does the patient really mean what he says or is he merely saying it for a quiet life, to satisfy someone else or because the advice and persuasion to which he has been subjected is such that he can no longer think and decide for himself?" In other words, "Is it a decision expressed in form only, not in reality?"

When considering the effect of outside influences, two aspects can be of crucial importance. First, the strength of will of the patient: one who is very tired, in pain, or depressed will be much less able to resist having his will overborne than one who is rested, free from pain, and cheerful. Second, the relationship of the "persuader" to the patient may be of crucial importance. The influence of parents on their children or of one spouse on the other can be, but is by no means necessarily, much stronger than would be the case in other relationships. Persuasion based upon religious belief can also be much more compelling and the fact that some arguments based upon religious beliefs are being deployed by someone in a very close relationship with the patient will give them added force and should alert the doctors to the possibility – no more – that the patient's capacity or will to decide has been overborne. In other words the patient should really mean what he says.'[2]

It will be seen from the above passage that the attending carers must ask themselves the following questions:

- Has the patient's expressed decision been influenced by some third party or parties? If so, who are these parties and what form did their influence take?
- Whatever the nature of the influence, did it overbear the independence of the patient or his own will? Factors to take into account in deciding this will include, but not be limited to, the nature of the relationship, that is, whether the relationship was one in which the third party might be

expected to be dominant, such as parent and child, or priest and church member, and the physical and mental fitness of the patient to withstand pressure.

• Does the patient really mean what he is saying?

These are unlikely to be easy matters to consider, particularly in the case of urgently needed treatment where there may be little time in which to undertake a detailed social inquiry. The issue requires difficult value judgments to be made about the nature of relationships, the effect of behaviour which may not have been witnessed or be part of a background history of which the carers have little or no knowledge. It is impossible to give more than general guidance about what to do without considering the facts of an individual case. Inevitably there will be many cases where more than one view of the facts could reasonably be taken.[3]

Where the patient's refusal appears to have been influenced unduly by others, it would, therefore, generally be prudent to seek the sanction of the court before proceeding wherever that is possible.

If a patient's life may be lost even in the time it might take to make an urgent court application, and the attending doctors are of the view after whatever inquiry is possible that the patient's will has been overborne by undue influence, then the doctors will be in a difficult position. If they give the treatment in question the patient may later complain that this was contrary to his competent refusal which had not, in fact, been vitiated by undue influence. In this situation the doctors will not be protected under s 5 MCA since the patient will not have lacked capacity (unless there was an impairment of, or a disturbance in the functioning of, the mind or brain), and they will have to rely instead on the principle of necessity, the ambit of which in the case of a patient with capacity is far from clear. Alternatively, a decision not to treat on the basis of a lack of consent may be criticised if the patient dies or suffers harm as a result and it is established that the refusal to consent was invalid by reason of undue influence. In a case of a conscious patient who has capacity but whose refusal to consent appears to be vitiated by undue influence, doctors may consider it preferable to give whatever treatment they consider necessary to save the patient's life.

1   The *Journal of the American Medical Association* reported a significantly higher death rate than a control population in those who graduated from Principia College in Elsah, III, a liberal arts college for Christian Scientists: 'Comparative longevity in a college cohort of Christian Scientists' 262 (12) *Journal of the American Medical Association* 1657–1658.
2   *Re T (adult: refusal of treatment)* [1993] Fam 95 at 113 per Lord Donaldson of Lymington MR and see **CHAPTER 1**: Consent – General, **PARA 1.32**.
3   *Re C (adult: refusal of treatment)* [1994] 1 WLR 290, where the Court of Appeal took a different view to the first-instance judge on whether there had been a vitiating influence.

Scope of the decision

11.9   The attending doctors will have to decide precisely what circumstances the refusal of a blood transfusion is intended by the patient to cover. Where the patient is still conscious and apparently competent the matter can obviously be discussed with him. Where the patient has become unconscious when the need for a transfusion actually arises, the position is more difficult.

The Jehovah's Witness of many years' standing who has calmly and carefully listened to the potential consequences of refusing this treatment and has maintained a refusal to contemplate a transfusion in any circumstances will be entitled to have his refusal respected.[1] A doctor is not entitled to assume once a particular need for a transfusion is perceived that the patient would not have maintained a refusal in those particular circumstances, if the advance refusal was clear and universal.[2] On the other hand, a refusal reported to the doctor by members of the family, apparently based on some unspecified will of God, might more easily be interpreted as not necessarily covering the situation actually facing the doctor. Where doctors are uncertain as to whether an advance decision to refuse treatment is valid and applicable an application should be made to the court to determine the issue. In the meantime, doctors will be able to provide treatment where it is necessary to preserve life or prevent a serious deterioration.[3]

1   See **CHAPTERS 2–4**.
2   *Re T (adult: refusal of treatment)* [1993] Fam 95 at 114 per Lord Donaldson of Lymington MR; see **PARA 11.13** below and see **CHAPTER 2**: Consent – Adults: **PARA 2.13–2.19**.
3   MCA, s 26(5).

The role of relatives and close friends

11.10   It is well established that family members, spouses and friends have no power to authorise or veto treatment on behalf of an adult patient who has been rendered incapable of making his own decision.[1] Nonetheless, anyone who has knowledge of the patient and his beliefs and wishes may have a role to play in providing information to the medical attendants and carers of the patient and thereby in assisting them to come to an informed decision. Where a patient is suspected to have been subjected to undue influence, or where the intended scope of the decision under debate is uncertain, those with personal knowledge of the patient may be able to give information which will clarify the position. Doctors and others are then faced with the invidious task of assessing the reliability of the information they are given. They will face the challenge of deciding the extent to which their informant's views have been coloured by his own personal convictions, rather than those of the patient, while ensuring that their own strong desire to provide life-saving treatment does not interfere in their own objective assessment of the situation. These are difficulties which few doctors have been trained to face. Therefore in cases likely to provoke dispute it would be prudent to seek legal advice. However undesirable it will be felt in many circumstances to introduce lawyers to treatment decisions, at least they have the training to define the issues and help in the objective assessment of evidence supplied by lay witnesses.

1   See **CHAPTER 3**, and MCA, s 4(6) and (7), **APPENDIX 1.1**: Mental Capacity Act 2005.

Recording of decision against medical advice

11.11   The validity of a patient's decision will not depend as a matter of law on whether or not it is recorded in writing, unless it is an advance decision in

223

relation to life-sustaining treatment.[1] However, it will always be desirable for any decision of a patient not to accept the treatment advised by doctors to prevent death or a serious deterioration in health to be entered in the patient's medical records, together with a statement, preferably signed by the patient, acknowledging that the decision is against the medical advice received and may be prejudicial to health. If the patient refuses to sign such a statement, the refusal to accept the recommended treatment and a record of the potential consequences should be confirmed in writing by the responsible doctor, and by some other professional, such as the ward sister, who has witnessed or participated in the advice given. A draft form is contained in the Appendices.[2] In the past, some forms used by hospitals have contained a disclaimer of liability. It may be thought that it is inappropriate to seek the patient's agreement to a legal position at what is likely to be a stressful time in any event, and when he will probably not have access to legal or independent medical advice. If the patient has been advised and treated in accordance with good medical practice, and his refusal to accept advice is properly recorded, it is unlikely that any liability will arise, whether or not a disclaimer has been signed. If a disclaimer is to be asked for, it should be visibly separated:

> 'from what really matters namely the declaration by the patient of his decision with a full appreciation of the possible consequences, the latter being expressed in the simplest possible terms and emphasised by a different and larger type face, by underlining, the employment of coloured print or otherwise.'[3]

1   MCA, s 24(5) and (6); see **APPENDIX 1.1**: Mental Capacity Act 2005. See **CHAPTER 2**: Consent – Adults: **PARA 2.13–2.19**. For advance decisions made before 1 October 2007, Mental Capacity Act 2005 (Transitional and Consequential Provisions) Order 2007, art 3.
2   See **APPENDIX 11.1**: Draft form for refusal of treatment, to be signed by the patient.
3   Per Lord Donaldson of Lymington MR in *Re T (adult: refusal of treatment)* [1993] Fam 95 at 115. Note also the Unfair Contract Terms Act 1977, s 2(1) (liability for negligence occasioning death or personal injury cannot be excluded).

C INCAPACITATED ADULTS

General principle

11.12   As with every other field of medical treatment, if a blood transfusion is thought to be required by an adult who currently lacks the capacity to consent to or refuse the treatment, it may be administered if the treatment is in the patient's best interests.[1] However, it may sometimes be easier to determine the patient's lack of capacity than to decide where a patient's best interests lie when a close relative or friend claims that the patient has made it very clear previously that he would never be willing to accept this form of treatment.

1   MCA, s 5(1), **APPENDIX 1.1**: Mental Capacity Act 2005 and see **CHAPTER 3**: Deciding for Others – Adults, **PARA 3.4**.

Advance decisions

11.13   A practitioner faced with a suggestion that an incapacitated patient in a life-threatening condition has previously expressed a determination not to have the one form of treatment he believes can save his life has an awesome responsibility. If he disregards the suggestion and proceeds to save the life of the patient, he may find he has condemned him to spiritual exile or even damnation and a fate far worse, in the patient's eyes, than physical death. On the other hand, if he complies with a purported advance refusal of treatment and allows the patient to die, subsequent information may indicate that the information was incorrect or that the patient's decision had been the result of undue pressure from others. Inevitably, decisions about the validity of advance treatment decisions will arise in cases thought to require urgent treatment when there is little or no time for leisurely and thorough enquiries into the history of the decision that has been communicated. While it has been suggested that doctors who have made honest mistakes in this field will be liable to actions for damages,[1] in reality a court is unlikely to find against a doctor who has acted honestly and in accordance with good medical practice or if it does, only for nominal damages. Nonetheless, wherever possible, the most careful consideration will be required to be given to the question of whether the patient has actually made an advance statement binding on attending doctors and carers.[2]

1 Per Staughton LJ in *Re T (adult: refusal of treatment)* [1993] Fam 95 at 122.
2 See **CHAPTERS 2–4**.

Reported oral advance decisions

11.14   It must be recognised that a patient who is an established member of a religion which is known to oppose certain forms of treatment, such as blood transfusions, may, but will not necessarily, have expressed an advance decision about that form of treatment. It would be erroneous without further enquiry to conclude from a simple report of a person belonging to a particular religion that he would adhere to all the tenets of that religion as expressed by the informant. After all, there is fierce debate within most religions about matters of doctrine and many give considerable scope for personal variations.[1] In assessing the available evidence the following points should be borne in mind:

- Careful enquiry into the views expressed by the patient must be undertaken, where this is possible. An advance refusal to accept a transfusion should not be rejected merely because it is not evidenced in writing, unless the transfusion is necessary to sustain life, in which case it is mandatory that the advance decision to refuse be in writing, but it may be difficult to determine the extent to which the patient merely expressed a general view, or made a statement intended to be complied with in the future.

- Reliable evidence should be required of a firm and clearly expressed intention to decline the proposed type of treatment in the type of circumstances now prevailing. A general reluctance would not be sufficient.

- There should be evidence of an understanding of the potential consequences of declining the treatment in question before it is accepted that the patient had expressed a binding advance refusal of treatment. The doctors may need to be aware of the general teaching of a particular religion about the efficacy of alternative methods of treatment. Such beliefs cannot be disregarded by doctors merely because they believe them to be wrong, but they should consider whether the patient made the advance statement in the knowledge that the medical profession might disagree with the church's view.[2]

● Those making the assessment on this issue should also seek assurance that at the time the statement relied on was made the patient had the capacity to make it and was not subjected to undue influence.

1   For example, Christian Scientists, although advocating prayer rather than medical treatment as a means of curing illness, do not condemn members who choose medical treatment.
2   Jehovah's Witnesses advocate a range of alternative therapies in the place of blood transfusions. In an appropriate case the attending doctors might wish to consider whether the patient had access to knowledge of the relative risks of the various treatments advocated.

The effect of uncertainty

11.15   What does the doctor do if left uncertain about any of these matters or if he simply has no information at all?

If there is no evidence that an advance statement was made, then the doctor should proceed as if there had been none. No liability will be incurred for carrying out treatment unless, at the time, the doctor is satisfied that an advance decision exists which is valid and applicable to the treatment. If there are reasonable grounds to believe that an advance decision may exist then doctors should, if possible, make reasonable efforts to find out what that decision was.[1] If, on the other hand, it is clear that such a statement was made, compliance with it cannot be excused on the ground that there is no information one way or the other about the existence of undue influence. To assume that there had been such a vitiating factor in the absence of evidence to the contrary would potentially open the practitioner to the charge of discriminating against an individual on the grounds of his religion. Before being entitled to rely on undue influence as a vitiating factor, the practitioner would have to be able to show evidence that it existed. Such evidence might exist where, for example, the statement was reported to the doctor by a parent or spouse who was a devout adherent of the religion in question after a long and private meeting with a patient in a weak condition.[2]

Even though there may be no evidence that the patient made the statement in the knowledge of opinions contrary to those expressed by the church, it is doubtful that a practitioner would usually be entitled to ignore the statement on the ground that he could not be satisfied that the patient understood the nature and effect of the decision. The exception would be if it could be argued that the advance decision was inapplicable under MCA s 25(4)(c).[3] This provides that an advance decision is not applicable to the treatment in question if there are reasonable grounds for believing that circumstances exist which the patient did not anticipate at the time of the advance decision and which would have affected his decision had he anticipated them.[4] The use of the word 'anticipate', which usually denotes some future event, as opposed to the word 'know', suggests that such an argument may not succeed where the true position is that the patient was simply unaware of information at the time of his decision. It should be emphasised that there is no authority on this issue, and if in doubt it would probably be advisable to apply to the court to determine the applicability of the advance decision.

1   MCA Code of Practice, para 9.49.
2   For example the facts of *Re T (adult: refusal of treatment)* [1993] Fam 95, where it was remarked (at 111): '(g) The matrimonial history ... suggests that Miss T's mother is a deeply committed Jehovah's Witness, who would regard her daughter's eternal salvation as more important and more in her daughter's best interests, than lengthening her terrestrial life span. (h) We do not know what the mother said to Miss T, because she has not chosen to tell the court, but it appears to be the fact that on the two occasions when Miss T raised the issue of blood transfusions, she did so suddenly and "out of the blue" without inquiry from the hospital staff and immediately following occasions when she had been alone with her mother.'
3   See **APPENDIX 1.1**: Mental Capacity Act 2005.
4   **CHAPTER 2**: Consent – Adults, **PARA 2.14**.

Written declarations

11.16   These issues may be easier to resolve if the patient has made a written declaration. The focus of the investigation can then be on the circumstances in which that statement came to be made. The same questions which are relevant in the case of an alleged oral advance decision are to be considered.[1] Ideally, the document will have been made after the patient has participated in a full discussion of the issues with the attending doctors so that the latter can be fully aware of the patient's wishes, and have had the opportunity to give the patient the benefit of their advice.[2] If a written declaration is produced by someone other than the patient, the doctors will need to be satisfied of its authenticity. A copy should be kept in the patient's records. Those who have made advance decisions complain sometimes that the copies given to medical practitioners are frequently not kept in the records and are thus not made accessible to all who might need to know that an advance decision has been made.

1   See **PARA 11.14** above.
2   If specific treatment for a specific condition is contemplated a form similar to that in **APPENDIX 11.1**: Draft Form for refusal of treatment to be signed by the patient can be used. Otherwise an advance decision form such as the precedent in **APPENDIX 2.1**: Draft Advance Decision would be appropriate.

D CHILDREN

General principle

11.17   Generally the consent of one parent (or whoever has parental responsibility) will be sufficient authority for treatment, even if the other objects, whether on religious or other grounds. In the case of proposed circumcision or sterilisation, however, such a disagreement will mean that the dispute should be referred to the court before treatment is given.[1] The courts have frequently been faced with cases of conflict between parents with strong religious convictions against blood transfusions and doctors and other carers who wish to administer what they regard to be life-saving treatment.[2] The almost invariable outcome has been that the court will authorise the treatment as being in the best interests of the child. In effect the court will do so where there is clear evidence that the child's condition requires a blood transfusion without which treatment will be unsuccessful and harm will be suffered by the child as a result, whatever the parent's views might be. As stated in *Prince v Massachusetts:*

> 'Parents may be free to become martyrs themselves, but it does not follow that they are free in identical circumstances to make martyrs of their children before they have reached the age of full and legal discretion when they can make choices for themselves.'[3]

Consultation with the parents, nevertheless, will be encouraged, as will consideration of reasonable alternatives to blood transfusions.[4] In any decision to override the views of one or both parents, adequate account must be taken of their rights to family life, and to manifest their religion under Arts 8 and 9 of the European Convention.[5] These rights have to be balanced against the welfare of the child and the equivalent rights of the other parent.[6]

1   *Re J (child's religious upbringing and circumcision)* [2000] 1 FLR 571 at 577. Whilst immunisation is included, it is unclear what other cases should fall within the category of requiring court approval. It is suggested that they may comprise any 'non-therapeutic' treatment which could cause important irreversible changes to the child's physical abilities. And see **CHAPTER 4**: Deciding for Others – Children, **PARA 4.1** and generally see **CHAPTER 5**: Going to Court.
2   *Re E (a minor)* [1992] 2 FCR 219; *Re O (a minor) (medical treatment)* [1993] 2 FLR 149; *Re R (a minor) (medical treatment)* [1993] 2 FLR 757; *Re S (a minor) (refusal of medical treatment)* [1995] 1 FCR 604.
3   321 US Reports 158 (1944): quoted by Ward J in *Re E (a minor)* [1993] 1 FLR 386 at 394, and, as stated by Ward J at 394, the court 'should be very slow to allow an infant to martyr himself'. See **CHAPTER 4**: Deciding for Others – Children, **PARA 4.09**.
4   The form of order taken from *Re R (a minor) (medical treatment)* [1993] 2 FLR 757 in **APPENDIX 9.6**: Draft Specific Issue Order for Administration of Blood Products to Child.
5   See **PARA 11.2** above.
6   See *Re J* (N1 above).

Best interests

11.18   Doctors faced with a refusal of parents to consent to a blood transfusion to save a child patient's life should act in the child's best interests.[1] If it is possible to apply to a court for an order approving the treatment, then this should be done. Judges of the family courts have immense experience and far greater powers than doctors to assess the best interests of children. The doctor faced with the immediacy of the need for a course of medical treatment is not always in the best position to obtain, let alone assess, all the relevant information. For example, if the child might be ostracised by its parents and community if given blood, and there might be some chance of recovery with an alternative form of treatment, then a difficult judgment has to be made. Similarly, if only a very poor quality of life is likely to be enjoyed by the child even with the proposed treatment, then there might be arguments for withholding it. Parental refusals seen as unreasonable by doctors will not always be rejected by the court.[2]

The consequences of overriding the parents' views will be taken into account. Where there is some medical opinion supporting doubts expressed by the parents as to the efficacy or risks of proposed treatment, greater weight may be given to the parental view than where medical opinion is unanimous. Therefore, it should not be automatically assumed that the medical view is the correct one.[3]

1   See **CHAPTER 4**: Deciding for Others – Children and in particular **PARA 4.15**.
2   See, in a different treatment context, Re *T (a minor) (wardship: medical treatment)* [1997] 1 WLR 242.
3   It is interesting that in the USA a large number of states provide that a child is not to be deemed abused or neglected merely because he is receiving treatment by spiritual means alone in accordance with the tenets of a recognised religion (for example, Alabama Code: §13A-13-6: Endangering Children). This is felt to accord with the constitutional guarantee of protection of religious practice from intrusion by government. This prompted a challenge in *Pediatrics*, the official journal of the American Academy of Pediatrics (Religious Exemptions From Child Abuse Statutes, Vol 81, No 1: pp 169–171, January 1988). A further article in April 1998 concluded that when faith healing is used to the exclusion of medical treatment, 'the number of preventable child fatalities and the associated suffering are substantial and warrant public concern. Existing laws may be inadequate to protect children from this form of medical neglect.' (Child Fatalities From Religion-motivated Medical Neglect, *Pediatrics*, Vol 101, No 4 April 1998, pp 625–629).

The *'Gillick* competent' child

11.19   Where the child is old and mature enough to understand the nature and effect of the treatment and the consequences of refusing it, it may be competent in law to make treatment decisions for itself, but both the parents and the court will still retain the power to override such a decision where to do so is in the best interests of the child.[1] In such a case it would be unwise of the doctors to proceed to treatment without the consent of either the parents or the court exercising its inherent jurisdiction. An advance decision to refuse medical treatment may be made only by a person aged 18 or over.[2] Where a child is approaching the age of 18 its refusal may be determinative if to allow treatment would merely achieve a postponement for a short time of an inevitable death because the child, on reaching 18, would then exercise its right to refuse the treatment.[3]

1   *Re R (a minor) (wardship: consent to treatment)* [1992] Fam 11; *Re W (a minor)(medical treatment: court's jurisdiction)* [1993] Fam 64; *Re E (a minor)* [1993] 1 FLR 386 and see **CHAPTER 4**: Deciding for Others – Children, **PARA 4.6**.
2   MCA, s 24(1), see **APPENDIX 1.1**: Mental Capacity Act 2005; and see **CHAPTER 5**: Going to Court, **PARA 5.6**.
3   *Re P (a minor)* [2004] 2 FLR 1117.

E PROCEDURAL ISSUES WITH CHILDREN'S APPLICATIONS[1]

Anticipation

11.20   In any case of potential conflict between medical and parental opinion, it is obviously important that the issue is addressed as far ahead of the actual time when a decision becomes vital as is possible. Practitioners should be constantly alert to the possibility that parents may hold particular views about certain types of treatment such as blood transfusions. Such issues should become apparent during careful history taking and discussion of the child's condition with the parents. In practice the significant problems for NHS Trusts in such cases are more often created by procrastination over taking advice or obtaining objective evidence than by questions concerning substantive merits.

1   See **CHAPTER 5**: Going to Court.

Notice and consultation

11.21   Where there is a potential serious difference of opinion as to the correct course of action between the attending doctors and the parents, consideration must be given to whether an application should be made to the court.[1] The fact that such a step may be taken should usually be shared with the parents unless it is clearly not in the child's interests that they should be informed. They are entitled to the opportunity to obtain advice of their own, second medical opinions and so on. It must constantly be borne in mind that whatever the outcome, they will remain the parents of the child, and, in most cases, will retain responsibility for its care. All possible steps should be taken to prevent parents from becoming alienated from the therapeutic process.

1   For the procedures to be adopted, see **CHAPTER 5**: Going to Court.

Evidence

11.22   On issuing any application it is necessary to set out the issues for the court and explain why the application is being made. Evidence should be obtained as quickly as possible. However, an application should not necessarily be delayed pending receipt of all the evidence. It is important – as discussed in **CHAPTER 5** – to ensure that CAFCASS and all appropriate parties are involved as quickly as possible. Relevant evidence for a hearing at a minimum will include medical evidence of the child's condition, the reasons why the disputed treatment is needed, in addition to a full account of the parental or other objections, and any other information thought to be relevant to an assessment of the child's interests. It must be remembered that *all* relevant information should be put forward, whether or not it appears to assist the case to be advanced. These should not be regarded as adversarial proceedings, but an engagement of the court in the process of caring for a vulnerable child.

Change of circumstance

11.23   Medical conditions frequently change unexpectedly. New medical techniques are regularly discovered or found to be more effective than previously thought. Authority from the court or from parents to proceed with a particular form of treatment should not be taken as exempting the medical attendants from continuing to review the condition of the patient and whether that chosen treatment remains in his best interests. Should there be a change of circumstances and it becomes desirable to vary the treatment plan, whoever gave the prevailing authority to treat must be approached again for the matter to be reconsidered, unless the authority explicitly covers what it is now desired to do. The form of order suggested in the Appendices[1] would avoid the need to refer back to the court in many situations.

1   See **APPENDIX 11.3**: *Draft Specific Issue Order for Administration of Blood Products to Child.*

F CONCLUSION

11.24   The right of a competent adult to make medical treatment decisions for himself on the basis of religious conviction has long been recognised by the common law and is reinforced by the provisions of the MCA. Whenever such an issue arises, or may arise, the treating professionals should make an early and thorough assessment of the validity and scope of any refusal of treatment, taking legal advice where necessary. If the courts may be required to make a determination then an application should be made in good time, avoiding, where possible, the need to conduct a hasty hearing where the court cannot, for reasons of urgency or the patient's condition, be presented with the best evidence.

Where the patient is a child the parents have no absolute right to make medical treatment decisions on religious (or any other) grounds. Where parents refuse medical treatment on religious grounds it will be necessary to balance the welfare of the child against the parents' rights to family life and to manifest their religion. Often, where life-saving measures are required, this exercise will result in the treatment in question being given to the child. As with adult patients, though, it is important that the treating professionals give full consideration to the issues at an early stage, so that a timely application to court can be made where necessary.

For updating material and hyperlinks related to this chapter, see: www.3serjeantsinn.com/mtdl/religious

---

Chapter 12

Permanent Vegetative State

A   Introduction 12.1
B   Legal principles 12.2
      The *Bland* decision 12.3
      The problem with 'act' and 'omission' 12.4
      European Convention on Human Rights 12.5
      Continuing treatment is an assault 12.6
      Extending *Bland* to other cases 12.7
      Advance directives/prior consent 12.8
      Summary 12.9
C   Medical issues 12.10
      Imaging 12.11
      Rehabilitation and time to allow for a recovery 12.12
      Cases outside the RCP guidelines 12.13
D   Role of the family 12.14
E   Is an application to court required? 12.15
      Consequences of withholding nutrition and hydration without court approval 12.16
F   Application to court 12.17
      Confidentiality 12.18
      Evidence 12.19
G   Emergency cases 12.20
      Critique of *Frenchay* approach 12.21
H   Children 12.22
I   Doctors who disagree in principle 12.23
J   Conclusion 12.24

A INTRODUCTION

12.1   Permanent Vegetative State[1] ('PVS') has been described as a 'twilight zone of suspended animation where death commences while life, in some form, continues.'[2] Patients in PVS are in a state lacking all consciousness, with no prospect of recovery.[3] It was estimated at the time of the the *Bland* decision in 1993 that there were over 1,000 patients who were in PVS in Britain.[4] Whether cared for in hospital or at home, there is an immense human cost in caring for

233

these patients. Family members are unable to mourn for a loved one who has departed: instead they have the enduring pain of watching a 'living death.' There is also the significant burden and strain placed on those nursing such a patient. Further, there are substantial economic costs in caring for patients who have, by definition, no prospect of any meaningful human existence.

> 'Given that there are limited resources available for medical care, is it right to devote money to sustaining the lives of those who are, and always will be, unaware of their own existence rather than to treating those who, in a real sense, can be benefited, e.g. those deprived of dialysis for want of resources?'[5]

Family members cannot consent to treatment on behalf of an unconscious adult: under English law no-one has the power to consent for an incompetent adult patient.[6] Thus, an unconscious patient must be treated in accordance with his 'best interests.' The advent of the Mental Capacity Act 2005 ('MCA') has not altered this aspect of English common law.

Once a patient has an established diagnosis of PVS, two major ethical problems face doctors and family members: the first is whether active treatment should be provided to save the patient in the event of an illness and the second is whether artificial feeding and hydration should be withdrawn, thereby allowing the patient to die. In essence, both issues raise the same fundamental question: whether the PVS patient's life is so devoid of value that it should be allowed to end without the medical intervention afforded to other patients. Nonetheless, it is the second issue (the withdrawal of feeding and hydration) which has been the most controversial. As discussed elsewhere, feeding and hydration are not viewed in the same way as other medical interventions.[7]

Headlines such as 'Shock at court ruling which lets coma woman 'starve'[8] have followed hearings where it has been declared lawful to withdraw feeding and hydration. Pro-Life pressure groups have attacked in strong terms attempts at withdrawal of feeding. Mike Willis, chairman of the Pro-Life Alliance, has stated:

> 'As for this idea of considering hydration as a treatment, it's a basic human need and you wouldn't deny it to a dog.'[9]

Janet Allen of 'SOS-NHS Patients in Danger' has stated:

> 'Giving water is not treatment – that's not a medicine, it's the stuff of life.'[10]

Lord Mustill in *Bland* noted that it was a 'striking fact' that in 20 out of the 39 American states which have legislated in favour of 'living wills' the legislation specifically excluded termination of life by the withdrawal of nourishment and hydration.[11]

Opposition to withdrawal of treatment in these cases stems from the absolute view that all human life is sacred and that it is therefore morally wrong to allow a PVS patient to die no matter how meaningless his existence or how bleak the prospect of recovery. Doctors, it is argued, should not therefore be allowed to withdraw the basic necessities of life – food and water – from a person merely for the emotional convenience of others or in order to release resources to others.

This position finds ostensible support in the wording of Art 2 of the European Convention on Human Rights.[12] However, courts in the United Kingdom have rejected an absolutist position even in the face of challenges under the Human Rights Act 1998[13] and have determined that not all human life is worth saving at all costs. *Bland* established that if the diagnosis of permanent vegetative state[14] is established a court will declare withdrawal of feeding and/or hydration lawful.

The underlying ethics of the *Bland* decision have been attacked by religious groups, pro-life campaigners and others. Similar cases in other countries have attracted even greater controversy. For example, in the US a lengthy series of court hearings concerning *Terri Schiavo*[15] was followed by remarkable last ditch legislative steps in the US Congress[16] to prevent withdrawal of her feeding tube. The medical position and issues surrounding the case are well summarised by Dr T Quill[17] who pleaded that:

'future courts and legislative bodies [should] put aside all the special interests and distractions and listen carefully to the patient's voice as expressed through family members and close friends. This voice is what counts the most, and in the Terri Schiavo case, it was largely drowned out by a very loud, self-interested public debate.'[18]

In Italy the Supreme Court permitted the withdrawal of feeding from *Eluana Englaro* (a 38 year old woman in PVS) in compliance with her parents' wishes. This prompted a national debate which ended in a political storm with Prime Minister Silvio Berlusconi accusing his President of being party to 'killing' Eluana by rejecting an emergency decree intended to force doctors to resume her feeding.[19]

Nevertheless, whilst the ethics are controversial, legal uncertainty in the UK is now only found in those cases where the condition does not match the established and recognised criteria for a PVS diagnosis.

The substantial difficulty for clinicians is in determining whether the PVS diagnosis has been established to an adequate degree of certainty. It is in this area of diagnosis that the second ground for challenging withdrawal of treatment in PVS cases has arisen, namely that it cannot be satisfactorily determined either that the condition is 'permanent' or that the patient is truly in a 'vegetative' state. Significant concern in relation to misdiagnosis of PVS has emerged within the medical profession[20] and this has intermittently received national publicity. For example, *The Sunday Times* headlined:

'Trapped inside their bodies, apparently switched off to the world, but still alive: they are the undead. Or so we thought. Forty per cent of patients in a 'vegetative state' are misdiagnosed.'[21]

Thus, given the justified concern about mis-diagnosis, before proceeding to a court hearing it is essential that all rehabilitative measures have been exhausted and that the diagnosis has been confirmed by at least two neurologists experienced in diagnosing PVS. The current Guidance from the Royal College of Physicians ('RCP') states that doctors should:

'take account of the views of the medical staff, other clinical staff (including clinical neurophysiologists, occupational therapists and physiotherapists with expertise in assessing disorders of consciousness), carers and relatives about the patient's reactions and responses. They should undertake their clinical assessments separately and write the details of their assessments and their conclusions in the notes. They should consider the results of the investigations which have been performed to clarify the cause of the condition. As the patient's position can affect responsiveness, it may be valuable to assess the patient in more than one position. It may be helpful for nursing staff and relatives to be present during the examination.'[22]

It is also recommended that careful consideration is given to a full structured assessment such as a SMART (Sensory Modality Assessment and Rehabilitation Technique) assessment.[23]

1   Paragraph 1.3 of the 'Vegetative State Guidance on diagnosis and management, Report of a working party of the Royal College of Physicians 2003': 'A patient in the vegetative state (VS) appears at times to be wakeful, with cycles of eye closure and eye opening resembling those of sleep and waking. However, close observation reveals no sign of awareness or of a "functioning mind": specifically, there is no evidence that the patient can perceive the environment or his own body, communicate with others or form intentions. As a rule, the patient can breathe spontaneously and has a stable circulation. The state may be a transient stage in the recovery from a coma or it may persist until death ...'

2   *Rasmussen v Fleming* 154 Ariz 207, 211, 741 P 2d 674, 678 (1987).

3   'Criteria for PVS Diagnosis', Treatment of patients in persistent vegetative state, Guidance from the BMA's Medical Ethics Department': ' ... The condition is distinguished from a state of low awareness and the minimally conscious (MCS) where patients show minimal but definite evidence of consciousness despite profound cognitive impairment. MCS patients, for example, may demonstrate eye movement to direct stimuli, even though their reactions may be inconsistent. Patients in the "locked-in syndrome" retain cognitive functioning but are unable to communicate other than by purposeful eye movement. Their condition disrupts the patient's ability to control the body's movements, effectively paralysing the patient.'

4   In *Airedale NHS Trust v Bland* [1993] AC 789, [1993] 2 WLR 316, [1993] 1 FLR 1026, HL [hereafter simply '*Bland*'], decided in February 1993, Lord Browne-Wilkinson indicated at [1993] AC 879B that the court had been informed that the number of PVS patients was between 1,000 and 1,500. The British charity Headway states now that 'There are normally just less than 100 people in the UK in PVS at any one time.' http://www.headway.org.uk/Coma-and-PVS.aspx .

5   *Bland* at 879D.

6   Save for circumstances in which a substituted decision-maker is authorised. See **CHAPTER 3**: Deciding for Others – Adults; and see also **PARA 12.8** below on advance directives/prior consent.

7   Despite the acceptance in *Bland* that artificial feeding and hydration are forms of medical treatment: see [1993] AC 789 at 857 and 870.

8   *Electronic Telegraph*, March 23, 1997.

9   *BBC News*, 23 June 23, 1999: http://news.bbc.co.uk/1/hi/health/376150.stm .

10 *Ibid.*

11 *Bland* [1993] AC 789 at 890F.

12 **PARA 12.5** below.

13 *An NHS Trust 'A' v Mrs 'M'* and *An NHS Trust 'B' v Mrs 'H'* [2001] 1 All ER 801, [2001] 1 FCR 406: see **PARA 12.5** below.

14 *Bland* in fact refers to 'persistent vegetative state': however, since the judgment, new guidelines (discussed below) have been issued, advocating the terminology 'permanent vegetative state' for patients such as Anthony Bland where there is no prospect of recovery from the vegetative state.

15 As the Respondent argued in written submissions to the US Supreme Court on 24 March 2005, the 'massive and intensive judicial (and now legislative) scrutiny of a patient's medical condition and intent is unprecedented in the annals of American jurisprudence'. It involved

eight years of litigation 'including a week-long trial ... fourteen appeals, and innumerable motions, petitions, and hearings in the Florida courts ... five suits in federal district court ...the enactment of unconstitutional state legislation to overturn the judgment of the state courts, which was struck down by the Florida Supreme Court ...' and four visits to the US Supreme Court (Respondent Michael Schiavo's Opposition to Application for An Injunction, 24 March 2005 pp 1- 2 http://fl1.findlaw.com/news.findlaw.com/hdocs/docs/schiavo/32405acluopp.pdf).

Post dating this summary and after the US Supreme Court refused to hear the emergency appeal on 24 March 2005: on 25 March 2005 a federal judge rejected a second appeal and a federal appeals court refused to overturn that decision on appeal; on 26 March 2005 a Florida state court rejected a further appeal; on 27 March 2005 the Florida Supreme Court rejected an emergency appeal; on 30 March a federal appeals court rejected a petition to have the feeding tube inserted and, finally the US Supreme Court refused to intervene for a sixth time. Terri Schiavo died the following day, 31 March 2005. http://news.bbc.co.uk/1/hi/world/americas/4358877.stm (31 March 2005).

16 Legislation was initiated and passed unopposed in the Senate by a voice vote on Sunday 20 March 2005 to allow the federal courts to intervene in preventing the withdrawal of Terri Schiavo's feeding tube. After summoning sufficient House members back from the Easter recess to provide a quorum, an identical bill was then passed in the House of Representatives at 12.42am on Monday 21 March 2005. President Bush was awakened shortly afterwards at his ranch in Crawford, Texas to sign the bill into law which he did while standing in a hallway at around 1.08am. In a speech later that day, President Bush declared: '... in extraordinary circumstances like this, it is wisest to always err on the side of life.' http://www.nytimes.com/2005/03/21/politics/21debate.html (21 March 2005) and http://www.nytimes.com/2005/03/22/national/22bush.html (22 March 2005).

17 'Terri Schiavo — A Tragedy Compounded', N Engl J Med (April 2005); 352(16): 1630.

18 *Ibid.* at 1633.

19 http://www.timesonline.co.uk/tol/news/world/europe/article5701289.ece (February 10, 2009).

20 For example, K Andrews, L Murphy, R Munday and C Littlewood, 'Misdiagnosis of the vegetative state: retrospective study in a rehabilitation unit' British Medical Journal 1996, p 313 and Helen Gill–Thwaites, 'Lotteries, loopholes and luck: Misdiagnosis in the vegetative state patient,' Brain Injury, December 2006; 20 (13–14); 1321–1328; and see **PARA 12.10** below.

21 http://www.timesonline.co.uk/tol/life_and_style/health/article3004892.ece (December 9, 2007).

22 RCP guidance (see **N1** above) at para 3.3.

23 Gill-Thwaites article (see **N18** above); see also **PARA 12.10** below.

B LEGAL PRINCIPLES

12.2   The law does not consider PVS patients to be dead: irreversible loss of consciousness by itself does *not* equate with death of the individual; death occurs when there is no longer any brain stem function.[1] In PVS patients the brain stem is still functioning. The legal duty of a doctor is to ensure that those in his care receive adequate care and nourishment. In usual circumstances a failure by a doctor to provide adequate feeding and hydration resulting in a patient's death would result in a manslaughter charge. Thus, what is the legal rationale for allowing withdrawal of feeding/hydration of PVS patients?

1   *Re A* [1992] 3 Med LR 303; see also *An NHS Trust 'A' v Mrs 'M'* and *An NHS Trust 'B' v Mrs 'H'* [2001] 1 All ER 801; [2001] 1 FCR 406. For a full discussion of the complexities of this determination see **CHAPTER 14**: The End of Life and in particular **PARA 14.6–14.8**.

The *Bland* decision

12.3   In short, the legal position following *Bland*[1] is that it is lawful to withdraw nutrition and hydration from a patient who is in PVS. If a court determines that the PVS diagnosis is correct, a declaration allowing the withdrawal of feeding/hydration is likely to be granted.

This simple statement belies the substantial ethical and legal debate behind the decision in *Bland*. Whilst in determining how to deal with vegetative patients the key is to be satisfied of the PVS diagnosis, it is worthwhile exploring the reasoning behind the *Bland* decision because it casts light on how English law reconciles the withdrawal of life-saving treatment with its opposition to euthanasia. In particular it provides guidance in the approach to 'near-PVS' cases or those cases where the British Medical Association's ('BMA') or RCP Guidelines for PVS are not met.

The House of Lords concluded that the sanctity of life is not absolute: there is no absolute duty to prolong life. The principle underlying that determination is the view that an unconscious or incompetent person should not have to be subjected to what a rational and conscious person would reject. Thus, a rational person, it is argued, would not wish to be kept alive in a vegetative state as 'a person who has no conscious being at all'.[2]

However, in reaching this 'rational' conclusion it was necessary for the Law Lords to address how such action can be taken without being construed as euthanasia. The problem is simple: a PVS patient is not dead and has all the rights of other human beings. Consequently, taking his life would be a homicide.[3] If a child is starved to death by his parents, that would amount to a homicide. They are under a duty to feed the child. Their omission to feed the child renders them liable for the consequences. If a doctor administered a lethal injection to a PVS patient, again that would be homicide. Thus the legal dilemma here is: why is the failure to continue to feed a PVS patient not a homicide?

The House of Lords, in determining why withdrawal of feeding does not constitute homicide, found it necessary to distinguish between an act and an omission:

'To act is to cross the Rubicon which runs between on the one hand the care of the living patient and on the other hand euthanasia.'[4]

An omission to act cannot be an offence unless one is under a duty to act. Those caring for a patient are usually under a duty to act: they have a duty to give food and drink to those in their care. If they do not do so and the patient dies, they have committed a homicide (usually manslaughter but if the requisite intent were proved, murder).[5]

However, a medical practitioner is no longer under a duty to feed or hydrate a patient when it is established that no benefit at all would be conferred by continuance; that is, it is not in the patient's 'best interests'. This 'best interests' test was often formulated as 'acting towards the patient in accordance with a responsible body of medical opinion': the *Bolam*[6] test:

' ... on an application to the court for a declaration that the discontinuance of medical care will be lawful, the court's only concern will be to be satisfied that the doctor's decision to discontinue is in accordance with a respectable body of medical opinion and that it is reasonable.'[7]

This would lead to the conclusion that the critical question is not what the court considers is in the patient's best interest but whether the doctor's belief (that the medical care should be withdrawn) is reasonable and bona fide. Given this rationale, it could be argued that a more precise way of formulating the duty is: a medical practitioner is no longer under a duty to feed or hydrate when it is established that a responsible body of medical opinion (a *Bolam* responsible body) supports the determination that no benefit at all would be conferred by treatment being continued.

It is suggested that this is not the intended result of *Bland*. The requirement that this type of case be considered by the court before treatment is withdrawn does not suggest that in all cases where the patient would die as a result, the judge's function is to be a mere rubber stamp for the medical profession. As stated by the then Master of the Rolls in *Frenchay*:

'It is, I think, important that there should not be a belief that what the doctor says is the patient's best interest is the patient's best interest. For my part I would certainly reserve to the court the ultimate power and duty to review the doctor's decision in the light of all the facts.'[8]

Further, not all the Law Lords approached 'best interests' on the *Bolam* basis. For example, Lord Mustill approached 'best interests' not through assessing the question of whether objectively the doctor's determination is reasonable and bona fide but by assessing the question of what (objectively) was in Anthony Bland's best interests. Thus a 'real' 'best interests' test was applied: Lord Mustill determined that the withdrawal of feeding was objectively the best option for Anthony Bland rather than merely being an option supported by a body of medical opinion. This is akin to the position in child cases in which the court determines what is the best option for the child, rather than merely declaring that a given course of treatment is lawful because it is *Bolam* reasonable. The advent of the MCA means that this must be the approach which is now adopted for adults: a true 'best interests' assessment is required.

Thus, if there is no longer a duty to continue to feed or hydrate a patient, then no criminal or civil liability results from the omission to continue feeding and hydrating. Applied to a PVS patient, this produces the following results.

Initially, it is appropriate to treat a vegetative patient if only to stabilise the patient's condition while an assessment of his condition and prognosis is completed. The basis for treating such an unconscious patient who can neither give nor withhold consent is that the practitioner is acting in the patient's 'best interests.' At first 'best interests' usually requires that the patient be treated and kept alive by artificial feeding and hydration.

However, a vegetative patient's 'best interests' may change. While there may be a potential benefit in initial treatment, once it is established that there is no prospect of recovery for the vegetative patient and that continuing treatment is futile, the position changes. Existence in a vegetative state with no prospect of recovery is not a benefit. Lord Mustill commented:

'The continued treatment of Anthony Bland can no longer serve to maintain that combination of manifold characteristics which we call a personality.'

239

Lord Goff stated:

'It is the futility of the treatment which justifies its termination.'[9]

Further, if the diagnosis is correct, there will be no detrimental consequences for the PVS patient in the withdrawal of feeding or hydration: he has no consciousness, is not sensate and is not losing any opportunity for recovery.

Such an analysis of the patient's 'best interests' dictates that there is no longer a duty to feed and hydrate the patient. Any subsequent failure to feed or hydrate legally is not an act; it is merely an omission. Once the diagnosis is determined, given that those caring are no longer under any duty to feed or hydrate the patient, that omission does not constitute homicide. The operative cause of the patient's death will be the original accident or condition that caused the vegetative state in the first place.

The underlying rationale is: why should artificial feeding and hydration be different from other forms of medical treatment? Lord Goff stated:

'Indeed, the function of artificial feeding in the case of Anthony, by means of a nasogastric tube, is to provide a form of life support analogous to that provided by a ventilator which artificially breathes air in and out of the lungs of a patient incapable of breathing normally, thereby enabling oxygen to reach the bloodstream.'[10]

Regardless of the criticisms, the law is now clear: where the court is satisfied that a justifiable and firm diagnosis of irreversible PVS has been made, feeding and hydration can be withdrawn.[11]

However, before doing so an application should be made to the Court of Protection, seeking the court's approval.[12] A failure to do so would leave a clinician exposed to a risk of a criminal prosecution.

1   *Re A* [1992] 3 Med LR 303; see also *An NHS Trust 'A' v Mrs 'M'* and *An NHS Trust 'B' v Mrs 'H'* [2001] 1 All ER 801; [2001] 1 FCR 406.
2   Sir Thomas Bingham MR in *Frenchay Healthcare NHS Trust v S* [1994] 1 WLR 601, [1994] 2 All ER 403, [1994] 1 FLR 485.
3   The term 'homicide' is used here to connote the unlawful killing of another whether in law it comprises 'murder' or 'manslaughter'.
4   Lord Goff at [1993] AC 865.
5   *R v Gibbins and Proctor* (1918) 13 Cr App R 134, cited in *Bland*.
6   *Bolam v Friern Hospital Management Committee* [1957] 1 WLR 582.
7   Per Lord Browne-Wilkinson at [1993] AC 883. See also *A Hospital v SW (Represented by the Official Solicitor as Litigation Friend) and A PCT* [2007] EWHC 425 (Fam), [2007] LS Law Medical 273. Sir Mark Potter P held that a medical practitioner was under no duty to treat such a patient where there was a large body of informed responsible medical opinion that continuance would be of no benefit.
8   *Frenchay Healthcare NHS Trust v S* [1994] 1 WLR 601, [1994] 2 All ER 403.
9   [1993] AC 789 per Lord Mustill at 899 and Lord Goff at 869.
10 Ibid. at 870. The BMA has stated in its publication, 'End of Life decisions: views of the BMA' (August 2009), 'The BMA does not believe that it is appropriate to prolong life at all costs, with regard to its quality or the burdens of intervention.'
11 Also: *B NHS Trust v J* [2006] EWHC 3152 (Fam), [2007] 94 BMLR 15 in which Sir Mark Potter P granted a declaration that it was in the best interests of a patient, who was in PVS, to undergo a course of drug treatment over a period of three days to determine whether any beneficial effect resulted, before making any further declaration as to the lawfulness of discontinuing medical treatment.

12 See also the 'British Medical Association's MCA tool kit' http://www.bma.org.uk/images/ ConsentToolKit2008_tcm41–175551.pdf ; see paras 6.18, 8.18 and 8.19 of the MCA 2005 Code of Practice.

The problem with 'act' and 'omission'

12.4   The withdrawal of feeding is deemed legally not to be an act. The distinction has not been free from criticism. Hoffmann LJ considered that it:

'leads to barren arguments over whether the withdrawal of equipment from the body is a positive act or an omission to keep it in place.'[1]

Returning to the example given earlier: why is it an 'act' which hastens death if an outsider comes in and removes the patient's feeding tube? The removal of the feeding tube is an 'act' when done by an outsider but paradoxically is an 'omission' when done by someone who used to have a duty to the patient. The outsider has no duty. The doctor now has no duty. How then can the act of pulling out the tube be an 'omission' in one person's hands and an 'act' in another's?

The explanation given by Lord Goff was that the outsider is actively stopping the medical treatment:

'I also agree that the doctor's conduct is to be differentiated from that of, for example, an interloper who maliciously switches off a life support machine because, although the interloper may perform exactly the same act as the doctor who discontinues life support, his doing so constitutes interference with the life-prolonging treatment then being administered by the doctor. Accordingly, whereas the doctor, in discontinuing life support, is simply allowing his patient to die of his pre-existing condition, the interloper is actively intervening to stop the doctor from prolonging the patient's life, and such conduct cannot possibly be categorised as an omission.'[2]

An alternative might be that the outsider would be under a duty not to interfere with the patient's medical treatment. Thus, the removal of the feeding tube by the outsider would comprise criminal homicide because he was under a duty not to intervene.

1   [1993] AC 789 at 831, CA.
2   *Ibid.* at 866, HL.

European Convention on Human Rights

12.5   Article 2 of the European Convention on Human Rights provides:

'Everyone's right to life shall be protected by law. No one shall be deprived of his life intentionally save in the execution of a sentence of a court following his conviction of a crime for which this penalty is provided by law.'

It was suggested that the common law position would not survive the advent of the Human Rights Act 1998 ('HRA')[1] which established direct liability on public authorities for breach of the European Convention on Human Rights: the absolute terms of Art 2, protecting the right to life, prohibited death by withdrawal of artificial and nutrition. However, in *An NHS Trust 'A' v Mrs 'M'* and *An NHS Trust 'B' v Mrs 'H'* the President rejected the view that the *Bland* approach was incompatible with Art 2.[2] Both patients M and H fell within the RCP definition of the PVS. The patients' families supported the Trusts' applications to withdraw artificial feeding and the Official Solicitor acting for the patients themselves agreed that withdrawal was in their best interests and did not violate Art 2.

The President concluded, first, that both patients were 'alive' within the meaning of Art 2.

Secondly, the President rejected an argument by the Trusts that the intention in withdrawing artificial nutrition and hydration was not to bring about the patient's death and agreed with the Official Solicitor's position that the intention here would be to end life. The Trusts had argued that the purpose of the withdrawal of treatment would not be to kill, therefore the intention would not be to kill. The intention was simply to withdraw futile treatment. Reliance was placed on Brooke LJ in *Re A (children) (conjoined twins: surgical separation):*[3]

> 'I do not consider that the *Woollin* extension [4] of the meaning of the word 'intention' is appropriate when determining whether a doctor who performed a separation operation on conjoined twins in circumstances like these was intentionally killing the twin whose life was to be sacrificed. The doctor's purpose in performing the operation was to save life, even if the extinction of another life was a virtual certainty. Like Robert Walker LJ I do not consider that the adoption of an autonomous meaning of the word 'intentionally' in Article 2(1) of the Convention need have any effect on the interpretation of the concept of 'intention' in our national law, which has at long last been settled by the House of Lords in *Woollin*.'

Reliance was also placed on Walker LJ in *Re A:*[5]

> 'The Convention is to be construed as an autonomous text, without regard to any special rules of English law, and the word 'intentionally' in Article 2(1) must be given its natural and ordinary meaning. In my judgment the word, construed in that way, applies only to cases where the purpose of the prohibited action is to cause death. It does not import any prohibition of the proposed operation [on the conjoined twins] other than those which are to be found in the common law of England.'

Concern was expressed by the Trusts in argument that a ruling that the intention in the PVS situation was to kill would impact on the doctrine of double effect. This doctrine serves to relieve doctors of criminal responsibility in circumstances where pain-relieving medication is given which is for pain relief but also has the effect of causing a premature death.[6] The President however stressed that:

> 'This judgment is dealing only with the situation where treatment is to be discontinued and is not concerned with nor relevant to acts by doctors or

other members of the health service, such as the giving of palliative drugs to a terminally-ill patient, which might have the effect of shortening his life.'[7]

Thirdly, the President determined that, whilst the intention in withdrawing hydration and nutrition was to cause death, such withdrawal did not amount to an 'intentional deprivation of life' within Art 2. The President noted the view in *Widmer v Switzerland*[8] in which the Commission[9] had concluded that Art 2 does not require that 'passive euthanasia' – by which a person is allowed to die by not being given treatment – be a crime.[10] Further, in *Association X v United Kingdom*[11] the Commission determined that where a small number of children died as a result of a vaccination scheme whose aim was to protect the health of society, their deaths could not be considered to be as a result of an intentional deprivation of life within Art 2(1).

The President stressed the importance of the autonomy of the patient. Treatment contrary to a patient's best interests violates that right to autonomy. Article 8 of the Convention defends that right: the moral and bodily integrity of a person should be protected from unjustified assault.[12] Given that for M and H ceasing medical treatment was in their best interests, it cannot be said that their death following the discontinuance of such treatment amounts to an intentional deprivation of life. By analogy there cannot be a duty in every case 'to take steps indefinitely, until the patient's body could no longer sustain treatment, irrespective of the circumstances or the prognosis'. Thus, the President accepted that there was not an intentional deprivation of life here:

> 'Although the intention in withdrawing artificial nutrition and hydration in PVS cases is to hasten death, in my judgment the phrase 'deprivation of life' must import a deliberate act, as opposed to an omission, by someone acting on behalf of the state, which results in death. **A responsible decision by a medical team not to provide treatment at the initial stage could not amount to intentional deprivation of life by the state**. Such a decision based on clinical judgment is an omission to act. The death of the patient is the result of the illness or injury from which he suffered and that cannot be described as a deprivation. It may be relevant to look at the reasons for the clinical decision in the light of the positive obligation of the state to safeguard life, but in my judgment, it cannot be regarded as falling within the negative obligation to refrain from taking life intentionally. I cannot see the difference between that situation and a decision to discontinue treatment which is no longer in the best interests of the patient and would therefore be a violation of his autonomy, even though that discontinuance will have the effect of shortening the life of the patient.'[13]

Fourthly, the President considered the positive obligation on the State to protect life.[14] In *Osman v United Kingdom*[15] it was stated:

> 'The first sentence of Article 2(1) enjoins the State not only to refrain from the intentional and unlawful taking of life, but also to take appropriate steps to safeguard the lives of those within its jurisdiction.'[16]

However, the obligation to prevent harm:

'must be interpreted in a way which does not impose an impossible or disproportionate burden on the authorities.'[17]

The President noted that the standard to be applied in assessing this positive obligation bore a 'close resemblance' to the English common law negligence standard. Thus, where a responsible clinical decision is made, on grounds of the patient's best interests, to withhold treatment which is in accordance with a respectable body of medical opinion, 'the state's positive obligation under Article 2 is, in my view, discharged'. In summary:

'Article 2 therefore imposes a positive obligation to give life-sustaining treatment in circumstances where, according to responsible medical opinion, such treatment is in the best interests of the patient but does not impose an absolute obligation to treat if such treatment would be futile.'[18]

Finally, the President did not consider that Art 3 of the Convention applied to M or H. Article 3 provides that:

'No one shall be subjected to torture or to inhuman or degrading treatment or punishment.'

This was considered in two areas. First, Alert[19] had argued that the withdrawal of treatment itself violated Art 3. The President determined that the withdrawal of futile medical treatment could not be seen as torture or as punishment. Further, given that the withdrawal is for a benign purpose in accordance with the best interests of the patient, it was not inhuman or degrading treatment.[20]

Secondly, the Trusts had argued that, given the broad approach to the definition of 'degrading treatment' in *D v United Kingdom*,[21] Art 3 should be invoked in order to ensure protection of a PVS patient's right to human dignity: enforcing the continuation of life as a biological machine with no cognition was inhuman; allowing a family to witness their loved one in such an abhorrent state was degrading. Cazalet J had determined (two months before) that:

'In *D v UK* ... it was held that Article 3 of the Convention which requires that a person is not subjected to inhuman or degrading treatment includes the right to die with dignity. It is that right ... which is to be protected through the declaration that I propose to make in this case.'[22]

The issue was also addressed by Lynch J in *The Matter of A Ward of Court*[23] who sought to reconcile withdrawal of feeding from a PVS patient with the Irish Constitution's requirement that the State:

'respect, and as far as practicable, defend and vindicate the personal rights of the citizen ... [and] in particular, by its laws protect as best it may from unjust attack ... the life, person ... of every citizen.'[24]

Lynch J stated that:

'The State undoubtedly has an interest in preserving life but this interest is not absolute in the sense that life must be preserved and prolonged at all costs and no matter what the circumstances. Death is a natural part of life. All humanity is mortal and death comes in the ordinary course of nature and this aspect of nature must be respected as well as its life-giving aspect ... A person has a right to be allowed to die in accordance with nature ...'

Lynch J further noted that the right to life whilst ranking 'first in the hierarchy of personal rights' may nevertheless be 'subjected to the citizen's right of autonomy or self-determination or privacy or dignity'. Thus, the constitution did not preclude the court determining withdrawal of feeding was in the patient's best interests.

The President, however, rejected the applicability of Art 3 to the withdrawal of treatment from a PVS patient because a victim has to be aware of the purported inhuman or degrading treatment he or she is experiencing: an insensate PVS patient has no feelings and no comprehension and thus there can be no violation of Art 3. The President did, in accord with Lynch J, assess the appropriate scope of Art 2 by reference to Art 8, which protects patient autonomy.[25]

In deciding that the *Bland* decision was in accord with the values of democratic societies, the President noted whilst 'the jurisdictional basis varies and thought processes differ' the ultimate conclusion in *Bland* that withdrawal of nutrition and hydration was lawful had been accepted in many parts of the world.[26]

In *An NHS Trust 'A' v Mrs 'M'* and *An NHS Trust 'B' v Mrs 'H'* the families supported the Trust's approach. Thus the case does not determine to what extent the right to family life under Art 8 impacts on the decisions to be made in this area. However, it is suggested that ultimately the assessment to be made is the same: is the withdrawal in the patient's best interests? The President – whilst not deciding the question – doubted whether a family has rights in this area under Art 8 separate from the rights of the patient.

Thomas J in *Auckland Area HB v AG*[27] summed up the importance of balancing human rights in this area. It was important, he stated, to set against the right to life 'another set of values which are central to our concept of life; values of human dignity and personal privacy':

> 'Medical science and technology has advanced for a fundamental purpose; the purpose of benefiting the life and health of those who turn to medicine to be healed. It surely was never intended that it be used to prolong biological life in patients bereft of the prospect of returning to an even limited exercise of human life ... Nor, surely, was modern medical science ever developed to be used inhumanly. To do so is not consistent with its fundamental purpose.'[28]

Subsequently in *Burke*, the Court of Appeal approved the dictum of Munby J. at first instance that:

> 'There is a very strong presumption in favour of taking all steps which will prolong life and save in exceptional circumstances or where the patient is dying the best interests of the patient will normally require such steps to be taken. In case of doubt, that doubt falls to be resolved in favour of the preservation of life but the obligation is not absolute. Important as the sanctity of life is, it may have to take second place to human dignity.'[29]

1   Came into force: 2 October 2000.
2   [2001] 1 All ER 801, [2001] 1 FCR 4062 the first case to consider the impact on medical treatment jurisprudence of the implementation of the HRA and was probably the first case decided in the High Court under the HRA.
3   [2000] 4 All ER 961.

4   In English law murder occurs when a life is ended by the intentional act of another. Further, causing death in circumstances where the defendant appreciates that death or serious harm is a virtually certain consequence of his positive act is also murder. (The 'foresight' test in *R v Woollin* [1999] AC 82.)

5   [2000] 4 All ER 961.

6   *Re A (children) conjoined twins: surgical separation)* [2001] 2 WLR 480 per Ward, Brooke and Robert Walker LJJ.

7   See N2, para 31.

8   No 20527/92 (1993).

9   This does not therefore represent a decision and merely provides some guidance as to the likely approach in the European courts.

10 Also note *Dec of Verieraltungsgericht Bremmen* of 9 November 1959, cited in *Fawcett* No 1287/61 (p 36) a West German case in which it was held that a doctor did not infringe Art 2 by giving an overdose of drugs to the terminally-ill.

11 (1978) 14 DR 31.

12 *X and Y v Netherlands* (1985) 8 EHRR 235; see also *X v Austria* and the ECJ decision in *the HIV case* cited at footnotes 1 and 2 of Nys, 'Physician Involvement in a Patient's Death – a Continental European Perspective' (1999) Med L Rev 7(2) at p 209. See also *Peters v Netherlands* (1994) 77A DR 75 at 79, indicating that unwanted medical intervention (the taking of urine samples) is an infringement of Art 8.

13 See N2, para 30 [emphasis added].

14 The positive obligation is: 'Everyone's right to life shall be protected by law'. The negative obligation is: 'No one shall be deprived of his life intentionally.'

15 (1998) 29 EHRR 245, para 115.

16 Harris, O'Boyle (et al), p 38: 'The first sentence of Article 2(1) ... establishes a positive obligation for states to make adequate provision in their law for the protection of human life.'

17 *Osman v United Kingdom* (1998) 29 EHRR 245, para 116.

18 See N2, para 37.

19 A 'pro-life' organisation whose attempt to be heard at the hearing was rejected by the President.

20 Noting *V and T v United Kingdom* (1999) 30 EHRR 121; *Herczegfalvy v Austria* (1992) 15 EHRR 437 ('as a general rule, a measure which is a therapeutic necessity, cannot be regarded as inhuman or degrading. The Court may nevertheless satisfy itself that the medical necessity has been convincingly shown to exist').

21 (1997) 24 EHRR 423 ('the Court must reserve to itself sufficient flexibility to address the application of that Article in other contexts which might arise. It is not therefore prevented from scrutinising an applicant's claim under Art 3 where the source of the risk of proscribed treatment in the receiving country stems from factors which cannot engage either directly or indirectly the responsibility of the public authorities of that country, or which, taken alone, do not in themselves infringe the standards of that Article. To limit the application of Art 3 in this manner would be to undermine the absolute character of its protections').

22 *A National Health Service Trust v D* [2000] 2 FCR 577.

23 (5 May 1995) High Court of the Republic of Ireland.

24 Article 40, s 3 of the Irish Constitution (Bunreacht Na hÉireann).

25 See N2, para 41.

26 See Grubb (et al), 'Reporting on the Persistent Vegetative State' (1998) Med L Rev 6(2) at 161–210; Scotland: *Law Hospitals NHS Trust v Lord Advocate* [1996] 2 FLR 407; Republic of Ireland: *Re A Ward of Court* [1995] 2 IRLM 901; New Zealand: *Auckland Area HB v AG* [1993] 1 NZLR 235, Thomas J; South Africa: *Clark v Hurst* [1992] (4) SA 630 cited in Grubb (et al) at p 185. Also note in Germany the Supreme Court determined that 'the withdrawal of treatment or care which leads to death may be done consistently with a patient's rights: indeed may be a vindication of them even where there is a constitutionally protected right to life'. Cited in Nys, 'Physician Involvement in a Patient's Death – a Continental European Perspective' (1999) Med L Rev 7(2) 209 at 227.

27 [1993] I NZLR 235 per Thomas J.

28 [1993] I NZLR 235 at 245.

29 *R (Burke) v. The General Medical Council* [2005] EWCA 1003 at para 61; see also *Re OT* [2009] EWHC 633 (Fam).

Continuing treatment is an assault

12.6   Theoretical complications arise from the Law Lords' determination that it is no longer in a PVS patient's best interests to continue feeding and hydration. As a PVS patient is unconscious and incompetent, the only lawful basis on which treatment in any form can be provided is if it is in his 'best interests'. Given that feeding and hydration have been determined to be no longer in the patient's best interests, then any continued feeding and hydration is an assault.[1]

This will largely be a theoretical problem: the PVS patient will not sue, although it is conceivable that a concerned relative could mount an action in the patient's name. After his death, it might be open to his estate to sue for the additional loss of amenity caused by the assault.

Given the medical debate concerning the nature of the PVS condition and the difficulties of diagnosis, the problem can partially be addressed by allowing that there must be a period of time when it is in the patient's best interests for his condition, prognosis and long-term interests to be subjected to the most rigorous assessment. It might also be argued that there will be a period during which it would be *Bolam* reasonable either to continue feeding or to cease feeding a patient. In such a situation no liability can flow from feeding during that time. However, the problem will still arise if the vegetative state continues for so long that no body of responsible medical opinion would consider that it was reasonable to continue feeding/hydration.[2] On the basis of the *Bland* analysis, the continued feeding and hydration at that stage would amount to an assault on the patient.

1   *Bland* [1993] AC 789 per Lord Browne-Wilkinson at 883: 'If there comes a stage where the responsible doctor comes to the reasonable conclusion (which accords with the views of a responsible body of medical opinion) that further continuance of an intrusive life support system is not in the best interests of the patient, he can no longer lawfully continue that life support system: to do so would constitute the crime of battery and the tort of trespass to the person.'

2   It has been held by the High Court that a doctor is under no duty to continue to treat a PVS patient where there was a large body of informed, responsible medical opinion that continuance (of treatment) would be of no benefit, as would be the case where the patient was in a vegetative state with no prospect of recovery. *A Hospital v SW* [2007] EWHC 425 (Fam); [2007] LS Law Medical 273.

Extending *Bland* to other cases

12.7   Given the concerns expressed about the withdrawal of feeding being 'backdoor euthanasia', the Law Lords in *Bland* were keen to emphasise that Anthony Bland's was an exceptional case: for example, Lord Browne-Wilkinson noted that it was:

'an extreme case where it can be overwhelmingly proved that the patient is and will remain insensate: he neither feels pain from treatment nor will feel pain in dying and has no prospect of any medical care improving his condition.'[1]

Lord Mustill stressed that he was not saying that he would support discontinuance of feeding in a patient with 'glimmerings of awareness.'[2]

Nonetheless, it appears that some doctors and carers have erroneously relied on *Bland*³ to withdraw normal oral feeding in patients who cannot be described as in PVS or even 'near-PVS'. *The Times* in January 1999 ran an exposé into allegations that doctors caring for elderly patients were 'giving nature a helping hand' by withholding intravenous drips from dehydrated patients and allowing them to die. It was reported that by January 1999 the number of known cases where this had occurred was 60.⁴

Thus the *Bland* decision itself is attacked as having opened the door to euthanasia:

> '[The reasoning in *Bland* was] sophistry. Bland wasn't dying. And feeding wasn't treatment, though it might require invasive procedures – after all, what is the illness being treated? Hunger? Living? And so now – surprise – patients being fed orally are also being refused food and water: inevitable once the Bland judges made it legal to starve patients to death.'⁵

The *Bland* decision expressly does not warrant or support 'mercy killing' of patients. Families, clinicians and Trusts must be alert to attempts by individuals to extend withdrawal of feeding and hydration to circumstances well beyond those of vegetative patients. No doctor should attempt to extend withdrawal of feeding and hydration beyond PVS patients without first seeking a definitive court ruling. To do otherwise risks criminal sanctions for the individual and a substantial erosion of public faith in the profession as a whole. The BMA's guidance on withdrawing and withholding artificial nutrition and hydration⁶ is clear. Oral nutrition and hydration 'should continue to be offered to all patients who are able to swallow.' Where swallowing is either impossible or very difficult, the decision about whether to withhold or withdraw nutrition and hydration should be made 'in consultation with relatives, in close discussion with the team of people involved in the care of the patient and in the BMA's view, with independent advice from another doctor.'

1   [1993] AC 789 at 885.
2   *Ibid*. at 899.
3   *Ibid*.
4   Also note the investigation in the *Daily Telegraph* in November/December 1999.
5   See above.
6   'End of life – withdrawing and withholding artificial nutrition and hydration' (BMA, published March 2007).

Advance directives/prior consent

12.8   Can a patient consent in advance to the withdrawal of feeding and hydration? Limits are placed by law on an individual's power to consent to actions which will injure him or which are otherwise morally unacceptable. Under English law a person does not have full autonomy to allow someone to assault his person: moral limits are set.¹ A doctor is not entitled to kill someone merely because he consents to be killed.

The principle that an unconscious or incompetent person should not have to be subjected to what a rational and conscious person would reject provides an answer. Just as with other forms of medical treatment, a competent adult is able to refuse consent to artificial hydration and feeding. In *Secretary of State for the Home Department v Robb*[2] a prisoner of sound mind and understanding went on hunger strike. The Home Office, prison officials, physicians and nursing staff responsible for his care could lawfully observe and abide by his refusal to receive nutrition and could lawfully abstain from providing hydration and nutrition. The Home Secretary was not under any duty to prolong the respondent's life.

Thus, if in advance a mentally competent individual indicates by way of a validly made advanced directive that should they deteriorate to a vegetative state they do not consent to the continuation of artificial feeding or hydration, that wish should be given effect. However, to be effective the advance directive must:

1) be in writing (it can be written by someone else or recorded in healthcare notes);
2) be signed and witnessed; [3] and
3) state clearly that the decision applies even if the author's life is at risk.[4]

Healthcare professionals will be protected from liability if they:

- treat a person because, having taken all practical and appropriate steps to find out if the person has made an advance decision to refuse treatment, they do not know or are not satisfied that a valid and applicable advance decision exists;[5]
- stop or withhold treatment because they reasonably believe that an advance decision exists, and that it is valid and applicable.[6]

In order to establish whether an advance decision is valid and applicable, healthcare professionals must try to find out if the person:

- has done anything that clearly goes against their advance decision;
- has withdrawn their decision;
- has subsequently conferred the power to make that decision on an attorney;[7]
- would have changed their decision if they had known more about the current circumstances.[8]

It is advisable in all circumstances to seek a declaration from the court in relation to the validity and application of any advance directive prior to discontinuance in order to ensure the legal validity of the patient's advanced expression.[9]

The General Medical Council's draft guidance 'End of life treatment and care: Good practice in decision-making. A draft for consultation' states that doctors 'must make a record of the decisions made about a patient's treatment and care, and who was consulted in relation to those decisions'.[10]

1   *R v Brown* [1993] 2 WLR 556 considered whether consent by the victim could amount to a defence to a charge of assault in relation to certain sado–masochistic practices. It was held that it was not in the public interest that a person should wound or cause actual bodily harm to another for no good reason and, in the absence of such a reason, the victim's consent afforded no defence to a charge. See Chapter 1: Consent – General, **PARA 1.9**.
2   [1995] Fam 127, [1995] 1 FLR 412, [1995] 1 All ER 677 per Thorpe J.
3   MCA, s 25(6): see **APPENDIX 1.1**: Mental Capacity Act 2005.

4 s 25(5)(a).
5 ss 24–26; and Chapter 9 of the MCA Code.
6 s 26(3).
7 s 25(2).
8 s 25(4).
9 See **APPENDIX 12.4** for a helpful flowchart demonstrating an approach to Advance Directives from 'Advance Decisions to Refuse Treatment, A Guide for Health and Social Care Professionals' published by the National Council for Palliative Care and the National Health Service.
10 See para 62 of the Draft Guidance. A period of consultation concerning end of life treatment (of which the draft guidance is part) closed on 13 July 2009. At the time of this publication going to press, the final version of the Guidance had not been published.

Summary

12.9   The legality of the withdrawal of feeding in *Bland* was resolved by analysing whether the doctor should or should not continue treatment and not by an assessment of whether the doctor should take a course which in fact causes or accelerates the patient's death.[1]

Not continuing feeding is an omission, not an act. Criminal liability for the consequence of an omission to act can arise only when there is a duty to act. Here, because continuing treatment is no longer in the patient's best interests, there is no continuing duty to act; that is, there is no duty on the doctors to continue feeding. Thus, if death follows a failure to feed, that death is not the criminal (or civil) responsibility of the doctor: the cause of the death is legally the original disease or trauma which caused the vegetative state.

1 Lord Mustill felt it was not a question of whether the patient's 'best interests' are in terminating life: it has to be a question of whether continued treatment is in the best interests of the patient.

C MEDICAL ISSUES

12.10   The granting of a declaration by the court permitting withdrawal of life-supporting treatment will turn on whether the court is satisfied that the diagnosis of PVS is correct. Once that determination is made, following *Bland*, only one result will generally follow, namely that withdrawal of feeding is lawful.[1] There has been significant anxiety about whether the diagnosis of PVS is being accurately applied in British hospitals. Permanent Vegetative State by definition indicates that that there is no prospect of recovery.[2]

Significant public concern was expressed following the well-publicised recovery of Andrew Devine. It was reported that Devine had begun communicating with his family eight years after being diagnosed as being in PVS. He suffered brain damage when he was crushed during the Hillsborough football stadium disaster. He could now respond to questions by pressing an electronic pad with his finger. The case was reported as being 'likely to fuel the controversy about experts' ability to diagnose persistent vegetative state, and raise fresh doubts about right-to-die cases.'[3]

The press and public worries about mis-diagnosis are not ill founded. A retrospective study has been reported by Dr Keith Andrews (then Medical

Director, Royal Hospital for Neuro-disability, Putney, London and a neurologist at the forefront of rehabilitation of 'vegetative' patients) and others of forty patients with a diagnosis of vegetative state who were admitted to the Putney Brain Injury Rehabilitation Unit.[4] Of those, a staggering 42 per cent were found to be able to communicate and were therefore not vegetative. One patient who had been thought to be vegetative for seven years was in fact dictating letters to his wife within two weeks of admission. This paper provides a stark warning to clinicians, lawyers and judges about the necessity to ensure that the diagnosis is accurate. It is not within the scope of this book to give medical guidance on how to diagnose the condition. It will be instructive for clinicians to read *The Vegetative State: Persisting Problems, Putting the Vegetative State into Perspective* by Dr Keith Andrews. He stresses that the vegetative state is a:

> 'syndrome of clinical features not a pathological, anatomical or disease process diagnosis,'

and that the major problem of diagnosis is that the only way for a patient to demonstrate conscious awareness is by a motor act, but that the very severity of the patient's physical disabilities may prevent or mask any such demonstration of awareness.

Although the study was undertaken before the criteria for minimally conscious state were introduced in 2002,[5] little appears to have changed. A similar rate of misdiagnosis (41 per cent) was revealed in a study of 103 patients conducted in Belgian brain injury treatment centres between October 2005 and January 2007. The study revealed that 41 per cent of those patients (within the study) diagnosed as being in PVS were, in fact, in a minimally conscious state. It concluded that the rate of misdiagnosis has not changed substantially in the last 15 years and that standardised neurobehavioural assessment[6] is a more accurate means of assessment than clinical consensus.[7]

A further paper by Helen Gill-Thwaites, an occupational therapist also of the Royal Hospital for Neuro-disability,[8] described the many factors which contributed to the high rates of misdiagnosis in Vegetative State ('VS') patients; namely (1) the diverse range of differential diagnoses and definitions evident within medicine, law and the media; (2) assessors' knowledge, experience and availability; (3) the method of assessment; (4) the degree of involvement of family and carers in the assessment; and (5) the manner in which the patient has been managed. The paper's conclusions echo those of the Belgian study, calling for:

> 'clear and prescriptive internationally agreed mandatory guidelines and checklists [in order to] determine definitions, provide agreed levels of expertise among both the physician and the MDT, outline frequencies and types of assessments to be applied, ensure systematic family and carer involvement and stipulate the application of mandatory factors in respect of patients' management.'

It is abundantly clear that there is a need for acceptance and adoption of objective criteria against which patients can be assessed.

In *Bland* great emphasis was laid on compliance with the then BMA Guidelines for the diagnosis of PVS[9] which in particular emphasised that:

1)   every effort should be made at rehabilitation for at least six months after the injury;

2)   the diagnosis of irreversible PVS should not be considered confirmed until at least 12 months after the injury, with the effect that any decision to withhold life-prolonging treatment will be delayed for that period; (the Belgian study continues to stress the importance of the timing of a diagnosis, 'clinicians should recognise that diagnoses established during the acute stage tend to be transitional and may change over time as the injury sequelae resolve ... ');

3)   the diagnosis should be agreed by two other independent doctors; and

4)   generally, the wishes of the patient's immediate family should be given great weight.

The 2007 BMA Guidelines also suggest that:

1)   Rehabilitation is continued until the treating clinicians consider that it is no longer of benefit to the individual (as opposed to an arbitrary time limit being imposed).

2)   Specialist expert opinion should be sought to clarify this in each case.[10]

3)   The diagnosis of PVS should be confirmed by two doctors, one of whom should be a neurologist.[11]

4)   Nursing staff must be consulted about decisions to withdraw life-prolonging treatment, as they have particular expertise and close contact with the family. It must also be recognised that decisions to withdraw artificial nutrition and hydration from a PVS patient impose particular burdens on nursing staff.[12]

The RCP Guidelines also provide details of clinical features which occur commonly, features which are compatible with the diagnosis but are atypical and features which are incompatible with the diagnosis.[13] They warn that PVS patients may even display features which appear to reflect survival of 'islands' of cortex but which are no longer part of the coherent thalamo-cortical system required to generate awareness, for example, following a moving target for more than a second.[14] Dame Butler-Sloss in *An NHS Trust 'A' v Mrs 'M'* and *An NHS Trust 'B' v Mrs 'H'* provided the helpful description given by an expert regarding the difference between Permanent Vegetative State and a minimally conscious state:

'He said the way to look at this is, is there any evidence of a working mind, and that he was satisfied this was not a case of minimal awareness. There was no evidence in this case of a working mind but there were fragments of cortical activity at a reflex level and those fragments of cortical activity did not demonstrate any evidence in this case of a working mind ...'[15]

The RCP Guidelines provide clinical criteria in relation to the diagnosis of Vegetative State which indicate that the following criteria are usually met by patients in a vegetative state:

1)   The key requirement for diagnosis is that there must be no evidence of awareness of self or environment at any time; no response to visual,

auditory, tactile or noxious stimuli of a kind suggesting volition or conscious purpose, and no evidence of language comprehension or meaningful expression. These are all necessary conditions for the diagnosis.

2)   There are typically cycles of eye closure and eye opening giving the appearance of a sleep–wake cycle.

3)   Hypothalamic and brain-stem function are usually sufficiently preserved to ensure the maintenance of respiration and circulation.

Nonetheless, the Guidance indicates that the VS diagnosis is *excluded* in patients with:

(i)   discriminative perception;
(ii) purposeful actions; and
(iii) communicative actions.

1   It is impossible to say that the contrary result will never occur. However, the courts have yet to consider a case where it is known that the patient held strong pro-life convictions before losing capacity.

2   Compare the description (that is, 'no prospect of recovery') with that of a 'minimally conscious state' in which sufferers 'retain some capacity for cognitive processing and can activate similar brain networks, in response to painful stimulation; suggesting that they can experience pain'. 'Diagnostic accuracy of the vegetative and minimally conscious state: Clinical consensus versus standardised neurobehavioural assessment': *BMC Neurology* 2009, 9:35.

3   National newspaper and television coverage on 27 March 1997; quotation from the *British Media Review*.

4   K Andrews, L Murphy, R Munday and C Littlewood, 'Misdiagnosis of the vegetative state: retrospective study in a rehabilitation unit' 1996 *British Medical Journal*, p 313.

5   'The minimally conscious state: Definition and diagnostic criteria' *Neurology* 2002 58(3): 349–353.

6   The research team used the Coma Recovery Scale – Revised (CRS-R) which assesses auditory, visual, verbal and motor functions, as well as communication and arousal level. The test was specifically designed to differentiate between those patients with PVS and those in a minimally conscious state.

7   That is, a diagnosis reached by clinical consensus, according to the observations reported by each member of the clinical team, during structured and unstructured meetings.

8   Helen Gill–Thwaites, *'Lotteries, loopholes and luck: Misdiagnosis in the vegetative state patient'*, Brain Injury, December 2006; 20(13–14); 1321–1328.

9   *'A Discussion Paper on Treatment of Patients in Persistent Vegetative State'* issued in September 1992 by the Medical Ethics Committee of the British Medical Association.

10 'Review of treatment options', p 2.

11 'Initial assessment and treatment', p 2.

12 'Views of health professionals', p 3.

13 Para 2.4 of 'The Vegetative State, Guidance on diagnosis and management: Report of a working party of the Royal College of Physicians 2003'.

14 *Ibid.*

15 See **PARA 12.5** above, **N2**: para 12.

Imaging

12.11   Research suggests that neuroimaging can provide useful supportive information in diagnosing PVS after traumatic brain injury.[1] Thus, before seeking a court declaration, consideration should be given to whether imaging techniques should be undertaken to confirm the diagnosis.[2] The comprehensive review of neuroimaging of Skene and others concluded that:

'... evidence from fMRI [a functional magnetic resonance imaging test] that a patient who has been diagnosed as being in VS has even a low level of consciousness or awareness may be legally significant ... in deciding whether to withdraw life-sustaining treatment'

and

'Evidence of a positive response to fMRI may be considered relevant to the patient's diagnosis or prognosis, which in turn may be relevant in determining whether the continuation of treatment is 'futile'.'

1   'The persistent vegetative state after closed head injury: clinical and magnetic resonance imaging findings in 42 patients' (May 1998) J Neurosurg 88(5), 809–816; Kampfl, Schmutzhard, Franz *et al*, 'Prediction of recovery from post-traumatic vegetative state with cerebral magnetic-resonance imaging' (June 1998) *Lancet* 13, 351(9118) 1763–1767; MM Monti, MR Coleman and AM Owen, 'Neuroimaging and the vegetative state: resolving the behavioural assessment dilemma?' Ann NY Acad Sci 2009 Mar 1157 81–89.
2   Neuroimaging and the withdrawal of life-sustaining treatment from patients in vegetative state' (2009) Med L Rev 245.

Rehabilitation and time to allow for a recovery

12.12   The RCP guidance states that beyond one year following trauma, and beyond six months in non-trauma cases, the chances of regaining consciousness are extremely low. Patients in Vegetative State (lasting more than 4 weeks) should be observed for 12 months after head injury (traumatic brain injury) and 6 months after other causes before the vegetative state is judged to be permanent.[1]

It also states that there is no 'firm scientific evidence' that treatment, 'in terms of special medical, physiotherapeutic or rehabilitative activities', improves outcome of patients in a continuing vegetative state. Thus, the RCP provides no mandatory requirement that rehabilitative measures be undertaken for a specific period of time. However, the high level of misdiagnosis and recovery demonstrated at the Putney Brain Injury Rehabilitation Unit demonstrates the need for stronger and clearer general guidance as to the appropriate treatment and rehabilitative action to be applied in relation to apparently vegetative patients.

Thus, despite the definitive timescales outlined in the RCP guidance, a court may look sceptically on a diagnosis of PVS even if made after a year when there has been little or no attempt at rehabilitation. Detailed evidence from clinicians and nursing staff of attempts at communication and rehabilitation should be obtained for any court application.

1   The evidence accepted in *Bland* was that 'if a PVS patient shows no signs of recovery after six months, or at most a year, then there is no prospect whatever of any recovery.'.

Cases outside the RCP guidelines

12.13   In cases falling within the RCP guidelines it is unlikely that clinicians seeking a court declaration authorising withdrawal will face difficulties, provided that the diagnosis has been clearly and unequivocally made and confirmed by experts of sufficient standing. Cases outside the former RCP guidelines are more problematic.

The issue of whether feeding and hydration could be withdrawn in a patient who failed to meet the RCP criteria was addressed in *Re D (adult: medical treatment).*[1] The patient had nystagmus[2] in response to ice water caloric testing; was able to track movements with the eyes; and had a menace response.

Thus, these clinical features placed the patient outside the 'permanent vegetative state' condition then defined by the RCP. The evidence of Professor Jennett was that D was in a permanent vegetative state. The evidence of the two other neurologists was that the patient had no awareness but both were reluctant to diagnose PVS because the case did not match the old guidelines. D's mother commented that her daughter:

> 'was no longer the victim of a severe head injury; she is now the victim of medical technology.'[3]

On behalf of the Official Solicitor it was submitted that because the Guideline requirements of the Royal College of Physicians were not satisfied, it could not be determined that keeping the patient alive was futile and thus 'best interests' did not mandate withdrawal of feeding.

Although the case was determined by reference to the former Guidelines, it reasserted the importance of detailed evidence being available to the court concerning the patient and in particular the importance of reports from the clinicians and nurses in day-to-day contact with the patient. The President noted that 'every single witness – medical and ... nursing – have all made it clear that this patient has no awareness whatsoever'. He determined that she was in 'a living death' and that she was in PVS. He felt that allowing her to die would *not* extend the range of cases in which a declaration ought to be considered:

> 'The court recognises that no declaration to permit or to sanction the taking of so extreme a step could possibly be granted where there was any real possibility of meaningful life continuing to exist.'

As there was no evidence that D had a meaningful life and there was no prospect of recovery, a declaration permitting the clinicians *not* to re-establish feeding by gastrotomy[4] was granted. Following *Re D*, in *Re H (adult: medical treatment)*[5] the patient had 'visual tracking': this placed her outside the former RCP definition. However, both neurologists concluded that she fell within the international working party's definition and both were satisfied she was a vegetative state patient with no hope of recovery. The President commented that:

> 'It may be that a precise label is not of significant importance. This is ... a developing field for medical analysis.'[6]

The President also emphasised two key elements: first, that the patient was 'wholly unaware of herself or of her environment' and, second, that there was no possibility of change. Thus, notwithstanding that the former RCP criteria precluded the formal PVS diagnosis, the President determined that it was appropriate to grant a declaration in support of the discontinuance of feeding.

1   [1988] 1 FCR 498.
2   Involuntary rapid, rhythmic movement of the eyeball.
3   See N1 above at 502.
4   The gastrostomy tube had become detached.
5   [1998] 2 FLR 36.
6   *Ibid. at* 38.

D ROLE OF THE FAMILY

12.14   The courts have indicated that the views of the family members must be considered. They have recognised that not only have they the right to be heard as the patient's family, but because they may be in the best position to convey what a patient's wishes might have been.[1]

Care should be taken to note any information they have concerning the PVS patient's previously expressed wishes concerning what he would want to happen should he be in a vegetative state. The Official Solicitor's representative will usually interview the family members and others close to the patient.[2]

While it is 'good practice for the doctor to consult relatives,' their views are not determinative: as stated by Lord Goff of Chieveley in *Bland*, their Lordships were:

> 'firmly of the opinion that the relatives' views cannot be determinative of the treatment.'[3]

This view flows inevitably from the approach of English law to the incompetent adult: no-one has power to consent on behalf of an incompetent adult. All questions of the continuation or discontinuation must be assessed whether by doctors or finally by the courts on the basis of the 'best interests' test. Save for those empowered under the MCA to take substituted decisions, no individual, no matter how closely related, can override that determination. In *Re G (persistent vegetative state)*[4] the President granted a declaration that feeding and hydration should be withdrawn, notwithstanding that the application (in which the Trust and the patient's wife concurred) was not supported by the patient's mother.

Conversely, in *BHS Trust v J*,[5] the patient's mother, who supported the treating Trust's application to withdraw artificial nutrition and hydration, opposed the Official Solicitor's application to administer Zolpidem to her daughter. The benefits of the drug were uncertain, but it had been used on three patients (in supposed PVS) whose condition had improved. The mother's opposition was twofold. First, she believed that the withdrawal of artificial nutrition and hydration was in her daughter's best interests and in accordance with her wishes. Second, if her daughter awoke temporarily, she would realise her condition which would be deeply distressing for her. The President of the Family Division held that the trial of the drug (which was ultimately unsuccessful) should go ahead, even though the prospects of success were small.

1   *Trust A v M* [2005] EWHC 807 (Fam).
2   *Official Solicitor, Declaratory Proceedings: Medical and Welfare Decisions for Adults who Lack Capacity*, 26 July 2006.

3   [1993] AC 789 at 871.
4   [1995] 2 FCR 46.
5   [2006] EWHC 3152 (Fam), (2007) 94 BMLR 15. See also 'Intrathecal baclofen in patients with persistent vegetative state: 2 hypotheses.' *Arch Phys Med Rehab* 2009 Jul; 90 (7) 1245–9. The article describes the beneficial side effects of *Intrathecal baclofen* used for spasticity in 6 supposed PVS patients, which ranged from a mere increased alertness to full recovery of consciousness.

E IS AN APPLICATION TO COURT REQUIRED?

12.15   Before discontinuance of feeding or hydration in a PVS patient, an application must be made to the Court of Protection.[1]

1   *Practice Direction E – Applications relating to Serious Medical Treatment*, Court of Protection Rules 2007. See **CHAPTER 5**: Going to Court. Reproduced at **APPENDIX 5.4**.

Consequences of withholding nutrition and hydration without court approval

12.16   In relation to an adult, a court can merely declare that a given course of treatment or withdrawal of treatment would be lawful. Thus, in the absence of a prior court order, retrospective assessment of the withdrawal of feeding or hydration in a criminal or civil court after a patient dies will turn on whether the patient's 'best interests' mandated such withdrawal. Clinicians face the risk of professional[1] or even criminal[2] censure in the absence of a prior court declaration. Pro-life pressure groups and individuals are keen to challenge any perceived attacks on the sanctity of life.

Following the death of Anthony Bland, the Reverend James Morrow sought privately to prosecute the treating clinician for murder. Given the court's advance declaration that withdrawal was lawful, the magistrates refused to issue a summons on the information laid by the private individual. This decision was upheld by the Divisional Court. Staughton LJ indicated that the guidance in *Bland* should inhibit prosecution or if the matter went ahead the ruling of the House of Lords would be an answer to prosecution.

Thus, prudence dictates that a clinician should seek the determination of the court as to the validity of his intention to withhold nutrition and hydration from a patient to avoid the risk of being faced with a prosecution for murder or with disciplinary proceedings.

Further, 'best interests' connotes acting in accordance with a *Bolam* responsible body of opinion. Given that the courts have required a prior application and doctors' professional bodies have supported that requirement, is a doctor who does not seek court approval *Bolam* reasonable? Unless there is an exceptionally rapid emergency (and it should be stressed that the Court of Protection can respond very quickly indeed in medical treatment decision cases), a failure to apply is likely to be considered *not* in accordance with a *Bolam* body of opinion,[3] thereby placing the clinician at risk of criminal censure and his hospital at risk of a civil suit.

It should be emphasised that this requirement relates to cases where it is intended to withhold or withdraw nutrition from a patient in a permanent vegetative state, or a similar condition. Doctors are constantly having to make decisions about the withdrawal or withholding of ventilation and other life prolonging treatment from accident victims and other seriously ill patients. It has never been suggested that all such cases should be referred to the courts before such a decision is implemented.

1   For example, the suspension by the General Medical Council of GP Dr Ken Taylor for failing to listen to nurses and consult colleagues in relation to the withdrawal of nutrition from an elderly patient (March 1999).

2   For example, note the prosecution of Dr David Moor following the death of an elderly patient after pain-relieving morphine had been administered: he was acquitted.

3   It should be noted that establishing *Bolam* responsible conduct does not merely require proof that there is a body of opinion, but also proof that the body of opinion 'stands up to analysis' and is 'not unreasonable in the light of the state of medical knowledge at the time': *Joyce v Merton and Sutton and Wandsworth Health Authority* [1995] 6 Med LR 60.

F APPLICATION TO COURT

12.17   The first stage before making any application to court for withdrawal of feeding and hydration is to consider whether the patient expressed any wishes about how he wished to be treated in this situation. Is there a living will or any form of advanced directive?

The next stage is to consult the family and determine their wishes. The timing of any court application should be managed sensitively. Time should be given to the family to come to terms with the determination that the patient will not recover. If the family's agreement to discontinuance is initially not forthcoming, it is suggested that a significant period of time is allowed before forcing the issue to a court hearing.

The *Practice Note* indicates that applications must be made to the Court of Protection, seeking a declaration in the form that:

'P lacks capacity to make a decision in relation to the withdrawal of life-sustaining treatment,

That, having regards to the best interests of P, it is lawful for [name of healthcare provider] to withdraw the life-sustaining treatment from P.'[1]

The parties should be either the next-of-kin or other individual closely connected with the patient and must include the relevant health authority or NHS Trust.[2]

It is suggested that the Official Solicitor should be contacted as soon as it is known that an application to court is contemplated in order that steps can then be initiated as soon as possible to instruct an independent expert to examine the patient and enable the Official Solicitor's detailed report to be prepared. Such early notice may prove crucial should circumstances suddenly change as a result, for example, of an inability to maintain feeding and an urgent application to court is required.

1   See *Practice Direction E – Applications Relating to Serious Medical Treatment*, Part 9 Court of Protection Rules 2007. Reproduced at **APPENDIX 5.4**.

2   *Re S (hospital patient: court's jurisdiction)* [1996] Fam 1, CA.

Confidentiality

12.18 Hearings before the court in PVS cases will generally be in public, with appropriate anonymisation provisions,[1] but the court may order that the whole or part of any hearing is to be held in private.[2]

The court also has power to:

(a)   authorise the publication of information about a private hearing;

(b)   authorise persons to attend a private hearing;

(c)   exclude persons from attending either a private or public hearing; or

(d)   restrict or prohibit the publication of information about a private or public hearing.[3]

Thus:

●   the court may preserve the anonymity of other parties to the litigation, if necessary to avoid the risk of identification of the patient;

●   orders preserving the anonymity of the patient are capable of extending beyond the death of the patient until any successful application to have them discharged.

However, it must be stressed that any coroner's inquest will be conducted in open court without protection of the identity of the deceased and the family should be made aware of this when an application for a declaration is being made. Whether a hearing is in fact conducted is within the discretion of the coroner.

1   See **Chapter 5**: Going to Court.
2   *Ibid.*
3   *Practice Direction A – Hearings (Including Reporting Restrictions)* Court of Protection Rules, 2007 and Annex: Application for a Reporting Restriction Order.

Evidence

12.19 In *Bland* itself the Law Lords emphasised that the patient's lack of consciousness and absence of any prospects of recovery had been 'overwhelmingly proved.'[1] Convincing and detailed evidence must be produced to the court which demonstrates that there is no benefit to the patient in his continued existence.

Statements/reports should be obtained from the treating clinician and from those in the nursing staff with closest daily contact with the patient. The Official Solicitor will ensure that statements are obtained from material family members. The medical and nursing notes should be available and any entries which might be interpreted as indicating awareness must be explained.

It is important before embarking on any court application that, wherever possible, the hospital obtains a supportive independent report from at least one expert of standing in this field. The court will require evidence from at least two independent experts; one of these will be commissioned by the Official Solicitor. If the case raises particular complications of diagnosis and in particular if it falls outside the RCP guidance, it would be worthwhile the hospital commissioning two independent expert opinions itself, before seeking a declaration. Consideration should be given in all cases to obtaining the opinion of an independent expert in structured assessment, such as SMART, in addition to neurological evidence.

The expert neurological assessments should:

- be undertaken separately;
- involve consultation with clinical and nursing staff, relatives and carers;
- involve a formal neurological examination, preferably undertaken in the presence of nursing staff and relatives who have had the opportunity to observe the patient over a prolonged period.[2]

Both factual and expert evidence should be obtained, addressing the following issues:

- What is the history of the patient's condition?
- What is his current condition?
- What benefit is likely from any treatment?
- What rehabilitative steps have been taken and what impact would any such steps in the future have?
- What is the diagnosis?
- What imaging techniques have been undertaken (if any) and what imaging (if any) is proposed?
- What are the views concerning the proposed discontinuance of –
  - the treating clinician?
  - the nursing staff?
  - the family?
- How is any discontinuance of feeding/hydration going to be effected?
- If requested, why is a confidentiality order required in the terms requested?
- What steps are being taken to offer counselling to relatives and staff?

In particular, care should be taken to ensure that the experts address the following questions:[3]

- Is there any evidence of awareness of self or environment?
- Is there any prospect of improvement in the patient's condition?
- Does the patient meet the criteria for diagnosis of permanent vegetative state set out by the RCP guidance? [If he does not, specify why].
- Into which category of the Appendix to the International Working Party Report does the patient fall?
- Are there any comments concerning the patient's current medication (if any) and in particular is it possible that such medication may be (or may have been) masking or dampening signs of awareness?
- What are the risks/benefits of withdrawing any such medication?
- How long will the patient survive in his current state?
- How long would the patient survive if hydration and feeding were to be withdrawn?
- Is it – in the expert's clinical judgement – appropriate to discontinue artificial nutrition and hydration?
- Are there any recommendations concerning treatment and nursing care at such time?

All sources of information must be assessed before a final diagnosis of Permanent Vegetative State should be considered. Often family members can describe patients as appearing to '*suffer*': for the hospital, a clear response to this is required, explaining why the signs and symptoms viewed as '*suffering*' are not in fact indicative of any underlying awareness.

Prior to the final determination of the application there will ordinarily be a directions hearing at which:

- the involvement and precise role of the Official Solicitor will be determined;
- the nature of the necessary medical evidence will be established;
- any orders preserving confidentiality are likely to be made.

The scope of the evidence to be heard at the final hearing should be addressed at the directions appointment. The extent to which clinicians, nursing staff and family members will be required to give evidence will turn on the degree to which (a) there is evidence concerning the patient's previously expressed wishes (b) the diagnosis is open to debate and (c) there is a dispute between clinicians and family members about the proposed discontinuance.

At the final hearing, the court is likely to require as a minimum evidence from the independent experts instructed and the responsible clinician. If family members dispute the proposed discontinuance they should ensure – and they should be invited to ensure – that they have adequate representation at this hearing.

At the final hearing the judge will determine on the basis of the evidence and submissions by all interested parties whether or not to grant the declaration. As stated above, in cases where the diagnosis of PVS falls within RCP guidance it is likely that a declaration will be granted. Outside that Guidance each case will turn on its own merits and will face detailed scrutiny by the judge.

1   [1993] AC 789 at 885 per Lord Browne-Wilkinson.
2   Derived from the Official Solicitor's excellent instructions in *Re D* (9 November 2000, unreported per Johnson J).
3   *Ibid.*

G EMERGENCY CASES

12.20   In *Frenchay Healthcare NHS Trust v S*[1] a vegetative patient's gastrostomy tube had become dislodged. An urgent application came before the court. Time had not permitted independent examinations to be performed to assess the patient's condition. The Court of Appeal held that it was appropriate to grant a declaration authorising the hospital not to replace the gastrostomy tube. The court rejected the Official Solicitor's argument that the tube should be reinserted to allow independent opinions to be commissioned.

1   [1994] 2 All ER 403 and see *Re OT* [2009] EWHC 633 (Fam) in which Parker J rejected an a due process argument that the PVS case should not have been brought in an emergency and that the parents should have been permitted further time in order to present their case (para 78 – 94).

Critique of *Frenchay* approach

12.21   In *Bland* Lord Goff commented:

> 'Even so, where (for example) a patient is brought into hospital in such a condition that, without the benefit of a life support system, he will not continue to live, the decision has to be made whether or not to give him that benefit, if available. That decision can only be made in the best interests of the patient. No doubt, his best interests will ordinarily require that he should be placed on a life support system as soon as necessary, **if only to make an accurate assessment of his condition and a prognosis for the future.'** [1]

Thus, the House of Lords envisaged a situation whereby it can be in a patient's 'best interests' to continue treatment which may subsequently be demonstrated to be futile in order to allow an assessment of the patient's condition. It is submitted that this principle should be applied in an emergency situation such as *Frenchay*. It must be in the patient's 'best interests' to ensure that his condition is assessed adequately in accordance with the accepted guidelines. Thus, pending final determination of the diagnosis by independent examination, it cannot be determined that continued feeding is against the patient's 'best interests' and an assault.

Further, given that death by starvation is not instantaneous, a significant amount of information can in fact be placed before the court in a short space of time. In *Re D*[2] the court had detailed expert reports and evidence from clinicians and nurses, even though the hearing was on a Friday and the patient's gastrostomy tube had become detached on Tuesday.[3]

Thus, the court and the Official Solicitor can act at short notice. However, a Trust should gather careful evidence from clinicians and experts in order to establish the precise degree of urgency in each case.

1   [1993] AC 789 at 867F (emphasis added).
2   9 November 2000, unreported.
3   Also note the significant information obtained for the emergency hearing in *Re S* (30 November 1994, unreported) per Ward J; and note the short period of time in which evidence was gathered in the case of *Re H* (*An NHS Trust 'A' v Mrs 'M'* and *An NHS Trust 'B' v Mrs 'H'* (ibid).

H CHILDREN

12.22   Is the substantive and procedural position different if the PVS patient is a child? Usually a parent can provide valid consent for a child. If the child is unconscious a parent can provide consent for that child to undergo medical procedures. Nonetheless, even if a parent consents to discontinuance of feeding and hydration in a PVS child, an application should still be made to court in relation to this terminal step. The court can then objectively assess the question of 'best interests.'[1]

While suggested by the *Practice Note*, an application for wardship is no longer required. If there is no other reason to invoke the wardship jurisdiction then the application can simply be made within the inherent jurisdiction.

The procedure and evidence for such a hearing will be substantially the same as outlined above in relation to adults. The test for children is whether the proposed discontinuance is in the best interests of the child. As discussed above,[2] this is the same test as applied for adults.

1 See *Re OT* [2009] EWHC 633 (Fam).
2 See PARA **12.3** above.

I DOCTORS WHO DISAGREE IN PRINCIPLE

12.23 What steps should be taken by a doctor treating a PVS patient who is in principle against withdrawal of feeding/hydration? A doctor cannot be forced to undertake treatment with which he does not agree.[1] However, given that continued treatment of a patient in PVS could comprise an assault, the family of a PVS patient may be able to obtain an injunction ordering the cessation of the assault and the withdrawal of tube-feeding. Thus, a doctor who disagrees in principle with allowing the patient to die may wish to transfer the care of that patient to another doctor. However, before doing so, he must '[ensure] that arrangements have been made for another doctor to take over [his] role'[2] The General Medical Council does not consider that it is acceptable to 'withdraw from a patient's care if this would leave the patient, or colleagues with nowhere to turn.'

1 With *Re J (a minor) (child in care: medical treatment)* [1993] Fam 15.
2 Para 67 of the General Medical Council's Draft Paper for Consultation 'End of life treatment and care: Good practice in decision-making.'

J CONCLUSION

12.24 The substantive law in relation to PVS has changed little over recent years. The principles enunciated by the House of Lords in *Bland* still apply. In stark contrast, the rate of medical research into the diagnosis of the condition has been rapid. The disturbing level of mis-diagnosis mandates a cautious approach to the immediate acceptance of a PVS diagnosis by the court. It is essential that any application for withdrawal of artificial hydration and nutrition should be supported by convincing evidence that all reasonable treatment, assessment and rehabilitation measures have been undertaken. Any indications of possible consciousness, apparent either from medical records or from witness testimony, should be analysed and explained to determine whether they in fact are indicators of consciousness. Only once the diagnosis of PVS is clearly established should the final steps of withdrawal of life-sustaining hydration and nutrition be permitted and then only with permission of the court.

For updating material and hyperlinks related to this chapter, see: www.3serjeantsinn.com/mtdl/pvs

---

Chapter 13

Treatment of Suicidal Patients

A   Introduction 13.1
B   Basic definition 13.2
     What is suicide? 13.2
          An act 13.3
          An intention to act 13.4
          An understanding of the likely consequences 13.5
C   Statute 13.6
     European Convention on Human Rights 13.7
D   Refining the definition of suicide: failure to treat or feed 13.16
E   General principles 13.19
F   Practical problems 13.23
G   Autonomy v liability for failing to act 13.28
H   European Convention on Human Rights: duty to preserve life 13.39
I   General guidance 13.47
     Emergency situations 13.49
          Inadequate time to assess capacity 13.49
          Preventing a jump from a window 13.52
J   European Convention on Human Rights: the balance to be struck 13.54
K   Compulsorily detained patients 13.56
     Legal test in criticising a doctor's determination under s 63 of the Mental
     Health Act 1983 13.64
L   Guidance on approach to treatment 13.66
M   Conclusion 13.67

A INTRODUCTION

13.1   This chapter addresses the issue of the relative entitlements of patients
and medical attendants in relation to the control of suicidal behaviour in
hospital. Of all situations facing doctors and other hospital staff, this is the one
where they are most likely to have to make decisions without recourse to
advice, let alone the courts, although the latter may on occasion be available
and, indeed, play a necessary part in what occurs. The law on the treatment of
suicidal patients results in very difficult dilemmas for clinicians in reconciling
their duty to protect and treat patients with their obligation to respect patients'
autonomy.

B BASIC DEFINITION

What is suicide?

13.2   It is an intentional act of self-destruction committed in the knowledge of the probable consequences of the act.[1] Therefore, it requires the following ingredients.

1   *Clift v Schwabe* (1846) 3 CB 437 at 464; *Re Davis (deceased)* [1968] 1 QB 72.

An act

13.3   The vexed question of the distinction between acts and omissions has been discussed in the chapter on the withholding or withdrawing of treatment from PVS patients.[1] It appears that the distinction is relevant here.[2]

1   See **CHAPTER 12.**
2   Note discussion below at **PARA 13.16** in relation to *Secretary of State for the Home Department v Robb.*

An intention to act

13.4   By definition, suicide cannot be committed by a person who is, at the time of the act in question, incapable, either temporarily or permanently, of forming an intention, or of appreciating the quality of his actions.

An understanding of the likely consequences

13.5   This and the previously mentioned requirements do not necessarily mean that the individual must have the mental capacity required for consenting to and refusing medical treatment.[1] A person who is suffering from a depression may understand the consequences, but still wish for them. Thus, coroners' inquests may return a verdict of suicide while the balance of the deceased's mind was disturbed.

1   See **CHAPTER 1**: Consent – General.

C STATUTE

13.6   Until the passing of the Suicide Act 1961, the act of committing suicide was a crime, as was an attempt. Section 1 of the Act abolished that rule. Nevertheless, by s 2 it remains an offence to aid and abet suicide.[1] Therefore, it is criminally unlawful for anyone to seek to render assistance to a person wishing to kill himself, however moving their plight might be. In the medical context it is therefore clearly unlawful for a doctor knowingly to supply a patient with the means of committing suicide, intending thereby to help him to do so.

1   Suicide Act 1961, s 2.

European Convention on Human Rights

13.7   Does the Suicide Act 1961 contravene the European Convention on Human Rights?[1] The validity of s 2 of the Suicide Act 1961 was first considered by the European Commission on Human Rights in *R v United Kingdom*.[2] This was a challenge by a member of the Voluntary Euthanasia Society who was convicted of conspiracy to aid and abet a suicide. He argued that the section violated the right to privacy (Art 8) and the right to freedom of expression (Art 10). The Commission's view was that s 2 did not violate the right to privacy (Art 8) because the notionally private act of suicide encroached on the legitimate public interest of protecting life. Further, there was not a breach of freedom of expression (Art 10) on the ground that:[3]

> 'the State's legitimate interest in this area in taking measures to protect, against criminal behaviour, the life of its citizens particularly those who belong to especially vulnerable categories by reason of their age or infirmity'.

1   It should be noted that any challenge to the Act could not be made other than by seeking a declaration of incompatibility in the High Court (or by a challenge within criminal proceedings) – see *DPP v Kebeline* [1993] 3 WLR 972: as primary legislation, the courts have no power to override its effect unless and until it is repealed or amended by Parliament.
2   (1983) 33 DR 270. In Canada the constitutional 'right to life' was the basis for a challenge (albeit unsuccessful) to the Criminal Code which prohibited assisting suicide (*Rodriguez v British Columbia* (1994) 107 DLR (4th) 342).
3   (1983) 33 DR 270 at 272.

13.8   Section 2 of the Suicide Act 1961 was challenged again in *R (Pretty) v Director of Public Prosecutions*[1] on the basis that the operation of the section in preventing Mrs Pretty's assisted suicide violated her right to life (Art 2) and right to privacy (Art 8). Both claims were ultimately dismissed, confirming that Art 2 does not confer a right to die and stating that Art 8 was not engaged.[2] On appeal to Strasbourg[3] it was held that the manner in which one chooses to end one's own life, in order to avoid an undignified or distressing end, did engage the right to privacy (Art 8(1)). However, the operation of s 2, which allowed due regard to be given in each particular case to the public interest in bringing a prosecution, did not violate the right itself (Art 8(2)).

1   *R (Pretty) v DPP* [2002] 1 AC 800.
2   *Pretty* has now been overruled by *Purdy* (see discussion below). Compare with what Michael Freeman had previously stated: 'Article 2 is limited to protecting an individual's right to life, and whether it protects a person's right to decide how to live or how to die must be regarded as dubious given that the Convention separates the right to life (Art 2) from the right to security (Art 5).' ('Death, Dying and the HRA', 1999 52 *Current Legal Problems* 218).
3   *Pretty v United Kingdom* (2002) 35 EHRR 1.

13.9   A different approach to s 2 was adopted in *R (Purdy) v Director of Public Prosecutions*.[1] This time the challenge was on the basis that Art 8 was infringed by the refusal of the DPP to issue specific guidance as to the criteria which would be used in exercising his discretion under s 2(4), whether or not to prosecute an individual case of assisted suicide. The applicant did not seek to decriminalise assisted suicide but challenged the uncertainty as to whether or not an individual would, in fact, be prosecuted. On this basis the challenge was successful.

1   [2009] UKHL 45; [2009] LS Law Med.

13.10   Mrs Purdy, a sufferer of progressive multiple sclerosis, wished to have the assistance of her husband in travelling abroad to Switzerland where assisted suicide is lawful. She sought specific guidance from the DPP as to whether or not in such circumstances her husband was likely to face criminal prosecution. The House of Lords, overturning the Court of Appeal, held that Mrs Purdy's Art 8 rights were engaged (thereby overruling *Pretty*) and ruled that the current general guidance from the DPP failed to satisfy the Art 8(2) requirements of accessibility and foreseeability in assessing whether or not a prosecution of her husband was likely to follow after her death.[1]

1   By the time of the House of Lords' hearing in *Purdy* there had apparently been 115 cases where suicide had been successfully achieved abroad. To date there have been no prosecutions but only in the case of Daniel James did the DPP provide reasons as to why a prosecution had not taken place – 9 December 2008. For further discussion of *Purdy* see C Johnston's commentary at [2009] LS Law Med.

13.11   The decision of the House of Lords has not altered the substantive criminal law. It remains a criminal offence under s 2 to assist the suicide of another. However, s 2(1) was a special case, as stated by Lord Brown:

'There are not many crimes of which it can be said that their discouragement by the State may violate the fundamental human rights of others. Yet undoubtedly that is true in certain circumstances of the conduct criminalised by section 2(1) of the Suicide Act 1961.'[1]

Thus, the decision has confirmed that Art 8 encompasses an individual's right to manage his life and death and entitles that individual to be provided with sufficient guidance from the State as to how the discretion to prosecute the offence of assisted suicide will be exercised. The DPP was required to provide detailed and specific guidance on when prosecution was, or was not, likely to be in the public interest.

1   See **PARA 13.9, N1**; para 70.

13.12   Interim guidance was published by the DPP in September 2009. That guidance, which is reproduced here in full,[1] is to be subject to further public consultation. The guidance indicates that those who provide such assistance to the terminally ill on compassionate grounds are unlikely to face criminal prosecution. However, at this stage, it appears to be limited to close relatives or close personal friends of the dying person. Doctors, who occupy a very different and unique relationship with the terminally ill, are unlikely to fit easily into any such guidance.

1   See **APPENDIX 13.1** and for updates on this guidance see www.3serjeantsinn.com/mtdl/ suicide.

13.13   While Mrs Purdy's case worked its way through the legal system there were further legislative attempts to change the law on assisted suicide. The Assisted Dying for the Terminally Ill Bill 2005 was blocked in the House of Lords in 2006. That Bill would have included proposals which allowed doctors to provide the means for terminally ill patients to end their own lives. The BMA, whose members voted against euthanasia in June 2006, remained neutral on this issue.

13.14 This was followed by Lord Falconer's proposed amendment to the Coroners and Justice Bill which would have removed the threat of prosecution from those who go abroad to help an assisted suicide. The amendment, which called for the law to be waived if two doctors deemed the person in question terminally ill and competent to make the decision to end their life, described by some peers as ill defined, unsound and unnecessary, was defeated in the House of Lords on 7 July 2009 by 194 votes to 141. It resulted in considerable media interest. The strongly polarised views in the country were reflected in the debate in the House itself. For example, Baroness Campbell contended that sanctioning assisted suicide would make doctors and those helping disabled people think that death was what was wanted by disabled people:

'the very people who need every encouragement to live and not to succumb to society's prevalent view that our situation is so tragic, so burdensome, so insufferable that surely we must want to die.'[3]

Baroness Warnock responded:

'I think that there is confusion if we run the disabled as a class of people, members of society, into another class of people, the terminally ill, although they may overlap. There are two different concepts and we should not bring them together under the general heading of the vulnerable about whom we hear, in my experience, all too much. Being vulnerable is a judgment made by somebody about another person; in my experience, it is not a judgment that one ever makes about oneself. To be classified as vulnerable is to be regarded from a great height by lawyers or doctors, above all, or nurses. They deem one to be vulnerable. There is a very small category of people, of whom we have heard today, to which belong some of those people who have gone to Switzerland to commit suicide, who do not want to be categorised as vulnerable. They therefore make their own decision.'[4]

Further she dealt with the concern about selfish relations preying on the disabled or ill stating:

'Why should people ... put up with [the current state of the law] for the sake of other people who are in a quite different position, who may be disabled or under pressure from their nasty relations? ... We should go back to what this amendment is about and not fear the slippery slope. We should aim for the positive result of clarifying the law as it now stands.'[5]

There will undoubtedly be further attempts to change the substantive law.[6]

1   Report of the Select Committee on Medical Ethics, Vol 1, (HL Paper 21-I).
2   Government Response to the Report of the Select Committee on Medical Ethics (Cmnd 2553).
3   Hansard Vol 712 No 103 col 613 (7 July 2009).
4   *Ibid*, col 616.
5   *Ibid*, col 617.
6   A last ditch attempt by Lord Alderdice to amend the Coroners and Justice Bill in similar fashion to that of Lord Falconer's amendment failed. He withdrew it in the face of stiff opposition. Baroness O'Cathain argued that more help for the terminally ill should be provided by greater support for the hospice movement and that 'We must work towards that, but, in the mean time, please let us stop condoning, exulting and encouraging assisted suicide.' (Hansard Vol 713 No 123, Col 1085, 26 Oct 2009).

13.15 However, prior to Lord Falconer's proposed legislative changes, the Report of the House of Lords' Select Committee on Medical Ethics had concluded that there were 'no circumstances in which assisted suicide should be permitted'.[1] The report was accepted by the Government who commented that a change in the law to allow assisted suicide 'would be open to abuse and put the lives of the weak and vulnerable at risk'.[2] While Lord Falconer's amendments to the current law would have reflected the DPP's practice not to prosecute in such circumstances, it remains the case that, while Art 8 accepts the right of a person to decide when and how to die, it does not give an assistant immunity from prosecution under s 2. While, following the decision in *Purdy* and the issuing of the DPP's guidance, that position has changed in certain defined circumstances, it remains the case that doctors who do provide such assistance expose themselves to criminal prosecution and disciplinary sanction including erasure from the medical register.[3]

1   Report of the Select Committee on Medical Ethics, Vol 1, (HL Paper 21-I).
2   Government Response to the Report of the Select Committee on Medical Ethics (Cmnd 2553).
3   In 2006 a general practitioner was erased from the medical register for supplying sleeping tablets to a close friend so that the friend could commit suicide – *The Times*, 28 September.

D REFINING THE DEFINITION OF SUICIDE: FAILURE TO TREAT OR FEED

13.16 In *Airedale NHS Trust v Bland*[1] the House of Lords concluded that a competent patient who refuses to consent to treatment which would have the effect of prolonging his life and who by reason of the refusal subsequently dies does not commit suicide. It was stated that any doctor who complied with a patient's wishes in those circumstances cannot be said to be aiding and abetting suicide. This view was followed in *Secretary of State for the Home Department v Robb*,[2] in which it was determined that a prison hunger striker who starved himself to death was not thereby committing suicide. Thus, in considering whether the 'countervailing State interest' in preventing suicide should be set against the 'individual's right of self- determination' Thorpe J held that the State interest was inapplicable in this setting because the prisoner's:

'refusal of nutrition and medical treatment in the exercise of the right of self-determination does *not* constitute an act of suicide'.[3]

1   [1993] AC 789, HL (see **CHAPTER 12**).
2   [1995] 1 FLR 412.
3   [1995] 1 FLR 412 at 416D.

13.17 This seems a surprising conclusion. Just as someone who failed to feed a dependent child would be guilty of homicide, so it would seem to follow that someone who does not feed themselves is committing self-homicide. However, the determination in *Robb* that refusing nutrition is not an act of suicide follows from the decision in *Bland*[1] that providing food and drink comprises medical treatment. Nonetheless, this determination is an unnecessarily contrived answer to ensure the (necessary) result that doctors are not liable under s 2 of the Suicide Act 1961 in failing to provide treatment to patients who refuse consent. Further, *Robb* could be misconstrued as implying that in circumstances where a patient's acts or omissions can be construed as 'an act of suicide' it is by that reason alone lawful to treat or prevent that patient's 'act of suicide' and a failure to treat must comprise aiding and abetting suicide.

1   Applied, for example, in *B v Croydon Health Authority* [1995] 2 WLR 294, [1995] Fam 133.

13.18   The proposition in *Bland* would be better expressed as a doctor is not aiding or abetting suicide in circumstances where it is unlawful for him to act to prevent the suicide. If, in treating a patient without his consent, the doctor would be assaulting the patient, he cannot be held to have 'aided and abetted' a death when the law itself prevents any treatment. To assess the culpability of the doctor's acts or omissions solely in terms of the definition to be applied to the patient's actions is to downplay the importance of an adult's autonomy. A doctor cannot violate an adult's autonomy over his body to prevent his death, whether that death is the result of 'suicide' as defined by the courts or as a result of a refusal to be treated. It would be simpler to accept (contrary to *Robb*) that starving oneself to death is suicide but that, given a competent refusal of nutrition, no-one can lawfully act to prevent that suicide because to do so would be an assault. Thus, no-one can be guilty of aiding and abetting the patient's death.

E GENERAL PRINCIPLES

13.19   The general principles in approaching suicidal patients can be derived from our chapters on capacity and consent.[1] A distinction must clearly be drawn between the mentally well adult in possession of full capacity to make medical treatment decisions of importance, and others who lack such capacity or who are suffering from some degree of mental illness or disorder, whether or not that deprives them of capacity.

1   **CHAPTER 1**: Consent – General and **CHAPTER 2**: Consent – Adults.

13.20   In general, the law does not now seek to interfere in the actions of an adult possessing full capacity intended to cause that individual's own death. Indeed, in the case of *Re Z (an adult: capacity)*[1] a local authority was not obliged to take steps to prevent a vulnerable adult from travelling with her husband to Switzerland for the purposes of an assisted suicide. If there was a reasonable suspicion that providing such assistance may constitute a criminal offence the police should be informed who could then decide whether or not to take action. Hedley J stated:

> 'This case affords no basis for trying to ascertain the court's views about the rights or wrongs of suicide, assisted or otherwise. This case simply illustrates that a competent person is entitled to take their own decisions on these matters and that that person alone bears responsibility for any decision so taken. That is the essence of what some will regard as God-given free will and what others will describe as the innate right of self autonomy.'[2]

1   *Re Z (an adult: capacity); Local Authority v Z* [2004] EWHC 2817 Fam, *The Times,* December 9, 2004.
2   At para 21; see also P de Cruz, 'The Terminally Ill Adult Seeking Assisted Suicide Abroad' (2005) 13 Med L Rev 257.

13.21   Further, where it is clear that the suicidal actions are the result of a firm and irrevocable decision to end life, taken by an adult possessing the relevant degree of capacity, and that individual evinces a wish to be left to die, any attempt at resuscitation by a person knowing those facts may well be unlawful.[1] There is, however, nothing to prevent anyone doing all in their power to persuade a suicidally inclined person to change his mind and to take steps to avoid the individual acquiring the means of self destruction. In some circumstances there may be a duty owed to the suicidally inclined individual to take reasonable care to prevent him from obtaining the means to commit or attempt suicide.

13.22   In the case of children,[1] or adults lacking the appropriate degree of capacity, the position is quite different. Those responsible for their care may, and almost certainly must, take all reasonable steps in their best interests to prevent acts of suicide. Further, in treating such patients their best interests will generally mandate that doctors act to preserve their lives despite any refusal of consent. In relation to adults who have a mental illness or disorder, the law may allow treatment following a refusal of consent if the adult is detained under the Mental Health Act 1983 and the treatment is considered to be for the patient's mental illness or disorder. This is so even if the illness or disorder does not in fact deprive the adult of capacity. In relation to an unconscious patient whose wishes are not known, in an emergency situation, life-saving treatment can lawfully be administered on the legal ground of necessity.

1   A child might possess the relevant capacity under the *Gillick* principles, but those having parental responsibility would in any event have a right to seek to prevent suicide by a child. Further, the protective principles applied by the courts to restrict children's autonomy would certainly come into play here. For a more general discussion of these principles, see **CHAPTER 4**. The position of children is therefore considered here as being identical to others lacking legal capacity.

F PRACTICAL PROBLEMS

13.23   About 100,000 people present at hospital each year following acts of deliberate self-harm. In 2006 in England and Wales there were 24,000 cases of attempted suicide among teenagers.[1] Casualty officers are in the front line of the treatment of those who have attempted suicide. Often little thought is given to the legal basis on which such patients are treated. Three particular illustrations of the legal and ethical dilemmas may assist:

- First, if an adult presents at the Accident and Emergency Department with bleeding wounds having attempted to kill himself, and he says he does not want his wounds to be bound, would binding the wounds be unlawful?
- Second, if an adult patient who has been assessed as competent and is voluntarily in hospital, starts to run towards a window, would it be an unlawful assault for a doctor to rugby-tackle him to prevent him from jumping out of the window?
- Third, given that it is presumed that adults have capacity if, following a drugs overdose, an unconscious adult is taken by ambulance to the

Accident and Emergency Department, has he not thereby indicated that
he does not want to receive any treatment and that he wants to die?

1   There are 6,000 suicides per annum in England and Wales, across all age groups.

13.24   The last problem is the more easily addressed. Often, attempted
suicides are 'cries for help': the ultimate intention of the person is not in fact to
die. How then is a casualty officer to distinguish between patients who are
'genuine' suicides from those that are 'cries for help'? Quite simply, he cannot
and must therefore treat the patient on the basis of necessity. As discussed
above, in treating an unconscious patient, a doctor can provide such treatment
as is necessary to save the patient's life.[1]

1   This approach is supported by research findings on 34 'self-poisoners' which determined that
only around 40% of such patients themselves in fact expressed a wish to die: see James and
Hawton, 'Overdoses: Explanation and Attitudes in Self-Poisoners and Significant Others'
(1985) 146 *British Journal of Psychiatry* 481–485. And see **CHAPTER 3**: Deciding for Others –
Adults, **PARA 3.8**, **CHAPTER 6**: Restraint and Deprivation of Liberty, **PARA 6.3**.

13.25   As to the first problem – the conscious patient who refuses treatment
for his bleeding wounds – the general principle outlined above appears to
provide the simple answer that, unless the patient is known to be incompetent,
treatment is prohibited. In *Bland* it was asserted that the principle of sanctity of
life is not an absolute one:

'It does not compel a medical practitioner on pain of criminal sanctions to
treat a patient who will die if he does not, contrary to the express wishes of
the patient.'[1]

1   Page 1031A.

13.26   However, while it is easy for House of Lords judges and legal authors
to assert the paramountcy of autonomy, it is another for a doctor to watch
someone die. As stated by J A Strauss:

'What doctor will fail to render medical aid to a person who has cut his
pulses in a suicide attempt and is bleeding to death?'[1]

The solution might ostensibly be to argue that there is not adequate time to
assess competence, and thus the doctrine of necessity comes into play, thereby
mandating the treatment of the bleeding patient's wounds. However, in
assessing the legality of the act, this argument would appear to ignore the
doctrine of presumed capacity:[2] it is to be assumed that the person with
bleeding wounds has capacity to refuse consent unless the opposite is
established.

1   'Legal Questions Surrounding Hunger Strikes by Detainees and Prisoners' (1991) 10 Med L.
Rev 211–218.
2   See **CHAPTER 2**: Consent – General, **PARA 2.8**: presumption of capacity. *Kerrie Wooltorton*, a
26 year old suffering from depression, took poison intending to commit suicide. On being taken
to hospital she handed the doctors a 'living will' which instructed the medical staff to make her
comfortable but take no steps to save her life. Facing prosecution if they interfered, the doctors
allowed her to die. It is thought to be the first time a living will has been used to commit suicide.
(Daily Telegraph, 1 October 2009).

13.27   Nonetheless, as the cases of *Reeves*[1] and now *Savage v South Essex
Partnership NHS Foundation Trust*[2] establish, one can be liable for a failure to

protect even competent people from themselves. Thus, the casualty officer may feel that he is in the impossible situation that a failure to treat the patient may in fact render him liable to civil, disciplinary or even criminal sanctions. The doctor is placed between the rock of patient autonomy and the hard place of negligence litigation.

1   *Reeves v Commissioner of the Metropolitan Police* [2000] 1 AC 360.
2   [2009] 2 WLR 115.

G AUTONOMY V LIABILITY FOR FAILING TO ACT

13.28   More often than not – whether in textbooks or judgments – the question of suicidal patients' competence to refuse treatment is considered in a vacuum. We, however, feel it is unrealistic to address the question of a doctor's duty to respect a suicidal patient's refusal of treatment without also considering that doctor's liability for failure to protect a suicidal patient.

13.29   Generally the law will not impose a duty on a person to prevent someone else from self-inflicted harm. As stated by Lord Hoffmann in Reeves:

'This argument is based upon the sound intuition that there is a difference between protecting people against harm caused to them by third parties and protecting them against harm which they inflict upon themselves. It reflects the individualist philosophy of the common law. People of full age and sound understanding must look after themselves and take responsibility for their actions. This philosophy expresses itself in the fact that duties to safeguard from harm deliberately caused by others are unusual and a duty to protect a person of full understanding from causing harm to himself is very rare indeed.'[1]

1   See **PARA 13.27, N1** above at 368C.

13.30   However, as seen in *Reeves*[1], the courts will impose a duty on the police to take reasonable care to prevent known suicide risks from harming or killing themselves. Whether the duty goes further was analysed in the case of *Orange v Chief Constable of West Yorkshire*[2] where an argument that the specific duty to take reasonable steps to prevent harm extended to all prisoners was rejected by the Court of Appeal who confirmed that the specific duty only arose where the risk of self-harm was known or should have been known in an individual case.

In *Savage*[3] a similar duty to that defined in *Reeves* was imposed upon medical authorities under Art 2 to do all they reasonably can to prevent a suicide where there is a 'real and immediate risk to life' of a detained patient under their care and control. It is at least arguable that this duty extends to all vulnerable patients where the immediate risk of self-harm is, or should be, known. Surprisingly, capacity or soundness of mind does not appear to have any role in determining when liability will be imposed on a third party for a person's deliberate acts (albeit that these concepts will have a role in determining the degree of contributory negligence of the deceased[4]).

1   See **PARA 13.27, N1** above.
2   [2002] QB 347. The test was applied in *Smiley v Home Office* [2004] EWHC 240.

3   *Savage v South Essex Partnership NHS Foundation Trust* [2009] 2 WLR 115.
4   Or, as more accurately phrased in US jurisprudence: in assessing the 'comparative negligence' of the defendant doctors it will be necessary to assess the capacity and sanity of the patient. Put shortly, the saner the patient, the lower the percentage damages the defendant will have to pay. See also the House of Lords case of *Corr v IBC Vehicles Ltd* [2008] 2 WLR 499, where the deceased was not a known suicide risk at the time of the negligence and the issue of capacity went to the issue of contributory negligence and not primary liability.

13.31   If the duty of care is owed, courts will impose civil and may even impose criminal liability on doctors who fail to act to preserve life. In *Reeves* the police failed to relay vital information concerning the suicidal status of a prisoner in their charge. Civil liability ensued. In circumstances where the failure to provide appropriate, or any, care or protection is found to amount to a gross failure, criminal liability will follow.

13.32   But doctors faced with the dilemma of whether to treat or not to treat a patient with bleeding wounds may feel that the law here is not fair or consistent. The decision in *Reeves* does not adequately address the query raised by Michael Jones that as 'suicide is the supreme act of individual self-assertion':

> 'How can the law respect the individual's claim to self-determination, while at the same time making someone else legally responsible for failing to prevent a suicide attempt?'[1]

1   M A Jones, 'Saving the patient from himself', *Professional Negligence* (September 1990).

13.33   How can doctors successfully negotiate the line between autonomy and protection when the law appears to point in different directions depending on whether doctor's negligence or patient autonomy is the issue? In *Reeves*[1] the line was drawn as follows.

1   [2000] 1 AC 360. It should be stressed that this was in the context of patients/prisoners known to be a suicide risk.

13.34   First, a doctor will not be liable for a death resultant from a failure to act which stems from a competent patient's refusal of consent to the doctor's act: autonomy means that the doctor could not act to prevent death. In particular, *Re W (Adult: Refusal of Treatment)*[1] is a good example of how this principle is applied. It was held that a secure prisoner with capacity had the right to refuse treatment for a self-inflicted life-threatening wound. Once it was confirmed that the patient had sufficient capacity to comprehend the decision he had taken, he had the absolute right to refuse treatment for any reason (or even no reason at all) even where that decision would lead to his death.[2]

In *Brightwater Care Group v Rossiter* the Supreme Court of Western Australia respected the right of quadriplegic patient, Mr Rossiter, to refuse artificial nutrition and hydration, declaring that his care provider, Brightwater, was not under an obligation to continue to feed him.[3] Martin CJ stated:

> 'Mr Rossiter lacks the physical capacity to control his own destiny, but enjoys the mental capacity to make informed and insightful decisions in respect of his future treatment. In that latter respect he is not relevantly within 'the charge' of Brightwater. Rather, Brightwater is, in that respect, consistent with the well-established common law position to which I have referred, subject to Mr Rossiter's direction.'[4]

He concluded:

'... it seems to me to be absolutely clear that after he has been provided with full information with respect to the consequences of any decision he might make, Mr Rossiter has the right to determine and direct the extent of the continuing treatment in the sense that treatment cannot and should not be administered against his wishes. If, after the provision of full advice, he repeats his direction to Brightwater that they discontinue the provision of nutrition and hydration to him, Brightwater is under a legal obligation to comply with that direction.'[5]

1   [2002] EWHC 901 (Fam).
2   *Re Z* [2004] EWHC 2817. Where legal capacity had been found to be present there was no basis in law for prohibiting Mrs Z from taking her own life. As stated by Hedley J at para 14: 'In the circumstances here, Mrs Z's best interests are no business of mine.'
3   [2009] WASC 229 (20 August 2009).
4   *Ibid*, para 40.
5   *Ibid*, para 49.

13.35   Secondly, a doctor (and hospital or prison authorities) will be liable for a death resultant from a failure adequately to control the patient's environment (provided any such intervention would not have invaded the patient's autonomy). Hoffmann LJ stated:

'Autonomy means that every individual is sovereign over himself and cannot be denied the right to certain kinds of behaviour, even if intended to cause his own death. On this principle, if the deceased had decided to go on hunger strike, the police would not have been entitled to administer forcible feeding. But autonomy does not mean that he would have been entitled to demand to be given poison, or that the police would not have been entitled to control his environment in non-invasive ways calculated to make suicide more difficult. If this would not infringe the principle of autonomy, it cannot be infringed by the police being under a duty to take such steps.'[1]

And as stated by Jauncey LJ:

'If an individual can do to his own body what he wills, whether by positive act or neglect then there can be no duty on anyone else to prevent his so doing ... [T]he cases in which the principle has been recognised ... were cases in which prevention of injury to health or death would have involved an unlawful physical invasion of the individual's rights. In this case performance of the duty of care by closing the flap on the cell door from which the Deceased hanged himself would have involved no invasion of any rights of the deceased.'[2]

1   At 369B.
2   At 375B.

13.36   However, their Lordships' formulation – which defines permissible steps as those which do not interfere with patient autonomy – in fact leaves the line for doctors blurred. Excessive interference with a patient's environment could constitute an infringement of that patient's autonomy. In *Keenan v UK*[1] the European Commission on Human Rights, in considering the appropriate regime to safeguard prisoners' lives, noted that:

'it would run counter to other fundamental rights guaranteed under the Convention – the right to respect for private life and potentially the prohibition against torture and inhuman and degrading treatment – to impose a regime with the rigorous controls necessary to render any self-injurious attempts impossible.'[2]

1   (2001) 33 EHRR 38.
2   Paragraph 79.

13.37   The imposition of liability based on fine distinctions between acts and omissions troubled Kay J in *R v Dr Collins and Ashworth Hospital Authority, ex p Brady*.[1] The case concerned the 'Moors Murderer' Ian Brady. In the course of argument, the question was raised as to whether a prisoner who was engaged in a hunger-strike could be force-fed even if he had capacity and was not capable of being lawfully force-fed under s 63 of the Mental Health Act 1983. It was argued for the respondent that the right to self-determination was not absolute and that it had to be balanced against public interests[2] such as:

(1)   the preservation of life;
(2)   the prevention of suicide;
(3)   the maintenance of the integrity of the medical profession;
(4)   institutional discipline.[3]

1   [2000] Lloyd's Med LR 355 (discussed also in relation to the test under s 63 of the Mental Health Act 1983: see **CHAPTER 10**).
2   Note *Thor v Superior Court* (1993) 5 Cal 4th 725, Supreme Court of California (refusal of food by a quadriplegic prison inmate. Right of self-determination held to prevail. However, noted four potential countervailing state interests: 'preserving life, preventing suicide, maintaining the integrity of the medical profession and the protection of innocent third parties'). In *McNabb v. Department of Corrections* 163 Wn.2d 393 (2008) the Washington State Supreme Court held that the State's interests in applying a force-feeding policy to a prisoner outweighed his right to refuse artificial means of nutrition and hydration. Madsen J concurring said that a prisoner had 'no right to starve himself to death by refusing sustenance while in the custody of the State — this is not a privacy right that citizens of the state hold or expect to hold.' Sanders J dissented arguing 'this case is about 'the most comprehensive of rights and the right most valued by civilized men,' namely, 'the right to be let alone.'
3   It was argued that institutional discipline would be undermined 'if detained persons had the right to self-harm, or to commit suicide or to protest against their circumstances by the use of hunger strikes and the refusal of medical treatment'.

13.38   While Kay J ultimately determined that it was not possible on the facts of the case to decide the point, his observations are of interest. Kay J felt that if *Secretary of State for the Home Department v Robb*[1] stood alone, the respondent's argument would be difficult to sustain. However, the judge determined that the *Reeves* decision had an important impact on the jurisprudence in this area particularly in considering whether in fact autonomy should prevail. He stated:

'It would be somewhat odd if there is a duty to prevent suicide by an act (for example, the use of a knife left in a cell) but not even a power to intervene to prevent self-destruction by starvation. I can see no moral justification for the law indulging its fascination with the difference between acts and omissions in a context such as this and no logical need for it to do so.

It seems to me that if one were dealing with a physically fit man with capacity but who is detained in hospital for medical treatment for mental

277

illness or disorder, there should be circumstances in which state or public interests ... would properly prevail over a self-determined hunger strike so as to enable, even if not to require, intervention.'[2]

While stressing that he was not deciding the point, Kay J expressed the view that authority did not appear to require him to find that autonomy was paramount, stating:

'it would seem to me to be a matter for deep regret if the law has developed to a point in this area where the rights of a patient count for everything and other ethical values and institutional integrity count for nothing'.[3]

1   [1995] 1 FLR 412.
2   Paragraph 71.
3   Paragraph 73; we are, however, unaware of any cases in the English courts in which it has been determined that a capable person should not be allowed to starve him or herself to death because it offends the public interest. This includes a case involving one of the authors in which there was a significant public interest in an alleged murderer not starving himself to death before trial.

H EUROPEAN CONVENTION ON HUMAN RIGHTS: DUTY TO PRESERVE LIFE

13.39   Kay J's preferred approach is mirrored in the decisions under the European Convention. The Commission has held that force-feeding a prisoner who was on hunger strike was not a breach of the right to freedom from inhuman and degrading treatment (Art 3).[1] It concluded, given that Art 2 (the right to life) imposes 'in certain circumstances' a duty to take positive action to preserve life, that it was incumbent on the State in particular to take:

'active measure to save lives when the authorities have taken the person in question into their custody'.

However, the force-feeding of a prisoner in *Nevmerzhitsky v Ukraine*[2] was a breach of Art 3 where the detaining authorities had failed, at the time of providing the treatment, convincingly to demonstrate the medical necessity for such acts.

1   In *X v Germany* (1984) 7 EHRR 152 at 153.
2   (2006) 43 EHRR 32.

13.40   In *Keenan v UK*,[1] it was noted that Convention case law establishes that Art 2 (the right to life) is not exclusively concerned with intentional killing by the use of force by agents of the State but also imposes a positive obligation on the State to take appropriate steps to safeguard lives. The European Commission on Human Rights determined that prison authorities had an obligation under Art 2 to take appropriate steps to safeguard the lives of the prisoners under their control:

'When depriving an individual of his liberty, the authorities thereby assume a responsibility for his welfare, the individual's autonomy to undertake that responsibility for himself having been largely removed.'[2]

1   (2001) 33 EHRR CD 362. See also *R (Middleton) v West Somerset Coroner* [2004] 2 AC 182;
    R (Sacker) v West Yorkshire Coroner [2004] 1 WLR 796; *R (Takoushis) v Inner North London*
    Coroner [2006] 1 WLR 461.
2   Keenan N1 above, para 79.

13.41   The approach adopted in *Keenan*, imposing a positive obligation to protect prisoners whose lives are in danger, applies to patients detained under the Mental Health Act. In *Savage v South Essex Partnership NHS Foundation Trust*[1] the House of Lords considered the scope of Art 2 in a case where Mrs Savage, a paranoid schizophrenic, absconded from hospital and committed suicide while being detained for treatment under s 3 of the Mental Health Act.[2] In applying the reasoning in *Keenan* the court held that where the medical authority knew, or ought to have known, that an individual patient was a suicide risk and there was a 'real and immediate risk to life' Art 2 requires those caring for the patient to do all that could reasonably have been expected of them to prevent the suicide from occurring.

1   [2009] 2 WLR 115.
2   Ms Carol Savage was one of 165 who took their own life while receiving treatment as a
    psychiatric in-patient: 'National Confidential Inquiry into Suicide and Homicide by People
    with Mental Illness' (University of Manchester, 2008).

13.42   However, in *Keenan* the Commission recognised that limits have to be placed on the obligation to interfere and intervene. No regime which respects prisoners or patients as human beings can ensure that no attempts are made to self-harm. Just as in *Keenan,* the court in *Savage* was mindful of the competing claims of personal autonomy and the need to take these into account when considering the scope and nature of any interference required. It was in relation to those rights of liberty and autonomy that Baroness Hale observed:

' … the steps taken must be proportionate. If this is so in prison, it must even be more so in hospital, where the objectives of detention are therapeutic and protective rather than penal.'[1]

Lord Scott stated that it behove the hospital to:

' … respect their personal autonomy and to impose restrictions on them to the minimum extent of strictness consistent with the need to protect them from themselves … the hospital were, in my opinion, entitled, and perhaps bound, to allow Mrs Savage a degree of unsupervised freedom that did carry with it some risk that she might succeed in absconding. They were entitled to place a value on her quality of life in the Hospital and accord a degree of respect to her personal autonomy above that to which prisoners in custody could expect.'[2]

1   See **PARA 13.40** above, N1, para 100.
2   *Ibid,* para 13.

13.43   *Savage* only examined the scope of Art 2 in relation to detained patients. However, the reasoning in the judgments would apply equally to those patients admitted informally (as Mrs Savage originally was) and mentally vulnerable patients voluntarily admitted onto general wards.

13.44   In terms of imposing liability in any given case, the threshold for triggering the duty is high. There must be a risk to life. That risk must be real and immediate – in *Keenan* it was obvious that the risk of suicide was real but there was no particular indication on the day in question. Those responsible must also be aware of the risk at the time – not sooner or later.[1]

1   *Van Colle v Chief Constable of the Hertfordshire Police* [2009] 1 AC 225.

13.45   There is an interesting gap between the formulation of the legal test in *Savage* and the ability of professionals accurately to foresee and protect against such risk. As Neil Allen wrote:[1]

'Our inability to predict risk accurately was strikingly illustrated by the National Confidential Inquiry's findings: at their final point of contact, immediate suicide risk was estimated to be low or absent for 86 per cent of those already known to mental health services who committed suicide.'[2]

Intriguingly, Baroness Hale looked beyond the duty to detained patients to the possibility that Art 2 had implications for the protection of all people against an immediate risk of self-harm.[3] Again, this mirrors the observations of Kay LJ and dovetails with the common law doctrine of necessity.[4] It should be noted that *Savage* is a decision on its facts in considering the scope of Art 2 in relation to detained patients. As Lord Scott said:

' ... personal autonomy is entitled to respect subject only to whatever proportionate limitations may be placed by the law on that autonomy in the public interest. The prevention of suicide, no longer a criminal act, is not among those limitations.'[5]

1   'Saving Life and Respecting Death: A Savage Dilemma' (2009) 13(2) Med L Rev 262–273 (May 4, 2009).
2   Page 6.
3   In relation to the extent of such a duty note decision in *Orange* PARA **13.30** above.
4   N Allen (see N1 above) argues that the implications of *Savage* could mark a radical departure from the current common law position and impose a professional duty to act whenever a doctor is aware of a real and immediate risk to a particular man's life.
5   Paragraph 11.

13.46   Under the ECHR it is likely that new law will be created as the doctors' overarching professional duty to preserve life (and the State's obligation to do so) encapsulated in Art 2 vies with the right of patients seeking to determine what they perceive to be in their own interests as protected by Art 8.

I GENERAL GUIDANCE

13.47   There is a tension in the law between the desire to ensure that vulnerable people are afforded the best possible care and the defence of the right of autonomy. If what is at issue is a course of treatment that a competent adult refuses, then that refusal will be seen as absolute (save in relation to prisoners or persons detained under the Mental Health Act 1983). However, even in respect of competent adults, the law will impose a duty on doctors to ensure that a patient is not presented with the means of taking his life. Thus, great care will need to be exercised by doctors in controlling the environment of patients who are apparently suicidal or who have refused to be treated for the consequences of an act of self-harm.

13.48   In emergency situations where it is not possible to determine a patient's views (whether because he is unconscious or incoherent), life-saving treatment can be given under the doctrine of necessity. Where treatment or care relates to a child or an adult without capacity then 'best interests' will usually operate to render lawful treatment against the person's wishes. The only exception would relate to unusual circumstances in which it would be considered that saving the patient's life was not in his best interests. While it is impossible to predict all the situations when this dilemma will occur, it is likely that in nearly all the guidance of the court should be sought.

Emergency situations

Inadequate time to assess capacity

13.49   A particular difficulty arises on those occasions where there is no time adequately to assess capacity. The current state of the law implies that the doctrine of presumed capacity means that treatment of a patient following a refusal to consent would be an assault. However, it could be argued that:

- in circumstances where someone has presented having harmed himself the doctrine of presumed capacity should not apply: the person has engaged in an act which questions – although clearly does not negate – capacity;
- pending an assessment of capacity, the doctrine of necessity should therefore protect a doctor who takes the minimum steps necessary to preserve life.[1]

In these circumstances Art 2 requires the doctor to do all that can reasonably be expected to preserve life.

1   See Chapter 2: Consent – Adults, para 2.13–2.19 for the position in relation to advance directives. A patient now has the ability to set down clearly in advance his intentions about refusing future treatment in a directive, which complies with the necessary legal protections. That ability leads to a cogent argument that the *absence* of such a document could be used to support a role for the doctrine of necessity to trump the presumption of capacity in these emergency situations. See also the *Kerrie Wooltorton* news story referred to at **PARA 13.26, N2** above.

13.50   It should be stressed that this is an argument only and has not been tested in the courts. Support for such an approach is, however, found in *Savage* where the status of the patient requiring protection was not the key but the underlying vulnerability of the patient was.

13.51   The first problem set out above was: if an adult presents at the Accident and Emergency Department with bleeding wounds, having attempted to kill himself, and he says he does not want his wounds to be bound, would binding the wounds be unlawful? Applying this argument to that problem will often result in treatment of the patient. This proposed approach runs counter to the general thrust of the academic literature in this area which strongly supports autonomy, although the view of Strauss[1] is noted:

'Social disapproval of suicide is still strong in many societies. It is generally accepted that the conduct of a person such as a policeman – or any other person – who endeavours to prevent a prospective suicide from ending his life, is not only lawful but in fact praiseworthy. Such conduct would accordingly not constitute assault. Juridically the rescuer's act is justified on the basis of necessity.'[2]

In any event, even if the courts hereafter accept this approach, it will not negate the responsibility to ensure that all doctors are versed in the component elements of capacity: only in situations of dire emergency where no sensible answer to the s 3 capacity test[3] can be provided by the doctor should resort be had to the doctrine of necessity.

1   'Legal Questions Surrounding Hunger Strikes by Detainees and Prisoners' (1991) 10 Med Law 211–218.
2   Strauss also notes the view of Van Der Westhizen that, under South African law, there is an entitlement to save a person's life 'even if it is against the will of the person rescued'.
3   MCA s 26(2) now allows a doctor to raise as a defence to any charge of assault the assertion that he acted in good faith in ignorance of an advance refusal of treatment. See **CHAPTER 2**: Consent – Adults **PARA 2.17**. Note also the defence available to a doctor ('D') under MCA s 5(a) if (i) before doing the material act, D took reasonable steps to establish whether the patient lacked capacity in relation to the matter in question, and (ii) when doing that act, D reasonably believed that the patient lacked capacity in relation to the matter, and that it was in patients best interests for the act to be done. See **CHAPTER 3**: Deciding for Others – Adults, **PARA 3.4**.

Preventing a jump from a window

13.52   The second practical problem posed was: if an adult patient who has been assessed as competent and is voluntarily in hospital starts to run towards a window, would it be an unlawful assault for a doctor to rugby-tackle him to prevent him from jumping out the window? It is likely that the law would answer that question by stating that the action of rugby-tackling the patient was lawful. Again, the wider doctrine of necessity comes into play: it is potentially dangerous to others for a patient to jump out of a window. Thus in acting to prevent this suicide attempt the doctor is of necessity 'assaulting' the patient to prevent potential harm to others and is therefore acting lawfully.

13.53   Further, even in a differing factual scenario in which the focus would solely be on protecting the patient from himself – for example, in restraining a patient from using a blade on his wrists – the protective public policies behind the decision in *Reeves* and discussed in *Brady* (see **PARA 13.37** above) surely mandate physical intervention to prevent the act of suicide or self-harm. Given these public policy imperatives, justification again is found for the notional assault under the doctrine of necessity.

J   EUROPEAN CONVENTION ON HUMAN RIGHTS: THE BALANCE TO BE STRUCK

13.54   In assessing the approach of the law as to the difficult balance to be struck between individual self-determination and the need to protect the vulnerable, it should be noted that the Convention, by Art 2 (the right to life), imposes a positive obligation on the State to protect and preserve life.[1] In this context, and as described in *Savage*, there are discrete aspects to this obligation. First, there is a general duty to have proper systems in place for providing a safe health care service. Secondly, there is a duty to protect vulnerable individuals, at present those detained under the Mental Health Act, from a 'real and immediate risk' to their lives. This duty involves taking all reasonable steps to reduce that risk. This Art 2 obligation would provide support for a doctrine of necessity in taking steps immediately to preserve life – whether by preventing someone from jumping out of a window or binding up someone's bleeding wrists – even in circumstances which ostensibly do not accord with the general presumption of competence in English law. Thus, there is scope for using the Convention to argue for legitimate and limited departures from the otherwise immutable principle of autonomy. English law could be developed (or current law explained) in accordance with the reasoning of Justice Stevens in the US Supreme Court that:[2]

> ' ... the value to others of a person's life is far too precious to allow the individual to claim a constitutional entitlement to complete autonomy in making a decision to end that life.'

1   *McCann v UK* (1995) 21 EHRR 97 (Art 2(1) imposes a positive obligation on States both to refrain from taking life intentionally and to take appropriate steps to safeguard life). See also *Andronicou and Constantinou v Greece* (1998) 25 EHRR 491.
2   *Washington v Glucksberg* 521 US 702 (1997): the US Supreme Court declared that a Washington law prohibiting physician-based suicide was not unconstitutional.

13.55   There is support in *Savage* for such a development, although the comments of Lord Rodger, as already noted, are in the context of prisoners, and are yet to be worked out in the context of patients, vulnerable or otherwise:

> ' ... the need to respect the autonomy of prisoners remains. Nevertheless, so far as the individual prisoner or conscript is concerned, the immediacy of the danger to life means that, for the time being, there is, in practice, little room for considering other, more general, matters concerning his treatment. There will be time enough for them, if and when the danger to life has been overcome. In the meantime, the authorities' duty is to try to prevent the suicide.'[1]

1   See **PARA 13.41** above, N1, para 42.

K COMPULSORILY DETAINED PATIENTS

13.56   The extensive protections in place in relation to the treatment of patients compulsorily detained under the Mental Health Act 1983 are outside the scope of this book. However, no consideration of the issues concerning treating 'suicides' and those engaged in self-harm can be complete without reference to a doctor's power to treat those detained under the Act without their consent.

As detailed throughout this book, the law presents hospitals and doctors with difficult ethical and practical problems as to issues of capacity and consent. The major ethical problem is the need, if a patient lacks capacity, to determine whether treatment is in the patient's best interests. The major practical problem is the requirement for the doctor to determine whether or not a patient in fact has capacity. In relation to patients compulsorily detained under s 3 of the Mental Health Act 1983, the law ostensibly relieves the doctor of the practical problem of weighing up the difficult questions concerning whether a patient has capacity to refuse treatment. By s 63 of the Act a doctor can provide such a patient with treatment[1] for 'the mental disorder from which he is suffering' even if the patient has capacity and refuses to consent to the treatment.

1   Treatments specified under ss 57 or 58 (for example treatments destroying brain tissue; long-term administration of medicine) are not included.

13.57   The Court of Appeal in *B v Croydon Health Authority*[1] considered the meaning of this section: is treatment within s 63 limited to the core treatment directed at the mental disorder (for example, psychotherapy) or does it extend to treatment for the symptoms or consequences of a mental disorder?

B had a psychopathic disorder known as borderline personality disorder. She engaged in self-harming behaviour. She was compulsorily detained under s 3. Other methods of self-harming having been removed by the hospital, Ms B resorted to starvation. As her physical condition deteriorated, her doctor informed her that he would consider force-feeding to prevent her death.

Through the MIND representative at the hospital, Ms B sought legal assistance. She was granted an ex parte injunction restraining the hospital from feeding without consent. Following a hearing, which included evidence from Ms B herself, Thorpe J determined that:

(a)   Ms B had capacity to refuse to eat; and
(b)   nonetheless by s 63 it was lawful for the hospital to feed her by means of naso-gastric tube without her consent.

1   [1995] 1 All ER 683 and see **CHAPTER 10**: Feeding, **PARA 10.9**.

13.58   The Court of Appeal considered whether such tube feeding was treatment for Ms B's mental disorder. The Act defines 'medical treatment' as including 'nursing ... care, rehabilitation under medical supervision',[1] thus indicating a significant range of acts ancillary to core treatment. It was held that treatment within s 63 included nursing and care:

• concurrent with the core treatment; or
• as a necessary prerequisite to such treatment; or
• to prevent the patient from causing harm to himself; or
• to alleviate the consequences of the mental disorder.

As Ms B's self-harming behaviour and therefore her refusal to eat were products of her mental disorder, the proposed medical treatment, namely naso-gastric tube feeding, was treatment within s 63 and could be performed without the patient's consent.

1   Mental Health Act 1983, s 145(1).

13.59   The *B* decision was followed by *Re VS (Adult: Mental Disorder)*.[1] The patient had a history of trying to harm herself. She was formally admitted under s 3 of the Mental Health Act 1983. She refused liquid or food and there was a real risk that she could die from renal damage. The Trust sought a declaration declaring that forced tube feeding and/or intravenous hydration would be lawful. The court held that such treatment would be lawful: it was clear that she was suffering from a major depressive illness and her refusal to eat or drink was a product of this disorder; thus, by virtue of s 63 of the Mental Health Act 1983 it would be permissible for the hospital to hydrate or feed the patient artificially.

1   [1995] 3 Med L Rev 292.

13.60   Thus, a doctor can treat a detained patient who has capacity without his consent if the treatment is to alleviate the symptoms of a mental disorder. Relieving the symptoms of the mental disorder is just as much a part of treatment as relieving the underlying cause of the disorder and is treatment within s 63 of the Act.

Therefore, the suggestion in the BMJ by both Dalal and Sensky[1] that the Mental Health Act 1983 cannot authorise treatment for physical disorders is an over-simplification. While it is correct that detention under the Act is only lawful for the treatment of 'mental disorder', if a physical disorder or condition is the product or symptom of the mental disorder for which the patient is detained then medical treatment for that physical disorder or condition is lawful. Thus, bandaging the cut wrists of a suicidally depressed s 3 patient without consent is lawful by virtue of s 63.

1   Sensky, *British Medical Journal* (8 July 1995) 115–118.

13.61   The *B* decision, however, does not provide the doctor with *carte blanche* to override the patient's wishes. In *Re C (adult: refusal of medical treatment)*[1] a mental patient refused consent for his leg to be removed because of the presence of gangrene. The gangrene (and the patient's response to it) was wholly unconnected with his mental disorder. His refusal to consent to the proposed treatment could not therefore be overridden by the Act.

1   [1994] 1 WLR 290.

13.62   Further, while s 63 may seem to provide the doctor with an easy way out of the practical problems posed by consent and capacity issues, the reality is that for clinical and legal reasons these issues must be addressed even in relation to treatment authorised by s 63. The Mental Health Act Code of Practice[1] requires practitioners to consider whether the patient lacks capacity to consent in all cases. Further, in all cases 'sufficient information must be given to ensure that the patient understands the nature, likely effects and risks of … treatment including the likelihood of its success and any alternatives to it' and there must be a compelling reason, in the patient's interest, for not disclosing relevant information.

1   Chapter 15.

13.63   Thus, s 63 and the *B* decision merely provide a last resort for the treating clinician: treatment without consent should be considered only once endeavours to achieve the patient's consent have failed and once the doctor is satisfied that proceeding with the treatment in the absence of consent is in the patient's best interests.

Legal test in criticising a doctor's determination under s 63 of the Mental Health Act 1983

13.64 In *R v Dr Collins and Ashworth Hospital Authority, ex p Brady*[1] Kay J considered an application by the 'Moors Murderer' Ian Brady challenging:

'the continuing decision ... to force feed the Applicant, ... apparently made pursuant to section 63 of the Mental Health Act 1983'.[2]

In approaching the test for assessing the doctors' determination that force-feeding was appropriate under s 63, the applicant submitted that:

'the role of the court is to satisfy itself that force feeding was and is being applied to the Applicant "for the mental disorder from which he is suffering" and not just that Dr. Collins and his colleagues had reasonable grounds for considering it to be such'.[3]

The judge rejected this submission:[4] it was not for the judge to determine whether as a 'precedent fact' the feeding was for the mental disorder from which he is suffering. The judge simply had to determine whether or not the doctor's determination that it was for the mental disorder satisfied the *Wednesbury* reasonableness test,[5] namely whether it was a determination that a reasonable doctor could make. However, given that the feeding interfered with the applicant's human rights, it was necessary for the respondent to satisfy a higher evidential threshold, described in the case as the 'super-*Wednesbury* approach'. Kay J stated:

' ... it would be wholly undesirable if RMOs [Responsible Medical Officers] were challengeable in relation to section 63 on any basis other than the appropriate Wednesbury one ... Section 63 is about the clinical judgment of the RMO in relation to patients who, by definition, are being detained for medical treatment for their mental disorders. When a RMO is challenged by way of judicial review ... the test to be applied [under s 63] by this court is the appropriate *Wednesbury* one. That means, in the context of this and similar cases, what counsel referred to as the 'super-*Wednesbury* test' appropriate to human rights cases as set out in *R v Ministry of Defence, ex parte Smith*:[6]

'The court may not interfere with the exercise of an administrative discretion on substantive grounds save where the court is satisfied that the decision is unreasonable in the sense that it is beyond the range of responses open to a reasonable decision-maker. But in judging whether the decision-maker has exceeded the margin of appreciation the human rights context is important. The more substantial the interference with human rights, the more the court will require by way of justification before it is satisfied that the decision is reasonable in the sense outlined above.'

1 [2000] LS Law Medical 355.
2 See also **PARA 13.37** and **PARA 13.38** above.
3 See **N1**, para 27.
4 He stated, nonetheless, that he would have found for the respondent, even applying the applicant's proposed test. See also *R (on the application of Wilkinson) v RMO Broadmoor Hospital* [2001] EWCA Civ 1545 in relation to treatment without consent under s 58 of the

Mental Health Act where the court's review extended to full consideration of the evidence and deciding the matter for itself on the merits.

5   *Associated Provincial Picture Houses Ltd v Wednesbury Corporation* [1948] 1 KB 223.
6   [1996] QB 517 at 554 per Bingham MR.

13.65   On the facts of the case, Kay J noted the evidence from Brady's treating clinician that Brady's hunger strike was a product of his personality disorder and that, in response to being moved against his will, Brady:

> 'would feel the need to "do something" and "get his own back". He would also feel the need to re-establish his sense of control and address the wounds to his self-image and his narcissism – What better way to do this than through a hunger strike, which, as his past experience had shown him, allowed him to dictate the agenda for others, so taking control, and give him a "psychological boost"?'[1]

The doctors felt that the hunger strike was 'a florid example of his psychopathology in action'. Thus, the judge concluded that the treating doctors were acting reasonably in accordance with the 'super-*Wednesbury* test' in force-feeding him pursuant to s 63:

> 'The hunger strike is a manifestation or symptom of the personality disorder. The fact (if such it be) that a person without mental disorder could reach the same decision on a rational basis in similar circumstances does not avail the Applicant because he reached and persists in his decision because of his personality disorder.'[2]

1   See **PARA 13.64, N1**, para 40.
2   *Ibid*, para 44.

L GUIDANCE ON APPROACH TO TREATMENT

13.66   In general,[1] it remains the position that a doctor cannot force treatment on a competent patient who refuses that treatment. A doctor faced with such a refusal should ensure that he is satisfied that:

- the patient is competent to make the refusal (preferably with the assistance of a psychiatric assessment);
- the patient has received a detailed and explicit explanation of the consequences of any failure to consent;
- consideration has been given as to whether the patient should be detained under the Mental Health Act 1983;
- even if a patient is competently refusing treatment, if it is felt that he is at continuing risk of self-harm he should be placed in as safe an environment as possible.

If treatment is not given because of a competent adult's refusal to consent, great care should be taken to record the patient's determination. The patient should sign a record indicating that he has refused to consent. The refusal, and the information provided to the patient should, if possible, be witnessed by others.

In considering each case, in addressing the ethical dilemma and weighing up the litigation risk,[2] a doctor should err on the side of preserving life rather than allowing a patient to die.

The court's assistance should be sought if time permits[3] in relation to suicidal adults when capacity is in question or there is a difficult issue concerning 'best interests'.

The court's assistance should be sought in relation to 'suicidal' children when:

- parent/s have refused consent to life-saving treatment;
- a *Gillick* competent child[4] and his parent/s have refused consent to life-saving treatment;
- consideration is being given to not providing life-saving treatment following a suicide attempt under the doctrine of 'best interests'.

In the prison setting, court authorisation for forced intervention which overrides consent may be permitted in exceptional circumstances on the basis of the factors outlined in the *Brady* case, namely:

(1)   the preservation of life;
(2)   the prevention of suicide;
(3)   the maintenance of the integrity of the medical profession; and
(4)   institutional discipline.

1   Exceptional circumstances may arise in the treatment of prisoners or of patients detained under the Mental Health Act 1983.
2   *Malette v Shulman* [1991] 2 Med LR 162, where an Ontario court found for a Jehovah's Witness plaintiff who claimed assault on the ground that she had been given a blood transfusion without her consent. The court awarded $20,000 damages (about $28,000 or £16,000 at today's rates). This is a rare example of litigation founded on an assault derived from treatment against a refusal of consent which, if respected, would have resulted in the death of the patient. See also **CHAPTER 2**: Consent – Adults **PARA 2.17** and **CHAPTER 11**: Religious Objections to Treatment **PARA 11.2**.
3   It should be stressed that the Family Division of the High Court or the Court of Protection can act at very short notice.
4   Or child aged 17.

M CONCLUSION

13.67   The application of the law surrounding suicide demonstrates the interplay of the most basic, fundamental ethical principles and how they may well conflict. In particular, neither autonomy nor the sanctity of life is an absolute: one may gain precedence over the other, depending on the particular circumstances of the case and other competing, legitimate interests. In the case of *Brady*[1] Kay's reference to institutional integrity was unusual, but important, in that case.

1   See **PARA 13.37** above.

13.68   The law in this field is evolving and will continue to do so as the courts struggle in those areas where autonomy and the sanctity of life do conflict and the principles enshrined within Arts 2 and 8 of the European case law are being worked out.[1] While this may appear a minefield for the practising doctor, it should not be forgotten that acts taken to preserve life, objectively in the patient's interests, will often be justified under the doctrine of medical necessity and provide a defence to most actions.

1   See, in particular, *Savage*: **PARA 13.41** above.

13.69   Finally, the law in relation to assisted suicide continues to arouse much controversy. The State's position has been that the interest in protecting life outweighs any individual's interest in facilitating the suicide of another. *Purdy* is an important case in that it recognises an individual's right to regulate not only his life but also his death and potentially involve others in bringing about that end where it is compassionate to do so. In such circumstances a compassionate facilitator of someone's suicide will still technically be acting unlawfully but is unlikely to face prosecution on the ground that it is not in the public interest to pursue such a conviction.

13.70   Lord Falconer's proposed legislative amendment decriminalising assisted suicides in certain defined circumstances has been rejected but it is likely that there will be further attempts to change the criminal law and bring it into line with other European jurisdictions.

13.71   Indeed, it may seem odd to the reader to criminalise any person who assists another in a lawful act but it is important to remember that most people who contemplate suicide do so because they feel weak and vulnerable. The Director of Public Prosecution's guidance on when it will not be in the public interest to prosecute cases of assisted suicide is a first, albeit tentative, step to mark out those situations when it is ethically right to assist someone else's suicide. However, the doctor/patient relationship is unique. Doctors hold positions of great influence over their patients and the current interim guidance, quite properly, does not begin to cover such situations.[1] This is an area in which there are likely to be further significant developments.

1   Indeed a former GP and right-to-die campaigner is believed to face arrest over advice she gave a multiple sclerosis sufferer in relation to the use of equipment ordered over the internet. The MS sufferer was found dead 2 days after the advice. The case is thought to be a test of how the guidance will be implemented – *The Sunday Times* 27 September 2009.

For updating material and hyperlinks related to this chapter, see: www.3serjeantsinn.com/mtdl/suicide

Chapter 14

The End of Life

A   The definition of 'death' 14.1

B   The diagnosis of death 14.12

      Brain stem death 14.13

      Death following cessation of cardio-respiratory function 14.14

      Certification 14.17

      The 'process of dying' 14.18

C   After death 14.26

D   Application of 'work and skill' exception 14.29

E   Right of possession and disposal 14.35

F   The use and storage of human bodies and tissues 14.38

G   Conclusion 14.39

A THE DEFINITION OF 'DEATH'

14.1   The precise definition of 'death' has troubled the English courts surprisingly little. Until relatively recently, the generally accepted criterion for the diagnosis of death was the permanent absence of respiration and circulation.[1] With the arrival of methods of artificial ventilation and other means of resuscitation, together with the demands of organ transplant techniques, this definition has come under increasing scrutiny.

1   'Defining Death: US President's Commission for the study of ethical problems in medicine and biomedical and behavioral research' (1981), p 3.

14.2   Clearly, ascertaining whether a person is dead or alive is a matter of the utmost importance. The living, however badly disabled and however poor the prognosis, have all the legal, human and social rights attaching to that status,[1] whereas the dead have no such recognition, but, as will be seen below, have the status of a special type of property, subject to a particular set of rules.[2] Thus, actions which may be lawful after death will not be lawful before it, and vice versa. Whether an act or omission caused death will depend on the determination of death, and thus this will be highly material to issues of criminal and civil liability. It is not difficult to imagine circumstances in which, through natural causes, a patient is near or at the point of death and the issue is whether a medical or other intervention has caused death. It would then be very

291

important to establish whether at the moment of the intervention the patient was already legally dead.

1   Thus in *Airedale NHS Trust v Bland* [1993] AC 789 it was held not only that a patient in a permanent vegetative state was alive, but it was suggested that he had a right to be treated with dignity. Hoffmann LJ, in the Court of Appeal, referred to the need to respect a person's dignity as being based on a:
   'belief that quite irrespective of what the person concerned may think about it, it is wrong for someone to be humiliated or treated without respect for his value as a person' [at 826].'
   The right to such respect is now recognised by the incorporation of Articles 2 and 3 of the ECHR into domestic law.
2   See below from **PARA 14.26**.

14.3   There is no statutory definition of 'death' in the United Kingdom. In the USA, a Uniform Determination of Death Act was proposed which utilised the following definition:

'... either (1) irreversible cessation of circulatory and respiratory functions, or (2) irreversible cessation of all functions of the entire brain, including the brain stem.'[1]

This was adopted by a majority of the States, but has not been free from criticism.[2]

1   Uniform Determination of Death Act (1980), National Conference of Commissioners on Uniform State Laws.
2   'Brain Death – Well Settled yet Still Unresolved' *N Eng J M* (2001) 344:1244–1246.

14.4   In Australia, all but one of the States use the following definition: a person has died where there has occurred:

(a)   irreversible cessation of all function of the brain of the person; or
(b)   irreversible cessation of circulation of blood in the body of the person.[1]

Paradoxically a statutory definition of 'death' does not always help determine whether a person is alive. Thus in New South Wales it has been held that a baby would be properly found to have been 'born alive' for the purposes of a manslaughter case by 'any indicia of independent life' such as 'the evanescently persistent activity of the heart' even in the absence of any evidence of an ability to breathe without assistance and only 'tentative' evidence that the presence of a heart beat and circulation indicated a functioning brain stem. There was, it was considered, no need for consistency between the statute and the common law rule.[2]

1   Human Tissue Act 1985, s 27A (Tasmania); Death (Definition) Act 1983, s 3 (South Australia); Human Tissue Act 1983 (New South Wales); Human Tissue Act 1982, s 41 (Victoria); Human Tissue Transplant Act, s 23 (Northern Territories); Transplantation and Anatomy Act 1979, s 45 (ACT); Transplantation and Anatomy Act 1979, s 45 (Queensland).
2   *R v Iby* [2005] NSWCCA 178.

14.5   Generally the fact of death is proved by a death certificate or evidence from witnesses that an individual has been found to be dead, without much, if any, consideration of what that means. In 1981 the Court of Appeal rejected the argument that the withdrawal of life support from brain stem dead patients supervened to negate the causative effect of an earlier lethal injury.[1] While the court expressly stated that it was not deciding what constituted death, it recognised that modern medical techniques had blurred many of the conventional and traditional concepts of death,[2] and that there was then a body of medical opinion which considered that the only 'true test of death' was:

> 'the irreversible death of the brain stem, which controls the basic functions of the body such as breathing. When that occurs it is said the body has died, even though by mechanical means the lungs are being caused to operate and some circulation of blood is taking place'.[3]

However, the court also said that whatever test was applied to the facts before it, there was no doubt that the victim:

> 'died; that is to say, applying the traditional test, all body functions, breathing and heart beat and brain function came to an end, at the latest, soon after the ventilator was disconnected'.[4]

That undoubtedly suggests that the law recognises that the permanent cessation of all bodily functions, including respiration, circulation and brain function, constitutes death. That does not mean, and was not intended to mean, that this is the only permissible point at which death can be recognised. Thus the 'brain stem death' test accepts that death can occur even though the heart is still beating.

1   *R v Malcherek; R v Steel* [1981] 1 WLR 690.
2   *Ibid* at 694.
3   *Ibid* at 694.
4   *Ibid* at 694.

14.6   In 1990 the Family Division[1] explicitly recognised the 'brain stem death' test as indicating death for legal purposes: it was held that a child who was brain stem dead was not capable of being subject to the court's inherent jurisdiction over children. The court exercised its general declaratory jurisdiction to declare that the patient was dead and that it was lawful for life support to be withdrawn. In accepting the medical evidence before the court to the effect that the patient was brain stem dead, the judge appeared to accept the propriety of acting in accordance with the then current recommendation of the medical Royal Colleges.[2] Implicitly, therefore, the court treated the definition of death as a matter for medical opinion rather than an absolute concept fixed by immutable legal principle.

1   *Re A* (1992) 3 Med LR 303.
2   '*Diagnosis of Brain Stem Death*', Conference of Medical Royal Colleges and their Faculties in the United Kingdom, *BMJ* 1996: 2:11, 1187.

14.7   In 1993 the Northern Ireland Family Division[1] also accepted that death 'in the usual sense' terminated a wardship and that medically, and in law, brain stem death was accepted as death. However, where the deceased was a ward of court it was thought preferable for an application to be made for withdrawal of life support even though brain stem death had been confirmed. This decision has been criticised,[2] but in any event should not be regarded as undermining the proposition that brain stem death, as defined by the medical profession, is sufficient to constitute legal death.

1   *Re TC (A Minor)* High Court (NI) Family Division, McDermott LJ, 30 November 1993, reported in [1994] 2 Med L Rev 376.
2   *Ibid.*

14.8   In *Bland*[1] the House of Lords accepted that a patient in a permanent vegetative state was not dead, and in doing so endorsed the 'brain stem death' test:

'In the eyes of the medical world and of the law a person is not clinically dead so long as the brain stem retains its function.[2]

Until recently, there was no doubt what was life and what was death. A man was dead if he stopped breathing and his heart stopped beating. There was no artificial means of sustaining these indications of life for more than a short while. Death in the traditional sense was beyond human control. Apart from cases of unlawful homicide, death occurred automatically in the course of nature when the natural functions of the body failed to sustain the lungs and the heart.

Recent developments in medical science have fundamentally affected these previous certainties. In medicine, the cessation of breathing or of heartbeat is no longer death. By the use of a ventilator, lungs which in the unaided course of nature would have stopped breathing can be made to breathe, thereby sustaining the heartbeat. Those, like Anthony Bland, who would previously have died through inability to swallow food, can be kept alive by artificial feeding. This has led the medical profession to redefine death in terms of brain stem death, ie the death of that part of the brain without which the body cannot function at all without assistance. In some cases it is now apparently possible, with the use of the ventilator, to sustain a beating heart even though the brain stem, and therefore in medical terms the patient, is dead: the 'ventilated corpse'.

I do not refer to these factors because Anthony Bland is already dead, either medically or legally. His brain stem is alive and so is he; provided that he is artificially fed and the waste products evacuated from his body by skilled medical care, his body sustains its own life.'[3]

1   *Airedale NHS Trust v Bland* [1993] AC 789. See **CHAPTER 12**: Permanent Vegetative State.
2   *Ibid* at 856 per Lord Keith of Kinkel.
3   *Ibid* at 878 per Lord Browne-Wilkinson.

14.9   A recent definition of 'brain stem death' was contained in guidance issued by the Royal College of Paediatrics and Child Health:

'Brain death occurs when a child has sustained either (i) irreversible cessation of circulatory and respiratory functions or (ii) irreversible cessation of all functions of the entire brain including the brain stem. A determination of death must be made in accordance with accepted medical standards'[1]

Their guidance states that brain death must be diagnosed 'in the usual way' by two medical practitioners. It is stated, emphatically, that:

'Where brain-stem death is confirmed, the patient is by definition dead.'[2]

Since there has been an acceptance by the courts of brain stem death as defining death, it is necessary to ask whether it is the only acceptable definition. Frequently, death is still diagnosed by means other than the full 'brain stem death' test as recommended by the Royal Colleges. In many cases death will be obvious from the state in which a body is found, or from the time which has elapsed since the cessation of breathing and cardiac circulation. However, this does not mean that there need be two or more definitions of death; merely that there is more than one way of diagnosing it. Thus cessation of cardiac function for a sufficiently prolonged period to be considered irreversible may be evidence of brain stem death, as opposed to a second definition of death in itself. There is no legal authority in this jurisdiction which currently answers this question, but at least two distinguished academic commentators have expressed the view that there is only one legal definition of death and that is brain stem death.[3]

1   *Withholding or withdrawing life sustaining treatment in children: A framework for practice* (2004) RCPCH fn 2 p 10 and fn 30 p 28, see **APPENDIX 14.3**; see also *A code of practice for the diagnosis of brain stem death* (Department of Health, March 1998), p 3.
2   *Withholding or withdrawing life sustaining treatment in children: A framework for practice* (2004) RCPCH, p 28, para 3.1.3.
3   See Kennedy and Grubb, *Medical Law* (3rd ed, OUP, 2005) (edited by Prof Grubb), pp 2213–2214, and quoted there, Skegg, *Law Ethics and Medicine*.

14.10   The Academy of the Medical Royal Colleges has now published a revised Code of Practice[1] which seeks to define death arising in any circumstances and to make practical recommendations with regard to diagnosis. It emphasises the need to separate entirely the diagnosis of death from anything to do with organ donation and transplantation.[2] At first glance the definition offered is deceptively simple:

'Death entails the irreversible loss of those essential characteristics which are necessary to the existence of a living human person, and, thus, the definition of death should be regarded as the irreversible loss of the capacity for consciousness, combined with irreversible loss of the capacity to breathe.'[3]

While simple, it is not the same as a brain stem death definition, and links the absence of higher brain functions with the loss of the capacity to breathe, without, it is assumed, assistance (although this is not made explicit). Such a change has not been without its critics.[4]

1   *A Code of Practice for the Diagnosis and Confirmation of Death* (Academy of Medical Royal Colleges, October 2008).
2   *Ibid*, p 9.
3   *Ibid*, p 10.
4   'No-one with a scientific mind really believes you can diagnose death in these simplistic ways. By rushing to retrieve organs we are depriving ourselves of the simplest tool to diagnose death, which is the passage of time'. A retired consultant, David Evans, quoted in article 'Brain-death test dropped to boost organ donation' (Rogers, *Sunday Times*, 29 June 2008).

14.11   As will be seen, the recommendations made for the criteria by which death is to be confirmed may throw some doubt over what is meant by 'irreversible'. A condition might be considered irreversible because, whatever is done, it cannot be reversed, or because, although it might be reversed it is not intended or possible to do so. The Code appears to adopt the latter meaning, whereas some might argue that the point in time at which we recognise that life has ended should be when there is a physical state which we recognise as equating with death.

B THE DIAGNOSIS OF DEATH

14.12   Clearly, the confirmation that a patient has died, as judged by the brain stem death criteria, is a more complex matter than the diagnosis of death by the traditional criteria of the apparently irreversible absence of circulation and respiration. Given the demands for recoverable organs for transplant and the resulting perceived need for organ recovery to take place as soon as possible after the cessation of artificially maintained circulation, the means of diagnosing and confirming death have come under continued scrutiny. The point at which death occurs after both breathing and the heart stop has come under particularly detailed consideration. This is because of the need for certainty as to the earliest time at which it would be acceptable to start the process of removing organs for transplantation.

As set out above, the Academy of the Medical Royal Colleges, in its revised Code of Practice, has sought to define death and simplify its diagnosis while keeping separate the issues of organ donation and transplantation.[1]

The Code divides the criteria for diagnosing death into two categories: death following the irreversible cessation of brain stem function and death following cessation of cardio-respiratory function. Each of these requires separate consideration.

1   Above at **PARA 14.10**.

Brain stem death

14.13   The Code emphasises that the irreversible loss of consciousness by itself does *not* equate with death of the individual: thus, patients in a vegetative state are alive.[1] The difference is that such patients are capable of breathing without assistance, whereas those with an irreversible loss of brain stem function are not. Further, loss of brain stem function does not equate with the loss of all neurological activity, such as reflexes which are independent of the brain, but only those forms of consciousness associated with human life, and in particular the ability to feel, be aware of or to do anything. Where such residual activity exists, it will not do so for long because of rapid breakdown of other bodily functions.[2]

The Code sets out detailed recommendations for the process of diagnosis of brain stem death.[3]

1   See above.
2   *Code*, p 11.
3   *Ibid*, pp 13–20.

Death following cessation of cardio-respiratory function

14.14   The Code proposes that:

'Death can be diagnosed when a registered medical practitioner, or other appropriately trained and qualified individual, confirms the irreversible cessation of neurological (pupillary), cardiac and respiratory activity. Diagnosing death in this situation requires confirmation that there has been irreversible damage to the vital centres of the brain-stem, due to the length of time in which the circulation to the brain has been absent.'[1]

It is observed that there are no standardised criteria for the confirmation of death after cessation of cardio-respiratory function.

1   Code, p 11.

14.15   While the Code should be read in full for the detail,[1] in summary it recommends that the point at which death occurs is identified by the following conditions:[2]

- The simultaneous and irreversible onset of apnoea and unconsciousness in the absence of circulation.
- Full and extensive attempts at reversal of any contributing cause of the arrest have been made.
- Either the patient meets the criteria for not attempting cardiopulmonary resuscitation, or attempts at this have failed, or life-sustaining treatment has been withdrawn as not being in the patient's best interests, or contrary to a valid advance decision to refuse treatment.
- The patient should be observed for a minimum of five minutes to establish that irreversible cardio-respiratory arrest has occurred, usually by confirming the absence of a central pulse and/or heart sounds.
- Any spontaneous return of cardiac or respiratory activity within the period of observation should be followed by a further five minutes' observation from the next point of cardio-respiratory arrest.
- After five minutes of such arrest the absence of pupillary responses to light, of the corneal reflexes and of any motor response to supra-orbital pressure should be confirmed.
- The time of death will be recorded as the time at which these criteria are fulfilled.

1   See **APPENDIX 14.1** and **14.2** for further extracts from the Code and see http://www.aomrc.org.uk/aomrc/admin/reports/docs/DofD-final.pdf for the full Code.
2   Code, p 12.

14.16   While this Code was produced by a highly distinguished working party, it is not entirely clear, without further explanation, that it has arrived at a definition of death and a means of confirming death that will always be acceptable as a matter of law. We would highlight the following problems.

- There is a lack of clarity with regard to the neurological state required for death to have occurred. The recommended definition and means of diagnosing brain stem death derive from widely accepted criteria which have, as noted above, been commonly accepted by the courts as indicating legal death. The methods recommended for diagnosing death following cardio-respiratory arrest run the risk of giving rise to a second definition, as opposed to a second means of diagnosis. While neurological tests are recommended, they are not as apparently detailed as those required to confirm brain stem death. The suggested tests may be sufficient to demonstrate brain stem death in a patient who is not being artificially ventilated, following a five-minute cessation of circulation, but the paper does not say so. Judgments about the desirability of resuscitation should not be part of the process of determining whether death has occurred. While the Code's overall definition of death includes the criterion of irreversible loss of consciousness and of the capacity to breathe, the diagnostic tests include reference to an intent (on the part of a doctor, or others) not to permit resuscitation. We suggest that irreversibility in this context ought to refer to a physical state which is physiologically irreversible by any means, not merely irreversible because no-one intends to make the attempt. If, for whatever reason, a doctor intervened successfully to resuscitate a patient whose heart had stopped for more than five minutes, it could not be claimed that the patient had been dead before then, merely because until that moment no-one had intended or wanted to resuscitate and the required neurological tests had been carried out. These concerns are not entirely academic. In the US it has been reported that successful heart transplantation has been performed using hearts from two babies, whose life support had been withdrawn, and who were declared dead after cardio-respiratory function had stopped for 1.25 minutes.[2] It has been argued that the successful restarting of the heart in such circumstances shows that there had not been an irreversible cessation of function and that life was ended by organ removal.[3] It is not suggested that a similar procedure would be permitted under the AMRC's Code, but it may be that further consideration is required as to whether the requirement for irreversibility is adequately addressed or explained in the guidance.

- There should be no need to discourage attempts at restoring cerebral perfusion after confirmation of death if the diagnostic process truly establishes that cessation of cardio-respiratory and brain function is irreversible. The inclusion of this requirement is likely to make the lay reader at least wonder whether the diagnostic recommendations are as robust as they need to be in order to give assurance that death has truly taken place.

The desire of the authors of the Code to separate the definition of death from the process of organ donation must be applauded. Nevertheless, the insertion of doctors' subjective intentions about the desirability of further resuscitation into that definition creates troublesome uncertainty. While quantum physicists may be content that Schrödinger's cat was both dead and alive, this will not be an approach when applied to humans which will find favour with society or the courts.

1 Roucek *et al*, 'Pediatric Heart Transplantation after Declaration of Cardiocirculatory Death' (2008) *N Engl J Med* 359:7; 709.
2 Veatch, 'Donating Hearts after Cardiac Death' (2008) *N Engl J Med* 359: 672.

Certification

14.17   The Shipman Inquiry observed in 2003 that there is no legal requirement that the *fact* of death need be certified.[1] It recommended that such certification by a health professional be required in order, in part, to assist in the professional scrutiny of the circumstances of the death and to protect against the falsification of relevant facts. Dame Janet Smith was also critical of the system for the medical certification of the cause of death, which is required before any death can be registered. Detailed recommendations were made for reform of the certification and coronial systems. Governmental response to these recommendations has been hesitant with both Coroners and Death Certification Bills being published but not proceeded with. At the time of writing the Coroners and Justice Bill has received royal assent, but the Act is yet to be published in its final version.[2] Chapter 2 of the Bill, covering notification, certification and registration of death, establishes a framework to be supplemented by regulations. Medical examiners must be appointed by primary care trusts in England and local health boards in Wales and such examiners are intended to provide independent scrutiny of the certification of the cause of death. In addition to establishing this role, there is to be a new framework for certification with increased interaction between medical practitioners who have attended the deceased before his death (attending practitioners), medical examiners conducting their own inquiries into the cause of death in some circumstances, and referrals from the senior coroner to a medical examiner and from attending practitioners to medical examiners. Since the Act has yet to be published and regulations have yet to be put in place to expand on this framework, it would be unhelpful to elaborate more at this stage.

1   Shipman Inquiry: Third Report – The Certification of Death and the Investigation of Deaths by Coroners (Cmnd 5854, July 2003).
2   A hyperlink to the final form of the Coroners and Justice Act 2009 will be placed on www.3serjeantsinn.com/mtdl/end-of-life .

The 'process of dying'

14.18   Although, as we have seen, the process by which a diagnosis of death is reached has seen some flux, death remains commonly understood as a biological event, the timing of which can be determined. On the other hand, dying, that is the transition from life to death, is more difficult to grasp. A dying person, including a person very close to death, remains alive and therefore the object of legal protections, including the fundamental entitlement to be treated with dignity. If the dying person is capable of making decisions about his own death then respect for his autonomy requires that doctors provide life-prolonging treatment only if it is expressly requested.[1] If the patient is unable to take an active part in decision-making, a decision needs to be made, usually by doctors and, more rarely, by the courts, on when and how to end treatment. Similarly, such decisions must accord with the right to human dignity at the end of life.

1   See **CHAPTERS 1 AND 13** for further discussion.

14.19   End-of-life issues, such as assisted suicide, are frequently a matter of debate and it seems that increasing attention is being paid to the 'process of dying', including the provision of good-quality palliative care. In 2006/07 the first 'National Audit of the Care of the Dying in Hospitals in England' was carried out.[1] A second round took place in 2008/09.[2] In July 2008 the Department of Health published an 'End of Life Care Strategy',[3] described as the first comprehensive framework aimed at promoting high-quality care across the country for all adults approaching the end of life. By formalising the advance decision, the Mental Capacity Act 2005 can be seen to have extended the ways in which people can plan for a time when they are dying but may not have capacity to make decisions as to their treatment, particularly refusal of life-sustaining treatment. *Airedale NHS Trust v Bland*[4] provides a clear acknowledgement that when life-prolonging treatment is refused by a competent patient, and this refusal leads to that patient's death, this is not adjudged as suicide.

1   http://www.rcplondon.ac.uk/clinical-standards/ceeu/Documents/NCDAH-Summary-report.pdf .
2   Results can be found at http://www.mcpcil.org.uk/liverpool-care-pathway/.
3   http://www.dh.gov.uk/en/Publicationsandstatistics/Publications/
PublicationsPolicyAndGuidance/DH_086277, see also www.endoflifecareforadults.nhs.uk.
4   [1993] AC 789.

14.20   It is only in limited cases that the law becomes involved in the 'process of dying', for example where capacity is an issue, the patient is unable to indicate his intentions or there is no valid advance decision. While the courts have stressed that there is a strong presumption in favour of a course of action which will prolong life, this presumption is not irrebuttable.[1] It is recognised that there is a distinction between a dignified death and undignified treatment to preserve life. In highly fact-sensitive cases, often involving children as wards of the court, a close analysis of the benefits and burdens of continuing life-sustaining treatment has been undertaken.[2] In these cases concerning children, the focus has been on the 'best interests' of the child but the language of dignity has featured heavily in the judgments. In its 2004 'framework for practice', the Royal College of Paediatrics and Child Health has also identified and classified the variety of situations that the court has faced.[3]

1   *Wyatt v (1) Portsmouth Hospital NHS Trust (2) Charlotte Wyatt (by her Guardian CAFCASS)* [2005] 1 WLR 3995.
2   See, for example, *An NHS Trust v (1) MB (a Child by CAFCASS as guardian ad litem) (2) Mr and Mrs B* [2006] 2 FLR 319, where a detailed list of benefits and burdens was drawn up by the guardian *ad litem* and adopted by the court.
3   *Withholding or Withdrawing Life Sustaining Treatment in Children: A Framework for Practice* (2004) RCPCH, pp 10–11 (and see **APPENDIX 14.3**), which sets out five situations in which it may be ethical and legal to consider withholding or withdrawal of life-sustaining medical treatment: (1) The 'Brain-Dead' Child; (2) The 'Permanent Vegetative State'; (3) The 'No-Chance' Situation; (4) The 'No Purpose' Situation; and (5) The 'Unbearable' Situation. See **CHAPTER 4**: Deciding for Others – Children, **PARA 4.13**.

14.21   In *Re C (a Minor) (Wardship: Medical Treatment)* C, a young child, had a severe condition leading to brain damage. C had undergone palliative surgery but this was unable to restore brain function.[1] The court accepted that C was dying and the only question was how soon this would happen, since there was no medical treatment capable of altering that prognosis. Because of the high standard of care being given to C, the medical expert was unable to forecast how long she would live. The expert's view was that the goal should be to ease the child's suffering rather than to achieve a short prolongation of life. Therefore, treatment such as administering antibiotics in the event of infection or setting up a feeding regime, actions which would prolong a life that had no future, were considered by the expert as wrong. The expert's advice was followed by the court, with the practical result that C could be treated by the hospital to allow her life to come to an end peacefully and with dignity.

A similar conclusion was reached on the facts in *An NHS Trust v (1) MB (a Child by CAFCASS as guardian ad litem) (2) Mr & Mrs B.*[2] The child in this case suffered from degenerative and progressive spinal muscular atrophy. He required ventilation and could not swallow. Although he also suffered from epileptic fits, he was aware and conscious. The experts agreed that the child's prognosis was very poor and that death, even with continuation of the extant treatment, was inevitable. With such treatment the child may have survived for a small number of years or could die suddenly and soon. Applying the 'best interests' test, it was decided that ventilation should continue. However, the experts went on to identify a number of procedures that went beyond maintaining ventilation and required the positive infliction of pain. In the court's view in the event that these procedures were needed MB had moved naturally towards death and it would be in the child's best interest to withhold those procedures even though he would probably die. Holman J stated:

'... I do not enter the question of whether he is already "in the dying process" as stated by one [of the treating doctors]. Precisely because doctors and modern science have the capacity to prolong life or delay death, there may be medical, ethical and philosophical questions about when "the dying process" begins. But I do know that currently, between one day and the next he [MB] is not dying and does not die; although he may die suddenly on any day.'

1   [1990] 1 FLR 252.
2   (2006) 2 FLR 319.

14.22   In another case involving a seriously ill child,[1] the 'dying process' merged, in practical terms, into the provision of palliative care which itself has been described by the courts as:

'the treatment of distress where there is a low possibility of cure and the provision of comfort and improved quality of life so far as possible. The aim is not to prolong life but to provide the child and their family with support and care anticipating the child's death.'[2]

In this case a declaration was granted to the treating Hospital Trust in the following terms:

'K should continue to receive full non-life prolonging palliative care, offering relief of any distress with analgesic and anxiolytic medication and should be allowed to die in comfort and dignity.'

So, while it seems courts may be reluctant to acknowledge in express terms that a patient has embarked on the 'dying process', in cases where the courts do become involved, the reality is that declarations such as that above may be viewed as a tacit acceptance of it. However, there is clearly a real difference between recognising the inevitability of the dying process and the attendant concern with maintaining human dignity at the end of a life and a course of action aimed at accelerating death. Taylor LJ said in *Re J (a Minor)*: [3]

'There is no question of approving, even in the case of the most horrendous disability, a course aimed at terminating life or accelerating death. The court is concerned only with the circumstances in which steps should not be taken to prolong life.'[4]

1   *Re K (a Child)* (2006) 2 FLR 883, (2008) 99 BMLR 98.
2   At para 21.
3   [1991] Fam 33, [1991] 1 FLR 366, [1991] 2 WLR 140, [1990] 3 All ER 930, CA. Cited and approved in *A National Health Service Trust v D and Others* (2000) 2 FLR 677.
4   At 155. Thus in *re RB (a Child)* [2009] EWHC B26 (Fam) the court did not intervene when a father who had previously opposed withdrawal of ventilation from a seriously ill (but not brain damaged) baby agreed to such withdrawal after consideration of the medical evidence to the effect that the child's future life would be full of pain and distress.

14.23   The above cases reflect the court's role in overseeing the 'process of dying' at stages where death is not immediately imminent. The complexities of this kind of situation were further considered, both at first instance and in the Court of Appeal, in *R (on the application of Burke) v GMC and Disability Rights Commission and Others*[1] in the context of addressing the lawfulness of guidance contained in the GMC publication *Withholding and Withdrawal of Life-Prolonging Treatment – Good Practice in Decision-Making (2002)*[2] (the '2002 Guidance'). The appellant in *Burke* was concerned about the effect of para 81 of the 2002 Guidance which provided:

'Where death is not imminent, it usually will be appropriate to provide artificial nutrition or hydration. However, circumstances may arise where you [the doctor] judge that a patient's condition is so severe, the prognosis so poor, that providing artificial nutrition or hydration may cause suffering or be too burdensome in relation to the possible benefits.'

Expert evidence was given to the court that the provision of artificial nutrition could actually increase a patient's suffering to the extent that, having weighed the benefits and burdens of providing artificial nutrition, as well as considering the patient's wishes, it would be appropriate to withhold or withdraw such life-prolonging treatment even though this would lead to death and a case in which death was not otherwise imminent.[3]

1   [2005] QB 424, Munby J, and [2006] QB 273, CA, [2005] 3 WLR 1132, [2005] 2 FLR 1223. The applicant sought clarification of the circumstances in which artificial nutrition and hydration could lawfully be withdrawn and contended that the 2002 Guidance was unlawful. He did not want artificial nutrition and hydration to be withdrawn and was concerned that a decision to do so would be taken by clinicians on the basis that his life was not 'worth living'.
2   At the time of writing, the GMC has published a draft for consultation intended, at the end of the consultation period, to replace the 2002 Guidance: GMC, '*End of Life Treatment and Care: Good Practice in Decision-Making, a Draft for Consultation*' (2009).
3   See paras 18–20 at first instance and para 54 in the Court of Appeal. See further para 11 of the (2009) GMC consultation document, *ibid.*

14.24   The draft consultation document, to replace the 2002 Guidance, published by the GMC,[1] addresses the factual situation encountered in *Burke*. It provides the following guidance for situations in which a patient who has lost capacity requested a particular treatment while he had capacity:

'Where death is imminent (within a few days or within hours), and the burdens of continuing a potentially life-prolonging treatment outweigh any possible benefits to the patient, it will usually be appropriate to stop the treatment, while focusing on meeting the patient's needs for palliative care and effective symptom management. However, if the patient had previously requested that the treatment be continued in these circumstances, you should consider any harm that might be caused, on the one hand by going against the patient's wishes and on the other by continuing to provide the treatment. If significant disagreement arises between you and the patient's representative or those close to them, or members of the healthcare team, about what would be of overall benefit, you must take steps to resolve this.'[2]

1   See GMC, *End of Life Treatment and Care: Good Practice in Decision-Making, a Draft for Consultation* (2009).
2   *Ibid*, para 55. For guidance on how to resolve disagreements, doctors are referred to paras 77–78 of GMC '*Consent: Patients and Doctors Making Decisions Together*' (2008).

14.25   For medical practitioners the end stages of the 'dying process' raise further difficult legal and moral issues. For example, cases may arise where a patient with a severe traumatic brain injury is to become a non-heart beating organ donor[1] after a withdrawal of care decision. Leaving aside the difficult issues of obtaining appropriate consent for donation, optimal organ viability is clearly desirable in such cases. Therefore close attention needs to be paid to the dying process – immediate access to a surgical retrieval team needs to be organised and protective measures such as the administration of heparin and antibiotics may be needed. Since such measures may not be understood as in the patient's best interests, having no therapeutic effect, there is potential for conflict. Similarly, in cases where a decision is made to withdraw life-supporting care, any subsequent prolonging of such care to gain extra time to organise a retrieval team raises delicate issues for practitioners.[2]

1   Form of donation in circumstances where the deceased donor was not ventilated at the time of death. Donation therefore occurs once death is certified following cardio-respiratory arrest.
2   For more detailed consideration of organ donation, see **CHAPTER 15**.

C   AFTER DEATH

14.26   The legal status of a corpse was first considered in the late seventeenth and early eighteenth centuries in the context of grave robbing.[1] In more recent times, as a result of the Royal Liverpool Children's Inquiry[2] and the Bristol Royal Infirmary Inquiry,[3] there has been public scrutiny of the legal status of cadavers and of post-mortem practices.

1   For a more detailed history, see R Hardcastle, *Law and the Human Body, Property Rights, Ownership and Control* (2007).
2   See http://www.rlcinquiry.org.uk/.
3   See http://www.bristol-inquiry.org.uk/.

14.27   The general principle in English law is that there is no property in a body.[1] The question of whether or not a corpse or part of a corpse could be property was considered by the English courts in *R v Kelly*.[2] In this case anatomical specimens which had been dissected, fixed or preserved at the Royal College of Surgeons had been taken by the defendant. The issue for the Court of Appeal was whether the offence of theft could be made out, given that the Theft Act 1968 requires appropriation of property. It was accepted that:

> 'however questionable the historical origins of the principles, it has now been the common law for 150 years at least that neither a corpse, nor parts of a corpse, are in themselves and without more capable of being property protected by rights.'[3]

1   This was recently re-affirmed in *Burrows v HM Coroner for Preston* [2008] 2 FLR 1225. The Supreme Court of California has also held, in *Moore v Regents University of California* (1990) 793 P 2d 479, that the plaintiff had no property rights to cells taken from his body and used in medical research. However, it was also stated by the court that 'we do no purport to hold that excised cells can never be property for any purposes whatsoever'(at 493).
2   [1998] 3 All ER 741, referring to *R v Sharp* (1857) Dears & Bell 160. The historical background was considered recently in *Yearworth v North Bristol NHS Trust* [2009] EWCA Civ 37 at para 31, [2009] 2 All ER 986, [2009] 3 WLR 118.
3   *R v Kelly* [1998] 3 All ER 741 at 749 per Rose LJ.

14.28   There was no attempt to alter this principle in the Human Tissue Act 2004. However, there are two key qualifications at common law to the 'no property' in a corpse rule, these being (1) the application of a 'work and skill' exception;[1] and (2) the right of possession of a body for disposal.[2] These will be considered in turn.

1   The US courts have recognised property rights to dead bodies and materials removed from dead bodies without relying on a 'work and skill' exception.
2   It should also be noted that if it is necessary for a coroner to take possession of a body for the purposes of his enquiries, he has an absolute right at common law to possession of this body until the inquest is completed, see *R v Bristol Coroner, ex parte Kerr* [1974] QB 652.

D   APPLICATION OF 'WORK AND SKILL' EXCEPTION

14.29   This caveat to the 'no property' principle was forged in a decision of the High Court of Australia in *Doodeward v Spence*.[1] The police had confiscated and refused to return the corpse of a pair of still-born conjoined twins which had been preserved and displayed by the plaintiff. Griffith CJ said:

> 'So far as it constitutes property, a human body, or a portion of a human body, is capable by law of becoming the subject of property ... When a person has by the lawful exercise of work or skill dealt with a human body in his lawful possession so that it has acquired some attributes differentiating it from a mere corpse awaiting burial, he acquires a right to retain possession of it, at least against any person not entitled to have it delivered to him for the purposes of burial.'[2]

1   (1908) 6 CLR 406 Aust HC; see also *Williams v Williams* [1882] 20 Ch D 659.
2   At p 414.

14.30   Barton J was prepared to agree that an action did lie in relation to a still-born foetus but did not wish to cast doubt on the general rule that an unburied corpse was not the subject of property. Higgins J dissented on the basis that no-one could have property in another human being, whether living or dead. Although Griffith CJ went furthest in his judgment, the limits of this apparent exception were not fully explored because he considered it unnecessary to give an exhaustive enumeration of the circumstances under which a right to possess a human body or body parts may be acquired. Whatever the source and extent of this exception, it has been recognised and followed by the English courts. In *Dobson v North Tyneside Health Authority and Another*[1] Peter Gibson LJ considered *Doodeward* and asked whether, on the facts before him, the 'work' done on the body part (a brain removed during a post-mortem and preserved in paraffin) was sufficient to transform it into an item that could be the subject of possessory rights. It was found that there was nothing to suggest that the preservation of a brain after post-mortem was:

'on a par with stuffing or embalming a corpse or preserving an anatomical or pathological specimen for a scientific collection or with preserving a human freak such as a double headed foetus that had some value for exhibition purposes.'[2]

This does nothing to clarify the extent of the 'work' required to be done before the 'work and skill' exception will apply. One commentator has noted that preservation of the foetus was deemed sufficient in *Doodeward* while in *Dobson* fixing (akin to preservation) was not and has gone on to suggest that the different treatment lies in an intention to create a novel item with a use of its own.[3]

1   [1997] 1 WLR 596, [1996] 4 All ER 474. For further consideration of this case, see (1997) Med LR 110.
2   *Ibid*, at 601.
3   See the commentary at (1998) 6 Med LR 247.

14.31   In spite of the uncertain boundaries, this approach to body parts from a corpse was accepted in *R v Kelly*[1] and Lord Justice Rose, giving judgment for the Court of Appeal, raised the possibility of further development of this exception:

'Furthermore the common law does not stand still. It may be that if, on some future occasion, the question arises, the Courts will hold that human body parts are capable of being property for the purposes of section 4 [of the Theft Act 1968], even without the acquisition of different attributes, if they have a use of significant beyond their mere existence. This may be so if, for example, they are intended for use in an organ transplant operation, for the extraction of DNA or, for that matter, as an exhibit in a trial.'[2]

Two points of distinction between *Doodeward* and *Kelly* should be noted. First, *Doodeward* seemed to be concerned with the right to possession rather than ownership, whereas *Kelly* asked whether the human specimens could be property. Secondly, the specimens in *Kelly* had originated in living persons while the corpse in *Doodeward* was that of a still-born foetus and thus had never actually been alive.[3] As discussed in **CHAPTER 8**: Abortion, in English law a foetus does not have any independent legal rights or legal status.[4] Nevertheless *Doodeward* is taken as authority for the proposition that there is no property in a dead body (unless it falls into the 'work and skill' exception). It is suggested that there is some conceptual legal difficulty with reconciling this proposition with the facts of *Doodeward*, given that the foetus never achieved the status of a living, and therefore dead, human being in the first place.[5]

Further examination of this 'work and skill' exception[6] was undertaken more recently in *Yearworth v North Bristol NHS Trust*,[7] with the court expressing dissatisfaction with the existing formulation. The appellant cancer patients had had sperm samples banked at a fertility unit of a hospital run by the defendant Trust, on the basis that forthcoming chemotherapy might cause infertility. These samples were damaged when the storage equipment failed. Claims were brought for psychiatric injury or mental distress caused by learning of the loss of the sperm samples. Clearly the court was dealing here with products from a living human body but it was acknowledged that the easiest course would nevertheless have been to apply the *Doodeward* exception; storing the sperm in liquid nitrogen was an application to the sperm of work and skill which conferred on it a substantially different attribute.[8] However, this was not the line of reasoning adopted:

'... we are not content to see the common law in this area founded upon the principle in *Doodeward*, which was devised as an exception to a principle, itself of exceptional character, relating to the ownership of a human corpse. Such ancestry does not commend it as a solid foundation. Moreover a distinction between the capacity to own body parts or products which have, and which have not, been subject to the exercise of work or skill is not entirely logical.'[9]

1   [1998] 3 All ER 741.
2   At 750. It appears that Lord Justice Rose did not consider that *Dobson* would be included within the scope of this *obiter* comment even though the brain in that case had been required for forensic examination within the context of a medical negligence action.
3   As pointed out in *The Inquiry into the Management of Care of Children Receiving Complex Heart Surgery at The Bristol Royal Infirmary* (Interim Report, Removal and Retention of Material), Annex B, Part III, para 124.
4   See further, in the context of abortion, *Paton v British Pregnancy Advisory Trustees* [1979] 1 QB 276; *C v S* [1987] 1 All ER 1230. See **CHAPTER 8**: Abortion, **PARA 8.24**.
5   It could be seen that Barton J's judgment was limited to a still-born child and not a once-living child. However, such an analysis fails to deal with the problem that such a foetus is not considered a human being in English law.
6   Considered and approved again by Gage J in *In Re Organ Retention Group Litigation* [2005] QB 506: see, for example, paras 160 and 257.
7   (2009) LS Law Medical 126.
8   *Ibid*, at para 45(c).
9   *Ibid*, }at para 45(d).

14.32   In reaching the conclusion that the men had ownership of the sperm for the purposes of their claim, the court emphasised a number of factors including the sole object of the ejaculation of the sperm being that it might be used later for their benefit, and that the men had retained the right to require destruction of the sperm at any time. It was considered that the latter represented a fundamental feature of ownership.

14.33   The authorities in this area are therefore somewhat in flux – on one hand the Court of Appeal (Criminal Division) in *R v Kelly* seemed to build on *Doodeward* in opening the way for ownership of future body parts beyond the confines of the 'work and skill' exception. In a slightly different manner, the Court of Appeal (Civil Division) appears to have sought to discard the formulation of this exception entirely, even if the decision did not relate to cadaveric body parts. It is reasonable to assume that future consideration of these kinds of cases will provide fertile ground for arguments of ownership not restricted to the 'work and skill' exception.

14.34 *Yearworth* may also be seen as complicating the following enquiry: if corpses and body parts can be property, then in whom does that property vest? The claims in *Re Organ* Retention *Group Litigation*[1] were brought by parents of deceased children on whom post-mortems had been performed in order to establish the cause of death (these were not coroner directed post-mortems). In respect of one of the claims, Gage J stated that the parents:

> 'did not, at any stage, obtain the right to possess the organs retained from [the deceased child]. In my opinion, following the post-mortem, the hospital acquired proprietary and possessory rights to the organs. Once the pathologists had by their work and skill removed the organs and prepared blocks and slides for histological examination those organs and the blocks and slides came within the Doodeward exception ...'[2]

Thus the suggestion is that whatever property rights do come into being as a result of work being done on the body parts, these vest in the person carrying out this work, probably because he is the first possessor. However, on this analysis possessory rights to the sperm in *Yearwood* would have vested in the clinicians or technicians and not the men themselves. The answer may lie in identifying the intentions of the persons from whom the tissue is taken, if alive, but those of the persons applying work and skill, to a dead body or tissue from it.

1 [2005] QB 506.
2 *Ibid*, at para 257.

E RIGHT OF POSSESSION AND DISPOSAL

14.35 Individuals may have a right to possess a corpse for the purposes of burial. It is arguable that for most purposes this is more appropriately viewed as correlative of the obligation to dispose of a deceased person's body. In *Williams v Williams*[1] it was acknowledged that the duty of disposal leads to a right to possession of a corpse until its lawful disposition.[2] However, this does not extend to a right to have organs that have lawfully been removed from a body, whether for post-mortem or other purposes, returned prior to the disposition.[3]

1 (1882) 20 Ch D 659.
2 See also *Dobson*, per Peter Gibson at 600, who affirmed the general principle that persons charged by law with interring the body have a right to the custody and possession of it until it is properly buried.
3 In *re Organ Retention Group Litigation* [2005] QB 506.

14.36 At common law the right of possession of a body for the purposes of burial falls to the deceased's personal representative or the executor of his will this is in preference to the surviving spouse or next-of-kin (unless he fulfils one of these roles).[1] In cases where no personal representative or executor has been appointed, the person with the best right to the grant of administration takes precedence. This situation was considered in *Burrows v HM Coroner for Preston*,[2] in which the court was required to determine who had the right to make funeral arrangements for the deceased teenager. The deceased had lived with his uncle for a number of years because his natural mother was a heroin addict. The deceased's mother wanted him to be buried while his uncle preferred cremation in accordance with the deceased's expressed wish. The court's approach to this dispute was as follows:

- There is no property in a body but various people have rights and duties in relation to its disposal.
- The deceased's personal representative, executor of the will and administrator of the estate have a right to determine the mode and place of disposal.
- The personal representative's claim to the body will usually oust other claims.[3]
- Where a personal representative is not appointed, the person with the best right to the grant of administration takes precedence. Where there are two or more persons ranking equally then the dispute must be decided on a practical basis.
- The domestic law, in r 22 of the Non-Contentious Probate Rules 1987, is clear about how to decide precedence.[4]
- However, if there is a dispute about who should have the right to possession of the body for the purposes of disposal, s 116 of the Senior Courts Act 1981 enables the court to appoint some other person as administrator and so displace the normal rules of priority. The exercise of such a power would be very rare.[5]
- In such situations two questions should be asked. First, whether there are any special circumstances which may displace the order of priority in r 22, and secondly, whether it is necessary and expedient, by reason of those special circumstances, to displace the normal order of priority.

In deciding whether the deceased's uncle should be appointed as administrator (thus displacing the normal rules) the court took into account, as special circumstances, the deceased's clear wish to be cremated and went on to state that in as much as domestic law said that the views of the deceased could be ignored, this was no longer good law.[6] The court also considered the right to privacy and family life under Art 8 of the ECHR.

1   Although see *R v Gwynedd County Council, ex parte B* [1992] 3 All ER 317, [1991] 2 FLR 365, which has been cited as authority for the proposition that the right to arrange disposal of remains of a child vests exclusively in the parents.
2   [2008] 2 FLR 1225.
3   The court stated that in some cases statute might entitle the coroner or possibly a hospital or local authority to make claims on the body.
4   Application of these Rules in this case would have given priority to the deceased's natural mother.
5   Citing *Buchanan v Milton* [1999] 2 FLR 844 Fam Div.
6   Applying *X v Germany* (8741/79) (unreported, March 10, 1981, Eur Comm HR) and *Dodsbo v Sweden* (2007) 45 EHRR 22, ECHR. In *Hartstone v Gardner* [2008] 2 FLR 1681 the

deceased's own wishes as to the place of his burial and the reasonable wishes and requirements of his family and friends were considered.

14.37   The right to possession has been expanded to include a coroner's right to possession of a body when this is part of his enquiries in this role.[1] Further, in some situations it may be that the occupier of the premises where the deceased died, has a right to dispose of the body.[2]

1   *R v Bristol Coroner, ex parte Kerr* [1974] QB 652.
2   See, for example, *University Hospital Lewisham NHS Trust v Hamuth* [2006] EWHC 1609 (Ch), [2006] Inquest LR 141, in which the NHS Trust was granted a declaration that it was lawfully in possession of the deceased's body and could make arrangements to dispose of it in a lawful manner. This was against the background of a dispute over the validity of the deceased's will, the prompt resolution of which was not likely.

F   THE USE AND STORAGE OF HUMAN BODIES AND TISSUES

14.38   The Human Tissue Act 2004 is now the governing legislation for issues relating to whole-body donation and the taking, storage and use of human organs and tissues.[1] This legislation, discussed in greater detail in **CHAPTER 15**, covers the removal of material from the bodies of deceased persons as well as from living persons. Consent from an appropriate person is the touchstone to this Act and such consent is required for the storage and use of whole bodies and the removal, storage and use of relevant material from the body of a deceased person.[2] 'Relevant material' is defined in s 53 as any material consisting of, or including, human cells, with the exception of gametes, embryos outside the body[3] and hair and nails from a living person.

1   The Act repeals and replaces the Human Tissue Act 1961, the Anatomy Act 1984 and the Human Organs Transplant Act 1989 as they relate to England and Wales and the corresponding legislation in Northern Ireland.
2   Consent is also required for the storage and use of relevant material from a living person.

G   CONCLUSION

14.39   It might be thought that a concept as fundamental as death should be capable of clear and easily comprehensible definition. The need for such a definition is obvious: death marks the point at which the bundle of rights and obligations attached to a living human being ceases. Unfortunately, advances in medical knowledge and techniques mean this is not so. The task of achieving a practical definition is complicated by the conflict between the medical recognition of death as a process and the law's need to identify a point in time when death occurs. In part the perceived need for sophisticated criteria, capable of being established only by skilled medical diagnosis, may be thought to have been driven by the demand for a wider pool of candidates for organ and tissue donation. It would be unfortunate if this laudable aim resulted in an erosion of the recognition afforded to the need for protection of the living.

The status of a dead body is now also the subject of increasing attention. When the only conceivable legitimate interest in possession of a body was in arranging for decent disposal, following, if necessary, some form of forensic investigation, it was understandable that the rights and obligations of interested parties could be loosely defined. However the increase in the benefits that can be obtained from organs and tissues of the dead, and the increased demand for recognition of a wide variety of religious and other beliefs, have combined to result in a requirement for a much more detailed definition of the rights and obligations associated with dead bodies. The law is in a state of development in this regard.

For updating material and hyperlinks related to this chapter, see: www.3serjeantsinn.com/mtdl/end-of-life

Chapter 15

Human Organ and Tissue Donation[1]

A   Introduction 15.1
B   The common law 15.2
C   The Human Tissue Act 2004 15.3
     Donations by living persons 15.8
          'Domino' transplants 15.9
          Consent 15.10
          Incompetent adults 15.11
          Children 15.12
          Best interests 15.13
          Approval by the Human Tissue Authority 15.14
          Types of donations by living donors 15.15
          Consent – children 15.16
          Consent – adults 15.17
     Preservation of organs after death 15.18
     Preparatory steps taken before death 15.19
D   Conclusion 15.20

A INTRODUCTION

15.1   The ability to transplant organs and other tissue to patients has dramatically transformed the life expectancy and quality of life of many patients. An increasing range of procedures has now become possible, from heart transplants to 'face' transplants. The success of such procedures brings with it an ever-increasing demand for organs and tissue and, inevitably, a shortage. Understandably, this has led to continual challenges to the legal and ethical boundaries of what is permissible. While animal organs and tissue can, in some circumstances, be used, in principle such procedures may be considered in the context of any other, more routine, form of medical treatment and raise the same issues of consent and propriety. Accordingly, no separate consideration is given to those issues in this chapter. Organs and tissues obtained from human beings, whether living or dead, raise special issues which are considered here. These issues principally concern the means by which organs and tissue are obtained and cross the boundaries of life and death. Thus the use of organs taken from a dead person may be governed by decisions made by that person before his death. Questions may arise as to what may or should be done to prepare a donor's organs for donation in anticipation of death. After death, disputes may occur as to the storage and use of organs or tissue. Above all, there is a need for as much legal clarity as possible so that doctors, other medical staff, potential donors and their families can feel confidence in the process. Failing this, there is a danger that the supply of tissues and organs will diminish rather than increase. This chapter looks specifically at the legal requirements for organ donation and transplantation in England and Wales.[1] The principal legislation, the Human Tissue Act 2004, also governs the donation and use of human tissue for other purposes, such as research and anatomical display, but these are beyond the scope of this book. Necessarily this chapter focuses on the process of organ donation, as the transplant of organs and tissue into a recipient is covered by the general legal principles governing consent to medical treatment dealt with elsewhere in this book.

1   There is separate legislation in Scotland- the Human Tissue (Scotland) Act 2006.

B THE COMMON LAW

15.2   As was observed in 1977 by the Australian Law Reform Commission,[1] the common law offers no rule or principle dealing with human tissue transplants as such. The Commission pointed to the complications caused in this area by the common law concept that invasive medical treatment, however beneficial, is regarded as an assault unless legitimated by consent and the common law criminal offence of maim.[2] Thus it is not entirely clear that at common law the consent of a mentally competent adult to the removal for the benefit of another of one of two healthy kidneys, or even regenerative tissue, the removal of which will leave a scar, would provide a defence to the surgeon undertaking the procedure: it is at least open to question whether it would be for the benefit of the donor, however willing. Even more difficult questions arise at common law with regard to whether it is lawful for a parent to consent to such a procedure on a child or other person lacking the capacity to consent. There are further problems arising with regard to the use of organs and tissue from a dead body. The common law provides few practical answers. Fortunately, Parliament has intervened and this area is now largely, but not entirely, governed by statute, comprehensive Codes of Practice and the Human Tissue Authority ('the Authority').[3]

1   Australian Law Reform Commission, *Human Tissue Transplants*, Report No 7 (1977), pp 22–25.
2   See **CHAPTER 1**: Consent – General for the general principles and requirements for consent in medical treatment.
3   Human Tissue Act 2004. The Human Tissue Authority has now issued nine Codes of Practice all of which can be found on its website: http://www.hta.gov.uk . The first edition, issued in 2006, had six Codes and were revised to reflect the experience of the Human Tissue Authority. The revised Codes came into force on 15th September 2009. The principal Codes referred to in this chapter are Code of Practice 1 – Consent, and Code of Practice 2 – Donation of Solid Organs for Transplantation (Human Tissue Authority, September 2009). In this chapter these will be referred to as Code on Consent and Code on Donation respectively, unless expressly stated otherwise. For updating material and hyperlinks related to this chapter, see: www.3serjeantsinn.com/mtdl/donation .

C THE HUMAN TISSUE ACT 2004

15.3 It is now unlawful for 'transplantable material', as defined in the Act, to be removed from the body of a living person with the intention that it be used for transplantation, or used for that purpose, knowing that the person from whom the material is, or has been, removed is alive, or where it might reasonably be expected that the person removing the material had that knowledge, unless the requirements of the Act are complied with. The offence so created is not a particularly serious one: it is a summary offence in respect of which the maximum sentence is 51 weeks' imprisonment or a fine.

The first edition of the Code of Practice on Donation of Organs, Tissue and Cells for Transplantation[1] suggested that the removal of an organ, part organ or tissue from a living human continued to be governed by the common law.[2] This was true in the sense that the principles of common law still governed the nature of the consent required. However, the regulations made under the Act require various procedures to be undertaken in order for the removal to be lawful, including the obtaining of permission from the Authority.[3] This is now recognised to a degree in the Code on Consent.[4]

1   Issued by the Human Tissue Authority in July 2006, now superseded.
2   *Ibid*, para 22.
3   See below.
4   Code on Consent, paras 27 and 42.

15.4 'Transplantable material' is defined[1] for this purpose as material removed from the body of a living person with the intention of it being transplanted into another person, where that material is:

* an organ or part of an organ if it is to be used for the same purpose as the entire organ in a human body, unless removed from the body of a living person for the primary purpose of the medical treatment of that person, for instance if an organ were removed for the purpose of surgery;
* bone marrow and peripheral blood cells, but only when removed from the body of an adult lacking capacity to consent or a child who is not competent to do so.

1   Human Tissue Act 2004 (Persons who Lack Capacity to Consent and Transplants) Regulations 2006 (SI 2006/1659), reg 9.

15.5 No criminal offence is created by the Act in relation to the removal or use of organs from the body of a dead person. There are, however, various common law offences which are likely to make any activity in this regard not authorised under the Act perilous.[1]

1   For example, it is an indictable offence to dispose of a dead body for the purpose of dissection without lawful authority: *R v Lynn* (1 Leach 497); *R v Cundick* (1822) Dow & Ry NP 13.

15.6 Leaving aside criminal offences, the following, among other, activities are lawful if done with 'appropriate consent' and for the purpose of transplantation:

* the storage and use of a body of a deceased person;
* the removal, for storage, from the body of a deceased person of relevant material;

- the storage and use of any relevant material which has come from a human body (by which must be meant the body of a living person).

15.7 The provisions relating to donations from living persons and those occurring after death are considered separately below.

Donations by living persons

15.8 It is a criminal offence to remove material knowingly from a living person for the purpose of transplantation, to use such material knowing it has come from a living person, unless permitted under the Act.[1] By regulation,[2] certain activities are permitted, subject to strict conditions.

1 Human Tissue Act 2004, s 33.
2 Human Tissue Act 2004, s 33; Human Tissue Act 2004 (Persons who Lack Capacity to Consent and Transplants) Regulations 2006 (SI 2006/1659), Part 3.

'Domino' transplants

15.9 Organs (but not bone marrow or blood stem cells) which have been removed for the primary purpose of treating the persons from whom they have been removed, may lawfully be transplanted into another person and are exempted from the requirements of the Act.

The Authority describes such procedures as 'non-directed domino organ donation'. It advises that as a matter of good practice the prospective donor should be asked to agree to the use of the organ, that an application form is prepared by the donor's clinician and signed by the donor, and that after the transplant the recipient's clinician completes all the relevant documentation. However approval of the Authority is not required.[1] As in at least some circumstances[2] a patient will retain proprietary rights over organs and tissue removed from his body it is suggested that the obtaining of his consent is not only good practice but potentially a legal requirement.

The activities rendered lawful by the Act, but controlled under it, are the removal of material from the body of a living person with the intention that it be transplanted into the body of another person where the material consists of:

- an organ, or parts of an organ, if to be used for the same purpose as the entire organ in the human body, except where the primary purpose of removal is the treatment of the person from whom the material is taken;
- in the case only of adults who lack capacity or children who are not competent, only bone marrow and peripheral blood stem cells, taken from such persons,[3] provided 'appropriate consent' has been obtained,[4] and the requirements of the regulations are complied with.[5]

Commercial dealings in organs for transplant and trafficking are criminal offences prohibited by the Act. However, the prohibition does not extend to activities licensed by the Authority or to the reasonable incidental expenses of the donor paid by a proper authority.[6]

1 Code on Donation, paras 27–28.
2 *Yearworth v North Bristol NHS Trust* [2009] EWCA 37.

3   SI 2006/1659, reg 10.
4   Section 1(1)(d) and (f), Schedule 1, para 7.
5   SI 2006/1659, Part 3.
6   Human Tissue Act 2004, s 32; Code on Consent, paras 42–46.

Consent

15.10   The Act provides that storage or use of any 'relevant material which has come from a human body' for the purpose of transplantation or transfusion to a living person may be lawful, but requires, among other things, 'appropriate consent'.

The Code of Practice points out that consent is a positive act[1] and that absence of a refusal does not equate with a consent.

In relation to consent for donation by a living donor the Act provides no definition or guidance as to what is required. Therefore the ordinary common law and statutory principles as described elsewhere in this book apply. The Human Tissue Authority's Code of Practice advises that consent from an adult is 'valid' if the person concerned:[2]

- is competent to give it;
- does so voluntarily; and
- is given full information about the procedure and its risks.[3]

The Code on Donation advises that obtaining valid consent presupposes that there is a process in which individuals, including partners, relatives and friends, may discuss the issues in full, ask questions and make an informed choice. It is advised that sufficient time is allowed for this process and surgeons should check before surgery that consent has not been withdrawn.[4]

1   Code on Consent, para 30 and Code on Donation, para 72.
2   Code on Donation, para 76.
3   The information that should be explained to the donor is set out in detail in the Code on Donation at para 90.
4   Code on Donation, para 73.

Incompetent adults

15.11   Where an adult lacks the capacity to consent to transplantation involving material from his body, consent is deemed to exist where the activity is done by a person acting in what he reasonably believes to be the adult's best interests.[1]

However, this provision has to be read alongside the requirement that an organ donation is one of the categories of case in which the decision is considered to be so serious that the matter has to be referred to the Court of Protection for it to be made.[2] Therefore in reality it is inevitably a matter for the court to decide whether a proposed donation is in the best interests of the adult, and it is unlikely that any practitioner will be found to have held a reasonable belief that an individual's best interests were served by organ donation without knowledge of a court order to that effect.

1   Human Tissue Act 2004 (Persons who Lack Capacity to Consent and Transplant) Regulations 2006 (SI 2006/1659), reg 3(1) and (2)(a).

2   Code on Donation, Appendix A, para A2; see also Mental Capacity Act Code of Practice (DCA 2007), para 6.18.

Children

15.12   A 'child' is defined for the purpose of the Human Tissue Act as a person under the age of 18.[1]

A child may have the capacity to consent at common law, in accordance with the principles recognised in *Gillick*.[2] The consent required for a proposed organ donation can be given by a child who is *Gillick* competent.[3] However, the Code on Donation states that children can only be considered as living donors in extremely rare circumstances.[4] Even where the child is competent it is probably good practice to consult the person with parental responsibility and to involve him/her in the child's decision-making process.[5] In any event court approval should be obtained, given the potentially serious consequences for the child.[6]

The person with parental responsibility may consent to a proposed donation by a child, but only if: [7]

●   there is not in force any decision of the child's to consent or not to consent to the proposed donation; and
●   the child is not competent to do so; or
●   the child, although competent, chooses not to do so.

The Act does not make it clear whether a decision of an incompetent child is capable of being 'in force' for this purpose. It is strongly arguable that a decision cannot be 'in force' unless it is competently made. In any event it is suggested that the circumstances in which the court or the Authority would ever impose the removal of an organ on an unwilling child must be very rare indeed.

Even where the person with parental responsibility is in a position to consent, any proposal for organ donation is non-therapeutic so far as the child is concerned and accordingly it is not lawful for a parent to consent to it unless satisfied that it is in the child's best interests to be a donor. As it will be very difficult for a parent to be objective about such an emotive issue, particularly where close family members are likely to be involved, some form of independent scrutiny will almost invariably be expected. Department of Health guidance suggests that where there is any doubt, court approval should be sought. [8] It is respectfully suggested by the authors that court referral should be almost invariable given the potentially serious consequences of organ donation for a child. This is recognised in the Code on Donation where it is advised that an application to the court will usually be made by the Trust wishing to carry out the procedure, or in some cases a person with parental responsibility if the donation is for a relative. The Code goes on to advise that a court ruling should be in place before the case is referred to the Authority for a decision on approval for the donation to proceed.[9] Different considerations may apply to more minor donation of tissue which is not within the scope of this chapter.

1   Section 54(1).
2   See **CHAPTER 4**: Deciding for Others – Children.
3   Section 2(2).
4   Code on Donation, para 47.

5   As advised in the Code of Practice- Donation or Organs, Tissue and Cells for Transplantation (Human Tissue Authority, July 2006), para 33.
6   Code on Donation, para 85 and Appendix A. Appendix A sets out guidance on requirements for court approval.
7   Section 2(3); Code on Donation, para 86.
8   Guide to Seeking Consent: Working with Children (DoH 2001): http://www.dh.gov.uk/en/ Publicationsandstatistics/Publications/PublicationsPolicyAndGuidance/DH_4007005.
9   Code on Donation, Appendix A, paras A8–A13.

Best interests

15.13   As demonstrated above, where a potential donor is incapable of giving a valid consent, whether as a child or as an incapacitated adult, it is necessary to consider whether the procedure is in that person's best interests. While the factual considerations may well differ between adults and children, in these circumstances it is suggested that identical principles apply to both.

Usually a medical procedure is performed on an adult or child incapable of giving consent only if it is intended that he derives some therapeutic benefit from it. Clearly, organ donation offers no such benefit to the donor and is associated with significant risks. Therefore it is unlikely that donation is ever in the best medical interests of a potential donor. However, that is not the only factor to be taken into account in deciding a person's best interests. It is well established that 'best interests' encompasses more than medical best interests and includes emotional, social and all other welfare issues.[1] Religious views may also be relevant.

Where a procedure of benefit to a third party is being considered, the only test of best interests is whether the procedure is of sufficient benefit to the potential donor to justify the risk inherent in it. In the case of bone marrow transplantation, approval was given for an adult lacking capacity to be a donor in *Re Y (Mental Patient: Bone Marrow Donation)*[2] on the ground that prolonging the life of the patient's mother was likely to be of benefit to her. However, the judge doubted that the case would act as a useful precedent where more intrusive surgery was required.[3] The judge referred to US cases[4] in which it appeared that:

- the key factor was the presence or absence of a benefit to the potential donor;
- a close relationship between intended donor and recipient was often considered to be a necessary factor;
- a sufficient benefit may be found in a psychological benefit from the potential for a continuing relationship.

In the case of a child who might benefit from the survival of a healthy parent to bring it up, or a sibling to provide a normal family life, it might be thought that the 'best interests' tests might be satisfied, depending on the degree of risk involved, but each case will be entirely dependent on its own facts.[5]

1   *Re A (Male Sterilisation)* [2000] 1 FLR 549 at 555; Code on Donation, Appendix A, para A9.
2   [1997] Fam 110 per Connell J.
3   *Ibid* at 116.
4   *Curran v Bosze* 566 NE 2d 1319 (1990).

5   For US cases in which organ/tissue donation has been sanctioned, see *Little v Little* 576 W 2d 493 (1979); *Strunk v Strunk* 445 SW 2d 145 (1969).

Approval by the Human Tissue Authority

15.14   In all cases of proposed donation by a living donor, the following steps must be taken:[1]

- the doctor with clinical responsibility for the donor must refer the case to the Human Tissue Authority;
- a person approved by the Authority must interview:
    - the donor;
    - if different, the person giving consent;
    - the recipient.

Such approved persons are called 'Independent Assessors' by the Authority. They are specially trained and accredited professionals and must be current (or recently retired) medical consultants, someone of equivalent registered professional status or a professional working in a hospital environment. They are usually based in hospitals with transplant units or referring nephrology units and act both as a representative of the Authority and as an advocate for the donor.[2]

The Assessor must then report a number of matters to the Authority, including:[3]

- whether there is any evidence of duress or coercion affecting the decision to consent;
- any evidence of an offer of a reward;
- any difficulties of communication with the person interviewed and an explanation of how those difficulties were overcome;
- the name and qualifications of the person giving consent;
- the capacity of the person interviewed to understand the nature of the medical procedure and its risks, and that consent may be withdrawn at any time before removal of the transplantable material;
- the information given to the potential donor (or other person giving consent) as to the nature of the medical procedure and the risk involved.[4]

The Assessor is expected to state whether it is recommended that the Authority approve the transplant.[5]

The Authority must take the report into account and decide if it is satisfied that:

- no reward has been or is to be given in contravention of the statutory prohibition;
- consent has been given or the removal is otherwise lawful.

The Code on Donation provides that all straightforward directed donations where the donor and recipient are genetically or emotionally related[6] can be assessed by the Authority Transplant Approvals Team. However this Team is able to refer complex cases (including those relating to newer types of organ transplant) to a panel for a decision.[7]

The decision of the Authority must be taken by a panel of no fewer than three members if:[8]

- the donor is a child, or an adult lacking capacity to consent and the material is an organ or part of an organ to be used to the same purpose;
- or the donor is an adult with capacity and the case involves 'paired donations', pooled donations' or a 'non-directed altruistic donation'.

These types of case are considered below.

The Authority must then notify the donor, recipient and doctor of its decision.

The Authority may reconsider its decision if required to do so by any such person or if satisfied that any material information it received was false or misleading or there has been a material change of circumstances. A person requiring reconsideration has a right to appear before and be heard by the meeting of the Authority at which the matter is reconsidered.[9]

1   SI 2006/1659, reg 11.
2   Code on Donation, para 61; Guidance for Transplant Teams and Independent Assessors – Living Donor Transplantation (Human Tissue Authority) and found at the Authority's website: https://www.hta.gov.uk.
3   SI 2006/1659, reg 11(8) and (9); Code on Donation, para 64; Guidance for Transplant Teams and Independent Assessors – Living Donor Transplantation (Human Tissue Authority) and found at on the Authority's website: https://www.hta.gov.uk .
4   Code on Donation, para 36.
5   Code on Donation, para 64.
6   See below.
7   Code on Donation, para 66.
8   SI 2006/1659, reg 12.
9   SI 2006/1659, regs 13, 14.

Types of donation by living donors

15.15   The Authority classifies living donations into three types:

Directed – genetically or emotionally related organ donation

This is a form of donation in which the potential donor wishes to donate an organ to a specific recipient who is genetically or 'emotionally' related to the donor. The Authority exercises a relatively loose control over this category in that a proposed donation does not usually have to be considered by its panel but only by the Executive unless it comes within one of the four categories which are required by the regulations to be considered by the panel. The regulations make no reference to 'emotional' relationships, and it is suggested it is not helpful to refer to relationships in such terms for this purpose.

Directed – paired/pooled organ donation

In some cases a close relation, friend or partner of a person in need of an organ transplant is willing to donate an organ but is found to be incompatible. In such circumstances it is sometimes possible to arrange for an exchange with another couple with the same problem. This is known as 'paired donation'. Where more than two couples are involved, the arrangement is described as a 'pooled donation'. Where a pair in such a situation indicates a willingness to undergo this type of donation that pair is registered and a match sought. If a match is found the Authority undertakes the process described above. The approval must be made by a panel of at least three members. The assessment of each pair is undertaken by separate independent assessors, but the reports are considered jointly by the Authority.[1]

Non-directed – altruistic organ donation

That is where a potential donor offers to donate an organ to anyone who might benefit, including a complete stranger. Again, the approval decision must be made by a panel of at least three Authority members. When interviewing the donor the assessor is required to ensure that there is a valid consent, that the donor is not subject to duress or financial inducement, and is aware that under no circumstances will either the donor or the recipient know the other's identity before the procedure. The Authority considers the case for approval before a potential recipient is looked for.[2]

Post-mortem donation

Provided that the activity is undertaken with 'appropriate consent', the Act[3] renders lawful the following activities for the purposes of transplantation:

- the storage of a dead body;
- its use;
- the removal from a dead body of relevant material;
- the storage of such material.

1 Code on Donation, paras 26, 38, 62, 65, 67, 92. For the Authority's process generally see paras 58–70 and Guidance for Transplant Teams and Independent Assessors – Living Donor Transplantation (Human Tissue Authority) and found at on the Authority's website: https://www.hta.gov.uk .

2 Code on Donation, paras 26, 38, 63, 67, 91, 92. See generally, Guidance for Transplant Teams and Independent Assessors – Living Donor Transplantation (Human Tissue Authority).[3] Section 1(1)(b) and (e); Schedule 1, para 7.

Consent – children

15.16   A child, if competent, may give a consent for organ donation after his death, and this will be effective if in force at the time of death.[1] Such a consent may be in writing, for example by way of registration on the Organ Donor Register, but it may also be given orally. Therefore an oral consent may be evidenced by a conversation with a relative or a nurse. Transplant co-ordinators are advised as a matter of good practice to discuss such a consent with parents and take their views into account.[2] The Code does not suggest, as it does in the case of the adult deceased, that a child's consent cannot be overridden as a matter of law by the parents or others. There is nothing in the Act to suggest that parents have a right of veto, but the tenor of the Code is that the views of parents should be respected.

If no such consent was given by the child, it may be provided by:

- a person having parental responsibility immediately before the death;
- or, if there is no such person, by a person in a 'qualifying relationship'. This includes spouses, partners, and 'friends of long standing' as well as close family relations.[3] Persons within the definition should be approached in the order in which they appear in the statutory definition, as consent should be obtained from the highest ranked person available.[4] Where persons in a qualifying relationship disagree, the view of the highest ranked prevails.[5] However, where there is strongly expressed dissent the clinicians may decide not to proceed in recognition of the sensitivity of the situation. The appropriate consent renders organ donation lawful if it is carried out, but it is not obligatory to do so. Great care must be taken not to impose one person's views on others and, where there is disagreement, the clinicians have to decide whether the benefits of proceeding are outweighed by strongly expressed objections.

1   Section 2(7).
2   Code on Consent, para 93.
3   Section 54(9).
4   Code on Consent, para 84.
5   Code on Consent, para 84.

Consent – adults

15.17   An adult may give a consent for organ donation after his death and this will be effective if in force at the time of death.[1] Such consent is commonly given by registration with the Organ Donor Register[2] but may also be contained in a will. However, the Act does not require consent for this purpose to be in writing at all.[3] Therefore transplant co-ordinators are advised not only to search the register but also to approach the deceased's family and close friends to establish his known wishes.

If such a consent is not in force at death it may be provided by:[4]

- a representative nominated under the Act: such a nomination may be general or limited to specified activities. The nomination may be in writing or orally. A written nomination must be signed, in the presence of at least one witness who attests the signature or be contained in a valid will. An oral nomination is valid only if given before two witnesses present at the same time. The nominee must be an adult and not of a description prescribed by regulations.
- a person in a qualifying relationship, if no other form of consent is available.[5]

While relatives should as a matter of good practice be consulted, they cannot overrule the expressed wishes of the deceased or of a nominated representative. However, it is recognised that there may be cases where proceeding with a donation against the opposition of relations and close friends may be inappropriate.[6]

1   Section 3(6).
2   http://www.uktransplant.org.uk/ukt/.

3   Section 3: written consent is required for certain other activities under the Act (public display
    and anatomical examination): see s 3(3) and (4).
4   Sections 3(6) and 4.
5   Section 3(6)–(8). 'Qualifying relationship' is defined as in **PARA 15.16** above.
6   Code on Consent, para 76.

Preservation of organs after death

15.18   The common law is of limited assistance with regard to the care and
treatment of dead bodies.[1] There is no right of property in a body,[2] with the
exception of a body or body part which has been subjected to the application of
special skill.[3] However, there will exist a right to possession of the body, if only
for the purpose of burial or cremation. Doctors can be in lawful possession of a
body following death until such time as control is handed over to the family or
whoever assumes responsibility for appropriate disposal of the remains. There
can, however, be a proprietary right over parts of a body or tissues or organs
which have been removed from it.[4] Where organs have been removed lawfully,
it appears that the right to possession is retained by the hospital responsible for
the removal.[5] It seems unlikely therefore that, for instance, the parent of a child
who consented in advance of death to organ donation, has a proprietary right
over the organ once removed.

The Human Tissue Act 2004 removes the doubt that may previously have
existed with regard to some activities ancillary to transplant procedures. It
expressly authorises the storage and use of bodies so long as 'appropriate
consent' has been obtained. While preservation is not specifically mentioned in
the Act, it is clearly intended to be authorised as a necessary part of the process
of storage.

It appears therefore that the attending clinicians may lawfully retain the body of
a person for the purpose of performing lawful activities authorised in pursuance
of the Human Tissue Act. It is suggested that these include the taking of
appropriate steps to preserve organs for transplant, even while they remain in
the body. The Code on Donation suggests that the Act authorises the
preservation of a body even if consent has not yet been obtained, in order for
steps to be taken to establish whether consent has been given or, if it has not
been, to obtain consent from a nominated representative or a qualifying
relation. In such circumstances the clinicians may take the minimum steps
needed to preserve the relevant material for transplantation using the least
invasive means and to retain the body for that purpose. However, such activities
must cease as soon as it is clear that no consent is going to be given.[6]

1   See Australian Law Commission, Report No 7, *Human Tissue Transplants*, (1977), paras 56–
    58.
2   *R v Kelly* [1999] QB 621, 630; *AB v Leeds Teaching Hospitals NHS Trust & Cardiff and Vale
    NHS Trust* [2004] EWHC 644 (QB) at para 135.
3   *Doodeward v Spence* (1908) 6 CLR 406, 413, 414; *AB* (N **2** above). **SEE CHAPTER 14**: End of
    Life.
4   *AB* (N **2** above) at paras 148 and 160. See also *Yearworth v North Bristol NHS Trust* [2009]
    EWCA 37. While *Yearworth* concerns the proprietary rights over tissue removed from a living
    patient, it is consistent with what is said here.
5   *AB* (N **2** above) at para 161. However, a duty of care may be owed to parents in relation to the
    taking of consent and similar matters.
6   Code on Donation, paras 123–132.

Preparatory steps taken before death

15.19   Until recently, most organ transplants have been achieved with organs taken from donors who have been kept on life-support machines and have eventually been declared dead by use of the 'brain stem death' test.[1] Increasing attention is now being paid to the possibility of obtaining organs from what are termed 'non-heart-beating donors'.[2] These are patients whom it is not appropriate to treat on life support machines, but whose death is predictable, and whose organs are considered available for removal once death has been determined, using criteria for death which refer to the irreversible cessation of cardiac and respiratory function.[3] Because of the fast rate at which organs deteriorate after death, the question arises whether it is lawful to take any steps prior to death in order to maximise the chances of preserving organs after death. These might range from the insertion of a cannula to facilitate venous access after death, to prolonging life by life-support techniques to allow the appropriate resources for organ harvesting and transplantation to be marshalled.

It is highly unlikely that such steps would be practicable or desirable at any time while a dying patient was actually conscious. However, it is possible that a prospective organ donor could consent in advance to such procedures. So long as what was proposed was unlikely to do harm to the patient, in the sense of shortening life or causing pain and suffering, it is suggested that such consent could lawfully be given and the steps lawfully taken.

Even if such consent has not been given but the patient is known to have consented to organ donation following death, the question could arise whether preparatory steps could lawfully be taken. If, as will occur in most cases, the patient is unconscious and therefore incapable of giving consent, the issue would be whether such steps could be considered to be in the patient's best interests. Clearly, as with organ donation itself, such steps would not be in the patient's best medical interests, but, as has been seen, the 'best interests' tests embraces many other considerations. It might be argued that action designed to maximise the prospects of fulfilling the patient's wishes with regard to organ donation would be in his best interests, so long as such action was not positively detrimental to the patient's own well-being and to his interest in a dignified death. At the time of writing it is understood that the Department of Health is intending to publish guidance on this sensitive issue, following a demand that the legal position be clarified.[4]

1   See Australian Law Commission, Report No 7, *Human Tissue Transplants*, (1977), paras 56–58. See **CHAPTER 14**.
2   For consensus guidance on practice in this area, see 'UK Guidance for Non-Heart Beating Donation' (2005) 95 *British Journal of Anaesthesia* 592–595.
3   *Ibid.*
4   See *Organs for Transplants* (Organ Donation Taskforce, DoH, January 2008), recommendation 3 and para 4.15; *Working Together to Save* Lives (Organ Donation Taskforce, DoH, October 2009) page 13.

D CONCLUSION

15.20   Organ and tissue transplantation raises issues of considerable social and ethical concern and there is an understandable demand for regulation and the outlawing of unacceptable practice. Rapid advances in what is technically and clinically possible in this field mean that the law is always in danger of being left behind. The perceived shortage of willing organ donors has increased pressure to ease the requirement of consent, to review the prohibition of 'selling' organs, and to find new ways of obtaining organs as quickly as possible after the death of the donor. This in turn has led to a reconsideration of the means of diagnosing death. It is no coincidence that the Human Tissue Authority has issued revised Codes of Practice within five years of the publication of the first version. Such demands mean that this is an area of law which is likely to be the subject of increasing court scrutiny. However the fundamental tenet of the law in this area is, and has to remain, consent along with the right of an individual to decide for himself what is done with his organs and tissue while alive, and to his body after death. The function of the law is to protect respect for that autonomy and to prevent abuse and exploitation of the vulnerable.

For updating material and hyperlinks related to this chapter, see: www.3serjeantsinn.com/mtdl/donation

---

Appendix 1.1

Mental Capacity Act 2005

PART 1 PERSONS WHO LACK CAPACITY

The principles

1 The principles

(1)   The following principles apply for the purposes of this Act.

(2)   A person must be assumed to have capacity unless it is established that he lacks capacity.

(3)   A person is not to be treated as unable to make a decision unless all practicable steps to help him to do so have been taken without success.

(4)   A person is not to be treated as unable to make a decision merely because he makes an unwise decision.

(5)   An act done, or decision made, under this Act for or on behalf of a person who lacks capacity must be done, or made, in his best interests.

(6)   Before the act is done, or the decision is made, regard must be had to whether the purpose for which it is needed can be as effectively achieved in a way that is less restrictive of the person's rights and freedom of action.

Preliminary

2 People who lack capacity

(1)   For the purposes of this Act, a person lacks capacity in relation to a matter if at the material time he is unable to make a decision for himself in relation to the matter because of an impairment of, or a disturbance in the functioning of, the mind or brain.

(2)   It does not matter whether the impairment or disturbance is permanent or temporary.

(3)   A lack of capacity cannot be established merely by reference to—

    (a)   a person's age or appearance, or

    (b)   a condition of his, or an aspect of his behaviour, which might lead others to make unjustified assumptions about his capacity.

(4)   In proceedings under this Act or any other enactment, any question whether a person lacks capacity within the meaning of this Act must be decided on the balance of probabilities.

(5)   No power which a person ('D') may exercise under this Act—

    (a)   in relation to a person who lacks capacity, or

    (b)   where D reasonably thinks that a person lacks capacity,

    is exercisable in relation to a person under 16.

(6)   Subsection (5) is subject to section 18(3).

3 Inability to make decisions

(1)   For the purposes of section 2, a person is unable to make a decision for himself if he is unable—
    (a)   to understand the information relevant to the decision,
    (b)   to retain that information,
    (c)   to use or weigh that information as part of the process of making the decision, or
    (d)   to communicate his decision (whether by talking, using sign language or any other means).

(2)   A person is not to be regarded as unable to understand the information relevant to a decision if he is able to understand an explanation of it given to him in a way that is appropriate to his circumstances (using simple language, visual aids or any other means).

(3)   The fact that a person is able to retain the information relevant to a decision for a short period only does not prevent him from being regarded as able to make the decision.

(4)   The information relevant to a decision includes information about the reasonably foreseeable consequences of—
    (a)   deciding one way or another, or
    (b)   failing to make the decision.

4 Best interests

(1)   In determining for the purposes of this Act what is in a person's best interests, the person making the determination must not make it merely on the basis of—
    (a)   the person's age or appearance, or
    (b)   a condition of his, or an aspect of his behaviour, which might lead others to make unjustified assumptions about what might be in his best interests.

(2)   The person making the determination must consider all the relevant circumstances and, in particular, take the following steps.

(3)   He must consider—
    (a)   whether it is likely that the person will at some time have capacity in relation to the matter in question, and
    (b)   if it appears likely that he will, when that is likely to be.

(4)   He must, so far as reasonably practicable, permit and encourage the person to participate, or to improve his ability to participate, as fully as possible in any act done for him and any decision affecting him.

(5)   Where the determination relates to life-sustaining treatment he must not, in considering whether the treatment is in the best interests of the person concerned, be motivated by a desire to bring about his death.

(6)   He must consider, so far as is reasonably ascertainable—
    (a)   the person's past and present wishes and feelings (and, in particular, any relevant written statement made by him when he had capacity),
    (b)   the beliefs and values that would be likely to influence his decision if he had capacity, and
    (c)   the other factors that he would be likely to consider if he were able to do so.

(7)   He must take into account, if it is practicable and appropriate to consult them, the views of—
    (a)   anyone named by the person as someone to be consulted on the matter in question or on matters of that kind,
    (b)   anyone engaged in caring for the person or interested in his welfare,
    (c)   any donee of a lasting power of attorney granted by the person, and

(d) any deputy appointed for the person by the court,

as to what would be in the person's best interests and, in particular, as to the matters mentioned in subsection (6).

(8)   The duties imposed by subsections (1) to (7) also apply in relation to the exercise of any powers which—

(a) are exercisable under a lasting power of attorney, or

(b) are exercisable by a person under this Act where he reasonably believes that another person lacks capacity.

(9)   In the case of an act done, or a decision made, by a person other than the court, there is sufficient compliance with this section if (having complied with the requirements of subsections (1) to (7)) he reasonably believes that what he does or decides is in the best interests of the person concerned.

(10)   'Life-sustaining treatment' means treatment which in the view of a person providing health care for the person concerned is necessary to sustain life.

(11)   'Relevant circumstances' are those—

(a) of which the person making the determination is aware, and

(b) which it would be reasonable to regard as relevant.

[4A Restriction on deprivation of liberty]

[(1)   This Act does not authorise any person ('D') to deprive any other person ('P') of his liberty.

(2)   But that is subject to—

(a) the following provisions of this section, and

(b) section 4B.

(3)   D may deprive P of his liberty if, by doing so, D is giving effect to a relevant decision of the court.

(4)   A relevant decision of the court is a decision made by an order under section 16(2)(a) in relation to a matter concerning P's personal welfare.

(5)   D may deprive P of his liberty if the deprivation is authorised by Schedule A1 (hospital and care home residents: deprivation of liberty).]

[4B Deprivation of liberty necessary for life-sustaining treatment etc]

[(1)   If the following conditions are met, D is authorised to deprive P of his liberty while a decision as respects any relevant issue is sought from the court.

(2)   The first condition is that there is a question about whether D is authorised to deprive P of his liberty under section 4A.

(3)   The second condition is that the deprivation of liberty—

(a) is wholly or partly for the purpose of—

(i)   giving P life-sustaining treatment, or

(ii)   doing any vital act, or

(b) consists wholly or partly of—

(i)   giving P life-sustaining treatment, or

(ii)   doing any vital act.

(4)   The third condition is that the deprivation of liberty is necessary in order to—

(a) give the life-sustaining treatment, or

(b) do the vital act.

(5)   A vital act is any act which the person doing it reasonably believes to be necessary to prevent a serious deterioration in P's condition.]

5 Acts in connection with care or treatment

(1)   If a person ('D') does an act in connection with the care or treatment of another person ('P'), the act is one to which this section applies if—

    (a) before doing the act, D takes reasonable steps to establish whether P lacks capacity in relation to the matter in question, and

    (b) when doing the act, D reasonably believes—

        (i)   that P lacks capacity in relation to the matter, and

        (ii) that it will be in P's best interests for the act to be done.

(2)   D does not incur any liability in relation to the act that he would not have incurred if P—

    (a) had had capacity to consent in relation to the matter, and

    (b) had consented to D's doing the act.

(3)   Nothing in this section excludes a person's civil liability for loss or damage, or his criminal liability, resulting from his negligence in doing the act.

(4)   Nothing in this section affects the operation of sections 24 to 26 (advance decisions to refuse treatment).

6 Section 5 acts: limitations

(1)   If D does an act that is intended to restrain P, it is not an act to which section 5 applies unless two further conditions are satisfied.

(2)   The first condition is that D reasonably believes that it is necessary to do the act in order to prevent harm to P.

(3)   The second is that the act is a proportionate response to—

    (a) the likelihood of P's suffering harm, and

    (b) the seriousness of that harm.

(4)   For the purposes of this section D restrains P if he—

    (a) uses, or threatens to use, force to secure the doing of an act which P resists, or

    (b) restricts P's liberty of movement, whether or not P resists.

(5)

(6)   Section 5 does not authorise a person to do an act which conflicts with a decision made, within the scope of his authority and in accordance with this Part, by—

    (a) a donee of a lasting power of attorney granted by P, or

    (b) a deputy appointed for P by the court.

(7)   But nothing in subsection (6) stops a person—

    (a) providing life-sustaining treatment, or

    (b) doing any act which he reasonably believes to be necessary to prevent a serious deterioration in P's condition,

while a decision as respects any relevant issue is sought from the court.

15 Power to make declarations

(1)   The court may make declarations as to—

    (a) whether a person has or lacks capacity to make a decision specified in the declaration;

    (b) whether a person has or lacks capacity to make decisions on such matters as are described in the declaration;

    (c) the lawfulness or otherwise of any act done, or yet to be done, in relation to that person.

(2)   'Act' includes an omission and a course of conduct.

16 Powers to make decisions and appoint deputies: general

(1)   This section applies if a person ('P') lacks capacity in relation to a matter or matters concerning—
        (a) P's personal welfare, or
        (b) P's property and affairs.

(2)   The court may—
        (a) by making an order, make the decision or decisions on P's behalf in relation to the matter or matters, or
        (b) appoint a person (a 'deputy') to make decisions on P's behalf in relation to the matter or matters.

(3)   The powers of the court under this section are subject to the provisions of this Act and, in particular, to sections 1 (the principles) and 4 (best interests).

(4)   When deciding whether it is in P's best interests to appoint a deputy, the court must have regard (in addition to the matters mentioned in section 4) to the principles that—
        (a) a decision by the court is to be preferred to the appointment of a deputy to make a decision, and
        (b) the powers conferred on a deputy should be as limited in scope and duration as is reasonably practicable in the circumstances.

(5)   The court may make such further orders or give such directions, and confer on a deputy such powers or impose on him such duties, as it thinks necessary or expedient for giving effect to, or otherwise in connection with, an order or appointment made by it under subsection (2).

(6)   Without prejudice to section 4, the court may make the order, give the directions or make the appointment on such terms as it considers are in P's best interests, even though no application is before the court for an order, directions or an appointment on those terms.

(7)   An order of the court may be varied or discharged by a subsequent order.

(8)   The court may, in particular, revoke the appointment of a deputy or vary the powers conferred on him if it is satisfied that the deputy—
        (a) has behaved, or is behaving, in a way that contravenes the authority conferred on him by the court or is not in P's best interests, or
        (b) proposes to behave in a way that would contravene that authority or would not be in P's best interests.

Advance decisions to refuse treatment

24 Advance decisions to refuse treatment: general

(1)   'Advance decision' means a decision made by a person ('P'), after he has reached 18 and when he has capacity to do so, that if—
        (a) at a later time and in such circumstances as he may specify, a specified treatment is proposed to be carried out or continued by a person providing health care for him, and
        (b) at that time he lacks capacity to consent to the carrying out or continuation of the treatment,
        the specified treatment is not to be carried out or continued.

(2)   For the purposes of subsection (1)(a), a decision may be regarded as specifying a treatment or circumstances even though expressed in layman's terms.

(3)   P may withdraw or alter an advance decision at any time when he has capacity to do so.

(4)   A withdrawal (including a partial withdrawal) need not be in writing.

(5)   An alteration of an advance decision need not be in writing (unless section 25(5) applies in relation to the decision resulting from the alteration).

25 Validity and applicability of advance decisions

(1)   An advance decision does not affect the liability which a person may incur for carrying out or continuing a treatment in relation to P unless the decision is at the material time—
   (a)   valid, and
   (b)   applicable to the treatment.

(2)   An advance decision is not valid if P—
   (a)   has withdrawn the decision at a time when he had capacity to do so,
   (b)   has, under a lasting power of attorney created after the advance decision was made, conferred authority on the donee (or, if more than one, any of them) to give or refuse consent to the treatment to which the advance decision relates, or
   (c)   has done anything else clearly inconsistent with the advance decision remaining his fixed decision.

(3)   An advance decision is not applicable to the treatment in question if at the material time P has capacity to give or refuse consent to it.

(4)   An advance decision is not applicable to the treatment in question if—
   (a)   that treatment is not the treatment specified in the advance decision,
   (b)   any circumstances specified in the advance decision are absent, or
   (c)   there are reasonable grounds for believing that circumstances exist which P did not anticipate at the time of the advance decision and which would have affected his decision had he anticipated them.

(5)   An advance decision is not applicable to life-sustaining treatment unless—
   (a)   the decision is verified by a statement by P to the effect that it is to apply to that treatment even if life is at risk, and
   (b)   the decision and statement comply with subsection (6).

(6)   A decision or statement complies with this subsection only if—
   (a)   it is in writing,
   (b)   it is signed by P or by another person in P's presence and by P's direction,
   (c)   the signature is made or acknowledged by P in the presence of a witness, and
   (d)   the witness signs it, or acknowledges his signature, in P's presence.

(7)   The existence of any lasting power of attorney other than one of a description mentioned in subsection (2)(b) does not prevent the advance decision from being regarded as valid and applicable.

26 Effect of advance decisions

(1)   If P has made an advance decision which is—
   (a)   valid, and
   (b)   applicable to a treatment,
the decision has effect as if he had made it, and had had capacity to make it, at the time when the question arises whether the treatment should be carried out or continued.

(2)   A person does not incur liability for carrying out or continuing the treatment unless, at the time, he is satisfied that an advance decision exists which is valid and applicable to the treatment.

(3)   A person does not incur liability for the consequences of withholding or withdrawing a treatment from P if, at the time, he reasonably believes that an advance decision exists which is valid and applicable to the treatment.

(4)   The court may make a declaration as to whether an advance decision—
    (a) exists;
    (b) is valid;
    (c) is applicable to a treatment.

(5)   Nothing in an apparent advance decision stops a person—
    (a) providing life-sustaining treatment, or
    (b) doing any act he reasonably believes to be necessary to prevent a serious deterioration in P's condition,
    while a decision as respects any relevant issue is sought from the court.

48 Interim orders and directions

(1)   The court may, pending the determination of an application to it in relation to a person ('P'), make an order or give directions in respect of any matter if—
    (a) there is reason to believe that P lacks capacity in relation to the matter,
    (b) the matter is one to which its powers under this Act extend, and
    (c) it is in P's best interests to make the order, or give the directions, without delay.

Appendix 1.2

DOH Consent Form 1

[NHS ORGANISATION NAME] CONSENT FORM 1

Patient agreement to investigation or treatment

Patient details (or pre-printed label)

Patient's surname/family name ....

Patient's first names ....

Date of birth ....

Responsible health professional ....

Job title ....

NHS number (or other identifier) ....

☐ Male   ☐ Female

Special requirements ....

(e g other language/other communication method)

To be retained in patient's notes

Patient identifier/label

Name of proposed procedure or course of treatment (include brief explanation if medical term not clear) ....

....

Statement of health professional (to be filled in by health professional with appropriate knowledge of proposed procedure, as specified in consent policy)

I have explained the procedure to the patient. In particular, I have explained:

The intended benefits ....

....

....

Serious or frequently occurring risks ....

....

....

Any extra procedures which may become necessary during the procedure

☐ blood transfusion ....

☐ other procedure (please specify) ....

....

I have also discussed what the procedure is likely to involve, the benefits and risks of any available alternative treatments (including no treatment) and any particular concerns of this patient.

☐ The following leaflet/tape has been provided ....

This procedure will involve:

☐ general and/or regional anaesthesia   ☐ local anaesthesia   ☐ sedation

Signed: .... Date ....

Name (PRINT) .... Job title ....

Contact details (if patient wishes to discuss options later)

....

Statement **of interpreter** (**where appropriate**)

I have interpreted the information above to the patient to the best of my ability and in a way in which I believe s/he can understand.

Signed .... Date ....

Name (PRINT) ....

Top copy accepted by patient: yes/no (please ring)

Statement of patient   **Patient identifier/label**

Please read this form carefully. If your treatment has been planned in advance, you should already have your own copy of page 2 which describes the benefits and risks of the proposed treatment. If not, you will be offered a copy now. If you have any further questions, do ask – we are here to help you. You have the right to change your mind at any time, including after you have signed this form.

I agree to the procedure or course of treatment described on this form.

I understand that you cannot give me a guarantee that a particular person will perform the procedure. The person will, however, have appropriate experience.

I understand that I will have the opportunity to discuss the details of anaesthesia with an anaesthetist before the procedure, unless the urgency of my situation prevents this. (This only applies to patients having general or regional anaesthesia.)

I understand that any procedure in addition to those described on this form will only be carried out if it is necessary to save my life or to prevent serious harm to my health.

I have been told about additional procedures which may become necessary during my treatment. I have listed below any procedures **which I do not wish to be carried out** without further discussion.

Patient's signature ....

Name (PRINT) ....

A witness should sign below if the patient is unable to sign but has indicated his or her consent. Young people/children may also like a parent to sign here (see notes).

Signature .... Date ....

Name (PRINT) ....

Confirmation of consent (to be completed by a health professional when the patient is admitted for the procedure, if the patient has signed the form in advance)

On behalf of the team treating the patient, I have confirmed with the patient that s/he has no further questions and wishes the procedure to go ahead.

Signed: .... Date ....

Name (PRINT) .... Job title ....

Important notes: (tick if applicable)

☐ See also advance directive/living will (e g Jehovah's Witness form)

☐ Patient has withdrawn consent (ask patient to sign /date here) ....

Guidance to health professionals (to be read in conjunction with consent policy)

What a consent form is for

This form documents the patient's agreement to go ahead with the investigation or treatment you have proposed. It is not a legal waiver – if patients, for example, do not receive enough information on which to base their decision, then the consent may not be valid, even though the form has been signed. Patients are also entitled to change their mind after signing the form, if they retain capacity to do so. The form should act as an *aide-memoire* to health professionals and patients, by providing a check-list of the kind of information patients should be offered, and by enabling the patient to have a written record of the main points discussed. In no way, however, should the written information provided for the patient be regarded as a substitute for face-to-face discussions with the patient.

The law on consent

See the Department of Health's *Reference guide to consent for examination or treatment* for a comprehensive summary of the law on consent (also available at www.doh.gov.uk/consent).

Who can give consent

Everyone aged 16 or more is presumed to be competent to give consent for themselves, unless the opposite is demonstrated. If a child under the age of 16 has 'sufficient understanding and intelligence to enable him or her to understand fully what is proposed', then he or she will be competent to give consent for himself or herself. Young people aged 16 and 17, and legally 'competent' younger children, may therefore sign this form for themselves, but may like a parent to countersign as well. If the child is not able to give consent for himself or herself, some-one with parental responsibility may do so on their behalf and a separate form is available for this purpose. Even where a child is able to give consent for himself or herself, you should always involve those with parental responsibility in the child's care, unless the child specifically asks you not to do so. If a patient is mentally competent to give consent but is physically unable to sign a form, you should complete this form as usual, and ask an independent witness to confirm that the patient has given consent orally or non-verbally.

When NOT to use this form

If the patient is 18 or over and is not legally competent to give consent, you should use form 4 (form for adults who are unable to consent to investigation or treatment) instead of this form. A patient will not be legally competent to give consent if:

- they are unable to comprehend and retain information material to the decision and/or
- they are unable to weigh and use this information in coming to a decision.

You should always take all reasonable steps (for example involving more specialist colleagues) to support a patient in making their own decision, before concluding that they are unable to do so.

Relatives **cannot** be asked to sign this form on behalf of an adult who is not legally competent to consent for himself or herself.

Information

Information about what the treatment will involve, its benefits and risks (including side-effects and complications) and the alternatives to the particular procedure proposed, is crucial for patients when making up their minds. The courts have stated that patients should be told about 'significant risks which would affect the judgement of a reasonable patient'. 'Significant' has not been legally defined, but the GMC requires doctors to tell patients about 'serious or frequently occurring' risks. In addition if patients make clear they have particular concerns about certain kinds of risk, you should make sure they are informed about these risks, even if they are very small or rare. You should always answer questions honestly. Sometimes, patients may make it clear that they do not want to have any information about the options, but want you to decide on their behalf. In such circumstances, you should do your best to ensure that the patient receives at least very basic information about what is proposed. Where information is refused, you should document this on page 2 of the form or in the patient's notes.

DOH Consent Form 2

[NHS ORGANISATION NAME] CONSENT FORM 2

Parental agreement to investigation or treatment for a child or young person

Patient details (or pre-printed label)

Patient's surname/family name ....

Patient's first names ....

Date of birth ....

Age ....

Responsible health professional ....

Job title ....

NHS number (or other identifier) ....

☐ Male   ☐ Female

Special requirements ....

(e g other language/other communication method)

To be retained in patient's notes

Patient identifier/label

Name of proposed procedure or course of treatment (include brief explanation if medical term not clear) ....
....

Statement of health professional (to be filled in by health professional with appropriate knowledge of proposed procedure, as specified in consent policy)

I have explained the procedure to the child and his or her parent(s). In particular, I have explained:

The intended benefits ....
....

Serious or frequently occurring risks ....
....
....

Any extra procedures which may become necessary during the procedure

☐ blood transfusion ....

☐ other procedure (please specify) ....

....

I have also discussed what the procedure is likely to involve, the benefits and risks of any available alternative treatments (including no treatment) and any particular concerns of this patient and his or her parents.

☐ The following leaflet/tape has been provided ....

This procedure will involve:

☐ general and/or regional anaesthesia   ☐ local anaesthesia   ☐ sedation

Signed: .... Date ....

Name (PRINT) .... Job title ....

Contact details (if child/parent wish to discuss options later) ....

....

Statement of interpreter (where appropriate)

I have interpreted the information above to the child and his or her parents to the best of my ability and in a way in which I believe they can understand.

Signed .... Date ....

Name (PRINT) ....

Top copy accepted by patient: yes/no (please ring)

Statement of parent   Patient identifier/label

Please read this form carefully. If the procedure has been planned in advance, you should already have your own copy of page 2 which describes the benefits and risks of the proposed treatment. If not, you will be offered a copy now. If you have any further questions, do ask – we are here to help you and your child. You have the right to change your mind at any time, including after you have signed this form.

I agree to the procedure or course of treatment described on this form and **I confirm** that I have 'parental responsibility' for this child.

I understand that you cannot give me a guarantee that a particular person will perform the procedure. The person will, however, have appropriate experience.

I understand that my child and I will have the opportunity to discuss the details of anaesthesia with an anaesthetist before the procedure, unless the urgency of the situation prevents this. (This only applies to children having general or regional anaesthesia.)

I understand hat any procedure in addition to those described on this form will only be carried out if it is necessary to save the life of my child or to prevent serious harm to his or her health.

I have been told about additional procedures which may become necessary during my child's treatment. I have listed below any **procedures which I do not wish to be carried out** without further discussion ....

....

....

Signature ....

Name (PRINT) .... Relationship to child ....

Child's agreement to treatment (if child wishes to sign)

I agree to have the treatment I have been told about.

Name .... Signature ....

Date ....

Confirmation of consent (to be completed by a health professional when the child is admitted for the procedure, if the parent/child have signed the form in advance)

On behalf of the team treating the patient, I have confirmed with the child and his or her parent(s) that they have no further questions and wish the procedure to go ahead.

Signed: .... Date ....

Name (PRINT) .... Job title ....

Important notes: (tick if applicable)

☐ See also advance directive/living will (e g Jehovah's Witness form)

☐ Parent has withdrawn consent (ask parent to sign /date here) ....

Guidance to health professionals (to be read in conjunction with consent policy)

This form

This form should be used to document consent to a child's treatment, where that consent is being given by a person with parental responsibility for the child. The term 'parent' has been used in this form as a shorthand for 'person with parental responsibility'. Where children are legally competent to consent for themselves (see below), they may sign the standard 'adult' consent form (form 1). There is space on that form for a parent to countersign if a competent child wishes them to do so.

Who can give consent

Everyone aged 16 or more is presumed to be competent to give consent for themselves, unless the opposite is demonstrated. The courts have stated that if a child under the age of 16 has "sufficient understanding and intelligence to enable him or her to understand fully what is proposed", then he or she will be competent to give consent for himself or herself. If children are not able to give consent for themselves, some-one with parental responsibility may do so on their behalf.

Although children acquire rights to give consent for themselves as they grow older, people with 'parental responsibility' for a child retain the right to give consent on the child's behalf until the child reaches the age of 18. Therefore, for a number of years, both the child and a person with parental responsibility have the right to give consent to the child's treatment. In law, health professionals only need the consent of one appropriate person before providing treatment. This means that in theory it is lawful to provide treatment to a child under 18 which a person with parental responsibility has authorised, even if the child refuses. As a matter of good practice, however, you should always seek a competent child's consent before providing treatment unless any delay involved in doing so would put the child's life or health at risk. Younger children should also be as involved as possible in decisions about their healthcare. Further advice is given in the Department's guidance *Seeking consent: working with children.* Any differences of opinion between the child and their parents, or between parents, should be clearly documented in the patient's notes.

Parental responsibility

The person(s) with parental responsibility will usually, but not invariably, be the child's birth parents. People with parental responsibility for a child include: the child's mother; the child's father if married to the mother at the child's conception, birth or later; a legally appointed guardian; the local authority if the child is on a care order; or a person named in a residence order in respect of the child. Fathers who have never been married to the child's mother will only have parental responsibility if they have acquired it through a court order or parental responsibility agreement (although this may change in the future).

Information

Information about what the treatment will involve, its benefits and risks (including side-effects and complications) and the alternatives to the particular procedure proposed, is crucial for children and their parents when making up their minds about treatment. The courts have stated that patients should be told about 'significant risks which would affect the judgement of a reasonable patient'. 'Significant' has not been legally defined, but the GMC requires doctors to tell patients about 'serious or frequently occurring' risks. In addition if patients make clear they have particular concerns about certain kinds of risk, you should make sure they are informed about these risks, even if they are very small or rare. You should always answer questions honestly.

Guidance on the law on consent

See the Department of Health publications *Reference guide to consent for examination or treatment* and Seeking *consent: working with children* for a comprehensive summary of the law on consent (also available at www.doh.gov.uk/consent).

Appendix 1.4

DOH Consent Form 3

[NHS ORGANISATION NAME] CONSENT FORM 3

Patient identifier/label

Patient/parental agreement to investigation or treatment

(procedures where consciousness not impaired)

Name of procedure (include brief explanation if medical term not clear)

....

....

....

Statement of health professional **(to be filled in by health professional with appropriate knowledge of proposed procedure, as specified in consent policy)**

I have explained the procedure to the patient/parent. In particular, I have explained:

The intended benefits ....

....

....

Serious or frequently occurring risks: ....

....

....

I have also discussed what the procedure is likely to involve, the benefits and risks of any available alternative treatments (including no treatment) and any particular concerns of those involved.

☐ The following leaflet/tape has been provided ....

Signed: .... Date ....

Name (PRINT) .... Job title ....

Statement of interpreter (where appropriate)

I have interpreted the information above to the patient/parent to the best of my ability and in a way in which I believe s/he/they can understand.

Signed .... Name (PRINT) ....

Statement of patient/person with parental responsibility for patient

I agree to the procedure described above.

I understand that you cannot give me a guarantee that a particular person will perform the procedure. The person will, however, have appropriate experience.

340

I understand that the procedure will/will not involve local anaesthesia.

Signature .... Date ....

Name (PRINT) .... Relationship to patient ....

Confirmation of consent (to be completed by a health professional when the patient is admitted for the procedure, if the patient/parent has signed the form in advance)

I have confirmed that the patient/parent has no further questions and wishes the procedure to go ahead.

Signed: .... Date ....

Name (PRINT) .... Job title ....

Top copy accepted by patient: yes/no (please ring)

Guidance to health professionals (to be read in conjunction with consent policy)

This form

This form documents the patient's agreement (or that of a person with parental responsibility for the patient) to go ahead with the investigation or treatment you have proposed. It is only designed for procedures where the patient is expected to remain alert throughout and where an anaesthetist is not involved in their care: for example for drug therapy where written consent is deemed appropriate. In other circumstances you should use either form 1 (for adults/competent children) or form 2 (parental consent for children/young people) as appropriate.

Consent forms are not legal waivers – if patients, for example, do not receive enough information on which to base their decision, then the consent may not be valid, even though the form has been signed. Patients also have every right to change their mind after signing the form.

Who can give consent

Everyone aged 16 or more is presumed to be competent to give consent for themselves, unless the opposite is demonstrated. If a child under the age of 16 has 'sufficient understanding and intelligence to enable him or her to understand fully what is proposed', then he or she will be competent to give consent for himself or herself. Young people aged 16 and 17, and legally 'competent' younger children, may therefore sign this form for themselves, if they wish. If the child is not able to give consent for himself or herself, some-one with parental responsibility may do so on their behalf. Even where a child is able to give consent for himself or herself, you should always involve those with parental responsibility in the child's care, unless the child specifically asks you not to do so. If a patient is mentally competent to give consent but is physically unable to sign a form, you should complete this form as usual, and ask an independent witness to confirm that the patient has given consent orally or non-verbally.

When NOT to use this form (see also 'This form' above)

If the patient is 18 or over and is not legally competent to give consent, you should use form 4 (form for adults who are unable to consent to investigation or treatment) instead of this form. A patient will not be legally competent to give consent if:

- they are unable to comprehend and retain information material to the decision and/or
- they are unable to weigh and use this information in coming to a decision.

You should always take all reasonable steps (for example involving more specialist colleagues) to support a patient in making their own decision, before concluding that they are unable to do so. Relatives **cannot** be asked to sign this form on behalf of an adult who is not legally competent to consent for himself or herself.

Information

Information about what the treatment will involve, its benefits and risks (including side-effects and complications) and the alternatives to the particular procedure proposed, is crucial for patients when making up their minds about treatment. The courts have stated that patients should be told about 'significant risks which would affect the judgement of a reasonable patient'. 'Significant' has not been legally defined, but the GMC requires doctors to tell patients about 'serious or frequently occurring' risks. In addition if patients make clear they have particular concerns about certain kinds of risk, you should make sure they are informed about these risks, even if they are very small or rare. You should always answer questions honestly. Sometimes, patients may make it clear that they do not want to have any information about the options, but want you to decide on their behalf. In such circumstances, you should do your best to ensure that the patient receives at least very basic information about what is proposed. Where information is refused, you should document this overleaf or in the patient's notes.

The law on consent

See the Department of Health's *Reference guide to consent for examination or treatment* for a comprehensive summary of the law on consent (also available at www.doh.gov.uk/consent).

Appendix 1.5

DOH Consent Form 4

[NHS ORGANISATION NAME] CONSENT FORM 4

Form for adults who are unable to consent to investigation or treatment

Patient details (or pre-printed label)

Patient's surname/family name ....

Patient's first names ....

Date of birth ....

Responsible health professional ....

Job title ....

NHS number (or other identifier) ....

☐ Male   ☐ Female

Special requirements ....

(e g other language/other communication method)

To be retained in patient's notes

Patient identifier/label

All sections to be completed by health professional proposing the procedure

A Details of procedure or course of treatment proposed

(NB see guidance to health professionals overleaf for details of situations where court approval must first be sought)

B Assessment of patient's capacity

I confirm that the patient lacks capacity to give or withhold consent to this procedure or course of treatment because:

☐ the patient is unable to comprehend and retain information material to the decision; and/or

☐ the patient is unable to use and weigh this information in the decision-making process; or

☐ the patient is unconscious

Further details (excluding where patient unconscious): for example how above judgements reached; which colleagues consulted; what attempts made to assist the patient make his or her own decision and why these were not successful.

C Assessment of patient's best interests

To the best of my knowledge, the patient has not refused this procedure in a valid advance directive. Where possible and appropriate, I have consulted with colleagues and those close to the patient, and I believe the procedure to be in the patient's best interests because:

(Where incapacity is likely to be temporary, for example if patient unconscious, or where patient has fluctuating capacity)

The treatment cannot wait until the patient recovers capacity because:

D Involvement of the patient's family and others close to the patient

The final responsibility for determining whether a procedure is in an incapacitated patient's best interests lies with the health professional performing the procedure. However, it is good practice to consult with those close to the patient (e g spouse/partner, family and friends, carer, supporter or advocate) unless you have good reason to believe that the patient would not have wished particular individuals to be consulted, or unless the urgency of their situation prevents this. 'Best interests' go far wider than 'best medical interests', and include factors such as the patient's wishes and beliefs when competent, their current wishes, their general well-being and their spiritual and religious welfare.

(to be signed by a person or persons close to the patient, if they wish)

I/We have been involved in a discussion with the relevant health professionals over the treatment of ....(patient's name). I/We understand that he/she is unable to give his/her own consent, based on the criteria set out in this form. I/We also understand that treatment can lawfully be provided if it is in his/her best interests to receive it.

Any other comments (including any concerns about decision)

Name .... Relationship to patient ....

Address (if not the same as patient ....

....

....

Signature .... Date ....

If a person close to the patient was not available in person, has this matter been discussed in any other way (e g over the telephone?)

☐ Yes   ☐ No

Details:

Signature of health professional proposing treatment

The above procedure is, in my clinical judgement, in the best interests of the patient, who lacks capacity to consent for himself or herself. Where possible and appropriate I have discussed the patient's condition with those close to him or her, and taken their knowledge of the patient's views and beliefs into account in determining his or her best interests.

I have/have not sought a second opinion.

Signature: .... Date ....

Name (PRINT) .... Job title ....

Where second opinion sought, s/he should sign below to confirm agreement:

Signature: .... Date ....

Name (PRINT) .... Job title ....

Guidance to health professionals (to be read in conjunction with consent policy)

This form should only be used where it would be usual to seek written consent but an adult patient (18 or over) lacks capacity to give or withhold consent to treatment. If an adult **has** capacity to accept or refuse treatment, you should use the standard consent form and respect any refusal. Where treatment is very urgent (for example if the patient is critically ill), it may not be feasible to fill in a form at the time, but you should document your clinical decisions appropriately afterwards. If treatment is being provided under the authority of Part IV of the *Mental Health Act 1983*, different legal provisions apply and you are required to fill in more specialised forms (although in some circumstances you may find it helpful to use this form as well). If the adult now lacks capacity, but has clearly refused particular treatment in advance of their loss of capacity (for example in an advance directive or 'living will'), then you must abide by that refusal if it was validly made and is applicable to the circumstances. For further information on the law on consent, see the Department of Health's *Reference guide to consent for examination or treatment* (www.doh.gov.uk/consent).

When treatment can be given to a patient who is unable to consent

For treatment to be given to a patient who is unable to consent, the following **must** apply:

* the patient must lack the capacity ('competence') to give or withhold consent to this procedure AND
* the procedure must be in the patient's best interests.

Capacity

A patient will lack capacity to consent to a particular intervention if he or she is:

* unable to comprehend and retain information material to the decision, especially as to the consequences of having, or not having, the intervention in question; and/or
* unable to use and weigh this information in the decision-making process.

Before making a judgement that a patient lacks capacity you must take all steps reasonable in the circumstances to assist the patient in taking their own decisions (this will clearly not apply if the patient is unconscious). This may involve explaining what is involved in very simple language, using pictures and communication and decision-aids as appropriate. People close to the patient (spouse/partner, family, friends and carers) may often be able to help, as may specialist colleagues such as speech and language therapists or learning disability teams, and independent advocates or supporters.

Capacity is 'decision-specific': a patient may lack capacity to take a particular complex decision, but be quite able to take other more straight-forward decisions or parts of decisions.

Appendix 1.5

Best interests

A patient's best interests are not limited to their best medical interests. Other factors which form part of the best interests decision include:

- the wishes and beliefs of the patient when competent
- their current wishes
- their general well-being
- their spiritual and religious welfare

Two incapacitated patients, whose *physical* condition is identical, may therefore have different best interests.

Unless the patient has clearly indicated that particular individuals should not be involved in their care, or unless the urgency of their situation prevents it, you should attempt to involve people close to the patient (spouse/partner, family and friends, carer, supporter or advocate) in the decision-making process. Those close to the patient cannot require you to provide particular treatment which you do not believe to be clinically appropriate. However they will know the patient much better than you do, and therefore are likely to be able to provide valuable information about the patient's wishes and values.

Second opinions and court involvement

Where treatment is complex and/or people close to the patient express doubts about the proposed treatment, a second opinion should be sought, unless the urgency of the patient's condition prevents this. Donation of regenerative tissue such as bone marrow, sterilisation for contraceptive purposes and withdrawal of artificial nutrition or hydration from a patient in PVS must never be undertaken without prior High Court approval. High Court approval can also be sought where there are doubts about the patient's capacity or best interests.

Appendix 1.6

DOH: Information to assist in amending consent forms

The following suggestions may help Trusts who have not already done so to amend their consent forms in the light of legislative and other changes. This is not a comprehensive list of all changes that Trusts may wish to make, which will be a matter for local decision. Trusts may wish to consult their own legal Departments about the suitability of their forms.

There are some global changes that can be made to the wording of the forms to reflect the Mental Capacity Act (MCA), most significantly the use of 'capacity' or 'lack the capacity' in place of 'competent' and the term 'advance decision to refuse treatment' in place of 'advance directive' or 'living will'.

Trusts may also want to include a reference to consent for the use of human tissue under the Human Tissue Act on some of the forms as appropriate.

The completion of consent forms is of course only part of the consent process and should only be carried out in the context of an informed discussion with the person giving consent with more detailed explanation given where necessary.

CONSENT FORM 1 – PATIENT AGREEMENT TO INVESTIGATION OR TREATMENT

- This form deals with people who have the capacity to consent to treatment and therefore is largely unaffected by the MCA.
- In the section 'statement of health professional', the wording about risks could be amended to reflect the *Chester v Afshar* judgment (see introduction of revised Reference guide to consent), so as to prompt health professionals to discuss 'significant, unavoidable or frequently occurring risks' with the patient rather than simply recording 'serious or frequently occurring risks' as at present.
- The information on page 4 could be updated to reflect the MCA, in particular the section on when the form would not be used, which could be amended in the following way:

'When NOT to use this form

If the patient is 18 or over and lacks the capacity to give consent, you should use form 4 (form for adults who lack the capacity to consent to investigation or treatment) instead of this form. A patient lacks capacity if they have an impairment of the mind or brain or disturbance affecting the way their mind or brain works and they cannot:

- understand information about the decision to be made
- retain that information in their mind
- use or weigh that information as part of the decision-making process, or
- communicate their decision (by talking, using sign language or any other means).

347

You should always take all reasonable steps (for example involving more specialist colleagues) to support a patient in making their own decision, before concluding that they are unable to do so.

Relatives **cannot** be asked to sign a form on behalf of an adult who lacks capacity to consent for themselves, unless they have been given the authority to so under a Lasting Power of Attorney or as a court appointed deputy.'

CONSENT FORM 2 – PARENTAL AGREEMENT TO INVESTIGATION OR TREATMENT FOR A CHILD OR YOUNG PERSON

- It may be useful to amend the title of the form and other reference to a parent to read 'parent (or person who has parental responsibility)'
- The section 'statement of health professional' – the wording about risks could be amended to reflect the *Chester v Afshar* judgment (see introduction of revised Reference guide to consent) for example to prompt health professionals to discuss 'significant, unavoidable or frequently occurring risks' with the patient rather than simply recording 'serious or frequently occurring risks' as at present.
- The information 'who can consent' on page 4 could be amended where it refers to young people who refuse consent (see 'Child or young person with capacity refusing treatment' in Chapter 3 of revised Reference guide to consent). The text could be amended along the following lines:

"Where a young person of 16 or 17 or a Gillick competent child under 16, refuses treatment, it is possible that such a refusal could be over-ruled if it would in all probability lead to the death of the child or to severe permanent injury. It would be prudent, to obtain a court declaration or decision if faced with a competent child or young person who is refusing to consent to treatment, to determine whether it is lawful to treat the child."

CONSENT FORM 3 – PATIENT/PARENTAL AGREEMENT TO INVESTIGATION OR TREATMENT

- Comments on use of terms and amendments to reflect the *Chester v Afshar* judgment as for forms 1 and 2 would also apply to this form.

CONSENT FORM 4 – FORM FOR ADULTS WHO ARE UNABLE TO CONSENT TO INVESTIGATION OR TREATMENT

- The MCA is of most relevance to this form and this is covered in chapter 2 of the revised Reference guide to consent.
- It may be useful to amend the title of the form to 'Form for adults who lack the capacity to consent to investigation or treatment'
- Section B will need to be amended to reflect the wording of the MCA, for example along the lines of:

'B Assessment of patient's capacity (in accordance with the Mental Capacity Act)

I confirm that the patient lacks capacity to give or withhold consent to this procedure or course of treatment because of an impairment of the mind or brain

348

or disturbance affecting the way their mind or brain works (for example, a disability, condition or trauma, or the effect of drugs or alcohol) and they cannot do one or more of the following:

- [ ] understand information about the procedure or course of treatment
- [ ] retain that information in their mind
- [ ] use or weigh that information as part of the decision-making process, or
- [ ] communicate their decision (by talking, using sign language or any other means)

Further details: for example how above judgements reached; which colleagues consulted; what attempts made to assist the patient make his or her own decision and why these were not successful.'

- Section C will need to reflect the elements health professionals will need to consider as part of a best interests assessment, for example along the following lines:

'C Assessment of patient's best interests

I am satisfied that the patient has not refused this procedure in a valid advance decision. As far as is reasonably possible, I have considered the person's past and present wishes and feelings (in particular if they have been written down) any beliefs and values that would be likely to influence the decision in question. As far as possible, I have consulted other people (those involved in caring for the patient, interested in their welfare or the patient has said should be consulted) as appropriate. I have considered the patient's best interests in accordance with the requirements of the Mental Capacity Act and believe the procedure to be in their best interests because:

(Where the lack of capacity is likely to be temporary ....)

The treatment cannot wait until the patient recovers capacity because: '

- Section D will need to reflect the fact that, unless the person has an attorney or deputy, the final responsibility for determining what is in a person's best interest will rest with the relevant health professional. However, the health professional must consult with those close to the patient (eg spouse/partner, family and friends, carer, supporter or advocate) as far as is practicable and as appropriate.
- Section D could also include a section on the involvement of an Independent Mental Capacity Advocate, for example along the lines of:

'Independent Mental Capacity Advocate (IMCA)

For decisions about serious medical treatment, where there is no one appropriate to consult other than paid staff, has an Independent Mental Capacity Advocate (IMCA) been instructed?

- [ ] Yes   - [ ] No

Details:

Signature .... Date .... '

- The form could include a new section E to cover patients who have an attorney or deputy, for example along the lines of:

'E The patient has an attorney or deputy

Where the patient has authorised an attorney to make decisions about the procedure in question under a Lasting Power of Attorney or a Court Appointed

Deputy has been authorised to make decisions about the procedure in question, the attorney or deputy will have the final responsibility for determining whether a procedure is in the patient's best interests.

Signature of attorney or deputy

I have been authorised to make decisions about the procedure in question under a Lasting Power of Attorney / as a Court Appointed Deputy (delete as appropriate). I have considered the relevant circumstances relating to the decision in question (see section C) and believe the procedure to be in the patient's best interests.

Any other comments (including the circumstances considered in assessing the patient's best interests)

Signature:.. etc'

- The information on page 4 will need to be amended in line with the changes made to the form and the MCA. The information below is given as a guide of the areas this information could cover:

'Guidance to health professionals

This form should only be used where it would be usual to seek written consent but an adult patient (16 or over) lacks capacity to give or withhold consent to treatment. If an adult **has** capacity to accept or refuse treatment, you should use the standard consent form and respect any refusal. Where treatment is very urgent (for example if the patient is critically ill), it may not be feasible to fill in a form at the time, but you should document your clinical decisions appropriately afterwards. If treatment is being provided under the authority of Part IV of the *Mental Health Act 1983*, different legal provisions apply and you are required to fill in more specialised forms (although in some circumstances you may find it helpful to use this form as well). If the adult now lacks capacity, but has made a valid advance decision to refuse treatment that is applicable to the proposed treatment then you must abide by that refusal. For further information on the law on consent, see the Department of Health's *Reference guide to consent for examination or treatment* (www.dh.gov.uk/consent).

When treatment can be given to a patient who lacks the capacity to consent

All decisions made on behalf of a patient who lacks capacity must be made in accordance with the Mental Capacity Act 2005. More information about the Act is given in the Code of Practice1[1]. Treatment can be given to a patient who is unable to consent, only if :

- the patient lacks the capacity to give or withhold consent to this procedure AND
- the procedure is in the patient's best interests.

1   Mental Capacity Act 2005 Code of Practice – www.publicguardian.gov.uk/mca/code-of-practice.htm

Capacity

A person lacks capacity if they have an impairment or disturbance (for example, a disability, condition or trauma, or the effect of drugs or alcohol) that affects the way their mind or brain works which means that they are unable to make a specific decision at the time it needs to be made. It does not matter if the impairment or disturbance is permanent or temporary. A person is unable to make a decision if they cannot do one or more of the following things:

- Understand the information given to them that is relevant to the decision.
- Retain that information long enough to be able to make the decision.
- Use or weigh up the information as part of the decision- making process.
- Communicate their decision – this could be by talking or using sign language and includes simple muscle movements such as blinking an eye or squeezing a hand.

You must take all steps reasonable in the circumstances to assist the patient in taking their own decisions. This may involve explaining what is involved in very simple language, using pictures and communication and decision-aids as appropriate. People close to the patient (spouse/partner, family, friends and carers) may often be able to help, as may specialist colleagues such as speech and language therapists or learning disability teams, and independent advocates (as distinct from an IMCA as set out below) or supporters. Sometimes it may be necessary for a formal assessment to be carried out by a suitably qualified professional.

Capacity is "decision-specific": a patient may lack capacity to take a particular complex decision, but be able to take other more straight-forward decisions or parts of decisions. Capacity can also fluctuate over time and you should consider whether the person is likely to regain capacity and if so whether the decision can wait until they regain capacity.

Best interests

The Mental Capacity Act requires that a health professional must consider all the relevant circumstances relating to the decision in question, including, as far as possible considering:

- the person's past and present wishes and feelings (in particular if they have been written down)
- any beliefs and values (e.g. religious, cultural or moral) that would be likely to influence the decision in question and any other relevant factors
- the other factors that the person would be likely to consider if they were able to do so.

When determining what is in a person's best interests a health professional must not make assumptions about someone's best interests merely on the basis of the person's age or appearance, condition or any aspect of their behaviour. If the decision concerns the provision or withdrawal of life-sustaining treatment the health professional must not be motivated by a desire to bring about the person's death.

The Act also requires that, as far as possible, health professionals must consult other people, if it is appropriate to do so, and take into account of their views as to what would be in the best interests of the person lacking capacity, especially anyone previously named by the person lacking capacity as someone to be consulted and anyone engaging in caring for patient and their family and friends.

Independent Mental Capacity Advocate (IMCA)

The Mental Capacity Act introduced a duty on the NHS to instruct an independent mental capacity advocate (IMCA) in serious medical treatment decisions when a person who lacks capacity to make a decision has no one who can speak for them, other than paid staff. IMCAs are not decision makers for the person who lacks capacity. They are there to support and represent that person and to ensure that decision making for people who lack capacity is done appropriately and in accordance with the Act.

Lasting Power of Attorney and Court Appointed Deputy

A person over the age of 18 can appoint an attorney to look after their health and welfare decisions, if they lack the capacity to make such decisions in the future. Under a Lasting Power of Attorney (LPA) the attorney can make decisions that are as valid as those made by the person themselves. The LPA may specify limits to the attorney's authority and the LPA must specify whether or not the attorney has the authority to make decisions about life-sustaining treatment. The attorney can only, therefore, make decisions as authorised in the LPA and must make decisions in the person's best interests.

The Court of Protection can appoint a deputy to make decisions on behalf of a person who lacks capacity. Deputies for personal welfare decisions will only be required in the most difficult cases where important and necessary actions cannot be carried out without the court's authority or where there is no other way of settling the matter in the best interests of the person who lacks capacity. If a deputy has been appointed to make treatment decisions on behalf of a person who lacks capacity then it is the deputy rather than the health professional who makes the treatment decision and the deputy must make decisions in the patient's best interests.

Second opinions and court involvement

Where treatment is complex and/or people close to the patient express doubts about the proposed treatment, a second opinion should be sought, unless the urgency of the patient's condition prevents this. The Court of Protection deals with serious decisions affecting personal welfare matters, including healthcare, which were previously dealt with by the High Court. Cases involving:

- decisions about the proposed withholding or withdrawal of artificial nutrition and hydration (ANH) from patients in a permanent vegetative state (PVS)
- cases involving organ, bone marrow or peripheral blood stem cell (PBSC) donation by an adult who lacks capacity to consent
- cases involving the proposed non-therapeutic sterilisation of a person who lacks capacity to consent to this (e.g. for contraceptive purposes) and
- all other cases where there is a doubt or dispute about whether a particular treatment will be in a person's best interests (include cases involving ethical dilemmas in untested areas)

should be referred to the Court for approval. The Court can be asked to make a decision in cases where there are doubts about the patient's capacity and also about the validity or applicability of an advance decision to refuse treatment.'

GMC: Good Medical Practice

DECISIONS ABOUT ACCESS TO MEDICAL CARE

7   The investigations or treatment you provide or arrange must be based on the assessment you and the patient make of their needs and priorities, and on your clinical judgement about the likely effectiveness of the treatment options. You must not refuse or delay treatment because you believe that a patient's actions have contributed to their condition. You must treat your patients with respect whatever their life choices and beliefs. You must not unfairly discriminate against them by allowing your personal views[1] to affect adversely your professional relationship with them or the treatment you provide or arrange. You should challenge colleagues if their behaviour does not comply with this guidance.[2]

1   This includes your views about a patient's age, colour, culture, disability, ethnic or national origin, gender, lifestyle, marital or parental status, race, religion or beliefs, sex, sexual orientation, or social or economic status.
2   See GMC guidance on valuing diversity.

8   If carrying out a particular procedure or giving advice about it conflicts with your religious or moral beliefs, and this conflict might affect the treatment or advice you provide, you must explain this to the patient and tell them they have the right to see another doctor. You must be satisfied that the patient has sufficient information to enable them to exercise that right. If it is not practical for a patient to arrange to see another doctor, you must ensure that arrangements are made for another suitably qualified colleague to take over your role.

CONSENT

36   You must be satisfied that you have consent or other valid authority before you undertake any examination or investigation, provide treatment or involve patients in teaching or research. Usually this will involve providing information to patients in a way they can understand, before asking for their consent. You must follow the guidance in *Seeking patients' consent: The ethical considerations,* which includes advice on children and patients who are not able to give consent.[1]

1   See GMC consent guidance and GMC research guidance paragraphs 15–29.

NHS: My advance decision to refuse treatment

My Name	Any distinguishing features in the event of unconsciousness
Address	Date of Birth
	Telephone Number

WHAT IS THIS DOCUMENT FOR?

This advance decision to refuse treatment has been written by me to specify in advance which treatments I don't want in the future. These are my decisions about my healthcare, in the event that I have lost mental capacity and can not consent to or refuse treatment. This advance decision replaces any previous advance decision I have made.

ADVICE TO THE READER

I have written this document to identify my advance decision. I would expect any health care professionals reading this document in the event I have lost capacity to check that my advance decision is valid and applicable, in the circumstances that exist at the time.

PLEASE CHECK

Please do not assume I have lost capacity before any actions are taken. I might need help and time to communicate.

If I have lost capacity please check the validity and applicability of this advance decision.

This advance decision becomes legally binding and must be followed if professionals are satisfied it is valid and applicable. Please help to share this information with people who are involved in my treatment and care and need to know about this.

Please also check if I have made any other statements about my preferences or decisions that might be relevant to my advance decision.

This advance decision does not refuse the offer and or provision of basic care, support and comfort.

My Name	

My advance decision to refuse treatment

I wish to refuse the following specific treatments:	In these circumstances:

(Note to the person making this statement: If you wish to refuse a treatment that is or may be life-sustaining, you must state in the box above that you are refusing that treatment even if your life is at risk as a result. An advance decision refusing life-sustaining treatment must be signed and witnessed).

My Signature (or nominated person)	Date of Signature
Witness	Witness Signature
Name	Telephone
Address	Date

Person to be contacted to discuss my wishes:	
Name	**Relationship**
Address	**Telephone**

I have discussed this with (e.g. name of Healthcare Professional)
Profession / Job Title Contact Details Date
I give permission for this document to be discussed with my relatives / carers **YES NO** (please circle one)
My General Practitioner is: (Name) Address Telephone
Optional Review Comment Date / Time Maker's Signature Witness Signature

The following list identifies which people have a copy and have been told about this Advance Decision to Refuse Treatment (and their contact details)

Name	Relationships	Telephone Number

Further Information (Optional)
I have written the following information that is important to me. It describes my hopes, fears and expectations of life and any potential health and social care problems. It does not directly affect my advance decision to refuse treatment but the reader might find it useful.

Appendix 4.1

Draft Originating Summons for Child Treatment Decision

IN THE HIGH COURT OF JUSTICE

Case No

FAMILY DIVISION

PRINCIPAL REGISTRY

IN THE MATTER OF: [NAME OF CHILD] [DOB]

AND IN THE MATTER OF THE INHERENT JURISDICTION OF THE HIGH COURT

AND IN THE MATTER OF THE CHILDREN ACT 1989

B E T W E E N:

BLANKSHIRE HEALTHCARE NHS TRUST

Plaintiff

– and –

[Name of child]

First Defendant

[Name of father]

Second Defendant

[Name of mother]

Third Defendant

ORIGINATING SUMMONS

Let all parties attend before Mr Justice Fairness at the Royal Courts of Justice, Strand, London on *[date]* at *[time]* for the hearing of the application of the Blankshire Healthcare NHS Trust for an Order:

1. That in the circumstances where the First Defendant cannot give her consent and where the Second and Third Defendants withhold their consent, it shall be lawful and in the First Defendant's best interests to carry out such operative and medical procedures on her as in the opinion of the consultant medical practitioners caring for the First Defendant are necessary for preserving her life and treating her leukaemia.

2. For the grounds of this originating summons see the attached affidavit and exhibits.

Appendix 4.2

Code of Practice Mental Health Act 1983 (revised 2008)

GENERAL CONSIDERATIONS

36.3 The legal framework governing the admission to hospital and treatment of children is complex, and it is important to remember a number of factors. Those responsible for the care of children and young people in hospital should be familiar with other relevant legislation, including the Children Acts 1989 and 2004, Mental Capacity Act 2005 (MCA), Family Law Reform Act 1969, Human Rights Act 1998 and the United Nations Convention on the Rights of the Child, as well as relevant case law, common law principles and relevant codes of practice.

36.4 When taking decisions under the Act about children and young people, the following should always be borne in mind:

- the best interests of the child or young person must always be a significant consideration;
- children and young people should always be kept as fully informed as possible, just as an adult would be, and should receive clear and detailed information concerning their care and treatment, explained in a way they can understand and in a format that is appropriate to their age;
- the child or young person's views, wishes and feelings should always be considered;
- any intervention in the life of a child or young person that is considered necessary by reason of their mental disorder should be the option that is least restrictive and least likely to expose them to the risk of any stigmatisation, consistent with effective care and treatment, and it should also result in the least possible separation from family, carers, friends and community or interruption of their education, as is consistent with their wellbeing;
- all children and young people should receive the same access to educational provision as their peers;
- children and young people have as much right to expect their dignity to be respected as anyone else; and
- children and young people have as much right to privacy and confidentiality as anyone else.

PEOPLE WITH PARENTAL RESPONSIBILITY

36.5 Those with parental responsibility will usually, but not always, be the parents of the child or young person. Legally, under the Children Act 1989, consent to treat a child or young person is needed from only one person with parental responsibility, although it is good practice to involve both parents and others close to the child or young person in the decision-making process. However, if one person with parental responsibility strongly disagreed with the decision to treat and was likely to challenge it in court, it might be appropriate to seek authorisation from the court before relying on the consent of another person with parental responsibility.

36.6 It is essential that those taking decisions under the Mental Health Act are clear about who has parental responsibility and that they always request copies of any court orders for reference on the child or young person's medical or social service file. These orders may include care orders, residence orders, contact orders, evidence of appointment as the child or young person's guardian, parental responsibility agreements or orders under section 4 of the Children Act and any order under wardship. If the parents of a child or young person are separated, and the child or young person is living with one parent, the person responsible for the care and treatment of the patient should try to establish whether there is a residence order and, if so, in whose favour.

36.7 Once it is established who has parental responsibility for the child or young person, the person responsible for the care and treatment of the patient must determine whether a person with parental responsibility has the capacity, within the meaning of the MCA, to take a decision about the child or young person's treatment and whether the decision is within the zone of parental control (see paragraphs 36.9–36.15).

CHILDREN LOOKED AFTER BY THE LOCAL AUTHORITY

36.8 Where children or young people are looked after by the local authority (see section 22 of the Children Act 1989), treatment decisions should usually be discussed with the parent or other person with parental responsibility who continues to have parental responsibility for the child. If a child or young person is voluntarily accommodated by the local authority, parents or other people with parental responsibility have the same rights and responsibilities in relation to treatment as they would otherwise. If the child or young person is subject to a care order, the parents (or others with parental responsibility) share parental responsibility with the local authority, and it will be a matter for negotiation and agreement between them as to who should be consulted about treatment decisions. However, local authorities can, in the exercise of their powers under section 33(3)(b) of the Children Act 1989, limit the extent to which parents (or others) may exercise their parental responsibility. (See also paragraphs 36.80–36.82 for the duties of local authorities in relation to hospital patients.)

ZONE OF PARENTAL CONTROL

36.9 People with parental responsibility may in certain circumstances (see below) consent on behalf of a child under 16 to them being given medical treatment or being admitted informally for such treatment. Even in these circumstances, mental health professionals can rely on such consent only where it is within what in this guidance is called the "zone of parental control". This may also apply to young people of 16 or 17 years of age who are given medical treatment for mental disorder and who lack the ability to consent for themselves, and to decisions about such young people being admitted for such treatment informally if they lack capacity. The concept of the zone of parental control derives largely from case law from the European Court of Human Rights in Strasbourg.[1] It is difficult to have clear rules about what may fall in the zone, when so much depends on the particular facts of each case. Certain guidelines are set out below, but where there is doubt professionals should take legal advice so that account may be taken of the most recent case law.

1   For example Nielsen v Denmark (1989) 11 EHRR 175.

36.10 In assessing whether a particular decision falls within the parameters of the zone of parental control, two key questions must be considered:

- firstly, is the decision one that a parent would be expected to make, having regard both to what is considered to be normal practice in our society and to any relevant human rights decisions made by the courts?; and
- secondly, are there no indications that the parent might not act in the best interests of the child or young person?

36.11 The less confident a professional is that they can answer both questions in the affirmative, the more likely it will be that the decision in question falls outside the zone.

36.12 The parameters of the zone will vary from one case to the next: they are determined not only by social norms, but also by the circumstances and dynamics of a specific parent and child or young person. In assessing where the boundaries lie in any particular case, and so whether a parent's consent may be relied upon, mental health professionals might find it helpful to consider the following factors:

- the nature and invasiveness of what is to be done to the patient (including the extent to which their liberty will be curtailed) – the more extreme the intervention, the more likely it will be that it falls outside the zone;
- whether the patient is resisting – treating a child or young person who is resisting needs more justification;
- the general social standards in force at the time concerning the sorts of decisions it is acceptable for parents to make – anything that goes beyond the kind of decisions parents routinely make will be more suspect;
- the age, maturity and understanding of the child or young person – the greater these are, the more likely it will be that it should be the child or young person who takes the decision; and
- the extent to which a parent's interests may conflict with those of the child or young person – this may suggest that the parent will not act in the child or young person's best interests.

36.13 For example, in a case where the parents had gone through a particularly acrimonious divorce, it might not be possible to separate the decision about whether to admit the child to hospital from the parents' own hostilities, and it might not be possible to treat the parents as able to make an impartial decision. It might also not be appropriate to rely on the consent of a parent in circumstances where the mental health of the child or young person has led to chronic battles over control in the home. In another case, there might be concerns about the mental capacity of the person with parental responsibility, and whether they have capacity to take a decision about the child's treatment.

36.14 It is also possible that a decision on treatment could be outside the zone of parental control simply because of the nature of the proposed treatment, e g where, like electroconvulsive therapy (ECT), it could be considered particularly invasive or controversial.

36.15 In any case where reliance could not be placed on the consent of a person with parental responsibility, or on that of the child or young person, consideration should be given to alternative ways to treat them. One way would be to apply to have the child or young person detained under the Mental Health Act, but this is available only where they meet all the criteria for such detention. In cases where they do not meet the criteria, it may be appropriate to seek authorisation from the court.

Appendix 4.3

Balance Sheet in *An NHS Trust v MB* [2006] EWHC 507 (Fam)

This balance sheet is taken from *An NHS Trust v MB* [2006] EWHC 507 (Fam) at 60.

Guardian's 'Balance Sheet' 8.3.2006

The columns below deal with the benefits and burdens for MB, associated with ventilatory support continuing.

BENEFITS	BURDENS
MB can see during those periods when he can open his eyes (but see note regarding visual clarity under burdens).	
Possible/probable recognition of his parents and siblings & some pleasure/comfort in their presence (extent of ability to experience pleasure uncertain).	MB cannot move his body, head, arms or legs, although has some very restricted 'flickering' movement in his thumbs and some of his fingers and possibly foot.
Possible/probable recognition of those caring for him & some pleasure/comfort in their presence (extent of his ability to experience pleasure uncertain).	He is therefore reliant on others to be moved periodically, at least 8 times a day to prevent skin soreness and discomfort.
Possibly/probably MB derives some comfort /pleasure from Barney the Dinosaur/Teddy.	He is likely to be suffering some positional discomfort despite being repositioned by nursing staff.
He has the sensation of touch and can feel gentle strokes and his hand being held.	MB cannot open his eyes fully and his difficulty in raising his eyelids is likely to progress.
He can hear and it should be assumed for balancing purposes that MB may have the ability to enjoy listening to voices/a story/music now or in the future.	MB's is able to follow and see. However his clarity of vision is uncertain, as he has both vertical and horizontal jerky movements (nystagmus) and his ability to focus is likely to be diminished (his pupils do not constrict).
	MB has lost his facial expression, except slight movement of his eyebrows.
	MB has lost the ability to communicate his needs and wishes to others. This is permanent.

	MB's limited ability to respond is not consistent and repeated and therefore cannot be relied upon as a means for communication as to his distress and pain levels, wishes and needs by the nurses and clinicians.
	MB has lost the ability to interact with others or his environment.
	He cannot swallow and is fed via a gastrostomy tube.
	He cannot cough or clear his own secretions and he undergoes suctioning from his mouth, nose and throat day and night. At a time when MB was able to show physical and facial reactions it was clear this distressed him. Dr S described this as 'profound discomfort'. He requires ET suctioning at least every 3–4 hours (6–8 times a day). Dr Jardine's enquiries regarding frequency of deep suctioning 4–6 times daily [C7]. Dr Hughes: at least once a day.
	MB has to be 'bagged' when deep suctioning occurs. This is an unpleasant experience and one which distressed him in the past when he was able to react physically.
	The clinicians and experts agree that the use of IV lines, blood sampling, deep suction, bagging and respiratory physiotherapy are likely to be distressing to MB. Thus they are kept to a minimum at present.
	The combination of being handled numerous times a day and undergoing the routine intensive and now for MB mundane procedures, whilst being unable to voice his wishes are considered to be 'intolerable' for MB (Dr S).
	Whilst blood testing has been minimised as much as possible, MB has to undergo blood testing about monthly and whenever there is a deterioration, a likely desaturation and infection at which time he will undergo more frequent blood tests. It is not always possible to give effective pain relief for this.

	He has lived all bar 7 weeks of his life in a high dependency unit or intensive care ward in hospital and is likely to have to remain in an intensive care environment.
	There is uncertainty as to whether pain relief and sedation levels are sufficient.
	It is difficult for MB to be held and cuddled by his parents because of his condition and his necessary connection to life sustaining equipment.
	The Future
	He will continue to suffer from infections, which if treated with antibiotics will require venous access and blood testing. He is likely to suffer at least 3–4 chest infections a year.
	Chest infections will involve increased secretions, more frequent deep suctioning, blood testing, IV access and increased ventilator pressures and 'intensive chest physio' therefore pain and distress for MB who will require increased doses of pain killers and sedation.
	Intravenous access is particularly difficult with MB and has required a number of attempts in the past. There are only a limited number of sites and gaining IV access is painful. In cases of urgency sedation/pain relief may not be possible.
	MB has to be handled numerous times during the day and night for both non painful as well as painful and distressing procedures listed above.
	If MB underwent a tracheostomy, he would have to undergo a general anaesthetic and the ordeal and stress of minor surgery in his weakened state.
	If MB receives LTIV
	He will continue to need suctioning, including deep suctioning, bagging, physiotherapy, splints, repositioning all of which are known to cause pain/ discomfort.

	There will be continuing neuro–muscular deterioration, he will loose the ability to open his eyelids within several months & his eyesight will deteriorate further.
	He will lose the ability to lower his eyebrow losing all ability to communicate any measure of pain, distress or upset.
	His contractures will worsen and scoliosis will develop, both these will cause discomfort and pain.
	There will be dysfunction of his autonomic system.
	He will need increasing amounts of oxygen and ventilation pressure, which of itself can be uncomfortable.
	MB would need high levels of sedation all the time because some of the procedures he will need are unpredictable and he cannot communicate his needs or distress adequately.
	The increasing need for sedation will reduce his awareness of pain as well as those experiences which give him comfort at present.
	CPR would cause pain and distress as well as possible injury.

Appendix 5.1

Practice Direction
Family Proceedings: Court Bundles
(Universal Practice to be applied in all
Courts other than the Family
Proceedings Court)

27 July 2006

[1]   The President of the Family Division has issued this practice direction to achieve consistency across the country in all family courts (other than the Family Proceedings Court) in the preparation of court bundles and in respect of other related matters.

Application of the practice direction

[2.1]   Except as specified in para [2.4], and subject to specific directions given in any particular case, the following practice applies to:

(a)   all hearings of whatever nature (including but not limited to hearings in family proceedings, Civil Procedure Rules 1998 Part 7 and Part 8 claims and appeals) before a judge of the Family Division of the High Court wherever the court may be sitting;

(b)   all hearings in family proceedings in the Royal Courts of Justice (RCJ);

(c)   all hearings in the Principal Registry of the Family Division (PRFD) at First Avenue House; and

(d)   all hearings in family proceedings in all other courts except for Family Proceedings Courts.

[2.2]   'Hearings' includes all appearances before a judge or district judge, whether with or without notice to other parties and whether for directions or for substantive relief.

[2.3]   This practice direction applies whether a bundle is being lodged for the first time or is being re-lodged for a further hearing (see para [9.2]).

[2.4]   This practice direction does not apply to:

(a)   cases listed for one hour or less at a court referred to in para [2.1](c) or [2.1](d); or

(b)   the hearing of any urgent application if and to the extent that it is impossible to comply with it.

[2.5]   The designated family judge responsible for any court referred to in paragraph [2.1](c) or [2.1(d)] may, after such consultation as is appropriate (but in the case of hearings in the PRFD at First Avenue House only with the agreement of the Senior District Judge), direct that in that court this practice direction shall apply to all family proceedings irrespective of the length of hearing.

Responsibility for the preparation of the bundle

[3.1] A bundle for the use of the court at the hearing shall be provided by the party in the position of applicant at the hearing (or, if there are cross-applications, by the party whose application was first in time) or, if that person is a litigant in person, by the first listed respondent who is not a litigant in person.

[3.2] The party preparing the bundle shall paginate it. If possible the contents of the bundle shall be agreed by all parties.

Contents of the bundle

[4.1] The bundle shall contain copies of all documents relevant to the hearing, in chronological order from the front of the bundle, paginated and indexed, and divided into separate sections (each section being separately paginated) as follows:

(a) preliminary documents (see para [4.2]) and any other case management documents required by any other practice direction;
(b) applications and orders;
(c) statements and affidavits (which must be dated in the top right corner of the front page);
(d) care plans (where appropriate);
(e) experts' reports and other reports (including those of a guardian, children's guardian or litigation friend); and
(f) other documents, divided into further sections as may be appropriate.

Copies of notes of contact visits should normally not be included in the bundle unless directed by a judge.

[4.2] At the commencement of the bundle there shall be inserted the following documents (the preliminary documents):

(i) an up to date summary of the background to the hearing confined to those matters which are relevant to the hearing and the management of the case and limited, if practicable, to one A4 page;
(ii) a statement of the issue or issues to be determined (1) at that hearing and (2) at the final hearing;
(iii) a position statement by each party including a summary of the order or directions sought by that party (1) at that hearing and (2) at the final hearing;
(iv) an up to date chronology, if it is a final hearing or if the summary under (i) is insufficient;
(v) skeleton arguments, if appropriate, with copies of all authorities relied on; and
(vi) a list of essential reading for that hearing.

[4.3] Each of the preliminary documents shall state on the front page immediately below the heading the date when it was prepared and the date of the hearing for which it was prepared.

[4.4] The summary of the background, statement of issues, chronology, position statement and any skeleton arguments shall be cross-referenced to the relevant pages of the bundle.

[4.5] The summary of the background, statement of issues, chronology and reading list shall in the case of a final hearing, and shall so far as practicable in the case of any other hearing, each consist of a single document in a form agreed by all parties. Where the parties disagree as to the content the fact of their disagreement and their differing contentions shall be set out at the appropriate places in the document.

[4.6] Where the nature of the hearing is such that a complete bundle of all documents is unnecessary, the bundle (which need not be repaginated) may comprise only those documents necessary for the hearing, but

- (i) the summary (para [4.2](i)) must commence with a statement that the bundle is limited or incomplete; and
- (ii) the bundle shall if reasonably practicable be in a form agreed by all parties.

[4.7] Where the bundle is re-lodged in accordance with para [9.2], before it is re-lodged:

- (a) the bundle shall be updated as appropriate; and
- (b) all superseded documents (and in particular all outdated summaries, statements of issues, chronologies, skeleton arguments and similar documents) shall be removed from the bundle.

Format of the bundle

[5.1] The bundle shall be contained in one or more A4 size ring binders or lever arch files (each lever arch file being limited to 350 pages).

[5.2] All ring binders and lever arch files shall have clearly marked on the front and the spine:

- (a) the title and number of the case;
- (b) the court where the case has been listed;
- (c) the hearing date and time;
- (d) if known, the name of the judge hearing the case; and
- (e) where there is more than one ring binder or lever arch file, a distinguishing letter (A, B, C etc).

Timetable for preparing and lodging the bundle

[6.1] The party preparing the bundle shall, whether or not the bundle has been agreed, provide a paginated index to all other parties not less than 4 working days before the hearing (in relation to a case management conference to which the provisions of the *Protocol for Judicial Case Management in Public Law Children Act Cases* [2003] 2 FLR 719 apply, not less than 5 working days before the case management conference).

[6.2] Where counsel is to be instructed at any hearing, a paginated bundle shall (if not already in counsel's possession) be delivered to counsel by the person instructing that counsel not less than 3 working days before the hearing.

[6.3] The bundle (with the exception of the preliminary documents if and insofar as they are not then available) shall be lodged with the court not less than 2 working days before the hearing, or at such other time as may be specified by the judge.

[6.4] The preliminary documents shall be lodged with the court no later than 11 am on the day before the hearing and, where the hearing is before a judge of the High Court and the name of the judge is known, shall at the same time be sent by email to the judge's clerk.

Lodging the bundle

[7.1] The bundle shall be lodged at the appropriate office. If the bundle is lodged in the wrong place the judge may:

(a)   treat the bundle as having not been lodged; and

(b)   take the steps referred to in para [12].

[7.2]   Unless the judge has given some other direction as to where the bundle in any particular case is to be lodged (for example a direction that the bundle is to be lodged with the judge's clerk) the bundle shall be lodged:

(a)   for hearings in the RCJ, in the office of the Clerk of the Rules, Room TM 9.09, Royal Courts of Justice, Strand, London WC2A 2LL (DX 44450 Strand);

(b)   for hearings in the PRFD at First Avenue House, at the List Office counter, 3rd floor, First Avenue House, 42/49 High Holborn, London, WC1V 6NP (DX 396 Chancery Lane); and

(c)   for hearings at any other court, at such place as may be designated by the designated family judge or other judge at that court and in default of any such designation at the court office of the court where the hearing is to take place.

[7.3]   Any bundle sent to the court by post, DX or courier shall be clearly addressed to the appropriate office and shall show the date and place of the hearing on the outside of any packaging as well as on the bundle itself.

Lodging the bundle — additional requirements for cases being heard at First Avenue House or at the RCJ

[8.1]   In the case of hearings at the RCJ or First Avenue House, parties shall:

(a)   if the bundle or preliminary documents are delivered personally, ensure that they obtain a receipt from the clerk accepting it or them; and

(b)   if the bundle or preliminary documents are sent by post or DX, ensure that they obtain proof of posting or despatch.

The receipt (or proof of posting or despatch, as the case may be) shall be brought to court on the day of the hearing and must be produced to the court if requested. If the receipt (or proof of posting or despatch) cannot be produced to the court the judge may: (i) treat the bundle as having not been lodged; and (ii) take the steps referred to in para [12].

[8.2]   For hearings at the RCJ:

(a)   bundles or preliminary documents delivered after 11 am on the day before the hearing will not be accepted by the Clerk of the Rules and shall be delivered:
   (i) in a case where the hearing is before a judge of the High Court, directly to the clerk of the judge hearing the case;
   (ii) in a case where the hearing is before a Circuit Judge, Deputy High Court Judge or Recorder, directly to the messenger at the Judge's entrance to the Queen's Building (with telephone notification to the personal assistant to the Designated Family Judge, 020 7947 7155, that this has been done).

(b)   upon learning before which judge a hearing is to take place, the clerk to counsel, or other advocate, representing the party in the position of applicant shall no later than 3 pm the day before the hearing:
   (i) in a case where the hearing is before a judge of the High Court, telephone the clerk of the judge hearing the case;
   (ii) in a case where the hearing is before a circuit judge, deputy high court judge or recorder, telephone the personal assistant to the designated family judge;
   to ascertain whether the judge has received the bundle (including the preliminary documents) and, if not, shall organise prompt delivery by the applicant's solicitor.

Removing and re-lodging the bundle

[9.1] Following completion of the hearing the party responsible for the bundle shall retrieve it from the court immediately or, if that is not practicable, shall collect it from the court within 5 working days. Bundles which are not collected in due time may be destroyed.

[9.2] The bundle shall be re-lodged for the next and any further hearings in accordance with the provisions of this practice direction and in a form which complies with para [4.7].

Time estimates

[10.1] In every case a time estimate (which shall be inserted at the front of the bundle) shall be prepared which shall so far as practicable be agreed by all parties and shall:

(a)   specify separately: (i) the time estimated to be required for judicial pre-reading; (ii) the time required for hearing all evidence and submissions; and (iii) the time estimated to be required for preparing and delivering judgment; and

(b)   be prepared on the basis that before they give evidence all witnesses will have read all relevant filed statements and reports.

[10.2] Once a case has been listed, any change in time estimates shall be notified immediately by telephone (and then immediately confirmed in writing):

(a)   in the case of hearings in the RCJ, to the Clerk of the Rules;

(b)   in the case of hearings in the PRFD at First Avenue House, to the List Officer at First Avenue House; and

(c)   in the case of hearings elsewhere, to the relevant listing officer.

Taking cases out of the list

[11] As soon as it becomes known that a hearing will no longer be effective, whether as a result of the parties reaching agreement or for any other reason, the parties and their representatives shall immediately notify the court by telephone and by letter. The letter, which shall wherever possible be a joint letter sent on behalf of all parties with their signatures applied or appended, shall include:

(a)   a short background summary of the case;

(b)   the written consent of each party who consents and, where a party does not consent, details of the steps which have been taken to obtain that party's consent and, where known, an explanation of why that consent has not been given;

(c)   a draft of the order being sought; and

(d)   enough information to enable the court to decide: (i) whether to take the case out of the list; and (ii) whether to make the proposed order.

Penalties for failure to comply with the practice direction

[12] Failure to comply with any part of this practice direction may result in the judge removing the case from the list or putting the case further back in the list and may also result in a "wasted costs" order in accordance with CPR, Part 48.7 or some other adverse costs order.

Commencement of the practice direction and application of other practice directions

[13] This practice direction replaces *Practice Direction (Family Proceedings: Court Bundles) (10 March 2000)* [2000] 1 WLR 737, [2000] 1 FLR 536 and shall have effect from 2 October 2006.

[14] Any reference in any other practice direction to *Practice Direction (Family Proceedings: Court Bundles) (10 March 2000)* shall be read as if substituted by a reference to this practice direction.

[15] This practice direction should where appropriate be read in conjunction with *Practice Direction (Family Proceedings: Human Rights)* [2000] 1 WLR 1782, [2000] 2 FLR 429 and with *Practice Direction (Care Cases: Judicial Continuity and Judicial Case Management)* appended to the *Protocol for Judicial Case Management in Public Law Children Act Cases.*

In particular, nothing in this practice direction is to be read as removing or altering any obligation to comply with the requirements of the *Public Law Protocol.*

This Practice Direction is issued:

(i)   in relation to family proceedings, by the President of the Family Division, as the nominee of the Lord Chief Justice, with the agreement of the Lord Chancellor; and

(ii)   to the extent that it applies to proceedings to which s 5 of the Civil Procedure Act 1997 applies, by the Master of the Rolls as the nominee of the Lord Chief Justice, with the agreement of the Lord Chancellor.

The Right Honourable Sir Mark Potter
President of the Family Division & Head of Family Justice

The Right Honourable Sir Anthony Clarke
Master of the Rolls & Head of Civil Justice

Appendix 5.2

List of Court of Protection Forms

Note r 61(2) of the Court of Protection Rules 2007: 'The appropriate forms must be used in the case to which they apply, with such variations as the case requires, but not so as to omit any information or guidance which any form gives to the intended recipient.'

The forms are available on the Court Service website. Go to–
www.hmcourts-service.gov.uk and select 'Forms and Guidance', or go direct to–
www.hmcourts-service.gov.uk/HMCSCourtFinder/FormFinder.do

Note that selecting 'Court of Protection' in the 'Work Type' box on the website does not produce all the Court of Protection forms. The better approach is to put 'COP' in the 'Form Title/Leaflet Title' box.

The title of the forms all have the prefix 'COP' (for Court of Protection) and a number. They are often referred to as 'cop 1' etc (as opposed to 'C.O.P 1').

The list of forms is as follows:

COP1:   Court of Protection Application Form
COP1A: Annex A – Supporting information for property and affairs applications
COP1B: Annex B – Supporting information for personal welfare applications
COP2:   Permission Form
COP3:   Assessment of capacity
COP4:   Deputy's declaration
COP5:   Acknowledgement of service / notification
COP7:   Application to object to the registration of a Lasting Power of Attorney
COP8:   Application relating to the registration of an Enduring Power or Attorney
COP9:   Application notice
COP10:   Application notice for applications to be joined as a party
COP12:   Special undertaking by trustees
COP14:   "Proceedings about you in the Court of Protection" [Form for notifying P]
COP15:   Notice that an application form has been issued
COP17:   Request for directions relating to an objection to the registration of an Enduring Power of Attorney
COP20:   Certificate of service / non-service / notification / non-notification
COP22:   Certificate of suitability of litigation friend
COP23:   Certificate of failure or refusal of witness to attend before an examiner
COP24:   Witness statement
COP25:   Affidavit
COP29:   Notice of hearing for committal order
COP30:   Notice of change of solicitor
COP31:   Notice of intention to file evidence by deposition
COP35:   Appellant's notice
COP36:   Respondent's Notice
COP37:   Skeleton Argument

There are also guidance notes to accompany the forms as well as the following general guidance:

COP42:   Making an application to the Court of Protection
COP43:   A guide for Deputies appointed by the Court of Protection

The following forms are for use in applications concerning the Deprivation of Liberty Safeguards under MCA s 21:

COPDLA: Application form – For urgent consideration
COPDLB: Declaration of exceptional urgency
COPDLC: Permission
COPDLD: Certificate of service/non-service/notification/non-notification
COPDLE: Acknowledgment of service/notification

Appendix 5.3

List of Court of Protection Practice Directions

The Court of Protection's Practice Directions are given under MCA, s 52 and are available on the HMCS website. Go to www.hmcourts-service.gov.uk, select 'Legal/Professional' from the left-hand side, then 'Practice Directions' from the left-hand side, then 'Court of Protection' from the right hand side; or go direct to www.hmcourts-service.gov.uk/cms/14705.htm .

Each Practice Direction is identified with a number, a letter and a title. The number is the Part of the Rules to which it relates. The Practice Directions relevant to each Part are each given a sequential letter.

The following is a complete list of the practice directions. Those likely to be of little or no relevance to any medical treatment cases are in square brackets. Those in bold are supplied as Appendices.

4A: Court documents
4B: Statements of truth
6A: Service
7A: Notifying P
8A: Permission
9A: The application form
9B: Notification of other persons that an application form has been issued
9C: Responding to an application
[9D: Applications by currently appointed deputies, attorneys and donees in relation to P's property and affairs]
9E: Applications relating to serious medical treatment [Appendix 5.4]
[9F: Applications relating to statutory wills, codicils, settlements and other dealings with P's property.]
[9G: Applications to appoint or discharge a trustee]
[9H: Applications relating to the registration of enduring powers of attorney]
10A: Applications within proceedings
10B: Urgent and interim applications [Appendix 5.5]
11A: Human Rights Act 1998
12A: Court's jurisdiction to be exercised by certain judges
12B: Procedure for disputing the court's jurisdiction
13A: Hearings (including reporting restrictions)
14A: Written evidence
14B: Admissions, evidence and depositions
[14C: Fees for examiners of the court]
14D: Witness summons
14E: Section 49 reports
15A: Expert evidence
17A: Litigation friend
18A: Change of solicitor
19A: Costs in the court of protection
20A: Appeals

21A: Contempt of court

[22A: Transitional provisions]

[22B: Transitory provisions]

[22C: Appeals against decisions made under Part 7 of the Mental Health Act 1983 or under the Enduring Powers of Attorney Act 1985 which are brought on or after commencement]

[23A: Request for directions where notice of objection prevents public guardian from registering enduring power of attorney]

23B: Where P ceases to lack capacity or dies

There is also a Practice Direction entitled 'Deprivation of liberty applications' supplementing Part 10A of the Court of Protection Rules. This should not be confused with Practice Direction A to Part 10 of the Rules (entitled 'Applications within proceedings') in the above list.

Appendix 5.4

Court of Protection Practice Direction 9E Practice Direction – How to start proceedings

This practice direction supplements Part 9 of the Court of Protection Rules 2007

PRACTICE DIRECTION E – APPLICATIONS RELATING TO SERIOUS MEDICAL TREATMENT

GENERAL

1.   Rule 71 enables a practice direction to make additional or different provision in relation to specified applications.

Applications to which this practice direction applies

2.   This practice direction sets out the procedure to be followed where the application concerns serious medical treatment in relation to P.

Meaning of 'serious medical treatment' in relation to the Rules and this practice direction

3.   Serious medical treatment means treatment which involves providing, withdrawing or withholding treatment in circumstances where:
   (a)   in a case where a single treatment is being proposed, there is a fine balance between its benefits to P and the burdens and risks it is likely to entail for him;
   (b)   in a case where there is a choice of treatments, a decision as to which one to use is finely balanced; or
   (c)   the treatment, procedure or investigation proposed would be likely to involve serious consequences for P.

4.   'Serious consequences' are those which could have a serious impact on P, either from the effects of the treatment, procedure or investigation itself or its wider implications. This may include treatments, procedures or investigations which:
   (a)   cause, or may cause, serious and prolonged pain, distress or side effects;
   (b)   have potentially major consequences for P; or
   (c)   have a serious impact on P's future life choices.

Matters which should be brought to the court

5.   Cases involving any of the following decisions should be regarded as serious medical treatment for the purpose of the Rules and this practice direction, and should be brought to the court:

    (a) decisions about the proposed withholding or withdrawal of artificial nutrition and hydration from a person in a permanent vegetative state or a minimally conscious state;

    (b) cases involving organ or bone marrow donation by a person who lacks capacity to consent; and

    (c) cases involving non-therapeutic sterilisation of a person who lacks capacity to consent.

6.   Examples of serious medical treatment may include:

    (a) certain terminations of pregnancy in relation to a person who lacks capacity to consent to such a procedure;

    (b) a medical procedure performed on a person who lacks capacity to consent to it, where the procedure is for the purpose of a donation to another person;

    (c) a medical procedure or treatment to be carried out on a person who lacks capacity to consent to it, where that procedure or treatment must be carried out using a degree of force to restrain the person concerned;

    (d) an experimental or innovative treatment for the benefit of a person who lacks capacity to consent to such treatment; and

    (e) a case involving an ethical dilemma in an untested area.

7.   There may be other procedures or treatments not contained in the list in paragraphs 5 and 6 above which can be regarded as serious medical treatment. Whether or not a procedure is regarded as serious medical treatment will depend on the circumstances and the consequences for the patient.

Consultation with the Official Solicitor

8.   Members of the Official Solicitor's staff are prepared to discuss applications in relation to serious medical treatment before an application is made. Any enquiries about adult medical and welfare cases should be addressed to a family and medical litigation lawyer at the Office of the Official Solicitor, 81 Chancery Lane, London WC2A 1DD, ph: 020 7911 7127, fax: 020 7911 7105, email: enquiries@offsol.gsi.gov.uk .

Parties to proceedings

9.   The person bringing the application will always be a party to proceedings, as will a respondent named in the application form who files an acknowledgment of service.[1] In cases involving issues as to serious medical treatment, an organisation which is, or will be, responsible for providing clinical or caring services to P should usually be named as a respondent in the application form (where it is not already the applicant in the proceedings).

    (Practice direction B accompanying Part 9 sets out the persons who are to be notified that an application form has been issued.)

10.   The court will consider whether anyone not already a party should be joined as a party to the proceedings. Other persons with sufficient interest may apply to be

joined as parties to the proceedings[2] and the court has a duty to identify at as early a stage as possible who the parties to the proceedings should be.[3]

1   Rule 73(1).
2   Rule 75.
3   Rule 5(2)(b)(ii).

Allocation of the case

11.   Where an application is made to the court in relation to:
    (a)   the lawfulness of withholding or withdrawing artificial nutrition and hydration from a person in a permanent vegetative state, or a minimally conscious state; or
    (b)   a case involving an ethical dilemma in an untested area,
    the proceedings (including permission, the giving of any directions, and any hearing) must be conducted by the President of the Court of Protection or by another judge nominated by the President.

12.   Where an application is made to the court in relation to serious medical treatment (other than that outlined in paragraph 11) the proceedings (including permission, the giving of any directions, and any hearing) must be conducted by a judge of the court who has been nominated as such by virtue of section 46(2)(a) to (c) of the Act (i.e. the President of the Family Division, the Chancellor or a puisne judge of the High Court).

Matters to be considered at the first directions hearing

13.   Unless the matter is one which needs to be disposed of urgently, the court will list it for a first directions hearing.

    (Practice direction B accompanying Part 10 sets out the procedure to be followed for urgent applications.)

14.   The court may give such directions as it considers appropriate. If the court has not already done so, it should in particular consider whether to do any or all of the following at the first directions hearing:
    (a)   decide whether P should be joined as party to the proceedings, and give directions to that effect;
    (b)   if P is to be joined as a party to the proceedings, decide whether the Official Solicitor should be invited to act as a litigation friend or whether some other person should be appointed as a litigation friend;
    (c)   identify anyone else who has been notified of the proceedings and who has filed an acknowledgment and applied to be joined as a party to proceedings, and consider that application; and
    (d)   set a timetable for the proceedings including, where possible, a date for the final hearing.

15.   The court should also consider whether to give any of the other directions listed in rule 85(2).

16.   The court will ordinarily make an order pursuant to rule 92 that any hearing shall be held in public, with restrictions to be imposed in relation to publication of information about the proceedings.

Declarations

17. Where a declaration is needed, the order sought should be in the following or similar terms:
    - That P lacks capacity to make a decision in relation to the (proposed medical treatment or procedure).
      E.g. 'That P lacks capacity to make a decision in relation to sterilisation by vasectomy'; and
    - That, having regard to the best interests of P, it is lawful for the (proposed medical treatment or procedure) to be carried out by (proposed healthcare provider).
18. Where the application is for the withdrawal of life-sustaining treatment, the order sought should be in the following or similar terms:
    - That P lacks capacity to consent to continued life-sustaining treatment measures (and specify what these are); and
    - That, having regard to the best interests of P, it is lawful for (name of healthcare provider) to withdraw the life-sustaining treatment from P.

Court of Protection
Practice Direction 10B
Practice Direction — Applications
within proceedings

This practice direction supplements Part 10 of the Court of Protection Rules 2007

PRACTICE DIRECTION B – URGENT AND INTERIM APPLICATIONS

Urgent applications and applications without notice

1. These fall into two categories:
    (a) applications where an application form has already been issued; and
    (b) applications where an application form has not yet been issued,
    and, in both cases, where notice of the application has not been given to the respondent(s).
2. Wherever possible, urgent applications should be made within court hours. These applications will normally be dealt with at court but cases of extreme urgency may be dealt with by telephone. Telephone contact may be made with the court during business hours on 084 5330 2900.
3. When it is not possible to apply within court hours, contact should be made with the security office at the Royal Courts of Justice on 020 7947 6000. The security officer should be informed of the nature of the case.
4. In some cases, urgent applications arise because applications to the court have not been pursued sufficiently promptly. This is undesirable, and should be avoided. A judge who has concerns that the facility for urgent applications may have been abused may require the applicant or the applicant's representative to attend at a subsequent hearing to provide an explanation for the delay.

Applications without notice

5. The applicant should take steps to advise the respondent(s) by telephone or in writing of the application, unless justice would be defeated if notice were given.
6. If an order is made without notice to any other party, the order will ordinarily contain:
    (a) an undertaking by the applicant to the court to serve the application notice, evidence in support and any order made on the respondent and any other person the court may direct as soon as practicable or as ordered by the court; and
    (b) a return date for a further hearing at which the other parties can be present.

Applications where an application form has already been issued

7.   An application notice using form COP9, evidence in support and a draft order should be filed with the court in advance of the hearing wherever possible. If the order sought is unusually long or complex, a disk containing the draft order sought should be made available to the court in a format compatible with the word processing software used by the court. (Queries in relation to software should be directed to a court officer.)

     (Practice direction A accompanying Part 10 sets out more detailed requirements in relation to an application notice.)

8.   If an application is made before the application notice has been filed, a draft order should be provided at the hearing, and the application notice and evidence in support must be filed with the court on the next working day or as ordered by the court.

Applications made before the issue of an application form

9.   Where the exceptional urgency of the matter requires, an application may be started without filing an application form if the court allows it (but where time permits an application should be made in writing). In such a case, an application may be made to the court orally. The court will require an undertaking that the application form in the terms of the oral application be filed on the next working day, or as required by the court.

10. An order made before the issue of the application form should state in the title after the names of the applicant and the respondent, 'the Applicant and Respondent in an Intended Application'.

Applications made by telephone

11. Where it is not possible to file an application form or notice, applications can be made by telephone in accordance with the contact details set out in paragraphs 2 and 3 of this practice direction.

Hearings conducted by telephone

12. When a hearing is to take place by telephone, if practical it should be conducted by tape-recorded conference call, and arranged (and paid for in the first instance) by the applicant. All parties and the judge should be informed that the call is being recorded by the service provider. The applicant should order a transcript of the hearing from the service provider.

Type of case may be indicated in the application notice

13. The applicant may indicate in the application notice that the application:
     (a)   is urgent;
     (b)   should be dealt with by a particular judge or level of judge within the court;
     (c)   requires a hearing; or
     (d)   any combination of the above.

Urgent cases in relation to serious medical treatment

14.   Practice direction E accompanying Part 9 sets out the procedure in relation to applications relating to serious medical treatment. Practice direction A accompanying Part 12 sets out the manner in which those cases are to be allocated.

Interim injunction applications

15.   Rule 82 enables the court to grant an interim injunction.

16.   Any judge of the court may vary or discharge an interim injunction granted by any judge of the court.

17.   Any order for an interim injunction must set out clearly what the respondent or any other person must or must not do. The order may contain an undertaking by the applicant to pay any damages which the respondent(s) sustains which the court considers the applicant should pay.

Appendix 5.6

Suggested directions to seek in an application form before the first directions hearing in a medical treatment case in the Court of Protection

- The Applicant shall have permission to make the application.
- [P – give name] is joined as a party (First Respondent) to these proceedings.
- The Official Solicitor shall be appointed, subject to his consent, as litigation friend to [P – give name].
- Upon the Official Solicitor so consenting, the requirement to notify P of the proceedings shall be dispensed with under r 49.
- The matter shall henceforth be heard by a judge of the Family Division of the High Court sitting as a nominated judge of the Court of Protection. The matter shall be transferred to the Royal Courts of Justice to be listed for a first directions hearing before such a judge by [insert date].

Appendix 5.7

Sample draft order for first directions hearing in a medical treatment case in the court of protection

NB: assume that the directions in Appendix 5.6 have already been made.

IN THE COURT OF PROTECTION   CASE NO: COP 12345678

IN THE MATTER OF THE MENTAL CAPACITY ACT 2005

IN THE MATTER OF MR P (DOB 1.1.1950)

B E T W E E N:

THE TRUST   Applicant

and

MR P

(by the Official Solicitor his Litigation Friend)

Person to whom the Application relates and

First Respondent

and

MRS P   Second Respondent

DRAFT ORDER ON BEHALF OF THE APPLICANT FOR HEARING ON 1.10.10

UPON HEARING Mr Able Drafter[1], Counsel for the Applicant; Miss Fancy Pleader, Counsel for the First Respondent; and Mr Technical Whizz, Counsel for the Second Respondent

UPON READING the documents in the hearing bundle

AND UPON the parties, institutions and witnesses being identified in a Schedule to this Order

IT IS DECLARED IN THE INTERIM THAT:

1. The First Respondent lacks capacity to make decisions about
    [   ].

2. Having regard to the First Respondent's best interests, it is lawful for
    [   ].

AND IT IS ORDERED THAT:

3.   Pursuant to paragraph 16 of Court of Protection Practice Direction 9E, this and future hearings shall be in public.

4.   For the purposes of these proceedings:
      (a) the First Applicant shall be referred to as "The Trust";
      (b) the First Respondent shall be referred to as "Mr P";
      (c) the Second Respondent shall be referred to as "Mrs P";
      (d) the establishment at which the First Respondent is currently being cared for shall be referred to as "the Unit";
      (e) the establishment at which it is proposed that the First Respondent will receive medical treatment shall be referred to as "the Hospital";
      (f) any witnesses, other than an expert witness, from whom evidence is adduced in these proceedings, whether by witness statement or otherwise in writing or orally, shall be referred to by the initial of their respective surname;
      (g) at trial any witnesses, other than expert witnesses, who give oral evidence shall be permitted not to disclose their respective name and address in open court.

5.   There shall be no report of this matter which identifies the First Respondent, whether by name, or by naming members of his family, giving her or their location, or naming, or giving the location of, the clinicians, healthcare professionals and/or the establishments which are or will be or have been responsible for his care or treatment.

6.   The Applicant shall by 4pm on [   ] serve paginated copies of its records concerning the First Respondent on the parties.

7.   The First Respondent's current and any previous GP shall by 4pm on [   ] serve paginated copies of its records concerning the First Respondent on the parties, and shall have liberty to apply, upon notice to the parties, to set aside or vary this paragraph of this order.

8.   The parties shall have permission jointly to instruct:
      (a) an expert psychiatrist to provide a report upon [eg capacity to litigate, capacity to make decisions about [   ]; matters relevant to best interests with regard to future management of [   ]]
      (b) an expert [of appropriate discipline] to provide a report upon [eg matters relevant to best interests with regard to future management of [   ]].

9.   The parties shall agree the identity of both of the above experts by 4pm on [   ].

10.   The parties shall agree the letters of instruction to the experts by 4pm on [   ] which shall be sent by [whichever party is most appropriate] to the experts by 4pm on [   ].

11.   The experts shall be permitted to see all documents filed and served in the case and to examine and interview the First Respondent.

12.   The experts' reports shall be filed and served on the parties by 4pm on [   ].

13.   The costs of the instruction of the above experts shall be shared equally between the parties and shall be a proper disbursement for the purposes of a public funding certificate.

14.   The Applicant and the Second Respondent shall each file and serve the factual evidence upon which they wish to rely by 4pm on [   ].

15.   The Official Solicitor shall have permission to file and serve a statement by 4pm on [   ].

16.   There shall be a further directions hearing with a time estimate of 1 hour before a Judge of the Family Division sitting as a nominated Judge of the Court of

Protection on [   ], unless the Applicant informs the Court by 4pm on [   ] that all parties agree that no hearing is required.

17. The parties shall file and serve their position statements and / or skeleton arguments for the final hearing by 4pm on [   ].

18. By 4pm on [   ] the Applicant shall circulate to the parties a draft index which shall be agreed if possible by 4pm on [   ].

19. The Applicant shall file and serve an agreed bundle for the final hearing by 4pm on [   ] (including a bundle for the witness box).

20. The matter shall be listed for final hearing in public on [   ] with a time estimate of [   ] before a Judge of the Family Division sitting as a nominated Judge of the Court of Protection.

21. The Applicant shall pay one half of the costs of the Official Solicitor of these proceedings, to be subject to detailed assessment if not agreed.

22. Liberty to apply.

SCHEDULE

Name	Party title	Referred to as
NEWTOWN NHS HOSPITAL TRUST	Applicant	The Trust
PETER PIPER	First Respondent	Mr P
PETRA PIPER	Second Respondent	Mrs P
DR V. CARING (Consultant Physician)		Dr C
OLDTOWN CENTRE, NEWTOWN		The Unit
NEWTOWN HOSPITAL, NEWTOWN		The Hospital

1   It is sometimes suggested that counsels' name should not appear. However, there is no universal practice. The authors consider it useful to include counsels' names, so that on future occasions (for example at a later directions hearing if an issue arises about what was said on an earlier occasion) one can see who represented the parties.

Appendix 5.8

Originating summons form

Originating summons

No ...... of **20**

IN THE HIGH COURT OF JUSTICE

PRINCIPAL REGISTRY OF THE FAMILY DIVISION

NOT FOR SERVICE OUT OF JURISDICTION

In the matter of

a minor

and in the matter of the Supreme Court Act 1981

Between   Plaintiff

and   Defendant

To

of

Let the defendant within 14 days after service of this summons on him, counting the day of service, return the accompanying Acknowledgment of Service to the Principal Registry of the Family Division

By this summons, which is issued on the application of the plaintiff

of the plaintiff claims against the defendant

The date of birth of the minor is

The present whereabouts of the minor are

The interest in, or relationship to, the minor of the plaintiff is

The interest in, or relationship to, the minor of the defendant is

See over
FD582

If the defendant does not acknowledge service, such judgment may be given or order made against or in relation to him as the Court may think just and expedient.

Dated the .... day of 20

NOTE: This summons may not be served later than 4 calendar months (or, if leave is required to effect service out of the jurisdiction, 6 months) beginning with the above date unless renewed by order of the Court.

This summons was taken out by ....

Of ....

[Solicitor for the said] Plaintiff whose address is as stated above.

IMPORTANT NOTICE: It is a contempt of Court, which may be punished by imprisonment, to take any child named in this summons out of England and Wales, even to Scotland, Northern Ireland, the Republic of Ireland, the Channel Islands or the Isle of Man, without the leave of the Court.

IMPORTANT

Directions for Acknowledgment of Service are given with the accompanying form

TO THE DEFENDANT(S) (Other than the minor)

TAKE NOTICE that, pursuant to Rule 5 of the Family Proceedings Rules

(1)   You must forthwith after being served with this summons lodge in the above-mentioned Registry a notice stating your address and the whereabouts of the minor (or, if it be the case, that you are unaware of the minor's whereabouts), and, unless the Court otherwise directs, you must serve a copy of such notice on the plaintiff; and

(2)   if you subsequently change your address or become aware of any change in the minor's whereabouts you must, unless the court otherwise directs, lodge in the above-mentioned Registry notice of your new address or of the new whereabouts of the minor, as the case may be, and serve a copy of such notice on every party.

Any notice required to be lodged in the above-mentioned Registry should be sent or delivered to the Chief Clerk, Principal Registry of the Family Division, Family Proceedings Department, First Avenue House, 42–49, High Holborn, London WC1V 6NP. The court office at the Principal Registry is open from 10.00am until 4.30pm on Mondays to Fridays.

Appendix 5.9

Example of information likely to be required in Acknowledgment of Service of Originating Summons

In the High Court of Justice

Principal Registry of the Family Division

Plaintiff

Defendant

(Your) (Defendant's) full name ....

(Do you) (Does the defendant) intend to contest:

the whole of the plaintiff's claim?   ☐

part of the plaintiff's claim?   ☐

none of the plaintiff's claim?   ☐

I acknowledge that (I have) (the defendant has) been served with a copy of the originating summons

Signed .... Date ....

Defendant (Solicitor for the defendant)

Address to which papers about this case should be sent:

....

....

Solicitor's ref. .... Telephone no. .... Fax no. ....

President's Direction (Representation of Children in Family Proceedings Pursuant to Family Proceedings Rules 1991, rule 9.5)

[1] The proper conduct and disposal of proceedings concerning a child which are not specified proceedings within the meaning of s 41 of the Children Act 1989 may require the child to be made a party. Rule 9.5 of the Family Proceedings Rules 1991 (FPR) provides for the appointment of a guardian ad litem (a guardian) for a child party unless the child is of sufficient understanding and can participate as a party in the proceedings without a guardian, as permitted by FPR r 9.2A.

[2] Making the child a party to the proceedings is a step that will be taken only in cases which involve an issue of significant difficulty and consequently will occur in only a minority of cases. Before taking the decision to make the child a party, consideration should be given to whether an alternative route might be preferable, such as asking an officer of the Children and Family Court Advisory and Support Service (CAFCASS) to carry out further work or by making a referral to social services or possibly, by obtaining expert evidence.

[3] The decision to make the child a party will always be exclusively that of the judge, made in the light of the facts and circumstances of the particular case. The following are offered, solely by way of guidance, as circumstances which may justify the making of an order:

[3.1] Where a CAFCASS officer has notified the court that in his opinion the child should be made a party (see FPR r 4.11B(6)).

[3.2] Where the child has a standpoint or interests which are inconsistent with or incapable of being represented by any of the adult parties.

[3.3] Where there is an intractable dispute over residence or contact, including where all contact has ceased, or where there is irrational but implacable hostility to contact or where the child may be suffering harm associated with the contact dispute.

[3.4] Where the views and wishes of the child cannot be adequately met by a report to the court.

[3.5] Where an older child is opposing a proposed course of action.

[3.6] Where there are complex medical or mental health issues to be determined or there are other unusually complex issues that necessitate separate representation of the child.

[3.7] Where there are international complications outside child abduction, in particular where it may be necessary for there to be discussions with overseas authorities or a foreign court.

[3.8] Where there are serious allegations of physical, sexual or other abuse in relation to the child or there are allegations of domestic violence not capable of being resolved with the help of a CAFCASS officer.

[3.9] Where the proceedings concern more than one child and the welfare of the children is in conflict or one child is in a particularly disadvantaged position.

[3.10] Where there is a contested issue about blood testing.

[4] It must be recognised that separate representation of the child may result in a delay in the resolution of the proceedings. When deciding whether to direct that a child be made a party, the court will take into account the risk of delay or other facts adverse to the welfare of the child. The court's primary consideration will be the best interests of the child.

[5] When a child is made a party and a guardian is to be appointed:

[5.1] Consideration should first be given to appointing an officer of CAFCASS as guardian. Before appointing an officer, the court will cause preliminary enquires to be made of CAFCASS. For the procedure, reference should be made to *CAFCASS Practice Note (Representation of Children in Family Proceedings Pursuant to Family Proceedings Rules 1991, Rule 9.5)* (6 April 2004) [2004] 1 FLR 1190.

[5.2] If CAFCASS is unable to provide a guardian without delay, or if for some other reason the appointment of a CAFCASS officer is not appropriate, FPR r 9.5(1) makes further provision for the appointment of a guardian.

[6] In cases proceeding in a county court, the court may, at the same time as deciding whether to join a child as a party, consider whether the nature of the case or the complexity or importance of the issues require transfer of the case to the High Court.

[7] Issued with the concurrence and approval of the Lord Chancellor.

Elizabeth Butler-Sloss

President
5 April 2004

Appendix 5.11

CAFCASS and the National Assembly for Wales Practice Note (Appointment of guardians in private law proceedings)

June 2006

Introduction:

[1] This Practice Note applies to both England and Wales and supersedes the *CAFCASS Practice Note (Representation of Children in Family Proceedings Pursuant to Family Proceedings Rules 1991, Rule 9.5)* [2004] 1 FLR 1190. It is issued with the approval of the President of the Family Division and should be read together with the President's Practice Direction dated 5 April 2004.

[2] The term 'CAFCASS Legal' throughout the Practice Note refers to the CAFCASS in house lawyers; the term 'the CAFCASS High Court Team' refers to the team of CAFCASS practitioners known by that name at the address given at para [11] below; the term 'CAFCASS CYMRU' refers to the division of the National Assembly for Wales to whom the functions of the Assembly under Part 4 of the Children Act 2004 have been delegated; the term 'Assembly lawyers' refers to lawyers employed by the National Assembly for Wales to provide legal advice, support and representation to Welsh family proceedings officers.

Appointment of CAFCASS officers and Welsh family proceedings officers in private law proceedings pursuant to r 9.5 of the Family Proceedings Rules 1991 (FPR 1991)

[3] Where the court has decided to appoint an officer of CAFCASS or Welsh family proceedings officer as guardian ad litem (guardian) the order should simply state that:

> '[name of the child] is made party to the proceedings and pursuant to rule 9.5 FPR an officer of CAFCASS/a Welsh family proceedings officer be appointed as his/her guardian.'

[4] Courts are to endeavour to send orders to CAFCASS or to CAFCASS CYMRU as appropriate on the day of the hearing but, in any event, no less than 2 working days following the hearing (or 2 working days following the order being received by the court office/associate). Where suitable arrangements exist, orders are to be sent by email. Where it is not possible to email orders they should be faxed or sent by first class post. Documents in adoption proceedings and Human Fertilisation and Embryology Act 1990 proceedings are not to be sent by email.

[5] The decision about which particular officer of CAFCASS or Welsh family proceedings officer to allocate as guardian is a matter for CAFCASS or CAFCASS CYMRU as appropriate. However, it is helpful if the court records whether there is any reason why any CAFCASS officer or Welsh family proceedings officer who has dealt with the matter so far should not continue to deal with it in the role of guardian.

County Court

[6]   In cases proceeding in the county court, the order making the r 9.5 appointment should be sent to the CAFCASS/CAFCASS CYMRU office responsible for private law cases in the area for which the child is currently living. For county court cases proceeding in the Principal Registry, the order and the court file should be sent to the CAFCASS office at the Principal Registry for referral to the relevant local office or directly to CAFCASS CYMRU.

[7]   The CAFCASS High Court Team does not undertake work proceeding in the county court.

High Court

[8]   In private law cases proceeding in the High Court where a guardian is appointed, the case will be referred either to the CAFCASS High Court Team (where child is resident in England); the Assembly lawyers (where child is resident in Wales) or to the relevant local CAFCASS office. Guidance as to which cases should be referred to the CAFCASS High Court Team/the Assembly lawyers is set out at para [10] below.

[9]   In proceedings brought under the Child Abduction and Custody Act 1985, the CAFCASS team based at the Principal Registry will continue to assist the High Court and provide reports in cases where the child is usually resident in England. Where the child is usually resident in Wales, the matter should be referred to the relevant regional office of CAFCASS CYMRU (National Office (North), Porthdy Grosvenor, 1 Grosvenor Road, Wrexham, LL11 1BS, telephone: 01978 368479; National Office (South), Llys y Delyn, 107–111 Cowbridge Road East, Cardiff, CF11 9AG, telephone: 02920 647 926).

[10]   The following categories of case involving an appointment pursuant to r 9.5 of the FPR 1991 or otherwise where the child is a party, should be referred to the CAFCASS High Court Team/Assembly lawyers:

10.1   reporting restriction orders arising in a children's case;

10.2   exceptionally complex adoption cases including exceptionally complex cases involving inter country adoption;

10.3   all medical treatment cases where the child is old enough to have views which need to be taken into account, or where there are particularly difficult ethical issues such as the withdrawal of treatment, unless the issue arises in existing proceedings already being handled locally when the preferred arrangement will usually be for the matter to continue to be dealt with locally but with additional advice provided by CAFCASS Legal/Assembly lawyers if necessary;

10.4   any free-standing human rights applications pursuant to s 7(1)(a) of the Human Rights Act 1998 in which it is thought that it may be possible and appropriate for any part to be played by CAFCASS/CAFCASS CYMRU or its officers;

10.5   exceptionally complex international cases particularly where there is a dispute as to which country's courts should have jurisdiction over the child's affairs;

10.6   applications in wardship and applications made under the High Court's inherent jurisdiction.

[11]   In cases referred to the CAFCASS High Court Team, a copy of the court file, including the order appointing the CAFCASS officer and the record of the court's reasons, should be sent for the attention of The Manager, CAFCASS High Court Team, 8th Floor, South Quay Plaza 3, 189 Marsh Wall, London, E14 9SH (fax no: 0207 510

7104) or by Document Exchange to DX 42691 Isle of Dogs. If the appointment is urgent, then the judge or a member of the Court Service is encouraged, if possible, to telephone on 020 7510 7089 to discuss the matter before an order is made.

[12] In cases referred to the Assembly lawyers a copy of the court file, including the order appointing the Welsh family proceedings officer and the record of the court's reasons, should be sent for the attention of the Social Care Team, Directorate of Legal Services, National Assembly for Wales, Cathays Park, Cardiff, CF10 3NQ (fax no: 02920 823834). If the appointment is urgent then the judge or a member of the Court Service is encouraged, if possible, to telephone on 02920 826813 to discuss the matter before an order is made.

[13] In cases falling outside the categories at para [10] above, the order making the appointment should be sent to the CAFCASS office/CAFCASS CYMRU office for the area where the child is currently living. The exception to this is cases proceeding in the Principal Registry when the order together with the court file should be sent to the CAFCASS office at the Principal Registry for referral to the relevant local office or directly to CAFCASS CYMRU.

[14] The office that is to be responsible for the matter will notify the court of the name and professional address and telephone number of the particular officer who will act as guardian. If for whatever reason there is likely to be any significant delay in an officer being made available CAFCASS/CAFCASS CYMRU will notify the court accordingly to enable the court to consider whether some other proper person should instead be appointed as guardian.

[15] If the officer to be appointed as guardian is a member of the CAFCASS High Court Team there may be no need for a solicitor for the child also to be appointed as the litigation may be conducted in house pursuant to s 15 of the Criminal Justice and Court Services Act 2000.

CAFCASS Legal or Assembly lawyers acting as advocate to the court

[16] CAFCASS Legal or Assembly lawyers may be invited to act or instruct counsel as advocate to the court in family proceedings in which the welfare of children is or may be in question.

Provision of general assistance by CAFCASS Legal and Assembly lawyers

[17] CAFCASS Legal and Assembly lawyers are available to offer advice to judges and other professionals engaged in family proceedings in which the welfare of children is or may be in question without necessarily being appointed as advocate to the court.

[18] Lawyers at CAFCASS Legal take it in turn to carry a mobile telephone through which they can be contacted any day of the year by the High Court out of hours duty judge if their help is needed, for instance in relation to a medical treatment emergency.

Anthony Douglas
Chief Executive
CAFCASS

Dafydd Ifans
Chief Executive
CAFCASS CYMRU

National Assembly for Wales

Appendix 5.12

President's Practice Direction (Applications for Reporting Restriction Orders)

18 March 2005

[1]   This direction applies to any application in the Family Division founded on European Convention rights (European Convention for the Protection of Human Rights and Fundamental Freedoms 1950) for an order restricting publication of information about children or incapacitated adults.

[2]   *Applications to be heard in the High Court*

Orders can only be made in the High Court and are normally dealt with by a judge of the Family Division. If the need for an order arises in existing proceedings in the county court, judges should either transfer the application to the High Court or consult their Family Division Liaison Judge. Where the matter is urgent, it can be heard by the Urgent Applications Judge of the Family Division (out of hours contact number 020 7947 6000).

[3]   *Service of Application on the national news media*

Section 12(2) of the Human Rights Act 1998 means that an injunction restricting the exercise of the right to freedom of expression must not be granted where the person against whom the application is made is neither present nor represented unless the court is satisfied (a) that the applicant has taken all practicable steps to notify the respondent, or (b) that there are compelling reasons why the respondent should not be notified.

Service of applications for reporting restriction orders on the national media can now be effected via the Press Association's CopyDirect service, to which national newspapers and broadcasters subscribe as a means of receiving notice of such applications.

The court will bear in mind that legal advisers to the media (i) are used to participating in hearings at very short notice where necessary; and (ii) are able to differentiate between information provided for legal purposes and information for editorial use. Service of applications via the CopyDirect service should henceforth be the norm.

The court retains the power to make without notice orders, but such cases will be exceptional, and an order will always give persons affected liberty to apply to vary or discharge it at short notice.

[4]   *Further guidance*

The *Practice Note (Official Solicitor: Deputy Director of Legal Services: CAFCASS: Applications For Reporting Restriction Orders)* 18 March 2005, [2005] 2 FLR 111 and issued jointly by the Official Solicitor and the Deputy Director of Legal Services, provides valuable guidance and should be followed.

[5]   Issued with the concurrence and approval of the Lord Chancellor.

Dame Elizabeth Butler-Sloss
President of the Family Division

Appendix 5.13

Practice Note
(Official Solicitor: Deputy Director of Legal Services: CAFCASS: Applications for Reporting Restriction Orders)

18 March 2005

[1]　This Note sets out recommended practice in relation to any application in the Family Division founded on European Convention rights (European Convention for the Protection of Human Rights and Fundamental Freedoms 1950) for an order which restricts freedom of expression. It is issued in conjunction with the *President's Practice Direction (Applications for Reporting Restriction Orders)* 18 March 2005, [2005] 2 FLR 120 and is subject to decisions of the courts. It applies directly to any proceedings in which the Children and Family Court Advisory and Support Service (CAFCASS) or the Official Solicitor represent a child or incapacitated adult, and follows discussions between the Official Solicitor, the Deputy Director of Legal Services CAFCASS, and representatives of media interests.

[2]　*Statutory Provisions*

An application founded on Convention rights need only be made where statutory provisions cannot provide adequate protection. Relevant provisions are Administration of Justice Act 1960, s 12(1); Children and Young Persons Act 1933, s 39; Contempt of Court Act 1981, s 11; Children Act 1989, s 8 (prohibited steps order preventing disclosure of information by parental figure) and s 97(2). While the *President's Practice Direction* is not aimed at applications under these provisions, s 12(2) of the Human Rights Act 1998 applies to any application for relief which might affect the exercise of the Convention right to freedom of expression and the procedures set out in this Note, including the arrangements for advance notification, can be used to secure compliance with this section in relation to any such application under these provisions.

An order founded on Convention rights may be required, for example, because:

–　the need for protection is not linked to particular court proceedings;
–　the statutory provisions do not prevent publication of all kinds of information;
–　an injunction is needed to prevent approaches to family, doctors or carers.

[3]　*Application and Evidence*

The application may be a freestanding claim brought under the Part 8 procedure in the Civil Procedure Rules 1998 or it may be made within existing proceedings to which either the CPR or Family Proceedings Rules 1991 apply. It may be appropriate to seek a direction under CPR r 39.2(4), where it applies, that the identity of a party or witness should not be disclosed, and for documents to be drafted identifying individuals by initials.

The applicant should prepare (a) the application/claim form (b) a witness statement justifying the need for an order (c) any legal submissions (d) a draft order and (e) an explanatory note.

Model Forms of Order and an example of an explanatory note are attached to this Practice Note and can be downloaded from the websites of either the Official Solicitor (www.offsol.demon.co.uk) or CAFCASS (www.cafcass.gov.uk).

In the rare event that it is not possible to draft such documentation in the time available before the hearing, the court is likely to require the applicant to file a statement at the earliest opportunity, setting out the information placed orally before the court.

Subject to any contrary direction of the court, this material should be made available on request to any person who is affected by the order: see *Kelly v British Broadcasting Corporation* [2001] Fam 59, [2001] 1 FLR 197.

[4] *Service of Application*

As required by the *President's Practice Direction*, advance notice should normally be given to the national media via the Press Association's CopyDirect service. Applicants should first telephone CopyDirect (tel no 0870 837 6429). Documentation should be sent either by fax (fax no 0870 837 6429) or to the email address provided by CopyDirect. CopyDirect will be responsible for notifying the individual media organisations. In the case of an application against the world at large this is sufficient service for the purposes of advance notice. The website — http://www.medialawyer.press.net/courtapplications gives details of the organisations represented and instructions for service of the application. Unless there is a particular reason not to do so, copies of all the documents referred to above should be served. If there is a reason for not serving some or all of the documents (or parts of them), the applicant should ensure sufficient detail is given to enable the media to make an informed decision as to whether it wishes to attend or be legally represented.

The CopyDirect service does not extend to local or regional media or magazines. If service of the application on any specific organisation or person not covered is required it should be effected directly. The Official Solicitor and CAFCASS Legal hold lists of contact details for many national and some regional news organisations, and these are posted on their websites.

[5] *The hearing*

Any application invoking Convention rights will involve a balancing of rights under Art 8 (right to respect for private and family life) and Art 10 (freedom of expression). There is no automatic precedence as between these Articles, and both are subject to qualification where (among other considerations) the rights of others are engaged. Section 12(4) of the Act requires the court to have particular regard to the importance of freedom of expression. It must also have regard to the extent to which material has or is about to become available to the public, the extent of the public interest in such material being published and the terms of any relevant privacy code (such as those of the Press Complaints Commission).

The court's approach is laid down in *Re S (Identification: Restrictions on Publication)* [2003] EWCA Civ 963, [2004] Fam 43, [2003] 2 FLR 1253 and *Re S (Identification: Restrictions on Publication)* [2004] UKHL 47, [2005] 1 FLR 591 and *Campbell v MGN Ltd* [2004] UKHL 22, [2004] UKHRR 648. Guidance on the application of s 12(3) is now also provided in *Cream Holdings Limited and Others v Banerjee and Another* [2004] UKHL 44, [2005] 1 AC 253.

[6] *Scope of Order*

Persons protected

The aim should be to protect the child or incapacitated adult, rather than to confer anonymity on other individuals or organisations. However, the order may include restrictions on identifying or approaching specified family members, carers, doctors or organisations in cases where the absence of such restriction is likely to prejudice their ability to care for the child or patient, or where identification of such persons might lead to identification of the child or patient and defeat the purpose of the order. In cases where the court receives expert evidence the identity of the experts (as opposed to treating clinicians) is not normally subject to restriction.

Identifying persons protected

Once an order has been made, the details of those protected by the order should normally be contained in the Schedule. In exceptional cases (for example *Leeds Teaching Hospital NHS Trust v A and B* [2003] EWHC 259 (QB), [2003] 1 FLR 1091) where it is not appropriate for details to be given, a description by reference to the facts of the case should be contained in the Schedule to enable those reading the order to identify whether a person is likely to be the subject of the order.

Information already in the public domain

Orders will not usually prohibit publication of material which is already in the public domain, other than in exceptional cases such as *Venables v News Group Newspapers Ltd and Others; Thompson v News Group Newspapers Ltd and Others* [2001] Fam 430, [2001] 2 WLR 1038, [2001] 1 FLR 791.

Duration of Order

Orders should last for no longer than is necessary to achieve the purpose for which they are made. The maximum extent of an order in a child case will usually be the child's 18th birthday. In the case of an incapacitated adult the order will normally end on death. In some cases a later date may be necessary, to protect safety or welfare, or the anonymity of other children who are named in the order and who are still under age, or to maintain the anonymity of doctors or carers after the death of a patient. see for example:

– 	*Re C (Adult Patient: Publicity)* [1996] 2 FLR 251;
– 	*Venables v News Group Newspapers Ltd and Others; Thompson v News Group Newspapers Ltd and Others* [2001] Fam 430, [2001] 2 WLR 1038, [2001] 1 FLR 791;
– 	*X (A Woman formerly known as Mary Bell) and Another v O'Brien and Others* [2003] EWHC QB 1101, [2003] 2 FCR 686.

Service of Orders

Service of orders should be effected in the usual way, i e by fax or by post. Contact details for the national press and broadcasters can be found at http://www.medialawyer.press.net/courtapplications.

[8] *Undertakings in damages*

The court will consider whether it is appropriate to require an applicant to give such an undertaking in an individual case, particularly when an order is made without notice, and will bear in mind the applicant's capacity to fulfil any such undertaking.

[9] *Explanatory notes*

It is helpful if applications and orders are accompanied by an explanatory note, from which persons served can readily understand the nature of the case. In any case where notice of an application has not been given, the explanatory note should explain why.

[10] *Advice and assistance*

Applicants or respondents are welcome to consult:

Deputy Director

CAFCASS Legal Services and Special Casework

8 floor, Wyndham House,

South Quay Plaza, London E14 9SH

DX: 42691 Isle of Dogs

Telephone: 020 7510 7080

Fax: 020 7510 7104

Email: legal@cafcass.gov.uk

Website: wvvw.cafcass.gov.uk

Official Solicitor

81 Chancery Lane

London WC2A 1D

Telephone: 020 7911 7127

Fax: 020 7911 7105

Email: enquiries@offsol.gsi.gov.uk

Website: www.offsol.demon.co.uk

Mike Hinchliffe

Deputy Director of Legal Services, CAFCASS

Laurence Oates

Official Solicitor

Attached

(1) Model Order

(2) Example of Explanatory Note

Appendix 5.13

(1) Model Order

IN THE HIGH COURT OF JUSTICE	**Case Number:**

FAMILY DIVISION

[PRINCIPAL REGISTRY]

BEFORE [*JUDGE*] IN PRIVATE

IN THE MATTER OF THE COURT'S INHERENT JURISDICTION

BETWEEN

[   ]

and

[   ]

REPORTING RESTRICTION ORDER

IMPORTANT

If you disobey this order you may be found guilty of contempt of court and may be sent to prison or be fined or have your assets seized. You should read the order carefully and are advised to consult a solicitor as soon as possible. You have the right to ask the Court to vary or discharge the order.

EXPLANATION

A   On [*date*] the Court considered an application for a reporting restriction order.

B   The following persons and/or organisations were represented before the Court:

         [*describe parties and their advocates*]

C   The Court read the following documents: [*list the documents*]

         and/or

         The Court directed the [Applicant/Claimant] to file a statement no later than [*date*] setting out the information presented to the court at the hearing.

         and/or

         The Court directed that copies of the attached Explanatory Note and [*list any other documents*] be made available by the [Applicant/Claimant] to any person affected by this Order.

[D   *In a case where an undertaking in damages is required by the Court:*

         The applicant gave an undertaking that if the Court later finds that this Order was obtained as a result of any deliberate or careless misrepresentation by the applicant, and that this has caused loss to any person served with the Order, and that that person should be compensated, the applicant will comply with any order the Court may make.]

E   *In the case of an order made without notice:*

         This order was made without notice to those affected by it, the Court having considered section 12(2) Human Rights Act 1998 and being satisfied (i) that the [Applicant/Claimant] has taken all practicable steps to notify persons affected and/or (ii) that there are compelling reasons for notice not being given, namely: [*set out the Court's reasons for making the order without notice*]

[F   *In the case of an application by a local authority:*

The Court granted permission to the applicant to apply for the exercise of the Court's inherent jurisdiction]

ORDER

1. *Duration*

Subject to any different order made in the meantime, this order shall have effect

[*in the case of an adult*] during the lifetime of the [Defendant], whose details are set out in Schedule 1 to this order.

[*in the case of a child*] until [date], the 18 birthday of the child whose details are set out in Schedule 1 to this order ('the Child').

2. *Who is bound*

This order binds all persons and all companies (whether acting by their directors, employees or agents or in any other way) who know that the order has been made.

3. *Publishing restrictions*

This order prohibits the publishing or broadcasting in any newspaper, magazine, public computer network, internet website, sound or television broadcast or cable or satellite programme service of:

(a)   the name and address of
  (i) the [Defendant/Child];
  (ii) [*in the case of a child*] the Child's parents ('the parents'), whose details are set out in Schedule 2 to this order;
  (iii) any individual having day-to-day care of or medical responsibility for the [Defendant/Child] ('a carer'), whose details are set out in Schedule 3 to this Order;
  (iv) any residential home or hospital, or other establishment in which the [Defendant/Child] is residing or being treated ('an establishment');

(b)   any picture being or including a picture of either the [Defendant/Child], a carer or an establishment;

(c)   any other particulars or information relating to the [Defendant/Child];

IF, BUT ONLY IF, such publication is likely to lead to the identification of the [Defendant/ Child] as being [*set out the feature of the situation which has led to the granting of the order*].

4. No publication of the text or a summary of this order (except for service of the order under paragraph 7 below) shall include any of the matters referred to in paragraph 3 above.

[5. *Restriction on seeking information*

This Order prohibits any person from seeking any information relating to the [Defendant/Child] [or the parents] or a carer from any of the following:

(a)   the [Defendant/Child];
[(b)   the parents];
(c)   a carer;
(d)   the staff or residents of an establishment.]

6. *What is not restricted by this Order*

Nothing in this Order shall prevent any person from:

(a) publishing information relating to any part of a hearing in a court in England and Wales (including a coroner's court) in which the court was sitting in public and did not itself make any order restricting publication.
(b) seeking or publishing information which is not restricted by paragraph 3 above.
(c) inquiring whether a person or place falls within paragraph 3(a) above.
(d) seeking information relating to the [Defendant/Child] while acting in a manner authorised by statute or by any court in England and Wales.
(e) seeking information from the responsible solicitor acting for any of the parties or any appointed press officer, whose details are set out in Schedule 4 to this order.
(f) seeking or receiving information from anyone who before the making of this order had previously approached that person with the purpose of volunteering information (but this paragraph will not make lawful the provision or receipt of private information which would otherwise be unlawful).
(g) publishing information which before the service on that person of this order was already in the public domain in England and Wales as a result of publication by another person in any newspaper, magazine, sound or television broadcast or cable or satellite programme service, or on the internet website of a media organisation operating within England and Wales.

7. Service

Copies of this Order endorsed with a notice warning of the consequences of disobedience shall be served by the [Applicant/Claimant] (and may be served by any other party to the proceedings)

(a) by service on such newspaper and sound or television broadcasting or cable or satellite or programme services as they think fit, by fax or first class post addressed to the editor (in the case of a newspaper) or senior news editor (in the case of a broadcasting or cable or satellite programme service) or website administrator (in the case of an internet website) and/or to their respective legal departments; and/or
(b) on such other persons as the parties may think fit, by personal service.

8. Further applications about this Order

The parties and any person affected by any of the restrictions in paragraphs 3–5 above may make application to vary or discharge it to a judge of the High Court on not less than [*48 hours*] notice to the parties.

SCHEDULE 1

[*The [Defendant/Child]'s Full Name:*

Born:

Address:]

or

[*Information enabling those affected by order to identify the Defendant/Child*]

SCHEDULE 2

[*Similar details of parents*]

SCHEDULE 3

[*Similar details of carers or other persons protected*]

SCHEDULE 4

[*Contact details of responsible solicitor and/or press officer*]

Date of Order:[   ]

(2) Example of Explanatory Note

NHS TRUST X v AB

Application for a Reporting Restriction Order

EXPLANATORY NOTE

1   AB is in a permanent vegetative state. An application has been made by the NHS Hospital Trust responsible for his care for the Court's approval of the withdrawal of artificial nutrition and hydration. This course is supported by AB's family.

2   On [date] the application will be heard by the President of the Family Division, who will give judgment in open court.

3   A Reporting Restriction Order has been [made/applied for] to protect AB's right to confidentiality in respect of his medical treatment. This does not restrict publication of information or discussion about the treatment of patients in a permanent vegetative state, provided that such publication is not likely to lead to the identification of AB, those caring for him, the NHS Trust concerned or the establishment at which he is being cared for.

Appendix 5.14

Practice Note
(Official Solicitor: Appointment in
Family Proceedings)

[1] This *Practice Note* supersedes *Practice Note* (*Official Solicitor: Appointment in Family Proceedings*) (4 December 1998) [1999] 1 FLR 310 issued by the Official Solicitor in relation to his appointment in family proceedings. It is issued in conjunction with a *Practice Note* dealing with the appointment of officers of CAFCASS Legal Services and Special Casework in family proceedings. This *Practice Note* is intended to be helpful guidance, but always subject to *Practice Directions*, decisions of the court and other legal guidance.

[2] The Children and Family Court Advisory and Support Service (CAFCASS) has responsibilities in relation to children in family proceedings in which their welfare is or may be in question (Criminal Justice and Court Services Act 2000, s 12). From 1 April 2001, the Official Solicitor will no longer represent children who are the subject of family proceedings (other than in very exceptional circumstances and after liaison with CAFCASS).

[3] This *Practice Note* summarises the continuing role of the Official Solicitor in family proceedings. Since there are no provisions for parties under disability in the Family Proceedings Courts (Children Act 1989) Rules 1991 (SI 1991/1395), the Official Solicitor can only act in the High Court or in a county court, pursuant to Part IX of the Family Proceedings Rules 1991 (SI 1991/1247). The Official Solicitor will shortly issue an updated *Practice Note* about his role for adults under disability who are the subject of declaratory proceedings in relation to their medical treatment or welfare.

Adults under disability

[4] The Official Solicitor will, in the absence of any other willing and suitable person, act as next friend or guardian ad litem of an adult party under disability, a 'patient'. 'Patient' means someone who is incapable by reason of mental disorder of managing and administering his property and affairs (Family Proceedings Rules 1991, r 9.1). Medical evidence will usually be required before the Official Solicitor can consent to act and his staff can provide a standard form of medical certificate. Where there are practical difficulties in obtaining such medical evidence, the Official Solicitor should be consulted.

Non-subject children

[5] Again in the absence of any other willing and suitable person, the Official Solicitor will act as next friend or guardian ad litem of a child party whose own welfare is not the subject of family proceedings (Family Proceedings Rules 1991, r 2.57, r 9.2 and r 9.5). The most common examples will be:

(a)   a child who is also the parent of a child, and who is a respondent to a Children Act 1989 or Adoption Act 1976 application. If a child respondent is already represented by a CAFCASS officer in pending proceedings of which he or she is the subject, then the Official Solicitor will liaise with CAFCASS to agree the most appropriate arrangements;

(b)   a child who wishes to make an application for a Children Act 1989 order naming another child (typically a contact order naming a sibling). The Official Solicitor will need to satisfy himself that the proposed proceedings would benefit the child applicant before proceeding;

(c)   a child witness to some disputed factual issue in a children case and who may require intervener status. In such circumstances the need for party status and legal representation should be weighed in the light of *Re H (Care Proceedings: Intervener)* [2000] 1 FLR 775;

(d)   a child party to a petition for a declaration of status under Part III of the Family Law Act 1986;

(e)   a child intervener in divorce or ancillary relief proceedings (r 2.57 or r 9.5);

(f)   a child applicant for, or respondent to, an application for an order under Part IV of the Family Law Act 1996. In the case of a child applicant, the Official Solicitor will need to satisfy himself that the proposed proceedings would benefit the child before pursuing them, with leave under Family Law Act 1996, s 43 if required.

[6]   Any children who are parties to Children Act 1989 or inherent jurisdiction proceedings may rely on the provisions of Family Proceedings Rules 1991, r 9.2A if they wish to instruct a solicitor without the intervention of a next friend or guardian ad litem. Rule 9.2A does not apply to Adoption Act 1976, Family Law Act 1986/1996 or Matrimonial Causes Act 1973 proceedings.

Older children who are also patients

[7]   Officers of CAFCASS will not be able to represent anyone who is over the age of 18. The Official Solicitor may therefore be the more appropriate next friend or guardian ad litem of a child who is also a patient and whose disability will persist beyond his or her eighteenth birthday, especially in non-emergency cases where the substantive hearing is unlikely to take place before the child's eighteenth birthday. The Official Solicitor may also be the more appropriate next friend or guardian ad litem in medical treatment cases such as sterilisation or vegetative state cases, in which his staff have particular expertise deriving from their continuing role for adult patients.

Advising the court

[8]   The Official Solicitor may be invited to act or instruct counsel as a friend of the court (amicus) if it appears to the court that such an invitation is more appropriately addressed to him rather than (or in addition to) CAFCASS Legal Services and Special Casework.

Liaison with CAFCASS

[9]   In cases of doubt or difficulty, staff of the Official Solicitor's office will liaise with staff of CAFCASS Legal Services and Special Casework to avoid duplication and ensure the most suitable arrangements are made.

Invitations to act in new cases

[10]   Solicitors who have been consulted by a child or an adult under disability (or by someone acting on their behalf, or concerned about their interests) should write to the Official Solicitor setting out the background to the proposed case and explaining why there is no other willing and suitable person to act as next friend or guardian ad litem. Where the person concerned is an adult, medical evidence in the standard form of the Official Solicitor's medical certificate should be provided.

Invitations to act in pending proceedings

[11]   Where a case is already before the court, an order appointing the Official Solicitor should be expressed as being made subject to his consent. The Official Solicitor aims to provide a response to any invitation within 10 working days. He will be unable to consent to act for an adult until satisfied that the party is a 'patient'. A further directions appointment after 28 days may therefore be helpful. If he accepts appointment the Official Solicitor will need time to prepare the case on behalf of the child or patient and may wish to make submissions about any substantive hearing date. The following documents should be forwarded to the Official Solicitor without delay:

(a)   a copy of the order inviting him to act (with a note of the reasons approved by the judge if appropriate);
(b)   the court file;
(c)   if available, a bundle with summary, statement of issues and chronology–(as required by President's *Practice Direction (Family Proceedings: Court Bundles)* (10 March 2000) [2000] 1 FLR 536).

Contacting the Official Solicitor

[12]   It is often helpful to discuss the question of appointment with the Official Solicitor or one of his staff by telephoning 020 7911 7127. Enquiries about family proceedings should be addressed to the Team Manager, Family Litigation.

The Official Solicitor's address is:
81 Chancery Lane
London
WC2A 1DD
DX 0012 London Chancery Lane
Fax: 020 7911 7105
Email: officialsolicitor@offsol.gsi.gov.uk

2 April 2001

LAURENCE OATES

Official Solicitor

Practice Note
(Official Solicitor, CAFCASS and the National Assembly for Wales: Urgent and Out of Hours Cases in the Family Division of the High Court)

28 July 2006

[1]   This Practice Note is issued jointly by the Official Solicitor, the Chief Executive of CAFCASS, and the Chief Executive of CAFCASS Cymru on behalf of the National Assembly for Wales. It describes the procedure to be followed in respect of urgent and out of hours cases in which a decision is sought by a judge of the Family Division of the High Court. It is issued with the approval of the President of the Family Division.

[2]   In some cases, urgent or out of hours applications become necessary because applications to the court have not been pursued sufficiently promptly. This is undesirable, in particular because urgent applications may be founded on incomplete evidence, inquiries and under-prepared advocacy, and should be avoided where possible. A judge who has concerns that the urgent or out of hours facilities may have been abused may require a representative of the claimant to attend at a subsequent directions hearing to provide an explanation.

[3]   Whenever possible, urgent applications should be made within court hours. The earliest possible liaison is required with the Clerk of the Rules. It will usually be possible to accommodate a genuinely urgent application (at least for initial directions) in the Family Division applications court, from which the matter may, if necessary and possible, be referred to another judge.

[4]   When it is not possible to apply within court hours, contact should be made with the security office at the Royal Courts of Justice (020 7947 6000) who will refer the matter to the urgent business officer. The urgent business officer can contact the duty judge. The judge may agree to hold a hearing, either convened at court or elsewhere, or by telephone. When the hearing is to take place by telephone it should be by tape-recorded conference call arranged (and paid for in the first instance) by the claimant's solicitors. Solicitors acting for NHS Trusts or other potential claimants should have standing arrangements with their telephone service providers under which such conference calls can be arranged. All parties (especially the judge) should be informed that the call is being recorded by the service provider. The claimant should order a transcript of the hearing from the service provider.

Adult Medical treatment and welfare cases

[5]   The Official Solicitor will act in urgent cases under the inherent jurisdiction concerning medical treatment to, or the welfare of, an adult who lacks capacity to make

decisions for himself or herself. His office should be contacted at the earliest possible opportunity if an urgent application is envisaged. Where cases arise out of hours the urgent business officer will be able to contact him or his representative. As with cases dealt with on a less urgent basis, evidence is required of incapacity and as to best interests. When written evidence is not available, oral evidence of incapacity must be available. When there is a telephone hearing, oral evidence must be given as part of the conference call.

[6]   When final evidence either as to capacity or best interests is not available, the court may be willing to grant an interim declaration (r 25.1(1)(b) of the Civil Procedure Rules 1998 (CPR) — *NHS Trust v T (Adult Patient: Refusal of Medical Treatment)* [2004] EWHC 1279 (Fam), [2005] 1 All ER 387). Evidence establishing on the balance of probability that the patient is under incapacity and that the treatment proposed is in his or her best interest must be adduced. An interim injunction to restrain treatment may be granted *Re C (Adult) (Refusal of Treatment)* [1994] 1 WLR 290, [1994] 1 FLR 31.

[7]   An adult patient must be a party and must be represented through a litigation friend (r 21.3 of the CPR). Notice of an application must be given to the patient (or his or her litigation friend). The claimant may be an NHS Trust, local authority, relative, carer, or the patient. The Official Solicitor stands ready to accept appointment as litigation friend (usually for the patient as defendant) if the conditions for his appointment are shown (either on an interim or final basis) to exist. Should a declaration be made without notice, it is of no effect and may be set aside — *St George's Healthcare NHS Trust v S; R (S) v Collins and Others* [1999] Fam 26, [1998] 2 FLR 728.

Children medical treatment and welfare cases

[8]   It may be desirable for a child who is the subject of such proceedings to be made a party and represented through a guardian ad litem (usually an officer of CAFCASS or a Welsh Family Proceedings Officer). CAFCASS and CAFCASS Cymru stand ready to arrange for an officer to accept appointment as guardian ad litem. They should be contacted at the earliest opportunity where an urgent application is envisaged. For urgent out of hours applications, the urgent business officer is able to contact a representative of CAFCASS. CAFCASS Cymru is not able to deal with cases that arise out of office hours and those cases should be referred to CAFCASS who will deal with the matter on behalf of CAFCASS Cymru until the next working day. A child of sufficient understanding to instruct his or her own solicitor should be made a party and given notice of any application.

[9]   Interim declarations/orders under the wardship jurisdiction (or the Children Act 1989) may be made on application either by an NHS Trust, a local authority, an interested adult (where necessary with the leave of the court) or by the child if he or she has sufficient understanding to make the application.

General Issues

[10]   Parents, carers or other necessary respondents should be given the opportunity to have independent legal advice or at least to have access to support or counselling

[11]   In suitable cases, application may be made for direction providing for anonymity of the parties and others involved in the matter in any order or subsequent listing of the case. Exceptionally, a reporting restriction order may be sought — see the *President's Practice Direction (Applications for Reporting Restriction Orders)* [2005] 2 FLR 120 issued on 18 March 2005.

[12] Either the Official Solicitor or CAFCASS, as the case may be, may be appointed by the court as advocate to the court — see Memorandum from the Lord Chief Justice and the Attorney-General reproduced in *The White Book Service 2006, Civil Procedure* (Sweet & Maxwell, 2006) at 39.8.2, especially at 39.8.5.

[13] Draft standard form orders for use in urgent and out of hours medical treatment cases are annexed to this note. They should be adapted to suit the individual circumstances of each case.

Consultation with CAFCASS, CAFCASS Cymru and the Official Solicitor

[14] Members of the Official Solicitor's legal staff, CAFCASS, and CAFCASS Cymru are prepared to discuss medical cases before proceedings are issued. In all cases in which the urgent and out of hours procedures are to be used it would be helpful if the Official Solicitor, CAFCASS or CAFCASS Cymru have had some advance notice of the application and its circumstances. Inquiries about adult medical and welfare cases should be addressed to a family and medical litigation lawyer at the office of the Official Solicitor, 81 Chancery Lane, London, WC2A, telephone 0207 911 7127, fax number: 0207 911 7105, email: enquiries@offsol.gsi.gov.uk. Inquiries about children medical cases should be directed to the duty lawyer at CAFCASS, 8th Floor, South Quay Plaza 3, 189 Marsh Wall, London, E14 9SH, telephone: 0207 510 7000, fax number: 0207 510 7104. Inquiries about children medical cases in Wales should be directed to the Social Care Team, Legal Services, National Assembly for Wales, Cathays Park, Cardiff, CF10 3NQ, telephone: 02920 826813, fax no: 02920 823834.

Laurence Oates

Official Solicitor

Anthony Douglas

Chief Executive CAFCASS

Dafydd Ifans

Chief Executive CAFCASS Cymru

National Assembly for Wales

ANNEX

OUT OF HOURS ADULT INTERIM DECLARATION AND DIRECTIONS

Claim No: ....

IN THE HIGH COURT OF JUSTICE

FAMILY DIVISION

.... REGISTRY

MR(S) JUSTICE ....

IN THE MATTER OF THE COURT'S INHERENT JURISTICTION

B E T W E E N:

<table>
<tr><td>.......... NHS TRUST</td><td>Claimant</td></tr>
<tr><td>— and —</td><td></td></tr>
<tr><td>.......... AB (by the official solicitor</td><td></td></tr>
<tr><td>as litigation friend)</td><td>Defendant</td></tr>
</table>

O R D E R

UPON HEARING .... of counsel for the claimant, and the [Deputy] Official Solicitor

UPON READING ....

(AND UPON HEARING oral evidence from ....)

(AND UPON the claimant undertaking by 4.00 pm on .... to issue a Claim Form under Part 8 of the Civil Procedure Rules 1998, to pay the necessary court fee and to file ....);

AND UPON the Official Solicitor, having consented, being appointed to act as the defendant's litigation friend;

IT IS ORDERED that:

1   this matter be listed for directions before the applications judge in London on .... at 10.30 am;

2   for the purposes of these proceedings:
    (a)   the proceedings shall be listed as 'NHS Trust A v Mr/Ms B';
    (b)   the Claimant shall be referred to as 'Trust A';
    (c)   the Defendant shall be referred to as 'Mr/Ms B';

3   further or alternative directions as to anonymity may be sought at the directions hearing;

4   the claimant shall keep the Official Solicitor informed of all material developments in the treatment and condition of the defendant.

IT IS DECLARED that with effect until the substantive hearing of this matter or further order:

(a)   the defendant lacks capacity to make medical treatment decisions relating to any need s/he may have to the treatment referred to in sub-paragraph (b) below;

(b)   it is lawful as being in the best interests of the defendant for the claimants, its servants or agents ....

(c)   it is lawful for the minimum necessary force to be used, if required, in the course of such treatment.

AND IT IS ORDERED:

(i)   [telephone applications] the claimant do obtain a transcript of the telephone hearing and (in the first instance at least) do pay the telephone service provider the cost of that transcript and of the telephone hearing;

(ii)   that the costs of this application be reserved.

Dated the .... day of .... /20...

OUT OF HOURS ADULT FINAL ORDER

Claim No: ....

IN THE HIGH COURT OF JUSTICE

FAMILY DIVISION

.... REGISTRY

MR(S) JUSTICE ....

IN THE MATTER OF THE COURT'S INHERENT JURISTICTION

B E T W E E N:

.... NHS TRUST   Claimant

— and —

.... AB (by the official solicitor as litigation friend)   Defendant

O R D E R

UPON HEARING .... of counsel for the claimant and the [Deputy] Official Solicitor

UPON READING ....

(AND UPON HEARING oral evidence from ....

[AND UPON the Claimant undertaking by 4.00 pm on .... to issue a Claim Form under Part 8 of the Civil Procedure Rules 1998, to pay the necessary court fee and to file]
....

AND UPON the Official Solicitor, having consented, being appointed to act as the defendant's litigation friend;

IT IS DECLARED THAT:

1   the defendant lacks capacity to make decisions about medical treatment in relation to ....;

2   It shall be lawful as being in the defendant's best interests:
        (a) for the defendant to undergo .... and such other treatment as may in the treating doctor's opinion be necessary for the purpose of treating the defendant's post-operative condition;
        (b) for the minimum necessary force to be used, if required, in the course of such treatment.

AND IT IS FURTHER ORDERED:

1   In the event of a material change in the existing circumstances occurring each party shall have liberty to apply for such further or other declaration or orders as may be just;
2   the claimant shall inform the Official Solicitor of the treatment carried out pursuant to this order within 48 hours of such treatment;
3   [telephone applications] the claimant do obtain a transcript of the telephone hearing and (in the first instance at least) do pay the telephone service provider the cost of that transcript and of the telephone hearing;
4   [the claimant shall pay (one half of) the Official Solicitor's costs in connection with these proceedings on the standard basis to be the subject of a detailed assessment if not agreed].

Dated the .... day of .... /20...

INTERIM DECLARATION AND DIRECTIONS: INHERENT JURISDICTION — CHILD

IN THE HIGH COURT OF JUSTICE

Case No: ....

FAMILY DIVISION

PRINCIPAL REGISTRY

Before .... IN PRIVATE

IN THE MATTER OF THE COURT'S INHERENT JURISDICTION

BETWEEN:

[NHS TRUST or LOCAL AUTHORITY]   Claimant

and

                                                                       First Defendant

and

[A child by an officer of CAFCASS/Welsh
family proceedings officer as his/her guardian ad litem]   Second Defendant

INTERIM ORDER

BEFORE the Honourable Mr/s Justice .... on the ....

The following persons and/or organisations were represented before the court:

[describe parties and their advocates]

[In the case of an application by a local authority: the court granted permission to the applicant to apply for the exercise of the court's inherent jurisdiction].

The court read the following documents:

[list the documents]

and/or

[[AND] UPON HEARING oral evidence from:

[list those giving oral evidence]]

[AND UPON the claimant undertaking by 4.00 pm on .... to issue and to file originating summons].

AND UPON [name of the child] being made a party to the proceedings and pursuant to r 9.5 of the Family Proceedings Rules 1991 an officer of CAFCASS/a Welsh family proceedings officer being appointed to act as his/her guardian ad litem;

IT IS ORDERED that:

1   this matter be listed for directions before the applications judge in London on .... at 10.30 am;
2   for the purposes of these proceedings:
      (a)   the proceedings shall be listed as 'NHS Trust A v Mr/Ms B' [or 'Local Authority A v Mr/Mrs B'];
      (b)   the claimant shall be referred to as 'Trust A' [or 'Local Authority; A'];
      (c)   the defendant parents shall be referred to as 'Mr/Ms B';
      (d)   the child should be referred to as 'C' ;
3   further or alternative directions as to anonymity may be sought at the directions hearing;
4   the claimant shall keep the guardian ad litem informed of all material developments in the treatment and condition of the child.

IT IS DECLARED that with effect until the substantive hearing of this matter or further order:

(a)   the child lacks capacity to make medical treatment decisions relating to any need s/he may have to the treatment referred to in sub-paragraph (b) below;
(b)   it is lawful as being in the child's best interests for the claimants, its servants or agents to [describe the treatment];
(c)   [it is lawful for the minimum necessary force to be used, if required, in the course of such treatment];
(d)   [the claimants shall generally furnish such treatment and nursing care as may be appropriate to ensure that the child suffers the least distress and retains the greatest dignity];
(e)   [notwithstanding the mother and the father's refusal to consent and the court finding that it is in their child's best interests, the claimant and/or the doctors having the responsibility for the care of the child may administer blood and/or blood products including blood transfusions, fresh frozen plasma and immunoglobulin should the same be deemed necessary in the professional opinion of those medically responsible for the child, without the parents' consent provided that, if and to the extent that it is reasonably practicable, the parents and/or any consultant or adviser proposed by the parents shall first be consulted to consider alternative forms of management and whether there are alternatives to the use of blood or blood products which would be clinically appropriate].

AND IT IS ORDERED that:

(i)   [telephone applications] the claimant do obtain a transcript of the telephone hearing and (in the first instance at least) do pay the telephone service provider the cost of that transcript and of the telephone hearing;
(ii)   that the costs of this application be reserved.

Dated the .... day of .... /20...

FINAL ORDER: INHERENT JURISDICTION CHILD

IN THE HIGH COURT OF JUSTICE

CASE NO: ....

FAMILY DIVISION

PRINCIPAL REGISTRY

Before .... IN PRIVATE

IN THE MATTER OF THE COURT'S INHERENT JURISDICTION

BETWEEN:

[NHS TRUST or LOCAL AUTHORITY]	Claimant
and	
[..........]	First Defendant
and	
[A child by an officer of CAFCASS/Welsh. Family Proceedings Officer as his/her guardian ad litem]	Second Defendant

ORDER

BEFORE the Honourable Mr/s Justice .... on the ....

The following persons and/or organisations were represented before the court:

[describe parties and their advocates]

[In the case of an application by a local authority where leave was not granted at an earlier hearing:

The court granted permission to the applicant to apply for the exercise of the court's inherent jurisdiction].

The court read the following documents:

[list the documents]

and/or

[AND UPON HEARING oral evidence from:

[list those giving oral evidence]]

[AND UPON the claimant undertaking by 4.00 pm on .... to issue

and to file originating summons].

AND UPON [name of the child] being made a party to the proceedings and pursuant to r 9.5 of the Family Proceedings Rules 1991 an officer of CAFCASS/Welsh Family Proceedings Officer being appointed to act aS his/her guardian ad litem;

IT IS DECLARED THAT:

1   The child lacks capacity to make decisions about medical treatment in relation to ....

2   It shall be lawful as being in the child's best interests:

          (a)   for the child to undergo .... and such other treatment as may in the treating doctor's opinion be necessary for the purpose of treating the child's post-operative condition;

(b) for the minimum necessary force to be used, if required, in the course of such treatment;

(c) [for the treating doctor generally to furnish such treatment and nursing case as may be appropriate to ensure that the child suffers the least distress and retains the greatest dignity];

(d) [notwithstanding the mother and the father's refusal to consent and the court finding that it is in their child's best interests, the claimant and/or the doctors having the responsibility for the care of the child may administer blood and/or blood products including blood transfusions, fresh frozen plasma and immunoglobulin should the same be deemed necessary in the professional opinion of those medically responsible for the child, without the parents' consent provided that, if and to the extent that it is reasonably practicable, the parents and/or any consultant or adviser proposed by the parents shall first be consulted to consider alternative forms of management and whether there are alternatives to the use of blood or blood products which would be clinically appropriate].

AND IT IS FURTHER ORDERED THAT:

3   In the event of a material change in the existing circumstances occurring each party shall have liberty to apply for such further or other declaration or orders as may be just;

4   the claimant shall inform CAFCASS Legal/CAFCASS Cymru of the treatment carried out pursuant to this order within 48 hours of such treatment;

5   [telephone applications] the claimant do obtain a transcript of the telephone hearing and (in the first instance at least) do pay the telephone service provider the cost of that transcript and of the telephone hearing;

6   the claimant shall pay (one half) of the costs of CAFCASS/CAFCASS Cymru in connection with these proceedings to be assessed if not agreed.

Dated the .... day of .... /20...

INTERIM ORDER: WARDSHIP

IN THE HIGH COURT OF JUSTICE

CASE NO: ....

FAMILY DIVISION

PRINCIPAL REGISTRY

Before .... IN PRIVATE

IN THE MATTER OF THE COURT'S INHERENT JURISDICTION AND IN THE MATTER OF AN APPLICATION FOR WARDSHIP

BETWEEN:

	Claimant
and	
	First Defendant
and	
[A child by an officer of CAFCASS/Welsh family proceedings officer as his/her guardian ad litem]	Second Defendant

ORDER

BEFORE the Honourable Mr/s Justice .... on the ....

The following persons and/or organisations were represented before the court:

[describe parties and their advocates]

[In the case of an application by a local authority:

The court granted permission to the applicant to apply for the exercise of the court's inherent jurisdiction].

The court read the following documents:

[list the documents]

and/or

[UPON HEARING oral evidence from:

[list those giving oral evidence]]

[AND UPON the claimant undertaking by 4.00 pm on .... to issue and to file originating summons].

AND UPON [name of the child] being made a party to the proceedings and pursuant to r 9.5 of the Family Proceedings Rules 1991 an officer of CAFCASS/a Welsh family proceedings officer being appointed to act as his/her guardian ad litem;

IT IS DECLARED THAT

1   It is in the best interests of the ward that ....

AND IT IS FURTHER ORDERED AND DIRECTED THAT:

2   this matter be listed for directions before the applications judge in London on .... at 10.30 am;

3   ....

AND IT IS ORDERED

(i)   [telephone applications] the claimant do obtain a transcript of the telephone hearing and (in the first instance at least) do pay the telephone service provider the cost of that transcript and of the telephone hearing;

(ii)   that the costs of this application be reserved.

Dated the .... day of .... /20...

REPORTING RESTRICTION ORDER

IN THE HIGH COURT OF JUSTICE

CASE NO: ....

FAMILY DIVISION

PRINCIPAL REGISTRY

Before .... IN PRIVATE

IN THE MATTER OF THE COURT'S INHERENT JURISDICTION

BETWEEN:

Claimant

and

First Defendant

and

[A child by an officer of CAFCASS/Welsh
family proceedings officer as his/her guardian ad litem]   Second Defendant

REPORTING RESTRICTION ORDER

IMPORTANT

If you disobey this order you may be found guilty of contempt of court and may be sent
to prison or be fined or have your assets seized. You should read the order carefully and
are advised to consult a solicitor as soon as possible. You have the right to ask the court to
vary or discharge the order.

Explanation:

A   On [date] the court considered an application for a reporting restriction order.
B   The following persons and/or organisations were represented before the Court;
       [describe parties and their advocates]
C   The court read the following documents: [list the documents]
       and/or

       The court directed the [applicant/claimant] to file a statement no later than
       [date] setting out the information presented to the court at the hearing.
       and/or

       The court directed that copies of the attached Explanatory Note and [list any
       other documents] be made available by the [applicant/claimant] to any person
       affected by this Order.

D   In the case where an undertaking in damages is required by the court

       The applicant gave an undertaking that if the court later finds that this Order
       was obtained as a result of any deliberate or careless misrepresentation by the
       applicant, and that this has caused loss to any person served with the Order,
       and that that person should be compensated, the applicant will comply with
       any order the court may make].

E   [In the case of an application by a local authority]

The court granted permission to the applicant to apply for the exercise of the court's
inherent jurisdiction].

ORDER

Child Party

1   UPON [name of the child] being made a party to the proceedings and pursuant
       to r 9.5 Family Proceedings Rules 1991 an officer of CAFCASS/a Welsh family
       proceedings officer being appointed to act as his/her Guardian ad litem;

2   *Duration*

       Subject to any different order made in the meantime, this order shall have
       effect until [date], the eighteenth birthday of the child whose details are set out
       in Schedule 1 to this Order ('the child').

3   *Who is bound*

This order binds all persons and all companies (whether acting by their directors, employees or agents or in any other way) who know that the order has been made.

4   *Publishing restrictions*

This order prohibits the publishing or broadcasting in any newspaper, magazine, public computer network, internet website, sound or television broadcast or cable or satellite programme service of:
(a)   The name and address of :
        (i)   the child;
        (ii)   the child's parents ('the parents'), whose details are set out in Schedule 2 to this order;
        (iii)   any individual having day-to-day care of or medical responsibility for the child 'a carer'), whose details are set out in Schedule 3 to this order;
        (iv)   any residential home or hospital, or other establishment in which the child is residing or being treated ('an establishment').
(b)   any picture being or including a picture of either the child or a carer or an establishment;
(c)   any other particulars or information relating to the child,
If, BUT ONLY IF, such publication is likely to lead to the identification of the child as being [set out the feature of the situation which has led to the granting of the order].

5   No publication of the text or a summary of this order (except for service of the order under paragraph 7, below) shall include any of the matters referred to in paragraph 4, above.

6   *Restriction on seeking information*

This order prohibits any person from seeking any information relating to the child [or the parents] or a carer of the child from any of the following:
(a)   the child
(b)   the parents
(c)   a carer
(d)   the staff or residents of an establishment

7   *What is not restricted by this order*

Nothing in this order shall prevent any person from:
(a)   publishing information relating to any part of a hearing in a court in England and Wales (including a coroner's court) in which the court was sitting in public and did not itself make any order restricting publication;
(b)   seeking or publishing information, which is not restricted by paragraph 4, above;
(c)   inquiring whether a person or place falls within paragraph 3(a), above;
(d)   seeking information relating to the child while acting in a manner authorised by statute or by any court in England and Wales;
(e)   seeking information from the solicitor acting for any of the parties or any appointed press officer, whose details are set out in Schedule 4 to this Order;
(f)   seeking or receiving information from anyone who before the making of this order had previously approached that person with the purpose of

volunteering information (but this paragraph will not make lawful the provision or receipt of private information which would otherwise be unlawful);

(g) publishing information which before the service on that person of this Order was already in the public domain in England and Wales as a result of publication by another person in any newspaper, magazine, sound or television broadcast or cable or satellite programme service, or on the internet website of a media organisation operating within England and Wales.

8   *Service*

Copies of this Order endorsed with a notice warning of the consequences of disobedience shall be served by the [applicant/claimant] (and may be served by any other party to the proceedings):

(a) by service on such newspaper and sound or television or cable or satellite or programme services as they think fit, by fax or first class post addressed to the editor (in the case of a newspaper) or senior news editor (in the case of a broadcasting or cable or satellite programme service) or website administrator (in the case of an internet website) and/or to their respective legal departments; and/or

(b) on such other persons as the parties may think fit, by personal service.

9   *Further applications about this Order*

The parties and any person affected by any of the restrictions in para- graphs 4–6 above may make application to vary or discharge it to a judge of the High Court on not less than [48 hours] notice to the parties.

10   *Costs*

(i) [telephone applications] the claimant do obtain a transcript of the telephone hearing and (in the first instance at least) do pay the telephone service provider the cost of that transcript and of the telephone hearing;

(ii) The claimant shall pay (one half) of the costs of CAFCASS Legal/ CAFCASS Cymru in connection with these proceedings to be assessed if not agreed.

SCHEDULE 1

[The child's full name:]

[Born:]

[Address:]

or

[Information enabling those affected by order to identify the child]

SCHEDULE 2

[Similar details of parents]

SCHEDULE 3

[Similar details of carers or other persons protected]

SCHEDULE 4

[Contact details of responsible solicitor and/or press officer]

Dated the .... day of ..../20...

Appendix 5.16

Sample draft order for first directions hearing in a medical treatment case concerning a minor in the High Court

CASE NO: FDxxxxxxxx

IN THE HIGH COURT OF JUSTICE

PRINCIPAL REGISTRY

FAMILY DIVISION

IN THE MATTER OF THE INHERENT JURISDICTION OF THE HIGH COURT

AND IN THE MATTER OF THE CHILDREN ACT 1989

AND IN THE MATTER OF BB (A CHILD) DOB 1.1.2000

B E T W E E N

THE TRUST

Plaintiff

and

(1) BB (A child by her guardian ad litem [name])

(2) MRS B

(3) MR B

Defendants

DRAFT ORDER
ON BEHALF OF THE PLAINTIFF
FOR HEARING ON 1.10.10

UPON HEARING Mr Able Drafter[1], Counsel for the Plaintiff; Miss Fancy Pleader, Counsel for the First Defendant; and Mr Technical Whizz, Counsel for the Second and Third Defendants

UPON READING the documents in the hearing bundle

IT IS DECLARED IN THE INTERIM THAT:

1.   The First Defendant by reason of her minority and [global developmental delay] lacks capacity to consent to or refuse medical treatment.

AND IT IS ORDERED THAT:

2.   For the purposes of these proceedings:

(a)   the plaintiff shall be referred to as 'The Trust';

(b)   the First Defendant shall be referred to as 'BB';

(c)   the Second Defendant shall be referred to as 'Mrs B';

(d)   the Third Defendant shall be referred to as 'Mr B'.

3.   BB is confirmed as a party (First Defendant) to the proceedings and pursuant to rule 9.5 Family Proceedings Rules 1991 an officer of CAFCASS is appointed as her guardian.

4.   The Plaintiff shall by 4pm on [   ] serve paginated copies of its records concerning the First Defendant on the parties.

5.   The First Defendant's current and any previous GP shall by 4pm on [   ] serve paginated copies of its records concerning the First Defendant on the parties, and shall have liberty to apply, upon notice to the parties, to vary or discharge this paragraph of this order.

6.   The parties shall have permission jointly to instruct an expert [of appropriate discipline] to provide a report upon [   ].

7.   The parties shall agree the identity of the above expert by 4pm on [   ].

8.   The parties agree the contents of the letters of instruction by 4pm on [   ] which shall be sent by [whichever party is most appropriate] to the experts by 4pm on [   ].

9.   The expert shall be permitted to see all documents filed and served in the case and to examine the First Defendant.

10.   The experts' report shall be filed and served on the parties by 4pm on [   ].

11.   The costs of the instruction of the above expert shall be shared equally between the parties and shall be a proper disbursement for the purposes of a public funding certificate.

12.   The Plaintiff and the Second and Third Defendants shall each file and serve the factual evidence upon which they wish to rely by 4pm on [   ].

13.   The First Defendant's guardian ad litem shall have permission to file and serve a statement by 4pm on [   ].

14.   There shall be a further directions hearing with a time estimate of 1 hour before a Judge of the Family Division.

15.   The parties shall file and serve their position statements and/or skeleton arguments for the final hearing by 4pm on [   ].

16.   The Applicant shall file and serve an agreed bundle for the final hearing by 4pm on [   ].

17.   The matter shall be listed for final hearing in public on [   ] with a time estimate of [   ] before a Judge of the Family Division.

18.   There shall be no order as to costs.

19.   Liberty to apply.

1   It is sometimes suggested that counsels' name should not appear. However, there is no universal practice. The authors consider it useful to include counsels' names, so that on future occasions (for example at a later directions hearing if an issue arises about what was said on an earlieroccasion) one can see who represented the parties.

Appendix 6.1

Order authorising a deprivation of liberty for rehabilitative treatment in a registered care home

<u>COURT OF PROTECTION</u>   <u>No: COP</u>

<u>IN THE MATTER OF THE MENTAL CAPACITY ACT 2005</u>

<u>IN THE MATTER OF FV (DOB 31.7.63)</u>

B E T W E E N

(1) A PCT

Applicant

– and –

(1) FV

(by her litigation friend, the Official Solicitor)

(2) A REGISTERED CARE HOME

<u>Respondents</u>

ORDER

UPON HEARING from the Counsel for the Applicant and Second Respondent and Counsel for the First Respondent

AND UPON reading all documents filed in this action and hearing evidence of Dr Z, Dr Y and Ms A.

IS HEREBY DECLARED that:

1.   By reason of her acquired brain injury FV does not have capacity to decide upon:
        (a)   where she should reside; and
        (b)   whether to undergo psychological and behavioural treatment.

2.   Notwithstanding FV's inability to consent, it shall be lawful and in her best interests for her treating clinicians and care workers including the Applicant's and Second Respondent's employees, servants or agents:
        (a)   to admit FV to the Registered Care Home, for the purpose of caring for her welfare and providing her with psychological, behavioural and psychiatric treatment;
        (b)   to provide her with psychological, behavioural and psychiatric treatment in accordance with the care plan dated 21.11.09 devised by the Care Home;
        (c)   for the responsible attending doctors, nurses, social workers, care assistants and healthcare staff and such other of the Applicants' and Second Respondent's employees servants or agents as may be appropriate and necessary:

(i)   to use such reasonable restraint as may be necessary in conveying FV to and preventing FV from leaving the Care Home, including measures that may amount to the deprivation of her liberty, for the purpose of caring for her welfare and providing her with psychological, behavioural and psychiatric treatment;

(ii)   generally to furnish such treatment and social care as may be appropriate to ensure that FV suffers the least distress and retains the greatest dignity.

Appendix 6.2

Interim Order providing for Court of Protection reviews of deprivation of liberty pending MCA DOLS authorisation

COURT OF PROTECTION   Case Number: COP

IN THE MATTER OF THE MENTAL CAPACITY ACT 2005

IN THE MATTER OF BD (DOB 21.9.83)

BETWEEN

A CITY COUNCIL   Applicant

– and –

(1)   BD

(By her litigation friend, the Official Solicitor)

(2)   A PCT

Respondents

(3)   A NHS TRUST

INTERIM ORDER

UPON HEARING Counsel for the Applicant Counsel for the Official Solicitor and Counsel for the Second and Third Respondent

AND UPON the Court reading the statement of Dr X dated 30 May 2009.

IT IS HEREBY DECLARED by way of interim order only and until further order that:

1.   BD lacks the capacity to
      (a) litigate;
      (b) make decisions regarding her financial affairs;
      (c) make decisions regarding her residence and care;

2.   Pending receipt of the further report of Dr X, as set out below, it is in BD's best interest to reside in the Hospital's Specialist Unit;

3.   Pending confirmation by Dr X that she is unable to detain BD pursuant to section 2 or 3 of the Mental Health Act 1983 and pending a Standard Authorisation pursuant to Schedule A1 of the MCA 2005 being obtained by the Applicant and/or the PCT it is lawful, being in BD's best interests for the Applicant and the PCT, by its employees or agents, to use reasonable and proportionate measures to:
      (a) transfer BD to the Specialist Unit.

(b) prevent BD from leaving the Specialist Unit in circumstances where she may be at risk.

AND IT IS FURTHER ORDERED that:

4. The declarations in paragraph 2 and 3 above shall cease to have effect on 31 August 2009 provided that a Standard Authorisation pursuant to Schedule A1 of the Mental Capacity Act 2005 has been made and shall take effect from 31 August 2009.

5. If no Authorisation has been supplied by 31 July 2009 the following review provisions shall apply:
    (i) A review hearing to be listed on the first available date after 31 July 2009 (time estimate 20 minutes) on a date to be agreed by the parties.
    (ii) A multi-disciplinary case review meeting to be held before the hearing and to which the Official Solicitor is invited.
    (iii) Not less than 14 days before the hearing the Applicant shall file and serve an updating statement by the social worker which shall include reports on BD's capacity and best interests.
    (iv) The Applicant will hold internal reviews of BD's capacity and best interests at least every 10 weeks from the date of this order.

6. The Official Solicitor's costs of dealing with the welfare and financial applications shall be paid by the deputy from BD's funds within 28 days of receipt of the invoice or fee note.

7. The matter of BD's health and welfare and placement is to be reviewed by the Court at the review hearing listed at paragraph 5(i).

Dated 28 June 2009

Appendix 6.3

Order permitting use of restraint

<u>COURT OF PROTECTION</u>

<u>IN THE MATTER OF THE MENTAL CAPACITY ACT 2005</u>

<u>IN THE MATTER OF CR (DOB 25.5.61)</u>

BETWEEN:

(1) NHS TRUST A

(2) NHS TRUST B

(3) A PCT

and

CR

(by the official solicitor as litigation friend)

Applicants

Respondent

ORDER

UPON HEARING from the Counsel for the Applicants and Counsel for the Respondent

AND UPON reading all documents and witness statements filed in this action

AND UPON hearing the oral evidence of Dr A, Ms B

AND UPON the Court having considered the dental treatment proposed for CR and the restraint measures proposed to be taken in providing such treatment

AND UPON the Court being satisfied that the Applicants have demonstrated that the treatment of CR's dental condition is a therapeutic necessity.

IT IS DECLARED THAT:

1.   CR lacks the requisite capacity to make decisions in respect of his dental healthcare and treatment.

2.   Notwithstanding CR's lack of capacity to consent thereto, it is in his best interests to undergo dental examination and treatment under general anaesthetic at Hospital B including, but not limited to:

    (a) examination and diagnostic assessment;

426

    (b) restorative periodontal and surgical treatment;

    (c) pre-, peri- and post-operative medical and nursing care associated with such treatment;

    (d) extraction of such teeth that are in the treating clinicians' opinion inappropriate for conservation in CR's case.

3.   It shall be lawful for the Applicants' staff, servants and agents to use such restraint as is deemed necessary by the clinical team in order to facilitate the transfer and treatment of CR, including but not limited to the use of emergency restraint belts and handcuffs.

4.   Such restraint shall be the minimum deemed necessary by the clinical team to protect the safety of CR and those involved in his transfer and treatment and shall be used in a manner to ensure he suffers the least distress and retains the greatest dignity possible in the circumstance.

5.   The Applicants do pay half of the Official Solicitor's costs (subject to detailed assessment if not agreed).

Appendix 6.4

Overview of deprivation of liberty safeguards

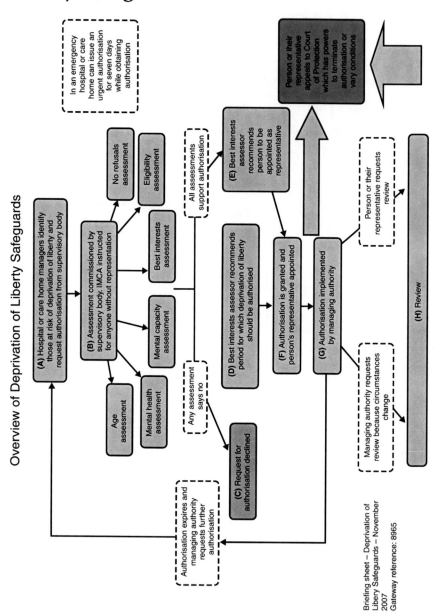

Overview of Deprivation of Liberty Safeguards

In an emergency hospital or care home can issue an urgent authorisation for seven days while obtaining authorisation

(A) Hospital or care home managers identify those at risk of deprivation of liberty and request authorisation from supervisory body

(B) Assessment commissioned by supervisory body. IMCA instructed for anyone without representation

Age assessment

Mental health assessment

Mental capacity assessment

Best interests assessment

No refusals assessment

Eligibility assessment

Any assessment says no

(C) Request for authorisation declined

All assessments support authorisation

(D) Best interests assessor recommends period for which deprivation of liberty should be authorised

(E) Best interests assessor recommends person to be appointed as representative

(F) Authorisation is granted and person's representative appointed

(G) Authorisation implemented by managing authority

Person or their representative appeals to Court of Protection which has powers to terminate authorisation or vary conditions

Person or their representative requests review

Managing authority requests review because circumstances change

(H) Review

Authorisation expires and managing authority requests further authorisation

Briefing sheet – Deprivation of Liberty Safeguards – November 2007
Gateway reference: 8965

Previous Consent Form (Sterilisation or Vasectomy) (DoH)

For sterilisation or vasectomy

Health Authority ....Patient's Surname ....

Hospital .... Other Names ....

Unit Number .... Date of Birth ....

Sex: (please tick) Male ☐ Female ☐

DOCTORS (*This part to be completed by doctor See notes on the reverse*)

TYPE OF OPERATION: STERILISATION OR VASECTOMY

Complete this part of the form

I confirm that I have explained the procedure and any anaesthetic (general/regional) required, to the patient in terms which in my judgement are suited to his/her understanding.

Signature .... Date ..../.../...

Name of doctor ....

PATIENT

1. Please read this form very carefully.
2. If there is anything that you don't understand about the explanation, or if you want more information, you should ask the doctor.
3. Please check that all the information on the form is correct. If it is, and you understand the explanation, then sign the form.

I am the patient

I agree	•	to have this operation, which has been explained to me by the doctor named on this form.
	•	to have the type of anaesthetic that I have been told about.
I understand	•	that the operation may not be done by the doctor who has been treating me so far.
	•	that the aim of the operation is to stop me having any children and it might not be possible to reverse the effects of the operation.
	•	that sterilisation/vasectomy can sometimes fail, and that there is a very small chance that I may become fertile again after some time.
	•	that any procedure in addition to the investigation or treatment described on this form will only be carried out if it is necessary and in my best interests and can be justified for medical reasons.
I have told	•	the doctor about any additional procedures I would not wish to be carried out straightaway without my having the opportunity to consider them first.
For vasectomy I understand	•	that I may remain fertile or become fertile again after some time.
	•	that I will have to use some other contraceptive method until 2 tests in a row show that I am not producing sperm, if I do not want to father any children.

Signature ....

NOTES TO:

Doctors, Dentists

A patient has a legal right to grant or withhold consent prior to examination or treatment. Patients should be given sufficient information, in a way they can understand, about the proposed treatment and the possible alternatives. Patients must be allowed to decide whether they will agree to the treatment and they may refuse or withdraw consent to treatment at any time. The patient's consent to treatment should be recorded on this form (further guidance is given in HC(90)22 (A Guide to Consent for Examination or Treatment.)

Patients

- The doctor is here to help you. He or she will explain the proposed procedure, which you are entitled to refuse. You can ask any questions and seek further information.
- You may ask for a relative, or friend, or a nurse to be present.
- Training health professionals is essential to the continuation of the health

service and improving the quality of care. Your treatment may provide an important opportunity for such training, where necessary under the careful supervision of a senior doctor. You may refuse any involvement in a formal training programme without this adversely affecting your care and treatment.

Appendix 7.2

Extracts from Previous Practice Note (Official Solicitor: Sterilisation)

[1996] 2 FLR 111

Sterilisation of minor — Mentally incompetent adult — Procedure — Applications to court — Parties — Evidence — Mental capacity — Consultation

The need for the prior sanction of a High Court judge

1. The sterilisation of a minor or a mentally incompetent adult ('the patient') will in virtually all cases require the prior sanction of a High Court judge: Re B (A Minor) (Wardship: Sterilisation) [1988] AC 199. [1987] 2 FLR 314; *Re F (Sterilisation: Mental Patient)* [1990] 2 AC 1, [1989] 2 FLR 376 ...

Evidence

8. The purpose of the proceedings is to establish whether or not the proposed sterilisation is in the best interests of the patient. The judge will require to be satisfied that those proposing sterilisation are seeking it in good faith and that their paramount concern is for the best interests of the patient rather than their own or the public's convenience. The proceedings will normally involve a thorough adversarial investigation of all possible viewpoints and any possible alternatives to sterilisation. Nevertheless, straightforward cases proceeding without dissent may be disposed of at the hearing for directions without oral evidence.

9. The Official Solicitor will in all cases, in whichever capacity he acts, carry out his own investigations, call his own witnesses and take whatever other steps appear to him to be necessary in order to ensure that all medical, psychological and social evaluations are conducted and that all relevant matters are properly canvassed before the court. Expert and other witnesses called in support of the proposed operation will be cross-examined and all reasonable arguments presented against sterilisation. The Official Solicitor will require to meet and interview the patient in private in all cases where he or she is able to express any views (however limited) about the case.

10. The Official Solicitor anticipates that the court will particularly require evidence clearly establishing the following:

Mental capacity

(1) That the patient is incapable of making her own decision about sterilisation and is unlikely to develop sufficiently to make an informed judgment about sterilisation in the foreseeable future, having regard to the most up-to-date medical knowledge in this field. In this connection it must be borne in mind that –

(i) the fact that a person is legally incompetent for some purposes does not mean that she necessarily lacks the capacity to make a decision about sterilisation; and

(ii) in the case of a minor her youth and potential for development may make it difficult or impossible to make the relevant finding of incapacity.

Risk of pregnancy

(2) That there is a need for contraception because the patient is fertile and is sexually active or is likely to engage in sexual activity in the foreseeable future. (Re W (Mental Patient: Sterilisation) [1993] 1 FLR 381.)

Potential psychological damage

(3) That the patient is likely if she becomes pregnant or gives birth to experience substantial trauma or psychological damage greater than that resulting from the sterilisation itself.

Alternative methods of contraception

(4) That there is no appropriate reversible method of contraception available having regard to the most up-to-date medical knowledge in this field.

OFFICIAL SOLICITOR

June 1996

Appendix 7.3

Draft Order for Declaration that Sterilisation of Adult is Lawful

1. It is declared that:
    (a) [Name of patient] lacks capacity to make a decision in relation to the operation of sterilisation proposed to be performed on [him or her] [describe here the nature of the procedure, e g namely by application of clips to her fallopian tubes];
    (b) Having regard to the best interests of [name of patient], it is lawful for the operation of sterilisation to be performed by [name of healthcare provider].
2. It is further ordered that in the event of a material change of circumstances occurring before the operation of sterilisation referred to above has been performed, any party (or the Official Solicitor) [1] may apply to the Court for such further or other declaration as may be just.

1 The explicit reference to the Official Solicitor should be added where, unusually, he has not previously been made a party to the proceedings.

Appendix 7.4

Draft Order Under Inherent Jurisdiction for Sterilisation of Child[1]

1.   It is ordered that there be leave to perform an operation of sterilisation on [name of child] [*describe here the nature of the procedure, e g namely by application of clips to her fallopian tubes*][2] and to carry out such post-operative treatment and care as may be in her best interests.

1   Based on the superseded *Practice Note (Official Solicitor: Sterilisation)* [1996] 2 FLR 111, reproduced at **APPENDIX 7.2** above.

2   Although the superseded *Practice Note (Official Solicitor: Sterilisation)* [1996] 2 FLR 111, reproduced at **APPENDIX 7.2** above, suggests that the description of the operation is optional, it is suggested that it should always be inserted. Even if sterilisation is in the patient's best interests and generally agreed to be so, there may still be controversy concerning the method used, such as hysterectomy.

Abortion Act 1967

1967 CHAPTER 87

An Act to amend and clarify the law relating to termination of pregnancy by registered medical practitioners

[27th October 1967]

BE IT ENACTED by the Queen's most Excellent Majesty, by and with the advice and consent of the Lords Spiritual and Temporal, and Commons, in this present Parliament assembled, and by the authority of the same, as follows:–

1 Medical termination of pregnancy

(1)   Subject to the provisions of this section, a person shall not be guilty of an offence under the law relating to abortion when a pregnancy is terminated by a registered medical practitioner if two registered medical practitioners are of the opinion, formed in good faith–

[(a)   that the pregnancy has not exceeded its twenty-fourth week and that the continuance of the pregnancy would involve risk, greater than if the pregnancy were terminated, of injury to the physical or mental health of the pregnant woman or any existing children of her family; or

(b)   that the termination is necessary to prevent grave permanent injury to the physical or mental health of the pregnant woman; or

(c)   that the continuance of the pregnancy would involve risk to the life of the pregnant woman, greater than if the pregnancy were terminated; or

(d)   that there is a substantial risk that if the child were born it would suffer from such physical or mental abnormalities as to be seriously handicapped].

(2)   In determining whether the continuance of a pregnancy would involve such risk of injury to health as is mentioned in paragraph (a) [or (b)] of subsection (1) of this section, account may be taken of the pregnant woman's actual or reasonably foreseeable environment.

(3)   Except as provided by subsection (4) of this section, any treatment for the termination of pregnancy must be carried out in a hospital vested in [the Secretary of State for the purposes of his functions under the [National Health Service Act 2006] or the National Health Service (Scotland) Act 1978 [or in a hospital vested in [a Primary Care Trust or] a National Health Service trust] [or an NHS foundation trust] or in a place approved for the purposes of this section by the Secretary of State].

[(3A) The power under subsection (3) of this section to approve a place includes power, in relation to treatment consisting primarily in the use of such medicines as may be specified in the approval and carried out in such manner as may be so specified, to approve a class of places.]

(4)   Subsection (3) of this section, and so much of subsection (1) as relates to the opinion of two registered medical practitioners, shall not apply to the

termination of a pregnancy by a registered medical practitioner in a case where he is of the opinion, formed in good faith, that the termination is immediately necessary to save the life or to prevent grave permanent injury to the physical or mental health of the pregnant woman.

2 Notification

(1)   The Minister of Health in respect of England and Wales, and the Secretary of State in respect of Scotland, shall by statutory instrument make regulations to provide–

   (a)   for requiring any such opinion as is referred to in section 1 of this Act to be certified by the practitioners or practitioner concerned in such form and at such time as may be prescribed by the regulations, and for requiring the preservation and disposal of certificates made for the purposes of the regulations;

   (b)   for requiring any registered medical practitioner who terminates a pregnancy to give notice of the termination and such other information relating to the termination as may be so prescribed;

   (c)   for prohibiting the disclosure, except to such persons or for such purposes as may be so prescribed, of notices given or information furnished pursuant to the regulations.

(2)   The information furnished in pursuance of regulations made by virtue of paragraph (b) of subsection (1) of this section shall be notified solely to the [Chief Medical Officer of the [Department of Health], or of the Welsh Office, or of the [Scottish Administration]].

(3)   Any person who wilfully contravenes or wilfully fails to comply with the requirements of regulations under subsection (1) of this section shall be liable on summary conviction to a fine not exceeding [level 5 on the standard scale].

(4)   Any statutory instrument made by virtue of this section shall be subject to annulment in pursuance of a resolution of either House of Parliament.

3 Application of Act to visiting forces etc

(1)   In relation to the termination of a pregnancy in a case where the following conditions are satisfied, that is to say–

   (a)   the treatment for termination of the pregnancy was carried out in a hospital controlled by the proper authorities of a body to which this section applies; and

   (b)   the pregnant woman had at the time of the treatment a relevant association with that body; and

   (c)   the treatment was carried out by a registered medical practitioner or a person who at the time of the treatment was a member of that body appointed as a medical practitioner for that body by the proper authorities of that body,

this Act shall have effect as if any reference in section 1 to a registered medical practitioner and to a hospital vested in [the Secretary of State] included respectively a reference to such a person as is mentioned in paragraph (c) of this subsection and to a hospital controlled as aforesaid, and as if section 2 were omitted.

(2)   The bodies to which this section applies are any force which is a visiting force within the meaning of any of the provisions of Part I of the Visiting Forces Act 1952 and any headquarters within the meaning of the Schedule to the

International Headquarters and Defence Organisations Act 1964; and for the purposes of this section–

    (a)   a woman shall be treated as having a relevant association at any time with a body to which this section applies if at that time—

        (i)   in the case of such a force as aforesaid, she had a relevant association within the meaning of the said Part I with the force; and

        (ii)   in the case of such a headquarters as aforesaid, she was a member of the headquarters or a dependant within the meaning of the Schedule aforesaid of such a member; and

    (b)   any reference to a member of a body to which this section applies shall be construed–

        (i)   in the case of such a force as aforesaid, as a reference to a member of or of a civilian component of that force within the meaning of the said Part I; and

        (ii)   in the case of such a headquarters as aforesaid, as a reference to a member of that headquarters within the meaning of the Schedule aforesaid.

4 Conscientious objection to participation in treatment

(1)   Subject to subsection (2) of this section, no person shall be under any duty, whether by contract or by any statutory or other legal requirement, to participate in any treatment authorised by this Act to which he has a conscientious objection:

Provided that in any legal proceedings the burden of proof of conscientious objection shall rest on the person claiming to rely on it.

(2)   Nothing in subsection (1) of this section shall affect any duty to participate in treatment which is necessary to save the life or to prevent grave permanent injury to the physical or mental health of a pregnant woman.

(3)   In any proceedings before a court in Scotland, a statement on oath by any person to the effect that he has a conscientious objection to participating in any treatment authorised by this Act shall be sufficient evidence for the purpose of discharging the burden of proof imposed upon him by subsection (1) of this section.

5 Supplementary provisions

[(1)   No offence under the Infant Life (Preservation) Act 1929 shall be committed by a registered medical practitioner who terminates a pregnancy in accordance with the provisions of this Act.]

(2)   For the purposes of the law relating to abortion, anything done with intent to procure [a woman's miscarriage (or, in the case of a woman carrying more than one foetus, her miscarriage of any foetus) is unlawfully done unless authorised by section 1 of this Act and, in the case of a woman carrying more than one foetus, anything done with intent to procure her miscarriage of any foetus is authorised by that section if–

    (a)   the ground for termination of the pregnancy specified in subsection (1)(d) of that section applies in relation to any foetus and the thing is done for the purpose of procuring the miscarriage of that foetus, or

    (b)   any of the other grounds for termination of the pregnancy specified in that section applies].

6 Interpretation

In this Act, the following expressions have meanings hereby assigned to them:–

"the law relating to abortion" means sections 58 and 59 of the Offences against the Person Act 1861, and any rule of law relating to the procurement of abortion;

7 Short title, commencement and extent

(1)   This Act may be cited as the Abortion Act 1967.
(2)   This Act shall come into force on the expiration of the period of six months beginning with the date on which it is passed.
(3)   This Act does not extend to Northern Ireland.

Appendix 8.2

Abortion Regulations 1991

1991 No 499

Made – 4th March 1991

Authority: Abortion Act 1967, s 2

1 Citation and commencement

(1)   These Regulations may be cited as the Abortion Regulations 1991, and shall come into force on 1st April 1991.
(2)   These Regulations extend to England and Wales only.

[2 Interpretation]

[In these Regulations–

"the Act" means the Abortion Act 1967;

['the Chief Medical Officer for Wales" means the Chief Medical Officer to the Welsh Assembly Government;]

"electronic communication" has the same meaning as in section 15 of the Electronic Communications Act 2000;

"practitioner" means a registered medical practitioner;

"solicitor" means a person who is qualified to act as a solicitor as provided by section 1 of the Solicitors Act 1974;

['the Statistics Board" means the Statistics Board established under section 1 of the Statistics and Registration Service Act 2007].]

3 Certificate of opinion

[(1)   Any opinion to which section 1 of the Act refers shall be certified–
    (a)   in the case of a pregnancy terminated in accordance with section 1(1) of the Act, either–
        (i)   in the form set out in Part I of Schedule 1 to these Regulations; or
        (ii)   in a certificate signed and dated by both practitioners jointly or in separate certificates signed and dated by each practitioner stating:–
        (a)the full name and address of each practitioner;
        (b)the full name and address of the pregnant woman;
        (c)whether or not each practitioner has seen or examined, or seen and examined, the pregnant woman; and
        (d)that each practitioner is of the opinion formed in good faith that at least one and the same ground mentioned in paragraph (a) to (d) of section 1(1) of the Act is fulfilled.

(b)   in the case of a pregnancy terminated in accordance with section 1(4) of the Act, either–
- (i)   in the form set out in Part II of Schedule 1 to these Regulations; or
- (ii)   in a certificate giving the full name and address of the practitioner and containing the full name and address of the pregnant woman and stating that the practitioner is of the opinion formed in good faith that one of the grounds mentioned in section 1(4) of the Act is fulfilled.]

(2)   Any certificate of an opinion referred to in section 1(1) of the Act shall be given before the commencement of the treatment for the termination of the pregnancy to which it relates.

(3)   Any certificate of an opinion referred to in section 1(4) of the Act shall be given before the commencement of the treatment for the termination of the pregnancy to which it relates or, if that is not reasonably practicable, not later than 24 hours after such termination.

(4)   Any such certificate as is referred to in paragraphs (2) and (3) of this regulation shall be preserved by the practitioner who terminated the pregnancy to which it relates for a period of not less than three years beginning with the date of the termination.

(5)   A certificate which is no longer to be preserved shall be destroyed by the person in whose custody it then is.

4 Notice of termination of pregnancy and information relating to the termination

(1)   Any practitioner who terminates a pregnancy in England or Wales shall give to the appropriate Chief Medical Officer–
- (a)   notice of the termination, and
- (b)   such other information relating to the termination as is specified in Schedule 2 to these Regulations,

and shall do so by sending them to him [within 14 days of the termination either in a sealed envelope or by an electronic communication transmitted by an electronic communications system used solely for the transfer of confidential information to him].

(2)   The appropriate Chief Medical Officer is–
- (a)   where the pregnancy was terminated in England, the Chief Medical Officer of the Department of Health, Richmond House, [79] Whitehall, London, SW1A 2NS; or
- (b)   where the pregnancy was terminated in Wales, the Chief Medical Officer [for Wales, [Welsh Assembly Government], Cathays Park, Cardiff, CF10 3NQ].

5 Restriction on disclosure of information

A notice given or any information furnished to a Chief Medical Officer in pursuance of these Regulations shall not be disclosed except that disclosure may be made–

(a)   for the purposes of carrying out their duties–
- (i)   to an officer of the Department of Health authorised by the Chief Medical Officer of that Department, or to an officer of [the Welsh Assembly Government] authorised by the Chief Medical Officer [for Wales], as the case may be, or
- [*(ii)   to the National Statistician duly appointed under section 5 of the Statistics*

          and Registration Service Act 2007 or an employee of the Statistics Board (established under section 1 of that Act) authorised by the National Statistician]

          [(ii) to the chairman of the Statistics Board or a member of the Statistics Board's staff who has been duly authorised by the chairman]; or

          [(iii) to an individual authorised by the Chief Medical Officer who is engaged in setting up, maintaining and supporting a computer system used for the purpose of recording, processing and holding such notice or information; or]

(b)   for the purposes of carrying out his duties in relation to offences under the Act or the law relating to abortion, to the Director of Public Prosecutions or a member of his staff authorised by him; or

(c)   for the purposes of investigating whether an offence has been committed under the Act or the law relating to abortion, to a police officer not below the rank of superintendent or a person authorised by him; or

(d)   pursuant to a court order, for the purposes of proceedings which have begun; or

(e)   for the purposes of bona fide scientific research; or

(f)   to the practitioner who terminated the pregnancy; or

(g)   to a practitioner, with the consent in writing of the woman whose pregnancy was terminated; or

(h)   when requested by the President of the General Medical Council for the purpose of investigating whether [the fitness to practise of the practitioner is impaired], to the President of the General Medical Council or a member of its staff authorised by him;

[(i)   to the woman whose pregnancy was terminated, on her supplying to the Chief Medical Officer written details of her date of birth, the date and place of the termination and a copy of the certificate of registration of her birth certified as a true copy of the original by a solicitor or a practitioner].

6 Revocations

The whole of the Regulations specified in Schedule 3 to these Regulations are revoked.

Appendix 8.3

Form of Certification under the Abortion Regulations 1991

Part I

IN CONFIDENCE

CERTIFICATE A

ABORTION ACT 1967

Not to be destroyed within three years of the date of operation

Certificate to be completed before an abortion is performed under Section 1(1) of the Act

I, ... (Name and qualifications of practitioner in block capitals) of

....

(Full address of practitioner)

Have/have not (delete as appropriate) seen/and examined (delete as appropriate) pregnant woman to whom this certificate relates at ....

(full address of place at which patient was seen or examined) on .... and I

....

(Name and qualifications of practitioner in block capitals) of ....

(Full address of practitioner) ....

Have/have not (delete as appropriate) seen/and examined (delete as appropriate) the pregnant woman to whom this certificate relates at ....

(Full address of place at which patient was seen or examined) on ....

We hereby certify that we are of the opinion, formed in good faith, that in the case of .... (Full name of pregnant woman in block capitals) of ....

(Usual place of residence of pregnant woman in block capitals)

(Ring appropriate letter(s))

A the continuance of the pregnancy would involve risk to the life of the pregnant woman greater than if the pregnancy were terminated;

B the termination is necessary to prevent grave permanent injury to the physical or mental health of the pregnant woman:

C the pregnancy has NOT exceeded its 24th week and that the continuance of the pregnancy would involve risk, greater than if the pregnancy were terminated, of injury to the physical or mental health of the pregnant woman;

D the pregnancy has NOT exceeded its 24th week and that the continuance of the pregnancy would involve risk, greater than if the pregnancy were terminated, of injury to the physical or mental health of any existing child(ren) of the family of the pregnant woman;

E there is a substantial risk that if the child were born it would suffer from such physical or mental abnormalities as to be seriously handicapped.

This certificate of opinion is given before the commencement of the treatment for the termination of pregnancy to which it refers and relates to the circumstances of the pregnant woman's individual case.

Signed .... Date ....

Signed .... Date ....

Form HSA1 (revised 1991)

Appendix 8.4

Form of Certification under the Abortion Regulations 1991: Emergency Case

Part II

IN CONFIDENCE

CERTIFICATE B

Not to be destroyed within three years of the date of operation

ABORTION ACT 1967

CERTIFICATE TO BE COMPLETED IN RELATION TO ABORTION PERFORMED IN EMERGENCY UNDER SECTION 1(4) OF THE ACT

I, ... (Name and qualifications of practitioner in block capitals) of ....

Hereby certify that I am/was (delete as appropriate) of the opinion formed in good faith that it is/was (delete as appropriate) necessary immediately to terminate the pregnancy of (Full address of practitioner)...

(Full name of pregnant woman in block capitals) of ....

(Usual place of residence of pregnant woman in block capitals)

(Ring appropriate number)

in order

1 to save the life of the pregnant woman; or

2 to prevent grave permanent injury to the physical or mental health of the pregnant woman.

This certificate of opinion is given-

(Ring appropriate letter)

A before the commencement of the treatment for the termination of the pregnancy to which it relates; or,

if that is not reasonably practicable, then

B not later than 24 hours after such termination.

Signed ....

Date ....

Form HSA2 – Crown copyright – produced by the Department of Health, January 2009.

Abortion Regulations 1991 Schedule 2

1991 No 499

[Information to be supplied in an Abortion Notification

1 Full name and address (including postcode) of the practitioner who terminated the pregnancy and the General Medical Council registration number of the practitioner.

2 In non-emergency cases particulars of the practitioners who gave a certificate of opinion pursuant to section 1(1) of the Act and whether they saw or examined, or saw and examined the patient before giving the certificate.

3 Patient's details–

(a)   patient's hospital or clinic number or National Health Service number or (if unavailable) patient's full name;
(b)   date of birth;
(c)   in the case of a patient resident in the United Kingdom, her full postcode or, if the postcode is unavailable, her address;
(d)   in the case of a patient resident outside the United Kingdom, her country of residence;
(e)   ethnicity (if disclosed by the patient);
(f)   marital status; and
(g)   parity.

4 Name and address of place of termination.

5 Whether the termination was paid for privately or not.

6 Date and method of foeticide if appropriate.

7 In a case where the termination is by surgery–

(a)   date of termination;
(b)   the method of termination used; and
(c)   in cases where the dates are different, the date of admission to the place of termination and the date of discharge from the place of termination.

8 In a case where the termination is by non-surgical means–

(a)   the date of treatment with antiprogestrone;
(b)   the date of treatment with prostaglandin;
(c   the date on which the termination is confirmed;
(d)   in cases where the place of treatment with prostaglandin is different from the place of treatment with antiprogestrone, the name and address at which the prostaglandin was administered;
(e)   details of other agents used and the date of administration; and
(f)   the date of discharge if an overnight stay is required.

9 Number of complete weeks of gestation.

10 The ground(s) certified for terminating the pregnancy contained in the certificate of opinion given pursuant to section 1(1) of the Act together with the following additional information in the case of–

(a)   the ground specified in paragraph (a), whether or not there was a risk to the patient's mental health and if not, her main medical conditions;

(b)   the grounds specified in paragraphs (b) and (c), the main medical condition(s) of the patient;

(c)   the ground specified in paragraph (d), any foetal abnormalities diagnosed, together with method of diagnosis used, and any other reasons for termination.

11 The ground(s) certified for terminating the pregnancy contained in the certificate of opinion given pursuant to section 1(4) of the Act and the patient's main medical conditions.

12 In cases of selective termination the original number of foetuses and the number of foetuses remaining.

13 Whether or not the patient was offered chlamydia screening.

14 Particulars of any complications experienced by the patient up to the date of discharge.

15 In the case of the death of the patient the date and cause of death.]

NOTES

Amendment

Substituted in relation to England by SI 2002/887, reg 6, Schedule and in relation to Wales by SI 2002/2879, reg 6, Schedule.

Appendix 8.6

Form of Notification for pregnancies terminated in England and Wales: Form HSA4

Form HSA4 (Revised Sept 2006)

ABORTION NOTIFICATION

ABORTION ACT 1967 – FORM OF NOTIFICATION FOR PREGNANCIES TERMINATED IN ENGLAND AND WALES

This form is to be COMPLETED BY THE PRACTITIONER TERMINATING THE PREGNANCY and sent in a sealed envelope within FOURTEEN DAYS of the termination to:

The Chief Medical Officer
Department of Health
Richmond House   OR
79 Whitehall
LONDON SW1A 2NS

The Chief Medical Officer
National Assembly for Wales
Cathays Park
CARDIFF CF10 3NQ
for pregnancies terminated in Wales

PLEASE USE BLOCK CAPITALS AND NUMERALS FOR DATES THROUGHOUT, KEEPING WITHIN THE BOXES
DO NOT CROSS THROUGH ANY BOXES THAT DO NOT NEED TO BE COMPLETED

❶ PRACTITIONER TERMINATING THE PREGNANCY

FULL NAME   I

PERMANENT   of
ADDRESS

GMC registration number

hereby give notice that I terminated the pregnancy of the woman identified overleaf, and to the best of my knowledge the particulars on this form are correct. I further certify that I joined/did not join* in giving HSA1 having seen/not seen* and examined/not examined* her before doing so.

Signature   Date

❷ CERTIFICATION   In all non-emergency cases state particulars of practitioners who joined in giving HSA1
a. To be completed in all cases.   b. Do not complete if the operating practitioner joined in giving Certificate HSA1.

FULL NAME(S)

PERMANENT
ADDRESS

Did the practitioner named at a. certify that s/he saw/and examined the pregnant woman before giving the certificate?   ☐ YES ☐ NO

Did the practitioner named at b. certify that s/he saw/and examined the pregnant woman before giving the certificate?   ☐ YES ☐ NO

* delete as appropriate

Page 1

448

❸ PATIENT'S DETAILS

a) PATIENT'S REFERENCE

Patient's hospital/clinic number or NHS number:

If not available enter full name below

➡

b) DATE OF BIRTH

In all cases enter date of birth

d   d   m   m   y   y   y   y

c) POSTCODE

For UK residents, state full postcode

➡

If full postcode is not available, enter complete address below

For non-UK residents, state country of residence

☐ Republic of Ireland

Other – state

d) ETHNICITY   Please state the patient's self-reported ethnicity where known:

White:
- ☐ British
- ☐ Irish
- ☐ Any other white background

Mixed:
- ☐ White and Black Caribbean
- ☐ White and Black African
- ☐ White and Asian
- ☐ Any other mixed background

Asian or Asian British:
- ☐ Indian
- ☐ Pakistani
- ☐ Bangladeshi
- ☐ Any other Asian background

Black or Black British:
- ☐ Caribbean
- ☐ African
- ☐ Any other Black background

Chinese or other ethnic group:
- ☐ Chinese
- ☐ Any other

Not known:
- ☐ Not Known

e) MARITAL STATUS   (tick appropriate box)

- ☐ Single (no partner)
- ☐ Single (with partner)
- ☐ Single (partner status not known)
- ☐ Married
- ☐ Widowed
- ☐ Civil Partnership
- ☐ Divorced
- ☐ Separated
- ☐ Not known

f) PARITY   Number of previous pregnancies resulting in:

Livebirths and stillbirths over 24 weeks	Spontaneous miscarriages and ectopic pregnancies	Legal terminations

P ☐☐ + ☐☐ + ☐   (enter number – if nil enter 0)

Page 2

449

Appendix 8.6

4 TREATMENT DETAILS

a) NAME AND ADDRESS OF PLACE OF TERMINATION INCLUDING PLACE OF TREATMENT WITH ANTIPROGESTERONE

Hospital/clinic code ☐ ☐ ☐ ☐ ☐

Please specify whether this was an NHS funded
or privately funded abortion

☐ NHS funded abortion   ☐ Privately funded abortion

b) FETICIDE

Where feticide used complete this section. Otherwise go to 4c or 4d as appropriate

(i) Date of feticide   ☐ ☐ ☐ ☐ 2 0 ☐

(ii) Method of feticide   [   ]

Please now complete 4c or 4d according to the method used to evacuate the uterus.

c) SURGICAL TERMINATIONS

TERMINATION   Date of termination   ☐ ☐ ☐ ☐ 2 0 ☐

If date of admission or discharge are different from date of termination, please enter dates below:

ADMISSION   Date of admission to place of termination   2 0 ☐

DISCHARGE   Date of discharge from place of termination   2 0 ☐

                                                            d d m m y y y y

State method used:

Vacuum aspiration/Suction ☐   Other surgical – specify: [   ]

Dilatation and Evacuation ☐

An evacuation of retained products of conception is not a termination and should not be entered.

Please now go to Section 5

d) MEDICAL TERMINATIONS

(i)   Date of treatment with Antiprogesterone   ☐ ☐ ☐ ☐ 2 0 ☐

(ii) Date of treatment with Prostaglandin   ☐ ☐ ☐ ☐ 2 0 ☐

(iii) Date termination confirmed   ☐ ☐ ☐ ☐ 2 0 ☐

                                                      d d m m y y y y

Name and address of place of treatment with Prostaglandin (if different from address at Section 4a)

Hospital/clinic code ☐ ☐ ☐ ☐ ☐

Medical Terminations – continued overleaf

Page 3

450

d) MEDICAL TERMINATIONS – continued

If other medical agents were used, specify:

(i) Date of treatment   (ii)   Medical agent used   (i)

					2	0		
d	d	m	m	y	y	y	y	

If an overnight stay was required please also complete date of discharge in Section 4(c) on page 3   (ii)

---

❺ GESTATION   Specify number of completed weeks

---

❻ GROUNDS   The certified ground(s) for terminating the pregnancy stated on HSA1 were: (tick appropriate box(es))

A ☐   that the continuance of the pregnancy would involve risk to the life of the pregnant woman greater than if the pregnancy were terminated.

B ☐   that the termination is necessary to prevent grave permanent injury to the physical or mental health of the pregnant woman.

> A or B state main medical condition(s)

C ☐   that the pregnancy has NOT exceeded its 24th week and that the continuance of the pregnancy would involve risk, greater than if the pregnancy were terminated, of injury to the physical or mental health of the pregnant woman (this includes pregnancies up to 24 weeks and 0 days).

Was there a risk to the woman's mental health?   ☐ YES   ☐ NO

If not, please state the main medical condition(s)

> State main medical condition(s)

D ☐   that the pregnancy has NOT exceeded its 24th week and that the continuance of the pregnancy would involve risk, greater than if the pregnancy were terminated, of injury to the physical or mental health of any existing child(ren) of the family of the pregnant woman (this includes pregnancies up to 24 weeks and 0 days).

E ☐   that there is a substantial risk that if the child were born it would suffer from such physical or mental abnormalities as to be seriously handicapped:

> State the abnormality or other reason for termination

For ground E cases only, state method(s) of diagnosis (tick appropriate box(es))

Amniocentesis ☐   Ultrasound ☐   Chorionic villus sampling ☐   Other – specify

Grounds – continued overleaf

Page 4

451

6 GROUNDS – continued

EMERGENCY ONLY Termination was immediately necessary, as stated on HSA2:

F ☐   to save the life of the pregnant woman OR

G ☐   to prevent grave permanent injury to the physical or mental health of the pregnant woman

F or G State main medical condition(s):

7 SELECTIVE TERMINATION   If this was a selective termination, state:

(i) original number of fetuses: ☐   (ii) number of fetuses reduced to: ☐

All other relevant sections of the form should also be completed

8 CHLAMYDIA SCREENING

Was screening for chlamydia offered?   ☐ YES   ☐ NO

9 COMPLICATIONS – up until the time of discharge (tick appropriate box(es))

None ☐   Haemorrhage ☐   Uterine Perforation ☐   Sepsis ☐

Other – specify:

An evacuation of retained products of conception is not a complication

10 DEATH OF WOMAN   In the case of death, specify:

DATE ☐ ☐ | ☐ ☐ | 2 0 ☐ ☐
         d d   m m   y y y y

State cause of death

**Please now send the form in a sealed envelope (HSA4ENV)
to the address shown on page 1**

Page 5

452

A guidance note to aid completion of this form may be found at
www.dh.gov.uk or requested from hsa4@dh.gsi.gov.uk

Supplies of forms HSA1, HSA2, HSA4 (27259) and HSA4ENV are available from:

Department of Health
PO Box 777
London
SE1 6XH

Fax: 01623 724 524

Or you can call the NHS Responseline on 08701 555 455

SAMPLE

Page 6

453

Sample text for sections 5.1 and 5.2 of the COP 1 Application Form, in relation to an application for a declaration that the court determine whether a termination is in an adult's best interests:

5.1 Please state the matter you want the court to decide?

1.   Whether P lacks capacity to decide between termination and continuation of her current pregnancy.
2.   P's best interests in relation to the termination or continuation of her current pregnancy.

5.2 Please state the order you are asking the court to make?

1.   That P lacks capacity to make a decision between termination and continuation of her current pregnancy.
2.   That, having regard to the best interests of P, it is lawful for her pregnancy to be terminated by [insert method of termination] by the applicant.
        Or
3.   That it is in P's best interests for her current pregnancy to continue.

5.3 How would the order benefit the person to whom the application relates?

It would ensure that a decision is taken in relation to P's pregnancy which is in her best interests.

Appendix 8.8

Draft order that it is in an adult's best interests to undergo a termination

(Assume that the hearing has been ordered to take place in public with reporting restrictions)

CASE NO xxxxxxxx

IN THE COURT OF PROTECTION

IN THE MATTER OF THE MENTAL CAPACITY ACT 2005

IN THE MATTER OF AB

BEFORE MR JUSTICE

SITTING ON [DATE]

B E T W E E N

AN NHS TRUST

Applicant

– and –

AB (by her litigation friend the Official Solicitor)

Respondent

DRAFT ORDER ON BEHALF OF APPLICANT

UPON HEARING [name of Counsel], counsel for the Applicant and [name of Counsel], counsel for the Respondent

UPON READING the hearing bundle

AND UPON HEARING evidence from Dr D

IT IS DECLARED THAT:

1. P lacks capacity to make a decision between termination and continuation of her current pregnancy.
2. Having regard to the best interests of P, it is lawful for her pregnancy to be terminated by [insert method of termination] by the Applicant.

AND IT IS ORDERED THAT:

1. There shall be liberty to apply in the event of a material change in the existing circumstances.
2. The Applicant shall pay half of the Official Solicitor's costs, to be subject to detailed assessment if not agreed.

Appendix 8.9

The law and ethics of abortion

BMA Views

Legal considerations

- England and Wales
- Scotland
- Northern Ireland

November 2007
http://www.bma.org.uk/images/lawethicsabortionnov07_tcm41-146867.pdf

1. Legal considerations
   1.1 The Law on abortion in England, Scotland and Wales
   1.2 The Law on abortion in Northern Ireland
   1.3 Conscientious Objection Clause
       1.3.1 Legal scope
       1.3.2 Distinction between legal and moral duties
       1.3.3 Conscientious objection applied to contraceptive services
   1.4 Early medical abortion
   1.5 Late abortion for fetal abnormality
   1.6 Selective abortion of multiple pregnancy
   1.7 Abortion on grounds of fetal sex
2. Ethical considerations
   2.1 Moral arguments
       2.1.1 Arguments used in support of abortion
       2.1.2 Arguments used against abortion
       2.1.3 Arguments used to support abortion in some circumstances
       2.1.4 The BMA's view on abortion
       2.1.5 Fetal pain
   2.2 Consent
       2.2.1 The competent adult.
       2.2.2 The incompetent adult
       2.2.3 Competent minors
       2.2.4 Incompetent minors
       2.2.5 Partners' views
   2.3 Confidentiality
       2.3.1 Adults
       2.3.2 Minors
3. Summary

Abortion is a very sensitive issue and one on which members of the BMA hold a wide diversity of views. Association policy, however, has been agreed at the BMA's annual representatives meeting (ARM)

456

1. LEGAL CONSIDERATIONS

Doctors must act in accordance with the law.

1.1 The law on abortion in England, Scotland and Wales

Abortion in England, Scotland and Wales is governed by the Abortion Act 1967 as amended by the Human Fertilisation and Embryology Act 1990. This states that a registered medical practitioner may lawfully terminate a pregnancy, in an NHS hospital or on premises approved for this purpose, if two registered medical practitioners are of the opinion, formed in good faith:

"(a)   that the pregnancy has not exceeded its twenty-fourth week and that the continuance of the pregnancy would involve risk, greater than if the pregnancy were terminated, of injury to the physical or mental health of the pregnant woman or any existing children of her family; or

(b)   that the termination is necessary to prevent grave permanent injury to the physical or mental health of the pregnant woman; or

(c)   that the continuance of the pregnancy would involve risk to the life of the pregnant woman, greater that if the pregnancy were terminated; or

(d)   that there is a substantial risk that if the child were born it would suffer from such physical or mental abnormalities as to be seriously handicapped."[1]

In addition, where a doctor "is of the opinion, formed in good faith, that the termination is immediately necessary to save the life or to prevent grave permanent injury to the physical or mental health of the pregnant woman" the opinion of a second registered medical practitioner is not required. Nor, in these limited circumstances, are there restrictions on where the procedure may be carried out.

The 1990 amendments to the Act removed pre-existing links with the Infant Life Preservation Act 1929 which had made it illegal to "destroy the life of a child capable of being born alive" with an assumption that a child was capable of being born alive after 28 weeks gestation. Thus, terminations carried out under sections 1(1)(b) to 1(1)(d) of the Act may be performed at any gestational age.

The question of what constitutes a "serious handicap" under section 1(1)(d) is not addressed in the legislation. It is a matter of clinical judgment and accepted practice. In assessing the seriousness of a handicap, the following criteria may be used:

- the probability of effective treatment, either in utero or after birth;
- the child's probable potential for self-awareness and potential ability to communicate with others; and
- the suffering that would be experienced by the child when born or by the people caring for the child.

1.2 The law on abortion in Northern Ireland

The Abortion Act 1967 does not extend to Northern Ireland. The law on abortion in Northern Ireland is different and is based on the Offences Against The Person Act 1861 which makes it an offence to "procure a miscarriage ... unlawfully". The *Bourne*[2] judgement of 1939, in which a London gynaecologist was found not guilty of an offence under this Act for performing an abortion on a 14 year old who was pregnant as a result of rape, was based on an interpretation of the word unlawfully in this Act. The defence argued, and the judge accepted, that in the particular circumstances of the case, the operation was not unlawful since continuation of the pregnancy would severely affect the young woman's mental health. In reaching this decision, the judge turned to the wording of the Infant Life (Preservation) Act 1929 which gave protection from prosecution if the act was carried out in good faith "for the purpose only of preserving the life of the mother". This formed the basis of the judgment and extended the grounds for a lawful abortion to include the mental and physical well-being of the woman. Whereas the law in England, Scotland and Wales is covered by the 1967 Act, Northern Ireland has been left with the task of interpreting this word "unlawfully" in the 1861 Offences Against the Person Act using also the 1945 Criminal Justice Act (Northern Ireland) (under which the 1929 Infant Life (Preservation) Act was applied to Northern Ireland) with the precedent set in *Bourne*.

It is known that abortions are carried out in Northern Ireland and that abortion is lawful in some circumstances. The cases of *K* and *A*[3] in 1993 and 1994 respectively confirm this but in the judgment in *A* the judge stated that:

> "The doctor's act is lawful where the continuance of the pregnancy would adversely affect the mental or physical health of the mother …The adverse effect must, however, be a real and serious one and it will always be a question of fact and degree whether the perceived effect of non termination is sufficiently grave to warrant terminating the unborn child".

Following a successful High Court Appeal by the Family Planning Association in October 2004, the Department of Health, Social Services and Public Safety (DHSSPS) was instructed by the Court to produce clear guidance for women and doctors on the circumstances in which abortion would be permissible. Final publication of this guidance is awaited at the time of writing in 2007.

The BMA has policy supporting the extension of the Abortion Act to Northern Ireland (Annual Representatives Meeting 1985 and 2003). In July 2007, however, the Westminster government clarified in a Parliamentary Answer that any changes in abortion legislation in Northern Ireland would have to be instigated by the Northern Irish public: "We are aware of a body of opinion in Northern Ireland that considers the current law on abortion to be either unsatisfactory or unclear, but we also recognise the strength of feeling for not changing the existing legislative provision. In such circumstances, the Government believe that any change to the law should only come about at the request of a broad cross-section of the people who live there."[4]

Doctors in Northern Ireland wishing to discuss particular cases or to seek advice on the law may contact the local BMA office.

1.3 Conscientious objection clause

1.3.1 Legal scope

The Abortion Act 1967 has a conscientious objection clause which permits doctors to refuse to participate in terminations but which obliges them to provide necessary treatment in an emergency when the woman's life may be jeopardised. The BMA supports the right of doctors to have a conscientious objection to termination of pregnancy and believes that such doctors should not be marginalised. Some doctors have complained of being harassed and discriminated against because of their conscientious objection to termination of pregnancy. There have also been reports of doctors, who carry out abortions, being subjected to harassment and abuse. The Association abhors all such behaviour and any BMA members who feel they are being pressured, abused or harassed because of their views about termination of pregnancy, should contact their regional office for advice and support.

The scope of the conscientious objection clause, in the 1967 Act, was clarified by a Parliamentary answer in December 1991.[5] This made clear that conscientious objection was only intended to be applied to participation in treatment, although hospital managers had been asked to apply the principle, at their discretion, to those ancillary staff who were involved in the handling of fetuses and fetal tissue.

The same view emerged from the House of Lords' decision in case of Janaway v Salford Health Authority[6] in 1988 when a doctor's secretary (Janaway) refused to type the referral letter for an abortion and claimed a conscientious objection under the Act. The House of Lords, in interpreting the word "participate" in this context, decided to give the word its ordinary and natural meaning – that is, that in order to claim conscientious exemption under section[4] of the Act, the objector had to be required to actually take part in administering treatment in a hospital or approved centre. In the same case the judge went on to say that "The regulations do not appear to contemplate that the signing of the certificate would form part of the treatment for the termination of pregnancy". This would seem to support the view that general practitioners cannot claim exemption from giving advice or performing the preparatory steps to arrange an abortion if the request for abortion meets the legal requirements. Such steps include referral to another doctor as appropriate. Doctors with a conscientious objection to abortion should make their views known to the patient and enable the patient to see another doctor without delay if that is the patient's wish. Although they may not impose their views on others who do not share them doctors with a conscientious objection may explain their views to the patient if invited to do so. The General Medical Council advises that:[7]

> 'If carrying out a particular procedure or giving advice about it conflicts with your religious or moral beliefs, and this conflict might affect the treatment or advice you provide, you must explain this to the patient and tell them they have the right to see another doctor. You must be satisfied that the patient has sufficient information to enable them to exercise that right. If it is not practical for a patient to arrange to see another doctor, you must ensure that arrangements are made for another suitably qualified colleague to take over your role.'

General practitioners with a conscientious objection, who are working in a group practice, may ask a partner to see patients seeking termination. Practices may wish to state in advance if GPs in their practice have a conscientious objection to abortion, for example in their practice leaflets.

The position of medical students was clarified in personal communication with the Department of Health which has been passed to the Association for information. This made clear that the conscientious objection clause can be used by students to opt out of witnessing abortions. The BMA's advice is that those who have a conscientious objection should disclose that fact to supervisors, managers or GP partners (whichever is appropriate) at as early a stage as possible so that this fact can be taken into account when planning provisions for patient care.

The Scottish Executive published guidance in September 2004 on the information about abortion that may be included in job advertisements, and descriptions and the questions that may be asked at interview.[8] At the time of writing there is no equivalent guidance for England and Wales.

1.3.2 Distinction between legal and moral duties

In some cases a distinction can be made between the legal and ethical obligations. Whilst noting the legal view, the BMA considers that some things which arguably fall outside the legal scope of the conscience clause, such as completion of the form for abortion, are arguably an integral part of the abortion procedure. In this case, the BMA considers that completion of a form for abortion falls morally within the scope of the conscience clause. Other preliminary procedures, such as clerking in the patient, are incidental to the termination and are considered outwith the scope of the conscience clause both legally and morally. Generally it will not be beneficial for women undergoing termination to be cared for by health professionals who feel distressed or unhappy about their involvement. Nevertheless where such tasks are unavoidable, health professionals must pursue a non-judgemental approach to the women concerned.

1.3.3 Conscientious objection applied to contraceptive services

There has, in the past, been some uncertainty about whether certain types of contraceptives, such as hormonal emergency contraception and intra uterine devices should be classed as abortifacients which could be issued only under the terms of the Abortion Act. This question was resolved by a Parliamentary answer in May 1983 in which it was clarified that the prevention of implantation does not constitute the "procuring of a miscarriage" within the terms of the Offences Against the Persons Act 1861.[9] This interpretation was tested and confirmed in the case of *R v HS Dhingra*[10] in 1991 and by a judicial review in 2002.

Judicial review on emergency hormonal contraception

The Society for the Protection of the Unborn Child applied for a judicial review of the decision of the Secretary of State for Health, in 2000, to make emergency contraception available from pharmacists without a prescription. The claimant contended that the "morning after pill" was not a contraceptive but an abortifacient because it procured a miscarriage within the meaning of the 1861 Offences Against the Persons Act. Its use, therefore, would only be lawful if prescribed by two doctors, as required by the Abortion Act 1967. The Secretary of State argued, however, that the meaning of "miscarriage" was the loss of a fertilised egg that had become implanted in the endometrium of the uterus. Since emergency hormonal contraception caused the loss of an egg before implantation, there was no miscarriage and therefore no criminal offence.

The High Court judge held that the decision turned on the meaning of "miscarriage" now and not its meaning in 1861. Today, miscarriage is taken to mean the termination of an established pregnancy and therefore the application was dismissed.

R v Secretary of State for Health[11]

Although, legally, the use of contraceptives designed to prevent implantation does not constitute an abortion, the BMA recognises that some doctors, believing that life begins at fertilisation, may have an ethical objection to their use. Doctors holding this view are not obliged to prescribe these forms of contraception but must ensure the patient has access to another doctor who will be willing to comply with the request; this may include a referral. Guidelines on the use of emergency contraception are available from the Faculty of Family Planning and Reproductive Health Care.[12]

1.4 Early medical abortion

Since 1991 mifepristone (formerly known as RU486) has been available in England, Scotland and Wales for early medical abortions. These must comply with the terms of the 1967 Act (as amended). A 1990 amendment to the Abortion Act specifies that the power to approve premises for termination of pregnancy includes the power to approve premises for the administration of medical terminations. Without this amendment, the administration of mifepristone would have been lawful only if carried out on premises approved for surgical terminations.

1.5 Late abortion for fetal abnormality

Under the law in England, Scotland and Wales, a pregnancy may be terminated at any gestation if there is a "substantial risk that if the child were born it would suffer from such physical or mental abnormalities as to be seriously handicapped". Practical guidelines for health professionals involved with terminations for fetal abnormality are available from the Royal College of Obstetricians & Gynaecologists.[13]

Women need to be given time to understand the nature and severity of fetal abnormality and, with the help of specialised counselling where appropriate, to reach a decision about how to proceed. The purpose of antenatal screening is to extend the choice available to the pregnant woman and to allow her to make an informed decision about whether to continue with the pregnancy or seek a termination. Women should not be rushed into making these important decisions but, if a firm decision is made to terminate the pregnancy, this should proceed without undue delay. Health and other appropriate professionals should provide support before and after the termination.

1.6 Selective abortion of multiple pregnancy

Until 1990 the legality of selective reduction of multiple pregnancies was unclear. This was clarified by section 37(5) of the Human Fertilisation & Embryology Act which amended the Abortion Act to explicitly include "in the case of a woman carrying more than one fetus, her miscarriage of any fetus". Thus, selective reduction of pregnancy would be lawful provided the circumstances matched the criteria for termination of pregnancy set out in the 1967 Act (as amended) and the procedure was carried out in an NHS hospital or premises approved for terminations. The same ethical and legal considerations apply to termination of all or part of a multiple pregnancy as to the termination of a singleton pregnancy. Under the new section 5(2) of the Abortion Act selective reduction of a multiple pregnancy may lawfully be performed if:

> "(a)   the ground for termination of the pregnancy specified in subsection (1)(d) of [section 1] applies in relation to any fetus and the thing is done for the purpose of procuring the miscarriage of that fetus; or
>
> (b)   any of the other grounds for termination of the pregnancy specified in that section applies"

Thus it has been suggested that a general risk of serious handicap to the fetuses, if the multiple pregnancy is not reduced, would not be covered by the Act and the risk must be to a specific fetus.[14] Alternately where there is an increased risk to the mother, as a result of the multiple pregnancy, the selective reduction may be lawful under section 1(1)(a), (b) or (c).

The BMA considers selective termination to be justifiable where the procedure is recommended for medical reasons. Women who have a multiple pregnancy should be carefully counselled where medical opinion is that continuation, without selective reduction, will result in the loss of all the fetuses but they cannot be compelled or pressured to accept selective abortion. The Association does not, however, consider it acceptable to choose which fetuses to abort on anything other than medical grounds. Where there are no medical indications for aborting particular fetuses, the choice should be a random one. The Association would not consider it acceptable, when making this decision, to accede to the parents' desire for a male or a female child.

1.7 Abortion on grounds of fetal sex

Fetal sex is not one of the criteria for abortion listed in the Abortion Act of 1967 and therefore termination on this ground alone has been challenged as outwith the law. There may be circumstances, however, in which termination of pregnancy on grounds of fetal sex would be lawful. It has been suggested that if two doctors, acting in good faith, formed the opinion that the pregnant woman's health or that of her existing children would be put at greater risk than if she terminated the pregnancy, the abortion would be arguably lawful under section 1(1)(a) of the Abortion Act. The Association believes that it is normally unethical to terminate a pregnancy on the grounds of fetal sex alone except in cases of severe x-linked disorders. The pregnant woman's views about the effect of the sex of the fetus on her situation and on her existing children should nevertheless be carefully considered. In some circumstances doctors may come to the conclusion that the effects are so severe as to provide ethical justification for a termination. They should be prepared to justify the decision if it were challenged.

2. ETHICAL CONSIDERATIONS

2.1 Moral arguments

People generally take one of three main stances on abortion: pro-abortion, anti-abortion and the middle ground that abortion is acceptable in some circumstances. The main arguments for each of these positions is set out below.

2.1.1 Arguments used in support of abortion

Those who support the wide availability of abortion consider that abortion is not wrong in itself and need not involve undesirable consequences. These arguments tend not to recognise fetal rights or to acknowledge the fetus to be a person. According to some, abortion is a matter of a woman's right to exercise control over her own body. Moralists who judge actions by their consequences alone could argue that abortion is equivalent to a deliberate failure to conceive a child and since contraception is widely available, abortion should be too. Some think that even if the fetus is a person, its rights are very limited and do not weigh significantly against the interests of people who have already been born, such as parents or existing children of the family.

Most people who support this position do so on the basis that the overriding principle is the woman's right to choose what happens to her body. This use of the language of "choice" conveys approval regardless of the type of pressures the individual faces and any constraints on her freedom to make a genuine choice.

2.1.2 Arguments used against abortion

Some people consider that abortion is wrong in any circumstances because it fails to recognise the rights of the fetus or because it challenges the notion of the sanctity of all human life.

Some argue that permitting abortion diminishes the respect society feels for other vulnerable humans, possibly leading to their involuntary euthanasia. Those who consider that an embryo, from the moment of conception, is a human being with full moral status, see abortion as killing in the same sense as the murder of any other person. Those who take this view cannot accept that women should be allowed to obtain abortion without legal repercussions, however difficult the lives of those women or their existing families are made as a result.

Such views may be based on religious or moral convictions that each human life has unassailable intrinsic value, which is not diminished by any impairment or suffering that may be involved for the individual living that life. It is also argued that abortion treats humans merely as a means to an end in that abortion can be seen as a discarding of a fetus in which the pregnant woman no longer has any interest. Many worry that the availability of abortion on grounds of fetal abnormality encourages prejudice towards any person with a handicap and insidiously creates the impression that the only valuable people are those who conform to some ill-defined stereotype of "normality".

Some people who oppose abortion in general, concede that it may be justifiable in very exceptional cases such as where it is the result of rape or the consequence of exploitation of a young girl or a mentally incompetent woman. Risk to the mother's life may be another justifiable exception but only where abortion is the only option. It would thus not be seen as justifiable to abort a fetus if the life of both fetus and mother could be saved by any other solution.

2.1.3 Arguments used to support abortion in some circumstances

Many people argue that abortion may be justified in a greater number of circumstances than those conceded by anti-abortionists but that it would be undesirable to allow abortion on demand. To do so might incur undesirable effects, such as encouraging irresponsible attitudes to contraception. It could also lead to a devaluation of the lives of viable fetuses and trivialise the potential psychological effects of abortion on women and on health professionals.

These types of argument are based on the premise that the embryo starts off without rights, although having a special status from conception in view of its potential for development, and that it acquires rights and status throughout its development. The notion of developing fetal rights and practical factors, such as the possible distress to the pregnant woman, nurses, doctors or other children in the family, gives rise to the view that early abortion is more acceptable than late abortion.

Some people support this position on pragmatic grounds, believing that abortions will always be sought by women who are desperate and that it is better for society to provide abortion services which are safe and which can be monitored and regulated, rather than to allow "back-street" practices.

2.1.4 The BMA's view on abortion

In the 1970s and 1980s the BMA approved policy statements supporting the 1967 Abortion Act as "a practical and humane piece of legislation" and calling for its expansion to Northern Ireland. The BMA does not consider that abortion is unethical but as with any act having profound moral implications, the justifications must be commensurate with the consequences. Patients are entitled to receive objective medical advice regardless of their doctor's personal views for or against abortion. Furthermore, a doctor could be sued for damages if, because of a failure to refer, a delay is caused which results in the woman being unable to obtain a termination.

At the BMA's Annual Representatives Meeting (ARM) in 2005, a detailed briefing paper on abortion time limits was prepared that considered the peer-reviewed published data on survival rates and the longer-term health of babies born at early gestation in the UK.[15] Doctors representing the membership debated the issue, voted, and concluded that there should be no reduction in the current 24-week limit under the Abortion Act 1967.

At the 2007 ARM the issue of first trimester abortion (up to around 13 weeks of pregnancy) was debated. As a result of this debate the BMA has policy that the Abortion Act 1967 should be amended so that first trimester abortion is available on the same basis as any other medical treatment – on the basis of informed consent. Therefore, first trimester abortions should not need the signature of two doctors' and women seeking such abortions should not need to meet specified medical criteria. The policy is based partly on the fact that, from a clinical perspective, abortion is safer carried out early in pregnancy. Given the relative risks of early abortion compared with pregnancy and childbirth, virtually all women seeking an abortion in the first trimester will meet the current medical criteria for abortion. If enacted, the proposed amendment would help to ensure that women seeking abortions are not exposed to unnecessary delays, and consequently, to later, more costly and higher risk procedures. BMA policy is clear that any changes in relation to first trimester abortion should not adversely impact upon the availability of later abortions.

2.1.5 Fetal pain

Whether, and at what stage, a fetus feels pain has been a matter of much debate and past practice has been partly influenced by Department of Health advice. Interpretation of the evidence on fetal pain is conflicting with some arguing that the fetus has the potential to feel pain at ten weeks' gestation[16], others arguing that it is unlikely to feel pain before 26 weeks gestation[17] and still others arguing for some unspecified gestational period in between.[18]

There is clearly a need for further research to provide more conclusive evidence about the experiences and sensations of the fetus in utero. In the meantime the BMA recommends that, when carrying out any surgical procedures (whether an abortion or a therapeutic intervention) on the fetus in utero, due consideration must be given to appropriate measures for minimising the risk of pain. This should include an assessment of the most recent evidence available. Even if there is no incontrovertible evidence that fetuses feel pain the use of pain relief, when carrying out invasive procedures, may to relieve the anxiety of the parents and of health professionals.

2.2 Consent

2.2.1 The competent adult

With consent to termination of pregnancy as with consent for other medical procedures, there are certain criteria which must be met in order for the consent to be valid. The woman must have sufficient competence to understand the procedure and its alternatives in broad terms and to make a decision, the consent must be voluntary and the decision must be made on the basis of sufficient, accurate information.

In England and Wales the Mental Capacity Act 2005 outlines a four-stage test of capacity. In order to be able to make a competent decision, an individual must be able to:

1. To understand the information relevant to the decision;
2. to retain the information relevant to the decision;
3. to use or weigh the information; and
4. to communicate the decision (by any means).

Where an individual fails one or more parts of this test, then they do not have the relevant capacity and the entire test is failed. This formulation is a good working test for assessing capacity to consent to or refuse medical treatment both in relation to adults and children.

2.2.2 Adults who lack capacity

Decision-making in relation to adults who lack the capacity to consent on their own behalf is governed in England and Wales by the Mental Capacity Act 2005, and in Scotland by the Adults With Incapacity (Scotland) Act 2000; in Northern Ireland, decisions are covered by the common law. A decision relating to a termination of pregnancy for an incapacitated adult would need to comply with the relevant legislation. The BMA has separate guidance on both pieces of legislation, however the relevant points with regard to abortion are outlined below.[19]

The central tenet of the English and Welsh legislation is the principle of "best interests" and in Scotland "benefit". Although the Adults with Incapacity (Scotland) Act uses the term "benefit", in the BMA's view it is likely that this term can be interpreted in a similar way to "best interests". If, however, health professionals working in Scotland were recommending an intervention in the incapacitated person's best interests that was unlikely to provide clinical benefit, they should consider taking legal advice.

Health professionals presented with a pregnant woman lacking the capacity to give a valid consent must use their professional judgment to assess her best interests. It is important to remember that an individual's best interests extend beyond medical best interests alone. The incapacitated persons' past and present wishes and feelings, beliefs and values should be taken into consideration. An essential part of the assessment of best interests will also involve a discussion with those close to the patient, including family, friends, carers, or a proxy decision maker, where practical and appropriate; and also bearing in mind the patients right to confidentiality (see below).

There is no mandatory requirement to seek court approval to perform an abortion on an adult who lacks capacity;[20] although in cases of doubt, it would be advisable to seek a second opinion. In the following circumstances, however, cases decisions should be referred to the court:

- where there is a dispute about capacity;
- where the patient may regain capacity during or shortly after pregnancy;
- where the decision of the medical team is not unanimous;
- where the patient, the potential father, or the patient's close family disagree with the decision;
- where the procedures under section 1 of the Abortion Act have not been followed; or
- where there are other exceptional circumstances, for example the pregnancy is the patient's last chance to conceive.[21]

The need for an abortion to be considered in respect of a women who lacks capacity may raise questions about that patient's ability to consent to sexual intercourse and is likely to require investigation as to whether a criminal offence has occurred. The BMA and Law Society have jointly issued guidance on the law relating to mental capacity and sexual relationships (chapter 10 of Assessment of Mental Capacity[22]). This recognises the right of mentally disordered people to enter voluntarily into sexual relationships but also focuses on the obligation to protect vulnerable adults from abusive relationships. If there are grounds to believe that the pregnancy has resulted from unlawful sexual intercourse (rape of an unwilling woman or one who is unable to consent), immediate steps must be taken to protect the woman (and others who may be at serious risk) from further possible abuse.

2.2.3 Competent minors

Any competent young person, regardless of age, can independently seek medical advice and give valid consent to medical treatment. This legal position was established in the

1985 House of Lords' ruling in the Gillick case.[23] Thus people under 16 are legally able to consent on their own behalf to any surgical, medical or dental procedure or treatment if, in the doctor's opinion, they are capable of understanding the nature and possible consequences of the procedure. It is clearly desirable for young people to have their parents' support for important and potentially life-changing decisions. Sometimes, however, young patients do not wish their parents to be informed of a medical consultation or its outcome and the doctor generally should not override patients' views. Doctors have an obligation, however, to encourage the patient voluntarily to involve parents. Young patients are likely to need help and support if the treatment sought has serious implications, such as contraception, abortion, or treatment for sexually transmitted disease. In very exceptional cases where the doctor has reason to believe that the pregnancy is the result of child abuse, incest or exploitation, a breach of confidentiality may be necessary and justifiable. The patient should be told in advance that secrecy in such cases cannot be guaranteed and must be offered appropriate help, counselling and support.

The main exception to these general rules is if the young woman is a ward of court, in which case the courts will need to approve a termination or other serious medical intervention. It is thus particularly important that it is always clear from the medical records that the child is a ward of court. Similarly if a young woman seeking termination is in care she should be encouraged to involve the local social services. If she refuses to consent to information being shared, legal advice should be sought before proceeding with the termination.

When consulted by a young woman under 16 requesting abortion the doctor should consider in particular:

- Whether the young woman understands the potential risks and possible longer-term effects of the proposed termination.
- Whether the young woman has sufficient maturity i.e. "Gillick competence" to make this decision and give a valid consent.
- Parental support. The value of parental support must be discussed with the patient. Doctors should encourage young people to discuss their situation with parents but must provide reassurance that their confidentiality will be maintained. If the young woman is unwilling to inform her parents of the consultation there may be another adult, perhaps an aunt or a friend of the family, in whom she would be prepared to confide. The importance of support during and after the termination should be discussed.
- Appropriate communications with the patient's own GP. If the doctor consulted is not the patient's own general practitioner, the young woman should be encouraged to consent to information being provide to her GP. It should be explained that this is in her own medical interest and an assurance given that confidentiality will be maintained but that, if she refuses, her wishes will be respected.

Requests by young people for abortion and contraceptive services, without parental involvement, can raise serious ethical dilemmas for doctors. The BMA takes the view that establishing a trusting relationship between the patient and doctor at this stage will do more to promote health than if doctors refuse to see young patients without parental consent. Further information is available in Confidentiality and Under 16s,[24] available from the BMA Medical Ethics Department.

The Department of Health has published guidance for health professionals on the provision of advice and treatment for people under 16, on contraception, sexual and reproductive health.[25]

2.2.4 Incompetent minors

If a young woman is pregnant and is not considered to be Gillick-competent she should be encouraged to involve her parents in decision-making and the parents may, legally, consent on her behalf. The word "parents" includes other holders of parental responsibility including, in relation to a child in care, the local authority. Relatives who are not holders of parental responsibility cannot consent to treatment for a minor. If the young woman refuses consent to parental involvement the Official Solicitor's office has advised that legal advice should be sought about whether the parents should be informed, against her wishes, and whether the termination can proceed. This may require an application to the courts.

2.2.5 Partners' views

The decision to terminate a pregnancy, within the broad framework accepted by society, rests with the woman and her doctors. Legally, the woman's spouse or partner has no right to demand or refuse a termination.[26] It is, however, good practice to encourage women to discuss such decisions with their partners. Where a woman refuses to share information with her partner, confidentiality must be maintained unless there are exceptional reasons to justify a breach of confidentiality.

2.3 Confidentiality

2.3.1 Adults

Patients have a right to expect that doctors will not disclose any personal health information to a third party without consent. Women seeking termination of pregnancy are likely to be particularly concerned about the confidentiality of this information and doctors should be sensitive to this.

Sometimes doctors are asked to remove information about previous terminations from a patient's medical records. The BMA advises doctors to be very wary of removing relevant medical information from a patient's record, especially if further consultations or treatment have arisen on the basis of this information. To remove relevant medical information may make the doctor's later decisions appear unsupported and could also be detrimental to the future care of the patient.

If the doctor consulted is not the patient's own general practitioner, the woman should be encouraged to consent to information being provided to her GP. If, however, she refuses to consent to the sharing of this information her wishes should be respected. Where such consent is withheld and the patient's GP is a fundholder, the procedure will be chargeable to the Health Authority in order to ensure that confidentiality is maintained.[27]

2.3.2 Minors

The duty of confidentiality owed to a person under 16 is as great as the duty owed to any other person. An explicit request by a patient that information should not be disclosed to particular people, or indeed to any third party, must be respected except in the most exceptional circumstances, for example, where the health, safety or welfare of some person would otherwise be at serious risk. The exceptions set out above, where the child is a ward of court, or is in care, should be noted.

3. SUMMARY

The Abortion Act requires doctors to make an assessment in the context of each case. They must assess the potential impact of the pregnancy and birth on the woman's physical and mental health and the well-being of existing siblings. Blanket rules cannot be applied to such sensitive and difficult decisions, which require an understanding of the woman's individual needs. A decision to terminate a pregnancy is never an easy one. In making these decisions, patients and doctors should ensure that the decision is supported by appropriate information and counselling about the options and implications.

© BMA November 2007

BMA members may contact: askBMA on 0870 60 60 828 or British Medical Association Department of Medical Ethics, BMA House, Tavistock Square, London WC1H 9JP Tel: 020 7383 6286 Fax: 020 7383 6233 Email: ethics@bma.org.uk

Non-members may contact: British Medical Association Public Affairs Department, BMA House Tavistock Square, London WC1H 9JP Tel: 020 7387 4499 Fax: 020 7383 6400 Email: info.public@bma.org.uk

REFERENCES

1. Abortion Act 1967 section 1.
2. *R v Bourne* [1939] 1 KB 687.
3. Lee S An A to K to Z of abortion law in Northern Ireland: abortion on remand in Furedi A (ed) The Abortion Law in Northern Ireland (1995) Family Planning Association Northern Ireland and SHEE1293.
4. House of Lords Hansard. 26 July 2007: col WA105.
5. Hansard, vol 201; No 37, Part II, 20 December 1991 col 355.
6. *Janaway v Salford* HA [1988], 3 All ER 1079 HL.
7. General Medical Council. Good Medical Practice. London: GMC, 2006; para 8.
8. Scottish Executive. Advertisements and job descriptions of doctors to hospital posts: termination of pregnancy. NHS Circular:PCS(DD)2004/8. Edinburgh: Scottish Executive, September 2004.
9. Hansard, 10 May 1983, Vol 42, No 112 Col 239.
10. *R v HS Dhingra* – Birmingham Crown Court Judgment 24 January 1991.
11. *R v Secretary of State for Health & (1) Schering Health Care Ltd (2) Family Planning Association (Interested Parties), ex parte John Smeaton (on behalf of the Society for the Protection of the Unborn Child)* [2002] EWHC 2410.
12. Faculty of Family Planning and Reproductive Health Care Clinical Effectiveness Unit. FFPRHC Guidance (April 2006) Emergency contraception. Journal of Family Planning and Reproductive Health Care 2006; 32(2): 121–128.
13. Royal College of Obstetricians & Gynaecologists. Further Issues Relating to Late Abortion, Fetal Viability and Registration of Births and Deaths. London: RCOG Press, 2001.
14. Morgan D & Lee RG. Blackstone's Guide to the Human Fertilisation & Embryology Act 1990. London: Blackstone, 1991.
15. British Medical Association. Abortion time limits: a briefing paper from the British Medical Association. London: BMA, 2005. Available at www.bma.org.uk/ap.nsf/Content/AbortionTimeLimits.
16. McCullagh P. Fetal Sentience. The All-Party Parliamentary Pro-Life Group, 1996.

17. Royal College of Obstetricians and Gynaecologists, Fetal Awareness. Report of a Working Party (October 1997) and Fitzgerald, M. Fetal Pain: An Update of Current Scientific Knowledge. Department of Health, May 1995

18. See, for example, Glover V, Fetal Stress and Pain Responses – The First Nine Months at a symposium arranged by the Women and Children's Welfare Fund Making the pre-born and premature comfortable and pain free. 10 November 1995.

19. British Medical Association. The Mental capacity Act 2005 – guidance for health professionals. London: BMA, 2007; and British Medical Association. Medical treatment for adults with incapacity: guidance on ethical and medico-legal issues in Scotland. London: BMA, 2007. Both available at www.bma.org.uk/ethics

20. Mason & McCall Smith. Law and Medical Ethics, Fourth Edition. London: Butterworths, 1994;121 and *Re SG (Adult Mental Patient: Abortion)* [1991] 2 FLR 329.

21. *D v An NHS Trust (Medical Treatment: Consent: Termination)* (2004) FLR 1110.

22. British Medical Association and The Law Society Assessment of Mental Capacity – Guidance for doctors and lawyers (Second Edition). London: BMJ Publishing, 2004.

23. *Gillick v West Norfolk & Wisbech Area Health Authority* [1986] AC 122.

24. British Medical Association. Confidentiality & Under 16s. London: BMA, 1994.

25. Department of Health. Best practice guidance for doctors and other health professionals on the provision of advice and treatment to young people under 16 on contraception, sexual and reproductive health. London: DH, July 2004.

26. Paton v British Pregnancy Advisory Service Trustees discussed in – Mason & McCall Smith. Law and Medical Ethics (Fourth Edition). London: Butterworths, 1994;118.

27. NHS Executive. Guidance on fundholder purchase of terminations of pregnancy, HSG(95)37, July 1995.

Royal College of Obstetricians and Gynaecologists Joint Guidance Further Issues Relating to Late Abortion, Fetal Viability and Registration of Births and Deaths

THE ATTENTION OF FELLOWS AND MEMBERS IS DRAWN TO THE FOLLOWING RELEVANT DOCUMENTS:

- RCOG report Termination of pregnancy for fetal abnormality in England, Wales and Scotland (Jan 1996);
- Joint Report of the RCOG/RCPCH Guidelines for screening, diagnosis and management of fetal abnormalities (Dec 1997);
- Report of the RCOG Ethics Committee Late termination of pregnancy for fetal abnormality: A consideration of the law and ethics (Mar 1998);
- The British Association of Perinatal Medicine Memorandum, November 1999 – Fetuses and Newborn Infants at the Threshold of Viability: A Framework for Practice.

LATE TERMINATION OF PREGNANCY

Late abortion can be an extremely traumatic event, not only for the patient but also for the attendant, medical and nursing staff. There are serious clinical, ethical and legal issues and the patient should be managed according to the recommendations in the RCOG report *Late termination of pregnancy for fetal abnormality in England, Wales and Scotland.*

Parents must receive sympathetic and supportive counselling before and particularly after the procedure. For all terminations at gestational age of more than 21 weeks and 6 days, the method chosen should ensure that the fetus is born dead. This should be undertaken by an appropriately trained practitioner. Intracardiac potassium chloride is the recommended method and the dose chosen should ensure that fetal asystole has been achieved. It should be confirmed by observing the fetal heart by an ultrasound scan for five minutes. Additionally, it is mandatory to confirm asystole by an ultrasound scan 30–60 minutes after the procedure, and definitely before the patient leaves hospital. Consideration can be given to abolishing fetal movements by the instillation of anaesthetic and/or muscle relaxant agents immediately prior to potassium chloride administration.

It is essential to have an agreed multidisciplinary management plan prior to late termination, taking account of issues such as conscientious objection. The multidisciplinary team should include, where appropriate, obstetricians, neonatologists, midwives and nursing staff. Where the patient chooses not to have feticide in the presence of a lethal abnormality, discussion must take place within the appropriate team, and the patient's wishes and agreement sought on the management of the fetus after birth.

ISSUES AROUND FETAL VIABILITY

The management of fetuses and newborn infants at the threshold of viability should be in accordance with the British Association of Perinatal Medicine's Framework for Practice. It is professionally acceptable not to attempt to support life in fetuses below the threshold of viability. It is extremely important to distinguish between physiological movements and signs of life, as well as being aware that observed movements may be of a reflex nature and not necessarily signs of life or viability.

REGISTRATION RESPONSIBILITIES

Where a fetus is born before the 24th week of gestation and did not breathe or show any signs of life, there is no provision for the event to be registered. However, the doctor or midwife who attended the delivery will need to issue a certificate or letter for the funeral director, cemetery or crematorium stating that the baby was born before the legal age of viability and showed no signs of life to allow a funeral to proceed, if that is the parents' wish. Where a child is born after 24 weeks but did not breathe or show any sign of life, and is therefore classified as a *stillbirth*, these must be registered within three months and the Registrar will allow a funeral to proceed. In the event of a child being born which shows signs of life but subsequently dies, both the birth and death need to be registered, irrespective of the gestation period of the child, and the Registrar will then issue a form to allow the funeral to proceed. The Registrar General's Office has confirmed that midwives are permitted to certify stillbirths only. In cases where there are any signs of life the baby must have been seen by a medical practitioner and that practitioner must sign the death certificate (otherwise it becomes a Coroner's case).

In situations where parents feel they are unable to act as informants to effect a registration, alternative informants, such as "present at the stillbirth" or "present at the death", are acceptable in order that registration can be achieved with as little distress to the family as possible.

(This advice was produced in collaboration with the Royal College of Midwives, the British Association of Perinatal Medicine and the Department of Health.)

Appendix 9.1

Court of Appeal Guidelines: *RE MB* Guidelines and *St George's Healthcare v S* Guidelines

RE MB (AN ADULT: MEDICAL TREATMENT)

[1997] 2 FCR 541, [1997] 2 FLR 426, CA

'Conclusions on capacity to decide

All the decisions made in the caesarean section cases to which we have referred arose in circumstances of urgency or extreme urgency. The evidence was in general limited in scope and the mother was not always represented as a party. With the exception of *Re S* (supra), in all the cases the court decided that the mother did not have the capacity to make the decision. In these extremely worrying situations, it is important to keep in mind the basic principles we have outlined, and the court should approach the crucial question of competence bearing the following considerations in mind. They are not intended to be determinative in every case, for the decision must inevitably depend upon the particular facts before the court.

1.   Every person is presumed to have the capacity to consent to or to refine medical treatment unless and until the presumption is rebutted.

2.   A competent woman who has the capacity to decide may for religious reasons, other reasons, for rational or irrational reasons or for no reason at all, choose not to have medical intervention, even though the consequence may be the death or serious handicap of the child she bears, or her own death. In that event the courts do not have the jurisdiction to declare medical intervention lawful and the question of her own best interests objectively considered, does not arise.

3.   Irrationality is here used to connote a decision which is so outrageous in its defiance of logic or of accepted moral standards that no sensible person who had applied his mind to the question to be decided it could have arrived at it. As Kennedy and Grubb (*Medical Law* (2nd edn, 1994)) point out, it might be otherwise if a decision is based on a misperception of reality (eg the blood is poisoned because it is red). Such a misperception will be more readily accepted to be a disorder of the mind. Although it might be thought that irrationality sits uneasily with competence to decide, panic, indecisiveness and irrationality in themselves do not as such amount to incompetence, but they may be symptoms or evidence of incompetence. The graver the consequences of the decision, the commensurately greater the level of competence is required to take the decision: *Re T* (supra), *Sidaway* (supra) at page 904 and *Gillick v West Norfolk and Wisbech Area Health Authority* [1986] 1 AC 112, 169 and 186.

4.   A person lacks capacity if some impairment or disturbance of mental functioning renders the person unable to make a decision whether to consent to or to refuse treatment: That inability to make a decision will occur when:

(*a*)   the patient is unable to comprehend and retain the information which is material to the decision, especially as to the likely consequences of having or not having the treatment in question.

(*b*)   the patient is unable to use the information and weigh it in the balance as part of the process of arriving at the decision. If as Thorpe J observed in *Re C* (supra), a compulsive disorder or phobia from which the patient suffers stifles belief in the information presented to her, then the decision may not be a true one. As Lord Cockburn CI put it in *Banks v Goodfellow* (1370) LB. 5 QB 549 at p 569: 'One object may be so forced upon the attention of the invalid as to shut out all others that might require consideration.'

5.   The 'temporary factors' mentioned by Lord Donaldson MR in Re T (supra) (confusion, shock, fatigue, pain or drugs) may completely erode capacity but those concerned must be satisfied that such factors are operating to such a degree that the ability to decide is absent.

6.   Another such influence may be panic induced by fear. Again careful scrutiny of the evidence is necessary because fear of an operation may be a rational reason for refusal to undergo it. Fear may be also, however, paralyse the will and thus destroy the capacity to make a decision.'

ST GEORGE'S HEALTHCARE NHS TRUST V S

[1999] Fam 26, [1998] 2 FCR 685, CA

30 July. The court handed down the following guidelines to replace those set out at the end of the judgment handed down on 7 May:

> 'We have now received written submissions from Mr Havers and Mr Gordon. We understand that MS's solicitor has taken soundings from the Royal College of Midwives, the Royal College of Nursing, the United Kingdom Central Council for Nursing, Midwifery and Health Visiting, the Law Society's mental health and disability subcommittee, MIND, the Association for Improvements in the Maternity Services, the National Childbirth Trust, the Maternity Alliance and the Association of Community Health Councils for England and Wales. We further understand that Mr Havers received comments from the British Medical Association, who in the available time have not had any practical opportunity to carry out a formal consultation process, and the Department of Health. We have also received a letter from the Head of Legal Services for Merton London Borough Council confirming that no submissions in relation to the proposed guidelines would be made 'as they do not appear to impact upon the role of an approved social worker.'

In the light of these written submissions we have considered the draft guidelines set out at the end of the judgment handed down on 7 May, which are now superseded.

The case highlighted some major problems which could arise for hospital authorities when a pregnant woman presented at hospital, the possible need for Caesarean surgery was diagnosed, and there was serious doubt about the patient's capacity to accept or decline treatment. To avoid any recurrence of the unsatisfactory events recorded in the judgment, and after consultations with the President of the Family Division and the Official Solicitor, and in the light of the written submissions from Mr Havers and Mr Gordon, we shall attempt to repeat and expand the advice given in *Re MB (an adult: medical treatment)* [1997] 2 FCR 541 [*see above*]. This advice also applies to any cases involving capacity when surgical or invasive treatment may be needed by a patient, whether female or male. References to 'she' and 'her' should be read accordingly. It also extends, where relevant, to medical practitioners and health professionals generally as well as to hospital authorities.

The guidelines depend on basic legal principles which we summarise:

(i)   They have no application where the patient is competent to accept or refuse treatment. In principle a patient may remain competent notwithstanding detention under the Mental Health Act 1983.

(ii) If the patient is competent and refuses consent to the treatment, an application to the High Court for a declaration would be pointless. In this situation the advice given to the patient should be recorded. For their own protection hospital authorities should seek unequivocal assurances from the patient (to be recorded in writing) that the refusal represents an informed decision, that is, that she understands the nature of and reasons for the proposed treatment, and the risks and likely prognosis involved in the decision to refuse or accept it. If the patient is unwilling to sign a written indication of this refusal, this too should be noted in writing. Such a written indication is merely a record for evidential purposes. It should not be confused with or regarded as a disclaimer.

(iii) If the patient is incapable of giving or refusing consent, either in the long term or temporarily (eg due to unconsciousness), the patient must be cared for according to the authority's judgment of the patient's best interests. Where the patient has given an advance directive, before becoming incapable, treatment and care should normally be subject to the advance directive. However, if there is reason to doubt the reliability of the advance directive (for example it may sensibly be thought not to apply to the circumstances which have arisen), then an application for a declaration may be made.

Concern over capacity

(iv) The authority should identify as soon as possible whether there is concern about a patient's competence to consent to or refuse treatment.

(v)   If the capacity of the patient is seriously in doubt it should be assessed as a matter of priority. In many such cases the patient's general practitioner or other responsible doctor may be sufficiently qualified to make the necessary assessment, but in serious or complex cases involving difficult issues about the future health and well being or even the life of the patient, the issue of capacity should be examined by an independent psychiatrist, ideally one approved under section 12(2) of the Mental Health Act 1983. If following this assessment there remains a serious doubt about the patient's competence, and the seriousness or complexity of the issues in the particular case may require the involvement of the court, the psychiatrist should further consider whether the patient is incapable by reason of mental disorder of managing her property or affairs. If so the patient may be unable to instruct a solicitor and will require a guardian ad litem in any court proceedings. The authority should seek legal advice as quickly as possible. If a declaration is to be sought the patient's solicitors should be informed immediately and if practicable they should have a proper opportunity to take instructions and apply for legal aid where necessary. Potential witnesses for the authority should be made aware of the criteria laid down in *Re MB (an adult: medical treatment)* [1997] 2 FCR 541 [*see above*] and this case, together with any guidance issued by the Department of Health and the British Medical Association.

(vi) If the patient is unable to instruct solicitors, or is believed to be incapable of doing so, the authority or its legal advisers must notify the Official Solicitor and invite him to act as guardian ad litem. If the Official Solicitor agrees he will no doubt wish, if possible, to arrange for the patient to be interviewed to ascertain her wishes and to explore the reasons for any refusal of treatment. The Official Solicitor can be contacted through the Urgent Court Business Officer out of office hours on (0171) 936 6000.

The hearing

(vii) The hearing before the judge should be inter partes. As the order made in her absence will not be binding on the patient unless she is represented either by a guardian ad litem (if incapable of giving instructions) or (if capable) by counsel or solicitor, a declaration granted ex parte is of no assistance to the authority. Although the Official Solicitor will not act for a patient if she is capable of instructing a solicitor, the court may in any event call on the Official Solicitor (who has considerable expertise in these matters) to assist as an amicus curiae.

(viii) It is axiomatic that the judge must be provided with accurate and all the relevant information. This should include the reasons for the proposed treatment, the risks involved in the proposed treatment, and in not proceeding with it, whether any alternative treatment exists, and the reason, if ascertainable, why the patient is refusing the proposed treatment. The judge will need sufficient information to reach an informed conclusion about the patient's capacity, and, where it arises, the issue of best interest.

(ix) The precise terms of any order should be recorded and approved by the judge before its terms are transmitted to the authority. The patient should be accurately informed of the precise terms.

(x) Applicants for emergency orders from the High Court made without first issuing and serving the relevant applications and evidence in support have a duty to comply with the procedural requirements (and pay the court fees) as soon as possible after the urgency hearing.

Conclusion

There may be occasions when, assuming a serious question arises about the competence of the patient, the situation facing the authority may be so urgent and the consequences so desperate that it is impracticable to attempt to comply with these guidelines. The guidelines should be approached for what they are, that is, guidelines. Where delay may itself cause serious damage to the patient's health or put her life at risk then formulaic compliance with these guidelines would be inappropriate.'

Appendix 9.2

Witness statement for patient opposing imposition of caesarean section

SAMPLE TEXT FOR INCLUSION IN A SOLICITOR'S WITNESS STATEMENT IN FORM COP 24, FOR THE PURPOSE OF AN URGENT APPLICATION TO THE COURT OF PROTECTION UNDER PRACTICE DIRECTION 10B, FOR A DECLARATION THAT IT WOULD BE UNLAWFUL FOR A CAESAREAN SECTION TO BE PERFORMED ON HER WITHOUT HER CONSENT

1. The Applicant seeks a declaration that she retains capacity to consent to or refuse medical treatment including treatment in connection with her current pregnancy and labour, alternatively that she made a valid advance decision to refuse to undergo a caesarean section operation, and for an injunction to restrain the Respondent from forcibly performing a caesarean section on her against her will.

2. The Respondent is an NHS Trust responsible for the management of the Blankshire Hospital.

3. The Applicant is a patient at the said hospital and is receiving treatment in connection with her current pregnancy and labour.

4. In the course of her attendance at the Respondent's ante-natal clinic on [date] the Applicant gave to Mr Deliverance, a consultant obstetrician, a written advance decision stating that she would not consent to any form of surgical delivery of her baby, and that such delivery should not be carried out if circumstances arose in which she lost capacity, as such procedure would be against her religious beliefs. At the time of making the advance decision and handing it to Mr Deliverance, the Applicant fully understood the potential consequences of such a decision, including the risk that either she or her baby might die or be seriously injured.

5. The Applicant is now in labour and has been advised by the attending doctor that they intend to perform a caesarean section on her to deliver her baby, whether or not she consents to such a procedure. The Applicant has repeated to the said doctor her unwillingness to have such an operation on religious grounds, but he has ignored her.

6. In the circumstances the Applicant seeks a declaration that she has capacity to make this decision for herself, alternatively that the advance decision was valid, and that a caesarean section in the absence of her consent would be unlawful.

7. Further details of the evidence relied on are set out in the appended witness statements and other documents.

Draft order preventing a caesarean section

IN THE COURT OF PROTECTION

IN THE MATTER OF THE MENTAL CAPACITY ACT 2005

IN THE MATTER OF CD

BEFORE MR JUSTICE W

SITTING ON [DATE]

B E T W E E N

CD

Applicant

– and –

AN NHS TRUST

Respondent

DRAFT ORDER ON BEHALF OF APPLICANT

UPON HEARING [name of Counsel], counsel for the Applicant and [name of Counsel], counsel for the Respondent

UPON READING the hearing bundle

AND UPON HEARING evidence from CD and Dr G

IT IS DECLARED THAT:

1. P has capacity to decide whether or not to have a caesarean section.
2. P made an advance decision dated X which is valid and applicable to a caesarean section in the existing circumstances.
3. It would be unlawful to perform a caesarean section upon her in the absence of her consent to such procedure.
   AND IT IS ORDERED THAT:
4. There shall be liberty to apply.
5. There shall be no order as to costs.

Witness statement for declaration that lawful to perform caesarian section

SAMPLE TEXT FOR INCLUSION IN A SOLICITOR'S WITNESS STATEMENT IN FORM COP 24, FOR THE PURPOSE OF AN URGENT APPLICATION TO THE COURT OF PROTECTION UNDER PRACTICE DIRECTION 10B, FOR A DECLARATION THAT IT WOULD BE LAWFUL FOR A CAESAREAN SECTION TO BE PERFORMED

1. This is an application for a declaration that:
   (a) P lacks capacity to decide whether to have a caesarean section and to make decisions generally about her care and treatment in connection with her present labour, and:
   (b) having regard to her best interests, it shall be lawful to provide her with such medical treatment in connection with her present labour, including if necessary caesarean section, the insertion of needles for intravenous infusions, and anaesthesia and such other treatment and care as may be necessary to cause her the least distress and to preserve for her the greatest dignity, and for the minimum necessary reasonable force to be used for such purposes.
2. The Applicant is an NHS Trust responsible for the management of the Blankshire District Hospital and the provision of obstetric services there.
3. P is a patient at the said hospital and is in the course of labour in her first pregnancy.
4. P lacks capacity to make decisions about her care during the said labour by reason of a phobia against the insertion of needles in any part of her body. The phobia has deprived her of the ability to retain or use treatment information.
5. The medical practitioners attending P are of the opinion that her baby must be delivered by caesarean section within the next 6 hours, to avoid dangers to the health of both P and her baby, but P has refused to consent to such a procedure on the grounds that she will not allow doctors to administer the necessary anaesthetic by use of any needle inserted in her body.
6. It is in P's best interests that the treatment advised by the attending medical practitioners be provided and therefore the Applicant seeks a declaration that such treatment is lawful.
7. Further details of the evidence relied on are set out in the appended witness statements and other documents.

Appendix 9.5

Draft declaration permitting caesarean section

CASE NO xxxxxxxx

IN THE COURT OF PROTECTION

IN THE MATTER OF THE MENTAL CAPACITY ACT 2005

IN THE MATTER OF EF

BEFORE MR JUSTICE W

SITTING ON [DATE]

B E T W E E N

AN NHS TRUST

Applicant

– and –

EF

Respondent

DRAFT ORDER ON BEHALF OF APPLICANT

UPON HEARING [name of Counsel], counsel for the Applicant and [name of Counsel], counsel for the Respondent

UPON READING [identify the documents read]

AND UPON HEARING evidence from Dr H

AND UPON the parties, institutions and witnesses being identified in a Schedule to this Order[1]

IT IS ORDERED THAT:

1. Pursuant to paragraph 16 of Court of Protection Practice Direction 9E, this and future hearings shall be in public.
2. The Applicant shall have permission to make the application.
3. EF is joined as a party to these proceedings.
4. The Official Solicitor, having consented, shall be appointed as litigation friend to EF.
5. The requirement to notify EF of the proceedings shall be dispensed with under r49.
6. For the purposes of these proceedings:
    (a) the First Applicant shall be referred to as 'An NHS Trust';
    (b) the Respondent shall be referred to as 'EF';
    (c) the establishment at which the Respondent is currently being cared for shall be referred to as 'the hospital';

(d) any witnesses, other than an expert witness, from whom evidence is adduced in these proceedings, whether by witness statement or otherwise in writing or orally, shall be referred to by the initial of their respective surname;

(e) any witnesses, other than expert witnesses, who give oral evidence shall be permitted not to disclose their respective name and address in open court.

7. There shall be no report of this matter which identifies the Respondent, whether by name, or by naming members of her family, giving her or their location, or naming, or giving the location of, the clinicians, healthcare professionals and/or the establishments which are or will be or have been responsible for her care or treatment.

8. There shall be liberty to apply.

9. The Applicant shall pay half of the Official Solicitor's costs, to be subject to detailed assessment if not agreed.

AND IT IS DECLARED THAT

10. EF lacks capacity to decide whether to have a caesarean section and to make decisions generally about her care and treatment in connection with her present labour.

11. Having regard to the best interests of EF, it is lawful until [time] on [date]:

(a) for the medical practitioners attending EF to carry out such treatment as may in their opinion be necessary for the purposes of EF's present labour, including if in their professional opinion it is necessary in her best interests, delivery by caesarean section, the insertion of needles for the purpose of intravenous infusions, and anaesthesia;

(b) for the minimum necessary reasonable force to be used in the course of such treatment;

(c) generally for EF to be furnished with such treatment and nursing care as may be appropriate to ensure that she suffers the least distress and retains the greatest dignity.

1 Schedule is not reproduced here: see suggested directions order in COP

Appendix 9.6

Draft Order Permitting Administration of Blood Products and Caesarean Section in the Case of a Minor – assume that the hearing has been in private

IN THE HIGH COURT OF JUSTICE   W141/96

FAMILY DIVISION

PRINCIPAL REGISTRY

Before

IN THE MATTER OF CHICAGO (a minor)

AND IN THE MATTER OF THE INHERENT JURISDICTION OF THE HIGH

COURT WITH RESPECT TO CHILDREN

BETWEEN:

WEST WING NHS TRUST   **Plaintiff**

– and –

CHICAGO (A minor, by her guardian and ad litem [ ])

First Defendant

and

MARY HOPE   **Second Defendant**

DRAFT ORDER ON BEHALF OF APPLICANT

UPON HEARING Counsel for the Plaintiff, First Defendant and Second Defendant

AND UPON hearing the evidence of the Second Defendant and Dr Ross and upon reading the evidence filed herein;

IT IS ORDERED THAT:

1.   If it is the professional opinion of those medically responsible for the First Defendant that she is in need of the administration of blood or blood products, it shall be lawful for her to be given such blood or blood products and any necessary ancillary treatment without her consent or the consent of her parents in any life-threatening situation during (*a*) the First Defendant's current pregnancy, labour and delivery: and (*b*) care for the First Defendant after delivery;

481

2.   If it is the professional opinion of those medically responsible for her care that it is necessary for the protection of the First Defendant that a caesarean section operation be performed, it shall be lawful to undertake such operation and any necessary ancillary treatment (including, in a life-threatening situation, the administration of blood or blood products) without the First Defendant's consent or the consent of her parents during the course of the First Defendant's current pregnancy, labour and delivery.

3.   There shall be no order as to costs.

Dated etc

Appendix 9.7

ROCG Guidelines 2006 Law and ethics in relation to court-authorised obstetric intervention

This is the second edition of this guideline. It updates and replaces the first edition published in 1994 and the supplement that was added in 1996.

1 PURPOSE AND SCOPE

The purpose of this guideline is to:

- clarify the position of the current law on Court-authorised obstetric intervention in competent and incompetent patients (or those with and without capacity) (sections 3 and 4)
- identify the ethical principles involved (section 5)
- provide guidance on best practice in how to prevent such conflicts and deal with them when they arise (section 6).

2 BACKGROUND

This guideline intentionally focuses on Court-authorised caesarean section because that is the dominant issue to have been brought to the Courts in the UK thus far.

Law and ethics are not synonymous. Although laws often consolidate ethical positions, it is quite possible to have unethical practice that is legal (and *vice versa*).

The legal and ethical principles that apply to caesarean section also apply to other possible interventions, such as intrauterine transfusion, cervical cerclage or medication in pregnancy.

This guideline is based on the fundamental premise in English law that the competent adult has the right to refuse treatment. Surgery without consent is, therefore, illegal.[1,2]

The major experience of Court-ordered intervention has so far been in the USA and Canada. The law of England and Wales relating to the fetus has been described as 'both unclear and confused'.[3] However, as far as the right of the fetus to live and its protection is concerned, an unborn child is not distinct from its mother. The question of whether a fetus is a separate person under European Human Rights Legislation has been reviewed.[4] The majority view of the Court was that Article 2 'Right to Life' did not apply to the fetus.

Although Court-authorised intervention in the UK remains an extremely rare event, it has occasionally occurred since the first case in 1992.[5] Details of relevant cases are summarised in Appendix 1 (Cases 4, 5 and 7).

Helpful guidelines were given by the Court of Appeal in 1998 as to suggested practice when declarations permitting intervention are sought.[6] The Court made it clear that it is unlikely to entertain an application for a declaration unless the capacity of the patient to consent to or to refuse the medical intervention is in issue.

The main ethical issues are maternal autonomy, bodily integrity, the interests of the fetus and the obligations of the mother and other caregivers.

3 THE LEGAL POSITION

The competent adult has the right to refuse treatment and surgery without consent is an assault in English law.[1,2] This has recently been confirmed: 'Where a competent patient makes it clear that he does not wish to receive treatment which is, objectively, in his best interests, it is unlawful for doctors to administer treatment. Personal autonomy or the right to self determination prevails'.[7] While concerned primarily with the law in the UK, relevant decisions from other jurisdictions are considered.

3.1 Consent and the capacity to make decisions

The usual rules relating to consent apply to pregnant women in the same way as to other patients. The NHS Management Executive's document, *A Guide to Consent for Examination or Treatment* (1990), states: 'Principles of consent are the same in maternity services as in other areas of medicine. It is important that the proposed care is discussed with the woman, preferably in the early antenatal period when any wishes she expresses should be recorded in the notes, but of course the patient may change her mind about these issues at any stage, including during labour'.[8]

The Department of Health defines capacity (or competence) to make decisions as the abilities 'to comprehend and retain information material to the decision, especially as to the consequences of having or not having the intervention in question' and ' to use and weigh this information in the decision making process'.[9] The guide emphasises:[10]

- The presumption is 'that every adult has the capacity to decide whether to consent to, or refuse, proposed medical intervention, unless it is shown that they cannot understand information presented in a clear way.'
- 'Capacity should not be confused with a health professional's assessment of the reasonableness of the patient's decision'. As long as she understands what it entails, the woman is entitled to make a decision based on her own religious belief or value system even if it seems to others to be irrational.'
- 'If an adult with capacity makes a voluntary and appropriately informed decision to refuse treatment this decision must be respected even where this may result in the death of the patient and/or the death of an unborn child, whatever the stage of the pregnancy'.

Under the new Mental Capacity Act 2005 (see section 3.5) 'a person lacks capacity in relation to a matter if at the material time he is unable to make a decision for himself in relation to the matter because of an impairment of, or a disturbance in the functioning of, the mind or brain.' And '... a person is unable to make decisions for himself if he is unable: to understand the information relevant to the decision; to retain that information; to use or weigh that information as part of the process of making the decision; or to communicate his decision (whether by talking, using sign language or other means)'.

3.2 Refusal of consent

Axiomatic to the patient's right to consent to treatment is the right to refuse treatment.[10] The Court of Appeal in the case of Re T (Appendix 1, Case 3)[11] affirmed that right whatever the rationality of the decision. However, for such refusal to be effective, doctors had to be satisfied that at the time of the refusal:

- the patient's capacity to decide had not been diminished by illness or medication or given on the basis of false assumptions or misinformation
- the patient's will had not been unduly influenced by another person
- any refusal had been directed to the relevant situation.

Only where a patient's refusal was ineffective could doctors treat in accordance with their clinical judgment of the patient's best interests.

This case affirms a patient's absolute right, properly exercised, to refuse medical treatment. The issue was reviewed again in 2002 in the case of *Ms B v an NHS Hospital Trust* (Appendix 1, Case 6) and the Court confirmed that 'if mental capacity is not in issue and the patient, having been given the relevant information and offered the available options, chooses to refuse the treatment, that decision has to be respected by the doctors.[12] Considerations that the best interests of the patient would indicate that the decision should be to consent to treatment are irrelevant'. In the case of *R (Burke) v GMC* the Court said, 'The relationship between doctor and patient usually begins with diagnosis and advice. The doctor will describe the treatment that he recommends or, if there are a number of alternative treatments that he would be prepared to administer in the interests of the patient, the choices available, their implications and his recommended option. In such circumstances the right to refuse a proposed treatment gives the patient what appears to be a positive option to choose an alternative. In truth, the right to choose is no more than a reflection of the fact that it is the doctor's duty to provide a treatment that he considers to be in the interests of the patient and that the patient is prepared to accept'.[7]

Usually children will be considered competent to make decisions on their own behalf when they are capable of understanding fully the nature of what is proposed[13] and, in general, a competent child's refusal should not be overridden, save in exceptional circumstances.[14] There is a distinction between consent to and refusal of treatment (covered by *Re R [1991]* and *Re W [1992]*).[15,16] Young people under the age of 18 years may not refuse treatment where someone with parental authority consents.

3.3 Possible exception to right to refuse consent

In *Re T [1992]*,[11] Lord Donaldson made one hypothetical exception in relation to pregnancy to the right of a competent patient to refuse medical treatment. He said: 'The only possible qualification is a case in which the choice may lead to the death of a viable fetus'. He stressed, however, that this was not the case and that when the situation arose the Court would be faced with a novel problem of considerable legal and ethical complexity. Despite this being an incidental remark tangential to the judicial opinion being given, it formed the basis of a decision in *Re S [1992]* to authorise a nonconsensual caesarean section.[5]

While the direct point has not been tested, there is considerable judicial authority to the effect that the interests of the fetus are necessarily subordinated to the rights of the pregnant woman. In *Paton v BPAS*,[17] Sir George Baker, President, said: 'The fetus cannot, in English law, in my view, have a right of its own at least until it is born and has a separate existence from its mother. That permeates the whole of the civil law of this country'.

More significant are the comments made in *Re F [1988]*,[18] when the Court considered whether it had the jurisdiction to make an unborn child a ward of Court. Details of the case and judicial statements regarding the decision not to allow wardship are presented in Case 2 in Appendix 1. Their lordships considered that allowing wardship would have meant unacceptable control over the mother's actions. Lord Justice Balcombe said: 'If the law is to be extended in this manner, so as to impose control over the mother of an unborn child, where such control may be necessary for the benefit of that child, then under our system of parliamentary democracy, it is for Parliament to decide whether such controls can be imposed and, if so, subject to what limitations or conditions'.

3.4 Court-authorised caesarean section, UK

In light of the above, concern has been expressed about the decision in Re S [1992] in which a declaration was given that 'a caesarean section and any necessary consequential treatment which the hospital and its staff proposed to perform on the patient could be lawfully performed despite the patient's refusal to give her consent being vital in the interests of the patient and her unborn child' (Appendix 1, Case 4).5 This case differs from others in respect of the threat to life of both the mother (in obstructed labour) and the baby.

Re S [1992][5] was not appealed. Can it be legally justified that a competent patient's wishes are overridden purportedly in her best interests? The justification provided by the case of *Re F [1988]* applies only in the case of incompetent adults,[19] and should certainly not be applied in the case of competent female patients. Indeed, even if the woman were unconscious, *Re F [1990]*[19] would only justify treating her if such treatment were in her best interests, either to save her life or to ensure improvement or prevent deterioration in her physical (or mental) health. This would not necessarily justify a caesarean section unless it fulfilled these criteria.

Re S [1992][5] is also out of step in elevating the status of the fetus in law to such an extent that its supposed rights become more important than its mother's. To do so is out of line with both previous case law and with the Congenital Disabilities (Civil Liabilities) Act 1976, which gives a child a right of action for damage caused in utero against everyone except its mother (with the exception of motor accidents, for which the mother is insured). Indeed, as Grubb points out,[20] the Law Commission, in its report on injuries to unborn children,[21] explicitly stated that a woman should not be liable for 'rash conduct during pregnancy' which causes harm to the unborn child. Rather, the intent of Parliament was to leave it up to the individual mother to decide how to act in the 'best interests' of her unborn child.

Moreover, there is no other precedent in law for forcing one person to use his or her body to save the life of another. In the American case of *McFall v Shimp* (Appendix 1, Case 1)[22] it was determined that a person could not be forced to give a potentially life saving bone marrow donation for his cousin even though his moral stance was heavily criticised. Thus, by extension, although a pregnant woman may well have an extremely strong ethical responsibility towards her unborn child, this does not mean that it is correct to use the law to enforce these responsibilities.

Two further cases have subsequently arisen; *Re MB [1997]* and *St George's Healthcare NHS Trust v S* (Appendix 1, Cases 5 and 7).[6,23] There were a number of cases in which clinicians used the Mental Health Act to section women as mentally disordered, in order to perform a physical procedure as supposed treatment for a mental disorder. Following the *Re MB [1997]* and *St George's Healthcare NHS Trust v S* decisions, it would be incorrect for clinicians to have the impression that the Mental Health Act is allowed to be used for this purpose.

In *Re MB [1997]*,[23] the appeal judgement gave guidance as to what should be done in cases where such emergency applications were made. It stated:

- It is a criminal and civil wrong to perform an operation of any sort without a patient's consent.
- All competent patients (including women in labour) have the right to refuse medical treatment for good, bad or even no reasons. The unborn child has no rights in law that complicate this fundamental proposition.
- Every person is presumed to have capacity to consent to or refuse medical treatment until the contrary is shown.
- Competent patients are those who have the capacity to take a decision to consent to operations. The test is whether they are able to:
    - comprehend and retain information material to the decision
    - weigh the information so as to reach a decision.
- Medical treatment can be undertaken in an emergency even where a patient lacks capacity to consent. The attendants then have a duty to act in the best interests of the patient, although the treatment given must be limited to that which is a necessity in the best interests of the patient.
- It would be inappropriate to ask the Courts to overrule an informed and competent woman's refusal of treatment.
- In cases of doubt the Court can be asked to give guidance.

Such emergency incidents by their very nature require urgent resolution and leave little time for deliberation or for seeking advice. Their rarity usually means that no one directly involved has previous experience of what to do in such circumstances. Conventional legal processes do not fit easily with the acuteness of the clinical situation in most of these cases and this has led to some criticism.[24] For example, applications were made without any representation of the patient or formal evidence being tendered. The Court was prepared to act on information relayed by telephone with no opportunity for cross examination of the witness.

In *St George's Healthcare NHS Trust v S [1998]*,[6] the Court suggested the practice to be followed when declarations from the Courts were being sought. These are summarised below (and given more fully in Box 1). It should, however, be noted that the guidelines have no application where the patient is competent to accept or refuse treatment. In principle, a patient may remain competent notwithstanding detention under the Mental Health Act 1983. It will be seen that the Court is unlikely to entertain an application for a declaration unless the capacity of the patient to consent to or refuse the medical intervention is an issue. Best practice includes:

- Any problem about mental capacity to consent to treatment should be identified as early as possible so that both the hospital and the patient can obtain legal advice and allow time for proper instructions from the patient.
- If the capacity of the patient is seriously in doubt it should be assessed as a matter of priority. In many such cases the patient's general practitioner or other responsible doctor may be sufficiently qualified to make the necessary assessment, but in serious or complex cases involving difficult issues about the future health and wellbeing or even the life of the patient, the issue of capacity should be examined by an independent psychiatrist.
- If, following this assessment, there remains a serious doubt as to the patient's competence, an application to the Court may need to be made. The trust should seek legal advice as quickly as possible and, if a declaration from the Court is to be sought, the patient's solicitors should be informed immediately.
- The hearing of the application should be held in the presence of both parties and representation of the woman in all cases (unless she does not wish to be). If she is unconscious an advocate for her best interests should be appointed.

487

3.5 The Mental Capacity Act 2005

The Mental Capacity Act 2005 was passed by Parliament after the cases relating to Court-authorised obstetric intervention were determined. As with all new legislation, it may be that during the early days of the Act more cases will come before the Court until there is some clarity as to interpretation of the Act's provisions.

The Mental Capacity Act states: 'A person must be assumed to have capacity unless it is established that he lacks capacity ... A person is not to be treated as unable to make a decision unless all practicable steps to help him to do so have been taken without success ... A person is not to be treated as unable to make a decision merely because he makes an unwise decision ... a person lacks capacity in relation to a matter if at the material time he is unable to make a decision for himself in relation to the matter because of an impairment of, or a disturbance in the functioning of, the mind or brain'.

So far as the inability to make decisions is concerned, the Mental Act states:

'(1)   a person is unable to make decisions for himself if he is unable:
- to understand the information relevant to the decision
- to retain that information
- to use or weigh that information as part of the process of making the decision, or
- to communicate his decision (whether by talking, using sign language or other means).

(2)   A person is not to be regarded as unable to understand the information relevant to a decision if he is able to understand an explanation of it given to him in a way that is appropriate to his circumstances (using simple language, visual aids or any other means).

(3)   The fact that a person is able to retain the information relevant to a decision for a short period only does not prevent him from being regarded as able to make the decision.

(4)   The information relevant to a decision includes information about the reasonably foreseeable consequences of:
(a)   deciding one way or another, or
(b)   failing to make the decision.'

Any act performed or decision made for or on behalf of a person who lacks capacity must be done or made in his best interests. In determining what is in the person's best interests and where it relates to life-sustaining treatment, the person making the determination 'must consider so far as is reasonably ascertainable:

(a)   the person's past and present wishes and feelings (and, in particular, any relevant written statement made by him when he had capacity)

(b)   the beliefs and values that would be likely to influence his decision if he had capacity, and

(c)   the other factors that he would be likely to consider if he were able to do so'.

Section 37 of the Mental Capacity Act 2005 seeks to address the issue of what should happen if an NHS body is 'proposing to provide, or secure the provision of, a serious medical treatment for a person ... who lacks capacity to consent to the treatment'. In such circumstances, the NHS body must instruct an independent mental capacity advocate to represent the patient. It remains to be seen how this section of the Act will operate in practice. It appears that the advocate will be able to challenge or assist in challenging a decision. It also appears that if the treatment needs to be given urgently the body can give the treatment without the advocate being appointed. Until the Act has come into force and there is greater clarity about the role of advocates clinicians would be advised to follow the St George's Guidelines.

4 THE PATIENT WHO DOES NOT HAVE CAPACITY TO MAKE DECISIONS

In the event of an adult patient being incompetent and in the absence of specific statutory authority under the 1983 Mental Health Act (see below), no one else, not even the next of kin, is in a position to give consent to treatment. The doctor's duty is to act in the best interests of the patient.[25] Not only is he or she justified in taking such steps as good medical practice demands, the doctor may even have a duty (per Lord Brandon) to administer treatment in such circumstances. Under the provisions of the Mental Health Act 1983 Section 63, 'The consent of the patient shall not be required for any medical treatment given to him for the mental disorder from which he is suffering if the treatment is given by or under the direction of the responsible medical officer'. It should be noted, however, that the medical treatment concerned must be for the mental disorder from which the patient is suffering as opposed to treatment for any other condition. As Section 63 of the Act only authorises nonconsensual treatment for a mental condition, not for a physical condition, it should not be used for enforced caesarean sections. Lord Donaldson said in *Re T [1992]*,[11] 'If an adult patient did not have capacity to decide at the time of the purported refusal and still does not have that capacity, it is the duty of the doctors to treat him in whatever way they consider, in the exercise of their clinical judgement, to be in his best interests'.

The underlying moral presumptions are first in favour of life and second in favour of a mother's normal will to do what is best for the fetus. For example, in the absence of an advance directive and with neurological evidence of brain death in the mother, it would be appropriate to act on behalf of the fetus.

4.1 Advance Directives (or 'living wills')

The Mental Capacity Act 2005 (Section 26) addresses the issue of Advance Directives. In summary, if the patient who does not have capacity at the time of proposed treatment has made an advance decision in writing in respect of treatment at a time when she had capacity, has not withdrawn it at a time when she had capacity to do so, and the decision specifies the treatment concerned, the decision has the effect as if she had made it and had capacity to make it at the time when the question about the treatment being carried out arises. However, an advance decision will not be applicable to the treatment in question if the treatment is not the treatment specified in the advance decision, any circumstances specified in the advance decision are absent or there are reasonable grounds for believing that circumstances exist which the patient did not anticipate at the time of the decision and which would have affected the decision.

The Court has power under the Act to make a declaration as to the validity and applicability of an advance decision. In the case of *R (Burke) v GMC*,[7] the Court said of the Mental Capacity Act: 'While Section 26 of that Act requires compliance with a valid advance directive to refuse treatment, Section 4 does no more than require this to be taken into consideration when considering what is in the best interests of a patient'.

In general, doctors are under duty to respect, in an advance directive, refusal of any procedure debarred to them by a patient's refusal of consent.[26,27] They are however, not obliged to honour a request for specific treatment in advance directives that they would hold to be contrary to professional judgement or personal conscience.

What then is the status of an advance directive in pregnancy? The BMA Code of Practice states: 'Women of childbearing age should be advised to consider the possibility of their advance statement or directive being invoked at a time when they are pregnant. A waiver covering pregnancy might be written into the statement' and: 'If an incapacitated pregnant woman presents with an apparently valid advance directive refusing treatment, legal advice should be sought to clarify the position'.[26]

The Law Commission reports: 'the majority of the US states with living will legislation set statutory limits to the effectiveness of any declarations during the maker's pregnancy'[28] and quotes a similar opinion from King's College London Centre of Medical Law and Ethics.[29]

The Law Commission continues: 'We do not, however, accept that a woman's right to determine the sorts of bodily interference which she will tolerate somehow evaporates as soon as she becomes pregnant. There can, on the other hand, be no objection to acknowledging that many women do in fact alter their views as to the interventions they find acceptable as a direct result of the fact that they are carrying a child. By analogy with cases where life might be needlessly shortened or lost it appears that a refusal, which did not mention the possibility that the life of a fetus might be endangered, would be likely to be found not to apply in circumstances where a treatment intended to save the life of the fetus was proposed. Women of child-bearing age should therefore be aware that they should address their minds to this possibility if they wish to make advance refusals of treatment'.

They suggest, 'The best way of balancing the continuing right of the patient to refuse such treatment with the public interest in preserving life is to create a statutory presumption in favour of the preservation of life. 'They recommend, 'In the absence of any indication to the contrary, it shall be presumed that an advance refusal of treatment does not apply in circumstances where those having the care of the person who made it consider that the refusal (a) endangers that person's life; or (b) if that person is a woman who is pregnant, the life of the fetus.' The Law Commission's recommendations are not legally binding. No statutory presumption in favour of society's interest in preserving life has been created by act of Parliament.

4.2 The patient who lacks capacity at the time of the proposed treatment but with whom the treatment has previously been discussed during the pregnancy and who at a time when she did have capacity, was fully informed, has refused it in advance

In such a case, Section 4(4) of the Mental Capacity Act 2005 will apply. Thus, 'Any act done or decision made for or on behalf of a person who lacks capacity must be done or made in his best interests'. In determining what is in the person's best interests and where it relates to life-sustaining treatment the person making the determination 'must consider so far as is reasonably ascertainable:

(a)   the person's past and present wishes and feelings (and, in particular, any relevant written statement made by him when he had capacity)
(b)   the beliefs and values that would be likely to influence his decision if he had capacity, and
(c)   the other factors that he would be likely to consider if he were able to do so'.

The mother's wishes should be respected in the same way as if she were conscious and competent. This may be at the expense of the fetus.

4.3 The patient who does not have capacity at the time of the proposed treatment but who made a valid advance directive relating to some form of treatment but with whom there has been no opportunity for discussion during the pregnancy

Section 26 of the Mental Capacity Act 2005 will apply (see above). Thus, it will be necessary to look at whether the treatment is the treatment that was specified, whether circumstances specified are or are not present and whether there are reasonable grounds for believing that circumstances exist which the patient did not anticipate at the time of making the directive which would have affected the decision if they had been anticipated.

Where there is no mention of pregnancy in the directive, the timing and content of the advance directive are relevant. If the document was drawn up before the pregnancy was known, and made no reference to pregnancy, the directive could be declared invalid because the circumstances at the critical time of decision were not clearly envisaged when the directive was made. The obstetrician, being uncertain of the intentions of the mother, would be free to allow more weight to the interest of the fetus. If the directive referred to pregnancy, or had been made after the pregnancy was known, that freedom would be denied. Whether a particular directive will be found invalid or not will depend on the facts of the case. To avoid ambiguity, women of childbearing age drawing up advance directives are advised to clarify their views regarding pregnancy.

4.4 The patient who does not have capacity where there is only a presumption of her refusal

One possible example would be if she belongs to a religious sect with relevant scruples. In such circumstances, the obstetrician may be advised to act in the patient's 'best interests' as stated in for example *T v T [1988]*[30] and *Re F [1990]*[19] and as now provided for by Section 4 of the Mental Capacity Act 2005.The previous wishes and feelings of the patient must be taken into account as well as the views of those who know her.

The condition for which the patient is on life support is relevant to any decision. If the condition were one of a trauma from which the patient might reasonably be expected to emerge, her own interest would be higher than if she were brainstem dead. In the latter case, the interests of the fetus would predominate. It would, thus, be appropriate to defer any decision to withdraw life support until intact independent survival was likely.

4.5 Refusal of intervention resulting in adverse outcome

As well as a common law duty of care towards an unborn child (confirmed by the Court of Appeal in *Burton v Islington HA: de Martell v Merton and Sutton HA [1992]*),[31] since July 1976, a third party has a statutory duty of care towards an unborn child who is subsequently born disabled, under the Congenital Disabilities (Civil Liability) Act of that year. However, a person is only liable towards a child, if he or she would, if sued in time, be liable in civil law to one or both of the child's parents.

This raises the question of a child damaged in utero or in the course of delivery as a result of maternal noncompliance. An obstetrician has a duty of care to a mother to exercise reasonable care for her wellbeing. Consider the following scenario: A woman who has capacity to consent to or refuse treatment, being fully informed about the potential risks and benefits of the proposed intervention, refuses to permit the obstetrician to act in such a way as to secure the interests of herself and of her unborn child. As a direct result, the child suffers damage. In this case, no unlawful act has been committed, because the obstetrician's duty is to respect the mother's wishes. To do otherwise would be to commit a battery. An obstetrician who complied with a mother's refusal of consent to a caesarean section would not incur legal liability towards the child, even if it suffered harm.

A crucial test is how well informed the woman was. It may be that, in the event of an adverse outcome, the woman or her family will claim in retrospect that, 'if she had truly understood the risks she would, of course, have consented to the procedure'. The best prospective defences against this are good communication, inter-professional team working and, most of all, meticulous record keeping (see the guidelines in *St George's Healthcare NHS Trust v S [1998]*).[6]

4.6 The Adults with Incapacity (Scotland) Act 2000

The position in Scotland is distinguished by The Adults with Incapacity (Scotland) Act 2000, which defines incapacity, provides a legal framework for decision making on behalf of incapable adults (in relation to medical treatment and research in Part 5 but also financial and property issues), clarifies the law for the carers of adults with incapacity and covers the power to appoint an attorney to look after finances and welfare. The definition of an adult in Scotland is 16 years. Incapacity is defined as being incapable of acting, making or communicating decisions, understanding decisions, or retaining memory of decision by reason of mental disorder or an inability to communicate by reason of physical disability (but not if the deficiency can be made good by the use of an aid e.g. hearing aid, computer screen).

In general, no intervention should be undertaken unless it will benefit the adult and the proposed benefit cannot readily be achieved without the intervention. The least restrictive option in terms of personal freedom consistent with the purpose of the intervention should be chosen. Account should be taken of the present and past wishes and feelings of the adult in so far as they may be ascertained; any personal welfare attorney; primary care giver; nearest relatives. The Act has been in place for several years but with no challenges in an obstetric situation as yet. Further information can be found at www.scotland.gov.uk/justice/incapacity.

5 ETHICAL PRINCIPLES

5.1 Unique relationship

The maternal–fetal relationship is unique. The doctor can benefit or harm the mother and the fetus but there is only access to one through the other. For the duration of pregnancy, the woman is the only person who can directly control what is done to her fetus. The fetus is totally reliant on the mother so long as it remains in utero. The protection of the fetus stands on her performance of her moral obligations, not on any legal right of its own.

5.2 Maternal obligations

The unique relationship between a mother and her embryo or fetus places on her a responsibility that increases as the pregnancy advances. The welfare of the child may well be dependent on her commitment to this unique obligation. The concern of parents for their offspring in utero is normally deep and genuine and many pregnant women more than fulfil their obligations, even to the extent of putting their own lives and health at risk.

The pregnant woman's actions and lifestyle may enhance or damage her fetus. There are many ways in which a mother can influence her fetus. Indirectly, she can accept or reject advice regarding drugs, alcohol, smoking, diet and also maternal examination and investigation. More directly related to the fetus, she alone decides whether to accept prenatal diagnosis and treatment, such as ultrasound scans, chorionic villus sampling, amniocentesis, fetal monitoring and caesarean section.

There are different views of the moral status of the fetus, which are contested and might lead to different views as to the extent of maternal obligations. The concept of 'the fetus as a patient' is confusing; it might be a description of a fetus inside its mother undergoing tests and treatment or it may refer to a person under the care of a doctor. The latter contains a moral assumption, but a fetus is not a person.

It has been argued that Court-authorised interventions are still not ethically justified even if we consider that fetuses have the same full moral status as their mothers and there were maternal duties to look after them.[32] A legal system of 'hands-off' pregnant women encourages altruism, attendance for care and better outcomes, whereas Court-authorised intervention relies on coercion and will inevitably drive women from care, causing worse outcomes.

The pregnant woman may have a different perspective from that of her professional adviser towards a recognised problem.[33] Some may have religious or other convictions that prevent them from accepting a particular course of action.

While doctors cannot force treatments on women, they can build trusting relationships, give advice and use the power of communication and persuasion (but not coercion). So long as a doctor does everything within his or her ability and professional limits, and the mother fully understands, then, if things go wrong, she alone shoulders the burdens of responsibility and guilt. Clearly, this is not to diminish the distress caused to obstetricians, and midwives, of being prevented from using their skills to act as usual to preserve life and health, and from witnessing avoidable tragedy.

5.3 Relationship between caregiver and patient

The aim of those who care for pregnant women must be to foster the greatest benefit to both the mother and fetus with the least risk to both.

Obstetricians must recognise the dual claims of the mother and her fetus. The mother may have separate interests from her future child. Obstetricians must inform and advise the family, using their training and experience in the best interests of both parties. When medical information and the possible options are communicated sensitively and effectively, the mother and her obstetrician can share both the decision and the responsibility for it.

There are limits to the accuracy and effectiveness of many diagnostic and therapeutic procedures during pregnancy and confinement and this should be discussed with the mother. For example, the methods for detecting fetal compromise antenatally and during labour are not always reliable indicators of a poor outcome. The fine indices that determine whether the dynamic process of labour will culminate in a normal outcome are difficult to measure.

In caring for the pregnant woman, an obstetrician must respect the woman's autonomy and her legal right to refuse any recommended course of action. He or she must also fulfil the professional obligation to promote the wellbeing of mother and child. In addition, the caring doctor will be attentive to the woman's reports and concerns about their experiences during pregnancy.[34]

In considering so-called 'non-compliance' in pregnancy,[34,35] a number of reasons for the rejection of a doctor's advice by the pregnant woman have been proposed as factors:

- The attitude of the doctor involved.
- The advice runs contrary to the woman's values.
- The doctor and patient fundamentally disagree about the grounds on which medical knowledge is based.
- The woman may question the specific knowledge on which the advice is based: this can arise as a result of the intrinsic lack of certainty of medical knowledge, very different advice being given on the same clinical issue by different doctors, past tragic failures (such as the use of thalidomide in pregnancy, or past personal or family experience).
- The patient may distrust doctors, fail to understand the issues or be afraid.
- There may be just too much advice 'and it is simply not practical for anyone to follow it all'.
- There may be other concerns and constraints on her life (such as demands of work, children or social circumstances such as poverty, being a single parent or having an uncaring or abusive partner).
- Sometimes the reasons for rejecting the advice may not be fully understood even by the woman herself.

Other ethics committees have reached similar conclusions.[36,37] The Ethics Committee of the American College of Obstetricians and Gynecologists advises that caregivers should refrain from performing procedures that are unwanted by a pregnant woman.[37] The use of judicial authority to implement treatment regimens in order to protect the fetus violates the pregnant woman's autonomy and should be avoided unless stringent criteria are met.

6 WHAT SHOULD THE OBSTETRICIAN DO?

The first question is whether the patient has capacity to consent to, or to refuse, treatment and is refusing recommended treatment. If the patient has capacity there is no action to be taken save for the making of meticulous notes. These must record:

- the unequivocal assurance from the patient that the refusal represents an informed decision
- that she understands the nature and reasons for the proposed treatment, and the risks and the likely outcome involved in the decision to refuse or accept it.

If the patient is unwilling to sign, an indication of this refusal too must be noted in writing.

If the patient's capacity is seriously in doubt, it should be assessed as a matter of priority by a medical practitioner experienced in such assessments (such as a consultant psychiatrist). If, following that assessment, there remains a serious doubt about the patient's competence, legal advice should be sought.

All NHS trusts should have an 'out of hours' contact number to enable legal advice to be obtained and to deal with this sort of situation. Those who may need to make use of the service must know the particular system that applies in each trust.

The number of times that it is necessary to apply to the Court is small; the law is relatively settled and in most, if not all, cases the Court would not need to be involved.

In the event that an Application to the Court has to be made, other issues need to be considered. Commonly, the Official Solicitor will need to be involved to ensure that the interests of anyone lacking mental capacity are represented. There are also questions as to what evidence needs to be put before the Judge and what precisely is being sought from the Court.

The Courts recognise that there is a need for an urgent response at any time and there is therefore at all times a duty Judge in the High Court who is available to hear such cases. In appropriate and urgent cases the Application will generally be dealt with by telephone rather than by way of a Court hearing.

The guidance from the Court in the case of *St Georges Healthcare NHS Trust v S [1998]* is set out in Box 1.6

Box 1. Suggested practice when declarations are sought from the Courts

1. The guidelines have no application where the patient is competent to accept or refuse treatment.

2. The Court is unlikely to entertain an application for a declaration unless the capacity of the patient to consent to or refuse the medical intervention is in issue.

3. Refusals should be recorded and authenticated in writing wherever possible. The hospital authorities should seek unequivocal assurances from the patient (to be recorded in writing) that the refusal represents an informed decision; that is, that she understands the nature of and reasons for the proposed treatment and the risks and likely prognosis involved in the decision to refuse or accept it. If the patient is unwilling to sign a written indication of this refusal, this too should be noted in writing.

4. For the time being, at least, the doctors ought to seek a ruling from the High Court on the issue of competence.

5. Those in charge should identify a potential problem as early as possible so that both the hospital and the patient can obtain legal advice. In this case, for instance, the problem was identified at the antenatal clinic.

6. It is highly desirable that, in any case where it is not an emergency, steps are taken to bring it before the Court, before it becomes an emergency, to remove the extra pressure from the parties and the Court and to enable proper instructions to be taken, particularly from the patient and where possible give the opportunity for the Court to hear oral evidence, if appropriate.

7. Both parties should be present at the hearing(s).

8. The mother should be represented in all cases, unless, exceptionally, she does not wish to be. If she is unconscious, she should have an advocate appointed by the Court to act in her best interests (known as 'guardian ad litem').

9. The Official Solicitor should be notified of all applications to the High Court. It would be helpful if, at least for the time being, in cases where he is not asked to be guardian ad litem, the Official Solicitor were prepared to continue to act as an adviser to the Court who is not a party to the case (amicus curiae).

10. If competence is in issue there should in general be some evidence, preferably but not necessarily from a psychiatrist, as to the competence of the patient.

11. Where time permits, the person identified to give the evidence as to capacity to consent to or refuse treatment should be made aware of the observations made in this judgement.

12. In order to be in a position to assess a patient's best interests, the judge should be provided, where possible and if time allows, with information about the circumstances of and relevant background material about the patient.

7 SUMMARY

- The management of pregnancy rests upon dual responsibilities of mothers and other caregivers. While the clear professional obligation of the obstetrician is under the sanction of law, the moral obligation of the mother is not. Normally both responsibilities are exercised in concert.
- The aim of those who care for pregnant women is to foster the greatest benefit to both mother and fetus with the least risk.
- The competent adult has the right to refuse treatment and surgery without consent is an assault.
- Doctors must recognise that medical advice is based on evidence that is seldom, if ever, infallible. It is the doctor's duty to provide appropriate information so that the pregnant woman can make an informed and thoughtful decision.
- Occasionally, problems arise when a pregnant woman and her doctor fundamentally disagree over action believed to be in the best interest of mother or fetus or when advice is in conflict with her religious scruples.
- Such circumstances are usually unexpected and the requirement of haste leaves little time for the case to be properly prepared and decided.
- The presumption is that every adult has the capacity to decide whether to consent to, or refuse, proposed medical intervention, unless it is shown that they cannot understand information presented in a clear way.
- Capacity should not be confused with a health professional's assessment of the reasonableness of the patient's decision.
- Although obligations to the fetus increase as it develops *in utero*, UK law does not grant it personal legal status. This comes from the time of birth.
- The law provides no restriction on a woman's freedom on account of her pregnancy. Any medical action requires her informed consent.
- Where conflict arises the doctor should seek help and advice from other professional colleagues and, with the patient's agreement, it may be appropriate to involve other members or friends of her family.
- A doctor must respect the competent pregnant woman's right to choose or refuse any particular recommended course of action while optimising care for both mother and fetus to the best of his or her ability. A doctor would not then be culpable if these endeavours were unsuccessful.
- The best defences against any retrospective claim that the woman did not fully understand the risks are good communication, interprofessional teamworking and, most of all, meticulous record keeping.
- It is inappropriate to invoke judicial intervention to overrule an informed and competent woman's refusal of a proposed medical treatment, even if it seems to others to be irrational.
- If an adult with capacity makes a voluntary and appropriately informed decision to refuse treatment this decision must be respected, even where this may result

in the death of the patient and/or the death of an unborn child, whatever the stage of the pregnancy.
- In an emergency (and in the absence of an advance directive) the obstetrician should act in what he or she considers to be the best interests of the woman.
- If the treatment had previously been fully discussed with the now incompetent woman when she was competent and she had refused it, her wishes should be respected, even at the expense of the fetus.
- When an advance directive specifies refusal of treatment during pregnancy this, too, should be honoured.
- If the advance directive does not mention pregnancy, the obstetrician should act in what he or she considers to be the best interests of the woman (and the fetus).
- Legal advice should be sought when the obstetrician has doubt or reservations.
- In all cases, consultation with senior colleagues is advisable and grounds for decisions and actions must be clearly set down.
- Any Court application must be supported by accurate and relevant information about the reasons for the proposed treatment, the risks involved, any alternatives, and the patient's reasons for refusal.
- The patient or her representative must have notice of the proceedings and an opportunity to put her case. The terms of any declaration must be communicated quickly and accurately to the woman.

APPENDIX 1

LEGAL PRECEDENTS (IN CHRONOLOGICAL ORDER)

CASE 1 1978 *MCFALL V SHIMP* [22]

A man was found to be the only person with compatible bone marrow to save his cousin's life. After some reflection, the first cousin declined to have the tissue removed, even in the knowledge that his cousin would probably die as a result. The issue went to Court. The Court, unsurprisingly, was unwilling to order the removal of the tissue, even though the cousin's moral culpability was criticised heavily. This is a critical distinction. Although a pregnant woman may well have an extremely strong ethical responsibility towards her unborn child, this does not mean that it is correct to use the law to enforce these responsibilities.

CASE 2 1988 *RE F (IN UTERO)* [18]

The case concerned a 36-year-old pregnant woman who suffered from severe mental disturbance, accompanied by occasional drug use. Her first son had been the subject of a care order and was being adopted by foster parents. The woman had a nomadic life style and the local authority became concerned when she disappeared from her flat and could not be located. Expressing concern for the welfare of her unborn child, the local authority sought to extend the wardship jurisdiction to the child *in utero*. The Court of Appeal was entirely opposed to this course of action.

Lord Justice Balcombe said, 'Since an unborn child has, ex hypothesi, no existence independent of its mother, the only purpose of extending the jurisdiction to include a fetus is to enable the mother's actions to be controlled ... indeed, that is the purpose of the present application.'

He cited Lowe,[38] who gave examples of how such control might operate in practice: 'It would mean, for example, that the mother would be unable to leave the jurisdiction without the Court's consent, the Court being charged to protect the fetus' welfare would surely have to order the mother to stop smoking, imbibing alcohol and indeed any activity which might be hazardous to the child. Taking it to the extreme, were the Court to be faced with saving the baby's life or the mother's, it would surely have to protect the baby's.'

Lord Justice Balcombe went on to consider that another possibility would be that the Court might be asked to order that the baby be delivered by caesarean section. He said: 'it would be intolerable to place a judge in the position of having to make such a decision without any guidance as to the principles on which his decision should be based. If the law is to be extended in this manner, so as to impose control over the mother of an unborn child, where such control may be necessary for the benefit of that child, then under our system of parliamentary democracy, it is for Parliament to decide whether such controls can be imposed and, if so, subject to what limitations or conditions'.

He went on to observe that, in such a sensitive field, affecting as it does the liberty of the individual, it was not for the judiciary to extend the law.

Additionally, Lord Justice May pointed to the 'insuperable difficulties' that would be caused if one sought to enforce any order in respect of an unborn child against its mother, if that mother failed to comply with the order. He said 'I cannot contemplate the Court ordering that this should be done by force, nor indeed is it possible to consider with any equanimity that the Court should seek to enforce an order by committal'. All three of their Lordships stressed that such a drastic extension of wardship jurisdiction to protect the fetus at the expense of the liberty of the mother would be a matter for Parliament. While this statement was not at the heart of the decision in the case, it is fairly persuasive.

CASE 3 1992 *RE T (ADULT: REFUSAL OF TREATMENT)*[11]

T was a 20-year-old woman who was injured in a road traffic accident when she was 34 weeks pregnant. On admission to hospital, her condition deteriorated. T, who had been brought up by her mother as a Jehovah's Witness, stated spontaneously to a nurse that she did not want a blood transfusion, having spent a period of time alone with her mother. T gave birth to a stillborn child. She reiterated her opposition to a blood transfusion. Her condition became critical and she was sedated and placed on a ventilator. Her father, supported by her boyfriend, applied to the Court for a declaration that it would not be unlawful for the hospital to administer a transfusion to her in the absence of her consent.

The Court of Appeal held that an adult patient was entitled to refuse consent to treatment, irrespective of the wisdom of the decision. However, for such refusal to be effective, doctors had to be satisfied that at the time of the refusal the patient's capacity to decide had not been diminished by illness or medication or given on the basis of false assumptions or misinformation, or that the patient's will had not been overborne by another's influence, and that any refusal had been directed to the situation which had become relevant. Only where a patient's refusal was ineffective could doctors treat in accordance with their clinical judgment of the patient's best interests. In T's situation, it was held that the effect of her condition, together with misinformation, rendered her refusal of consent ineffective.

Notwithstanding the outcome for the individual patient, this case affirms a patient's absolute right, properly exercised, to refuse medical treatment.

Lord Donaldson said 'An adult patient who suffers from no mental incapacity has an absolute right to choose whether to consent to medical treatment, to refuse it or to choose one rather than another of the treatments being offered'.

Lord Justice Butler Sloss said: 'A man or woman of full age and sound understanding may choose to reject medical advice and medical or surgical treatment either partially or in its entirety. A decision to refuse medical treatment by a patient capable of making the decision does not have to be sensible, rational or well considered'.

Agreeing with the reasoning of the Court of Appeal in Ontario [*T v T 1990*] in which a blood transfusion was given to an unconscious card-carrying Jehovah's Witness, she cited Robbins,[40] who said: 'At issue here is the freedom of the patient as an individual to exercise her right to refuse treatment and accept the consequences of her own decision. Competent adults ... are generally at liberty to refuse medical treatment even at the risk of death. The right to determine what shall be done with one's body is a fundamental right in our society. The concepts inherent in this right are the bedrock upon which the principles of self-determination and individual autonomy are based. Free individual choice in matters affecting this right should, in my opinion, be accorded very high priority'.

Likewise, Lord Justice Staughton said: 'An adult whose mental capacity is unimpaired has the right to decide for herself whether she will or will not receive medical or surgical treatment, even in circumstances where she is likely or even certain to die in the absence of treatment'.

CASE 4 1992 *RE S (ADULT: REFUSAL OF MEDICAL TREATMENT)* [5]

'Mrs S is 30 years of age, she is in labour with her third pregnancy. She was admitted to a hospital last Saturday with ruptured membranes and in spontaneous labour. She has continued in labour since. She is already 6 days overdue beyond the expected date of birth and she has now refused, on religious grounds, to submit herself to a caesarean section operation. She is supported in this by her husband. They are described as 'born again Christians' and are clearly quite sincere in their belief. I have heard the evidence of P, a Fellow of the Royal College of Surgeons, who is in charge of the patient at the hospital. He has given, succinctly and graphically, a description of the condition of this patient. Her situation is desperately serious, as is also the situation of the as yet unborn child. The child is in what is described as a position of "transverse lie" with the elbow projecting through the cervix and the head being on the right side. There is the gravest risk of a rupture of the uterus if the section is not carried out and the natural labour process is permitted to continue. The evidence of P is that we are concerned with "minutes rather than hours" and that this is a "life and death" situation. He has done his best, as have other surgeons and doctors at the hospital, to persuade the mother that the only means of saving her life, and also I emphasise the life of her unborn child, is to carry out a caesarean section operation. P is emphatic. He says it is absolutely the case that the baby cannot be born alive if a caesarean operation is not carried out. He has described the medical condition. I am not going to go into it in detail because of the pressure of time.'

After proceedings conducted in the absence of legal representation for Mrs S, lasting for under 2 hours, the President granted a declaration authorising treatment. He gave only two justifications for granting the declaration, namely: 'The fundamental question appears to have been left open by Lord Donaldson in *Re T (Adult: refusal of medical treatment)[1992]*[5] and ... there is no English authority which is directly in point'.

He also referred to: 'Some American authority, which suggests that, if this case were being heard in the American Courts, the answer would be likely to be in favour of granting a declaration in these circumstances' and cited *Re AC [1987]*[41] and *[1990]*.[42]

The reliance on the case of *Re AC [1987]*[41] and *[1990]*[42] was both extraordinary and, it has been submitted by a number of legal commentators, wrong. In the Columbia Court of Appeal's decision in *Re AC*, the majority departed from the Court's earlier decision in the case, and ruled that a caesarean section should not have been authorised on AC by the trial Court to save her unborn child. It was held that a full hearing was required involving legal representation of both parties before a Court could contemplate authorizing a procedure upon a pregnant woman who was refusing treatment. Rather, the correct approach was for the Court to determine whether the woman was competent, and if so what were her wishes. If she was not competent, the Court should apply a substituted judgment test to decide what she would have wanted in the circumstances. Judge Terry stated in *Re AC* that the woman's wishes would be determinative in virtually all cases. The Court left open whether there might be 'truly extraordinary or compelling reasons' to override the woman's wishes. The only possible justification for Sir Stephen Brown's decision could be an assumption by him that the facts of *Re S [1992]*[5] involved the truly exceptional case.

This seems unlikely, since even in *Re AC*, where the carrying out of a caesarean section was likely to affect the mother's health adversely (the pregnant woman had cancer and died 2 days after the caesarean), Judge Terry stated: 'Some may doubt that there could ever be a situation extraordinary or compelling enough to justify a massive intrusion into a person's body, such as a caesarean section, against the person's will'.

Martha Swartz[43] points out that the decision of the District of Columbia Court of Appeals which overturned the decision in *Re AC* only applied to Washington DC and elsewhere the overwhelming trend has, worryingly, been to override the pregnant woman's objections to treatment. Certainly, Sir Stephen Brown's reliance on *Re AC* has made the *Re S* judgement be regarded with considerable scepticism by legal commentators.

The *Re S* case has not been appealed. There is no legal justification for overriding a competent patient's wishes purportedly in her best interests. Thus, to the extent the declaration in *Re S* purports to be in the mother's vital interest, this must surely be wrong. The justification provided by the case of *Re F [1990]*[19] applies only in the case of incompetent adults and should certainly not be applied in the case of competent female patients. Indeed, even if the woman were unconscious, Re F would only justify treating her if such treatment were in her best interests, either to save her life or to ensure improvement or prevent deterioration in her physical (or mental) health. This would not necessarily justify a caesarean unless it fulfilled the above criteria.

CASE 5 1997 *RE MB*[22]

A caesarean section was planned for a footling breech presentation but the appellant withdrew consent in the anaesthetic room because of a fear of needles. The defendant health authority sought a decision from the Courts that it would be lawful to perform the caesarean section. A psychiatrist examined the patient and gave his opinion by telephone jointly to the solicitors for the hospital and the patient. In a telephone hearing that lasted from 9.25pm until 9.55pm,the judge decided that it would be lawful because the patient lacked capacity to decide. By this time, the emergency had abated because she went out of the incipient labour. An appeal was initiated by MB via her solicitors and in a hearing that lasted from 11.30pm until after 1am, the Court of Appeal upheld the decision, albeit reserving judgement. The following day she agreed to the induction of anaesthesia and a healthy male infant was born by operative delivery on that day.

As far as MB herself was concerned the Court of Appeal held:

1. The judge was right to hold that the appellant lacked capacity to consent; although generally she was perfectly competent, at the moment when confronted with the needle in the anaesthetic room, she panicked and for that moment she lacked capacity to take a decision whether or not to consent to the operation;

2. He had to make a finding as to what were the appellant's best interests and on the evidence he had reached a correct finding.

The Court then gave the guidance that was subsequently approved in *Re S* (see Case 6). Re MB remains a puzzling decision because it illustrates clearly both the legal principles and the way in which they are likely to be interpreted. At the time when the Court of Appeal decided that MB lacked capacity as a result of a temporary panic brought on by the sight of a needle, she was in fact on an antenatal ward out of sight of any needle. Her refusal was being presented by a QC to whom she was competent to give clear instructions that she did not want to have an operation if it involved a needle.

The Court's analysis of this issue was that she wanted the caesarean section; what she refused was not the surgical incision but only the prick of the anaesthetist's needle; she could not bring herself to undergo the section she desired because her fear of the needle at the moment of panic dominated all her thinking, rendering her incapable of taking any decision at all The Court pointed out that fear of an operation may be a rational reason for refusal; here, it paralysed the will, destroying the capacity to make a decision.

Furthermore, the guidance that in future cases this problem should be detected in the antenatal clinic and brought before the Court before any emergency has arisen implied that this was not an expedient devised for the facts of this case but the way in which such problems should be tackled in the future.

CASE 6 1997 *RE MS B V AN NHS TRUST*[12]

This was a case in which the main issue was whether Ms B had the capacity to make her own decision about her treatment in hospital. Underlying this important issue was the tragic story of an able and talented woman of 43 years of age who had suffered a devastating illness which had caused her to be tetraplegic and whose expressed wish was not to be kept artificially alive by use of a ventilator. The Court found that she did have capacity. In giving judgement, the Court restated the basic principles and offered additional guidelines in case a similar situation arose. These included the following: 'if there are difficulties in deciding whether the patient has sufficient mental capacity, particularly if the refusal may have grave consequences for the patient, it is most important that those considering the issue should not confuse the question of mental incapacity with the nature of the decision made by the patient, however grave the consequences. The view of the patient may reflect a difference in values rather than an absence of competence and the assessment of capacity should be approached with this firmly in mind. The doctors must not allow their emotional reaction to or strong disagreement with the decision of the patient to cloud their judgement in answering the primary question whether the patient has mental capacity to make the decision'.

CASE 7 1998 *ST GEORGE'S HEALTHCARE NHS TRUST V S*[6]

Guidelines were given by the Court of Appeal in July 1998, in relation to an appeal in the case of *St George's Healthcare NHS Trust v S, R v Collins and others, ex parte S*. The case of *S* had centred on the question of S's competence to decide on treatment, in this case whether or not to undergo the recommended caesarean section to control a case of severe pre-eclampsia. Incorrect submissions to the judge at the time had resulted in a decision to proceed to caesarean section against S's wishes. This decision was subsequently appealed against, being heard approximately 2 years later. The appeal against the decision allowing the caesarean section was allowed.

References

1 Wall J (1996) Tameside and Glossop Acute Services NHS Trust v CH [1996] 1 FLR 753.

2 Savage W. 'Caesarean section: who chooses – the woman or her doctor?' In: Dickenson D, editor. *Ethical Issues in Maternal-Fetal Medicine*. Cambridge: Cambridge University Press; 2002. p. 263–83.

3 Grubb A. *Principles of Medical Law*. 2nd ed. Oxford: Oxford University Press; 2004.

4 *Vo v France* (Application number 53924/00) [2004] 2 F.C.R. 577.

5 *Re S (Adult: refusal of medical treatment)* [1992] 4 All ER 671.

6 *St Georges Healthcare NHS Trust v S* [1998] 3 All ER 673.

7 *R (Burke) v GMC* [2005] EWCA Civ 1003.

8 NHS Management Executive. *A Guide to Consent for Examination or Treatment*. London: DH; 1990.

9 Department of Health. *Reference Guide to Consent for Examination or Treatment*. London: DH; 2001 [www.dh.gov.uk/PublicationsAndStatistics/ Publications/PublicationsPolicyAndGuidance/ PublicationsPolicyAndGuidanceArticle/fs/ en?CONTENT_ID=4006757&chk=snmdw8].

10 *[Tameside and Glossop Acute Services NHS Trust v CH (A Patient)* 1996]1 FLR 762.

11 *Re T (Adult: refusal of treatment)* [1992] 3 WLR 782.

12 *Ms B v an NHS Hospital Trust* [2002] EWHC 429 (Fam).

13 *Gillick v West Norfolk and Wisbech AHA* [1986] AC 112.

14 British Medical Association. *Consent, Rights and Choices in Health Care for Children and Young People*. London: BMJ Books; 2002.

15 *Re R (A Minor) (Wardship: Medical Treatment)* [1991]4 All ER 177.

16 *Re W (A Minor) (Medical Treatment)* [1993]4 All ER 627 (1993) 1 FLR 1.

17 *Paton v BPAS* [1979] 1 QB 276.

18 *Re F (in utero)* [1988] 2 All ER 193.

19 *Re F (mental patient: sterilisation)* [1990] 2 AC 1.

20 Grubb A. Refusal of medical treatment, III:The pregnant woman.*Dispatches, Centre of Medical Law and Ethics, King's College, London* 1993;3(3):1–3.

21 Law Commission. *Injuries to Unborn Children*. No. 60, CMND 5709. London: HMSO; 1974.

22 *McFall v Shimp* (1978) 10 Pa D&C 3d 90–92.

23 *Re: MB (an adult: medical treatment)* [1997] 2FCR 541.

24 Francis R. Consent. In: *Risk Management and Litigation in Obstetrics and Gynaecology*. Clements RV, Brennan D, editors. London: RSM Press and RCOG Press; 2001. p. 25–33.

25 Wood J (1988) in *T v T* [1988] Fam 52.

26   British Medical Association.*Advance Statements about Medical Treatment. Code of Practice*. London: BMA; 1995.

27   General Medical Council. *Seeking Patients' Consent: the Ethical Considerations*. London: GMC; 1988 [www.gmc-uk.org/guidance/library/consent.asp].

28   Law Commission. *Mental Incapacity*. London: Law Commission; 1995.

29   Kennedy I. *The Living Will: Consent to Treatment at the End of Life*. London: Age Concern, Institute of Gerontology and Centre of Medical Law and Ethics, Kings College London; 1998.

30   *T v T* [1988] Fam 52.

31   *Burton v Islington HA*: de Martell v Merton and Sutton HA [1992] 3 All ER 833.

32   Bewley S. Restricting the freedom of pregnant women. In: Dickenson D, editor. *Ethical Issues in Maternal–Fetal Medicine*. Cambridge: Cambridge University Press; 2002. p. 131–46.

33   Murray,TH. Moral obligations to the not yet born child. In: *The Worth of a Child*. Berkeley: University of California Press; 1996. p. 96–114.

34   Baylis F, Sherwin S. Judgements of non-compliance in pregnancy. In: Dickenson D, editor. *Ethical Issues in Maternal–Fetal Medicine*. Cambridge: Cambridge University Press; 2002. p. 285–301.

35   Jonsen AR. Ethical issues in compliance. In: Haynes B, Taylor DW, Sackett DL, editors. *Compliance in Health Care*. Baltimore: Johns Hopkins University Press; 1979. p. 113–20.

36   International Federation of Gynecology and Obstetrics. *Recommentations on Ethical Issues in Obstetrics and Gynecology by the FIGO Committee for the Ethical Aspects of Human Reproduction and Women's Health*. Geneva: FIGO; 2000. p. 36–7.

37   American College of Obstetrics and Gynecologists Committee on Ethics. Patient choice and the maternalfetal relationship.Washington DC:ACOG; 2002. p. 61–3.

38   Lowe 96 LQR 29 at 30.

39   *T v T* 1990.

40   Robbins JA (1990) *Malette v Shulman* [1990] 67 DLR (4th) 321.

41   *Re AC* (1987) 533 A 2d 611.

42   *Re AC* (1990) 573 A 2d 1235.

43   Swartz M. Pregnant woman vs. fetus: a dilemma for hospital ethics committees. *Camb Q Healthc Ethics* 1992;1(1):51–62.

Valid until September 2009 unless otherwise indicated

These guidelines were produced under the direction of the Ethics Committee of the Royal College of Obstetricians and Gynaecologists, as an educational aid to obstetricians and gynaecologists. These guidelines do not define a standard of care, nor is it intended to dictate an exclusive course of management. Variations of practice taking into account the needs of the individual patient, resources and limitations unique to the institution or type of practice may be appropriate.

Appendix 10.1

Draft Injunction Restraining Force-Feeding

UPON hearing counsel for the Claimant and counsel for the Defendant

AND UPON reading the application notice and the claim form

AND UPON   [the Court not being satisfied that the Claimant lacks capacity] or

[the Court being satisfied that although the Claimant lacks capacity it is not in her best interests to impose any form of medical treatment or care]

IT IS ORDERED THAT

1.   The Defendant, its servants or agents, be restrained from imposing any form of medical treatment or care, including naso-gastric feeding, on the Claimant without her consent until the trial of the action or further order of the court.
2.   The Defendant have permission to apply to discharge or vary this order on 24 hours' notice to the Claimant and the Official Solicitor.

Appendix 10.2

DSM-IV: Diagnostic criteria for eating disorders

Diagnostic and Statistical Manual of Mental Disorders (4th Edition, 1995) American Psychiatric Association

DIAGNOSTIC CRITERIA FOR ANOREXIA NERVOSA

(A) Refusal to maintain body weight at or above a minimally normal weight for age and height (eg, weight loss leading to maintenance of body weight less than 85% of that expected; or failure to make expected weight gain during period of growth, leading to body weight less than 85% of that expected).

(B) Intense fear of gaining weight or becoming fat, even though underweight.

(C) Disturbance in the way in which one's body weight or shape is experienced, undue influence of body weight or shape on self-evaluation, or denial of the seriousness of the current low body weight.

(D) In post-menarcheal. females, amenorrhea, ie the absence of at least three consecutive menstrual cycles. (A woman is considered to have amenorrhea if her periods occur only following hormone, eg estrogen, administration.)

Specify type:

Restricting Type: during the current episode of Anorexia Nervosa, the person has not regularly engaged in binge-eating or purging behaviour (ie self-induced vomiting or the misuse of laxatives, diuretics, or enemas).

Binge-Eating/Purging Type: during the current episode of Anorexia Nervosa, the person has regularly engaged in binge-eating or purging behaviour (ie, self-induced vomiting or the misuse of laxatives, diuretics, or enemas).

DIAGNOSTIC CRITERIA FOR BULIMIA NERVOSA

(A) Recurrent episodes of binge-eating. An episode of binge-eating is characterized by both of the following:
   (1) eating, in a discrete period of time (eg, within any 2-hour period), an amount of food that is definitely larger than most people would eat during a similar period of time and under similar circumstances;
   (2) a sense of lack of control over eating during the episode (eg, a feeling that one cannot stop eating or control what or how much one is eating).

(B) Recurrent inappropriate compensatory behaviour in order to prevent weight gain, such as self-induced vomiting; misuse of laxatives, diuretics, enemas, or other medications; fasting; or excessive exercise.

(C) The binge-eating and inappropriate compensatory behaviours both occur, on average, at least twice a week for three months.

505

(D)   Self-evaluation is unduly influenced by body shape and weight.
(E)   The disturbance does not occur exclusively during episodes of Anorexia Nervosa.

Specify type:

Purging Type: during the current episode of Bulimia Nervosa, the person has regularly engaged in self-induced vomiting or the misuse of laxatives, diuretics, or enemas.

Non-purging Type: during the current episode of Bulimia Nervosa, the person has used other inappropriate compensatory behaviours, such as fasting or excessive exercise, but has not regularly engaged in self-induced vomiting or the misuse of laxatives, diuretics, or enemas.

EATING DISORDER NOT OTHERWISE SPECIFIED

The Eating Disorder Not Otherwise Specified category is for disorders of eating that do not meet the criteria for any specific Eating Disorder. Examples include:

(1)   For females, all of the criteria for Anorexia Nervosa are met except that the individual has regular menses.
(2)   All of the criteria for Anorexia Nervosa are met except that, despite significant weight loss, the individual's current weight is in the normal range.
(3)   All of the criteria for Bulimia Nervosa are met except that the binge-eating and inappropriate compensatory mechanisms occur at a frequency of less than twice a week or for a duration of less than 3 months.
(4)   The regular use of inappropriate compensatory behaviour by an individual of normal body weight after eating small amounts of food (eg self-induced vomiting after the consumption of two cookies).
(5)   Repeatedly chewing and spitting out, but not swallowing, large amounts of food,
(6)   Binge-eating disorder: recurrent episodes of binge-eating in the absence of the regular use of inappropriate compensatory behaviours characteristic of Bulimia Nervosa.

Appendix 11.1

Draft Form for Refusal of Treatment to be Signed by the Patient

RECORD OF REFUSAL OF RECOMMENDED TREATMENT

Patient's name Susan Patient **Patient no.** AB1000

Address 15 Acacia Avenue, Blankton, Blankshire BL15 5PW

Ward Elderberry

Attending doctor Dr James Concern

Position Consultant physician **Date** 11th January 2010

STATEMENT OF PATIENT

I, the above-named patient, confirm that I have been advised by the medical practitioner whose name appears above that in order to prevent a deterioration in my health/ permanent injury/or death* I should receive the following treatment:

one or more blood transfusions as considered necessary by those providing me with medical treatment.

I understand that if I do not receive this treatment my health may deteriorate and that I may suffer serious permanent injury or die as a result.* I confirm that I am not willing to consent to such treatment being given to me now or in the future in spite of this.

I have reached this decision of my own free will and have not been subjected to improper pressure or persuasion of any kind.

I understand that I may change the decision recorded in this document at any time while I remain conscious and mentally competent by telling a doctor or nurse, but that if I lose consciousness or my mental competence, I will not then be able to do so.

Patient's signature Susan Patient

Witness' signature Alison Carer

Witness position/address Ward Sister, Elderberry Ward

STATEMENT OF ATTENDING DOCTOR

I, the above-named doctor, confirm that I have advised the above-named patient that the treatment specified above is required to prevent a deterioration in health/serious injury/ death* and that in my opinion the patient understands the advice I have given and is competent to make an independent decision about this medical treatment.

Doctor's signature J Concern **Date** 11/1/2010

* Delete as appropriate

Appendix 11.2

Draft Record of Refusal of Treatment to be Signed by Doctor

RECORD OF REFUSAL OF RECOMMENDED TREATMENT

Patient's name Susan Patient **Patient no.** AB1000

Address 15 Acacia Avenue, Blankton, Blankshire BL15 5PW

Ward Elderberry

Attending doctor Dr James Concern

Position Consultant physician

Date 11th January 2010

I, the above-named doctor, confirm that on the above date I have advised the patient whose name appears above that in order to prevent a deterioration in the patient's health/permanent injury, or death* he/she should receive the following treatment:

one or more blood transfusions as considered necessary

I have advised the patient that if he/she does not receive this treatment his/her health may deteriorate and that he/she may suffer serious permanent injury or die as a result.*

In spite of this advice the patient has refused to give consent to this treatment being given.

In my opinion the patient has not lost the capacity to make a decision to consent or refuse this treatment, and I know of no facts which suggest to me that the patient is acting under the undue influence of others.

I have explained to the patient that he/she may change the decision recorded in this document at any time while remaining conscious and mentally competent by telling a doctor or nurse, but that if he/she loses consciousness or mental competence, he/she will not then be able to do so.

The patient has refused to sign a statement confirming his/her decision and has maintained that refusal in spite of being shown a copy of this document.

Doctor's signature J Concern **Date** 11/1/2010

Witness' signature Alison Carer

Witness position/address Ward Sister, Elderberry Ward

*Delete as appropriate

Appendix 11.3

Draft Specific Issue Order for Administration of Blood Products to Child

IN THE HIGH COURT OF JUSTICE

FAMILY DIVISION

IN THE MATTER OF THE INHERERNT JURISDICTION OF THE COURT

AND IN THE MATTER OF THE SUPREME COURT ACT 1981

BETWEEN:

BLANKSHIRE NHS FOUNDATION TRUST

Claimant

AND

SUSAN PATIENT (A minor)

First Defendant

JOSEPH AND ANNABEL PATIENT

Second and Third Defendants

ORDER

UPON reading the application, witness statements and medical reports herein

AND UPON hearing the evidence of Mr and Mrs Patient, Dr Goodley

AND UPON hearing counsel for the Claimant and the Defendants

It is declared that:

1. In an immediately life-threatening situation, when it is the professional opinion of those medically responsible for the First Defendant that she is in need of the administration of blood and/or blood products, it shall be lawful for her to be given such blood and/or blood products without [her consent and/or without] the consent of her parents.
2. In any situation which is less than imminently life-threatening, those medically responsible for the First Defendant shall consult with [her and] her parents and will consider at every opportunity all alternative forms of management suggested by [her and] her parents. In the event that those medically responsible for the First Defendant conclude, after such consultation, that there is no reasonable alternative to the administration of blood and/or blood products, they

shall be at liberty to administer such blood and/or blood products without the consent of [the First Defendant or of] her parents.

3. For the avoidance of doubt, this Declaration shall take effect forthwith, notwithstanding that it has not yet been sealed by the Court.

4. There shall be liberty to all parties to apply.

Appendix 12.1

End-of-life decisions

VIEWS OF THE BMA

Contemporaneous requests for and refusal of treatment

Incapacitated patients

Advance refusals and requests

Withholding and withdrawing life-prolonging medical treatment

Assisted dying

Euthanasia

Physician-assisted suicide

Effects on health professionals

INTRODUCTION

The British Medical Association (BMA) has several publications dealing in detail with aspects of end-of-life decisions. These include chapters in its general textbook, *Medical Ethics Today* (2nd edition 2004), *Withdrawing and Withholding Life Prolonging Medical Treatment* (3rd edition 2007) and *Advance Decisions and Proxy Decision-Making in Medical Treatment and Research* (2007). This guideline summarises the BMA's views on three main issues:

- Contemporaneous and advance refusal of treatment
- Withholding and withdrawing life-prolonging medical treatment
- Assisted dying: euthanasia and assisted suicide

BACKGROUND TO BMA POLICIES

The BMA is a professional association for doctors. Its policies are formulated at its annual representative meeting where motions submitted by the BMA membership are debated. If approved, they become BMA policy.

End-of-life issues are frequently a matter of such debate, including concerns about the availability of good quality palliative care. In its policies, the BMA distinguishes between the right that every person has to be supported and cared for during the process of dying and requests that patients sometimes make that the doctor should deliberately hasten their death. The Association emphasises patients' clear and indisputable right to care and assistance while dying but does not believe that patients have a right to assistance to end their lives.

Many doctors worry that high profile media interest in other aspects of end-of-life treatment may detract attention from issues such as palliative care provision. In 2005, a House of Lords Select Committee[1] criticised the gaps in palliative care provision. It said services were inadequately resourced and unevenly spread. BMA members echoed this point. In 2006, the Government acknowledged that more investment was needed and pledged to double funds for palliative care services.[2] Nevertheless, a continuing matter of concern for the Association remains the uneven availability of good quality palliative care for patients who want it.

CONTEMPORANEOUS REQUESTS FOR AND REFUSAL OF TREATMENT

Patients with a terminal or degenerative condition are likely to be anxious about how their care will be managed and how choices are made. Sensitive discussion of their views about the options is useful in enabling those treating them to act in accordance with patients' wishes. While competent, patients decide for themselves what is in their best interests in terms of medical care. They may request or decline certain procedures or refuse life-prolonging treatment generally in certain circumstances. Requests should be taken into account but ultimately the clinician in charge of the patient's care decides which options are clinically appropriate to offer. Patients or their families cannot insist upon clinically inappropriate treatment being provided. It should be borne in mind, however, that the Appeal Court has said that it is always appropriate for doctors to comply with a request for artificial nutrition and hydration (ANH) from patients with mental capacity who are unable to accept nourishment in other ways.[3] The court made clear that this does not imply that patients can more generally insist upon receiving particular forms of treatment but that, as part of their duty of care, doctors must take reasonable steps to keep patients alive when this is the patients' known wish.

In terms of treatment refusal, the law and codes of ethical practice emphasise that adults with mental capacity can refuse medical treatment, including life-prolonging procedures. Where adult patients refuse procedures which are likely to benefit them, the BMA advises health professionals to ensure that there is no misunderstanding and provide information in a sensitive manner about the implications of refusal. Good communication is essential and may include exploration of alternative treatment options that might be acceptable to the patient. Ultimately, however, a refusal made by an adult with mental capacity must be respected.

INCAPACITATED PATIENTS

Decision-making in relation to adults who lack the capacity to consent on their own behalf is governed in England and Wales by the Mental Capacity Act 2005 (MCA), and in Scotland by the Adults with Incapacity (Scotland) Act 2000 (AWIA). In Northern Ireland, decisions are covered by the common law. Decisions with regard to incapacitated adults at the end of life must comply with the relevant legislation.

Both Acts incorporate previous good practice and common law in primary legislation. They do, however, introduce some new functions and responsibilities which health professionals treating patients who lack capacity, or may lack capacity, need to be aware of. Below is a brief outline of the new functions under the legislation, with regard to end of life decisions. More detailed guidance on the treatment of adults who lack capacity can be obtained from the BMA's website.[4]

Where it has been determined that a person lacks capacity, the principal tenet of both Acts is that treatment decisions must be made in the individual's best interests.[5] Identifying a person's best interests can be complex and will depend upon the circumstances of each case; it is important to remember that an assessment of best interests does not just mean medical best interests – it should also encompass, in so far as is practicable, a person's values and known wishes and beliefs. This may include any past written or verbal statement, made when the person had capacity, and discussion with those close to the patient.

In England, Wales and Scotland, individuals are entitled to nominate a proxy decision-maker, commonly referred to as a welfare attorney, to make health and welfare decisions on their behalf. The individual nominating a proxy decision-maker can set a variety of conditions on the exercise of the proxy's powers and the transfer of decision-making authority does not extend to refusing life-sustaining treatment unless this is explicitly stated. Anyone acting as a proxy decision-maker must make decisions based on the best interests of the incapacitated patient. Where there is a serious and irresolvable dispute between a health professional and a proxy decision-maker, the case can be referred for adjudication to the Court of Protection, in England and Wales, and in Scotland the Court of Session.

The MCA has also developed an advocacy scheme to support 'un-befriended' incapacitated adults. Where it is clear that a decision needs to be made on behalf of an incapacitated adult in relation to either serious medical treatment or place of residence and there is no one close to the adult, excluding paid carers, to provide advice or guidance, then the services of an independent mental capacity advocate (IMCA) will be engaged. IMCAs cannot give consent on behalf of incapacitated adults, but they must be consulted and their views taken into account when assessing a patient's best interests.

ADVANCE REFUSALS AND REQUESTS

The recording of advance decisions provides a mechanism for individuals with capacity to say what they would like to happen in the future if their mental capacity becomes impaired. An advance decision (sometimes known as a living will) can either be a statement authorising or requesting specific procedures, or a clear instruction refusing some or all medical procedures.

An advance decision can be a written document, a witnessed oral statement, a signed printed card, a smart card or a note of a particular discussion recorded in the patient's file. Advance decisions only come into consideration once patients lose their mental capacity, are unconscious or otherwise unable to communicate. Where there is a valid and legally binding refusal of treatment, that must be followed. Otherwise, doctors must act in the incapacitated patient's best interests. Evidence of an informed advance decision that does not meet the criteria for legal validity should nevertheless be taken into account when deciding what is in the individual patient's best interests.

In England and Wales, advance decisions are covered by the Mental Capacity Act. To be valid and legally binding the advance decision must be specific about the treatment that is being refused and the circumstances in which the refusal will apply. Where the patient's advance decision relates to a refusal of life-prolonging treatment this must be recorded in writing and witnessed. The patient must acknowledge in the written decision that they intend to refuse treatment even though this puts their life at risk.

In Scotland and Northern Ireland, advance decisions are not covered by statute but it is likely they are covered by common law. An advance refusal of treatment is likely to be binding in Scotland and Northern Ireland if the patient was an adult at the time the decision was made (16 years old in Scotland and 18 in Northern Ireland). The patient must have had capacity at the time the decision was made and the circumstances that have arisen must be those that were envisaged by the patient.

In all cases, doctors need to consider whether the advance decision fits the circumstances that now arise or if there is a major difference or has been a significant change from the scenario the patient anticipated. For example, if the advance refusal was made a long time ago, not updated and treatment options have altered, its validity should be questioned. In case of doubt, legal opinion should be sought.

Health professionals must abide by the terms of a patient's valid advance refusal but care is needed to ensure that the refusal of medical treatment is applicable to the circumstances which have subsequently occurred. Patients cannot demand or refuse anything in advance that they cannot demand or refuse when conscious and competent. Therefore, patients cannot refuse in advance compulsory treatment provided under the mental health legislation or demand euthanasia or assisted dying. Also although advance requests or authorisation of specific treatment can be helpful, they lack legal weight if clinicians assess that treatment to be inappropriate.

While the BMA recognises the advantages of advance decisions in terms of encouraging openness, dialogue and forward planning, it also draws attention to potential disadvantages. Health professionals and the public should be aware that treatment decisions are complex and practice is constantly evolving. If advance decisions are made a long time before capacity is lost, treatment options may have significantly changed. Over time, patients' views can also change about what constitutes a tolerable existence. Advance decisions cannot encompass unforeseen possibilities and options. Therefore, while upholding patients' rights to decide in advance, the BMA also emphasises that patients need to think carefully about the risks associated with committing themselves in advance.

Further guidance is available in the BMA's separate guidance note on advance decision making.[6]

WITHHOLDING AND WITHDRAWING LIFE-PROLONGING MEDICAL TREATMENT

Medical treatment can legally and ethically be withdrawn when it is futile, i e it is unable to produce the desired benefit, when it would not be in the patient's best interest to continue treatment (because, for example, it is simply prolonging the dying process) or when the patient has refused further treatment.

This is, however, a profoundly difficult area, as medical technology increasingly appears to blur the boundaries between life and death. This was illustrated in 1993 by the House of Lords deliberations in the case of Tony Bland.[7] In a persistent vegetative state (PVS) with no awareness of the world and no hope of recovery, Bland was not terminally ill but withdrawal of artificial nutrition would inevitably result in his death. Following judgments made in other jurisdictions and confirming that artificial nutrition constitutes a medical treatment, the House of Lords agreed that it could be withdrawn.

The BMA receives many enquiries about when to give, and when to stop giving, medical treatment which has the potential to prolong life. These enquiries prompted the Association to undertake a consultation in 1998 and subsequently publish guidance for health professionals.[8] The issues are difficult and complex, and doctors, patients and their families need reassurance that each individual decision is carefully thought through, is based on the best quality information available and follows a widely agreed procedure.

Medicine aims to restore or maintain patients' health by maximising benefit and minimising harm. When medical treatment or intervention fails, or ceases, to provide a net benefit to the patient, this primary goal of medicine cannot be realised and the justification for intervening is gone. Unless some other justification can be demonstrated, most people would accept that treatment should not be prolonged. The BMA does not believe that it is appropriate to prolong life at all costs, with no regard to its quality or the burdens of the intervention.

Technological developments continually extend the range of treatment options available to prolong life when organ or system failure would naturally result in death. Patients with progressive, degenerative conditions can have their lives prolonged considerably but this will not necessarily reverse a patient's disease. Other patients, for example those with very severe brain damage, may remain stable for many years if life-prolonging treatment is provided, but this may be with no hope of recovering more than very minimal levels of awareness of their surroundings. They may lack the ability to interact with others or the capacity for self-directed action. In such severely damaged patients, treatment or intervention to prolong life by artificial means may fail to provide sufficient benefit to justify the intervention and the proper course of action may be to withhold or withdraw further treatment.

The guiding principles underlying any such decision must be to protect the dignity, comfort and rights of the patient; to take into account any known wishes of the patient and the views of people close to patients who lack capacity. Communication and consultation are essential. A thorough clinical evaluation, including the initiation of treatment for a trial period if appropriate, must take place, so that the decision is based on as accurate as possible an assessment of the benefits, risks and burdens of the treatment for that particular patient. Where the treatment to be withheld or withdrawn is artificial nutrition and hydration, the General Medical Council requires that a second clinical opinion be sought before treatment is withdrawn or withheld from a patient who is not imminently dying.[9] Furthermore, in England, Wales and Northern Ireland, the withdrawal or withholding of ANH from a patient in a persistent vegetative state needs to be subject to court review. In Scotland, this is not obligatory but it is advisable to seek legal advice.

The BMA's guidance, contained in Withholding and withdrawing life-prolonging medical treatment, gives advice on the ethical, legal and clinical issues, and sets out safeguards for decision making. It indicates how the human rights legislation applies in this area. It also seeks to provide a coherent and comprehensive set of principles which apply to all decisions to withhold or withdraw life-prolonging treatment, which it is hoped will stimulate the development of local policies and guidelines.

Doctors considering withholding or withdrawing life-prolonging treatment can find detailed guidance in the BMA booklet. In any cases of doubt, legal advice should be sought. In England and Wales, legal advice can be sought from the Official Solicitor. Northern Ireland has its own Official Solicitor. In Scotland, advice can be sought from the Mental Welfare Commission or NHS Central Legal Office.

ASSISTED DYING

"Assisted dying" is a general term covering both euthanasia (where someone other than the patient administers a fatal dose) and assisted suicide (where patients are assisted to end their own lives).

Traditionally, the BMA opposed any form of assisted dying but in 2005 its annual representative meeting (its policy-making body) recognised that there were diverse opinions within society and the profession. It agreed that Parliament and society at large should decide the issue of possible legalisation. This meant that the BMA took a neutral stance on assisted dying (euthanasia and assisted suicide), agreeing not to oppose legislation which might alter the criminal law. If legal change occurred, the BMA was mandated to press for robust safeguards for patients and for doctors who did not wish to be involved in assisted dying. In 2006, however, BMA members voting at the annual meeting made clear that the majority opposed such legislation. Therefore the BMA dropped its neutral stance and again opposes all forms of assisted dying.

The current policy is that the BMA:

(i)   believes that the ongoing improvement in palliative care allows patients to die with dignity;

(ii)   insists that physician-assisted suicide should not be made legal in the UK;

(iii)   insists that voluntary euthanasia should not be made legal in the UK;

(iv)   insists that non-voluntary euthanasia should not be made legal in the UK; and,

(v)   insists that if euthanasia were legalised, there should be a clear demarcation between those doctors who would be involved in it and those who would not.

EUTHANASIA

Active and intentional termination of another person's life is morally and legally different to the withholding or withdrawal of treatment. Arguments for legalisation of euthanasia are generally based on arguments about competent individuals' rights to choose the manner of their demise or about cases where medicine is unable to control distressing terminal symptoms. Although the BMA respects the concept of individual autonomy, it argues that there are limits to what patients can choose if their choice will impact on other people.

Arguments against legalisation often focus on practical points. If euthanasia were an option, there might be pressure for all seriously ill people to consider it even if they would not otherwise entertain such an idea. Health professionals explaining options for the management of terminal illness would have to include an explanation of assisted dying. Patients might feel obliged to choose it for the wrong reasons, if they were worried about being a burden or concerned about the financial implications of a long terminal illness. Legalisation could generate anxiety for vulnerable, elderly, disabled or very ill patients.

PHYSICIAN-ASSISTED SUICIDE

The arguments for and against assisted suicide and physician assisted suicide are similar to those made in relation to euthanasia. Assisted suicide differs from euthanasia in that the individual retains control of the process, rather than the doctor or anyone else assisting.

In the past, the BMA made no attempt to distinguish between euthanasia and physician assisted suicide. The two were assumed to be the same, and BMA policy opposing the involvement of doctors in the intentional killing of patients was believed to cover the illegal act of assisting their suicide too.[10] Only in 1997 did BMA policy make specific reference to both physician assisted suicide and euthanasia. It recognised that there was a wide spectrum of views about both but opposed any changes in law to permit either.

In 1998 the BMA's Medical Ethics Department published a discussion paper asking whether the moral arguments about physician assisted suicide and euthanasia differ, and whether it is morally relevant that in physician assisted suicide the patient, not the doctor, is the main actor.[11] The same year, the BMA was mandated by its representative body to hold a conference "to promote the development of a consensus on physician assisted suicide." In March 2000, 50 BMA members, representing a range of medical specialties and professional seniority, met for two days of debate. They produced a consensus statement opposing physician assisted suicide, whilst recognising that the views of individuals within the profession covered a wide spectrum.

In Parliament between 2003–6, there were attempts to change the law prohibiting physician-assisted suicide. In 2003 Lord Joffe brought forward the first of three Bills attempting to legalise assisted dying in England and Wales. None have progressed to become law. The most recent was the 2005 Assisted Dying for the Terminally Ill Bill. In May 2006 this Bill received its second reading and Peers voted to delay it for six months. Lord Joffe pledged to reintroduce the Bill at a later date and the Government said it would not block a further hearing. In Scotland, a proposed similar Bill on Assisted Dying for which MSP Jeremy Purvis had sought support fell through lack of Parliamentary support in November 2005.

Like the arguments for euthanasia, the issue of physician assisted suicide is often portrayed as a question of "patient rights", "free choice" or "liberty of action". The BMA considers that this language of choice may belie the real pressures from family members or society in general which may be exerted if assisted suicide were legalised.

EFFECTS ON HEALTH PROFESSIONALS

While it is difficult, if not impossible, to predict the long-term effect of major social changes, the BMA would be concerned if health professionals were expected to participate in euthanasia or assisted suicide as a result of legal changes. Even if robust conscientious objection clauses were enacted, such a change could give rise to demoralisation among health professionals and ambiguity about their role. If it were part of a health professional's role and duty to assist with suicide and provide advice and counselling for people wishing to carry it out, the underpinning of much of medicine's efforts to improve individual quality of life might be undermined.

© BMA October 2007

For further information about these guidelines, BMA members may contact: askBMA on 0870 60 60 828 or British Medical Association Department of Medical Ethics, BMA House Tavistock Square, London WC1H 9JP Tel: 020 7383 6286 Fax: 020 7383 6233 Email: ethics@bma.org.uk

Non-members may contact: British Medical Association, Public Affairs Department, BMA House, Tavistock Square, London WC1H 9JP Tel: 020 7387 4499 Fax: 020 7383 6400 Email: info.public@bma.org.uk

REFERENCES

1   Report of the House of Lords Select Committee on the Assisted Dying for the Terminally Ill Bill.
2   Department of Health. White paper, Our health, our care, our say. (para 4. 102); 2006.
3   R (on the application of Burke) v General Medical Council [2005] 2 FLR 1223.
4   www.bma.org.uk/ethics
5   Although the Adults with Incapacity (Scotland) Act uses the term 'benefit', in the BMA's view it is likely that this term can be interpreted in a similar way to 'best interests'. If, however, health professionals working in Scotland were

recommending an intervention in the incapacitated person's best interests that was unlikely to provide clinical benefit, they should consider taking legal advice.

6   BMA. Advance Decisions and Proxy Decision-Making in Medical Treatment and Research. London: BMA, 2007.

7   Airedale NHS Trust v Bland [1993] AC 789

8   BMA. Withdrawing & withholding life prolonging medical treatment, 3rd edtn. London: BMA, 2007.

9   GMC. Withholding & withdrawing life-prolonging treatments: good practice in decision-making. London: GMC, 2002.

10   It is unlawful to aid, abet, counsel or procure a suicide under the Suicide Act 1961.

11   BMA. Euthanasia and physician assisted suicide: Do the moral arguments differ? London: BMA, April 1998. Available on the BMA website (www.bma.org.uk/ethics).

Appendix 12.2

Treatment of patients in persistent vegetative state

GUIDANCE FROM THE BMA'S MEDICAL ETHICS DEPARTMENT

Background
Terminology
Criteria for PVS diagnosis
Diagnosis
RCP clinical criteria
Misdiagnosis
Initial assessment and treatment
Review of treatment options
The views of the patient
The views of people close to the patient
Views of health professionals
Conscientious objection
The legal position
Pregnant PVS patients
Post mortem examinations

BACKGROUND

Persistent vegetative state (PVS) began to attract attention in the UK in the 1990s. In 1992–3, the first high profile PVS legal case, that of Tony Bland, progressed through the courts up to the House of Lords.[1] As is discussed below, the Bland case attracted considerable attention and established the current legal criteria in England, Wales and Northern Ireland for decisions about the withdrawal of life-prolonging treatment from such patients. It was followed in 1996 by the Law Hospital case in Scotland, described below.

Prior to the 1990s, there was little debate about PVS. Experts agreed that the condition was poorly understood. In 1992, the BMA produced a 26-page consultation paper on the subject[2] which was circulated widely and used as a resource in the Bland case. Among other things, the BMA paper highlighted the risk of a PVS diagnosis being made prematurely or on insufficient evidence. It emphasised that any lack of rigour in excluding other conditions carried serious dangers for patients: the main danger being that once assumed to be in an irrecoverable condition, such patients may face the removal of life-sustaining treatment, including artificial nutrition and hydration. The risk of premature diagnosis without other factors having been investigated was illustrated in the United States by some cases in which patients, deemed to be in PVS, recovered some functioning. Such was the case of 86-year old Carrie Coons who having been diagnosed as a PVS patient, regained sentience in April 1989 after a court had agreed that her feeding tube could be removed. Cases such as hers drew attention to the need to carry out far more exhaustive testing prior to categorising any patient as being in PVS.

1989 case of misdiagnosis

Carrie Coons, an 86-year old American was unconscious for four and a half months and diagnosed as being in PVS. Her gerontologist's request for tests to eliminate other factors which might have caused her condition was refused by the patient's family. Her relatives applied to court for feeding to be withdrawn. Although the diagnosis had been made without corroboration by a neurologist, the New York court agreed that her artificial nutrition should cease. The patient unexpectedly regained consciousness, however, after aggressive efforts by nurses to stimulate her.

TERMINOLOGY

Variations in terminology occur but BMA guidance refers to the "persistent vegetative state": 'persistent' indicates that the condition is a continuing one. The BMA has resisted the term 'permanent' vegetative state although it agrees that the condition should be seen as irrecoverable once all preliminary diagnostic steps (see below) have been taken and other factors eliminated.

In 1996, the Royal College of Physicians (RCP) issued initial guidance, distinguishing between 'continuing vegetative state' and 'permanent vegetative state'. The former was said to apply to patients prior to confirmation of the permanence of the condition. In 2003, the RCP published new guidance[3] which pointed out that the label 'permanent vegetative state' represents a prediction that the patient will definitely never recover awareness. It noted that such a prediction cannot be made with absolute certainty although the likelihood of recovery significantly diminishes with time.

Debate about the diagnosis and the possibility of recovery from it arose in 2006 when several highly publicised cases appeared to indicate that patients diagnosed as in PVS actually could regain awareness.

In Autumn 2006, trials on the use of zolpidem – a common ingredient in sleeping pills – were due to start in South Africa, involving such patients with severe brain injuries. This followed reports[4] that the drug appeared to temporarily stimulate the brain cells of patients previously thought to be in an irreversible vegetative state. The BMA continues to monitor such reports and awaits the findings of the study. In the meantime, the Association continues to stress the importance of trying all appropriate diagnostic tests prior to categorising any patient as being in PVS.

CRITERIA FOR PVS DIAGNOSIS

The persistent vegetative state presents particular medical, ethical and legal dilemmas because of the extreme nature of the condition, the difficulties associated with diagnosing it accurately and the risks of premature diagnosis. It results from severe damage to the cerebral cortex, resulting in destruction of tissue in the thinking, feeling part of the brain. Patients appear awake but show no psychologically meaningful responses to stimuli and it is common for cerebral atrophy to occur. The condition is distinguished from a state of low awareness and the minimally conscious state (MCS) where patients show minimal but definite evidence of consciousness despite profound cognitive impairment. MCS patients, for example, may demonstrate eye movement to direct stimuli, even though their reactions may be inconsistent. Patients in the "locked-in syndrome" retain cognitive functioning but are unable to communicate other than by purposeful eye movement. Their condition disrupts the patient's ability to control the body's movements, effectively paralysing the patient.

DIAGNOSIS

Although current methods of diagnosing PVS cannot be regarded as infallible, the 2003 RCP document includes a useful checklist for diagnosis. Steps must first be taken to eliminate other possibilities and clinicians must be aware of the dangers of prematurely diagnosing the patient's condition. Although it is impossible to make a confident diagnosis in all suspected PVS cases, new technologies can be helpful in some. New brain-imaging methods appear to offer the potential for identifying some patients who should not be categorised as being in PVS.

> In July 2005, a 23-year old patient remained unresponsive but with sleep-wake cycles after suffering severe traumatic brain injury in a road accident. She was judged to fulfil the criteria for the vegetative state. Five months after the accident, functional magnetic resonance imaging was used to record the patient's neural responses and her brain's ability to process language when she was spoken to. In a subsequent experiment, the patient was asked to imagine visiting rooms in her house or playing tennis. The brain activation patterns that were observed matched those of conscious control subjects. This indicated that despite the patient's apparent unresponsiveness to visual or auditory stimuli and lack of purposeful actions, she had retained the ability to process language and perform mental imagery tasks. The patient was not seen as typical, however, of the vegetative state, not least because she had suffered far fewer cerebral brain lesions.[5]

The RCP set out both the steps to be taken prior to diagnosis and diagnostic criteria:

- Establish cause of the condition
- Persisting effect of anaesthesia or drugs must be excluded
- Possibility of metabolic disturbance investigated
- Possibility of treatable structural cause should be excluded by brain imaging.

RCP CLINICAL CRITERIA:

- No evidence of awareness of self or environment

- No response to visual, auditory, tactile or other stimuli suggesting conscious purpose

- No use of language comprehension or meaningful expression

- An apparent sleep-wake cycle

- Hypothalamic and brainstem function continue, ensuring respiration and circulation.

Any purposeful movement or evidence of communication or awareness indicate that the patient is not in PVS. Research studies indicate that the level of metabolic functioning of the cerebral cortex of PVS patients is the level associated with deep surgical anaesthesia.

MISDIAGNOSIS

Since 1989, an enduring cause for concern has been the risk of misdiagnosis and the RCP document cites studies providing evidence of such errors. In the BMA's view, reports of alleged "recovery" from PVS are likely to indicate an original misdiagnosis. Nevertheless, the BMA continues to keep the evidence of recoveries under review.

INITIAL ASSESSMENT AND TREATMENT

A PVS diagnosis takes time. During the period of initial assessment, it is appropriate to provide aggressive medical treatment. The BMA believes that it is vital that stimulation and rehabilitation should be available for patients suspected of being in PVS as soon as their condition is stabilised. Clinicians should give active consideration to the wide range of specific measures which might effect some improvement in each individual case. Even if few patients improve as a result of being included in coma arousal programmes, the appropriateness of this and other options for each individual must be explored at an early stage. It is for clinical judgement to decide as to the most appropriate measures and the length of time they should be pursued.

High quality nursing care is needed to minimise the risks of complications. It is good medical practice to provide artificial nutrition and hydration to sustain any patient whose prognosis is uncertain. Medical treatments, including artificial nutrition and hydration, may be withdrawn at a later stage, after legal review of the case, if they are considered futile.

The BMA has consistently recommended that the diagnosis of irreversible PVS should not be considered confirmed (and therefore treatment not be withdrawn) until the patient has been insentient for at least 12 months. The Association recognises, however, that distinction can be drawn between different categories of PVS patient depending on factors such as the patient's age and the manner in which the damage to the brain occurred. For some categories, PVS can be diagnosed with considerable certainty within three months. Nevertheless, as an essential safety net the BMA recommends that decisions to withdraw treatment should only be considered when the patient has been insentient for 12 months.

The diagnosing clinician should also seek views from two other doctors, one of whom should be a neurologist. They should undertake their clinical assessments separately. In any case of doubt as to whether the patient's condition is irreversible, decisions about possible withdrawal of medical treatment must be deferred.

REVIEW OF TREATMENT OPTIONS

A high standard of nursing care, good nutrition and stimulation should be available to all unconscious patients. Rehabilitative measures should be continued until clinicians consider such measures can no longer benefit the individual patient. Specialised expertise should be sought to clarify this in each case.

If it is apparent at the end of the one-year period that the patient's condition is irreversible, consideration may be given to withdrawal of treatment. The BMA has published specific guidance on withdrawing and withholding life-prolonging treatment.[6] Such decisions for PVS patients should be based on the same principles as other patients.

Factors include a careful evaluation of all the evidence regarding the patient's diagnosis and prognosis, involvement of an independent specialist opinion, consideration of the anticipated benefits or burdens of the treatment, the patient's views if known and sensitive discussion with a proxy decision-maker, where applicable, and people close to the patient. In some cases, doctors may then recommend the withdrawal of all treatment including artificial nutrition and hydration. In England and Wales, an application must be first made to the courts. For specific advice, doctors can contact the Court of Protection. In Northern Ireland advice can be sought from the Official Solicitor and in Scotland, from the Mental Welfare Commission.

THE VIEWS OF THE PATIENT

Decision-making in relation to adults who lack the capacity to consent on their own behalf is governed in England and Wales by the Mental Capacity Act 2005, and in Scotland by the Adults with Incapacity (Scotland) Act 2000; in Northern Ireland, decisions are covered by the common law. The BMA has separate guidance relating to decision-making on behalf of people who lack capacity.[7]

In the absence of a valid advance refusal of treatment, treatment decisions for incompetent patients must be based on an assessment of the patient's best interests[8] which includes careful consideration of the patient's former views. These views may be ascertained through discussion with a proxy decision maker, the patients' relatives or, in some cases, may have been recorded in an advance decision.

THE VIEWS OF PEOPLE CLOSE TO THE PATIENT

In England, Wales and Scotland patients can appoint a proxy decision maker to make health and welfare decisions on their behalf. There are no such provisions in Northern Ireland. Whilst treatment decisions should always be discussed with proxy decision-makers, where practicable and appropriate, their decision-making power does not extend to decisions to withdraw artificial nutrition or hydration from patients in PVS, these decisions can only be taken by a court.

Regardless of whether a patient has appointed a proxy decision maker, it is good practice to consult the wishes of people close to the patient although their views alone do not necessarily determine treatment. If, however, the patient, when competent, specifically requested that certain people should not be consulted regarding treatment decisions, this should be respected once the patient loses capacity.

Relatives need time to accept and understand the prognosis. A decision to withhold life-prolonging treatment, such as artificial feeding, requires the cooperation of those emotionally close to the patient and those who provide the nursing care.

In England and Wales, there is a statutory advocacy scheme in place to support 'un-befriended' incapacitated adults. Where it is clear that a decision needs to be made on behalf of an incapacitated adult in relation to either serious medical treatment or place of residence, and there is no one close to the adult to provide advice or guidance, who is not a paid carer, then the services of an independent mental capacity advocate (IMCA) should be engaged.

VIEWS OF HEALTH PROFESSIONALS

Decisions to withdraw life-prolonging treatment should be deferred if there is disagreement within the health team about the diagnosis or prognosis. Nurses must be consulted since they have particular expertise and close contact with patients and their families. It must be recognised that decisions to withdraw artificial nutrition and hydration from a PVS patient impose particular burdens on nursing staff.

CONSCIENTIOUS OBJECTION

Any health professionals opposing the withdrawal of treatment on moral rather than clinical grounds, should not be marginalised or asked to act contrary to their conscience.

THE LEGAL POSITION

The legal position in England and Wales was clarified by the House of Lords in the Bland[9] case. This is likely to represent the law in Northern Ireland in the absence of any specific case law. The Lords confirmed the acceptability of life-prolonging treatment being withdrawn in some circumstances. In doing so, however, they recommended that all cases where the withdrawal of ANH was being considered from a patient in PVS, a court declaration should be sought.

> ### Bland case
>
> 17-year old Tony Bland was injured and the oxygen supply to his brain was interrupted in the Hillsborough football stadium tragedy in April 1989. He suffered irreversible brain damage and was diagnosed as being in PVS. Bland lacked cognitive function but breathed unaided. Unable to swallow, he was fed artificially by nasogastric tube. In 1992, an application was made to the court for a declaration that it would be lawful to discontinue artificial nutrition and hydration. The case went to the House of Lords which held that artificial feeding was a medical treatment that could be withdrawn along with other medical treatments that could no longer benefit the patient.

In Scotland, the Law Hospital[10] case of 1996 laid down a procedure whereby authority can be obtained from the Court of Session for the withdrawal of life-sustaining treatment from patients who are diagnosed as having been in PVS for at least 12 months. Either the hospital authorities or relatives can initiate a Petition to the court. It was made clear in the Law case that, in contrast to Bland, the court does not require each future PVS case to come before it before treatment is withdrawn. The decision whether to seek court authority must rest with those responsible for the patient's treatment, taking into account the relatives' views. It is expected, however, that difficult or exceptional cases will be brought before the court. Although court authority is not obligatory, the Lord Advocate has made clear that in Scotland anyone involved with withdrawal of treatment carried out with the authority of the court will be immune from prosecution.

PREGNANT PVS PATIENTS

The BMA recommends that no decision to withdraw treatment should be made within the first 12 months, thus the question of whether it is morally appropriate to keep a pregnant woman alive for the sake of her foetus alone does not arise. Each case must be considered on its merits, bearing in mind the known wishes of the patient and the benefits, drawbacks or invasiveness of the treatment options. In the BMA's view, coma arousal and other rehabilitative procedures should be equally available to pregnant comatose women as to other patients.

POST MORTEM EXAMINATIONS

It has sometimes been suggested that post mortems should routinely be carried out following the death of all patients diagnosed as having been in PVS in order to audit the accuracy of the diagnosis. Such a procedure could provide potentially helpful information if it could be shown that PVS can be definitely confirmed after death. The BMA has separate advice relating to the authorisation of post-mortem examinations and retention of human tissue.

For further information about these guidelines, BMA members may contact: askBMA on 0870 60 60 828 or British Medical Association Department of Medical Ethics, BMA House Tavistock Square, London WC1H 9JP Tel: 020 7383 6286 Fax: 020 7383 6233 Email: ethics@bma.org.uk

Non-members may contact: British Medical Association Public Affairs Department, BMA House Tavistock Square, London WC1H 9JP Tel: 020 7387 4499 Fax: 020 7383 6400 Email: info.public@bma.org.uk

REFERENCES

1   Airedale NHS Trust v Bland [1993] A.C. 789.
2   BMA, Medical Ethics Committee. Discussion paper on treatment of patients in persistent vegetative state. London: BMA, September 1992.
3   Royal College of Physicians. The Vegetative State: guidance on Diagnosis and Management. London: RCP, 2003.
4   Boggan S, "Reborn", The Guardian 12.09.2006.
5   Owen et al, Science 313, 1402, 2006.
6   BMA. Withdrawing & withholding life prolonging medical treatment, 3rd edtn. London: BMA, 2007.
7   BMA. The Mental Capacity Act 2005. Guidance for Health Professionals. London: BMA, March 2007; BMA. Medical treatment of adults who lack capacity: guidance on ethical and medico-legal issues in Scotland. London: BMA, October 2007. Both are available at: www.bma.org.uk/ethics
8   Although the Adults with Incapacity (Scotland) Act uses the term 'benefit', in the BMA's view it is likely that this term can be interpreted in a similar way to 'best interests'. If, however, health professionals working in Scotland were recommending an intervention in the incapacitated person's best interests that was unlikely to provide clinical benefit, they should consider taking legal advice.
9   Airedale NHS Trust v Bland [1993] A.C. 789.
10   Law Hospital v The Lord Advocate and Others, April 1996. 4

Appendix 12.3

The Vegetative State

GUIDANCE ON DIAGNOSIS AND MANAGEMENT

Report of a working party of the Royal College of Physicians

Royal College of Physicians 2003

This guidance has been endorsed by the Royal College of Physicians of Edinburgh and the Royal College of Physicians and Surgeons of Glasgow.

Readers will find the editorial by McLean in 2001 provides a helpful summary of the current medico-legal position, including differences between Scotland and England/Wales.[20] In Scotland, local advice should be sought from the Central Legal Office of the NHS in the Scottish Executive.

Royal College of Physicians of London 11 St Andrews Place, London NW1 4LE

Registered Charity No 210508

Copyright © 2003 Royal College of Physicians of London

ISBN 1 86016 186 3

Text edited and designed by the Publications Unit of the Royal College of Physicians

Printed in Great Britain by Sarum ColourView Group, Salisbury, Wiltshire

Members of the working party

1   Introduction
     Background
     Wakefulness without awareness
     Definitions
2   Criteria for the diagnosis of the vegetative state
     Preconditions
     Clinical criteria
     Clinical features
     Differential diagnosis
     The time course
3   Management of the vegetative state
     Medical care
     Assessment
     Re-assessment
     Final definitive diagnosis and decisions concerning life support
     A note on children and young persons (0–18)
Appendix 1 Checklist for the diagnosis of the permanent vegetative state
Appendix 2 Vignettes illustrating the definitions given in the report
Appendix 3 Information on the vegetative state for relatives, carers and friends
References

Members of the working party

David Bates MA FRCP, (Chair), Professor of Clinical Neurology, Royal Victoria Infirmary, Newcastle upon Tyne

Carol Black CBE MD PRCP, President, Royal College of Physicians (RCP)

Tim Evans MD FRCP, Chairman, RCP Critical Care Medicine Committee; Professor of Intensive Care Medicine, Royal Brompton Hospital, London

John Forsythe MD FRCS, Director, Transplant Unit, Royal Infirmary of Edinburgh

Elaine Gadd MB ChB MRCPsych, Department of Health

Ian Gilmore MD FRCP, Registrar, Royal College of Physicians

Andrew Grubb MA LLD FmedSci, Professor of Law, Cardiff Law School

Vic Larcher MA MB FRCP, Consultant Paediatrician, Queen Elizabeth Children's Service, Royal London Hospital

Lindsay McLellan MB FRCP, Professor of Neurological Rehabilitation, University of Southampton, Honorary Consultant in Neurology and Rehabilitation Medicine, Southampton General Hospital

Brian McGinnis OBE, Special Adviser, MENCAP, London

John Pickard FRCS, Professor of Neurosurgery, Consultant Neurosurgeon, Addenbrooke's Hospital, Cambridge

Roy Pounder MD DSC(Med) FRCP, Clinical Vice President, Royal College of Physicians

John Saunders MD FRCP, Honorary Secretary, RCP Ethical Issues in Medicine Committee; Consultant Physician, Nevill Hall Hospital, Abergavenny

Amanda Swain DipCOT SROT, National Adviser in Acquired Brain Injury,

Leonard Cheshire Foundation, London

Adam Zeman DM MRCP, Consultant Neurologist, Western General Hospital, Edinburgh

1 INTRODUCTION

Background

1.1 This guidance has been compiled to replace the recommendations published by the Royal College of Physicians in 1996,[1] in response to requests for clarification from the Official Solicitor. The guidance applies primarily to adult patients and older children in whom it is possible to apply the criteria for diagnosis discussed in the body of the document.

Wakefulness without awareness

1.2 Consciousness is an ambiguous term, encompassing both wakefulness and awareness. This distinction is crucial to the concept of the vegetative state, in which wakefulness recovers after brain injury without recovery of awareness.[2-5]

Definitions

The vegetative state

1.3 A patient in the vegetative state (VS) appears at times to be wakeful, with cycles of eye closure and eye opening resembling those of sleep and waking. However, close observation reveals no sign of awareness or of a 'functioning mind': specifically, there is no evidence that the patient can perceive the environment or his own body, communicate with others, or form intentions. As a rule, the patient can breathe spontaneously and has a stable circulation. The state may be a transient stage in the recovery from coma or it may persist until death. The vegetative state can follow a variety of severe insults to the brain, most commonly traumatic or hypoxicischaemic brain injuries.

1.4 The terms 'wakefulness' and 'awareness' require further clarification.

Wakefulness

1.5 Wakefulness refers to a state in which the eyes are open and there is a degree of motor arousal; it contrasts with sleep, a state of eye closure and motor quiescence. There are degrees of wakefulness. Wakefulness is normally associated with conscious awareness, but the VS indicates that wakefulness and awareness can be dissociated. This can occur because the brain systems controlling wakefulness, in the upper brainstem and thalamus, are largely distinct from those which mediate awareness.[6]

Awareness

1.6 Awareness refers to the ability to have, and the having of, experience of any kind. We are typically aware of our surroundings and of bodily sensations, but the contents of awareness can also include our memories, thoughts, emotions and intentions. Although understanding of the brain mechanisms of awareness is incomplete, structures in the cerebral hemispheres clearly play a key role. Awareness is not a single indivisible capacity: brain damage can selectively impair some aspects of awareness, leaving others intact. Many brain processes, including some in the cerebral cortex, occur in the absence of awareness.

1.7 There is no simple single clinical sign or laboratory test of awareness. Its presence must be deduced from a range of behaviours which indicate that an individual can perceive self and surroundings, frame intentions and communicate. As our techniques of assessment are fallible, we can never exclude the possibility of some awareness with complete certainty: this leaves open the possibility that some extremely simple forms of awareness may survive in the VS, including the experience of pain, although the available evidence suggests that this is not the case.[5,7,8]

The persistent vegetative state

1.8 This refers arbitrarily to a VS which has continued for four weeks or more (In the previous version of this guidance[1] this was referred to as the 'continuing vegetative state', to distinguish it more clearly from the permanent vegetative state: we have reverted here to the more widely used term but have avoided the ambiguous abbreviation 'PVS').

The permanent vegetative state (PVS)

1.9 When the VS is deemed permanent, a prediction is being made: that awareness will never recover. This prediction cannot be made with absolute certainty. However, as discussed below in para 2.8, the chances of regaining awareness diminish considerably as the time spent in the VS increases.

2 CRITERIA FOR DIAGNOSIS OF THE VEGETATIVE STATE

Preconditions

2.1 The following preconditions must apply before diagnosis of the VS can be considered.

1   The cause of the condition should be established as far as is possible. It may be due to acute cerebral injury, degenerative conditions, metabolic disorders, infections or developmental malformations.
2   The possibility that the persisting effects of sedative, anaesthetic or neuromuscular blocking drugs are responsible in whole or part should be considered. Drugs may have been the original cause of an acute cerebral injury, usually hypoxic, but their continuing direct effects must be excluded either by the passage of time or by appropriate laboratory tests.
3   The possibility that continuing metabolic disturbance is responsible for the clinical features must be considered and excluded. Metabolic disturbances may of course occur during the course of a VS.
4   The possibility that there is a treatable structural cause should be excluded by brain imaging.

Clinical criteria

2.2 The following criteria are usually met.

1   The key requirement for diagnosis is that there must be no evidence of awareness of self or environment at any time; no response to visual, auditory, tactile or noxious stimuli of a kind suggesting volition or conscious purpose; no evidence of language comprehension or meaningful expression. These are all necessary conditions for the diagnosis.
2   There are typically cycles of eye closure and eye opening giving the appearance of a sleep–wake cycle.
3   Hypothalamic and brain stem function are usually sufficiently preserved to ensure the maintenance of respiration and circulation.

2.3 Criteria 2 and 3 are usually satisfied by patients in the vegetative state but, unlike the first criterion, they are not obligatory (thus, for example, a patient with cerebral injuries sufficient to cause the vegetative state might, incidentally, have third nerve palsies preventing eye opening, or injuries to the chest or medulla affecting respiratory function).

Clinical features

2.4 It may be helpful to fill out the clinical picture by describing compatible clinical features which occur commonly, features which are compatible with the diagnosis but atypical, and features which are incompatible with the diagnosis.

1   *Compatible features* – As well as showing signs of a cycle of sleep and wakefulness, patients in the vegetative state may make a range of spontaneous movements including chewing, teeth grinding, swallowing, roving eye movements and purposeless limb movements; they may make facial movements such as smiles or grimaces, shed tears, or make grunting or groaning sounds for no discernible reason (it would be unusual for a patient to display the entire range of movements). They may react to a number of stimuli: brainstem reflexes can be present (pupillary, oculocephalic (doll's eye), corneal, oculovestibular (caloric) and gag); various stimuli, usually noxious or noisy, can both excite a generalised arousal response, with quickening of respiration, grimaces or limb movements, and cause the extensor or flexor withdrawal of a limb; patients' eyes may turn fleetingly to follow a moving object or towards a loud sound. Grasp reflexes may be present.

2   *Compatible but atypical features* – It is unusual for patients in a VS to follow a moving target for more than a fraction of a second, to fixate a target or to react to visual menace. However, all these behaviours have been described in patients whose clinical features are in all other respects typical of the VS.[5] Patients have also been described in whom isolated fragments of behaviour, such as the utterance of a single inappropriate word, occur in what otherwise appears to be a VS.[5,9] These features appear to reflect the survival of 'islands' of cortex which are no longer part of the coherent thalamo-cortical system required to generate awareness.[6] Epileptic seizures occur occasionally.[5] Features of these kinds should prompt careful reassessment of the diagnosis, but they do not in themselves negate the diagnosis of the VS.

3   *Incompatible features* – Evidence of discriminative perception, purposeful actions and communicative acts is incompatible with the diagnosis of the VS. Thus a smile in response to the arrival of a friend or relative, an attempt to reach out for an object or the appropriate use of language would all indicate the presence of a 'functioning mind' and the recovery of awareness, although such recovery is sometimes very limited.

Differential diagnosis

2.5 The VS must be distinguished from minimally conscious (or 'low awareness') states, states of life-long severe disability with preserved awareness, the locked-in syndrome, coma, and death confirmed by brainstem death testing (see Tables 1 and 2, page 6).

- *Minimally conscious state (MCS)* – The terms 'minimally conscious', 'minimally responsive' or 'low awareness' state refer to the condition of patients who show minimal but definite evidence of awareness despite profound cognitive impairment.10 Patients emerging from the VS often enter the MCS, which may be the end point of their improvement, or a staging post on the way to further recovery.

- *People with life-long severe disabilities* – Some people with severe intellectual disabilities, commonly accompanied by severe physical disabilities, have limited capacity to respond to the outside world; but those close to them are clear that they do communicate and are aware, and may indeed have a rich internal life. Such people should not be classed as vegetative.

- *Locked-in syndrome* – Locked-in syndrome results from brainstem pathology which disrupts the voluntary control of movement without abolishing either wakefulness or awareness. Patients who are 'locked in' are substantially paralysed but conscious, and can communicate using movements of the eyes or eyelids.

531

- *Coma* – Coma is a state of unconsciousness in which the eyes are closed and sleep-wake cycles absent. Coma is usually transient, lasting for hours or days: the VS is one possible outcome.
- *Death confirmed by brainstem death testing* – This implies the irreversible loss of all brain stem functions: it is followed by cardiac arrest, usually within hours or days, despite intensive care.

2.6 The above distinctions are made primarily on clinical grounds. Brain imaging with computed tomography (CT) or magnetic resonance imaging (MRI) often helps to clarify the cause of these clinical syndromes, but the findings on imaging are not specific. Cerebral atrophy is commonly seen in patients in the VS.

2.7 Sophisticated techniques used to assess cortical function – positron emission tomography (PET), electroencephalography (EEG), magnetoencephalography (MEG) and evoked potential (EP) studies – can be used to shed light on the physiology of the VS, but are not yet routine diagnostic tools. Their use is not required for diagnosis of the VS, which remains essentially clinical.

The time course

2.8 The prognosis of patients in the persistent VS is influenced by age, the underlying cause of the VS and its current duration. People in a VS one month after trauma stand a slightly better than even chance of regaining awareness; in cases of the VS due to non-traumatic causes, fewer than one-fifth of people in a VS at one month recover awareness. The chances of regaining awareness fall as time passes. Beyond one year following trauma, and beyond six months in non-traumatic cases, the chances of regaining consciousness are extremely low. In the very small number of well documented cases, recovery has usually been to a state of exceptionally severe disability.[3] Patients in the persistent VS should therefore be observed for 12 months after head injury (traumatic brain injury) and six months after other causes before the VS is judged to be 'permanent'.

Table 1 The Glasgow Coma Scale (GSC)

E Eye opening	M Motor function	V Verbal
1 None 2 To pain 3 To sound 4 Spontaneously	1 None 2 Extends to pain 3 Abnormal flexion to pain 4 Normal flexion to pain 5 Localises pain 6 Normal	1 None 2 Grunts 3 Inappropriate words 4 Confused 5 Oriented

Table 2 The differential diagnosis of the vegetative state

Condition	Vegetative state	Minimally conscious state	Locked-in syndrome	Coma	Death confirmed by brainstem tests
Awareness	Absent	Present	Present	Absent	Absent
Sleep-wake cycle	Present	Present	Present	Absent	Absent
Response to noxious stimuli	+/−	Present (in eyes only)	Present	+/−	Absent
Glasgow Coma Scale score	E4, M1–4, V1–2	E4, M1–5, V1–4	E4, M1, V1	E1–2, M1–4, V1–2	E1, M1–3, V1
Motor function	No purposeful movement	Some consistent or inconsistent verbal or purposeful motor behaviour	Volitional vertical eye movements or eyeblink preserved	No purposeful movement	None or only reflex spinal movement
Respiratory function	Typically preserved	Typically preserved	Typically preserved	Variable	Absent
EEG activity	Typically slow wave activity	Insufficient data	Typically normal	Typically slow wave activity	Typically absent
Cerebral metabolism (PET)	Severely reduced	Insufficient data	Mildly reduced	Moderately to severely reduced	Severely reduced or absent
Prognosis	Variable: if permanent, continued vegetative state or death	Variable	Depends on cause but full recovery unlikely	Recovery, vegetative state or death within weeks	Already dead

NB: as explained in the text, EEG and measures of cerebral metabolism are not required to make these clinical diagnoses.
EEG = electroencephalography; PET = positron emission tomography.

3 MANAGEMENT OF THE VEGETATIVE STATE

Medical care

3.1 Patients in the VS require a high quality of nursing care to avoid the preventable complications of their highly dependent state. Standard measures include adequate nutrition, often via a percutaneous endoscopic gastrostomy (PEG) tube, good skin care, passive joint exercises to minimise contractures, suction where necessary to help avoid aspiration, careful management of the doubly incontinent bladder and bowel, and attention to oral and dental hygiene. Until there is firm scientific evidence that treatment, in terms of specific medical, physiotherapeutic or rehabilitative activities, improves the outcome of patients in a VS, the use of these measures is a matter of clinical judgement. The medical and nursing staff must keep the relatives and carers well informed throughout the course of the VS.

Assessment

3.2 Both the initial diagnosis of the VS and the subsequent diagnosis of the permanent VS should be made with great care. There is evidence that the VS has been diagnosed in error.[11,12] The explanations for misdiagnosis include confusion about the meaning of the term, inadequate observation in suboptimal circumstances, failure to consult those who see most of the patient (especially family members), and the inherent difficulty of detecting signs of awareness in patients with major perceptual and motor impairments.

3.3 Thus, when the diagnosis of the permanent VS is being considered, it is essential that the patient should be examined by at least two doctors both of whom are experienced in assessing disorders of consciousness. They should take into account the views of the medical staff, other clinical staff (including clinical neuropsychologists, occupational therapists and physiotherapists with expertise in assessing disorders of consciousness), carers and relatives about the patient's reactions and responses. They should undertake their clinical assessments separately and write the details of their assessments and their conclusions in the notes. They should consider the results of the investigations which have been performed to clarify the cause of the condition. As the patient's physical position can affect responsiveness, it may be valuable to assess the patient in more than one position. It may be helpful for nursing staff and relatives to be present during the examination.

Re-assessment

3.4 There is no urgency in making the diagnosis of the permanent VS. If there is any uncertainty in the mind of the assessor, the diagnosis should not be made and the patient should be reassessed after an interval. Structured observation may help to reveal signs of awareness in doubtful cases.[13–15] The key consideration in making the diagnosis is whether the patient might be aware to some degree: it is always important to seek the views of nursing staff, relatives and carers on this issue.

Final definitive diagnosis and decisions concerning life support

3.5 When the diagnosis of a permanent VS has been made by establishing the cause of the syndrome so far as possible, by confirming the patient's clinical state and by the passage of time, recovery cannot reasonably be expected, and further therapy is futile. It merely prolongs an insentient life for the patient and a hopeless vigil entailing major emotional costs for relatives and carers.

3.6 In these circumstances, the clinical team, with the help of colleagues when required, should review the evidence formally. When the diagnosis of a permanent VS is considered definite, it should be discussed sensitively with relatives, who should then be given time to consider the implications, including the possibility of withdrawing artificial means of administering nutrition and hydration. At present, in England and Wales, the courts require that the decision to withdraw nutrition and hydration should be referred to them before any action is taken. In Scotland, although the court does not require that it be involved prior to any action being taken, as a result of the Lord Advocate's advice following the Law Hospital case,[16] it would be prudent for a doctor to seek the authority of the Court of Session in order to guarantee that the Lord Advocate would not initiate a criminal prosecution.

3.7 A decision to withdraw other life-sustaining medication, such as insulin for diabetes, may also need to be referred to the courts because the legal position is uncertain. By contrast, decisions not to intervene with cardio-pulmonary resuscitation, antibiotics, dialysis or insulin can be taken clinically, in the best interests of the patient, after full discussion with those concerned.

3.8 Where a patient has made a valid and applicable advance directive indicating their refusal of continuing treatment, this must be respected. If not, efforts should be made to establish what the patient's views and preferences might have been, to help to make a decision in his or her best interests.

3.9 As indicated earlier, one cannot ever be certain that a patient in the VS is wholly unaware, although the available evidence supports this supposition. In view of this small but undeniable element of uncertainty, it is reasonable to administer sedation when hydration and nutrition are withdrawn to eliminate the possibility of suffering, however remote. The normal standards of palliative care should be observed to ensure the dignity of the death.

A note on children and young persons (0–18 years)

3.10 Formal diagnosis of the permanent vegetative state in children in the UK is rare. However, there is evidence to suggest that older children (older than circa 10 years) behave clinically and prognostically in a similar fashion to adults. For younger children, in whom survival may be poorer than in older children, greater account must be taken of the child's potentially evolving developmental capabilities. For reasons of this kind, the diagnosis can seldom be made unequivocally under the age of one year. However, there seems no reason why the guidance contained in this document should not be applied to children over the age of ten years, and it can be used with appropriate caution in children between one and ten years.

3.11 Where withdrawal or witholding of life-sustaining treatment is being contemplated in children,clinicians should refer to guidance from professional regulatory bodies.[17–19]

APPENDIX 1

Checklist for the diagnosis of the permanent vegetative state

The diagnosis of the permanent vegetative state requires prolonged observation, experience in the assessment of disorders of consciousness,[5] and discussion with relatives and with medical and paramedical staff. It cannot be made by following a simple protocol. However, we hope that this checklist will be of some practical help by highlighting the key steps on the way to the diagnosis.

1   Has at least one year elapsed since the onset in cases due to head injury?

or

2   Have at least six months elapsed since the onset in cases due to other causes?
3   Has the cause been established? (It should be established 'as far as possible'.)
4   Have effects of drugs been excluded?
5   Have effects of metabolic disturbance been excluded?
6   Has the possibility of a treatable structural cause been excluded by brain imaging?
7   Have two doctors who are experienced in the assessment of disorders of consciousness, independently confirmed that there is no evidence of:
   • awareness of self or environment
   • purposeful movement
   • any attempt to communicate?
8   Do medical staff, nursing staff and other therapists agree?
9   Do family and friends agree?*
10   In case of doubt, has an expert clinical neuropsychological assessment been carried out?

Where the answer is 'yes' to all these questions, the diagnosis of the permanent vegetative state is confirmed.

First assessing doctor: Name Qualifications Signature Date	**Second assessing doctor:** Name Qualifications Signature Date

* Sometimes, even when all other members of the family and friends of the patient are in agreement, one individual may be unable to agree with the general conclusion that the patient lacks awareness. Any evidence of awareness should be examined very seriously, but in these circumstances the continuing disagreement of one individual with the conclusion of health professionals and others close to the patient is not a bar to the diagnosis of the permanent vegetative state.

APPENDIX 2

Vignettes illustrating the definitions given in the report

Hour-to-hour and day-to-day fluctuations in responsiveness are common in patients in minimally responsive states and during slow emergence from coma. Understanding the meaning of spontaneous movements and movements occurring in response to stimulation (for example to touch and sound) requires (a) careful observations over a period of several weeks, and (b) considerable experience in their interpretation.

These four brief vignettes are not comprehensive, nor are they a substitute for the formal definitions given in the report, but they are intended as illustrations of how these definitions might apply in practice. These subjects have all been in the state described for 12 months.

1. A man aged 22 with a severe traumatic brain injury and lower limb fractures, with spasticity in all limbs

He was on an artificial ventilator for the first six weeks after the injury, at which time spontaneous breathing and apparent 'sleep–wake' cycles were re-established. When 'asleep', he can be 'woken' by touch or by a loud noise; he blinks repeatedly in response to repeated noise (eg hand claps) for however long they are continued. His eyes are usually directed straight ahead but they sometimes make spontaneous movements; they do not, however, follow the faces of family members who approach and talk to him. He does not chew and swallow food placed in his mouth. When being washed or dressed there is no response but when his spastic limbs are stretched by the physiotherapist, after ten seconds or so a general increase in muscle tone occurs, sometimes accompanied by grimacing and occasionally groaning. Similar levels of responsiveness are seen irrespective of who touches or speaks to him; he shows no evidence of apprehension or discomfort when the physiotherapist first begins to handle him. During periods of urinary or respiratory infection his level of responsiveness usually diminishes, plateauing at the previous level when the infection is over.

Comment: The lack of discriminating responses to environmental or bodily stimuli is consistent with permanent VS.

2. A woman aged 34 who suffered severe brain damage in a near-drowning accident

When 'awake' her eyes are divergent. Usually there is no movement of the eyes in response to sounds, but family members have noticed that when she is 'awake' in calm surroundings, her left eye appears to follow her ten-year-old son when he speaks to her. This response, however, lasts for only a few seconds and after three or four repetitions it disappears; it cannot be elicited again for 30 minutes and sometimes not until the next day. When the patient is unwell with an infection, or if showing frequent limb spasms (which may be a prelude to opening of the bowels and bladder), no eye responses occur. There are no other consistent responses to stimulation but nursing staff have noticed over the past two months an apparent relaxation in spastic muscle tone in her when they move her arms to wash her, making their task a little easier.

Comment: The combination of discriminating responses to environmental and bodily stimuli with a changing level of responsiveness over the past two months suggests the possibility of a minimally conscious state, and therefore a further two-month period of observation is required.

3. A man aged 38 who was found unconscious after taking an overdose of antidepressant drugs

A year ago, two months after admission to hospital, he had shown early signs of emergence from coma (following people with his eyes, reliably squeezing his right hand to command and occasionally mouthing single words when in apparent discomfort). However, at this point he developed a serious urinary tract infection during which he had a prolonged episode of status epilepticus, requiring anticonvulsant drug treatment. Subsequently only reflex patterns of responses have been seen. Two months ago his anticonvulsant drugs were withdrawn, since when there has been no change in his level of responsiveness.

Comment: The history suggests a further episode of hypoxic brain damage during the episode of status epilepticus. Two months is ample time for any sedative effects of the anticonvulsant drugs to have disappeared and the observed pattern of responsiveness is now consistent with permanent VS.

4. A woman aged 25 injured in a high-speed road accident, resulting in coma and the need for assisted ventilation lasting three weeks

Three months after spontaneous respiration had returned, she started to show movements of the right arm and leg and grinding of the teeth, principally in response to noxious stimuli (e g having a blood sample taken, being stretched by the physiotherapist, or having a foot-drop splint applied in order to prevent calf muscle contractures). At times she would consistently follow certain members of staff and family members with her eyes for periods of up to five minutes but at other times her eyes would remain closed. Ward staff have noticed that each time she has been formally assessed by the visiting neurologist, her eyes have closed within 1–2 minutes of his arrival and she then makes no signs or responses indicating any conscious awareness and her face remains expressionless until after he has left. When the physiotherapist first enters her room she usually grinds her teeth and the limbs stiffen. When in bed or sat in a chair she has not been observed to make any limb movements for which a volitional purpose could be deduced, but in the gymnasium, moving her to an upright position or rolling her over a ball reliably induces an increased state of alertness with more visual tracking and apparent 'protective' volitional (not reflex) movements of the right arm; in this aroused state she might smile when teased by the therapists.

Comment: In this case, eye closure might sometimes represent a volitional withdrawal response to unwanted stimuli. The evidence of consistent discrimination in the range of responses made to different individuals varying with the state of arousal suggests the presence of awareness.

APPENDIX 3

Information on the vegetative state for relatives, carers and friends

For relatives, carers and friends of people who have suffered a major brain injury and are diagnosed as being in a vegetative state, life will inevitably be stressful and upsetting. Any confusion or uncertainty over what is being done for the patients, what they can and cannot feel, and what the outcome might be, will add to the strain. The information provided here is designed to help clarify these issues.

It may be of some comfort to know that

- rigorous standards have been laid down for the diagnosis and care of people in a vegetative state
- these standards are based on a considerable body of research evidence
- decisions on a patient's care are based on careful assessment of all the available evidence
- the patient's comfort and freedom from pain are top priorities.

What is a vegetative state?

People in a vegetative state show no sign of awareness or of a functioning mind. They are unaware of what is happening to or around them and have no control over what they are doing.

Before doctors can consider making a diagnosis of vegetative state, certain conditions have to be met:

1   Every effort has been made to find out the cause.
2   Any treatable cause (e g a tumour) has been ruled out.
3   Possible effects of drugs have been assessed and ruled out.

Then, in the patient there must be:

- no evidence of awareness of the self or the environment at any time
- no response of any kind suggesting intention, will or conscious purpose
- no evidence of understanding or meaningful expression.

Are brain scans needed to make the diagnosis of vegetative state?

Techniques like electroencephalography (EEG) and positron emission tomography (PET) are not needed to make a diagnosis of vegetative state. However, simple brain imaging should be performed to ensure that there is no unexpected treatable cause (this will generally have been done anyway).

What movements do people in a vegetative state usually make?

In most people in a vegetative state, there are cycles of eye closing and eye opening giving the appearance of sleeping and waking. Most people have normal circulation and can breathe without aid.

Patients in a vegetative state may make a range of spontaneous movements including chewing, teeth grinding, swallowing, roving eye movements and purposeless limb movements. They may make facial movements such as smiles or grimaces, shed tears, or make grunting or groaning sounds for no obvious reason. They may react automatically by reflex responses to various stimuli: for example, they may gag when being fed, or their eyes may move when their head is turned from side to side. Things like noise can also cause a response, such as faster breathing, grimaces or movement of limbs. Their eyes may turn fleetingly to follow a moving object or person, or towards a loud sound, and their hands may appear to grasp objects placed in them. **None of these responses require conscious awareness.**

In addition to occasionally following moving objects or people with their eyes, patients in a vegetative state have also been known to utter a single inappropriate word. Behaviour of this kind should lead to a careful search for awareness, but responses like these may occur because small 'islands' in the brain have survived but they are no longer able to work together to generate awareness.

What can hospital staff do for patients in a vegetative state?

Staff will carefully monitor and record patients' responses on a daily basis.

They will give high-quality nursing care to avoid any preventable complications developing. This care will include things like adequate nutrition (often via a feeding tube), good skin care, joint exercises, careful management of bowel and bladder incontinence, and oral and dental hygiene.

It is generally regarded as good practice to approach patients in a vegetative state as though they do have some awareness, but this is a precautionary measure in case someone should begin to show consciousness.

What can relatives, friends and carers do for someone in a vegetative state?

Those close to the patient can help healthcare staff by reporting their own observations about the patient and also by providing information about the previous personality and experience of the patient, as this will help ensure that staff approach the patient in an appropriate way if consciousness does begin to recover.

There is no evidence that constant stimulation of someone who is in a vegetative state can bring about improvement in the long-term outcome.

What is the outlook for people in a vegetative state?

The outlook for people in a vegetative state is influenced by their age, the underlying cause of the vegetative state and its current duration. Broadly speaking, the longer the state persists, the less chance there is of recovery. At one month after a traumatic brain injury (for example, a car crash), people in a vegetative state stand a better than 50% chance of regaining awareness. At the same stage, only 20% of those whose vegetative state is due to non-traumatic causes (for example, a stroke) recover awareness.

What is a permanent vegetative state?

Beyond one year following trauma, and beyond six months in non-traumatic cases, the chances of regaining consciousness are extremely low. So at this point patients are considered to be in a permanent vegetative state. The very small number of people worldwide who have recovered at this stage have been exceptionally severely disabled.

How do doctors make the diagnosis of permanent vegetative state?

First of all, the patient must have been in a vegetative state for at least twelve months if they had a traumatic injury to the head, and for at least six months if they had non-traumatic brain damage (for example, as a result of a heart attack).

Then all possible treatable causes of the state must have been ruled out. The patient then has to be examined by at least two doctors who are both experienced in assessing this kind of disorder. They must conduct their assessments independently of one another, and write their results in the notes. As the patient's physical position can affect responsiveness, the doctors may assess the patient in more than one position. They should take into account views about the patient's reactions and responses from the medical staff involved (e g nurses), from other clinical staff (e g physiotherapists with experience in making such assessments), and from those close to the patient.

If the two doctors think that the patient is in a permanent vegetative state, then they will discuss their opinion with other medical staff, nursing staff, therapists and those close to the patient. If there is broad agreement, then a diagnosis of permanent vegetative state will be made, meaning that the evidence indicates that the patient will never recover their awareness.

The diagnosis of permanent vegetative state will not be rushed. If there is any doubt about it, the patient will be re-assessed at a later date. In doubtful cases, the staff may use structured observation (watching closely for specific time periods at set intervals) to try to see if there are any signs of awareness in the patient.

How are decisions made about withdrawing nutritional support?

When the diagnosis of a permanent vegetative state has been made, it may be decided that recovery cannot reasonably be expected and that continued support and treatment is futile. Prolonging an insentient life would have no benefit for the patient, and would mean a hopeless vigil with major emotional costs for those close to the patient.

In these circumstances, the medical team, with the help of colleagues when required, will formally review the evidence. After confirming the diagnosis of a permanent vegetative state, they will discuss this with those close to the patient, and give them time to consider the implications, including the possibility of withdrawing the means of providing food and water.

At present, any decision to stop giving food and water by tube must be referred to the courts before any action can be taken.

A decision to withdraw life-sustaining medication, such as insulin for diabetes, is also likely to be referred to the courts.

On the other hand, decisions not to use intensive resuscitation in the case of a heart attack, or not to use antibiotics or dialysis, can be taken by doctors, in the best interests of the patient, after full discussion with all those concerned but without going to court.

The legal system in England and Wales differs from that in Scotland where the medical teams will act according to Scottish law.

What about the person's previously stated wishes or advance directives?

If the person has made a valid advance directive which fits these circumstances, indicating their refusal of continuing treatment, including tube feeding, this must be respected. If not, doctors will try to establish what the patient's views and preferences might have been, to help to make a decision in his or her best interests.

A dignified end

If the decision is taken to withdraw life support, every effort will be made to ensure that the person dies with dignity, and that the wishes of those close to the patient are respected, including having all the privacy and time that they require at the end.

Although it is extremely unlikely that the person can feel any pain, he or she will be given sedation if hydration and nutrition are withdrawn. This will eliminate any possibility of suffering, however remote.

Children and young people

These notes also apply to children over the age of ten, although formal diagnosis of permanent vegetative state in children in the UK is rare. In younger children, the brain is at a stage of development where new connections may be forming even in the absence of consciousness. A definite diagnosis of vegetative state can thus seldom be made in babies and young children.

REFERENCES

1   Royal College of Physicians. *The permanent vegetative state.* A working party report. London: RCP, 1996.

2   Jennett B, Plum F. Persistent vegetative state after brain damage. *Lancet* 1972; i:734–7.

3   The Multi-Society Task Force on PVS. Medical aspects of the persistent vegetative state, in two parts. *N Engl J Med* 1994; **330**:1499–1508, 1572–9.

4   *International working party report on the vegetative state.* London: Royal Hospital for Neuro-disability, 1996.

5   Jennett B. *The vegetative state.* Cambridge: Cambridge University Press, 2002.

6   Zeman A. Consciousness. *Brain* 2001; **124**:1263–89.

7   Zeman A. Persistent vegetative state. *Lancet* 1997; **350**:795–9.

8   Laureys S, Berre J, Goldman S. Cerebral function in coma, vegetative state, minimally conscious state, locked-in syndrome, and brain death. *Yearbook of Intensive Care and Emergency Medicine* 2001: 386–96.

9   Schiff ND, Ribary U, Moreno DR, Beattie B *et al*. Residual cerebral activity and behavioural fragments can remain in the persistently vegetative brain. *Brain* 2002; **125**:1210–34.

10   Giacino JT, Ashwal S, Childs N, Cranford R *et al*. The minimally conscious state: definition and diagnostic criteria. *Neurology* 2001; **58**:349–53.

11   Childs N, Mercer WN, Childs HW. Accuracy of diagnosis of the persistent vegetative state. *Neurology* 1993; **43**:1465–7.

12   Andrews K, Murphy L, Munday R, Littlewood C. Misdiagnosis of the vegetative state: retrospective study in a rehabilitation unit. *BMJ* 1996; **313**:13–16.

13   McMillan TM. Neuropsychological assessment after severe head injury in a case of life or death. *Brain Injury* 1996; **11**:483–90.

14   Gill-Thwaites H, Munday R. The sensory modality assessment and rehabilitation technique (SMART): a comprehensive and integrated assessment and treatment protocol for the vegetative state and minimally responsive patient. *Neuropsychol Rehabil* 1999; **9**:305–20.

15   Shiel A, Horn S, Wilson BA, Watson MJ, Campbell MJ, McLellan DL. The Wessex Head Injury Matrix (WHIM) Main Scale: a preliminary report on a scale to assess and monitor patient recovery after severe head injury. *Clin Rehabil* 2000; **14**:408–16.

16   1996 SLT848 and 1996 SLT859.

17   Royal College of Paediatrics and Child Health. *Withholding and withdrawing life-sustaining treatment in children: a framework for practice.* London: RCPCH, 1997.

18   British Medical Association. *Withholding and withdrawing life-prolonging medical treatment: guidance for decision making*, 2nd edn. London: BMJ Books, 2001.

19   General Medical Council. *Witholding and withdrawing life-prolonging treatments: good practice in decision making.* London: GMC, 2002.

20   McLean S. Permanent vegetative state and the law. *J Neurol Neurosurg Psych* 2001; **71** (Suppl 1):i26–i27.

Appendix 12.4

The process for making best interest decisions in serious medical conditions in patients over 18 years

Start by assuming that the patient has capacity. If there is doubt, proceed to the two stage test of capacity:

Stage 1: Does the person have an impairment of, or a disturbance in the functioning of, their mind or brain?

Stage 2: Does the impairment or disturbance mean that the person is unable to make a specific decision when they need to? Their capacity for this decision can be assessed by four functional tests:

1. **Can they understand the information?** *NB. this must be imparted in a way the patient can understand*
2. **Can they retain the information?** *NB. This only needs to be long enough to use and weigh the information*
3. **Can they use or weigh up that information?** *NB. They must be able to show that they are able to consider the benefits and burdens of the alternatives to the proposed treatment*
4. **Can they communicate their decision?** *NB. The carers must try every method possible to enable this*

The result of each step of this assessment should be documented, ideally by quoting the patient.

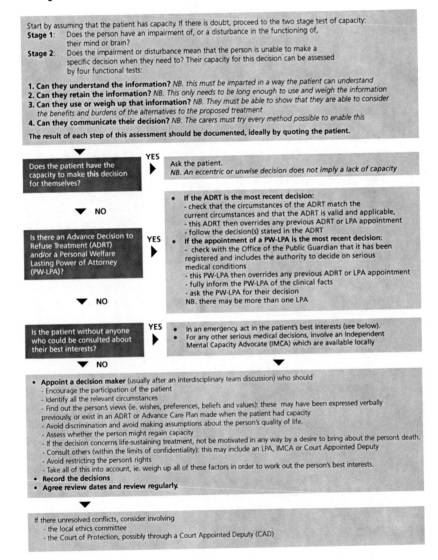

Does the patient have the capacity to make **this** decision for themselves?

YES ▶ Ask the patient.
NB. An eccentric or unwise decision does not imply a lack of capacity

▼ **NO**

Is there an Advance Decision to Refuse Treatment (ADRT) and/or a Personal Welfare Lasting Power of Attorney (PW-LPA)?

YES ▶
- **If the ADRT is the most recent decision:**
  - check that the circumstances of the ADRT match the current circumstances and that the ADRT is valid and applicable,
  - this ADRT then overrides any previous ADRT or LPA appointment
  - follow the decision(s) stated in the ADRT
- **If the appointment of a PW-LPA is the most recent decision:**
  - check with the Office of the Public Guardian that it has been registered and includes the authority to decide on serious medical conditions
  - this PW-LPA then overrides any previous ADRT or LPA appointment
  - fully inform the PW-LPA of the clinical facts
  - ask the PW-LPA for their decision
  - NB. there may be more than one LPA

▼ **NO**

Is the patient without anyone who could be consulted about their best interests?

YES ▶
- In an emergency, act in the patient's best interests (see below).
- For any other serious medical decisions, involve an Independent Mental Capacity Advocate (IMCA) which are available locally

▼ **NO**

- **Appoint a decision maker** (usually after an interdisciplinary team discussion) who should
  - Encourage the participation of the patient
  - Identify all the relevant circumstances
  - Find out the person's views (ie. wishes, preferences, beliefs and values): these may have been expressed verbally previously, or exist in an ADRT or Advance Care Plan made when the patient had capacity
  - Avoid discrimination and avoid making assumptions about the person's quality of life.
  - Assess whether the person might regain capacity
  - If the decision concerns life-sustaining treatment, not be motivated in any way by a desire to bring about the person's death.
  - Consult others (within the limits of confidentiality): this may include an LPA, IMCA or Court Appointed Deputy
  - Avoid restricting the person's rights
  - Take all of this into account, ie. weigh up all of these factors in order to work out the person's best interests.
- **Record the decisions**
- **Agree review dates and review regularly.**

▼

If there unresolved conflicts, consider involving
- the local ethics committee
- the Court of Protection, possibly through a Court Appointed Deputy (CAD)

V16 © 2008. Regnard C. From: Regnard, Dean & Hockley; A guide to Symptom Relief in Palliative Care 6th ed, Oxford: Radcliffe Publishing

Appendix 13.1

DPP Interim policy for prosecutors in respect of cases of assisted suicide

INTRODUCTION

1   A person commits an offence if he or she aids, abets, counsels or procures [referred to in this policy as 'assists'] the suicide of another, or the attempt by another to commit suicide. The consent of the Director of Public Prosecutions [DPP] is required before an individual may be prosecuted.

2   While the DPP can issue a policy which sets out the factors he will take into account in deciding whether to prosecute in individual cases, only Parliament can change the law on assisted suicide. The DPP cannot assure a person in advance of committing a crime that a prosecution will not be brought, and nothing in this policy can be taken to amount to such an assurance.

3   It has never been the rule that a prosecution will automatically follow whenever an offence is believed to have been committed. The way in which prosecutors make their decisions in all cases whether or not to prosecute is set out in the Code for Crown Prosecutors. However, the courts have decided that prosecutors should have further guidance setting out additional factors that may be relevant when deciding whether a prosecution for assisted suicide is needed in the public interest in a particular case.

4   For the purposes of this policy, the term 'victim' is used to describe the person who may have committed or attempted to commit suicide. Not everyone may agree that this is an appropriate description but in the context of the criminal law it is probably the most suitable term to use.

5   This policy applies when the acts that allegedly constitute the assistance are committed in England and Wales; the suicide or attempted suicide may occur anywhere in the world, including in England and Wales.

THE INVESTIGATION

6   The police are responsible for investigating all cases of assisted suicide and they are encouraged to ask for the advice of prosecutors at an early stage and throughout their enquiries to ensure that all appropriate lines of investigation have been undertaken. Prosecutors should only make a decision when they have all the relevant material that is reasonably capable of being obtained after a full and thorough investigation.

THE DECISION-MAKING PROCESS

7   Prosecutors will apply the Code for Crown Prosecutors in making their decisions: there must be sufficient evidence to provide a realistic prospect of conviction in respect of an offence of assisted suicide. If there is sufficient

evidence, prosecutors should consider whether a prosecution is needed in the public interest.

8   The factors taken into account in deciding whether a prosecution is needed in the public interest also determine whether or not the DPP will consent to a prosecution.

THE EVIDENTIAL STAGE

9   A person commits the offence of assisted suicide if he or she aids, abets, counsels or procures the suicide of another, or an attempt by another to commit suicide.

10   For the evidential stage to be satisfied, the prosecution must prove that:
   • the victim committed or attempted to commit suicide; and
   • the suspect assisted them in doing so.

11   The prosecution also has to prove that the suspect intended to assist the victim to commit or attempt to commit suicide and that the suspect knew that those acts were capable of assisting the victim to commit suicide.

12   The act of suicide requires the victim to take his or her own life. It remains murder or manslaughter to cause the death of someone who wishes to commit suicide but is unable to do so for him or herself. Even genuine and clear expressions of intent from someone who wishes to end his or her life do not entitle another person, even acting wholly out of compassion, to carry out those wishes if the person who wishes to commit suicide is asleep or is not conscious.

13   It is possible in law to attempt to assist a suicide. This means that there may be an offence committed even where a suicide does not occur or where there is not an attempt to commit suicide. Whether there is sufficient evidence of an attempt to assist suicide will depend on the factual circumstances of the case.

THE PUBLIC INTEREST STAGE

14   Prosecutors must consider the public interest factors set out in the Code for Crown Prosecutors and the factors set out in this policy.

15   Deciding on the public interest is not simply a matter of adding up the number of factors on each side and seeing which side has the greater number. Each case must be considered on its own facts and on its own merits. Prosecutors must decide the importance of each public interest factor in the circumstances of each case and go on to make an overall assessment. It is quite possible that one factor alone may outweigh a number of other factors which tend in the opposite direction.

16   Some public interest factors set out below appear in both lists, because their presence or absence is either a factor in favour of or against prosecution, to be taken into consideration in each case. Others are only either a factor in favour of or against prosecution and they therefore only appear in the appropriate list.

17   It may sometimes be the case that the only source of information about the circumstances of the suicide and the state of mind of the victim is the suspect. Prosecutors and investigators should make sure that they pursue all reasonable lines of further enquiry in order to obtain, wherever possible, independent verification of the suspect's account.

18   Once all reasonable enquiries are completed, if prosecutors are doubtful about the suspect's account of the circumstances of the suicide and the state of mind of

the victim which are relevant to any factor set out below, they should conclude that they do not have sufficient information in support of that factor.

Public interest factors in favour of prosecution

19   The public interest factors in favour of prosecution are set out below.
    (1)   The victim was under 18 years of age.
    (2)   The victim's capacity to reach an informed decision was adversely affected by a recognised mental illness or learning difficulty.
    (3)   The victim did not have a clear, settled and informed wish to commit suicide; for example, the victim's history suggests that his or her wish to commit suicide was temporary or subject to change.
    (4)   The victim did not indicate unequivocally to the suspect that he or she wished to commit suicide.
    (5)   The victim did not ask personally on his or her own initiative for the assistance of the suspect.
    (6)   The victim did not have:
        •   a terminal illness; or
        •   a severe and incurable physical disability; or
        •   a severe degenerative physical condition;
    from which there was no possibility of recovery.
    (7)   The suspect was not wholly motivated by compassion; for example, the suspect was motivated by the prospect that they or a person closely connected to them stood to gain in some way from the death of the victim.
    (8)   The suspect persuaded, pressured or maliciously encouraged the victim to commit suicide, or exercised improper influence in the victim's decision to do so; and did not take reasonable steps to ensure that any other person did not do so.
    (9)   The victim was physically able to undertake the act that constituted the assistance him or herself.
    (10) The suspect was not the spouse, partner or a close relative or a close personal friend of the victim.
    (11) The suspect was unknown to the victim and assisted by providing specific information via, for example, a website or publication, to the victim to assist him or her in committing suicide.
    (12) The suspect gave assistance to more than one victim who were not known to each other.
    (13) The suspect was paid by the victim or those close to the victim for their assistance.
    (14) The suspect was paid to care for the victim in a care/nursing home environment.
    (15) The suspect was aware that the victim intended to commit suicide in a public place where it was reasonable to think that members of the public may be present.
    (16) The suspect was a member of an organisation or group, the principal purpose of which is to provide a physical environment [whether for payment or not] in which to allow another to commit suicide ...
20   In most cases, factors (1) to (8) above will carry more weight than the other factors in deciding that a prosecution is needed in the public interest.

Public interest factors against prosecution

21   The public interest factors against prosecution are set out below.

(1) The victim had a clear, settled and informed wish to commit suicide.

(2) The victim indicated unequivocally to the suspect that he or she wished to commit suicide.

(3) The victim asked personally on his or her own initiative for the assistance of the suspect.

(4) The victim had:
- a terminal illness; or
- a severe and incurable physical disability; or
- a severe degenerative physical condition;

from which there was no possibility of recovery.

(5) The suspect was wholly motivated by compassion.

(6) The suspect was the spouse, partner or a close relative or a close personal friend of the victim, within the context of a long-term and supportive relationship.

(7) The actions of the suspect, although sufficient to come within the definition of the offence, were of only minor assistance or influence, or the assistance which the suspect provided was as a consequence of his or her usual lawful employment.

(8) The victim was physically unable to undertake the act that constituted the assistance him or herself.

(9) The suspect had sought to dissuade the victim from taking the course of action which resulted in his or her suicide.

(10) The victim has considered and pursued to a reasonable extent recognised treatment and care options.

(11) The victim had previously attempted to commit suicide and was likely to try to do so again.

(12) The actions of the suspect may be characterised as reluctant assistance in the face of a determined wish on the part of the victim to commit suicide.

(13) The suspect fully assisted the police in their enquiries into the circumstances of the suicide or the attempt and his or her part in providing assistance ...

22   In most cases, factors (1) to (7) above will carry more weight than the other factors in deciding that a prosecution is not needed in the public interest ...

23   The evidence to support these factors must be sufficiently close in time to the assistance to allow the prosecutor reasonably to infer that the factors remained operative at that time. This is particularly important at the start of the specific chain of events that immediately lead to the suicide or the attempt.

24   These lists of public interest factors are not exhaustive and each case must be considered on its own facts and on its own merits.

HANDLING ARRANGEMENTS

25   Cases of assisted suicide are dealt with in Special Crime Division in CPS Headquarters. The Head of that Division reports directly to the DPP.

26   Any prosecutor outside Special Crime Division of Headquarters therefore who receives any enquiry or case involving an allegation of assisted suicide should ensure that the Head of Special Crime Division is notified.

27   This interim policy comes into effect on the day of its publication and is to be applied in all current and future cases. It will be reviewed in the light of the public consultation exercise currently being undertaken ...

Appendix 14.1

Extracts from 'A code of practice for the diagnosis and confirmation of death' (Academy of Medical Royal Colleges, 2008)[1]

2. DIAGNOSIS AND CONFIRMATION OF DEATH

Death entails the irreversible loss of those essential characteristics which are necessary to the existence of a living human person and, thus, the definition of death should be regarded as the irreversible loss of the capacity for consciousness, combined with irreversible loss of the capacity to breathe. This may be secondary to a wide range of underlying problems in the body, for example, cardiac arrest.

Death following the irreversible cessation of brain-stem function

2.1 The irreversible cessation of brain-stem function whether induced by intra-cranial events or the result of extra-cranial phenomena, such as hypoxia, will produce this clinical state and therefore irreversible cessation of the integrative function of the brain-stem equates with the death of the individual and allows the medical practitioner to diagnose death.

Three things should be noted in this regard:

First, the irreversible loss of the capacity for consciousness does not by itself entail individual death. Patients in the vegetative state (VS) have also lost this capacity (see section 6.9). The difference between them and patients who are declared dead by virtue of irreversible cessation of brain-stem function is that the latter cannot continue to breathe unaided without respiratory support, along with other life-sustaining biological interventions. This also means that even if the body of the deceased remains on respiratory support, the loss of integrated biological function will inevitably lead to deterioration and organ necrosis within a short time.

Second, the diagnosis of death because of cessation of brain-stem function does not entail the cessation of all neurological activity in the brain. What does follow from such a diagnosis is that none of these potential activities indicates any form of consciousness associated with human life, particularly the ability to feel, to be aware of, or to do, anything. Where such residual activity exists, it will not do so for long due to the rapid breakdown of other bodily functions.

Third, there may also be some residual reflex movement of the limbs after such a diagnosis. However, as this movement is independent of the brain and is controlled through the spinal cord, it is neither indicative of the ability to feel, be aware of, or to respond to, any stimulus, nor to sustain respiration or allow other bodily functions to continue.

548

In short, while there are some ways in which parts of the body may continue to show signs of biological activity after a diagnosis of irreversible cessation of brain-stem function, these have no moral relevance to the declaration of death for the purpose of the immediate withdrawal of all forms of supportive therapy. It is for this reason that patients with such activity can no longer benefit from supportive treatment and legal certification of their death is appropriate.

The current position in law is that there is no statutory definition of death in the United Kingdom. Subsequent to the proposal of the 'brain death criteria' by the Conference of Medical Royal Colleges in 1976, the courts in England and Northern Ireland have adopted these criteria as part of the law for the diagnosis of death. There is no reason to believe that courts in other parts of the United Kingdom would not follow this approach.

Section 26(2)(d) of the Human Tissue Act 2004 empowers the Human Tissue Authority to develop a series of Codes of Practice, including the definition of death for the purposes of that Act only. The Codes published thus far are available at www.hta.gov.uk/guidance/codes_of_practice.cfm

Death following cessation of cardiorespiratory function

2.2 For people suffering cardiorespiratory arrest (including failed resuscitation), death can be diagnosed when a registered medical practitioner, or other appropriately trained and qualified individual, confirms the irreversible cessation of neurological (pupillary), cardiac and respiratory activity. Diagnosing death in this situation requires confirmation that there has been irreversible damage to the vital centres in the brain-stem, due to the length of time in which the circulation to the brain has been absent.

3. DIAGNOSING AND CONFIRMING DEATH AFTER CARDIORESPIRATORY ARREST

Confirmation of death is as important in the large number of patients in whom death is expected, either in the primary care setting or in hospital, as it is in cases of unexpected death. Death after cardiorespiratory arrest has long been identified by the simultaneous and irreversible onset of apnoea, unconsciousness and absence of the circulation. In these circumstances irreversible cessation of brain-stem function rapidly ensues. However, unlike confirmation of death using neurological assessment of cessation of brain-stem reflexes (section 6), there are currently no standardised criteria for the confirmation of death following irreversible cessation of cardiorespiratory function. As a result current practice varies from confirming death as soon as the heart stops of its own accord, or when attempts at cardiopulmonary resuscitation are abandoned, to waiting ten minutes or longer after the onset of asystole and apnoea. While such practice continues to be appropriate, particularly within primary care, the increasing practice of non-heartbeating organ donation has also focused attention on the need in a hospital setting, for a standard approach to confirming death.

Whilst dying is a process rather than an event, a definition of when the process reaches the point (death) at which a living human being ceases to exist is necessary to allow the confirmation of death without an unnecessary and potentially distressing delay. This is especially so within a primary or secondary care environment, where clear signs that are pathognomonic of death (hypostasis, rigor mortis) are present. However, in the absence of such signs, we recommend that the point after cardiorespiratory arrest at which death of a living human being occurs is identified by the following conditions:

- The simultaneous and irreversible onset of apnoea and unconsciousness in the absence of the circulation

- Full and extensive attempts at reversal of any contributing cause to the cardiorespiratory arrest have been made. Such factors, which include body temperature, endocrine, metabolic and biochemical abnormalities, are considered under section 5
- One of the following is fulfilled:
  - the individual meets the criteria for not attempting cardiopulmonary resuscitation
  - attempts at cardiopulmonary resuscitation have failed
  - treatment aimed at sustaining life has been withdrawn because it has been decided to be of no further benefit to the patient and not in his/her best interest to continue and/or is in respect of the patient's wishes via an advance decision to refuse treatment
- The individual should be observed by the person responsible for confirming death for a minimum of five minutes to establish that irreversible cardiorespiratory arrest has occurred. The absence of mechanical cardiac function is normally confirmed using a combination of the following:
  - absence of a central pulse on palpation
  - absence of heart sounds on auscultation

These criteria will normally suffice in the primary care setting. However, their use can be supplemented in the hospital setting by one or more of the following:
  - asystole on a continuous ECG display
  - absence of pulsatile flow using direct intra-arterial pressure monitoring
  - absence of contractile activity using echocardiography
- Any spontaneous return of cardiac or respiratory activity during this period of observation should prompt a further five minutes observation from the next point of cardiorespiratory arrest
- After five minutes of continued cardiorespiratory arrest the absence of the pupillary responses to light, of the corneal reflexes, and of any motor response to supra-orbital pressure should be confirmed
- The time of death is recorded as the time at which these criteria are fulfilled.

It is obviously inappropriate to initiate any intervention that has the potential to restore cerebral perfusion after death has been confirmed ...

5. CONDITIONS NECESSARY FOR THE DIAGNOSIS AND CONFIRMATION OF DEATH[1]

All of the following conditions must be fulfilled to allow the diagnosis of death following irreversible cessation of brain-stem function to be undertaken.

Aetiology of irreversible brain damage

5.1 There should be no doubt that the patient's condition is due to irreversible brain damage of known aetiology. It may be obvious within hours of a primary intra-cranial event such as a severe head injury or spontaneous intra-cranial haemorrhage that the condition is irreversible. When, however, a patient has suffered primarily from cardiac arrest or severe circulatory insufficiency with an ill-defined period of cerebral hypoxia or a cerebral air or fat embolism, it may take longer to establish the diagnosis and to be confident of the prognosis. If significant diagnostic uncertainties remain, brain-stem testing cannot be undertaken. However, there are patients in whom a final diagnosis for the cause of cessation of brain-stem function is never fully established despite extensive investigation (e.g., following presumed hypoxic brain injury, cerebral air or fat embolism, drug overdose, encephalitis). In this situation brain-stem testing should be undertaken only if, after continuing clinical observation and investigation, there is no possibility of a reversible or treatable underlying cause being present.

Exclusion of potentially reversible causes of coma

5.2 The patient is deeply comatose, unresponsive and apnoeic, with his/her lungs being artificially ventilated.

There should be no evidence that this state is due to depressant drugs

5.2.1 The action of narcotics, hypnotics and tranquillisers may be prolonged, particularly when hypothermia coexists or in the presence of renal or hepatic failure. Similarly in infants and children, altered metabolism and excretion of drugs should be taken into account. Some sedatives (e.g., the benzodiazepines) and analgesics are markedly cumulative and persistent in their actions and are commonly used as anticonvulsants or to assist synchronisation with mechanical ventilators.

It is therefore essential that the recent history of what drugs have been ingested or administered should be carefully reviewed and any possibility of intoxication being the cause of, or contributing to, the patient's comatose state should preclude a diagnosis of death. It is important to recognise that, in some patients, hypoxia may have followed the ingestion of a drug, but in this situation the criteria for death will not be applicable until such a time as the primary effects of the drug have been excluded as a continuing cause of the unresponsiveness. Excluding the effects of sedative drugs, however, may be difficult.

The length of time between discontinuation of depressant drugs and undertaking brain-stem testing depends on several factors including total dose, duration of treatment, the underlying renal and hepatic function and the availability of measurement of drug concentrations. If assays of thiopentone are available, it is recommended that brain-stem testing should not be undertaken if the level is >5mg/L. If levels are not available then determining an adequate duration to exclude the effects of depressant drugs will involve prediction according to pharmacokinetic principles in both adults and children.

If opioids or benzodiazepines are thought to be contributing to the coma, specific antagonists such as naloxone or anexate should be used. If midazolam levels are available brain-stem testing should not be undertaken if the level is >10μg/L. In other circumstances, residual sedative effects must be predicted according to pharmacokinetic principles in both adults and children. If there is any doubt, specific drug levels should be measured before proceeding. In exceptional circumstances, if the effects of sedation cannot be excluded, ancillary investigations may be necessary to confirm the diagnosis (see section 6.7).

Primary hypothermia as the cause of unconsciousness must have been excluded

5.2.2 Temperatures between 32–34°C are occasionally associated with an impaired level of consciousness but brain-stem reflexes tend to be lost if the temperature falls below 28°C. These deficits are potentially reversible. In clinical practice, patients remain awake and conscious with temperatures >34°C unless other factors are present. We therefore recommend that the core temperature should be greater than 34°C at the time of testing.

Potentially reversible circulatory, metabolic and endocrine disturbances must have been excluded as the cause of the continuation of unconsciousness

5.2.3 While trying to provide broad guidance on the magnitude of metabolic and endocrine disorders which are likely to influence the testing of brain-stem reflexes, it is essential to bear in mind that the most important factor is the establishment of an unequivocal cause for the individual's unconsciousness.

It is recognised that circulatory, metabolic and endocrine disturbances (e.g., hypernatraemia, diabetes insipidus) are likely accompaniments of death as a result of cessation of brain-stem function. It is important to emphasise that these may be the effect rather than the cause of cessation of brain-stem function and do not preclude the diagnosis of death by neurological testing of brain-stem reflexes. Furthermore it may be detrimental to correct such abnormalities too rapidly and, equally, to delay testing of brain-stem reflexes unnecessarily, simply because of strict adherence to the requirement to attain a predetermined blood electrolyte concentration. It is necessary to maintain circulation and respiration prior to testing. The mean arterial pressure should be consistently >60mmHg with maintenance of normocarbia and avoidance of hypoxia, acidaemia or alkalaemia ($PaCO2$ <6.0KPa, $PaO2$ >10KPa and pH 7.35 –7.45)

As guidance, we would emphasise that the effects of hyponatraemia depend on the rate of its development but it is rare for patients to become unresponsive if the serum sodium concentration is 115mmol/L or above. If severe hyponatraemia is corrected too rapidly the patient may develop unresponsive, but potentially reversible coma due to central pontine myelinolysis. Sodium levels above 160mmol/L are associated with unresponsiveness and this should be borne in mind if the primary cause of coma prior to testing is uncertain.

Profoundly low levels of serum potassium may cause myopathy and levels below 1mmol/L have been reported to cause flaccid quadriplegia. Whilst there is no clear evidence concerning the central effects of hypokalaemia, as a guide we would recommend that testing of brain-stem reflexes should not be undertaken in the face of a serum potassium concentration below 2mmol/L.

Similarly, profound elevation or lowering of phosphate or magnesium may be associated with severe neuromuscular weakness that may culminate in flaccid quadriplegia. Although there is little evidence to suggest a central component or to guide the clinician in determining at what levels brain-stem testing can safely be undertaken, clinically significant weakness is unlikely unless levels of magnesium or phosphate are <0.5 or >3.0mmol/L. In addition a peripheral nerve stimulator should be used to ensure that there is good neuromuscular transmission and some muscle response.

Hyperglycaemia in diabetic ketoacidosis or hyperosmolar non-ketotic coma may cause a state of unresponsiveness which mimics irreversible cessation of brain-stem function, but this state is extremely unlikely with blood glucose levels less than 20mmol/L. Severe hypoglycaemia is associated with coma or stupor and testing of brain-stem reflexes should not be undertaken if the glucose level is below 3.0mmol/L. Since blood glucose concentrations change rapidly in critically ill patients, a blood sugar measurement should always be made immediately prior to the testing of brain-stem reflexes. Patients in thyroid storm may present in acute coma or with acute thyrotoxic myopathy. Myxoedema may also cause a deep unresponsive coma. Addisonian crisis may be associated with severe neuromuscular weakness causing an acute ascending paralysis or encephalopathy proceeding to coma. These conditions are extremely rare and unlikely to co-exist in the presence of known primary pathologies. If there is any clinical reason to expect these disturbances then it is obligatory to ensure appropriate hormonal assays are undertaken.

Exclusion of potentially reversible causes of apnoea

5.3 The patient is being maintained on the ventilator because spontaneous respiration has ceased. Relaxants (neuromuscular blocking agents) and other drugs must have been excluded as the cause of respiratory inadequacy or failure. Immobility, unresponsiveness and lack of spontaneous respiration may be due to the use of neuromuscular blocking drugs and the persistence of their effects should be excluded by confirmation of the presence of deep-tendon reflexes or by the demonstration of adequate neuromuscular conduction with a conventional nerve stimulator. Persistent effects of hypnotics or narcotics must be excluded as the cause of respiratory failure. Profound neuromuscular weakness resembling the absence of brain-stem reflexes may occur as a consequence of a number of neurological disorders emphasising the importance of establishing a clear diagnosis of irremediable brain damage of known aetiology.

When coma follows a head injury, the presence of a cervical spine injury must be excluded in the usual way using clinical criteria, plain X-rays, CT and MRI scans as indicated. If there are reasons to suspect that an underlying high cervical spine injury and associated cord injury are causing the apnoea, then the apnoea test (see section 6.1.6) becomes invalid. In this rare scenario, cessation of brain-stem function can be established only by confirming the absence of other brain-stem reflexes and by using ancillary investigations (see section 6.7....).

1   Footnotes from the original document have not been included in this Appendix. See http://www.aomrc.org.uk/aomrc/admin/reports/docs/DofD-final.pdf for the full Code.

A code of practice for the diagnosis and confirmation of death (Academy of Medical Royal Colleges, 2008)

APPENDIX 1

Procedure for the diagnosis and confirmation of cessation of brain-stem function by neurological testing of brain-stem reflexes

Diagnosis is to be made by two doctors who have been registered for more than five years and are competent in the procedure. At least one should be a consultant. Testing should be undertaken by the doctors together and must always be performed completely and successfully on two occasions in total.

Patient Name:	Unit No:
Pre-conditions	

Are you satisfied that the patient suffers from a condition that has led to irreversible brain damage?

Specify the condition:	
Dr A:	Dr B:
Time of onset of unresponsive coma:	
Dr A:	Dr B:

Are you satisfied that potentially reversible causes for the patient's condition have been adequately excluded, in particular:

	Dr A:	Dr B:
Depressant drugs		
Neuromuscular blocking drugs		
Hypothermia		
Metabolic or endocrine disturbances		

Tests for absence of brain-stem function	1st set of tests	2nd set of tests	1st set of tests	2nd set of tests
Do the pupils react to light?				
Are there corneal reflexes?				
Is there eye movement on caloric testing?				
Are there motor responses in the cranial nerve distribution in response to stimulation of face, limbs or trunk?				
Is the gag reflex present?				
Is there a cough reflex?				
Have the recommendations concerning testing for apnoea been followed?				
Were there any respiratory movements seen?				

Date and time of first set of tests:	
Date and time of second set of tests:	
Dr A signature:	Dr B signature:
Status:	Status:

Appendix 14.3

Extracts from 'Withholding or withdrawing life sustaining treatment in children'
A framework for practice

Second edition May 2004

Royal College of Paediatrics and Child Health

SUMMARY

The RCPCH acknowledges that all members of the child health team, in partnership with parents, have a duty to act in the best interests of the child. This includes sustaining life, and restoring health to an acceptable standard. However there are circumstances in which treatments that merely sustain 'life' neither restore health nor confer other benefit and hence are no longer in the child's best interests.

There are five situations where it may be ethical and legal to consider withholding or withdrawal of life sustaining medical treatment[1]:

1. *The 'Brain Dead' Child*[2]. In the older child[3] where criteria of brain-stem death are agreed by two practitioners in the usual way[4] it may still be technically feasible to provide basal cardio-respiratory support by means of ventilation and intensive care. It is agreed within the profession that treatment in such circumstances is futile and the withdrawal of current medical treatment is appropriate.

2. *The 'Permanent Vegetative' State*[5,6] The child who develops a permanent vegetative state following insults, such as trauma or hypoxia, is reliant on others for all care and does not react or relate with the outside world. It may be appropriate to withdraw or withhold life-sustaining treatment.

3. *The 'No Chance' Situation.* The child has such severe disease that life-sustaining treatment simply delays death without significant alleviation of suffering. Treatment to sustain life is inappropriate.

4. *The 'No purpose' Situation.* Although the patient may be able to survive with treatment, the degree of physical or mental impairment will be so great that it is unreasonable to expect them to bear it.

5. *The 'Unbearable' Situation.* The child and/or family feel that in the face of progressive and irreversible illness further treatment is more than can be borne. They wish to have a particular treatment withdrawn or to refuse further treatment irrespective of the medical opinion that it maybe of some benefit.

In situations that do not fit with these five categories, or where there is uncertainty about the degree of future impairment or disagreement, the child's life should always be safeguarded in the best way possible by all in the Health Care Team, until these issues are resolved.

Decisions must never be rushed and must always be made by the team with all evidence available. In emergencies it is often doctors in training who are called to resuscitate. Rigid rules, even for conditions which seem hopeless, should be avoided, and life sustaining treatment should be administered and continued until a senior or more experienced doctor arrives.

The decision to withhold or withdraw life sustaining therapy should always be associated with consideration of the child's overall palliative or terminal care needs. These include symptom alleviation and care, which maintains human dignity and comfort.

1. INTRODUCTION

All members of the Child's Health Care Team[7], together with the parents (see section 2.5), have the common purposes of restoring health and sustaining the life of the child[8]. Advancing technology makes it possible to achieve these objectives in circumstances previously regarded as hopeless. However treatments exist that may promote and sustain life but confer no foreseeable benefit for the child. Such treatments may sometimes cause suffering to the child and the family. The background to all treatments, now and in the future, must be that they should be in the child's best interests.

It is clear that many professionals, patients and families need some help in making the difficult decisions on when and how life sustaining treatment is to be withheld or withdrawn. The purpose of this document is to provide practical help, framed within the existing law, and upholding the rights of children. As such this document is not intended to be prescriptive or specific but to enable decision making with the child's best interests at heart in a framework of good medical practice. It is unrealistic to expect complete consensus therefore the aim is to seek as much common ground as possible, while acknowledging sincerely held differences of opinion.

To this end the Ethics Advisory Committee of the Royal College of Paediatrics and Child Health (EAC-RCPCH) has defined five categories in which the withholding or withdrawal of life sustaining medical treatment might be appropriate and in which the goals of care are redirected. These are setout in the preceding summary. In no circumstances is it appropriate to withdraw palliative care designed to make the patient comfortable.

2. BACKGROUND CONSIDERATIONS

To withhold or withdraw

2.1 Withholding or withdrawing life sustaining treatment does not imply that a child will receive no care. It should rather signal a change in focus towards palliative care making sure that the rest of the child's life is as comfortable as possible.

Ethically the withholding and the withdrawal of life sustaining treatment are equivalent but emotionally they are sometimes poles apart. If the decision from the outset is that any treatment other than palliative care would not be in the child's interests, then the decision requires that no resuscitative action is taken. On the other hand if the decision is taken after treatment intended to continue life has been instituted, the decision will lead to a change in the treatment plan with active withdrawal of life sustaining treatment with emphasis on palliative care. Some paediatricians and parents find the second course psychologically and emotionally the more difficult but on the other hand in this situation it may be easier for the parents to believe that everything possible has been done.

In acute situations it is always necessary to give life-sustaining treatment first and to review this when enough information is available, from more experienced opinion or following the evolution of the clinical state or in the light of investigations. Neonates should almost always be resuscitated in the labour ward, particularly if there has been no prior discussion. Withholding or withdrawal decisions should be made by experienced senior staff.

In critical care areas[9] there should be frequent review of all decisions including those related to provision of life sustaining treatment. There should be a willingness to change with changing circumstances.

The extent of withholding and withdrawal of care in paediatric practice

2.2 There is substantial evidence that it is common and accepted practice to withdraw life-sustaining care where parents and medical staff believe that the distress incurred by such care outweighs the benefits.

Neonatal practice

2.2.1 Recent statistics show that discussions with parents about limitation and possible withdrawal of treatment may occur in up to 70% of deaths in UK neonatal intensive care units.[10]

Examples of clinical situations where treatment may not be started, may be discontinued, or may be limited include:

- Non-resuscitation of a baby at birth with a congenital abnormality that is incompatible with survival, such as the absence of a large part of the brain (anencephaly).
- Non-resuscitation of a baby born with a confirmed gestational age of 23 weeks or less when parents accept the neonatologist's opinion that survival would be so likely to be associated with severe neurological impairment that the many weeks of intensive care cannot be justified.
- Withdrawal of artificial ventilation from a baby who has suffered birth asphyxia and in whom investigation has revealed profound brain damage.

Practice later in childhood

2.2.2 Withdrawal of treatment in paediatric intensive care units accounts for between 43% and 72% of deaths[11] in the UK and other countries where it has been studied.

In the management of children with chronic conditions outside intensive care similar decisions are also made but much fewer data are available[12]. At least 12 in 10,000 children are living with a life-threatening condition in this country[13]. Many of these children receive palliative care at home where choices to withhold invasive and intensive interventions are made regularly[14].

Examples in later childhood might include:

- The withholding of antibiotics to treat pneumonia or other life threatening infection in the case of a seriously neurologically impaired child or child suffering from a terminal illness. In contrast, antibiotics might be used for a non-fatal infection which is causing distress, such as a painful middle ear infection (acute otitis media). This latter step would represent an important element of good palliative care.
- The paediatric neurologist might consider the appropriateness of ventilator care in an infant with progressive respiratory failure from anterior horn cell disease[15]. He or she might consider withdrawing all life sustaining care from a severely injured child where brain stem responses are absent on two occasions.
- When there is no expectation of a cure being achievable the paediatric oncologist might withhold antibiotics in a child with multiple secondary deposits of tumour. He might also withdraw chemotherapy in leukaemia if the child had previously suffered frequent relapse and the course of therapy was giving little benefit.

The ethical framework

2.3 No single ethical framework is likely to embrace all views on questions of withholding or withdrawing treatment but the EAC-RCPCH were mindful of a number of ethical theories and principles in shaping their recommendations.

Fundamental principles

2.3.1 The EAC-RCPCH believes that three fundamental principles apply:

2.3.1.1 *Duty of Care and the Partnership of Care*. Granted the compelling presumption in favour of life, the Health Care Team has a duty of care with the primary intention of sustaining life and restoring their patients to health. Whether or not the child can be restored to health, there is an absolute duty to comfort and to cherish the child and to prevent pain and suffering.

In fulfilling the obligations imposed by the duty of care, the Health Care Team and parents will enter a partnership of care, whose function is to serve the best interests of the child. This duty of care also involves respecting the ascertainable wishes and views of children in the light of their knowledge, understanding and experience. Children should be informed and listened to so that they can participate as fully as possible in decision making.

2.3.1.2 *The Legal Duty* All Health Care professionals are bound to fulfil their duty of care within the framework of the law. The law governing issues of withdrawal or with-holding treatment is complex and arguably inconsistent, but it is clear that any practice or treatment given with the primary intention of causing death is unlawful.

The Children Act (England and Wales, 1989; Scotland, 1995) provides an overall statutory framework for the provision of children's welfare and services but makes no specific provision concerning withholding or withdrawing treatment. It does however, provide *inter alia* that:

- The child's welfare is paramount.
- Particular regard is paid to the ascertainable wishes and feelings of the child.
- Children of sufficient maturity and understanding may be allowed to refuse medical or psychiatric examination or other assessment (but only for the

purposes of a child assessment order [section 43(8)] or an emergency protection order [section 44(7)].)

However, the Act also introduces the concept of parental responsibility (section 2.5). Those with parental responsibility may make decisions on behalf of children provided that they act in their child's best interests. Parental responsibility can be acquired under the Act by people who are not the child's natural parents. This increases the number of people who could be involved in making decisions about children. Judgements under the common law would appear to allow a child who is able to understand fully the nature and purpose of medical treatment to consent. By inference, it would seem that the child could refuse life saving or life sustaining treatment, but decisions of the Court of Appeal *re R and re* W[16] have established that those with parental responsibility can over-ride a child's refusal even if the child concerned is capable of fully understanding the consequences of the decision. In cases of disagreement, a court can be asked to consider whether continuing treatment would be in the best interests of the child and can override the objections of both parents and competent children.

A number of judgements on withholding or withdrawing life sustaining treatment have established that:

- There is no obligation to give treatment which is futile and burdensome – indeed this could be regarded as an assault on the child.
- Treatment goals may be changed in the case of children who are dying.
- Feeding and other medical treatment may be withdrawn in patients in whom the vegetative state is thought to be permanent (but in each case, it is suggested that legal advice should be taken).
- Treatment may be withdrawn from patients if continuation is not in their best interests.

Decisions concerning withholding or withdrawing treatment in the best interests of the child would probably need to fulfil the Bolam test[17]. That is, a responsible body of professional opinion would be of the view that it was not in the best interests of the child to continue treatment for reasons that are logical and stand up to analysis.

2.3.1.3 *Respect for Children's Rights* The United Nations Convention on the Rights of the Child (1989), which has been ratified by the British Government, sets out fundamental principles which govern how children should be treated. The following are the most relevant for the purposes of this document:

- Article 3 states that action affecting children should have 'their best interests' as a primary consideration.
- Article 24 confirms the right of the child to the highest obtainable standards of health and to facilities for the treatment of illness and the rehabilitation of health.
- Article 13 confirms the child's right of freedom of expression and to seek, receive and impart information and ideas of all kinds.
- Article 12, affirms that 'a child who is capable of forming his/her view has the right to express those views freely on all matters affecting the child, the views of the child being given due weight in accordance with the age and maturity of the child'.

The Convention also affirms the right of families to be given all necessary support in caring for their child and in the performance of their child rearing responsibilities.

Axioms on which to base practice

2.3.2 From these fundamental principles flow a number of general axioms which may govern practice. These are:

2.3.2.1 There is no significant ethical difference between withdrawing (stopping) and withholding treatments, given the same ethical objective.

2.3.2.2 Optimal ethical decision-making concerning children requires open and timely communication between members of the Health Care Team and the child and family, respecting their values and beliefs and the fundamental principles of ethics and human rights.

2.3.2.3 Parents may ethically and legally decide on behalf of children who are unable, for whatever reason, to express preferences, unless they are clearly acting against the child's best interest or are unable, unwilling or persistently unavailable to make decisions on behalf of their child.

2.3.2.4 The wishes of a child who has obtained sufficient understanding and experience in the evaluation of treatment options should be given substantial consideration in the decision making process.

2.3.2.5 The antecedent wishes and preferences of the child, if known, should also carry considerable weight given that conditions at the time for action match those envisaged in advance.

2.3.2.6 In general, resolution of disagreement should be by discussion, consultation and consensus.

2.3.2.7 The duty of care is not an absolute duty to preserve life by all means. There is no obligation to provide life sustaining treatment if:

- its use is inconsistent with the aims and objectives of an appropriate treatment plan
- the benefits of that treatment no longer outweigh the burden to the patient.

2.3.2.8 It is ethical to withdraw life sustaining treatment if refused by a competent child; or from children who are unable to express wishes and preference when the HealthCare Team and parent/carers agree that such treatment is not in the child's best interests.

2.3.2.9 A redirection of management from life sustaining treatment to palliation represents a change in beneficial aims and objectives and does not constitute a withdrawal of care.

2.3.2.10 The range of life sustaining treatments is wide and will vary with the individual circumstances of the patient. It is never permissible to withdraw procedures designed to alleviate pain or promote comfort.

2.3.2.11 There is a distinction to be drawn between treatment of the dying patient and euthanasia. When a dying patient is receiving palliative care, the underlying cause of death is the disease process. In euthanasia, the intended action is to cause death.

2.3.2.12 It follows that use of medication and other treatments which may incidentally hasten death may be justified if their primary aim is to relieve suffering. The EAC-RCPCH does not support the concept of euthanasia.

2.3.2.13 Legal intervention should be considered when disputes between the HealthCare Team, the child, parents and carers cannot be resolved by attempts to achieve consensus.

The Legal Framework

2.4 The courts have accepted that it is lawful to withdraw life-prolonging treatment when the quality of life the child would have to endure if given the treatment would be so afflicted as to be intolerable to the child[18]. Although there has not yet been a case involving a child, the implementation of the Human Rights Act 1998 has not altered the courts' view that withdrawing such treatment in appropriate cases is consistent with patients' human rights.

Although it is necessary and fundamental to practice within the framework of the law, the EAC-RCPCH believe it is important to define best practice in relation to the interests of the family and the child rather than presenting the minimum legal requirement. We must look at what is legally permitted and required, but also at what is ethically appropriate, which may exceed the minimum standards set by law.

If a doctor wishes to continue treatment of a very ill child, but there is room for reasonable doubt about the benefit, the doctor may be in a difficult position if he continues when the parents have withheld or withdrawn consent. A court might say that the doctor did not act in the child's best interests. In cases of dispute it is good practice to consult the court[19]. In the meantime, the treatment should be given in the expectation that the court will support the action.

The legal context behind a child's consent

2.4.1 In England and Wales in 1985, the Gillick ruling established that children who are capable of fully understanding the implications of their decisions can give valid consent and that parents have rights only in so far as these enable them to exercise responsibilities to benefit their children. More recent court rulings in 1991 and 1992 have retreated from the original Gillick level of respect for the competent child's views; they have reaffirmed parents' rights of consent as a necessary legal protection when doctors care for minors. The courts have previously regarded the appropriateness of enforcing treatment on resisting children as an ethical not a legal matter[20].

However, case law in relation to adults suggests that imposing treatment in such circumstances may constitute 'inhuman and degrading treatment' that breaches human rights unless it is 'medically necessary' to do so. It is accepted that 'medical necessity' can be present even when a decision is controversial, but the concept has not yet been further defined by the courts.

The 1969 Family Law Reform Act respects consenting decisions of young people aged over16 years as if they are adults, but not necessarily dissenting decisions. A dissenting child at any age is likely to have his or her views overridden. This is despite the 1989 Children's Act and the UN Convention, which both take a broad view of involving even 'non-competent' children (who may nevertheless hold important and informed views) into decision making. Such views can help adults to make more informed decisions.

The Convention of the Rights of the Child

2.4.2 The United Nations Convention on the Rights of the Child (1989) cannot be directly applied in UK courts, but ratification means that Governments undertake to honour the Convention and to report regularly to the United Nations on their progress in implementing children's rights. The Convention states that actions affecting children must have the 'best interests of the child' as a primary consideration (Article 3). It also enshrines 'the right of the child to enjoyment of the highest attainable standard of health and to facilities for the treatment of illness and the rehabilitation of health' (Article 24) subject to the resources available (Article4). The Convention also respects the child's right 'to freedom of expression (including) freedom to seek, receive and impart information and ideas of all kinds, regardless of frontiers' and in 'media of the child's choice' whether language, drawings and visual aids, or through other kinds of communications (Article 13).

Like English law, the Convention respects the rights of all children to form and express their view and states that "the child who is capable of forming his or her own views has the right to express those views freely on all matters affecting the child, the views of the child being given due weight in accordance with the age and maturing of the child".

Thus the Convention addresses the child's right to share in decision-making, but does not address questions of the child being the main or sole decider about proposed health care. The Convention does not affect any state laws which go further than the Convention (Article41). English law has gone further, in recognising the rights of competent children to make decisions in certain circumstances[21].

Euthanasia[22]

2.4.3 Withdrawal of life sustaining treatment in appropriate circumstances is not seen by the courts as active killing, nor as a breach of the right of life under article 2 of the European Convention on Human Rights[23].

Where withdrawal of ventilatory support does not lead to death, it must be made clear that euthanasia is not appropriate and that palliative care should be offered. The lives of unexpected survivors, even when badly disabled, should be respected and they should be cared for appropriately.

Some clinicians consider euthanasia acceptable practice: others believe that it is never acceptable. The Committee acknowledges the debate about euthanasia and changing clinical practice in some countries will continue to receive public attention[24]. The EAC-RCPCH does not support euthanasia.

Giving a medicine with the primary intent to hasten death is unlawful. Giving a medicine to relieve suffering which may, as a side effect, hasten death is lawful and can be appropriate.

It is recognised in English and Scottish law that increasing doses of analgesia necessary for control of pain or distress may shorten life. The giving of opioids is for the benefit of the patient during life not in order to cause or hasten death.

Parental responsibilities[25]

2.5 Under the UN Convention on the Rights of the Child the State has a duty to support parents in this responsibility. It is the duty of the parents to act for the child and in the best interests of the child. The parents will always be participants in the care and decision making. The child will be involved to a degree appropriate for their experience and condition.

Although parents act for the child, they often feel unsure of where they can go for extra advice outside the immediate Health Care Team and their decisions may be altered by the way in which the information is presented to them. Sometimes there may be a need for an advocate not connected with the medical team. Such a person may not only be able to interpret medical information to parents and child in understandable language, but – more importantly – assist the parents or child in conveying their views accurately to the professionals.

If the local authority achieves a care order it gains parental responsibility and the power to restrict the natural parents' authority or that of any other person who would normally carry such authority. Parents can appeal to the High Court and to the Court of Appeal.

2.6.

Involving Children

Competence

2.6.1 Children's competence is related to their experience as well as their developmental stage. Very young children who have had two courses of chemotherapy or two organ transplants will often have more informed views about proposals for a third course of treatment than adult patients who are considering such treatment for the first time. Other young children have no experience of decision making and their framework of values remains unformed.

The EAC-RCPCH believes that there should be a presumption of competence, unless a child is obviously incompetent e.g. extreme immaturity. It should be a duty of the professionals to assess the individual child's competency for decision making. Good practice goes beyond observing minimum legal standards (see 2.4.1) and takes account of higher ethical standards of respect for young children's views, as well as concern for their welfare. Open and timely communication between the young patient, family and members of the Health Care Team is central to informed and ethical decision-making. The EAC-RCPCH sees differences between:

1. informing children,
2. listening to them,
3. taking account of their views so that these can influence decisions, and
4. respecting the competent child as the main decider about proposed health care interventions.

These four levels involve different degrees of competence. The child's rights to be informed and to express views (levels 1 and 2) are conditioned only by the child being able to understand information and to form and express personal views.

Good Practice in Involving Children

2.6.2 The account taken of children's views (see above) varies according to how informed and wise each view is thought to be, and how much the adults concerned respect children's wishes and feelings. Respect for a child's view, including their wish to refuse further interventions, has been quite widely advocated[26]. Children are increasingly involved in social and nursing decisions about how their treatment is administered.

The real difficulties arise with the most troubling questions: What is the best course of treatment? When does life become not worth living? When is hope of benefit too slight to justify treatment? Such questions can increase doubts about how far it is wise or kind to inform and involve children. When does the child's wish become decisive? How far should parents' refusal to allow the child to be informed or involved be respected? There may be conflicts between children's rights based on competence and parental and medical views. How can children's competence, with their ability to cope with distressing news and to make decisions, be assessed taking account of their best interests? Varied ways of communicating with children and of respecting their physical and mental feelings, beyond cognitive and strictly verbal approaches, are being used. They need to be more widely reported and explained.

In many cases children have no views about proposed care (such as when they are babies, or when illness, injury or disability limit their understanding). In other cases, children prefer others to decide for them; although this apparent preference should be checked and not assumed. Some children want to influence decisions or to be the main decider. Experienced young patients with severe illness or disability may decide that life is not worth living, e.g. those with anorexia or severe mental illness may ask for less enforced treatments. In the latter group, assessments of competence are particularly complicated and it is often assumed that parents or courts know best.

Impairment and Disability[27]

2.7 One of the most challenging and difficult areas involves the question of withholding or withdrawing life sustaining treatment for children with severe impairment. (section 3.1.3)

In 1991 the Court of Appeal accepted that it is lawful to withdraw life-prolonging treatment when the quality of life the child would have to endure, if given the treatment, would be so afflicted as to be intolerable to the child[28]. The court recognised that a quality of life which could be considered intolerable to an able-bodied person, would not necessarily be unacceptable to a child who has been born disabled. The EAC-RCPCH believes that this means when there is little or no prospect of meaningful interaction with others or the environment. In this situation no reasonable person would want to lead such a life, nor impose on a doctor a duty actively to strive to bring it about.

Living with disability

2.7.1 Many people with severe impairment describe a life of high quality and say they are happy to be living it. Impairment is not incompatible with a life of quality. Children and adults may not view their residual disability as negatively as some able-bodied people do, provided adequate support is available. It is important that society does not devalue disabled people or those living with severe impairments. **The EAC-RCPCH strongly believes that the provision of care to those with disability should not be reduced and there must always be a commitment to the provision of high quality care for those with disability.** Sadly there are indications such children have been discriminated against when they compete for acute surgery[29].

There is a degree of impairment which includes a loss of awareness and an inability to interact. Perhaps this is intolerable disability. Spastic quadriplegia with very severe cognitive and sensory deficits might be one such condition. The burden is not only for the child but also the parents or their surrogates, and society must also determine how best to share it.

Disability

2.7.2 This is a matter of individual perception. What is tolerable for one person might well be intolerable for another. It is important in counselling to avoid over pessimistic views about life with disability. It is also important to recognise that while some people with disabilities are able to live fulfilled lives others with the same level of disability feel that life is not worth living. It is particularly difficult to assess the acceptability of a disability in the child.

'Very serious handicap' is a term that parents may use when facing a particularly bleak outcome.

An intolerable disability

2.7.3 A severe/intolerable disability is indefinable; there are ways of making it more tolerable, and an individual sufferer, even with extreme disability, may still attach some value to existence. Judgements on disability are bound up in people's fears and attitudes and can be altered by a change in the environment. Note:

- Intolerable may mean "that which cannot be borne" or "that which people should not be asked to bear".
- An individual may believe that he/she is an intolerable burden
- An impossibly poor existence may not be recognised by the individual, depending on that person's cognition.

It is possible to envisage a level of disability that doctors believe to be intolerable, i.e. no reasonable person would want to live with it, and yet an individual sufferer may attach value to their existence.

3 THE PROCESS OF DECISION MAKING

Consideration of withdrawal

3.1 In general, the outcome for a clinical problem at the time of presentation is uncertain. The team must wait until enough **information** (not feelings) about the child's clinical condition and other relevant matters to enable a clear decision on whether or not further treatment is appropriate. **All remediable causes for the child's condition must be excluded**. e.g. drugs, metabolic encephalopathy.

The EAC-RCPCH believes however that it is sufficient to have a reasonable belief that a particular outcome is likely and that absolute certainty may be neither possible nor always necessary.

Decision Making

3.1.1 In medicine there are two extremes: where death is certain and where cure is certain. Between these extremes exists uncertainty, and whether or not intervention is worthwhile is a value judgement based on prediction of outcome. Deciding what outcome is intolerable or treatment is unbearable is an intrinsic part of the decision making.

All members of the Health Care Team need to feel part of the decision making process in that their views should be listened to and accorded due weight. Most recognise that the latter will depend on their knowledge, understanding and experience. This applies to both clinical and moral matters. However greater openness between disciplines and grades will facilitate greater understanding of individual roles and responsibilities and enhance the sense of corporate moral responsibility.

Decisions should be made with the parents on the basis of knowledge and trust. Parents and children may have a greater perception of their roles and responsibilities as agents indecision making than professionals acknowledge. In order to maximise active participation of parents and children in the decision-making process, clinical teams need to ascertain the tolerance of parents and children for assuming responsibility and work within that. This should enhance their ability to live with the decision they have made.

Ultimately, the clinical team carries the corporate moral responsibility for decision making, which is an expression of their moral and legal duties as health care professionals. Teams can develop this moral responsibility by reasoning together.

Second opinion

3.1.2 There may however be circumstances when an independent consultation with another clinician or ethics committee may be helpful.

Paediatricians may seek further opinions to enable parents and children to come to terms with prognosis and to provide reassurance for themselves. In practice a decision to withdraw treatment is usually a matter of consensus rather than an individual decision. However, many major medical decisions require a second opinion for legal reasons as well as clinical assurance, e.g. termination of pregnancy, brain stem death. Obtaining a second opinion as to the advisability of withdrawing life sustaining treatment is not a legal requirement but there maybe circumstances in which it may highlight the appropriateness of the process of decision making. The circumstances where a second opinion **should** be sought are discussed in section 3.4.

Circumstances of withholding or withdrawal of treatment

3.1.3 *The Brain Dead Child*[30]. When brain stem death is confirmed, the patient is by definition dead. Within the patient organs may function due to extraordinary medical assistance: such assistance can appropriately be withdrawn. Brain death must be diagnosed in the usual way by two medical practitioners.

The 'Permanent Vegetative State' (PVS)[31]. The vegetative state may follow insults such as trauma or hypoxia. It may persist i.e. be present for four weeks or more or become permanent in that it is predicted that recovery of awareness will never occur. The child in such a state shows no awareness, does not react or relate with the outside world and is reliant on others for all care. Diagnosis in children as in adults depends on the fulfilment of clinical criteria and requires appropriate assessment. In such circumstances treatment, inclusive of tube feeding, may[32] be withdrawn whilst making the patient comfortable by nursing care.

The 'No Chance' Situation. Treatment delays death but neither improves life's quality nor potential. Needlessly prolonging treatment in these circumstances is futile and burdensome and not in the best interests of the patient; hence there is no legal obligation for a doctor to provide it. Indeed, if this is done knowingly (futile treatment) it may constitute an assault or 'inhuman and degrading treatment' under Article 3 of the European Convention on Human Rights. Consider for example a child with progressive metastatic malignant disease whose life would not benefit from chemotherapy or other forms of treatment aimed at cure.

The 'No Purpose' Situation. In these circumstances the child may be able to survive with treatment, but there are reasons to believe that giving treatment may not be in the child's best interest. For example, the child may develop or already have such a degree of irreversible impairment that it would be unreasonable to expect them to bear it. Continuing treatment might leave the child in a worse condition than already exists with the likelihood of further deterioration leading to an 'impossibly poor life'. The child may not be capable now or in the future of taking part in decision making or other self directed activity.

In all the above circumstances it is appropriate to consider withholding or withdrawing treatment. If it is likely that future life will be 'impossibly poor' then treatment might reasonably be withheld. If such a life already exists and there is likelihood of it continuing without foreseeable improvement, treatment might reasonably be withdrawn.

The 'Unbearable Situation'. This situation occurs when the child and/or family feel that further treatment is more than can borne they may wish to have treatment withdrawn or to refuse further treatment irrespective of the medical opinion that it may be of some benefit.

Clinical responsibilities of the Health Care Team

3.2 Treatment generally requires co-operation. The Health Care Team must always act in the child's best interests. The Health Care Team must not inflict treatment on children just because a treatment becomes available, but always introduce treatments for the benefit of the child, withdrawing them when they are no longer of benefit.

The clinical team will almost always have to start from a premise of uncertainty. It is crucial to wait until enough information is available to decide on the individual outcome. It is recognized that such delay may become a source of tension within the Team. This information must include a clear diagnosis where possible and an awareness of the likely prognosis, given an appraisal of the possible therapeutic options. Decisions to stop or withhold certain treatments will almost always be based on probabilities rather than certainties. Some children whose medical treatment is withdrawn go on to survive[33] and it is not a wrong decision if this is the outcome. Treatment is withdrawn because it is futile but not with the intention that to do so will bring about death. Continuing support, respect and palliative care is required for the unexpected survivor. In the situation where treatment is being withheld the Team need to be flexible in the face of changing circumstances.

Range of treatments

3.2.1 There are many different types and intensities of therapy that it may be appropriate to consider withdrawing or withholding, depending on the severity of the illness or the situation. These may include experimental therapies which are currently not validated by research evidence, cardiopulmonary resuscitation, mechanical ventilation, intravenous inotropic agents, antibiotics, artificial nutrition and intravenous hydration.

Feeding is a particularly emotive area for parents and staff, and opinions vary regarding withholding and withdrawal of feeding. The role of assisted feeding for an infant or child (bynasogastric tube or gastrostomy) should be considered very carefully and discussed fully with the family. It may be entirely appropriate, for example, in a child with a swallowing disorder due to a slowly progressive neurodegenerative disease, but would rarely be introduced for a child with rapidly progressive, disseminated malignant disease. In other circumstances, its withdrawal can be accepted if it is well managed[34].

Muscle relaxants

3.2.2 The use of paralysing agents prior to withdrawal of ventilatory support can be viewed in a similar way. In some situations, such as severe lung disease, synchrony with a mechanical ventilator which is a necessary part of effective treatment, can only be achieved by administering a muscle paralysing agent in addition to sedatives and analgesics.

If it subsequently becomes appropriate to consider withdrawal of ventilation, it is important to remember that there is a difference between managing the process and ensuring death. It may not be in the child's best interests to withdraw the paralysing drugs before discontinuing ventilation, as this action would subject the child to a period of sub-optimal ventilation leading up to withdrawal of ventilatory treatment. Thus, when a decision is made to withdraw mechanical ventilation, a paralysing agent necessarily prescribed for prior treatment may bead ministered up to (but not beyond) the point that respiratory support is withdrawn. It would however be unlawful to prescribe a paralysing agent prior to withdrawal of treatment simply to avoid terminal gasping which sometimes occurs as ventilation is withdrawn, a situation which should be managed with more appropriate and specific treatment to relieve distress.

In the case of a child with severe brain injury, it is unlikely that a paralysing agent would be required to facilitate curative treatment. As no paralysing agent was required at that stage, such a drug should not be introduced for withdrawal of treatment.

In a child with severe cardiopulmonary failure where paralysing agents have been required to ensure effective ventilation during treatment, death will be inevitable with or without paralysis. In these circumstances, there is no need to stop the paralysing agent prior to withdrawal of treatment.

Palliative Care

3.2.3 The clinical team has a duty always to offer palliative care to children with life-threatening and life-limiting illnesses. It may begin whenever it becomes apparent that the illness may result in premature death. It can be provided alongside treatments aimed to cure or significantly prolong life and should continue as the main focus of care when these treatments are withdrawn or withheld[35]. Palliative care should respect the child's dignity and consider their physical needs including the relief of pain and other symptoms, and also address the emotional, social and spiritual needs of both the child and their family. All these aspects of palliative care can be provided wherever a child and family are cared for – whether in hospital, at home or in a children's hospice. Careful planning and communication is needed to ensure continuity of care for the child, particularly when they are moving between hospital and home. A key worker (often the paediatric community nurse) is essential to co-ordinate this, especially where it is anticipated that palliative care may be needed for an extended period of time and involve a number of health care professionals. If the illness is prolonged respite care should be available.

3.3

Communication

Within the Health Care Team

3.3.1 When the issue to withhold or withdraw treatment is raised, all members of the clinical team should have an opportunity to voice their feelings and opinions. The weight given to each individual's views should take their experience into account. Some may feel afraid to voice their opinion, so sympathetic encouragement is important. Some units require the whole team to express an opinion and also require unanimity; in others the issue is discussed openly but not everyone may be expected to contribute. It is perhaps unrealistic and may not be in the child's best interests to expect unanimity in support of decisions to withdraw or withhold treatment in all cases. The consultant in charge of the case should lead the decision making process and always bears the final responsibility for the chosen course of action. Team discussions about the patient are a necessary learning experience for the whole team. Senior members should promote this by interpreting information that is shared from their previous experience, but also by considering any new interpretations fairly.

Decisions to withdraw or withhold life-sustaining treatment should be clearly understood and documented by the clinical team.

With the family

3.3.2 When withdrawal is an option that has been raised by the clinical team, the consultant and a senior colleague (nurse or social worker) should, at an early stage and either together or separately, discuss the fact that the issue is to be considered with parents[36]. The child, as far as he or she is able, their wider family (e g siblings) and any other individual (religious or social) whom the parents or child nominate should also be involved. For full involvement, the parents (and child if appropriate), must have adequate information and adequate time to understand and assess it, with time also to obtain alternate advice if they so wish. Siblings can have important insights into the feelings of their sick brother or sister. The final decision is made with the consent of the parents though the clinical team must take the main responsibility for the decision. (see 3.1.1.) This can help to alleviate the burden of guilt that some parents feel.

A full record of communication with the family should be written in the clinical record on all occasions. 'Do not attempt resuscitation' orders and decisions to withhold or withdraw life sustaining treatment must be clearly recorded in the child's clinical notes together with a written account of the process and factors leading to this decision.

After the death of the child, the consultant in charge and the nurse most involved should offer to see the parents, to discuss the death and the result of the post mortem examination[37] if it is available. A copy of such a report should be given to the parents on request. The parents may wish to meet with other members of the clinical team and such a meeting should be arranged by the consultant or the nursing staff. Valuable continuing support may be given by an involved social worker.

Communication with Primary Health Care and Community Services

3.3.3 When a decision is being made with a family about withdrawing or withholding life sustaining treatment, it will usually be appropriate to include the primary health care team and local paediatric professionals in the discussion, especially if they have known the child and family well. If they are not part of the ongoing discussion it is essential to keep them well informed of decisions and particularly of the child's death.

In some situations families may prefer to care for their child at home. This may be when the focus of care becomes palliative and some period of time at home is anticipated. Occasionally the family may elect to have intensive treatment withdrawn at home or take the child's body home after death. Careful communication and arrangements, according to the circumstances, need to be made between the primary health care team, the children's community nursing service or local palliative care team and their local paediatric unit. This will ensure that there is adequate support available, good continuity of care and that plans for a time of crisis are understood by all those involved.

Levels of community services still vary in different parts of the country but families will need 24 hour access to paediatric care and advice and local teams will need 24 hour access to advice and expertise in symptom management in palliative care. Families also need to know that they have a hospital bed available at any time if they need it.

Resolution of different opinions

3.4 Where there is a lack of agreement within the team or between the team and the family it is important to analyse its origins. It is possible that these reflect different understandings of the issues and that more time to consider them and better communication will resolve the tension. If there is anxiety about the degree of certainty behind the medical facts it should be considered whether any further investigation might help to resolve this. Input from religious advisors or other important sources of support to the family may be helpful. However, personal beliefs may dictate that some individuals decide in a particular way whatever the circumstances.

Unanimity on the part of the Health Care Team is not essential (see 3.3.1). Resolving a difference of opinion between the team and the family is essential and may occasionally require additional input. Under these circumstances the family should still be fully supported by the team.

Medical Input

3.4.1 The involvement of another senior clinician may help in the communication of bad news or in decision making. This could come from within the team if the main issue is one of uncertainty, but if there is a more fundamental disagreement between the family and the team or there has been an erosion of trust, an expert opinion from outside the unit/hospital may be preferred. This could be organised by the consultant responsible for the care of the child. To secure greater confidence in the independence of the second opinion, the family may wish to arrange this themselves with the help of their general practitioner. The family should be at liberty to change clinician and move to another consultant if this is possible.

Legal Input

3.4.2 In most cases, with effective communication and adequate time, the health care team and parents will come to agree. If this does not prove possible and other efforts to resolve the situation are not successful then the courts should be consulted. Every NHS Trust has a legal adviser and it should be possible to obtain legal advice through the hospital management structure. Another source of advice is the CAFCASS Legal Services (Children and Family Court Advisory and Support Service) can be telephoned for advice which will help clarify the need for court involvement. In the rare situation that court assistance is deemed necessary, the parents or their representative should be notified as soon as possible of such intended action. Legal support for medical matters would usually be sought from a judge in a High Court. At such a hearing parents must be able to express their own views and seek alternative opinion.

Clinical Ethics Committees

3.4.3 The number of Clinical Ethics Committees established in the UK is increasing. The function of such committees may include discussion, analysis and advice on individual cases as well as contribution to policymaking, teaching, training and research.

In our opinion the factors which are likely to result in best decision making in individual cases are factual knowledge of the problems and of the circumstances of the patient concerned and good relationships between the parties involved. Ethics Committees may be too remote from the individual case to understand all the nuances involved, too ready to reach a consensus and may lack an innovative approach to problems. There are fears that they may limit freedoms and create further bureaucracy around patient care. However they may bring significant analytical skills and may have important mediation and conciliatory functions and may serve to protect patients' rights.

If Clinical Ethics Committees are to be used to discuss cases in a proactive fashion they need to be easily convened and to develop supportive and educational functions.

Various models of functioning are possible:

1) It may be obligatory to consult a committee and to accept its recommendations;
2) It may be obligatory to consult but not to accept recommendations, and
3) Both consultation with the committee and the acceptance of its recommendations are optional.

In practice models 1 and 2 are seldom used and 3 is the most appropriate for individual case discussion.

Any UK Clinical Ethics Committee needs to retain its independence so as to secure its moral integrity. It is not clear how this is to be protected in the current Hospital and Primary Care Trust since both may be considered to have some financial interest in the decisions made. It is not clear how these tensions will develop in the future or what means may be used to reduce them. Whichever model of Clinical Ethics Committee is created, it remains the case that legal and professional responsibility for decision making still rests with the consultant in charge of the case.

It is possible that Clinical Ethics Committees may have a role if there is an appeal against a decision to withdraw or withhold treatment made in another Trust and an independent analysis of the case is required.

4. BEREAVEMENT

Families

4.1 The death of a child is one of the most devastating experiences that a parent can have and the quality of care at the end of life and after the child's death can have a major impact on the family's grieving[38].

Each hospital should have a policy in place for when a child dies and provide information which should be readily available for staff which includes details about asking for post mortems, the needs of different cultures and the provision of mementos for the family. There should also be information which can be given to families on the immediate practical details they will need for registering the death and making funeral arrangements and also for the future on how they may feel and how they can access support.

It is important to provide follow-up for parents after the death of a child. Sometimes due to the pressures of acute medical care this is promised but not fulfilled. Sometimes it is helpful for families if this is undertaken by a home visit. Contact between 1–2 months later gives the opportunity to discuss the results of a post mortem or investigations that may shed more light on the circumstances surrounding the death, to answer families' medical questions and to explore their feelings. Some teams are able to offer continuing, but gradually diminishing contact with acknowledgement of special anniversaries such as the child's birthday and date of death.

Grief is a normal reaction to bereavement and sometimes professionals seek to medicalise grief and intervene inappropriately. Many families will find their own support in different ways and at different times. Families should be given access to information from both staff and voluntary organisations to enable them to make choices from the support and services available. More counselling from support organisations or other forms of therapy can be offered to families requesting such help.

The Health Care Team

4.2 Like the parents, individuals in the health care team will experience a wide range of emotions, both in the short term and over time. Work pressures can interfere with the resolution of these issues and failure to address them can lead to stress, sickness, lowered morale and divisions within the team. All staff may need support but many may not know how to acknowledge or approach this need. Discussion sessions can be helpful but they may be complicated by questions of status, social taboos or defensive behaviour and protection. Senior doctors may find it difficult to share their stresses and uncertainties with trainees and nursing staff. Certain groups may be specifically vulnerable e.g. night staff. Each person has different needs and they may gain support from more senior staff, professional support workers, friends, partners, chaplains and others. Some are helped by maintaining contact with the families and by going to the funeral although both of these can also bring new stresses. Even with a formal support network the appropriate individuals are not always available when they are most needed.

Dealing well with these issues will have a beneficial effect on staff morale and should reduce staff sickness and turnover. Management need to be aware that resources allocated in this area will support their staff, benefit the organisation and improve health care delivery.

5. THE FUTURE

Training

5.1 All clinical staff and nurses should have access to continuing education in communication, ethics and the subject of withdrawing and withholding care. Such areas now have a more prominent role in medical and nursing curricula. It has been recognised in the GMC Guidance on Training Tomorrow's Doctors and in a scientifically based education it is essential that the psychological and spiritual dimensions of care are fully considered. Hospitals may also consider having an educational clinical ethics forum that periodically meets to review difficult cases[39], and child bereavement organisations and parent support groups should be used in providing some of this training. Finally the assessment of ethical issues, communication, knowledge and approaches should continue to form a mandatory part of the assessment of competence in clinical training.

Resources

5.2 Although clinicians do not and should not give paramount importance to resources in decisions about care, such considerations have always entered into discussions about treatment options. With limited available money in the NHS, offering expensive treatment inevitably uses funds that may have been better used elsewhere. The EAC-RCPCH do not feel that decisions about the sort of child who would be offered intensive care should be resource motivated but should be determined by whether such care was appropriate.

Research/audit

5.3 It is vital for units involved in work where withholding or withdrawal of life sustaining treatment is practised not only to conduct self-audit over the outcome of their care but also to obtain feedback from the affected families[40]. As perspectives may change with time, such surveys should aim to be continuous, over a period of years.

How can children's competence, their ability to cope with distressing news, and their ability to make decisions be assessed? In many British hospitals varied ways of communicating with children, beyond cognitive and strictly verbal approaches, are being used[41]. These need to be more widely reported and explained.

Research has been done and more is needed amongst disabled people to determine what degrees of disability they would think of as too burdensome to risk for others. Undoubtedly this is an area where it will be difficult to reach a consensus as the burden of disability depends on different perceptions.

The UK Census[42] has confirmed that one in ten children are classed as from minority ethnic groups and therefore decisions on the withdrawal of treatment need to be underpinned by an understanding of cultural 'diversity'. This is a relatively under-researched area.

Clinical Ethics Service

5.4 While there is agreement that support, guidance, teaching and training in these sensitive areas are required for all staff there is as yet no consensus as to how these aims are to be achieved and how the impact of providing ethical support is to be evaluated. A greater interest in qualitative research and the interface between the Humanities and Medicine may provide the necessary impetus and tools to accomplish this task. The establishment of a UK Clinical Ethics Network[43] will provide a forum for exchange of ideas, methodologies and protocols and also support for those attempting to establish, maintain or validate their service.

6. CONCLUSIONS

There are some circumstances in which the continuation of medical attempts to cure are either manifestly futile or inflict unbearable suffering on the child. Professionals, trained to restore health, often feel that they have failed patients whose problems persist despite active treatment. However, in some circumstances, to continue life sustaining treatment is to offer care that is no longer in the child's best interest.

Appropriate withdrawal of treatment will depend on accurate knowledge of the condition and sound inter-relationships with and around the child. Good judgement will usually involve consultation. Conflicting emotions can affect the balance of both parental and professional judgement. The availability of professionals who can address this conflict could be helpful in explaining and defusing areas of potential tension. Decisions should never be hurried and there should always be respect for the child's life and a responsibility to relieve suffering. The lives of those with severe disabilities, whether physical or mental, are to be highly valued. All who relate to those with disability should offer them the best personal, and professional care.

1   Withdrawal of curative medical treatment should signal the initiation of palliative care if this has not already been introduced. see section 3.2.4.
2   Definition – Brain death occurs when a child has sustained either (i) irreversible cessation of circulatory and respiratory functions or (ii) irreversible cessation of all functions of the entire

brain including the brain stem. A determination of death must be made in accordance with accepted medical standards.

3   Original definitions of brain death were not applied to neonates as criteria were thought to be affected by brain immaturity.

4   Task force for the determination of brain death in children. "Guidelines for the determination of brain death in children." *Annals of Neurology.* (1987) **21**:616–617. *Pediatrics.* (1987) **80**:298–299.

5   *The vegetative state – guidance on diagnosis and management.* A Report of a working party of the Royal College of Clinical Medicine (2003)**3**: 249–254. Defines the vegatative state and uses the terms "persistent" to mean a vegetative state that has persisted for four weeks or more and "permanent" when the vegetative state is deemed to be permanent and it is predicted that awareness will never recover.

6   "The persistent vegetative state." Conference of Medical Royal Colleges and their Faculties of the United Kingdom. *Journal of the Royal College of Physicians, London.* (1996) **30**: 119–121.

7   The Health Care Team consists of nursing staff, play specialists, educational specialists, medical staff (inclusive of the General Practitioner), and staff from the professions allied to medicine. The team would in all cases work closely with the parents and the child.

8   As endorsed by the Children Act (England and Wales 1989; Scotland 1995) and United Nations Convention on the Rights of the Child 1989

9   Critical care areas include A&E, labour ward and intensive care units.

10   McHaffie HS et al. *Crucial Decisions at the beginning of Life.* Radcliffe Medical Press (2001).

11   McCallum DE, Byrne P and Bruera E. "How children die in hospital." *J Pain Symptom Management.* (2000) **20**:417–23. Keenan SP, Busche KD, Chen LM et al. "Withdrawal and withholding of life support in the intensive care unit: a comparison of teaching and community hospitals." The Southwestern Ontario Critical Care Research Network.*Crit. Care. Medicine* (1998); **26** (2)245–51. Goh AY and Mok Q. "Identifying futility in a paediatric critical care setting: a prospective." *Arch Dis Child.*(2001) **84**: 265–8. Cuttini. M et al. "End-of-life decisions in neonatal intensive care: physicians' self reported practices in seven European countries." *Lancet.* (2000)**355**: 2112–2118.

12   Liben S, Goldman A. "Homecare for children with life threatening illness." *J of Palliative Care* (1998) **14**: 33–38.

13   *A Guide to the Development of Children's Palliative Care Services. Report of a Joint Working Party of the Association for Children with Life-threatening or Terminal Conditions and their Families and the Royal College of Paediatrics and Child Health.* September 2003.

14   Goldman A, Beardsmore A, Hunt J. "Palliative Care for Children with Cancer – home hospital or hospice?" *ArchDis Child* (1990) **65**:641–643. Lewis M. "The Lifetimes Service: a model for children with life-threatening illnesses and their families." *Paediatric Nursing.* (1999) **11**:21–23.

15   Hardart MKM, Truog RD. "Spinal muscular atrophy – Type 1." *Arch. Dis. Child.* (2003) **88**:848–850.

16   Re R (1991) 4 All ER 177, 185 Re W (1992) 4 A11 ER 627, 633

17   Bolam v Friern HMC (1957)2 All ER 118

18   Re J (1991) Fam 33 and Re c (1998) 1FLR 384; NHS Trust v M: NHS Trust v H (2001) 2FLR 367

19   Matters regarding health would normally be considered in a High Court. Court "orders" can only prohibit an intervention or authorise one if deemed medically expedient and in the patient's interests. They cannot oblige doctors to any specific medical intervention. In Scotland a doctor must take responsibility for his treatment decisions and the courts have little or no authority to give sanction to such decisions in advance.

20   Re R (1991) 4 All ER 177, 185 Re W (1992) 4 All ER 627, 633. R (On the Application of Wilkinson) v Broadmoor SHA (2002) 1 WLR 419.R (On the Application of N) v Dr M (2003) 1 FCR 124

21   Gillick v Wisbech & W Norfolk AHA (1985) 3 All ER 402; Children Act 1989. part V, 43, 44.

22   Definition – Causing death by intended lethal action, but for the relief of suffering

23   Airedale NHS Trust v Bland (1993)1 All ER 821; NHS Trust v M; NHS Trust v H (2001) 2 FLR 367

24 Cuttini, M. et al. "Should euthanasia be legal? An international survey of neonatal intensive care units staff."*Arch. Dis.Child* (2004) **89**:F19-F24. Lagercrantz, H. "Commentary on paper Cuttini et al." *Arch. Dis. Child.*(2004) **89**:F2. Cooke, RW "Commentary on paper Cuttini et al." *Arch. Dis.Child* (2004) **89**:F3.

25 A child's mother automatically has parental responsibility. A father does not have parental responsibility unless he has married the mother, or made a parental responsibility agreement with her, or obtained a court order granting him parental responsibility, or fathers whose name appears on the birth certificate for children born after 12 December 2003. However, it would be good practice for both parents to be fully involved in decision making as far as possible, whether or not the father has parental responsibility. Other individuals can obtain parental responsibility by court order, or by being appointed as a guardian on the death of a parent.

26 For example: Fradd E. "Tug of love." *Nursing Times* (1988) **88**:32–5. Warner J. "Commentary. Early experiences of heart lung transplantation in cystic fibrosis." *Arch Dis Child* (1989) **64**:9–13. Goodwin M, Alderson P. "Contradictions within concepts of children's rights." In *J of Children's Rights* (1989) **1**:303–13. British Medical Association *Consent, Rights and Choices in Health Care for Children and Young People* London: BMJ Books (2001).

27 Definitions – An impairment describes a pathological process such as spina bifida, a disability is the consequence of an impairment and a handicap the social consequence of the impairment or disability. Handicap is a disability of body or mind which interferes with the ability to lead a normal life or to benefit from a normal education. This may constitute a breach of the Disability Discrimination Act 1995 and also the Human Rights Act 1998. A recent example of this is the case of Glass v The United Kingdom in the European Court of Human Rights, 2004.

28 Re J (1991) Fam 33.

29 Smith GF et al. "The rights of infants with Down's syndrome." *JAMA* (1984) **251**:229. Bull *et. al.* Should management of complete atrioventricular canal defects be influenced by co-existent Down's syndrome. *Lancet.* (1985) ii: 1147–1149. A heart for Jo. *The Guardian Weekend.* 10.8.96. Controversy over disabled girl's death in casualty unit. *The Sunday Telegraph.* 29.12.96. R v Central Birmingham HA ex parte Walker (1987)3 BMLR 32.

30 Definition – Brain death occurs when a child has sustained either (i) irreversible cessation of circulatory and respiratory functions or (ii) irreversible cessation of all functions of the entire brain including the brain stem. A determination of death must be made in accordance with accepted medical standards.

31 Definition – A state of unawareness of self and environment in which the patient breathes spontaneously, has a stable circulation and shows cycles of eye closure and eye opening which simulates sleep and waking, for a period of 12 months following a head injury or 6 months following other causes of brain damage.

32 The legal judgement on Bland (Airedale NHS Trust v Bland (1993) 1 All ER 821) suggests that in this situation tube feeding is itself an assault and so it should be withdrawn. In paediatric practice this is less clear – see 3.1.4.

33 Vernon DD et al. Modes of death in the paediatric intensive care unit: withdrawal and limitation of support care. *Critical Care Medicine* (1993) **21**:1798–1802. Mink RB and Pollock MM. Resuscitation and withdrawal of therapyin paediatric intensive care. *Pediatrics* (1992) **89**:961–963. Lantos JD *et al.* Do-not-resuscitate orders in a children's hospital. *Critical Care Medicine* (1993) **21**:52–55. Ryan CA *et al.* No resuscitation and withdrawal of therapy in a neonatal and paediatric intensive care unit in Canada. *J Pediatr* (1993) **123**:534–538. Martinot A et al. All modes of death in a French paediatric intensive care unit. *Proceedings of the European Society for Pediatric Intensive Care.* (1994). Levetown M *et al.* Limitations and withdrawals of medical interventions in pediatric critical care. *JAMA* (1994) **272**:1271–5. Balfour-Lynn IM and Tasker RC. Futility and death in paediatric medical intensive care. *J Med Ethics* (1996)**22**:279–281.

34 Airedale NHS Trust v Bland (1993) 1 All ER 821

35 *Palliative Care for Young People. Report of the Joint Working Party of ACT* (The Association for Children with Life-Threatening or Terminal Conditions and their Families), the National Council for Hospice and Specialist Palliative Care Services and the Scottish Partnership Agency for Palliative and Cancer Care. 2001.

36 Greig-Midlane. H. "The parents perspective of withdrawing treatment" BMJ (2001)323:390.

37 No matter how careful the diagnosis during life, the EAC-RCPCH believes that a request for a post mortem is always appropriate. Information from postmortem consolidates and confirms the diagnosis during life providing certainty for the parents and the clinical team. The results should be given to the parents as soon as it is possible.

38 Chiswick M. "Parents' end of Life decisions in neonatal practice" *Arch. Dis. Child* (2001) **85**: F1–3. McHaffie HE, Laing IA, Lloyd DJ "Follow-up on bereaved parents after treatment withdrawal from newborns" *Arch.Dis.Child* (2001) **84**:F125–128.

39 Larcher VF, Lask B, McCarthy J, "Paediatrics at the cutting edge: do we need clinical ethics committees?" *J MedEthics* (1997) **23**: 245–249

40 Alderson P, Montgomery J *Health Care Choices – Making Decisions with Children.* London: Institute of Public Policy Research, 1996. Alderson P. *Children's consent to surgery.* Buckingham: Open University Press,1993.

41 Saigal S et al. Pediatric Research Abstracts. Abstract 225, (1995)**37**:40A. and Abstract 1654, (1996) **39**:378A.

42 Sheikh A, Gatrad AR. "Children and Young Families". In *Ethnicity, Health and Primary Care,* Ed. Kai J. Chapter 16 p. 151. Oxford: Oxford University Press, 2003. UK Census England and Wales www.pro.gov.uk

43 www.ethics-network.org.uk

Index

Abortion 8.1–8.31
  Abortion Act 1967 8.4
  Abortion Act conditions 8.6–8.18
    certification of medical
      opinion 8.10
    conscientious objection 8.6
    grounds 8.11–8.17
    multiple foetuses 8.7
    procedure performed by
      medical practitioner 8.9
    risk of injury to mother 8.11–.814
    risk to life of pregnant
      woman 8.16
    substantial risk of child
      being seriously
      handicapped 8.17
    successful procedure 8.8
    termination necessary to
      prevent grave permanent
      injury 8.15
  best interests 8.24
  consent of patient 8.19–8.30
    children 8.21
    competent adults 8.20
    incompetent adults 8.22
  considerations for court 8.28–8.30
    best interests 8.30
    capacity 8.29
    statutory position 8.28
  determining competence 8.23
  evidence 8.26–8.30
  Human Fertilisation and
    Embryology Act 1990 8.5
  Infant Life (Preservation)
    Act 1929 8.3
  making application 8.26
  Offences Against the Person
    Act 1861 8.2
  place of treatment 8.18
  procedure 8.26–8.30
  settled law 8.31

Abortion – *contd*
  statutory framework 8.1–8.5
  timing of applications 8.27
  use of force
    non-consensual incompetent
      patients 8.25
Acknowledgment of service
  High Court 5.54
Adults
  consent 2.1–2.20 *see also* consent
  deciding for others *see*
    Deciding for others
  meaning 2.1
Advance directives/decisions 2.13–2.19
  consent, and 2.13–2.19
  duration 2.18
  form 2.15
  general principle 2.13
  informed refusal 2.16
  knowledge 2.17
  records 2.19
  requirements 2.14
Appeals
  Court of Protection, from 5.39
  High Court, from 5.61
Assault
  continuing treatment as 12.6

Best interests 3.13
  abortion, and 8.30
  balance of competing factors 3.14
  determination of 3.13
  financial interests 3.15
  human organ and tissue
    donation 15.13
  interests to be considered 3.15
  intolerability, and 3.13
  medical issues 3.14
  participation of patient 3.13
  permanent vegetative state 12.3

Best interests – *contd*
  previously held beliefs and
      feelings 3.13
  refusal of treatment by child,
      and 4.6
  relevant circumstances 3.13
  religious objections, and 11.18
  restraint, and 6.25
  seriously ill infant 4.15
  sterilisation 7.8, 7.9, 7.22
  suicide, and 13.56
  tensions between family
      members and treating
      staff 3.15
  termination of pregnancy 8.24
Blood transfusions
  religious objections *see*
      Religious objections
Bundles
  Family Division Practice
      Directions 5.16

Caesarean section cases 9.4–9.13
  capacity 9.9
  competence of pregnant
      women, and 9.6
  foetus, interests of 9.11
  needle phobias 9.7
  procedure 9.12
  Re MB 9.8
  reasonable force 9.10
  *St George's Healthcare NHS
      Trust v S* 9.13
  *Thameside and Glossop Acute
      Services NHS Trust v CH* 9.5
  will of mother, and 9.4
CAFCASS 5.11
Capacity 2.2–2.10
  assessment 2.2–2.6
  concern over 2.8
  consent, and 1.33, 2.2–2.10
  definition 2.2–2.6
  extent of 2.6
  presumption of 2.8
      reasonable steps 2.8
  relevant mental capacity 2.2
  retaining information 2.4
  temporary incapacity 2.7
  understanding information 2.3
  weighing information as part of
      decision-making process 2.5
Change of mind
  consent, and 2.12

Children 4.1–4.17
  abortion, and 8.21
  capacity to consent 4.2–4.4
      children of 16 and over 4.2
      children under 16 4.3
      Gillick test 4.3
      judgment of 4.3
      parental responsibilities,
          persons with 4.4
      parents 4.4
      presumption 4.2
  compulsory treatment 4.7
  consent, and 4.1
  deciding for 4.1–4.17
  defendants, as 5.50
  feeding *see* Feeding
  human organ and tissue
      donation 15.16
  meaning 4.1
  organ and tissue donation 15.12
  permanent vegetative state 12.22
  refusal of treatment 4.5–4.10
      best interests, and 4.6
      children over 16 4.6
      children under 16 4.8
      children with *Gillick*
          competence 4.6
      court, and 4.10
      judging competence 4.6
      parents 4.9
  religious objections *see*
      Religious objections
  rights of 4.7
  seriously ill infants *see*
      Seriously ill infants
  sterilisation *see* Sterilisation
  suicide, and 13.22
Comprehension
  consent, and 1.14
Compulsory treatment
  children, and 4.7
Consent 1.1–1.38
  adults 2.1–2.20
      absolute nature of consent 2.9
      autonomy of patient 2.20
      treatment must be lawful 2.10
  advance directives/decisions 2.13–
          2.19 *see also*
          Advance
          directives/decisions
  capacity 1.33, 2.2–2.10 *see also*
          Capacity
  change of mind 2.12

Consent – *contd*
children *see* Children
communication of 1.15–1.18
comprehension 1.14
conduct, and 1.18
duration of authority 1.35, 1.36
duress, and 1.32
fraud, and 1.31
GMC guidance 1.38
human organ and tissue
  donation *see* Human organ
  and tissue donation
information about risks *see*
  Risks, information about
informed, no doctrine of 1.19
intention 1.13
legality of treatment, and 1.1
limited proxy of 3.3
oral 1.17
proposal to treat 1.3–1.9 *see also*
  Proposal to treat
refusal of treatment 2.11
scope of authority 1.34
state of mind 1.13, 1.14
sterilisation, and 7.1
undue influence, and 1.32
vitiating factors 1.30–1.33
withdrawal of authority 1.37
written 1.16

Contraception
sterilisation, and 7.12

Costs
Court of Protection 5.38
High Court 5.60

Counselling
religious objections, and 11.7

Court of Protection
aims of bringing proceedings 5.15
appeals 5.39
cases where no jurisdiction 5.4
constitutional issues 5.19
costs 5.38
deprivation of liberty 5.33
different age cut-offs for
  different types of case 5.6
final hearings 5.17, 5.37
first hearing 5.36
general approach 5.22
High Court, overlapping
  jurisdiction 5.5
initial directions 5.32
judges 5.20
jurisdiction 5.3–5.6

Court of Protection – *contd*
level of judge 5.32
litigation friend 5.29
location 5.20
medical treatment decisions,
  power to make 5.23
privacy 5.28
publicity 5.28
notification of proceedings 5.31
permission to start
  proceedings 5.30
points to consider before
  starting proceedings 5.29–5.33
power to consent to treatment 3.14
procedural points 5.9–5.18
respondents 5.31
serious medical treatment:
  Practice Direction 5.24
cases which should be
  brought to court 5.27
procedural matters 5.26
16 to 17 year olds 5.5
sources of procedural rules and
  guidance 5.21
starting proceedings-non-
  urgent 5.34
starting proceedings-urgent 5.35
subsequent directions hearings 5.36
timing of proceedings 5.9
typing up order 5.18
urgency of case 5.10
who should bring proceedings 5.13–
  5.15

Courts 5.1–5.63
identifying 5.2–5.8
jurisdiction 5.2
power to order treatment 3.1
procedure 5.2–5.8
public law issues 5.7
refusal of treatment
  children, and 4.10

Death 14.1–14.39
Academy of Medical Royal
  Colleges definition 14.10
after 14.26–14.28
American definition 14.3
Australian definition 14.4
bodies, use and storage 14.38
brain stem death 14.6, 14.7–14.9,
  14.13
certification 14.17

Death – *contd*
   cessation of cardio-respiratory
      function 14.14–14.16
   definition 14.1–14.11
   diagnosis of 14.12–14.25
   disposal of corpse 14.35–14.37
   human tissue, use and storage 14.38
   identification of point of death 14.15,
      14.16
   importance of defining 14.2
   'irreversible' 14.11
   no property in body 14.27, 14.28–
      14.34
     body parts 14.29–14.34
     vesting or property, and 14.34
     work and skill exceptions 14.29–
      14.34
   permanent cessation of all
      bodily functions 14.5
   possession of corpse 14.35–14.37
   process of dying 14.18–14.25
     court, role of 14.23
     GMC draft consultation
      document 14.24
     law, and 14.20
     legal and moral issues 14.25
     palliative care 14.19, 14.21, 14.22
   proof of 14.5
   sophisticated criteria for
      definition 14.39
Deciding for others 3.1–3.18
   adults 3.1.3.18
   adults with capacity, and 3.5–3.7
   adults without capacity 3.8–3.17
   best interests, determination of 3.13
   capable adult's wishes must be
      respected 3.2
   children *see* Children
   Court of Protection 3.14
   court, power to order
      treatment 3.1
   force and restraint, use of 3.16
   interests to be considered 3.15
   limited proxy of consent 3.3
   medical issues 3.14
   Mental Capacity Act 2005 3.9
   necessity 3.8
   obligation to treat in
      accordance with expressed
      wishes 3.6
   obstetric treatment in interests
      of viable foetus 3.7

Deciding for others – *contd*
   power to treat in incapable
      person's best interests 3.4
   records 3.11
   scope of power to treat 3.12
   temporary incapacity 3.10
Deliberate killing
   seriously ill infants 4.12
Deprivation of liberty
   agent of state, by 5.32
   authorised under MCA 6.8–6.10
   authorising 6.38
   borderline cases 6.36
   'Bournewood gap' 6.27–6.30
   common law 6.5
   court authorisation 6.39, 6.40
   DOLS procedure 6.41–6.44 *see also*
          DOLS procedure
   factors to be considered 6.31
   facts, decision on 6.31
   identifying 6.37
   lawful detention 6.27–6.30
   MCA or MHA, whether 6.45–6.48
   meaning 6.31–6.36
   mental health, and 6.2
   objective element 6.32, 6.33
   overlapping legislative
      schemes 6.45–6.48
   purpose of 6.34
   statutory basis 6.4
   subjective element 6.32
DOLS procedure 6.41–6.44
   'Byzantine in the extreme' 6.44
   Managing Authority, and 6.42
   MCA or MHA, whether 6.45–6.48
   standard authorisation 6.43
Duress
   consent, and 1.32

Eating disorders *see also* Feeding

Feeding 10.1–10.11
   adults 10.7–10.11
   adults lacking capacity to
      consent 10.8
   children 10.2–10.6
     aged 16 and 17 10.3
     court's jurisdiction, exercise
      of 10.5
     Gillick competence, and 10.4
     procedure 10.6
     under 16 10.2
   competent adults 10.7

Feeding – *contd*
  competent adults detained
      under Mental Health
      Act 1983 10.9
  declaration 10.10
  eating disorders 10.1
  injunction 10.11
  procedure 10.10, 10.11
Financial interests
  best interests, and 3.15
Force, use of 3.16
Fraud
  consent, and 1.31
Freedom of association
  sterilisation, and 7.15

High Court
  acknowledgment of service 5.54
  aims of bringing proceedings 5.15
  appeals 5.61
  cases which should be brought
      to court 5.44
  costs 5.60
  Court of Protection,
      overlapping jurisdiction 5.5
  defendants 5.49–5.52
    body responsible for
        treatment or care 5.49
    child 5.50
    local authority 5.52
    parents 5.51
  Family Division Practice
      Direction on bundles 5.16
  final hearings 5.17, 5.59
  first hearing 5.58
  general issues 5.44
  imposing treatment despite
      competent refusal 5.48
  inherent jurisdiction: vulnerable
      adults 5.62
  jurisdiction 5.40
  local authority issues 5.47
  originating summons 5.54
  parental issues 5.46
  privacy 5.57
  procedural points 5.9–5.18
  procedure 5.43
  publicity 5.57
  regional hearings 5.42
  rules 5.43
  starting proceedings –
      non-urgent 5.53–5.55
  starting proceedings – urgent 5.56

High Court – *contd*
  subsequent directions hearings 5.58
  timing of proceedings 5.9
  typing up order 5.18
  urgency of case 5.10
  who should bring proceedings 5.13–
      5.15
Human organ and tissue
      donation 15.1–15.19
  altruistic organ donation 15.15
  best interests 15.13
  children 15.12
  common law 15.2
  consent 15.10
    adults 15.17
    children 15.16
  domino transplants 15.9
  genetically or emotionally
      related organ donation 15.15
  Human Tissue Act 2004 15.2–15.19
  Human Tissue Authority,
      approval by 15.14
  incompetent adults 15.11
  lawful activities 15.6
  living donation, types of 15.15
  living persons, donations by 15.8–
      15.17
  paired/pooled organ donation 15.15
  post-mortem donation 15.15
  preparatory steps taken before
      death 15.19
  preservation of organs after
      death 15.18
  transplantable material 15.2, 15.4
Human tissue
  use and storage 14.38

Injunction
  feeding, and 10.11
Intention
  consent, and 1.13
Intolerability
  best interests, and 3.13

Litigation friend 5.29
Living wills *see* Advance
      Directives/Decisions

Mental Capacity Act 2005 3.9

Necessity
  treatment out of 3.8

Needle phobias
pregnancy, and 9.7

Obstetrics *see also* Pregnancies
compulsory 9.3
patient and foetal rights 9.2
Official Solicitor 5.11
Originating summons
High Court 5.54

Parent
consent to treatment of child 4.4
defendants, as 5.51
refusal of treatment for child 4.9
best interests, and 4.9
limits on power 4.9
weight to be given to views 4.9
Permanent vegetative state 12.1–12.24
'act' 12.4
advance directives 12.8
application to court 12.17–12.19
confidentiality 12.18
evidence 12.19
best interests 12.3
Bland 12.3
extending to other cases 12.7
BMA guidelines for diagnosis 12.10
cases outside RCP guidelines 12.13
children 12.22
clear guidance, need for 12.24
continuing treatment as assault 12.6
court, application to 12.15, 12.16
diagnosis 12.1
doctors who disagree in
principle 12.23
emergencies 12.20
critique of *Frenchay*
approach 12.21
European Convention on
Human Rights 12.5
family, role of 12.14
imaging 12.11
legal principles 12.2–12.9
meaning 12.1
medical issues 12.10–12.13
mis-diagnosis 12.10
'omission' 12.4
criminal liability, and 12.9
prior consent 12.8
reasonable and bona fide
belief 12.3
rehabilitation 12.12
sanctity of life 12.3

Permanent vegetative state – *contd*
time to allow for recovery 12.12
withholding nutrition without
court approval 12.16
Pregnancies 9.1–9.27
advance directives 9.16
application to court for
directions 9.14
Caesarean section cases *see*
Caesarean section cases
comatose women 9.17
compulsory obstetrics 9.3
Court of Appeal guidelines 9.14–9.17
legal background 9.2–9.13
managing 9.1–9.27
Mental Capacity Act 2005 9.15
patient and foetal rights in
obstetrics 9.2
permanent vegetative state,
and 9.17
procedure for patients 9.27
sterilisation, and 7.14
suggested procedure for
obstetric units 9.18–9.26
advance directive 9.22
advice to patients about
possible loss of
capacity 9.21
assessment of capacity 9.19–9.26
assessment where capacity in
doubt 9.23
compliance with Court of
Appeal guidelines 9.25
contingency planning for
court application 9.24
continual advice to patient 9.26
psychiatric referral 9.23
surgical deliveries 9.1
Proposal to treat 1.3–1.9
alternative forms of treatment 1.5
communication of 1.10–1.12
compelling doctor to treat 1.6
consent, and 1.3–1.9
formulation 1.3
irrational decisions by care
providers 1.7
resources 1.8
risks 1.4
treatment demanded by patient 1.9
Public law issues
courts, and 5.7

Records
significance of 3.11

Refusal of treatment 2.11
Rehabilitation
    permanent vegetative state,
        and 12.12
Religious objections 11.1–11.23
    ability to understand
        information relevant to
        decision 11.5
    ability to use or weigh
        information 11.6
    blood transfusions 11.1
    children 11.17–11.23
        anticipation 11.20
        best interests 11.18
        change of circumstance 11.23
        consent of parent 11.17
        consultation 11.21
        evidence 11.22
        Gillick competence 11.19
        notice 11.21
        procedural issues 11.20–11.23
    close friends, role of 11.10
    competent adults 11.2–11.11
    confirmation that patient is
        mentally competent 11.4
    counselling 11.7
    incapacitated adults 11.12–11.16
        advance decisions 11.13–11.15
        written declarations 11.16
    recording of decision against
        medical advice 11.11
    relatives, role of 11.10
    scope of decision 11.9
    steps to be taken 11.3–11.6
    undue influence 11.8
Restraint, use of 3.16
    alternative treatment 6.24
    Article 3 ECHR, and 6.11–6.14
    authorised under MCA 6.8–6.10
    best, interests, and 6.25
    common law 6.5
    'degrading' treatment 6.13
        meaning 6.6
    mental health, and 6.2
    practical issues 6.22–6.26
    proportionality 6.15–6.21
        case law 6.15–6.21
        life and death situations 6.19–6.21
        torture, and 6.20
    reasonable and proportionate 6.3
    statutory basis 6.4
    trespass to the person, and 6.7

Risks, information about 1.19–1.29
    alternative forms of treatment,
        information about 1.28
    delegation 1.25
    duty of care 1.20–1.24
        Article 8 1.21
        common law 1.20
        current practice in UK 1.23, 1.24
        other jurisdictions 1.22
    duty to answer questions 1.26, 1.27
    informed consent, doctrine of 1.19
    known comparative outcomes 1.29

Serious medical treatment
    meaning 5.25
Seriously ill infants 4.11–4.16
    best interests 4.15
        court's approach 4.15
        intolerability 4.15
    complexity of law 4.17
    deliberate killing 4.12
    treatment dilemmas 4.11
    withholding treatment 4.13
        Article 2 right to life, and 4.14
        brain death 4.13
        no chance situation 4.13
        no purpose situation 4.13
        permanent vegetative state 4.13
        practical guidance 4.16
        unbearable situation 4.13
Sexual contact, risk of
    sterilisation, and 7.11
Sterilisation 7.1–7.23
    adults lacking capacity to
        consent 7.7–7.18
    best interests 7.8
        capacity 7.7
        general application of
            principle 7.9
    capacity of patient 7.10
    children 7.20–7.23
        best interests 7.22
        CAFCASS 7.23
        evidence from carers 7.23
        learning disabilities 7.21
        no learning disabilities 7.20
        Official Solicitor, and 7.23
        pregnancy, and 7.21
        procedure 7.23
    competent patient 7.2–7.19
    consent 7.1
    contraception, availability of 7.12
    counselling, need for 7.13

Index

Sterilisation – *contd*
  freedom of association 7.15
  general rule 7.2
  immediacy of risks 7.18
  informed consent 7.3
  male patients 7.17
  nature of 7.1
  partner/spouse, role of 7.4
  paternalistic attitudes 7.1
  pregnancy, risks of 7.14
  preparation, need for 7.13
  procedure 7.5, 7.19
  sexual contact, risk of 7.11
  standard of care, and 7.16
  therapeutic 7.8
Suicide 13.1–13.71
  act 13.3
  adults, lacking capacity 13.22
  Assisted Dying for the
    Terminally Ill Bill 2005 13.13
  autonomy, and 13.25, 13.26, 13.27,
    13.34
  autonomy and liability for
    failing to act 13.28–13.38
  capacity, and 13.19
  children 13.22
  Coroners and Justice Bill 13.14,
    13.15
  'cries for help' 13.24
  criteria for prosecution 13.9–13.11
    interim guidance 13.12
  compulsorily detained
    patients 13.56–13.65
    alleviating symptoms of
      mental disorder 13.60–13.63
    best interests 13.56
    legal test in criticising
      doctor's determination 13.64,
      13.65
  decision as to 13.21
  distinction between acts and
    omissions 13.37, 13.38
  duty to prevent 13.30, 13.31
  emergency situations 13.49–13.53

Suicide – *contd*
  European Convention on
    Human Rights 13.7, 13.39–
      13.46
    balance to be struck 13.54, 13.55
    duty to preserve life 13.39–13.46
    risk prediction, and 13.45
  failure to control patient's
    environment 13.35, 13.36
  failure to treat or feed 13.16–13.18
  free will, and 13.20
  general guidance 13.47–14.53
  general principles 13.19–13.22
  guidance on approach to
    treatment 13.66
  inadequate time to assess
    capacity 13.49–13.51
  individual self-assertion, as 13.32
  intention to act 13.4
  interplay of ethical principles 13.67
  legal and ethical dilemmas 13.23
  liability for failure to protect 13.28–
    13.38
  meaning 13.2
  practical problems 13.23–13.27
  Pretty case 13.8
  preventing jump from window 13.52,
    13.53
  refining definition 13.16–13.18
  refusal of treatment 13.25
  Suicide Act 1961 13.6
  tube feeding, and 13.57, 13.58, 13.59
  understanding of likely
    consequences 13.5

Temporary incapacity 2.7, 3.10

Undue influence
  consent, and 1.32
  religious objections, and 11.8

Viable foetus
  freedom from physical
    invasion, and 3.7

Withholding treatment
  seriously ill infants 4.13